ROUTLEDGE HANDBOOK OF ELECTION LAW

Governments need rules, institutions, and processes to translate the will of the people into functioning democracies. Election laws are the rules that make that happen. Yet across the world various countries have crafted different rules regarding how elections are conducted, who gets to vote, who is allowed to run for office, what role political parties have, and what place money has in the financing of campaigns and candidates. The *Routledge Handbook of Election Law* is the first major cross-national comparative reference book surveying the electoral practices and law of the major and emerging democracies across the world. It brings together the leading international scholars on election law and democracy, examining specific issues, topics, or the regions of the world when it comes to rules, institutions, and processes regarding how they run their elections. The result is a rich volume of research furthering the legal and political science knowledge about democracies and the challenges they face. Scholars interested in election law and democracy, as well as election officials, will find the *Routledge Handbook of Election Law* an essential reference book.

David Schultz is Hamline University Distinguished Professor in the departments of Political Science, Legal Studies, and Environmental Studies, and a Professor of Law at the University of Minnesota.

Jurij Toplak is Professor of Law and Head of Department at the University of Maribor, the Executive Vice-President of the Alma Mater Europaea, Slovenia, and a recurring visiting professor at Fordham University School of Law. He is a member of the European Academy of Sciences and Arts.

ROUTLEDGE HANDBOOK OF ELECTION LAW

Edited by David Schultz and Jurij Toplak

Routledge
Taylor & Francis Group
LONDON AND NEW YORK

Cover image: rrmf13

First published 2023
by Routledge
4 Park Square, Milton Park, Abingdon, Oxon OX14 4RN

and by Routledge
605 Third Avenue, New York, NY 10158

Routledge is an imprint of the Taylor & Francis Group, an informa business

British Library Cataloguing-in-Publication Data
A catalogue record for this book is available from the British Library

Library of Congress Cataloging-in-Publication Data
Names: Schultz, David A. (David Andrew), 1958-editor. |
Toplak, Jurij, editor.
Title: Routledge handbook of election law/edited by David Schultz and Jurij Toplak.
Description: Abingdon, Oxon; New York, NY: Routledge, 2022. |
Includes bibliographical references and index. |
Identifiers: LCCN 2021060997 | ISBN 9781138393363 (hardcover) |
ISBN 9781032183053 (paperback) | ISBN 9780429401800 (ebook)
Subjects: LCSH: Election law.
Classification: LCC K3293 .R68 2022 | DDC 342/.07–dc23/eng/20220429
LC record available at https://lccn.loc.gov/2021060997

ISBN: 978-1-138-39336-3 (hbk)
ISBN: 978-1-032-18305-3 (pbk)
ISBN: 978-0-429-40180-0 (ebk)

DOI: 10.4324/9780429401800

Typeset in Bembo
by Deanta Global Publishing Services, Chennai, India

To
Jerry Pomper,
a great scholar of elections.
David Schultz

To
Živana.
You encourage and inspire me.
I can work, because you
take care of everything else.
Jurij Toplak

CONTENTS

TABLES

FIGURES

CONTRIBUTORS

Jordi Barrat i Esteve is a professor of constitutional law at Rovira i Virgili University. His research focuses on the legal analysis of electoral processes, capacity building aspects, and the use of new technologies.

Enira Bronitskaya is a Belarusian human rights expert and activist. She focuses on electoral observation, election law, and disability law. She holds a master degree in European law from Bordeaux University.

Ali Çarkoğlu is a professor at the Department of International Relations (CASE) of Koç University in Istanbul, Turkey.

Drude Dahlerup is a professor of political science at Stockholm University and an honorary professor at Roskilde University. Professor Dahlerup is a pioneer of gender research in political science and an expert on women's political representation.

Inese Druviete is former program director at the Riga Graduate School of Law. She was a Fulbright-Shuman fellow specializing in competition and technology law.

Ugochukwu Ezeh is a doctoral candidate in the Faculty of Law at the University of Oxford, where he also earned an MPhil in Law (with Distinction) as a Weidenfeld-Hoffmann scholar. He was an Oxford Human Rights Hub Research Fellow at Rhodes University.

Lenita Freidenvall is an associate professor and senior lecturer in political science at Stockholm University, specializing in political representation, candidate selection, and gender quotas, and is co-director of the Women Politics Research Network.

Djordje Gardašević is an associate professor at the Faculty of the Law, University of Zagreb. He has been a member of the Croatian Association for Constitutional Law, the International Political Science Association (IPSA), and the American Political Science Association (APSA).

Holly Ann Garnett is an associate professor of political science at the Royal Military College of Canada in Kingston, Ontario, and Queen's University. She is co-director of the Electoral Integrity Project.

M. V. Rajeev Gowda is a former member of India's parliament (Rajya Sabha) and Chairman of the Indian National Congress party's Research Department. He teaches occasionally at the Indian Institute of Management Bangalore, Kautilya School of Public Policy and the Indian School of Business.

Klemen Jaklič is professor of Constitutional Law and judge at the Constitutional Court of Slovenia. He taught for a decade at Harvard University and is the author of *Constitutional Pluralism in the EU* (OUP 2014).

Toby S. James is a professor of politics and public policy in the School of Politics, Philosophy, Language and Communication Studies at the University of East Anglia, UK. He is co-director of the Electoral Integrity Project and editor-in-chief of *Policy Studies*.

Robert Krimmer holds the ERA-Chair Professorship of e-Governance within Skytte Institute at the University of Tartu in Estonia.

Mathieu Leloup works at the Faculty of Law of the University of Antwerp as a PhD assistant in constitutional and administrative law. His interests are human rights law, constitutional law, and the separation of powers.

Hassan Nasir Mirbahar is a democratic governance expert with over 15 years of experience in electoral support, parliamentary strengthening, and human rights. He has been working with the Democracy Reporting International, and the United Nations Development Programme (UNDP).

Erik Johan Mobrand is an associate professor at the Graduate School of International Studies, Seoul National University. He researches politics in South Korea and Asia.

Steven J. Mulroy is the Bredesen Professor of Law at Cecil C. Humphreys School of the Law, University of Memphis. He is the author of the book *Rethinking U.S. Election Law: Unskewing The System* and a member of the American Law Institute.

Pippa Norris is the Paul F. McGuire Lecturer in Comparative Politics at the John F. Kennedy School of Government, Harvard University, and founding director of the Electoral Integrity Project, director of the Global Party Survey, co-director of the TrustGov Project, and on the executive of the World Values Survey.

Graeme Orr is a professor in law at the University of Queensland, Australia. The law of politics, in particular electoral regulation, is his primary research expertise.

Hannah Roberts is an independent election and governance consultant with over 20 years of experience. She has worked on election-related projects for various international organizations worldwide, including in Europe, Canada, Afghanistan, Nigeria, Kenya, and Pakistan.

Mark E. Rush is Waxberg Professor of politics and law, and director of the Center for International Education at Washington and Lee University. He writes extensively on US politics, comparative constitutional law, elections, democracy, and global affairs.

Mohd Azizuddin Mohd Sani is a professor of politics and international relations at the School of International Studies (SOIS), Universiti Utara Malaysia (UUM) and adjunct visiting professor at the Faculty of Liberal Arts and Sciences, Taylor's University Malaysia.

Varun Santhosh is a Senior Private Secretary to the Chairman, Parliamentary Standing Committee on Science, Technology, Environment and Climate Change in the Parliament of India (Rajya Sabha).

Emily Schnurr is an assistant professor at the political science department of Bradley University. She teaches Introduction to American Government, and Women and Politics.

David Schultz is Hamline University Distinguished Professor in the departments of political science, legal studies, and environmental studies, and a professor of law at the University of Minnesota.

Ēriks Kristians Selga is a PhD candidate at the university of Hong Kong. His research focuses on technologically-enabled regulation.

Maša Setnikar is a doctoral candidate and a researcher at the Catholic Institute, Slovenia. She has authored and co-authored several research papers and articles.

Alexander Shlyk is the Special Representative for Elections of Sviatlana Tsikhanouskaya, the Belarusian opposition leader. He was the head of the election department of the OSCE's Office for Democratic Institutions and Human Rights (ODIHR) and managed election-related activities across the OSCE region.

Barbara Jouan Stonestreet has worked as a lawyer for the French National Commission on Campaign Accounts and Political Party Financing and as an international political finance expert for various international organizations worldwide.

Jurij Toplak is a professor of law and head of department at the University of Maribor, the executive vice-president of the Alma Mater Europaea, Slovenia, and a recurring visiting professor at Fordham University School of Law, New York. He is a member of the European Academy of Sciences and Arts.

Daniela Urosa is an adjunct professor at the Boston College Law School and International Ally Professor at the Andrés Bello Catholic University, Caracas, Venezuela. Urosa has researched and written extensively in constitutional law, administrative law, electoral law, and human rights, mainly focused on Latin America.

Bob Watt is a retired professor of election law. He formerly worked at the University of Essex and the University of Buckingham.

ACKNOWLEDGEMENTS

We would like to thank Daniel Siter for his invaluable assistance in helping us get the final version of this project completed. Thanks also go to our many law students in our election law seminars who stimulated our thought on this topic. Of course, there are literally scores of academics and scholars whom we have benefitted from in terms of their research that has inspired us, and of course Daniel Lowenstein who really invented the field of election law. Finally, thank you to Alison Kirk who first invited us to produce this book and whose patience through the pandemic was very much appreciated.

1
INTRODUCTION

David Schultz and Jurij Toplak

Just a few years ago, it appeared that democracy was on the ascent across the world. The fall of the Berlin Wall in 1989 and the collapse of the Soviet Union in 1991 signaled to Francis Fukuyama (1992) that the end of history had arrived. Liberal democracy was triumphant, and its rivals had been vanquished, losers in the ideological Cold War. Liberal democracy was the last standing meta-narrative (Barber, 1996), a survivor of what Samuel Huntington (2011) called the clash of civilizations.

By 1991, it certainly looked as if the promises of the French Revolution – liberté, égalité, fraternité – was upon us. As George Hegel (2011) and Karl Marx (2014) had posited from different ideological positions, democracy was the inexorable destiny of the world. Across Africa, for example, the ranks of democratic states had swelled. In Europe, the conversion of formerly communist or totalitarian states to democracies was dramatic. In 1972, according to Freedom House, the number of free countries (a surrogate for democracies) stood at 44 out of 148 states (29.73%). Another 36 (24.3%) were partially free, and 68 (45.95%) were unfree. By 2008, these numbers had become 90 out of 193 (46.6%) free, 60 partially free (31.1%), and 43 (22.28%) unfree. Yet, by 2020, democracy was in retreat: 83 (42.56%) free, 63 (32.31%) partially free, and 49 (25.13%) not free (Freedom House, 2020).

Indeed, from its high point in 2008, democracy and freedom were now in retreat. There were accounts of people in countries such as Hungary and Poland questioning liberal democracy. The Russian Federation and Turkey were seen as backpedaling on basic freedoms. Hong Kong's democracy was losing out to China. The 2020 parliamentary elections in Venezuela were characterized by many as far from free and fair. In 2021, Myanmar faced a military coup, and Uganda experienced a contested election. Elsewhere in the world, democratic regimes were being challenged, exacerbated by the pressures of the Covid-19 pandemic and its attendant economic and public health crises. Nor did it seem, at least in the short term, that the spirit of the French Revolution or the hope for democracy of Fukuyama, Hegel, and Marx was destined or certain.

From the vantage point of the beginning of the third decade of the twenty-first century, many scholars are wondering if the promise of democracy has died – a light that has failed according to some authors (Krastev and Holmes, 2020). Many culprits are to blame. Perhaps rising inequality, neo-liberalism, and globalization undermine support for democracy. Maybe it is the rise of strong men and elites no longer committed to democracy. Perhaps it is the

DOI: 10.4324/9780429401800-1

decline of the US as a global power, the tepid commitment to human rights under the Trump administration, or even the reputational damage of the January 6, 2021 insurrection at the US Capitol that has lessened America's resolve to defend global democracy.

Another theory for this challenging of democracy focuses on the role that election law plays in creating and maintaining democracies. Election law is the body of legal norms that connects democratic theory to practice, the connective tissue that makes democracy work. It is the system of rules that decides who gets to vote, participate, and run for office, as well as how to hold elections and determine who gets to serve once elected. Election law can be a tool to give authoritarian regimes an air of legitimacy, but it can also be the vehicle to enable democratic regimes.

There is a large body of research that examines the prerequisites, or determinants, for democracy (Schultz, 2019). The range of factors is extensive, including economic equality, a free press, elite or mass support for democratic values, a commitment to a democratic political culture, and a range of other institutional, sociological, and economic factors. But one should not forget about the formal requisites of a democracy such as constitutions that call for checks on political power, protection of individual rights, and an independent judiciary. All contribute to building and maintaining democracies.

However, most studies overlook the role of election law. Prior to perhaps 1990, few scholars thought hard about election law. While there were international organizations that thought about human rights in terms of its connections to voting and ballot access, or in terms of vote counting and election processes, the idea of election law as an independent body of law and set of institutions that enabled democracy did not really exist. In fact, as an academic study or field, it did not really exist until it was pioneered by the American scholar Daniel Lowenstein (1994), whose case book *Election Law* gave definition to this field of study. Its discovery may have been a consequence of the fall of the Berlin Wall and the USSR. For suddenly there was a need to create a new body of law to replace that of the fallen regimes, which clearly had not been democratic. It was akin to the states that had to abandon their centrally-planned economies and build up markets almost ab initio.

In the last 30 years, election law has come to be seen as critical to the forging of democracies. Studies reveal at least two primary findings. One, there are common challenges faced by all regimes that aspire to be democracies. Two, there are common standards or practices that one can learn from and implement that help to promote democracies. The purpose of this volume is to provide a resource that catalogs, classifies, and summarizes both.

Across the world, democratic regimes face common problems. These issues perhaps start with the right to vote and voting procedures. Questions that thus would need answering include the following: Who is entitled to franchise? What proof is needed to cast a ballot? What provisions are in place to prevent fraud? Attached to voting rights would be questions regarding the conduct of elections. By that, how does voting occur? What types of technologies or procedures are in place to record and tabulate votes? Who does the tabulation or runs the elections? Are they centrally administered or locally controlled? Are the staff who administer the elections independent? If not, who controls and appoints them? Are independent monitors permitted as observers? Election law is not simply about the original casting of the ballot, but rather encompasses the management and administration of elections.

Another set of issues involves the regulation of political parties. What rights do parties have? Who can join them? There are further questions regarding ballot access for them or individual candidates. If there are dominant or major parties, how does the law treat minor parties, or what are called third parties in the US?

Moreover, there is the financing of campaigns and elections. Of course, there is the actual cost of administering elections, which is generally seen as a governmental expense. But parties, candidates, and other groups may also expend money for campaigns. Who can give or spend money? How much can they give or spend? For what purposes? Are there limits on business or union expenditures? Is the financing limited to citizens or nations? How does the law treat differences between bribes and legitimate expenses?

Furthermore, election law must address campaign tactics. Can one actively spend money on media advertising? Where does social media fit in? Who can campaign? Where can they campaign and under what conditions? Can one make false claims during an election or actually lie, and, if so, what are the remedies for such actions? Are there limits on when campaigning occurs?

Most democracies, in theory, are premised upon the idea of majority rule. Yet, few have ascribed to a pure and absolute theory of this concept. Elections need to respect minority voices. How do democracies balance majority rule and minority rights? For example, how can a country ensure that historically marginalized groups, such as women or ethnic minorities, participate fairly as candidates and voters? Are quotas a reasonable way to address historical discrimination? Moreover, might different electoral systems make a difference in terms of representation? Across the world, first-past-the-post, rank choice voting, proportional voting, and single- versus multi-member districts offer a range of possibilities. Increasingly, especially since the problem first surfaced in the US in the 1960s, when its Supreme Court addressed the problem of mal-districting or malapportionment, other countries in the world are similarly grappling with this problem, and their courts are stepping in to prevent gerrymandering as a tool of disenfranchising groups or individuals.

Beyond global issues, specific regions and even countries face unique challenges. As the world's largest democracy, India simply has a problem of scale in conducting elections that involve hundreds of millions of people over several weeks. Advanced democracies are differently situated than new democracies. Countries with colonial legacies are different than those without such recent histories. Even among states that are post-communist, those in the Baltics are differently positioned from those in the Caucuses. Multilingual or multi-ethnic states also differ.

Finally, all regimes in the world that aspire to being democracies must ask themselves if they are promoting an overall sense of integrity, transparency, and reliability in their electoral systems. On one level, do their own citizens trust and respect the electoral process and outcomes, and do they enjoy international standards? In the end, for states aspiring to be democracies, are their electoral systems producing real democratic regimes, whatever that term ultimately means? Can election rules make a difference in producing democratic regimes?

This handbook collects leading scholars and studies on election law. It assembles the most current research on the state of the relations between election law and democracy, seeking to understand how the former enables and strengthens the latter. For scholars, practitioners, and advocates, this handbook serves as a reference book on the state of what we know about the ways in which election law and rules facilitate and build democratic political systems and the challenges that remain.

REFERENCES

Barber, B. J. (1996). *Jihad vs. McWorld: Terrorism's challenge to democracy*. New York: Ballantine Books.

Freedom House. (2020). *Freedom in the world 2020*. Washington, DC: Freedom House.

Fukuyama, F. (1992). *The end of history and the last man*. New York: The Free Press.

Hegel, G. W. F. (2011). *Lectures on the philosophy of history*. Aalten, Netherlands: WordBridge Publishing.

Huntington, S. P. (2011). *The clash of civilizations and the remaking of the world order*. New York: Simon & Schuster.

Krastev, I., & Holmes, S. (2020). *The light that failed: Why the West is losing the fight for democracy*. New York: Pegasus Books.
Lowenstein, D. H. (1994). *Election law: Cases and materials*. Durham, NC: Carolina Academic Press.
Marx, K., & Engels, F. (2014). *The communist manifesto*. Moscow, Russia: International Publisher.
Schultz, D. A. (2019). Democracy and constitutional law: A preliminary political science perspective. In B. Kantaria (ed.), *Constitutionalism: Achievements and challenges*. Tbilisi, Georgia: Caucasus International University.

2
DEMOCRATIC THEORY AND ELECTION LAW

David Schultz

Introduction

Election law is the jurisprudence that puts constitutional democratic principles into action. Election laws are the rules in a country that determine who gets to vote and how, how campaigns are financed, the rights of political parties and interest groups, who gets to run for office, how elections are conducted, who oversees or administers elections, and how to resolve disputes when there are disagreements about election outcomes or violations. All countries of the world have election rules or principles, whether in their constitutions or laws.

Election law is thus the body of law or collection of rules that dictate how campaigns and elections operate. A country's election laws are not neutral. Instead, they are guided by a collection of values or principles that help resolve critical questions when making election laws, administering elections, and indirectly how courts and other regulatory bodies or tribunals resolve election disputes. In countries that are not free, election law either favors one party, interest, or perhaps person, or possibly the rules are formally enacted but not substantively enforced. But in free societies, election law serves to put democratic values into practice, enabling the people to govern themselves through elections. Appropriate election law rules, if enacted and enforced, can help support and sustain democracies.

But to understand how election law enables democracy, two questions have to be addressed: 1) What are the values that define a democracy? and 2) do formal rules of democracy, such as the right to vote, promote democracy?

Defining Democracy

The concept "democracy" is very old, dating back to Plato and the ancient Greeks ("δημοκρα τια") who saw it as a rule by the masses (Pennock, 1979). More modern notions of democracy have labeled it a form of popular government where the people rule, either directly or indirectly, through their representatives based upon the principle of majority rule. Huntington declares the essence of democracy as one in which representatives are chosen by the people in fair, honest, and competitive elections (Huntington, 1991, 7).

Democracy is also an open concept with its own history. If democracy originally meant direct rule by people, as its first wave according to Dahl (1989), it has gone through additional

DOI: 10.4324/9780429401800-2

phases since then, including the transition from direct to representational democracy. Moreover, the exact values that democracy represents also have changed such that they may now include a cluster that includes voting equality, effective participation, enlightened understanding, control of the agenda, and inclusion (Dahl, 1956). Dahl's criteria are similar to what other democratic theorists have described the requisites or values central to describing the purpose of a democracy as including general discussions of democratic theories and criteria used to evaluate regimes (Pennock, 1979; Sartori, 1987). Additionally, the concept of democracy, at least modern conceptions of it starting in the seventeenth century, has also been interconnected with the concepts of constitutionalism and liberalism.

Constitutions and constitutionalism are ancient concepts. They are also open concepts (Goldstein & Schultz, 2015). By that, like many other concepts, they have both a fixed and open meaning, with their exact notion carrying with them their own history. While the usage of the term πολιτεία goes back to ancient Greece, what the term actually means has changed over time. For the ancient Greeks, πολιτεία, politeia, or constitution referred not just to the formal institutions of the government, but also to the character or spirit of a nation. For Aristotle and many of the other ancients, governments could be typologized into several forms such as democracy, aristocracy, and monarchy, along with their perversions or corruptions. A constitution simply meant what constituted a state. With Montesquieu (1949, 1973), a constitution appeared more to refer to a broader spirit of a nation, not simply the formal institutions of government. Constitutions had a broader reference to the entire political and cultural apparatus that defined a state. Even Hegel seemed to view a constitution in that way (Schultz, 1990).

This classical notion of constitutions and constitutionalism included two views. One, as noted, believed that constitutions were more than simply about the governmental apparatus or rules that defined the formal institutions of the state. The second view held that a constitution did not have to be democratic. Constitutions could constitute states that were clearly anti-democratic. Modern conceptions of constitutionalism have associated the term with democracy; however, the two terms are not synonymous (Dworkin, 1995; Habermas, 2001; McHugh, 2002). According to the Comparative Constitutions Project (n.d.), all states in the world, except for Yemen, have a constitution. An initial examination of these 190 constitutions with Freedom House rankings produces interesting result. Freedom House (2018) overall ranks countries as free, partially free, and not free. Using this classification, 85 countries are free, 57 partially free, and 48 not free. Having a constitution does not guarantee that a state is democratic. Something more is required.

While constitutionalism historically evolved with democracy, the two also evolved alongside a third concept – liberalism. "Liberalism" is often traced to John Locke (1986), and it represents a set of political values committed to the protection of individual rights, polities instituted on the basis of the consent of the governed, and a notion of a limited government (Pennock & Chapman, 1983; DeRuggiero, 1959; Ashcraft, 1986). Liberalism, especially as it evolved and developed in the writings of Jeremy Bentham, James and John Stuart Mill, and the philosophical radicals (Halèvy, 1955), added a new dimension to the concept of democracy. If democracy as it had thus far evolved before liberalism meant either unqualified majority rule or it was understood within a classical republican framework that prioritized equality over personal liberties, it now took on greater emphasis to respect minority rights.

The significance of the evolution of liberalism, alongside some versions of democracy and constitutionalism, produced a theory of democracy not committed to unqualified majority rule. It came to mean a more restrained form, perhaps one more consistent with the notions of constitutionalism that emphasized limits on the government, presumably to respect majority rule tempered by minority rights.

Liberal constitutional democracy evolved as a Western European concept. This is significant for several reasons. One, it is possible to distinguish liberal democracy from other forms that are more populist and do not include respect for minority or individual rights. Political leaders such as Victor Orban in Hungary have argued for "illiberal democracy," or a conception of government that allows for popular rule, but not necessarily support for individual or minority rights. Second, it is possible that the concept of democracy might have more variegated meanings or, conversely, that it might be a concept in its liberal form that is only suitable or applicable to certain countries in the world. By that, efforts to explain the reason that democracy has not flourished or done well in Africa, for example, might be rooted in the reality that democracy is more than simply formal institutions or government (Schultz, 2019a). Instead, as a host of scholars have contended, there may be cultural, economic, and social pre- or co-requisites for democracies to form. By that, a real democracy needs other institutions and values in order for it to be sustained (Adagbabiri, 2015; Alexander, 2007; Almond & Verba, 1993; Ceaser, 1993; Huntington, 1956; Huntington, 1984; Lipset, 1959, 1960; Needler, 1968; Neubauer, 1967). For example, there is little correlation between having a formal constitution and being a free society, and there is also little evidence that mere textual recitation or more individual rights in a constitution alone indicate that a country is more free or democratic (Schultz, 2019b). Formal constitutional provisions are only part of a package of requisites for democracy.

Defining Democracy's Values

Acknowledging the limits of formalism and the possible biases in what constitutes a democracy, the following questions arise: 1) What does this form of government mean? and 2) how is election law related to it? As noted above, Robert Dahl (1989) argues that democracy embodies the values of voting equality, effective participation, enlightened understanding, control of the agenda, and inclusion.

Theorists generally agree that democracy supports the idea of some sort of equality (Pennock; Sartori, 58–9, 342–4). Now, there are significant debates regarding what type of equality is demanded of a democratic society. Dahl himself argues for both a procedural or formal sense of equality before the law, as well as substantive equality in terms of economic resources (Dahl, 1956, 1971, 1976, 1989, 83). Others have also described various meanings of equality as essential to democracy (Locke, 1996, 4, 54, 123; Rousseau, 1977, 96; Mill, 1956, 48–50; Dworkin, 1978). Theorists such as John Rawls have rendered similar claims, contending that a liberal democracy adhering to his two principles of justice – equal liberty for all consistent with like liberty for others, and the structuring of economic inequalities, so that they are of benefit to the least advantaged representative person in society – demand something approaching an equality both in terms of economic conditions and equality before the law (Rawls, 1971, 1993). A more general discussion of the role of equality in modern western political thought can be found in Rawls (2007).

With Dahl, the concept of equality entails two important concepts. The first is the notion of individual moral autonomy (Dahl, 1989, 97). For many democratic theorists, democracy begins with the idea of individual liberty or freedom. For John Locke, the idea that government derives its justification from a social contract and consent of the people is a powerful metaphor to enabling a theory about limited government. The government derives its just ends (as it states in the American Declaration of Independence) from the people. Other theorists, such as Jean-Jacques Rousseau and Immanuel Kant, echo similar thoughts. For Rousseau, the concept that freedom resides in conforming to the general will is an important one. It is here, where the people get to make the laws that will govern them, that one gets a sense of Rousseauian democracy (Rousseau, 1973). For Kant, Rawls, and Dworkin, the very notion of autonomy – living according to rules that one has legislated for herself – is the purist notion of what a democracy is (Kant, 1991, 1978; Rawls, 1971, 252–4; Dworkin, 1978). It is self-rule. It is where the people, as French political theorist Jean Bodin stated, are sovereign (2003). Democracies are where the people hold political power, either directly or indirectly, and generally, at least in the United States, are viewed as the ultimate source of authority.

Thus, for a democracy, personal autonomy or liberty of some fashion is required. That autonomy is also one that is shared equally. As Jeremy Bentham and other nineteenth-century philosophers would declare, each person should count as one and not more than one (Bentham, 1948; Halévy, 1955, 139, 147). Democracies mean that each person has an equal voice, and the equal freedom to act upon that voice. Thus, Rawls may be correct in describing the first principle of justice as perhaps also the first rule of a democracy, namely that each person is entitled to "the most extensive basic liberty compatible with similar liberty for others" (Rawls, 1971, 60). Later in his 2007 book, *Political Liberalism*, he refines this statement to declare that "each person has an equal claim to a fully adequate scheme of equal basic rights and liberties" (Rawls, 2007, 5). In reformulating the way that he does in his latter book, Rawls makes it clear that democracy embraces both concepts of equality or equal voice and the personal liberty to act on this voice.

But exactly what the liberty and equality extend to is a matter of contention. Moreover, how deep that equal voice is, also remains a matter of dispute in a democracy. At the very least, it appears to extend to formal voting, with each person given the same opportunity to cast a vote for a candidate or issue of her choice. Yet, even in declaring this proposition, many questions remain. Who is allowed to vote, over what matter, and when? Is voting for representatives the sum total of what equality is about, or is something else required? All of these are important questions, perhaps partially answered by the other criteria or values that Dahl describes.

The second criteria or value of a democracy is effective participation. What does effective participation mean? Here, Dahl describes this requirement as giving citizens a way to express their views on the final outcome of a choice, including time to place questions on the agenda and the chance to opt for one outcome over another. It also includes giving voters choice at decisive points in the decision-making process (Dahl, 1989, 109). Of course, it would be meaningless to say that one has effective participation in making choices, if the critical choices are already made before one gets to act. If the agenda has already been set, for example, or if items are kept off the agenda, the range of potential choices is already narrowed (Bachrach & Baratz, 1962, 947; Schattschneider, 1960, 20–47). Effective participation means a voice both over a range of issues that are important, as well as temporally early and late enough in the decision-making process, to ensure that the choices are meaningful and can really affect outcomes.

A third value that Dahl describes as essential for a democracy is enlightened understanding (1989, 111–2). It would be naive to say that one has a right to vote or make choices, but that one has no right to gather the information necessary to make informed choices. At some point along the way, there is a belief or need for citizens to gather information, talk to others, share ideas, or even work together if the idea of effective participation is to mean anything. James Madison would claim in *Federalist* 47 and 49 that "all government rests on opinion" (Hamilton, Madison & Jay, 1937, 329). The people have a right to form opinions about public matters. To do so requires that the people know something, that they gather information, and that they are informed. It is the concept that the people can rule, but only if they have access to an education that makes it possible for them to be informed. John Stuart Mill also believed in the importance of education as critical to self-governance, with his *On Liberty* often seen as the classic defense of freedom of thought and expression in the pursuit of truth.

Enlightened understanding also refers to the idea that political choices are more than simply raw expressions of preferences. Yes, political scientists will often describe voting choices as based on self-interest or pure economics – "Are you better off now than four years ago?". But even to be guided by self-interest requires knowledge of preferences and of how different options better serve them. John Stuart Mill emphasized the role that political participation can play in educating people (Mill, 1951, 252–5; Thompson, 1979, 137–41). The process of being exposed to other people and ideas educates one, hopefully producing a more refined set of choices that may transcend raw self-interest. Civic engagement builds social capital and trust, facilitating cooperation (Putnam, 2001). Collective action or decision-making is educative. Alexis de Tocqueville (1988), in *Democracy in America*, described the people of the United States as acting from self-interest rightly understood (De Tocqueville, 525). It was an enlightened self-interest that made America work because service on juries or participation in voluntary associations educated individuals to how to make better choices (De Tocqueville, 189–95).

What the concept of enlightened understanding is about then, on one level, is education and information-gathering. It is amassing the necessary information to make good political choices. But it is also about the marketplace of ideas. It is the concept that, in a free society, no one is the final arbiter of truth and that, as John Stuart Mill described it in *On Liberty*, the clash of competing ideas tests competing proposals, producing relevant and important information needed to make choices and yield the truth (Mill, 104–111). Democracy means then that no one is the final imprimatur of truth and that all opinions and diversity of thought should be tolerated. Democracy is part of a process or a decision-making system to locate and define the truth (Locke, 1983; Marshall, 2006; Habermas, 1991).

The fourth requisite, according to Dahl, for a democracy is control of the agenda (1989, 112–4). This value has already been spoken of above. Control of the agenda means that the people get to decide what will be decided. They get to make the choices over who the elected leaders are and, with that, what are the major issues and perhaps ideas that they want pursued in furtherance of their concept of the good. The idea of "We the people" or popular sovereignty is the idea that power belongs to the people. This point is captured by Jefferson's and the Declaration of Independence's idea in the second paragraph that the people have a right to form and disband governments ("Governments are instituted among Men, deriving their just powers from the consent of the governed"), which was appropriated from John Locke's theory of the social contract. If the people have a right to create their own government based on consent, they then have the right to decide the direction of the government. They get to decide for themselves what the government will do.

Buried within this idea of control of the agenda is the concept of majority rule. Again, this idea seems to come from John Locke (Locke, 1996, 140; Kendall, 1965). But majority rule suggests that the decision-making system that defines the agenda is also determined by the majority. This speaks to the notion that there has to be some mechanism of deciding what to do when everyone does not agree. While in the initial forming of the social contract or political society, Locke emphasizes unanimous consent as the precondition for membership. Once it is in operation, he relies both upon the concept of tacit consent and majority rule to continue to enforce the rules and laws (Pateman, 1988; Mills, 1999). Majority rule recognizes the reality that not everyone agrees and that there will be disagreement. What does one do when disagreement exists? Lacking a better mechanism, whatever 50% + 1 of the population wants seems to be the answer.

But, even with Locke, majoritarian control of the agenda at all critical stages of the decision-making process does not mean that the majority gets its way over all matters. For Locke, political society is instituted to protect certain natural rights of life, liberty, and estate (Locke, *Second*

Treatise, 87). These natural rights serve as a limit on governmental power, along with the terms of the original contract. Thus, majority rule is tempered by respect for minority rights. Majority rule means that they may not ever vote to limit the rights of the minority. This principle will be discussed latter on as an important qualification upon the American conception of democracy.

Another qualification imposed upon the control of the agenda is the idea of a representative government. Dahl describes how the movement from a small face-to-face direct democracy to a representative democracy was the second transformation in democratic theory (Dahl, 1989, 28). As communities grew, it no longer became practical for everyone to huddle in the town square and deliberate upon the issues (Dahl & Tufte, 1973). John Stuart Mill makes a similar argument in *Considerations on Representative Government*:

> From these accumulated considerations it is evident that the only government which can fully satisfy all the exigencies of the social state is one in which the whole people participate; that any participation, even in the smallest public function, is useful; that the participation should everywhere be as great as the general degree of improvement of the community will allow; and that nothing less can be ultimately desirable than the admission of all to a share in the sovereign power of the state. But since all cannot, in a community exceeding a single small town, participate personally in any but some very minor portions of the public business, it follows that the ideal type of a perfect government must be representative.
>
> *(Mill, 1951, 291–2)*

The ideal, of course, would be a government in which all of us participate. But, for all practical purposes, that is not possible. Time alone prevents all from deliberating or speaking on the issues of the day. Instead, some type of mechanism is needed in larger communities to make decisions – thus elections for representatives. Joseph Schumpeter (2015, 269–73) describes democracy as a process in which elites compete for the votes of citizens, seeking the authority to make decisions for them.[1] Representative government alters the concept of control of the agenda to mean, primarily, the voting for individuals who will then make policy or choices for the people. Thus, an important value of agenda control is enabling free and fair elections that make such a process possible. Of course, in some situations, such as with ballot propositions that include initiatives and referendums, direct democracy is possible. Conversely, in the age of the internet, maybe an electronic commonwealth is also possible (Abramson, Arterton, & Orren, 1990). Many states and communities do allow the public directly to vote on matters ranging from taxes to the amending of a constitution. All of these types of votes are a form of direct democracy and, in many cases, especially with initiatives that perhaps allow the people to place propositions on the ballot, this is clear control of the agenda. For reasons to be described later, however, ballot initiatives may only offer the illusion of direct democracy and majority control of the agenda.

A final value or criteria for a polyarchy, according to Dahl, is the principle of inclusion (Dahl, 1989, 119–21). The principle of inclusion asks who gets to have a voice in the affairs of the government and what constitutes a voice. Begin first with who gets to speak. One answer is to say that the right to speak is limited to citizens of a country or of a specific jurisdiction. This seems to make sense. A privilege of citizenship is the right to participate and make decisions for the community. After all, we do not want perhaps foreigners or worse, enemies, making decisions for us. The parallel is to a club. A club is a voluntary association and only those who are members should presumably be allowed to vote or make decisions for the club. A political society is similar to a large club and perhaps the same rule should apply. Thus, perhaps only those who are citizens should be allowed to have a voice. Yet, even this principle is highly contestable. For many years democratic states precluded women from voting; currently many bar those convicted of certain crimes from voting; most states prevent non-citizens from voting and other political activities; and minimum age for suffrage or running for office is the norm.

Another way to approach the question of who is included in terms of being allowed a voice (besides voting) is to say that all persons are entitled to speak. Why is this a critical distinction? To say that only citizens get a voice may deny a role to critical speakers in a democracy. Do political parties get a voice? How about interest groups or unions or corporations? None of them are citizens but, in some cases, they are persons for the purpose of being involved in campaigns and elections. But, even if not persons, should they be allowed to speak?

The other issue that complicates the matter on who gets to speak or who is included is to ask what does one do when included or what does it mean to have a voice or speak. Voting is, perhaps, the most important or common answer when discussing what it means to have a voice. But it is not the only form of voice that exists. A voice might also include simply talking and urging others to vote or take a particular political position. But voice or inclusion in the political system could include a range of activities that include attending rallies, volunteering for a candidate, raising money for a candidate or cause, and giving money to support a candidate or a cause (Verba & Nie, 1972; Rosenstone & Hansen, 2002). In asking whom should be included in the political process, it may also be critical to ask how they are included.

Let's return to the idea of only a citizen being allowed to have a voice. Assume we limit voting to citizens. Should non-citizens be denied the right to volunteer on a campaign, attend a political rally, or engage in other activities such as give money? Should non-citizens be barred from voting and giving money to candidates for federal office, even if nothing prevents them from volunteering or engaging in other political activities? How or why is this line drawn? Maybe the idea is that only citizens should directly be able to influence elections and giving money and voting count as direct influence. Or perhaps the reason is that there is a general principle – preventing foreign influence on elections – and, for good or bad, the line is drawn at voting and money.

Now think about it yet another way, pondering the claim that only biological persons should be given a voice in politics. Does that mean, as suggested earlier, that political parties, interest groups, corporations, and unions should be barred from all types of activities? Clearly, they cannot vote. But should they also be prevented from airing their views on important political matters? Should they be given the right to contribute or expend money for political purposes? Moreover, should that right extend both directly to giving to candidates or only indirectly? Or should it only extend, if at all, to general issues of public concern? All of these questions raise critical questions about free speech, rights of organizations, and what types of activities they should be allowed to engage in. Inclusion in the political process or the polity is thus not an easy question to define or summarize.

The point of the above discussion is that Robert Dahl's five values are perhaps not the sum of those essential to defining requisites for a democracy. One might argue that concepts such as federalism are important. By that, some would contend that political power needs to be divided up into some types of units along geographic regions. While some countries are not federal, but unitary, in design, federalism in large countries might make sense in terms of how it maximizes opportunities for individuals to secure the five values. Breaking a large polity up into smaller units or jurisdictions makes it easier for citizens to have a meaningful voice or feel like they are included or have control over the agenda. Additionally, perhaps another critical democratic value is adherence to the rule of law (Schultz, 2008; Dyzenhaus, 2006). Setting principled maxims for how controversies are to be handled – such as adhering to Aristotle's principle that equals are treated equally or likes treated alike – is important. Confining government discretion is important, and it also perhaps suggests that some concept of limited government and constitutionalism may be a requisite or value of a democracy.

Finally, for many, especially the pluralist writers of the 1950s such as David Truman and Seymour Martin Lipset (1960), diversity in values and allegiances are important to the protection of freedom. Still others would assert that democracy needs a robust civil society to serve as a buffer on the economy and the polity (Putnam, 2001; Putnam, Leonardi, & Nanetti, 1993; Dahl, 1961, 1968, 138–66, 1989, 262–4; Almond & Verba, 1965). This is a political culture, perhaps, that encapsulates all of the values listed above or maybe it is a culture distinct from these values – a culture that sustains or respects the above values. The point is that there may be other values needed to make democracy work, and it is also not clear what Dahl's five criteria or values always mean in practice.

But, of course, there are two other points to think about when discussing the values of a democracy. One is that values do not exist in isolation, but are perhaps in tension with one another (Pennock, 16–17). Second, the values are given meaning by the institutions that support them. Values such as effective participation and control of the agenda, for example, may come into conflict. Giving all the millions of people or voters in democracies such as the United States, France, or India control of the agenda or a meaningful voice may be impractical. Thus, the need to do tradeoffs and conclude that participation may need to be limited in some situations or confined to perhaps simply to representatives. Or another way to think about it is that tradeoffs may need to be made for different participants or activities. In the United States in *Burson v. Freeman*, 504 US 191 (1992), the Supreme Court had to confront clashing First Amendment rights. In one instance, there was the right to vote and, in the other, the right of free expression. Here the issue was a law the prohibited political campaigning within 100 feet of a voting booth. This ban was instituted in order to prevent voter intimidation at the polls. The court upheld the law, noting that there was a tradeoff that had to be effected here between contending rights.

Burson highlights the problem for democratic theory and then election law. Tradeoffs need to be made, and values cannot be evaluated in isolation from one another. One task of a democratic theory and of election law is to effect and define the tradeoffs. It is to decide who gets to participate or have a voice in what and for what purposes. It is to decide what it means to have free and fair elections viewed in the context of the rights of others to advocate their positions. It is the tradeoff or relationship between the use of one's economic resources and how they are converted into political influence.

Election Law and Democracy

Democracy is about values, but it is also about a set of institutions and practices that enable democratic values. For Dahl, each of the five criteria that he articulates comes with specific institutions that must be in operation (Dahl, 1989, 222). To achieve voting equality, Dahl stipulates that there needs to be elected officials and free and fair elections. Enlightened understanding requires freedom of expression, alternative information, and associational autonomy. Dahl's list of institutions run the range from a free press, voting systems, and elected officials to rights to run for office. Dahl's list is not exhaustive and, in many ways, what he considers to be institutions is strange. Saying a "right to run for office" is an institution is odd. Perhaps the right to run for office is a value effected be it primary or secondary effected to controlling the agenda or securing effective participation. Or perhaps something like the right to run for office is a measure or part of an index that measures inclusion or participation. This is where election law comes in.

Election law are the rules that enable values for a regime to be called a democracy. Election law is the connective tissue, so to speak, linking values and theories to institutions. Election laws are the rules that tell us how the game of democracy is played. It is the job of policy-makers and the courts to create rules for democracy and define the tradeoffs that must be made. Ultimately, though, the people are the judge of how well the institutions work.

What specific clauses or rules of election law best promote democracy? Empirically, one can partially test this question. The Comparative Constitutions Project has examined and classified constitutional clauses for all states of the world, producing 665 variables. Among those clauses are many that address election law type issues, such as the right to vote, rights of political parties, protection for free elections, and many other types of provisions generally associated with democracies. This database has been merged with the most recent Freedom House classification of regimes. National data on all these clauses allows for empirical testing: What specific type of constitutional clauses regarding election law issues promote or enable democracy? Being able to examine this question from an empirical political science perspective would enhance legal research into how election laws impact democracy and, perhaps, affect campaigns and elections and influence political participation, among other things.

In order to perform this empirical testing, three tasks were performed. First, Freedom House classifies states across the world as free, partially free, and not free. States designated as "free" could be considered as a form of a democracy. The most recent Freedom House regime classification was merged with the Comparative Constitutions Project data set. Second, since democracies are associated with rights, regimes classification was examined in conjunction with the number of rights found in a state's constitution. Third, for each of Dahl's five values, a specific variable from the Comparative Constitutions Project was used to operationalize it. Thus, voting equality was tested with whether there was a constitutional clause guaranteeing free elections (variable 445); effective participation with whether there was a clause providing for universal franchise (variable 430); enlightened understanding with a clause protecting freedom of expression (variable 611); control of the agenda with whether the people had a right to vote for the chief executive of the country (variable 89, answer number 2); and inclusion with whether the constitution provided for a right to form political parties (variable 414). It is possible that other variables might also be good or better ones to operationalize Dahl's variables. However, for the purposes of this initial study, these are the five that were selected. It is also possible that constitutional clauses are not an adequate way to measure constitutional values or criteria.

Examination of these constitutional clauses addressing election issues in relation to regime classification is suggestive of the type of research that could or should be done to see which types of provisions best promote democracies. Of course, what this database does not include are sub-constitutional election laws or statutes that are important to the regulation of campaigns and elections. Given these limitations, what do we know?

First, Table 2.1 averages out the number of rights per regime type. Surprisingly, partially free and not free regimes have on average more rights than free states.

Table 2.1 Average Number of Rights per Regime Type

Free	47.11
Partially Free	56.05
Not Free	48.06

Source: Comparative Constitutions Project (2016, April 8). *Constitution rankings*. Retrieved May 13, 2019, from http://comparativeconstitutionsproject.org/ccp-rankings/.

This point is reinforced when correlating the number of rights with the PR Freedom House regime ranking produces a r^2 of 0.025. While somewhat confusing because the Freedom House scale indicates countries are less free the higher their number on a scale of one to seven, the r^2 is essentially flat (or correcting for coding errors, it is really -0.025). Similarly, the correlation between the CL ranking and number of rights listed in a constitution is 0.028 (-0.028), again essentially flat. Third, doing a correlation between how a state is ranked as free, partially free, and not free and the number of rights listed in the constitution produces a 0.05 (-0.05) r^2. Finally, in a correlation between the number of rights listed in a constitution and the overall aggregate score (0–100, with a higher number being freer), the r^2 is -0.03. Therefore, no matter how analyzed, there is no correlation between the number of rights prescribed in a state's constitution and how free (democratic) it is.

Turning more specifically to election law type of clauses, consider three variables: 1) Does the constitution guarantee a universal right to vote?; 2) does the constitution guarantee a right for political parties to exist?; and 3) does the constitution guarantee free elections. Tables 2.2 and 2.3 provide a breakdown, by regime type, of the number and then percentage of state constitutions that affirmatively provide for each of these protections.

Many of the constitutions are silent on issues such as voting or party rights and fair elections. Among democracies, the United States is one such example. For many regimes either constitutional court decisions or laws might address these topics. But, nonetheless, it is still interesting to note little connection between regime type and constitutional clauses on election matters generally connected to democracies. For example, when it comes to guarantees of free expression or elections, non-free states are more likely to provide for constitutional protections. In everything, partially and non-free states do better constitutionally than do free regimes across the board. More specifically, when regime type and Dahl's criteria of equality, effective participation, and inclusion were tested with the chosen constitutional variables, the correlations were -0.22, -0.04, and 0.01 respectively. Meaning that there is effectively no connection. (Enlightened understanding and control of agenda could not be correlated with regime type because an insufficient number of constitutional clauses specifically address these issues.)

A more complete or thorough analysis of constitutional clauses could and should be done. But looking simply at these five major ones speaks to the limits of formal constitutional clauses when it comes to promoting democracies or democratic elections. This is not refutation that election laws or rules are immaterial to promoting democracy – statutory provisions and con-

Table 2.2 Regime Type and Constitutional Clauses Promoting Democracy

		Dahl's Five Criteria				
		Effective Participation	*Inclusion*	*Voting Equality*	*Enlightened Understanding*	*Control Agenda*
Regime Type	*Number*	*Vote*	*Parties*	*Free Elections*	*Express*	*Elect Leader*
Free	86	36	27	46	58	26
Partially Free	56	31	33	37	43	31
Not Free	49	25	21	35	35	23

Source: Freedom House (2018). *Freedom in the world 2018.* Retrieved May 13, 2019 from https://freedomhouse.org/report/freedom-world-2018-table-country-scores.

Table 2.3 Regime Type and Constitutional Clauses Promoting Democracy: Percentages

		Dahl's Five Criteria				
		Effective Participation	*Inclusion*	*Voting Equality*	*Enlightened Understanding*	*Control Agenda*
Regime Type	*Number*	*Vote*	*Parties*	*Free Elections*	*Express*	*Elect Leader*
Free	86	41.90%	31.40%	53.50%	58.10%	30.20%
Partially Free	56	55.40%	58.90%	66.10%	76.80%	55.40%
Not Free	49	51%	42.90%	71.40%	71.40%	46.90%

Source: Freedom House (2018). *Freedom in the world 2018.* Retrieved May 13, 2019 from https://freedomhouse.org/report/freedom-world-2018-table-country-scores.

stitutional court decisions do perhaps matter. But one needs also to understand the extent to which constitutional clauses, constitutional court decisions, and election laws are substantively followed and why, and not look simply to formalism to determine how election laws are connected to democracy. As noted earlier, there may be other economic, political, and social pre- or co-requisites working in conjunction with election law rules that impact, influence, or link all of them to democracy.

Conclusion

Presumably, election laws matter both in terms of how campaigns and elections are run, both also in terms of the type of political regimes that they produce. This chapter has focused mainly on how constitutional clauses regarding election law advance democracy. The results suggest that mere constitutional clauses alone are not strongly determinative of what constitutes a democratic regime. This is not to say that constitutions have no impact on democracy, but clearly more research is needed to explore the way election laws promote specific regimes, including democracy. The results here suggest, perhaps, inadequacies in how or what democracies are and which states should be so classified, how to operationalize democracy from a constitutional perspective, and the need to examine the impact of constitutional court, statutory provisions, and political culture or other values when it comes to explaining how and whether campaigns and elections promote democracy.

Note

1 *See also:* Peter Bachrach, *The Theory of Democratic Elitism: A Critique* (Boston: Little, Brown & Company, 1967) for criticism of this democratic revisionism or elite-driven model of politics.

References

Abramson, J. B., Arterton, F. C., & Orren, G. R. (1990). *The electronic commonwealth: The impact of new media technologies on democratic politics*. New York: Basic Books.

Adagbabiri, M. (2015). Constitutionalism and democracy: A critical perspective. *International Journal of Humanities and Social Science, 5*(12), 108–114. Retrieved from http://www.ijhssnet.com/journals/Vol_5_No_12_December_2015/13.pdf

Alexander, L. (2007). Constitutionalism and democracy: Understanding the relation. Legal Studies Research Paper Series. Research paper No. 07–121.
Ashcraft, R. (1986). *Revolutionary politics and Locke's Two Treatises of Government*. Princeton, NJ: Princeton University Press.
Bachrach, P., & Baratz, M. S. (1962). Two faces of power. *American Political Science Review*, *56*(4), 947–952. doi: 10.2307/1952796
Bentham, J. (1948). *An introduction to the principles of morals and legislation*. New York: Hafner Publishing.
Bodin, J. (2003). *On sovereignty: Four chapters from the six books of the commonwealth* (trans. J. Franklin). New York: Cambridge University Press.
Burson v. Freeman. (1992). 504 U.S. 191.
Ceaser, J. W. (1993). Reconstructing political science. In S. L. Elkin & K. E. Soltan (Eds.), *A new constitutionalism: Designing political institutions for a good society*. Chicago, IL: University of Chicago Press.
Dahl, R. A. (1956). *A preface to democracy theory*. Chicago, IL: University of Chicago Press.
Dahl, R. A. (1971). *Polyarchy: Participation and opposition*. New Haven, CT: Yale University Press.
Dahl, R. A. (1976). *Democracy in the United States: Promise and performance*. New Haven: Yale University Press.
Dahl, R. A. (1989). *Democracy and its critics*. New Haven, CT: Yale University Press.
Dahl, R. A., & Tufte, E. R. (1973). *Size and democracy*. Stanford, CA: Stanford University Press.
De Ruggiero, G. (1959). *The history of European liberalism*. Boston, MA: Beacon Press.
De Tocqueville, A. (1988). *Democracy in America* (trans. G. Lawrence). New York: Perennial Library.
Dworkin, R. (1978). *Taking rights seriously*. Cambridge, MA: Harvard University Press.
Dworkin, R. (1995). Constitutionalism and democracy: Political theory and the American Constitution. *The European Journal of Philosophy*, *3*(1), 2–11. Retrieved from http://www.jstor.org/stable/194230
Dyzenhaus, D. (2006). *The constitution of law: Legality in a time of emergency*. New York: Cambridge University Press.
Freedom House. (2018). Freedom in the world 2018. Retrieved May 13, 2019 from https://freedomhouse.org/report/freedom-world-2018-table-country-scores
Goldstein, L. J., & Schultz, D. (2015). *Conceptual tension: Essays on kinship, politics, and individualism*. Lanham, MD: Lexington Books.
Habermas, J. (1991). *The structural transformation of the public sphere: An inquiry into a category of bourgeois society*. Cambridge, MA: MIT Press.
Habermas, J. (2001). Constitutional democracy: A paradoxical union of contradictory principles? *Political Theory*, *29*(6), 766–781. doi: 10.1177/0090591701029006002
Halèvy, E. (1955). *The growth of philosophic radicalism*. Boston, MA: The Beacon Press.
Hamilton, A., Madison, J., & Jay, J. (1937). *The federalist*. New York: Modern Library.
Huntington, S. P. (1956). Civilian control and the constitution. *American Political Science Review*, *50*(3), 676–699. doi: 10.2307/1951551
Huntington, S. P. (1984). Will more countries become democratic? *Political Science Review*, *99*(2), 193–199. doi: 10.2307/2150402
Huntington, S. P. (1991). *The third wave: Democratization in the late twentieth century*. Norman, OK: University of Oklahoma Press.
Kant, I. (1969). *Foundations of the metaphysics of morals* (trans. L. W. Beck). Indianapolis, IN: Bobbs-Merrill Publishing.
Kant, I. (1978). Foundation of the metaphysics of morals. In R. P. Wolff (Ed.), Indianapolis, IN: Bobbs-Merrill Publishing.
Kant, I. (1991). *The metaphysics of morals* (trans. M. J. Gregor). Cambridge: Cambridge University Press.
Kendall, W. (1965). *John Locke and the doctrine of majority-rule*. Urbana, IL: University of Illinois Press.
Lipset, S. M. (1959). Some social requisites of democracy: Economic development and political legitimacy. *The American Political Science Review*, *53*(1), 69–105. Retrieved from https://scholar.harvard.edu/files/levitsky/files/lipset_1959.pdf
Lipset, S. M. (1960). *Political man: The social basis of politics*. Garden City; NY: Anchor Books.
Locke, J. (1996). *Two treatises of government*. New York: Cambridge University Press.
Marshall, J. (2006). *John Locke, toleration and early enlightenment culture*. New York: Cambridge University Press.
McHugh, J. T. (2002). *Comparative constitutional traditions*. New York: Peter Lang Publishing.
Mill, J. S. (1951). *Representative government in utilitarianism, liberty, and representative government*. New York: E.P. Dutton & Company, Inc.
Mills, C. W. (1999). *The racial contract*. Ithaca, NY: Cornell University Press.

Montesquieu, B. D. (1949). *The spirit of the laws* (trans. T. Nugent). New York: Hafner Press.
Montesquieu, B. D. (1973). *Persian letters*. New York: Penguin.
Needler, M. C. (1968). Political development and socioeconomic development: The case of Latin America. *The American Political Science Review, 62*(3), 889–897. doi: 10.2307/1953438
Neubauer, D. E. (1967). Some conditions of democracy. *The American Political Science Review, 61*(4), 1002–1009. doi: 10.2307/1953402
Pateman, C. (1988). *The sexual contract*. Stanford, CA: Stanford University Press.
Pennock, J. R. (1979). *Democratic political theory*. Princeton, NJ: Princeton University Press.
Pennock, J. R., & Chapman, J. W. (1983). *Liberal democracy*. New York: New York University Press.
Putnam, R. (2001). *Bowling alone, the collapse and revival of American community*. New York: Simon & Schuster.
Putnam, R., Leonardi, R., & Nanetti, R. (1993). *Making democracy work: Civic traditions in modern Italy*. Princeton, NJ: Princeton University Press.
Rawls, J. (1971). *A theory of justice*. Cambridge, MA: Harvard University Press.
Rawls, J. (1993). *Political liberalism*. New York: Columbia University Press.
Rawls, J. (2007). *Lectures on the history of political philosophy*. Cambridge, MA: Belknap Press.
Rosenstone, S. J., & Hansen, J. M. (2002). *Mobilization, participation, and democracy in America*. New York: Pearson.
Rousseau, J. J. (1977). *The social contract*. New York: Penguin.
Sartori, G. S. (1987). *The theory of democracy revisited, 2 volumes*. Chatham, NJ: Chatham House Publishers.
Schattschneider, E. E. (1960). *The semi-sovereign people*. New York: Holt, Rinehart & Winston.
Schultz, D. (1990). Hegel's constitutionalism. *4 COMMONWEALTH, 26*, 26–38.
Schultz, D. (2008). Democracy on trial: Terrorism, crime, and national security policy in a post 9–11 world. *Golden Gate Law Review, 38*. Retrieved from http://works.bepress.com/david_schultz/11/
Schultz, D. A. (2019a). Democracy and constitutional law: A preliminary political science perspective. Forthcoming in B. Kantaria (Ed.), *Constitutionalism: Achievements and challenges*. Tbilisi, Georgia: Caucasus International University.
Schultz, D. A. (2019b). Reflections on the prospects for democracy in Africa and on the impediments to that happening. Forthcoming *Development Management*.
Schumpeter, J. (2015). *Capitalism, socialism and democracy*. New York: Routledge.
Thompson, D. F. (1979). *John Stuart Mill and representative government*. Princeton, NJ: Princeton University Press.
Verba, S., & Norman, H. N. (1972). *Participation in America: Political democracy and social equality*. New York: Harper & Row.

3

REPRESENTATIVE GOVERNMENT AND ELECTIONS

Mark E. Rush

Introduction: Representative Government and Elections in the Twenty-First Century

The study of elections, democracy, and representative government is characterized by tension and contradiction among values and aspirations that would seem to be complimentary. But, in fact, they frequently clash with or at least constrain one another. On the one hand, we aspire to conduct free and fair elections that provide voters with meaningful choices on election day. On the other, to ensure the "fair and effective representation" (*Reynolds v. Sims*, 1964) of more than just a majority of a society's voters, interests, and constituencies, we must place constraints on the workings of elections, so that they generate governments that are truly representative of a society's diversity and responsive to the popular will. Accordingly, what might seem to be as simple and straightforward a notion as what Lincoln described at Gettysburg as "government of the people, by the people, for the people" becomes remarkably complex and contentious.

It is difficult to ascertain "the will of the people" from election results because there are countless formulas used to count votes and allocate them into legislative seats (Gallagher, 1992). Each bears an implicit or even explicit algorithmic bias that can alter the outcome or, at least, the "meaning" of an election. For example, votes may be channeled to a binary outcome if they are cast in a simple referendum. They also may be cast in a detailed rank-ordering in an election using the single transferable vote. A territory may be divided up into election districts or serve simply as one large constituency. Each district may be represented by only one legislator or a slate of legislators. Depending on the purpose of the vote, the number of choices, how the votes are aggregated and translated into legislative seats, and the manner in which votes are counted, "the will of the people" can change drastically.

Scholars continue to debate which electoral system is the fairest, most accurate, or simply the best means of choosing a government (Amy, 2002). Regardless of the evidence collected in support of one system or another, if critics believe that their interests would be better served under another electoral arrangement, they will allege that the system is a "gerrymander" insofar as it favors some interests at the expense of others. Accordingly, scholars continue to debate what fair representation should entail for majorities and minorities. Even if a legislature is a perfect microcosm of the society that elected it, minority groups may still feel aggrieved if they have no say in governing.

 DOI: 10.4324/9780429401800-3

These issues address the nature of representation and representative government and comprise the principal part of this chapter. In the conclusion, I turn to discuss how changes in the context in which elections are conducted affect our understanding of democracy and representation. These changes have resulted from technological advances, legal reforms, and, paradoxically, the democratization of politics and political power. Since the early twentieth century, American democracy has undergone an inexorable shift towards decentralization of control over elections and governmental processes (Rauch, 2016; Rauch & La Raza, 2019). What began as a movement to combat corruption and make government more transparent and responsive to the people has resulted in the exact opposite. Rauch argues that government is now more distant from and less responsive to the people and that political power is more private and less accountable (DeMuth, 2019).

At a minimum, in the United States, the role and power of political parties – without which, E. E. Schattschneider said, democracy is "unthinkable" (2003, 1) – have been diminished (Rauch, 2016; Rauch & La Raza, 2019; Issacharoff, 2017). But this is not simply an American phenomenon. In his study of western democracies, Peter Mair lamented that, over the 60-year period from 1950–2010, election turnout had fallen, party membership had fallen, elections had become more volatile, and parties had less control over nominations and campaign spending. Democracy, said Mair, had been "refined to downgrade its popular component" (Mair, 2013, 12). Across the western democracies, Mair said, "the shift from popular to constitutional democracy and the concomitant downgrading of politics and electoral processes" were the result of the same dismantling of the political parties that Rauch (2016) describes.

Paradoxically, the changes that embodied a democratization of political power away from political parties have been accompanied by what scholars refer to as backsliding away from democracy towards authoritarianism and populism (Mounk, 2018; Luce, 2017). Scholars from around the world continue to publish worried analyses about the fragile state of democracy (Diamond, 2019; Freedom House, 2019). Political power has become more privatized and, as a result, democracy and elections seem to matter less. With this as background, I begin with a review of the concepts of representation and representative government to get a better sense of "what democracy is and is not" (Schmitter & Karl, 1991) in order to create a framework for ongoing analysis of elections and representation in the twenty-first century.

Basics of Representation and Representative Government

The notion of democratic representation is so complex that it took Hanna Pitkin some 300 pages to parse. Near the end of her seminal work *The Concept of Representation* (Pitkin, 1972), she threw her hands up in resignation and said:

> Perhaps representation in politics is only a fiction, a myth forming part of the folklore of our society. Or, perhaps representation must be redefined to fit our politics; perhaps we must simply accept the fact that what we have been calling representative government is in reality just party competition for office.
>
> *(Pitkin, 1972, 221)*

Pitkin (1972) offers this thought in a final chapter in which she concludes that the concept of representation "is a continuous tension between ideal and achievement" (p. 240). Though she had dedicated the book to developing a taxonomy of the numerous dimensions of representation, in the end, the taxonomy did not enable her to set forth a simple, clear definition.

The fundamental challenge, she noted, was that the representative relationship between a principal and an agent takes two forms that are not complementary. According to Pitkin (1972), the fundamental question was: "Should (must) a representative do what his constituents want, and be bound by mandates or instructions from them; or should (must) he be free to act as seems best to him in pursuit of their welfare?" (p. 145).

Pitkin's dichotomy offers a simple, ideal vision upon which to expand analysis. The mandate vision of representation resonates with sending one's attorney to do one's bidding or defend one's interests or desires. The independence vision allows the representative more leeway, perhaps even to sacrifice some of the principal's desires in order to protect his or her interests. In the mandate case, the representative's goal is to pursue what the agent wants; with independence, the representative can pursue what the agent needs.

The simplicity of this dichotomy disappears once a representative is selected by a plural constituency. Unless the constituents are unanimous, the representative will not be able to say for sure what the constituents' desires and needs are. On the one hand, the representative could speak only on behalf of the majority. This would leave the minority with no representation (unless it can be argued that other representatives speak virtually for those constituents). On the other hand, if the representative speaks for all constituents, then he or she operates inescapably in Pitkin's independence mode. Under these circumstances, a representative may support or ignore any or all constituent desires in order to address all of their needs or, perhaps, a greater good.

These are unsurprising considerations: Legislators must play multifaceted roles (Pitkin, 1972, 147). However, Pitkin's analysis forces us to consider the purpose of elections and what the role should be of individual representatives, as well as of the government as a whole. In short, we must address what seems to be a simple question: What is the role and function of and what can one realistically expect from representative democracy? John Stuart Mill and Edmund Burke engaged in a vicarious debate about the answers to these questions.

In *Considerations of Representative Government* (Mill, 1861), John Stuart Mill argued that elections should produce a legislature that is a microcosm of the polity. He called for the enfranchisement of women, plural voting, and nationwide proportional representation to ensure that the government represented all aspects of British society. He insisted that "it is an essential part of democracy that minorities should be adequately represented. No real democracy, nothing but a false show of democracy, is possible without it" (Mill, VII). The more accurately the legislators represented all of the opinions in a nation, the better the government would perform (Mill, VIII). Accordingly, the legislature should be:

> an arena in which not only the general opinion of the nation, but that of every section of it, and as far as possible of every eminent individual whom it contains, can produce itself in full light and challenge discussion; where every person in the country may count upon finding somebody who speaks his mind, as well or better than he could speak it himself – not to friends and partisans exclusively, but in the face of opponents, to be tested by adverse controversy; where those whose opinion is overruled, feel satisfied that it is heard, and set aside not by a mere act of will, but for what are thought superior reasons, and commend themselves as such to the representatives of the majority of the nation.
>
> *(Mill, V)*

Despite the inclusive nature of his vision, Mill placed limits on the popular capacity to govern. Parliament was, said Mill, "radically unfit" for governing, despite its representative capacity. The proper role of a representative assembly was:

> to watch and control the government: to throw the light of publicity on its acts; to compel a full exposition and justification of all of them which one considers questionable; to censure them if found condemnable, and, if the men who compose the government abuse their trust, or fulfill it in a manner which conflicts with the deliberate sense of the nation, to expel them from office and either expressly or virtually appoint their successors.
>
> *(Mill, V)*

He distinguished between the parliament and the government (that is, the prime minister's cabinet and the executive branch). Parliament – the assembled representatives – would debate issues and inform and watch over the executive. But, at the end of the day, parliamentarians did not govern. They were elected to voice their constituents' demands, but they could not guarantee their satisfaction. Governing instead took place in the cabinet.

For Mill, representative elections offer voters a chance to be heard and to return or remove a government, but little else. Voters choose among representatives and their parties to find the one or ones closest to their own opinions. Thus, the legislature would look like all of the people. The government would serve their collective interests. But it would not necessarily serve any of their particular desires.

In contrast, Edmund Burke saw himself (and all elected representatives) as an independent agent – a governor. Elections gave voters the opportunity to choose among the best potential governors of the nation. They were not agents of particular constituencies:

> Parliament is not a *Congress* of Ambassadors from different and hostile interests; which interests each must maintain, as an Agent and Advocate, against other Agents and Advocates; but Parliament is a *deliberative* Assembly of *one* Nation, with *one* Interest, that of the whole; where, not local Purposes, not local Prejudices ought to guide, but the general Good, resulting from the general Reason of the whole. You chuse [sic] a Member indeed; but when you have chosen him, he is not Member of Bristol, but he is a Member of *Parliament*.
>
> *(Burke, 1774, 4.1.25)*

In Burke's vision, elections serve no representative purpose. Voters choose among candidates on the basis of who would be the best governors. In Mill's vision, voters do choose actual representatives. But, in the end, Mill and Burke share the same vision of parliament: Its job is to govern in the nation's best interest – not in the interest of discrete or local ones.

From Theory to Practice

Mill and Burke address the role of particular representatives and the role of a government. However, they leave open the questions concerning how representatives should be chosen and how the government should be constituted. Clearly, both entail elections. But there are numerous electoral formulae and elections can take place in one, large, national constituency, or in regional units such as states, provinces, etc. Insofar as combinations of different electoral formulae and different methods of national organization can generate radically different election results (and, therefore, different governments), we now are faced with two questions: 1) What constitutes fair representation? and 2) what constitutes effective representation?

The first addresses *who* should be elected. The second addresses *how much and what kind of power* elective representatives should have. The two emphases exist in tension.

This was manifest in in an early attempt by the US Supreme Court to set forth a vision of a fair democratic process in *Reynolds v. Sims* (1964). Speaking for the court, Chief Justice Earl Warren asserted that all voters must be treated equally. Therefore, they are entitled to have their votes all count the same.

> Legislators represent people, not trees or acres. Legislators are elected by voters, not farms or cities or economic interests. As long as ours is a representative form of government, and our legislatures are those instruments of government elected directly by and directly representative of the people, the right to *elect legislators in a free and unimpaired fashion* is a bedrock of our political system...if a State should provide that the votes of citizens in one part of the State should be given two times, or five times, or 10 times the weight of votes of citizens in another part of the State, it could hardly be contended that the right to vote of those residing in the disfavored areas had not been effectively diluted.
>
> (Reynolds v. Sims*, p. 562. Emphasis added.)*

Yet this attempt to connect voter equality with fair representation for democracy served only to muddy the waters. This is clear in his shift from a discussion of equally weighted votes to equally influential voters.

> Full and effective participation by all citizens in state government requires, therefore, that each citizen have an equally effective voice in the election of members of his state legislature. Modern and viable state government needs, and the Constitution demands, no less. Logically, in a society ostensibly grounded on representative government, it would seem reasonable that a majority of the people of a State could elect a majority of that State's legislators...With respect to the allocation of legislative representation, all voters, as citizens of a State, stand in the same relation regardless of where they live. Any suggested criteria for the differentiation of citizens are insufficient to justify any discrimination, as to the weight of their votes, unless relevant to the permissible purposes of legislative apportionment. Since the achieving of fair and effective representation for all citizens is concededly the basic aim of legislative apportionment, we conclude that the Equal Protection Clause guarantees the opportunity for equal participation by all voters in the election of state legislators.
>
> *(p. 565–6)*

In this passage, Warren conflates elements of representation theory and democracy that do not always complement one another. Equality of individual voting power and majority rule are basic components of democratic theory. But, without more, they can work to the detriment of effective representation for voters or groups that are not part of the governing majority.

In contrast, the Supreme Court of Canada offered a more nuanced view of representation and democracy some 27 years later in *Ref. Re Prov. Electoral Boundaries (Sask.)* ([1991] 2 SCR 158). There, the court stated:

> the purpose of the right to vote enshrined in s. 3 of the *Charter* is not equality of voting power *per se*, but the right to "effective representation." Ours is a representative democracy. Each citizen is entitled to be represented in government. Representation comprehends the idea of having a voice in the deliberations of government as well as the idea of the right to bring one's grievances and concerns to the attention of

> one's government representative...; elected representatives function in two roles -- legislative and what has been termed the "ombudsman role."...What are the conditions of effective representation? The first is relative parity of voting power...But parity of voting power, though of prime importance, is not the only factor to be taken into account in ensuring effective representation...Notwithstanding the fact that the value of a citizen's vote should not be unduly diluted, it is a practical fact that effective representation often cannot be achieved without taking into account countervailing factors...Factors like geography, community history, community interests and minority representation may need to be taken into account to ensure that our legislative assemblies effectively represent the diversity of our social mosaic. These are but examples of considerations which may justify departure from absolute voter parity in the pursuit of more effective representation; the list is not closed.
>
> *(p. 183–4)*

While the Canadian court offered a clearer acknowledgment of the complexities of representation, it did not address the rights of minorities. How to balance voter parity, majority rule, and effective representation for all?

James Madison offered a practical answer to this in *Federalist* 10. He called for a large, extended republic that would ensure the representation of a multitude of interests. This would protect all minority groups by weakening and destabilizing majorities:

> Extend the sphere [of government], and you take in a greater variety of parties and interests; you make it less probable that a majority of the whole will have a common motive to invade the rights of other citizens; or if such a common motive exists, it will be more difficult for all who feel it to discover their own strength, and to act in unison with each other.
>
> *(Congress.gov, n.d.)*

In a diverse society, Madison envisioned that no one group or coalition of groups would be able to govern for very long. As a result, he assumed that groups would alternate in power and, in the long run, all groups would be represented and have a share of governing authority (thereby rendering their fair representation effective).

He advocated what Arend Lijphart called the "consensus" model of democracy (2012). It is premised on the belief that representative democracy entails more than fair representation or majority rule. Instead, it assumes that "all who are affected by a decision should have the chance to participate in making that decision either directly or through chosen representatives" (2012, 30). To this end, there are numerous mechanisms that can enhance the capacity of minorities either to check or join a governing majority. Systems of proportional representation (see below) will enhance the likelihood that a legislature will be as diverse as Mill and Madison envision. Dispersing governmental power across branches of government that can check one another will also enhance the likelihood that minorities can check a majority (Lijphart, 2012, 30–45). But, regardless of the systemic features that are designed to ensure minority representation, it still may be the case that some groups are either so small or have such a "discrete and insular" (Ely, 1980) agenda that they are never able to join a governing coalition. In such circumstances, the electoral process would be "locked up" (Issacharoff & Pildes, 1998) by a majority and minority electoral success would lead to nothing more than "token" representation.

Lani Guinier (1991) addressed this in her criticism of the manner in which the United States implemented the Voting Rights Act of 1965 (42 USC 1973) to ensure minority representation in state legislatures and the US Congress. The principal mechanism for protecting minority representation in the United States has been the use of specially-designed election districts in which members of a minority group comprise a majority (or, at least, a critical proportion) of the voting population. In other nations, systems of proportional representation achieve the same ends.

The election of minority representatives is necessary for democracy. But it is not sufficient because it ignores the need to broaden "the base of participation and fundamentally reforming the substance of political decisions" (Guinier, 1991, 1080). Thus, she contended, mere representation "may not necessarily result in more responsive government" (p. 1080) because the electoral success of minority legislators does not necessarily enhance the fortunes or the quality of elections of their constituents (p. 1134). To ensure that minorities can participate meaningfully, they must be given additional power that enables them to affect or even occasionally control the process of government. There is no uncontroversial way to achieve this aim because it creates the possibility of minority rule – in addition to minority representation.

Allocating Power and Allocating Votes

The allocation of fair and effective representation is based on two considerations: To whom is power allocated and by what formula? In some nations, such as Israel, elections are held in one, national electoral district and governing power is, therefore, allocated from one, national constituency. In federal nations, power is allocated among multiple electoral "districts" such as states, provinces, or other subnational regions. Unless these subnational districts are equal in size, no representational formula – by which votes are translated into seats – will produce truly fair results. For voters in some regions will have relatively more voting power per capita than others (cf. Toplak, 2008).

Systems such as this manifest what Richard Katz refers to as "mandated" or "tolerated" malapportionment (1998, 250) because, invariably, smaller states are overrepresented in the federal legislature. While the practice of overrepresenting small states can produce counter-majoritarian election results and legislative practices, it is common throughout the world in federal systems.[1] In such nations, smaller states (in Canada and Spain they are called provinces; in Germany, they are Länder; in the European Parliament, they are the nations themselves) are frequently overrepresented in national legislatures and have much more voting power per capita than larger ones. In the US, Wyoming voters have much more per capita voting power than Californians. Belgians punch above their electoral weight in the EU when compared to Germans. In Canada, residents of Nunavut have much more voting power per capita than Ontarians (Rush, 2007, 2019).

These disparities in voting power are set by constitutional rule. In Australia, all states have 12 senators regardless of their populations (Senate – Parliament of Australia, n.d.). In the Canadian Parliament, seats are allocated among provinces via an "electoral quotient." Yet, the function of that formula is qualified by "grandfather clauses" that state, for example, that no province will have fewer seats in the House of Commons than it has in the Senate. Also, no province will have fewer seats than it had in 1985 (Elections Canada, n.d.). In Spain, all provinces are guaranteed two seats in the Congress of Deputies (Election Resources on the Internet, n.d.).

The justification for and function of such systems echoes Guinier's concerns about the fate of minority groups and their capacity to have more than token representation in legislative bodies, as well as Lijphart's support for the consensus model of democracy. But, in some cases, this can produce winners of elections with fewer votes than the opposition. Perhaps the best recent example of this was in the US Electoral College. In the US presidential elections of 2000 and 2016, the winning Republican candidates were elected because they won a majority of the Electoral College vote, despite receiving a minority of the popular vote. These perverse election results were due to the fact that votes in the Electoral College are based on the allocation of power (and small states' disproportionate representation) in the House of Representatives and Senate (US Census Bureau; Klein, 2018).

Allocating Votes: Electoral System Design and Algorithmic Bias

The allocation of seats to provinces or political parties in a legislature is determined by a mathematical formula. No matter how carefully such electoral formulae are designed, at some point, someone will benefit from them disproportionally and others will suffer (Katz, 1998). Apportionment formulae compare in their impact to the electoral formulae by which proportional representation systems convert votes into legislative seats (Farrell, 2011). Variations in how electoral formulae convert votes into seats can have fatal impacts on the fates of particular candidates or political parties. The following examples (adapted from Farrell, 2011) demonstrate this.

In a hypothetical election with 100,000 votes (see Table 3.1), five political parties contest ten seats. In this first example, we use the "largest remainder" method of allocating seats. If we assume, for simplicity's sake that one seat "costs" 10,000 votes (100,000 voters/ten seats), the results of the election will be as follows. Each party will gain one seat for each whole multiple of 10,000 votes it receives. Based on this, eight of ten seats will be allocated immediately. The remaining two seats will be awarded to the parties with the largest remainder of votes. This is known as the "largest remainder" method of seat allocation.

In comparison, in the "Highest Average" method, vote totals for each party are divided by successively higher divisors. This process generates a table of "priority values," as demonstrated in Table 3.2. Seats are allocated starting with the highest priority value and continuing on to the

Table 3.1 Largest Remainder Seat Allocation Method

Party	*Votes*	*First Seat Allocation*	*Remaining Votes*	*Second Seat Allocation*	*Final Seat Total*	*% of Vote to % of Seats*
Republican	38,000	3	8,000	1	4	38%/40%
Democratic	23,000	2	3,000	0	2	23%/20%
Reform	21,000	2	1,000	0	2	21%/20%
Green	12,000	1	2,000	0	1	12%/10%
Moll	6,000	0	6,000	1	1	6%/10%

Table 3.2 Highest Average Seat Allocation Method

Party	*Votes*	*1*	*2*	*3*	*4*
Republican	38,000	*38,000 (1)*	*19,000 (4)*	*12,666.67 (5)*	*9,500 (10)*
Democratic	23,000	*23,000 (2)*	*11,500 (7)*	*7,666.67 (9)*	5,750
Reform	21,000	*21,000 (3)*	*10,500 (8)*	7,000	5,250
Green	12,000	*12,000 (6)*	6,000	4,000	3,000
Moll	6,000	6,000	3,000	2,000	1,500

second, third, fourth highest, etc. until all seats are filled. Thus, in this example, the Republicans receive the first seat, the Democrats receive the second, and so forth.

The difference between the two methods is clear in the fate of the Moll party. It receives one seat using the largest remainder method. However, it remains without representation in the highest average system. This begs, but does not answer the question: Which formula is fairer?

The formulae in both methods can vary significantly. In some countries, the divisors are not consecutive. In others, they are not integers. For example, the formula to apportion seats in the US House of Representatives uses the following divisor:

$$\sqrt{(n(n-1))}$$

The simplicity of these formulae belies any suggestion that there is a conscious partisan bias built into them. Yet, it is clear that they have different impacts. As the fate of the Moll party indicates, different formulae can generate different election results from the same vote totals or different apportionment of legislative seats.

Of course, electoral systems can be manipulated to disadvantage any group of voters. In the United States, the sordid history of redrawing election district lines to favor one party or the other has produced a catalog of bizarrely-shaped electoral districts (Griffith, 2018). In countries that use proportional representation, it is possible to manipulate electoral competition and deny representation to particular groups simply by altering the number of seats in an election district (Rae, 1995). If a party consistently polls 20% of the vote, it can be denied representation if there are only three seats in the district. Similarly, if a nation uses single-member electoral districts or has a unitary executive, minority groups will always be at a disadvantage (*Holder v. Hall*, 1994).

In sum, there is no such thing as a perfectly fair or bias-free means of converting votes into representative seats in a legislature. Electoral formulae – like any other algorithm – inevitably and inescapably manifest intentional or unintentional bias. In some cases, such as Katz's mandated malapportionment, the bias is consciously built into a system to protect minorities, regions, etc. In others, the bias may be due to nothing more than the shifting preferences of voters among candidates and parties and the extent to which every electoral system must have some threshold of representation based on the number of seats and the allocation formula. Insofar as electoral formula bias is inescapable, there can be no unassailable definition of what constitutes "fair" representation. Perhaps, as Pitkin suggested, representative government really is just "party competition for office" (Pitkin, 1972, 221). If so, then we are left to consider whether the electoral marketplace promotes fair competition.

Representation and the Political Marketplace

In general, scholars have compared free and fair elections that offer voters meaningful choices among distinct candidates to an economic market that is free of monopolies, artificial barriers to entry, etc. (Issacharoff & Pildes, 1997). In the same way that there is no real choice in an economic market controlled by a monopoly or other form of cartel, there is no real democratic choice in elections if voters' choices are limited unfairly or their votes are rendered meaningless by electoral formulae. If the electoral marketplace is free of collusion, corruption, monopoly, barriers to entry, etc., then democratic elections can generate legitimate, meaningful representative outcomes. However, what constitutes a free electoral marketplace? Bauer (2017) suggests that a free electoral market would be comprised at least of the following:

- No artificial restrictions on the quality of candidates, meaning candidates who answer the requirements of a diverse and informed debate and from among whom would emerge capable public officials (openness to entry);
- Fair opportunity for adequate campaign funding, reflected in a reasonable expectation that, in some relation to candidates' message and the quality of their campaign, candidates can raise what they need to compete but would not be overwhelmed by fundraising pressures (efficiency and openness to entry);
- Flexibility within the system to allow for competition among candidates, parties, consultants, and others to experiment with and develop effective avenues for voter contact and persuasion (efficiency and innovation); and
- Sufficient availability of information about the candidates, parties, and other actors to allow voters to understand who is standing for or against which policies or positions, which is an objective consistent with the desire most candidates have to "control" the communication of their message, so that they have some prospect of defining for the voter what they stand for (Bauer, 2017, 895–6).

To ensure that these conditions are met, government must oversee the political marketplace to keep it operating smoothly.

Scholars and courts have struggled to identify an ideal balance between enabling a government to administer a fair, open, and orderly political marketplace, while simultaneously ensuring that those who control the government do not surreptitiously give themselves an unfair advantage. The US Supreme Court articulated the complexity of maintaining this balance in *Anderson v. Celebrezze* (1983):

> It is to be expected that a voter hopes to find on the ballot a candidate who comes near to reflecting his policy preferences on contemporary issues. The right to vote is heavily burdened if that vote may be cast only for major-party candidates at a time when other parties or other candidates are clamoring for a place on the ballot. The exclusion of candidates also burdens voters' freedom of association, because an election campaign is an effective platform for the expression of views on the issues of the day, and a candidate serves as a rallying point for like-minded citizens.
>
> *(p. 787–8)*

On the other hand, there is such a thing as too much choice or a marketplace that is so "free" that it is chaotic and confusing. As the court noted:

> We have recognized that, as a practical matter, there must be a substantial regulation of elections if they are to be fair and honest and if some sort of order, rather than chaos, is to accompany the democratic processes. To achieve these necessary objectives, States have enacted comprehensive and sometimes complex election codes. Each provision of these schemes, whether it governs the registration and qualifications of voters, the selection and eligibility of candidates, or the voting process itself, inevitably affects – at least to some degree – the individual's right to vote and his right to associate with others for political ends.
>
> *(p. 788)*

Thus, "as a practical matter, there must be a substantial regulation of elections if they are to be fair and honest and if some sort of order, rather than chaos, is to accompany the democratic process" (p. 788).

Of course, if government has such power, it can also control competition and, therefore, render elections less meaningful and party competition meaningless. But what constitutes meaningful competition? The United States Supreme Court has addressed this question with regard to laws that limit candidate and party access to ballots. In *Timmons v. Twin Cities Area New Party* (1997), the court upheld a law banning candidates from being listed more than once on a ballot (even though they were endorsed by more than one party). While this rule was in place ostensibly to minimize voter confusion, the New Party contended that it was a clandestine move by the major parties to prevent minor parties from gaining support and, for all intents and purposes, entrenching a duopoly of Democrats and Republicans (Hasen, 1997). While this was a plausible argument, the court stated: "States certainly have an interest in protecting the integrity, fairness, and efficiency of their ballots and election processes as means for electing public officials. [Therefore a] state may prevent "frivolous or fraudulent candidacies" [and] states have an interest in preventing "misrepresentation" (Timmons, 364–365). But, one person's prevention of frivolous candidates is another's formation of a cartel and creation of barriers to entry.

In their study of European political parties, Katz and Mair (1995) described the evolution of "cartel" parties that, instead of competing for office, collude and become "agents of the state" and "employ resources of the state to ensure their own survival" (p. 5) while rendering competition for office a meaningless charade:

> the state, which is invaded by the parties, and the rules of which are determined by the parties, becomes a fount of resources through which these parties not only help to ensure their own survival, but through which they can also enhance their capacity to resist challenges from newly mobilized alternatives. The state, in this sense, becomes an institutionalized structure of support, sustaining insiders while excluding outsiders. No longer simple brokers between civil society and the state, the parties now become absorbed by the state. From having first assumed the role of trustees, and then later of delegates, and then later again, in the heyday of the catch-all party, of entrepreneurs, parties have now become semi-state agencies.
>
> *(Katz & Mair, 1995, 16)*

In addition to behaving as cartels, many European parties now have much smaller memberships (Scarrow & Gezgor, 2010; Biezen, Mair, & Poguntke, 2012). As a result, they "have all but abandoned any pretensions to being mass organizations" (van Biezen et al., 42).

Bawn et al. draw the same conclusions about political parties in the United States:

> to posit that American politics is mainly organized by election-minded politicians, as the textbook view of American politics does, is to miss its essence. Organized combat among groups that aim to control policy-making is closer to the heart of the matter.
>
> *(Bawn et al., 2012, 591)*

Echoing Katz and Mair, they argue, what remains of the once dominant political party organizations are:

> coalitions of interest groups and activists seeking to capture and use government for their particular goals, which range from material self-interest to high-minded idealism.

> The coalition of policy-demanding groups develops an agenda of mutually acceptable policies, insists on the nomination of candidates with a demonstrated commitment to its program, and works to elect these candidates to office.
>
> *(Katz & Mair, 1995, 571)*

Faintly echoing Pitkin's description of representation, Bawn et al. acknowledge that "electoral competition does constrain groupcentric parties to be somewhat responsive to citizen preferences, but they cede as little policy to voters as possible. Parties mainly push their own agendas and aim to get voters to go along" (p. 572).

These disheartening visions of the diminished role of political parties (without which, Schattschneider said, democracy is "unthinkable" (1942, 1) and elections is made only worse by the acknowledgement that the evolution of campaign spending laws now allows private interests to dominate campaign spending as never before. The absence of any real constraints on private independent electoral expenditures has amplified the chaotic aspect of elections and shifted the balance of power in the political universe. As the Bipartisan Policy Center (2019) reported, spending by private entities such as super PACS and other nonprofits accounted for only 48% of spending in federal elections in 2010, but it accounted for 78% in 2016 (p. 31). Similarly, European elections suffer the same threat posed by the power of private spending (OECD, 2016).

Regardless of whether one see parties as Bawn et al. or Katz and Mair described them, both models suggest that the parties and elected officials are less dependent on voters and elections than democratic theorists such as Pitkin, Mill, Burke, Madison, etc. would suggest or hope. To the extent that private interests exercise increasing control over political parties and dominate campaign spending, seeking to prevent Guinier's token representation through a more meaningful electoral and legislative process would seem to matter less if, at the end of the day, power in a democracy has flowed to private unaccountable interests.

Conclusion: Representative Democracy in the Twenty-First Century

Democratic legitimacy still depends on, at least, the perception that elections generate governments that are representative of the people's wishes, even if "the will of the people" depends on the formula by which their votes are counted and converted into legislative seats. If Pitkin's "party competition for office" takes place in a free political market according to rules that voters and critics regard as fair, then, at least, a government can claim a legitimate power to rule, despite ongoing controversies about which electoral formula is the fairest. Twenty-first-century scholars must now confront the fact that debates about representative government occur in a political universe where private power seems to be overtaking and rivaling the public power of government.

Note

1 For a count of federal nations, see, e.g., www.cs.mcgill.ca/~rwest/wikispeedia/wpcd/wp/l/List_of_countries_by_system_of_government.htm; see also http://www.forumfed.org/countries/.

References

Amy, D. J. (2002). *Real choices / new voices: How proportional representation elections could revitalize American democracy* (2nd ed). New York: Columbia University Press.

Bauer, R. (2017). The parties' struggles in the political market: Can regulation solve this problem - Should it, and if so, how. *Houston Law Review*, 54(4), 881–910.

Bawn, K., Cohen, M., Karol, D., Masket, S., Noel, H., & Zaller, J. (2012). A theory of political parties: Groups, policy demands and nominations in American politics. *Perspectives on Politics, 10*(3), 571–597. doi: 10.1017/S1537592712001624

Bipartisan Policy Center. (2019). Campaign Finance in the United-States. Retrieved January 12, 2020 from https://bipartisanpolicy.org/wp-content/uploads/2019/03/BPC-Democracy-Campaign-Finance-in-the-United-States.pdf

Burke, E. (1774). Speech to Electors at Bristol. 3 November 1774. Retrieved January 12, 2020 from http://press-pubs.uchicago.edu/founders/documents/v1ch13s7.html

Congress.gov. (n.d.). The federalist papers. Retrieved January 12, 2020 from https://www.congress.gov/resources/display/content/The+Federalist+Papers

DeMuth, C. (2019). Trumpism, nationalism and conservatism. *Claremont Review of Books, 19*, 32–41.

Diamond, L. J. (2019). *Ill winds: Saving democracy from Russian rage, Chinese ambition, and American complacency*. New York: Penguin Press.

Election resources on the internet: Elections to the Spanish Congress of Deputies. (n.d.). Retrieved January 20, 2020 from http://electionresources.org/es/index_en.html

Elections Canada. (n.d.). *The representation formula*. Retrieved January 20, 2020 from https://www.elections.ca/content.aspx?section=res&dir=cir/red/ form&document=index&lang=e

Ely, J. H. (1980). *Democracy and distrust: A theory of judicial review* (Revised ed.). Cambridge, MA; London: Harvard University Press.

Farrell, D. M. (2011). *Electoral systems: A comparative introduction* (2nd ed.). London: Red Globe Press.

Freedom House. (2019). Freedom in the world 2019. Retrieved from https://freedomhouse.org/report/freedom-world/freedom-world-2019

Gallagher, M. (1992). Comparing proportional representation electoral systems: Quotas, thresholds, paradoxes and majorities. *British Journal of Political Science, 22*(4), 469–496. doi: 10.1017/S0007123400006499

Griffith, E. C. (2018). *The rise and development of the gerrymander*. Sagwan Press.

Guinier, L. (1991). The triumph of tokenism: The Voting Rights Act and the theory of Black electoral success. *Michigan Law Review, 89*(5), 1077–1154. doi: 10.2307/1289550

Hasen, R. L. (1997). Entrenching the duopoly: Why the Supreme Court should not allow the states to protect the Democrats and Republicans from political competition. *Supreme Court Review*, 331–372.

Issacharoff, S. (2017). Outsourcing politics: The hostile takeover of our hollowed-out political parties. The Twenty-First Annual Frankel Lecture: Address. *Houston Law Review, 54*(4), 845–880.

Issacharoff, S., & Pildes, R. H. (1998). Politics as markets: Partisan lockups of the Democratic Process Symposium: Law and the political process. *Stanford Law Review, 50*(3), 643–717.

Katz, R. S. (1998). Malapportionment and gerrymandering in other countries and electoral systems. In M. E. Rush (Ed.), *Voting rights and redistricting in the United States* (pp. 245–261). Westport, CT: Greenwood Press.

Katz, R. S., & Mair, P. (1995). Changing models of party organization and party democracy: The emergence of the cartel party. *Party Politics, 1*(1), 5–28.

Klein, E. (2018). The rigging of American politics. Vox. Retrieved from https://www.vox.com/policy-and-politics/2018/10/16/17951596/kavanaugh-trump-senate-impeachment-avenatti-democrats-2020-supreme-court

Lijphart, Arend. (2012). *Patterns of democracy: Government forms and performance in thirty-six countries.* 2d. Edition. New Haven, CT: Yale University Press.

Luce, E. (2017). *The retreat of Western liberalism (First Grove Atlantic hardcover edition).* New York: Atlantic Monthly Press.

Mair, P. (2013). *Ruling the void: The hollowing of Western democracy*. London: Verso.

Mill, J. S. (1861). Considerations on representative government. Retrieved January 12, 2020 from https://www.gutenberg.org/files/5669/5669-h/5669-h.htm

Mounk, Y. (2018). *The people vs. democracy: Why our freedom is in danger and how to save it.* Cambridge, MA: Harvard University Press.

OECD. (2016). Financing democracy: Funding political parties and election campaigns and the risk of policy capture. OECD Library. Retrieved from https://read.oecd-ilibrary.org/governance/financing-democracy_9789264249455-en

Pitkin, H. F. (1972). *The concept of representation (1st US edition)*. Berkeley, CA: University of California Press.

Rae, D. W. (1995). Using district magnitude to regulate political party competition. *Journal of Economic Perspectives, 9*(1), 65–75. Retrieved from https://www.jstor.org/stable/2138355

Rauch, J. (2016). How American politics went insane. *The Atlantic.* Retrieved January 20, 2020 from https://www.theatlantic.com/magazine/archive/2016/07/how-american-politics-went-insane/485570/
Rauch, J., & La Raja, R. (2019). Too much democracy Is bad for democracy. *The Atlantic.* Retrieved January 20, 2020 from https://www.theatlantic.com/magazine/archive/2019/12/too-much-democracy-is-bad-for-democracy/600766/
Rush, M. (2007). Voting power in federal systems: Spain as a case study. *PS: Political Science & Politics*, *40*(4), 715–720. Retrieved from https://www.jstor.org/stable/20452056
Rush, M. (2019). The Electoral College will never make everyone happy. *The Conversation.* Retrieved January 12, 2020 from http://theconversation.com/the-electoral-college-will-never-make-everyone-happy-119724
Rush, M. E. (Ed.). (1998). *Voting rights and redistricting in the United States.* Westport, CT: Greenwood Press.
Scarrow, S. E., & Gezgor, B. (2010). Declining memberships, changing members? European political party members in a new era. *Party Politics*, *19*(6), 823–43. doi: 10.1177/1354068809346078
Schattschneider, E. (2003). *Party government* (1st ed.). London: Routledge.
Schmitter, P. C., & Karl, T. L. (1991). What democracy is...And is not. *Journal of Democracy*, 2(3), 75–88. doi: 10.1353/jod.1991.0033
Senate – Parliament of Australia. (n.d.). Retrieved January 20, 2020 from https://www.aph.gov.au/About_Parliament/Senate
Toplak, J. (2008). Equal voting weight of all: Finally "One Person, One Vote" from Hawaii to Maine? *Temple Law Review*, *81*(1), 123–176.
Van Biezen, I., Mair, P., & Poguntke, T. (2012). Going, going...gone? The decline of party membership in contemporary Europe. *European Journal of Political Research*, *51*(1), 24–56. doi: 10.1111/j.1475-6765.2011.01995.x

Court Cases

United States

Anderson v. Celebrezze, 460 US 780 (1983)
Holder v. *Hall*, 512 U.s. 874 (1994
Reynolds v. Sims, 377 US 533 (1964)
Timmons v. Twin Cities Area New Party, 520 US 351 (1997)

Canada

Reference. Re: Provincial Electoral Boundaries (Sask.) [1991] 2 SCR 158

4
VOTING RIGHTS AND LIMITATIONS

Djordje Gardašević and Jurij Toplak

Introduction

In this chapter, we provide an overview of the most common restrictions imposed by legislation on the right to vote, as well as on the right to stand as a candidate for election. Voting rights can be restricted on the basis of age, place of residence, citizenship, criminal conviction, bankruptcy, physical or mental disability, knowledge of a certain language, status as a member of the military, or for other reasons. Some of them may be viewed as legitimate and inevitable, while others may not. Some of them have been upheld by the highest national courts and international tribunals. Others have been declared inadmissible.

Restrictions on the Right to Vote

Minimum Age Requirements

Election to public office limits to those within a specified age range the right to cast a vote and the right to stand for election. A minimum age is always set for the voters, as well as for those who wish to be candidates. Only rarely is a maximum age specified.[1]

In some democracies, such as in Croatia and Slovenia, a person may vote or run for any office when he or she turns 18. In some other democracies, the voting age may be different from the age that must be attained before standing as a candidate. The argument here is that it takes someone with more maturity and experience to administer a public office than to vote for someone to administer that same office.[2] The age that must be attained before a person may stand as a candidate usually rises with the importance of the office in question.[3]

The Council of Europe is striving to enforce an all-European standard according to which the minimum voting age would not exceed 18 years of age and the age required for running for a public office would not be higher than 25.[4]

The Residency Requirement

Many national or local laws around the globe require residents to live within the country or relevant jurisdiction for a certain amount of time before they qualify to vote or before they qualify to stand for election. Some democracies and government entities require voters to reside

 DOI: 10.4324/9780429401800-4

in the jurisdiction for a week or two; in others, this residency requirement may be extended to several years. Governments usually contend that such long periods are needed to reduce the possibility of nonresidents temporarily invading the district and falsely swearing that they are residents. Another government argument is that residency-duration requirements further the goal of having "knowledgeable voters." A long residency requirement provides some assurance that the new voter has become a member of the community and that, as such, has a common interest in all matters pertaining to its government and is therefore likely to exercise this right more responsibly.[5] Constitutional and supreme courts, however, have often struck down lengthy residency requirements.

The United States Supreme Court, for instance, has effectively put an end to lengthy residency requirements with the *Dunn v. Blumstein*[6] decision. The court annulled a Tennessee law requiring voters to reside in the state for a year before being allowed to vote. The court stressed that a 30-day residency requirement would be sufficient to give the government the possibility to check whether the new voter was a bona fide resident.[7] In a subsequent case, *Burns v. Fortson*, the United States Supreme Court invalidated Georgia's 50-day residency requirement and indicated that "the 50-day registration period approaches the outer constitutional limits in this area."[8] Currently, US state residency requirements vary from zero to thirty-two days.[9]

In Europe, somewhat lengthier residency requirements are accepted. In its Code of Good Practice in Electoral Matters, adopted in October 2002, the Venice Commission states that a residence requirement may be imposed as a condition of voting, but that it should not exceed six months.[10] In Northern Ireland, for instance, a period of three months' residence is required before an elector is registered. The law's intention in this case is to discourage residents in the Republic of Ireland moving across the border to vote in Northern Ireland elections.

In Montenegro, citizens are required to reside in the country for 24 months before being entitled to vote. The compliance of the Montenegrin law with the European standards has been evaluated by the Venice Commission (2005). In the commission's opinion,

> as far as international standards are concerned, a lesser requirement (say of 6 months) would surely fall within the state's margin of appreciation. A limit of 12 months might also be acceptable at Strasbourg, depending on the reasons advanced for imposing the limit.
>
> *(Venice Commission, 2005, § 63)*

The European Court of Human Rights addressed the residency issue in the 2005 *Py v. France*[11] decision. In this case, the court upheld a ten-year residence requirement in New Caledonia for the election of the Congress of New Caledonia due to very special circumstances. The applicant, a French citizen living in France, worked a few years in New Caledonia and was refused participation in elections. He alleged that the restriction imposed on his right to take part in the elections had violated the right to free elections. According to the French government, the reason for bringing in a residence condition was to ensure that the consultations would reflect the will of "interested" persons and that the result would not be altered by a massive vote cast by recent arrivals to the territory who had no solid links to it. The court found that New Caledonia's current status amounted to a transitional phase prior to acquisition of full sovereignty and the ten-year residency requirement was part of a process of self-determination. After a tormented political and institutional history, the ten-year residence condition became a key factor in settling what had become a deadly conflict. In the court's opinion, the history and status of New Caledonia were such that they could be regarded as amounting to "local requirements" of a kind, warranting the restrictions imposed on the applicant's right to vote.[12]

In a 1997 Italian case,[13] the European Court of Human Rights ruled that a four-year uninterrupted residence requirement was not, in itself, contrary to Article 3 Protocol No. 1 and might be legitimate. However, in view of the court's more recent decisions and the Council of Europe's expressed opinions, it is doubtful that the 1997 case would be decided the same way today.

In 1979, the European Commission ruled that a British national, employed by the European Communities in Brussels, was not allowed to vote in British national elections on the grounds that she was not a resident of United Kingdom.[14] Her application was declared inadmissible on the grounds that the applicant has voluntarily taken up residence abroad.

The durational residence requirements imposed for standing as a candidate are usually longer than the ones imposed for voting. In the United States, for instance, the residency requirements for state governors and state legislators vary from zero up to ten years, with most falling between two and five years.[15] The residence requirements for exercising the right to vote, as we saw earlier, are not longer than 30 days. Many of the European democracies also impose residency requirements for the people who wish to run for office. The European Court of Human Rights has ruled on the Ukrainian residency requirement of five years in the case of *Melnychenko v. Ukraine.*[16] The applicant, a Ukrainian citizen, left his country for fear of political persecution, had been living for five years in the United States, and his passport named Kiev as his residence. His candidature for parliamentary elections was rejected by the Ukrainian government. The court ruled that the imposition of a residence requirement for exercising the right to stand for election was not, per se, unreasonable or arbitrary. According to the court, even more restrictive conditions might be imposed. However, the court also took into consideration a Ukrainian law that required candidates to give their address "as contained in the ordinary citizen's passport" and so ruled that legal residence, rather than habitual residence, should be taken into consideration when evaluating the legitimacy of candidacies in Ukraine.[17] The judges concluded that Ukraine violated the European Convention of Human Rights when it did not allow the applicant to run for election.

In another case, the applicant challenged a Macedonian law requiring presidential candidates to reside in Macedonia continuously for ten years within the 15-year period prior to the elections. The applicant in this case had resided continuously for almost eight years in Macedonia and his candidature was rejected. The court rejected the application on the grounds that presidential election laws are not covered by the European Convention of Human Rights.[18]

The 2005 Council of Europe's resolution invites member states to "grant electoral rights to all their citizens (nationals), without imposing residency requirements."[19]

Prisoners' Right to Vote

The European Court of Human Rights has ruled in several important cases involving prisoners' right to vote. In the early cases, the applications by the prisoners who were denied the right to vote were, in general, rejected.

In *Patrick Holland v. Ireland,*[20] for instance, where, since there was no provision permitting a serving prisoner to vote in prison, the applicant, who was sentenced to seven years for possessing explosives, was *de facto* deprived of the vote. The commission found that the suspension of the right to vote did not thwart the free expression of the opinion of the people in the choice of the legislature and could not be considered arbitrary in the circumstances of the case.

In *Labita v. Italy,*[21] the applicant was charged with collaborating with the Mafia in 1992. As a part of "special preventive measures" taken against people suspected of belonging to Mafia, he was disenfranchised. Although he was acquitted in 1995, his voting rights were not reinstated until 1997. The government maintained that the measure was intended to prevent the Mafia from exercising any influence over elected bodies. In view of the real risk that persons suspected of belonging to the Mafia might exercise their right to vote in favor of other members of the Mafia, the temporary disenfranchisement of the applicant was, according to the government, justifiable. But, in the view of the fact that the applicant was disenfranchised *after* he was acquitted, the court found his disenfranchisement to violate the convention.

In another case, *M.D.U. v. Italy*,[22] the applicant had been convicted of fiscal fraud offences and sentenced to three years' imprisonment, with the additional penalty of prohibition of exercising public functions for two years. The court found this measure to be within the state's "wide margin of appreciation."

Since, in *Labita*, the court found that disenfranchisement of alleged Mafiosos under "special preventive measures" presented violation of the convention, but in *M.D.U.* upheld an additional penalty of prohibition on voting for two years, it was logical to question the scope of the state's "margin of appreciation" to ban prisoner voting. Out of the 43 convention parties examined, 25 imposed some sort of restrictions on prisoner voting rights.[23] With more than half of the states disenfranchising at least some of their convicted felons, and with the court's frequent emphasis on states having "wide margin of appreciation" in the area of elections, it was interesting to observe how the court would rule on disenfranchisement cases falling somewhere between the two Italian cases.

Just few months after the *M.D.U.* decision, the court faced a British law under which "[a] convicted person during the time that he is detained in a penal institution in pursuance of his sentence…is legally incapable of voting at any parliamentary or local election."[24] Contrary to the upheld Italian practice, British law imposed a blanket restriction on all convicted prisoners. It applied automatically to all such prisoners, irrespective of the length of their sentence and irrespective of the nature or gravity of their offence.[25] The government defended the law, claiming that "the disenfranchisement of a convicted prisoner was considered as part of his punishment and that it aimed to enhance civic responsibility." It also argued that the measure "only affected those who had been convicted of crimes sufficiently serious" and "as soon as prisoners ceased to be detained the legal incapacity was removed."[26]

In its chamber decision *Hirst v. the United Kingdom*,[27] the court repeated that the right to vote is "central to democracy and the rule of law," but it is "not absolute and may be subject to limitations." It also repeated that "the Contracting States have a wide margin of appreciation in this sphere." But the court

> has to satisfy itself that the [limitations] do not curtail the rights in question to such an extent as to impair their very essence and deprive them of their effectiveness; that they are imposed in pursuit of a legitimate aim; and that the means employed are not disproportionate.[28]

The court relied on ICCPR,[29] United Nations Human Rights Committee opinion,[30] European Prison Rules,[31] Venice Commission's Code of Good Practices in Electoral Matters,[32] jurisprudence of the South African Constitutional Court,[33] and the Supreme Court of Canada *Sauvé* decisions.[34] The court concluded that the convention does not guarantee the right to vote to every prisoner but, at the same time, the British ban on prisoner voting rights was contrary to the convention.

According to the chamber decision, therefore, the convention does not absolutely prohibit restrictions on prisoner voting rights. It does, however, prohibit an "absolute bar on voting by any serving prisoner in any circumstances" and the "imposition of an automatic and blanket restriction on convicted prisoners' franchise." From the court's repeated emphasis on the importance of prisoner rehabilitation,[35] it might well be concluded that disenfranchisement of ex-prisoners would not be upheld by the court.

In 2005, the Grand Chamber of the European Court of Human Rights confirmed that the British blanket ban on prisoner voting violates the convention, stressing that

> [a]ny departure from the principle of universal suffrage risks undermining the democratic validity of the legislature thus elected and the laws which it promulgates. Exclusion of any groups or categories of the general population must accordingly be reconcilable with the underlying purposes of Article 3 of Protocol No. 1.[36]

It confirmed that, although disenfranchisement of prisoners might constitute a pursuit of a government's legitimate aim, the blanket ban on all prisoner voting was a disproportionate measure and, therefore, constituted a violation of the convention. By holding that "the severe measure of disenfranchisement must...not be undertaken lightly and the principle of proportionality requires a discernible and sufficient link between the sanction and the conduct and circumstances of the individual concerned," the court made it quite difficult for member states to disenfranchise prisoners without violating the convention at the same time.

The decision has been criticized by numerous scholars within and outside Europe. Most notably, it upset American critics since there is a lively debate going on in United States over prisoners' right to vote. One of the arguments against the decision is that the court selectively relied on comparative experiences, looking to decisions of Canada and South Africa, but not to the United States.[37] According to Roger Alford, professor of law at Pepperdine University,

> the case is an alarming example of an international tribunal finding an individual right where none exists, interpreting that right broadly to require felon suffrage, ignoring historical roots, rejecting the democratic preferences in 60 percent of Contracting States, and selectively relying on comparative experiences to reach the desired result.
>
> *(Alford, 2005; see Blomhoff, 2005)*

Despite the *Hirst* ruling, prisoners in United Kingdom still do not have the right to vote. The Council of Ministers, which supervises the judgments' implementation, closed the case after 13 years in 2019. The closing of the case has been described as "an assault on the values to which democratic states ascribe and a hollow victory for the protection of rights" (Adams, 2019).

Meanwhile, the European Court of Human Rights issued several other decisions on prisoners' right to vote. In its 2010 decision, *Frodl v. Austria*, the court made it even harder for the governments to restrict voting rights of convicted persons. The court ruled that there needs to be a "direct link between the facts on which a conviction is based and the sanction of disenfranchisement."[38] A prisoner's right to vote could thus be taken away only in limited cases, for example, when a prisoner was imprisoned as a result of abuse of a public position or a threat to undermine the rule of law or democratic foundations.[39] The court also stated that disenfranchisement of the prisoner "should preferably be imposed not by operation of a law but by the decision of a judge following judicial proceedings."[40] The other case involved Franco Scoppola, an Italian citizen, who was convicted to 30 years for killing his wife and injuring his son. Based on a severity of the crime committed, under Italian law, he was also automatically disenfranchised. Relying on the *Frodl* decision, the chamber ruling found violation of the convention. The case was referred to the Grand Chamber of the European Court of Human Rights. The Grand Chamber rowed back considerably from the reasoning in *Frodl*. It ruled that having criteria for disenfranchisement in the legislation and not leaving the balancing to the judge does not violate the convention.[41] According to the court, the state may decide either to leave it to the courts to determine the proportionality of a measure restricting convicted prisoners' voting rights, or to incorporate relevant provisions into their laws.[42] The intervention of a judge is thus not mandatory in the disenfranchisement process. Consequently, the court ruled that voting rights of the Italian prisoner were not violated.

Disenfranchisement on the Basis of Bankruptcy

In a number of cases,[43] the European Court has ruled that disenfranchisement, being a measure taken against a bankrupt individual, presented an illegitimate restriction on voting rights. The court has observed that the measure serves no purpose other than to belittle such persons, penalizing them simply for having declared insolvency, irrespective of whether they have committed an offence. Furthermore, the court has pointed out that, far from being a privilege, voting is a right protected by the convention. The court has therefore held unanimously in all these cases that there had been a violation of Article 3 of protocol No. 1 of the European Convention of Human Rights.

Voting Rights of Persons with Disabilities

Legislation is often designed only with healthy voters in mind. Polling places are not wheelchair-accessible, or ballots are designed in such a way that visually impaired voters cannot read them. Since voters with physical and mental disabilities, including blind voters and elderly, are often unable to cast votes in the normal way, these voters need special arrangements that facilitate their voting. Elderly voters and voters with disabilities are continuously pressing on legislators and fighting in the courtrooms to gain equal access to voting. In some countries, they have been quite successful. In United States, as early as 1984, special laws were enacted to facilitate voting by the elderly and the disabled.[44] By 1994, all American polling places were said to be accessible to persons with disabilities and the elderly.[45] After the 2002 Help America Vote Act (HAVA) was adopted, billions of dollars were spent in order to facilitate voting by disabled persons.[46] Help America Vote Act has required all polling places to be accessible and equipped with machines that provide persons with disabilities the same opportunity for access and participation, including privacy and independence, that other voters receive.

Yet the current situation and legislation still attracts a lot of criticism by commentators and academia, which argue that disabled voters in the United States are still treated as second-class citizens on Election Day (Stone, 1998; Waterstone, 2003; Weis, 2004; Mercurio, 2004). For decades, some researchers have been proposing remote internet voting for persons with disabilities (Stone, 1998; Mercurio, 2004) while others have proposed the introduction of special arrangements for the blind (Harrington, 1999; Van Hagen, 2005) or elderly (LaFratta & Lake, 2001).

European democracies vary a lot when it comes to the regulation of disabled persons' voting rights. In most of them, polling stations and ballots were not accessible until the United Nation Convention on the Rights of Persons with Disabilities came into force in 2008. Under Article 8 of the Convention, state parties should ensure accessible buildings, indoor and outdoor facilities, information, communications, and other services.[47] Under Article 29 of the Convention, state parties undertake "protecting the right of persons with disabilities to vote by secret ballot."[48] This does not mean, however, that the voter is prohibited from having the assistance of another person while voting, if he or she so wishes. This is made clear by Art. 29 (a)(iii) of the

Convention, under which a voter is, besides voting privately and independently, allowed to have assistance in voting by a person of their own choice. All of the European Union member states, as well as the European Union itself, have ratified the convention.

The Convention on the Rights of Persons with Disabilities has triggered legal reforms in many European democracies. Constitutions and legislation in many democracies, particularly in the Western European ones, were amended and now they require polling stations to be accessible and assure secret ballot for disabled voters. In France, Sweden, and the Netherlands, however, the secret ballot is still not assured to the disabled. In these countries, disabled voters can appoint a proxy, and this person visits a polling station and casts ballot instead of the voter.[49]

In Eastern European democracies, on the other hand, not much has changed. Though the convention was ratified by many Eastern European democracies, it has still not been implemented in many. Two court proceedings took place in Slovenia, in which disabled voters claimed that legislation and practices violate their rights under the Convention on the Rights of Persons with Disabilities. In one of them, the Constitutional Court ruled that the rights of disabled persons were not violated, although only three percent of the polling stations were accessible. According to the court, disabled voters' rights are not violated when legislation gives them the possibility to follow a complicated administrative procedure to have their names moved from an inaccessible polling station's voter list to that of an accessible polling station.[50] In a different case, the Administrative Court ruled that a blind voter's rights were not violated, although neither voting machines nor Braille ballots were provided. A blind voter was told by the court that the government is not bound to assure an *absolutely secret ballot*, but only a *secret ballot* and that having someone else cast a ballot for him still counts as *secret*.[51]

In the *Toplak and Mrak v. Slovenia* judgment, issued in 2021, the Strasbourg-based court found no violation in only partly accessible polling stations, and in voters not being able to fill their ballots without revealing votes to other persons.[52]

In 2010, the European Court of Human Rights issued an important decision on the voting rights of persons with disabilities.[53] A Hungarian citizen, who suffered from manic depression, had been placed under partial guardianship for that reason. Under the Hungarian Constitution, all persons under guardianship were disenfranchised. The European Court held unanimously that such an absolute ban violated the right to free elections of Article 3 of Protocol 1 ECHR. In its reasoning, the court relied heavily on the UN Convention on the Rights of Persons with Disabilities, although Hungary had not yet ratified it at the time of elections in question. The decision is particularly important for extending the discrimination provision of the European Convention of Human Rights to disabled persons and for recognizing, for the first time, the right to vote of disabled persons.

In two recent judgments, *Strøbje and Rosenlind v. Denmark* and *Caamaño Valle v. Spain*, the European court found no violation in disenfranchisement of voters with intellectual disabilities.[54]

In addition to the first Protocol to the European Convention of Human Rights, there are several recommendations and other documents[55] published by the Council of Europe that guarantee disabled persons access to voting. See particularly the recommendation of April 5, 2006, which recommends to member states, among others, that they "ensure that voting procedures and facilities are appropriate and accessible to people with disabilities so that they are able to exercise their democratic rights, and allow, where necessary, the provision of assistance in voting."[56]

Compulsory Voting and the Right Not to Vote

Compulsory voting is a practice that requires citizens to vote in elections or to attend a polling place to get their name crossed off the electoral roll. Because of the secret ballot, people can only be compelled to cast ballots, whether they choose to vote formally or not. If an eligible voter does not attend a polling place, that person may be subject to fine, community service, imprisonment, or disenfranchisement in the case that he does not appear in the polling place. About thirty democracies require their citizens to vote, among them Australia, Austria (presidential elections only), Belgium, Greece, Luxemburg, Turkey, Argentina, and Brazil. Some commentators argue that voting should not be compulsory, as people have a "right not to vote" (Lardy, 2004).

The European Commission addressed the question of compulsory voting in 1972. At that time, voting in the Austrian parliamentary and presidential elections was mandatory.[57] The case was brought by an Austrian citizen challenging the Austrian federal law on presidential elections.[58] The challenge, under Article P1-3, was dismissed since the article did not cover presidential elections. The commission, however, evaluated compliance of the Austrian compulsory voting with the Convention's Article 9 on the freedom of thought, conscience, and religion. The court ruled that a system of compulsory voting for those of majority age does not violate the right to freedom of conscience, provided that electors are free to hand in a blank or spoiled ballot. Although the compliance of compulsory voting with the Article P1-3 has not been evaluated, commentators agree that the decision would be the same as that reached in the Austrian case (Baston & Ritchie, 2004).

The Right to Stand for Election and Ballot Access

The Strasbourg Court faced the limitations on running for office in several different cases. British law posed restrictions on the involvement of senior local government officers in certain types of political activity, inter alia, running for certain offices.[59] In Greece, most of the civil and public servants were not allowed to stand as candidates in elections. Under the Greek Constitution,[60] a person who has held a senior position as a public servant for more than three months during the three years preceding the election cannot be elected to parliament. Two complaints to the court were filed by several different civil servants, mostly employed by state television, who were elected and declared official winners, but were consequently disqualified.[61] In both cases, the court held that the state's aim to secure the political impartiality of state officers was legitimate. In the British case, the court took into consideration the fact that restrictions only operate for as long as the applicants occupy politically restricted posts.[62] According to the court, "any of the applicants wishing to run for elected office is at liberty to resign from his post."[63]

Moreover, in a more recent case involving the right to stand for election, the court ruled that the requirement that candidates have knowledge of certain language constitutes a state's legitimate aim and is not necessarily an unacceptable infringement of the right to stand for election. The applicant, a member of Russian minority in Latvia, was struck off the list of candidates on the grounds that she did not speak Latvian well enough, although she possessed the official certificate of an "upper-level" knowledge of the Latvian language.[64]

One of the most interesting questions in the ECHR jurisprudence is whether one can be denied the right to stand for election on account of one's previous activities. In two of these cases, the commission declared inadmissible applications from persons who had been convicted, following the Second World War, of collaboration with the enemy or "uncitizen-like conduct" and, on that account, were permanently deprived of the right to vote.[65] Similarly, in the case of *Van Wambeke v. Belgium*,[66] the commission declared inadmissible, on the same grounds, an application from a former member of the Waffen-SS, convicted of treason in 1945, who complained that he had been unable to take part in the elections to the European Parliament in 1989. In the case of *Glimmerveen and Hagenbeek v. the Netherlands*,[67] the commission declared inadmissible two applications concerning the refusal to allow the applicants, who were the leaders of a proscribed organization with racist and xenophobic tendencies, to stand for election.

Probably the most controversial of the ballot-access decisions was *Ždanoka v. Latvia.*[68] The European Court of Human Rights had to decide whether the applicant's denial of the right to stand for election on the grounds that she had been a member of the Communist Party over a decade before the election in question complied with the protocol. The applicant, Tatjana Ždanoka, later a member of the European parliament, had been a member of the Communist Party at the time of Latvian independence in 1990, and she had been elected a member of the Supreme Council of the Soviet Socialist Republic of Latvia. After the declaration of Latvia's independence in May 1990, the Communist Party, which had taken part in two attempted *coups d'etat*, was declared unconstitutional and then dissolved. Five years later, Latvia enacted electoral legislation making persons who had "actively participated" in the activities of the Communist Party after January 13, 1991 ineligible to take part in elections.[69] When the applicant tried to run for the Latvian parliament, both in 1998 and 2002, her candidature was declared inadmissible.

In 2004, the European Court of Human Rights held that Latvia violated the First Protocol by not allowing Tatjana Ždanoka to run for office. The decision, however, was not definite and, in 2006, the Grand Chamber of the Court reversed the previous court's judgment. It held, by thirteen votes to four, that there had been no violation of the convention. Judge Rozakis and especially Judge Zupančič wrote strongly dissenting opinions.

In its majority opinion, the court recognized the right of the state to take certain measures to protect itself and to protect democracy.[70] It explicitly acknowledged the legitimacy of the concept of a "democracy capable of defending itself."[71] According to the court:

> pluralism and democracy are based on a compromise that requires various concessions by individuals, who must sometimes be prepared to limit some of their freedoms so as to ensure the greater stability of the country as a whole. The problem, which is then posed is that of achieving a compromise between the requirements of defending democratic society on one hand and protecting individual rights on the other. Every time a state intends to rely on the principle of "a democracy capable of defending itself" in order to justify interference with individual rights, it must carefully evaluate the scope and consequences of the measure under consideration, to ensure that the aforementioned balance is achieved.[72]

The court's assessment was that the Communist Party of Latvia could pose a real threat to Latvian democracy. It reiterated its *Refah partisi and Others* judgment: "The Court considers that a State cannot be required to wait, before intervening, until a political party has seized power and begun to take concrete steps to implement a policy incompatible with the standards of the Convention and democracy"[73]

When evaluating the compliance of the Latvian law with the convention, the court relied on several older decisions, wherein the European Commission was required to consider whether the decision to withdraw an individual's "active" or "passive" election rights on account of his or her previous activities constituted a violation of Article 3 of Protocol No. 1.[74] It must be emphasized, however, that these cases involved convicted war criminals and felons, while Mrs. Ždanoka was never convicted of a felony, but only took an active role in the Communist Party.

It is also relevant in this context to note that Article 3 of Protocol No. 1, or indeed other convention provisions, do not prevent, in principle, the contracting states from introducing general policy schemes by way of legislative measures whereby a certain category or group of individuals is treated differently from others, provided that the interference with the rights of the statutory category or group as a whole can be justified under the convention. See, in the context of a legislative ban on a police officer from engaging in political activities, the *Rekvényi v. Hungary*[75] judgment. Here, no violation of the convention was found in that the domestic legislation at issue was adjudged to be sufficiently clear and precise as to the definition of the categories of persons affected (members of the armed forces, police and security services) and, as to the scope of the application of the impugned statutory restriction, the statute's underlying purpose of excluding the whole group from political activities being compatible with the proportionality requirements under Articles 10 and 11 of the Convention.[76] In both the *Rekvényi* and *Ždanoka* decisions, however, the court stated that these limitations were acceptable only for the transitional post-communist period. For two decades, Toplak (2001) has argued that the post-communist period in Hungary and Slovenia is over and that the constitutional ban on the police officers' party membership should be repealed.

Notes

1 In United States, the maximum age is set for the elective judicial offices. See, for instance, *Trafelet v. Thompson* 444 US 906 (1979). A group of judges and registered voters challenged the Illinois Compulsory Retirement of Judges Act, which provided that a judge is automatically retired after the first general election following his or her seventieth birthday. The voters asserted that the act violated their rights under the equal protection clause by discriminatorily denying them the opportunity to vote for the candidates of their choice. The court concluded that it was entirely rational for the legislature to believe that the most satisfactory way to ensure a vigorous judiciary was to impose a maximum age limitation. (Bott, p. 59).

2 On the minimum age requirements in United States, see Bott, pp. 58–62.

3 The US Constitution sets forth the following minimum age requirements for an individual to be a candidate for a federal elective office: 35 years for president; 30 years for a US senator; and 25 years for a member of the House of Representatives. US Const. Art. II par. 1, cl. 5; US Const. Art. I par. 3, cl. 3; US Const. Art. I par. 2, cl. 2.

4 The Council of Europe Resolution 1459 (2005) reads in part: "11. The Assembly therefore invites: i. the Council of Europe member and observer states concerned to: *a.* reduce minimum age requirements for active and passive electoral rights to 18 years for the right to vote and 25 years for the right to stand as candidates." *Resolution 1459 (2005) "Abolition of restrictions on the right to vote."* Adopted by the Parliamentary Assembly of the Council of Europe on June 24, 2005 (24th Sitting).

5 Bott, *supra* note 31, at 8. (discussing *Dunn v. Blumstein*, 405 US 330 (1972).)

6 *Dunn v. Blumstein*, 405 US 330 (1972).

7 *Dunn v. Blumstein*, 405 US 330, 349 (1972).

8 *Burns v. Fortson*, 410 US 686, 687 (1973), cited in Bott, p. 8.

9 See the Table 1.2 "Voter Requirements – State Residency and Registration Laws" in Bott, pp. 9–12.

10 Code of Good Practice in Electoral Matters, Cf. I.1.1c.

11 *Py v. France*, no. 66289/01, ECHR 2005.

12 *Py v. France*, no. 66289/01, ECHR 2005.

13 *Polacco and Garofalo v. Italy*, 15.9.1997, DR 90-A 5.

14 *X v. United Kingdom* (1979) 15 DR 137.

15 See the Table 2.1 "Residency Requirements for Certain State Candidates." Bott, pp. 63–67.

16 *Melnychenko v. Ukraine*, no. 17707/02, ECHR 2004.

17 *Melnychenko v. Ukraine*, no. 17707/02, ECHR 2004.

18 *Boškoski v. the former Yugoslav Republic of Macedonia* (dec.), no. 11676/04, ECHR 2004-VI.

19 Art. 11(b) of the Resolution 1459 (2005) "Abolition of restrictions on the right to vote" adopted by the Parliamentary Assembly on June 24, 2005.

20 *Patrick Holland v. Ireland*, no. 24827/94, Commission decision of April 14, 1998, DR 93, p. 15.

21 *Labita v. Italy* [GC], no. 26772/95, ECHR 2000-IV.

22 *M.D.U. v. Italy*, no. 58540/00, decision of January 28, 2003.

23 Of the states examined, 18 countries allowed prisoners to vote without restriction (Albania, Azerbaijan, Croatia, the Czech Republic, Denmark, Finland, the Former Yugoslav Republic of Macedonia,

Germany, Iceland, Lithuania, Moldova, Montenegro, the Netherlands, Portugal, Slovenia, Sweden, Switzerland, and Ukraine); in 13 states, all prisoners were barred from or unable to vote (Armenia, Belgium, Bulgaria, Cyprus, Estonia, Georgia, Hungary, Ireland, Russia, Serbia, Slovakia, Turkey, and the United Kingdom); while, in 14 states, the right to vote of prisoners could be limited in some other way (Austria, Bosnia and Herzegovina, France, Greece, Italy, Latvia, Liechtenstein, Luxembourg, Malta, Norway, Poland, Romania, and Spain). *Hirst v. the United Kingdom (no. 2)* [GC], no. 74025/01, § 33-34, ECHR 2005.

24 Section 3 of the Representation of the People Act 1983.

25 *Hirst v. the United Kingdom (no. 2)*, no. 74025/01, § 49, March 30, 2004.

26 *Id.*, § 34. The applicant John Hirst was charged with manslaughter, pleaded guilty, and was convicted for life with a possibility of parole.

27 *Hirst v. the United Kingdom (no. 2)*, no. 74025/01, March 30, 2004.

28 *Id.*, § 36.

29 Art. 25 provides: "Every citizen shall have the right and the opportunity, without any of the distinctions mentioned in Article 2 [race, colour, sex, language, religion, political or other opinion, national or social origin, property, birth or other status] and without unreasonable restrictions: (a) to take part in the conduct of public affairs, directly or through freely chosen representatives; (b) to vote" Art. 10 in part provides: "1. All persons deprived of their liberty shall be treated with humanity and with respect for the inherent dignity of the human person…3. The penitentiary system shall comprise treatment of prisoners the essential aim of which shall be their reformation and social rehabilitation." Cited in *Hirst v. the United Kingdom (no. 2)*, no. 74025/01, § 22, March 30, 2004.

30 In the General Comment (No. 25(57)), adopted by the Human Rights Committee under Article 40(4) of the ICCPR dated August 27, 1996, the committee stated, inter alia, concerning the right guaranteed under Article 25: "14. In their reports, State parties should indicate and explain the legislative provisions which would deprive citizens of their right to vote. The grounds for such deprivation should be objective and reasonable. If conviction for an offence is a basis for suspending the right to vote, the period of suspension should be proportionate to the offence and the sentence. Persons who are deprived of liberty but who have not been convicted should not be excluded from exercising the right to vote."

31 European Prison Rules (1987, *Recommendation R(87)3*, Council of Europe) reads in part: "64. Imprisonment is by the deprivation of liberty a punishment in itself. The conditions of imprisonment and the prison regimes shall not, therefore, except as incidental to justifiable segregation or the maintenance of discipline, aggravate the suffering inherent in this."

32 The European Commission for Democracy through Law (the Venice Commission) adopted the code in 2002 and submitted it to the Parliamentary Assembly of the Council of Europe. It includes the commission's guidelines as to the circumstances in which there may be deprivation of the right to vote or to be elected: "d. …(i.) provision may be made for depriving individuals of their right to vote and to be elected, but only subject to the following cumulative conditions; (ii.) it must be provided for by law; (iii.) the proportionality principle must be observed; conditions for disenfranchising individuals of the right to stand for election may be less strict than for disenfranchising them; (iv.) The deprivation must be based on mental incapacity or a criminal conviction for a serious offence. (v.) Furthermore, the withdrawal of political rights or finding of mental incapacity may only be imposed by express decision of a court of law." *Hirst v. the United Kingdom (no. 2)*, no. 74025/01, § 24, March 30, 2004.

33 *August and another v. Electoral Commission and others* (CCT8/99: 1999 (3) SA 1).

34 In 1992, the Canadian Supreme Court unanimously struck down a legislative provision barring all prisoners from voting (*Sauvé v. Canada (No. 1)* [1992] 2 SCR 438). Amendments were introduced limiting the ban to prisoners serving a sentence of two years or more. Then, the Supreme Court, on October 31, 2002 in *Sauvé v. the Attorney General of Canada (No. 2)*, held by five votes to four that the amendment, which denied the right to vote to every person imprisoned in a correctional institution serving a sentence of two years or more, was unconstitutional.

35 See primarily § 46: "There is much force in the arguments of the majority in Sauvé that removal of the vote in fact runs counter to the rehabilitation of the offender as a law-abiding member of the community and undermines the authority of the law as derived from a legislature which the community, as a whole, votes into power." See also § 22 (citing ICCPR), § 26 (quoting *Sauvé* case majority opinion given by McLachlin C.J).

36 *Hirst v. the United Kingdom (no. 2)* [GC], no. 74025/01, § 62, ECHR 2005.

37 See *Richardson v. Ramirez*, 418 US 24 (1974).

38 *Frodl v. Austria*, no. 20201/04, § 28, ECHR 2010.
39 Id., § 26.
40 Id., § 28.
41 *Scoppola v. Italy (No. 3)* [GC], 126/05, ECHR 2012.
42 Id., § 102.
43 See *Albanese v. Italy*, no. 77924/01, 23 March 2006; *Vitiello v. Italy*, no. 77962/01, 23 March 2006; *Campagnano v. Italy*, no. 77955/01, 23 March 2006; *Pantuso v. Italy*, no. 21120/02, 24 May 2006; *Bova v. Italy*, no. 25513/02, 24 May 2006.
44 In 1984, the US Congress enacted the *Voting Accessibility for the Elderly and Handicapped Act* 42 USC subsection 1973ee (VAEHA) in order to "promote the fundamental right to vote by improving access for handicapped and elderly individuals to registration facilities and polling places for Federal elections."
45 *Voting: A Constitutional Right for All Citizens: A Guidebook to Assist Election Officials to Achieve Equal Access for All Citizens to the Polling Place and to the Ballot.* National Organization on Disability and National Task Force on Accessible Elections, 1999, p. 3. See this publicaton for detailed standards that have been set as to what defines an "accessible" polling place.
46 *Help America Vote Act* (HAVA), Pub.L. 107-252 passed on October 29, 2002.
47 Art. 9 of the United Nations Convention on the Rights of Persons with Disabilities.
48 Art. 29 (a)(ii) of the United Nations Convention on the Rights of Persons with Disabilities.
49 In France and the Netherlands, anyone can be appointed as a proxy voter. In Sweden, the persons who can act as messengers are: (a) Voter's spouse or cohabitee and the voter's spouse's or cohabitee's children; (b) those who professionally or in a similar way provide the voter with care or who otherwise assist the voter in personal affairs; (c) those who have been specially appointed by the local government to be messengers; (d) postmen employed by Swedish Post (only in rural areas of Sweden); employees at the remand centre or a penal institution. The Swedish Election Act (2005: 837), Chapter 7, Section 5.
50 Constitutional Court of Slovenia decision U-I-25/10 of November 11, 2010.
51 Administrative Court of Slovenia decision II U 137/2012 of May 23, 2012.
52 *Toplak and Mrak v. Slovenia*, no. 34591/19, 42545/19, 26 October 2021.
53 *Alajos Kiss v. Hungary*, no. 38832/06, May 20, 2010.
54 *Strøbje and Rosenlind v. Denmark*, no. 25802/18 27338/18, February 2, 2021, and *Caamaño Valle v. Spain*, no. 43564/17, May 11, 2021.
55 See the revised *European Social Charter*, adopted by the Committee of Ministers on April 1–4, 1996 and opened for signature on May 3, 1996, provides in its Article 15, entitled "Right of persons with disabilities to independence, social integration and participation in the life of the community":

"With a view to ensuring to persons with disabilities, irrespective of age and the nature and origin of their disabilities, the effective exercise of the right to independence, social integration and participation in the life of the community, the Parties undertake, in particular: 3. to promote their full social integration and participation in the life of the community, in particular through measures, including technical aids, aiming to overcome barriers to communication and mobility and enabling access to transport, housing, cultural activities and leisure."

56 Recommendation No. Rec(2006)5 of the Committee of Ministers of April 5, 2006 on the Council of Europe Action Plan to promote the rights and full participation of people with disabilities in society. This recommendation identifies a comprehensive set of objectives and specific actions to be implemented by Member States in this area. As regards participation in political and public life, Recommendation No. Rec(2006)5 states:

"The participation of all citizens in political and public life and the democratic process is essential for the development of democratic societies. Society needs to reflect the diversity of its citizens and benefit from their varied experience and knowledge. It is therefore important that people with disabilities can exercise their rights to vote and to participate in such activities."

57 The mandatory voting for the elections to the Austrian National Council was abolished in 1992. Until then, each province was entitled to regulate mandatory voting in the respective provincial election laws. Styria, Tyrol, and Vorarlberg were the last provinces to exercise compulsory voting. They did so until 1992. As for the presidential elections, a nation-wide duty to vote existed until 1982. Subsequently, it was up to the provinces whether or not they required the exercise of the voting right. During the elections to the office of Federal President in 2004, only the province of Tyrol still had a provision governing compulsory voting. However, said provision was abolished in the same year, shortly after the elections. Federal Ministry of the Interior of Austria website at www.bmi.gv.at/wahlen/elections _compulsorey_voting.asp.

58 *Bundespräsidentenwahlgesetz 1971*, BGBI, No 57/1971.
59 *Ahmed and Others v. the United Kingdom*, judgment of September 2, 1998, *Reports of Judgments and Decisions* 1998-VI, § 75.
60 Art. 56 § 3 of the Constitution of Greece.
61 *Gitonas and Others v. Greece*, judgment of July 1, 1997, *Reports of Judgments and Decisions* 1997-IV. See also subsequent repetitive cases, *Karchimakis v. Greece* (dec.), no. 40429/98, September 10, 1998 and *Stratakis v. Greece* (dec.), no. 39709/98, September 10, 1998.
62 *Ahmed and Others v. the United Kingdom*, judgment of September 2, 1998, *Reports of Judgments and Decisions* 1998-VI, § 75.
63 *Ahmed and Others v. the United Kingdom*, judgment of September 2, 1998, *Reports of Judgments and Decisions* 1998-VI, § 75. In this case, the court applied its standard "proportionality test." Accordingly, the court first determined whether there had been an interference with the right and then determined whether the interference was justified. Answering this, the Court used a three-step test: (a) were the interferences "prescribed by law"; (b) did the state pursue a "legitimate aim"; and, finally, (c) was the interference with the right "necessary in a democratic society," therefore proportional to the aim pursued.
64 *Podkolzina v. Latvia*, no. 46726/99, ECHR 2002-II.
65 *X. v. the Netherlands* (no. 6573/74, Commission decision of December 19, 1974, DR 1, p. 88) and *X. v. Belgium* (no. 8701/79, Commission decision of December 3, 1979, DR 18, p.250). Discussed in *Ždanoka v. Latvia* [GC], no. 58278/00, § 109, ECHR 2006.
66 *Van Wambeke v. Belgium* (dec.), no. 16692/90, April 12, 1991.
67 *Glimmerveen and Hagenbeek v. the Netherlands* (dec.), nos. 8348/78 and 8406/78, October 11, 1979, DR 18, p. 187.
68 *Ždanoka v. Latvia* [GC], 58278/00 [2006] ECHR 231 (16 March 2006) (Grand Chamber decision). *Ždanoka v. Latvia*, no. 58278/00, § 109, ECHR 2004 (Chamber Decision).
69 Section 4 of the Latvian Parliamentary Elections Act (Saeimas velešanu likums) of May 25, 1995 reads: "All Latvian citizens who have reached the age of 21 on the date of the elections may be elected to Parliament, on condition that they are not concerned by one of the restrictions provided for in section 5 of the present law." Section 5 reads in part: "The following may not stand as candidates in elections or be elected to Parliament…(6) persons who actively participated [darbojušas] after 13 January 1991 in the [Communist Party of the Soviet Union (Communist Party of Latvia)], the Internationalist Front of Workers of the Latvian SSR, the United Council of Labour Collectives, the Organisation of War and Labour Veterans or the Latvian Public Rescue Committee, or in their regional committees."
70 "In order to guarantee the stability and effectiveness of a democratic system, the State may be required to take specific measures to protect itself" *Ždanoka v. Latvia* [GC], 58278/00 [2006] ECHR 231 (March 16, 2006), § 100.
71 *Ždanoka v. Latvia* [GC], 58278/00 [2006] ECHR 231 (March 16, 2006), § 100. The court relies on the judgement of *Vogt v. Germany*, judgment of September 26, 1995, Series A no. 323.
72 *Ždanoka v. Latvia* [GC], no. 58278/00, § 100, ECHR 2006. Here, the court relies on *United Communist Party of Turkey and Others v. Turkey*, judgment of January 30, 1998, *Reports of Judgments and Decisions* 1998-I, pp. 21–22, § 45-46, and *Refah Partisi (the Welfare Party) and Others v. Turkey* [GC], nos. 41340/98, 41342/98, 41343/98 and 41344/98, § 86, ECHR 2003-II.
73 *Ždanoka v. Latvia* [GC], no. 58278/00, § 101, ECHR 2006.
74 Among these are above mentioned *X v. the Netherlands, X. v. Belgium, Van Wambeke v. Belgium*, and *Glimmervee and Hagenbeek v. the Netherlands*.
75 *Rekvényi v. Hungary* [GC], no. 25390/94, ECHR 1999-III.
76 *Ždanoka v. Latvia* [GC], no. 58278/00, § 102–103, ECHR 2006.

References

Adams, E. (n.d.). Prisoners' voting rights: Case closed? *U.K. Const. L. Blog*. January 30, 2019. Available at https://ukconstitutionallaw.org/

Alford, R. (2005). Opinio Juris. October 13, 2005. Available at http://lawofnations.blogspot.com/2005/10/civic-death-penalty-violates-european.html

Baston, L., & Ritchie, K. (2004). *Turning out or turning off: An analysis of political disengagement and what can be done about it* (pp. 35–37). Electoral Reform Society.

Blomhoff, J. (2005). Hirst v. UK. *ComparativeLawBlog*. October 6 2005. Available at http://comparativelawblog.blogspot.com/2005/10/hirst-v-uk-grand-chamber-of-echr-rules.html

European Court of Human Rights. (2021). *Toplak and Mrak v. Slovenia* (applications no. 34591/19, 2545/19). Retrieved October 26, 2021 from https://hudoc.echr.coe.int/eng?i=001-212693

Harrington, J. C. (1999). Pencils within reach and a walkman or two: Making the secret ballot available to voters who are blind or have other physical disabilities: A chronology of litigation history, theory, and results. *Tex. F. on C.L. & C.R.*, *4*, 87.

LaFratta, B., & Lake, J. (2001). Inside the voting booth: Ensuring the intent of the elderly voter. *Elder L.J.*, *9*, 141.

Lardy, H. (2004). Is there a right not to vote? *Oxford Journal of Legal Studies*, *24*, 303–321 (arguing that there is no such a thing as a right not to vote).

Mercurio, B. (2004). Democracy in decline: Can internet voting save the electoral process? *J. Marshall J. Computer & Info. L.*, *22*, 409.

Stone, P. A. (1998). Electronic ballot boxes: Legal obstacles to voting over the internet. *McGeorge L. Rev.* *29*, 953.

Toplak, J. (2001). *Enake politične pravice za vse: tudi policiste in vojake. Pravna praksa*, *20*(26–27), 10–12.

Van Hagen, E. (2005). The not-so-secret ballot: How Washington fails to provide a secret vote for impaired voters as required by The Washington State Constitution. *Wash. L. Rev.*, *80*, 787.

Venice Commission (2005). European commission for democracy through law. Opinion on the compatibility of the existing legislation in Montenegro concerning the organisation of referendums with applicable international standards. Adopted by the Venice commission at its 65th plenary session, Venice, December 16–17, 2005. Available at http://www.venice.coe.int/docs/2005/CDL-AD(2005)041-e.asp.

Waterstone, M. (2003). Constitutional and statutory voting rights for people with disabilities (*symposium: Development in disability rights*). *Stan. L. & Pol'y Rev*, *14*, 353.

Weis, C. J. (2004). Why the help America vote act fails to help disabled Americans vote. *N.Y.U. J. Legis. & Pub. Pol'y*, *8*, 421.

5

ELECTORAL MANAGEMENT

Toby S. James and Holly Ann Garnett

Introduction

Over 500 election officials were reported to have died delivering the combined Indonesian elections in April 2019. The cause was not election violence or riots from competing forces trying to seize power, but heart attacks, hepatic comas, strokes, and respiratory failures, as employees labored under extremely difficult conditions, according to the Ministry of Health (Manafe & Yasmin, 2019). Although the precise number of deaths attributable to the election has been debated, the case shone a light on the much-overlooked area of how elections are run and who runs them (BBC News, 2019).

The challenge of running elections amounts to the largest peacetime logistical operation, with the highest possible stakes. The Indonesian election involved over seven million officials, 810,000 polling stations, and 193 million voters. The process included transporting votes from remote parts of the country via boat or horseback (BBC News, 2019). Indonesia was the world's third-largest democracy at the time and might appear to be an extreme case, but the challenges of organizing an election are echoed across the globe. They have become a central concern of policy makers, practitioners, and the public. Inquiries have been set up to identify the nature, causes, and consequences of electoral management problems in countries such as the United States (Bauer & Ginsberg, 2014) and at the international level (Global Commission on Elections, 2012).

Scholarly attention had been much slower, but this has changed significantly over recent years. Academic interest took off in the US in light of troubled elections such as the 2000 US presidential election. The expanding work of the international community in the field of electoral assistance has left a heavy imprint of grey literature on best practice (Carothers, 2003) and scholarship on that work (Lührmann, 2018). Cross-national work on electoral management has also ploughed new lines of enquiry (Garnett, 2017; Garnett, 2019a; James, 2020; James et al., 2019).

This chapter provides an overview of the state of the art of scholarly knowledge on electoral management. After introducing the concept, it explains the variety of state and non-state organizations that are involved in delivering elections. Next, it considers how "successful" electoral management has been conceptualized and measured. The factors that are thought to shape electoral management quality are explained, before the conclusion considers the consequences for the design of election law.

 DOI: 10.4324/9780429401800-5

Defining Electoral Management

Despite the obvious challenge of running elections, it has traditionally not been the focus of academic inquiry. Instead, scholars have paid more attention to the design of other electoral institutions or the political behavior of voters. It is a universal truth of public management, however, that once a decision has been made to provide a public service, the equally difficult task that remains is to implement the policy. Once electoral laws have been decided by governments and parliaments, public officials have the ominous task of implementing these decisions.

Electoral management is, therefore, the implementation of the electoral process (James, 2020). This implementation process involves a number of tasks (James et al., 2019) including:

- *Organizing the electoral process.* This could range from pre-election registration and campaigning and party and candidate registration to the actual voting on election day and post-election vote counting;
- *Monitoring electoral conduct throughout the electoral process.* This includes monitoring the political party/candidates' campaigns and media in the lead-up to elections, enforcing regulations regarding voter and party eligibility, campaign finance, campaign and media conduct, vote count, and tallying procedures, etc.;
- *Certifying election results.* Certification is undertaken by declaring electoral outcomes.

This list of tasks, however, is not exhaustive. Electoral officials conduct a wide range of other tasks, as diverse as the institutions that run elections.

Importantly, electoral management involves not only implementation, but also some degree of decision-making (James, 2020). The organization of polling stations, count venues, and electoral registration processes inevitably involves many meso- and micro- level decisions for practitioners as how best to the implement law. Even in countries where law is precise in detail and expansive in coverage, electoral officials have some freedom to consider how the election is organized. Electoral management is also surrounded by broader political debates and decisions such as funding. As with every public service, public management is surrounded by and inseparable from politics.

Electoral Management Bodies

Who runs elections? Identifying the organizations that deliver elections cross-nationally is no easy task, as organizational terminology does not always travel well across languages and political systems. The term "electoral commission" is used in many countries to refer to the organization that we might expect to be running elections. However, in some countries, the task of organizing elections partly rests with the government itself, or with units of sub-national government.

The term electoral management body[1] was usefully defined in International IDEA's *Electoral Management Handbook* as "an organization or body that has the sole purpose of, and is legally responsible for, managing some or all of the elements that are essential for the conduct of elections and direct democracy instruments" (Catt et al., 2014, 5). But, in many instances, these tasks might be shared across many organizations. For example, the Electoral Commission of Malta is responsible for maintaining and publishing the electoral registers.[2] These electoral registers, however, are based on information generated by Identify Malta, which also publishes the voter ID cards used at elections. The handbook recommends that all such organizations playing a role should be considered EMBs.

There have been some attempts to classify electoral management bodies. Initial approaches in this regard involved focusing on organizational structure. Rafael Lopez-Pintor (2000, 21–30)'s seminal report for the UNDP suggested that there five different types. The International IDEA typology condensed this to three: Governmental, independent, and mixed models. The governmental model involves elections being organized and managed by an executive branch through a ministry and/or local authorities. Cited examples of this included Denmark, Switzerland, and the UK. An independent model involves elections run by EMBs that had statutorily independence from the government. Contemporary examples included Estonia, Nigeria, and Thailand. Meanwhile, a mixed model involves some combination of these of governmental and non-governmental bodies. The International IDEA Handbook on Electoral Management Design classified every country according to this framework (Catt et al., 2014). These data have been hugely influential and are often cited in quantitative studies on electoral as a key independent variable (Birch, 2008; Norris, 2015).

One alternative approach to classification has been developed using policy network theory. The concept of electoral management government networks is used by James (2020, 87–196) to refer not only to the constellation of actors involved in delivering elections, but also to the relationships among them. Electoral management is thus defined in functional terms – identifying the actors who contribute towards the actual process of running the election, rather than institutional terms, which would involve simply looking at the statutorily designated organization for running elections. Actors who are formally part of civil society might be playing a role in organizing elections through voter registration drives, but they are not EMBs since they form part of civil society. International actors might also play an important role in shaping or directly delivering elections.

Borrowing from the concept of policy networks in broader public administration literatures (Rhodes & Marsh, 1992), the electoral networked governance approach seeks to identify types of network based on the diversity of actors involved in delivery partnerships, the degree of contestation, and power relationships. A typology has been proposed based on qualitative case studies to suggest some ideal type networks:

- *Closed statist.* These are found in autocratic regimes wherein the number of actors involved in running elections is very limited. Power is centralized through top-down control and there is an absence of open debate about electoral management for fear of state repression;
- *Contested statist.* These are autocratic or competitive authoritarian regimes in which there is some contestation and a greater variety of actors – but some ultimate hegemony for the ruling party or elite;
- *Mature governmental.* In this network type, elections are delivered by a single or collection of state organizations. There tends to be little civil society interest in the management of elections – and so a "silent consensus" might exist about how elections are run;
- *Asymmetric network.* A greater variety of actors are involved in proactively delivering elections, and there is considerable contestation about how elections should be run. Power remains consolidated with government, however;
- *Pluralistic collaborative.* At this extreme, there is a wide variety of actors and views, but power is also widely dispersed.

Electoral Management Quality

How do we know good electoral management when we see it? Elections are often surrounded by claims and counterclaims from members of the public, government, opposition, and international community that there were (not) defects with the election. Data on electoral management quality

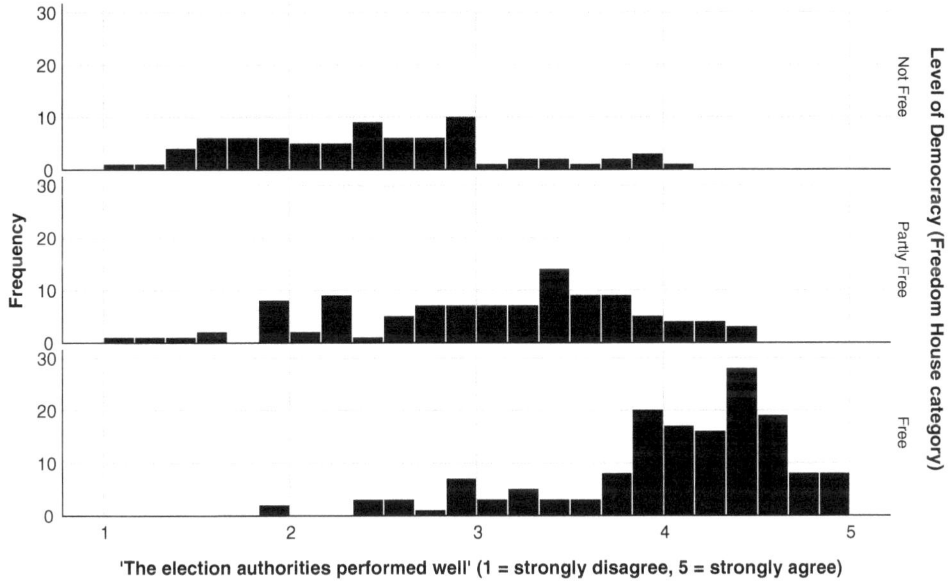

Figure 5.1 The Performance of Electoral Authorities in 166 Countries, From July 1, 2012 to December 31, 2018.

Source: The Electoral Integrity Project.

was initially quicker to emerge than more detailed elaborations of the underlying concepts. The international community increasingly undertook evaluations of elections through observation missions as election monitoring became established as an international norm (Hyde, 2011b). Unweighted data from the Quality of Elections Database (Kelley, 2011), based on these reports, suggests that problems with electoral management were present on the day of elections in 15.2% of contests between 1977 and 2004 (Kelley, 2011). More recently, the Electoral Integrity Project undertook surveys of academic experts around the world to ask their opinion about the performance of electoral authorities amongst a range of other questions about election quality. Figure 5.1 summarizes the responses for elections from 2012 to 2018 on a five-point scale. This suggests divergence in the quality of electoral management even within different types of political regimes.

But what is "good" performance? These measures don't, in themselves, answer that question without any elaboration and defining of our concepts.

One approach is to define good quality electoral management in terms of compliance with international standards (Norris, 2013a, b). Norris, for example, defines electoral integrity in general as "respecting international standards and global norms governing the appropriate conduct of elections" (Norris, 2015, 4). Most famously, Article 21(3) of the Universal Declaration of Human Rights states that:

> The will of the people shall be the basis of the authority of government; this will shall be expressed in periodic and genuine elections which shall be by universal and equal suffrage and shall be held by secret vote or by equivalent free voting procedures.
>
> *(UN General Assembly, 1948)*

Since then, the variety of international agreements have proliferated. There is also a "grey" policy literature that has been established by organizations such as the UNDP, International

IDEA, International Foundation for Electoral Systems (IFES), and the Carter Center (see, for example: Carter Center, 2014). Although these documents and agreements were designed to relate to electoral integrity in general, many shape our understanding of what "good" electoral management might involve and, therefore, could be used in the assessment of electoral management quality in any given jurisdiction.

A crucial advantage of this approach is that, by pointing out shortcomings in a country's electoral management against international norms and obligations, enforceability might be easier. It might be easier to gain consensus about the way forward, if there were an external set of practices that actors have signed up to. In the corridors of power in the UN, political theorists such as Robert Dahl may be less well known and their work is relatively abstract. However, states would be aware of the commitments that they have made about running elections well.

There are weaknesses with the approach, however. Firstly, as Norris herself points out, "'normative' authority is understood to derive from the body of human rights treaties and conventions in the international community; not directly from principles of democracy" (Norris, 2015, 4). There is, therefore, no room to guarantee that the international norms themselves are virtuous – or scope for research and practitioners to identify better practices in the future in light of new evidence or changed circumstances. Secondly, international agreements are themselves silent on key aspects of electoral management. Few say little, for example, about the completeness and accuracy of electoral registers, the funding of elections, and the management of workforces. International agreements and standards are useful instruments for incentivizing and tilting the behavior of states towards elections (James, 2020, 161–96), but are not necessarily good measures of electoral management *per se*.

A second, more detailed approach, is set out in the Electoral Performance Index (EPI). A concern about the management of elections was deep rooted in American history, but became especially strong after the 2000 US presidential election. Heather Gerken (2009) argued that an index would incentivize states to perform better and encourage accountability of electoral officials. This vision was realized through the work first of the Pew Center and later the MIT Election Data & Science Lab. The EPI was first launched in 2013, developed to assess the quality of electoral administration in US states. It was then updated and published quantitative measures of performance for each state in the 2016 elections. An overall index was based on 17 measures, including the number of mail ballots rejected, provisional ballots cast, voting wait times, residual vote rates, and turnout (MEDSL, 2018b). The rankings allowed changes to be identified with an objective measure over time and other patterns to emerge. For example, the 2016 index showed that states have increasingly made voter registration available online and that improvements had been made in wait times. In 2016, no state had an average wait-time to vote of over 20 minutes (MEDSL, 2018a).

The EPI presented a major step forward in assessing the quality of electoral management in the US. Gathering data along the lines undertaken by the Electoral Performance Index (EPI) becomes much more difficult at a cross-national level, however, because comparable information is rarely available. Relying on data collected by EMBs themselves is often patchy and incomplete. Some public surveys on perceptions of election quality exist, including modules of the Comparative Study of Electoral Systems, the World Values Survey, and some Global Barometer surveys. However, the public may not be deeply aware of the technical management of electoral processes or may be biased by other considerations, most notably whether their preferred candidate won the election (Anderson & Tverdova, 2001).

On the cross-national level, different approaches may thus be used in evaluating electoral management quality. Public administration scholarship offers an alternative way forward.

Evaluating public services has long been a concern of public administration, but it became an extended line of scholarship as new public management became influential in the Anglosphere (Hood, 1991) and internationally in an era of aid conditionality in the 1990s (Leftwich, 1993). Initial frameworks focused on the three Es: Economy, efficiency, and effectiveness. However, later models brought more nuanced ways to assess public services (Boyne, 2002). There are a variety of other factors that should be taken into consideration.

A third approach, which built on these methods for assessing public services is the PROSeS model (James, 2020, 59–86). The PROSeS model frames analysis around five dimensions of electoral management. The process design refers to whether decisions are made about managing elections with public participation, probity, and accountability. The allocation of resources is also considered alongside service outputs, outcomes, and stakeholder satisfaction. The model allows close cross-national comparison between jurisdictions to identify strengths and weaknesses in performance through mixed methods. A comparison of the UK and Canada from 2011to 2018 revealed many similarities in terms of performance (James, 2020). However, the Canadian system provided clearer systems of accountability in the process design, greater transparency with resource investment, more convenient services, less frequent service denials to voters, and higher satisfaction with citizens. The UK system, by comparison, was found to be economically efficient, had fewer rejected ballots, and did not exhibit the same accuracy enforcement issues as Canada – though this might be due to a lack of critical examination. A general lesson might be that centralized systems produce transparency accountability – but are more costly.

Organizational Features and Practices

What then shapes the quality of electoral management? To date, several factors have been explored. Most notably, a recent special issue of the *International Political Science Review* on the organizational approach to electoral management describes seven dimensions of EMBs: centralization, independence, capacity, scope, division of tasks, relation to external actors, and the use of technology (James et al., 2019). Many of these dimensions will be discussed here.

Centralization

Electoral management can be delivered in a highly centralized way through a single organization. In Canada, for example, Elections Canada is a single body responsible for running federal elections. Alternatively, it can be delivered in a very decentralized way. The law for UK parliamentary elections is set by parliament. The officials responsible for implementing it have historically been spread over 400 different local government units.

Failings in electoral integrity have often been attributed to decentralized management. These claims are predominately focused on the US, where decentralization is blamed for variations in the voter's experience of election administration. Gerken (2009, 1585–6) has suggested that "localism" has been the cause of many American problems and can make reform difficult to achieve. Pastor has claimed that the US system has been "decentralized to the point of being dysfunctional" (Pastor 2006, 273; also see Pastor, 2004). The most cited advantage of centralized systems is, therefore, consistent experiences for the voter (Guess, 2009; Catt et al., 2014, 17; James, 2017; James, 2020, 221–40; Pastor, 2004; Pastor, 2006). However, decentralized forms of election management may also have some unique advantages. Guess (2009) suggests that they often allow more responsive service delivery for diverse local needs and that they enable innovation. International IDEA's *Electoral Management Design Handbook* states that they can "ensure continuity" and "enhance inclusiveness and transparency in electoral management" (Catt et al.,

2014, 17). They have also been found to make better use of electoral officials' "knowledge of their local area" (James, 2017, 2020, 221–40).

Workforces

As the illustrative vignette of Indonesia at the start of this chapter illustrates, vast volumes of personnel are required in the immediate period surrounding polling day. The terminology used to refer to different types of staff vary from country to country. It is common, however, to refer to electoral officials at a more senior or long-term level and, at the grassroots level, to refer to the poll workers, who are needed to set up polling stations, greet voters, hand out ballot papers, and ensure voting secrecy and order in the polling station. At the end of the day, these employees may also seal ballot boxes and begin the process of counting the ballots, or transferring ballot boxes to counting locations. Even in countries where electronic voting machines are used, such as in India, they perform equivalent roles. Presiding officers are required to oversee the management of polling stations. Counting clerks are needed to count the ballots, often adjudicating between correctly completed ballot papers and those that are unclear. In addition to these short-term employees, there also tends to be a much smaller permanent workforce that is responsible for the strategic planning of elections.

The selection and nature of the short-term workforces varies enormously. They might be government employees who are seconded from other departments in the short-term, as they traditionally have been in India. They might be citizens who are compelled to undertake the task as a civic duty, as they are in Germany or Spain. Or they might be "stipend volunteers," who receive some payment for their work, as tends to be the case in the US and UK (Clark & James, 2016). Finding sufficient quality and quantity of poll workers can be a problem. Burden and Milyo (2015) report that just under half of all US jurisdictions, between 2008 and 2012, had difficulty in finding sufficient numbers of poll workers. Such problems are not confined only to American experience. but are also experienced elsewhere (Burden & Milyo, 2015; Clark & James, 2016; OSCE/ODIHR, 2008).

The size and nature of permanent workforces also varies by country. A global survey of EMBs workforces, with data collected in 2016–2017, reported that the largest workforces found were 15,000 in Mexico's Instituto Nacional Electoral, followed by 4,000 in Iraq's Independent High Electoral Commission. But most countries do not have one large national body running elections; rather, more tend to have lightly staffed central organizations. The Swiss Federal Chancellery Political Rights Section, for example, had only ten permanent staff members on the national level (James 2019, 367–7). The small nature of some teams can be explained by the fact that officials might be working on elections in other organizations, such as a devolved local government unit.

The importance of staff in the electoral process should be self-evident. Scholarship within public policy has taught that even the best-designed policies from above can go wrong at the implementation stage (Sabatier & Mazmanian, 1983). Street-level bureaucrats have considerable discretion and opportunity to implement policies differently (Lipsky, 1980). This is also the case in electoral administration. The public service that poll workers provide to electors can directly help shape public confidence in the electoral process (Hall, Quin Monson, & Patterson, 2009). The actions of those who are managing the electoral process have considerable consequences for electoral integrity. Research on the permanent workforces shows that the recruitment practices and workplace conditions make a considerable difference not only to the employees themselves, but also to the quality of the election. One cross-national study showed how EMBs that enable greater opportunities for employees to be involved in decision-making processes ran elections better, while recruitment practices, job satisfaction, and levels of stress were are also important (James, 2019).

Statutory Independence

As mentioned earlier, some of the first research on election management bodies focused on their legal independence from government, classifying them as either government departments or independent agencies. These studies assumed that independence, or impartiality, is vital to ensuring that political interests do not tamper with elections (Birch, 2008; Elklit & Reynolds, 2005; Kerevel, 2009; Mozaffar & Schedler, 2002; van Aaken, 2009). However, empirical research linking this formal independence to electoral integrity, here measured as public confidence in election, was initially underdeveloped (Birch, 2008). Van Ham and Lindberg (2015), however, have recently advanced the debate by suggesting that this relationship may be conditional on the quality of governance in a country and key differences between the role of independence in established and transitional democracies.

One key area of recent study has been the delineation between *de facto*, or actual independence of EMBs, and their *de jure* or formal legal independence. Van Ham and Garnett (2019) expand the study of EMB *de facto* independence to four components: Institutional independence, which refers to formal-legal independence as written into election law or the constitution; personnel independence, which refers to the appointment and removal mechanisms for key personnel; financial independence, which refers to control of budgets; and functional independence, which considers the scope of tasks within an EMBs jurisdiction. Their research finds that these dimensions of *de facto* independence relate strongly to overall electoral integrity, in a way that *de jure* independence does not. Meanwhile, James uses policy network theory to argue that that, while the effects of formal independence is sometimes unclear, independence provides EMBs with important strategic tactics for them to use in guarding the integrity of the electoral process against an aggressive government seeking to make changes to electoral management for partisan interest (James 2020, 87–159).

Resources and Capacity

The resources that any public organization has available to it is understandably likely to affect its performance. Many debates about the quality of public services, therefore, often focus on underfunding, especially during periods of economic austerity (Lodge & Hood, 2012). Research on electoral management has sought to explore the determinants of levels of funding of electoral services either within countries (Clark, 2019) or at a cross-national level (Garnett, 2019a; James, 2020, 252–65; López-Pintor & Fischer, 2005). The most common approach is to identify the budget size of EMBs. Different measures of spending have been introduced to measure the spending on each eligible member of the electorate or how much is spent on different voting methods (Krimmer et al., 2019). An alternative to measuring budget sizes is to measure capacity through other means. Garnett (2019a), for example, uses a website content analysis as a proxy for EMB capacity, considering whether indications of the major functions of EMBs appear on their websites.

The research seems clear that resources can make a difference to electoral management quality and that electoral officials are commonly without the resources that they require. The provision of resources has been linked to whether electoral officials can meet performance standards (Clark, 2015). When available funds are cut, there can be cuts in the quality of service to the voter, with "extras" such as voter outreach activities rolled back (James & Jervier, 2017).

Work has equally shown what the most cost-effective way of running elections are. Krimmer et al. (2019), for example, show how using remote internet voting can be a particularly cost-effective way of running elections.

If funding is so important, why is it sometimes restricted? Politics can be one reason. Mohr et al. (2019) analyzed spending on election in North Carolina from 1994 to 2014. They identified political influences as having a strong role in shaping how much the purse-string holders, in this case Republican county commissions, spent. Spend significantly declined once the county electorate reached a sufficient Republican majority. Drawing from interviews with experienced practitioners from other countries, however, James (2020, 252–65) identifies other causes such as practitioners communicating their needs to purse-string holders such as ministers, unpredictable costs, and the lack of contingency planning. Problems are, therefore, not the direct result of insufficient resources – but the advocacy and preparation for the unforeseen circumstances.

Electoral Assistance

Another line of research has focused on how the international community assists countries in building their own capacity to run elections or monitor their progress through electoral assistance programs. James traces how the period since the 1980s has seen a rapid growth in transgovernmental networks that sought to develop best practices and shape policy (James 2020, 160–96).

Foreign assistance often includes two major components: Capacity-building and election observation. Election observation has received a fair amount of empirical study in recent years (Hyde, 2011a; Hyde & Pallister, 2014; Kelley, 2012; van Aaken, 2009). These interventions are focused on measuring the impartiality and fairness of an election, usually on election day (though some observation missions have extended to the pre- and post-electoral periods). However, observers, as the name suggests, are there to observe: They are unable to directly intervene when problems, be they security, fraud, or technical errors. They instead report these concerns and publish their findings, which can then be acted upon by the domestic government or international organizations.

Capacity-building programs, on the other hand, can directly tackle the challenges of electoral integrity "on the ground" in ways that observation cannot. Technical electoral assistance often comes from international organizations and foreign governments, which assist local EMBs, governments, and civil society organizations in the tasks important to running a free and fair election. This may include working with the EMB or civil society organizations to educate votes, working with legislators to review and amend electoral laws, or helping the EMB to put in place systems to register voters (Kennedy & Fischer, 2000). This may also include in-person support from experienced professionals (including electoral officials and security services), training courses and programs, donations of technology or other resources, research and consulting services, and funding of programs aimed at specific goals. Some of the major providers include international organizations, including the United Nations Development Programme (UNDP), the Organization of American States (OAS), the International Foundation for Electoral Systems (IFES), and the International Institute for Democracy and Electoral Assistance (IDEA), to name only a few. This capacity-building support may also be provided by regional networks of EMBs, private enterprises, or on a bilateral basis, such as through a country's aid budget or, in the case of the Australian Election Commission's International Services Programme, as a peer-to-peer program managed by a foreign EMB (Mohr et al., 2019).

There are very few academic studies on the success of capacity-building programs, perhaps largely due to the difficulty of measuring "success" in such a complex environment. As such, most study of the impact of electoral assistance has been done in the process of evaluating specific programs, using imperfect retrospective qualitative and quantitative study (Australian Government Department of Foreign Affairs and International Trade, 2013; International Foundation for Electoral Systems, 2009; Nelson, 2015; USAID, 2014).

In one of the few cross-national studies, Borzyskowski (2016) considers which countries are likely to receive electoral assistance and finds that countries are less likely to request assistance under autocratic conditions, and when there are already strong electoral institutions. International organizations are less likely to provide assistance when there is a lack of domestic political will or a high chance the program cannot be fully implemented. These findings, although unsurprising, do point to electoral assistance as part of larger political questions surrounding the will for electoral integrity, and the needs of both domestic and international actors in the provision of electoral assistance.

Technology and Cyber Security

A final area of study that has experienced a resurgence in recent years is the use of technology in elections, including cyber-security (Garnett & James, 2020). Research in this area has traditionally focused on the use of e- and i-voting systems. There remains a number of concerns about the use of emerging technologies in elections, particularly surrounding issues such as the reliability and longevity of technology (Cetinkaya & Cetinkaya, 2007; Keller et al., 2004; McCormack, 2016); the privacy and security of vote choice (Gritzalis, 2003; Keller et al., 2004); and the potential implications of the use of e- and i-voting on public trust (Alvarez, Katz & Pomares, 2011; Atkeson & Saunders, 2007). Recent concerns about the potential for hacking of voting technology, whether by foreign or domestic actors, has made this issue re-emerge on the public and scholarly agenda (Garnett & James, 2020, forthcoming).

But most election management bodies use technology in all stages of the electoral cycle, not just on election day (Law Commission, 2012; Loeber, 2017). This notably includes online or digital voter registration systems. For example, biometric registration systems have been established in many countries to address the challenges of registering large populations where accurate existing population registers or identity documents do not exist (Piccolino, 2016). Online registration systems have also been tested in a variety of jurisdictions and remain vulnerable in regards to public trust (Garnett, 2019b), but also to interference by foreign or domestic actors, such as distributed denial of service, whereby the service is flooded with fake requests, preventing legitimate users from accessing it (Tenove et al., 2018). For example, the crash of the voter registration site for the Brexit referendum may have been influenced by false rumors about the need for voters to re-register, or a distributed denial-of-service, which was not ruled out as a possible cause of the crash (House of Commons Public Administration and Constitutional Affairs Committee, 2017).

In addition to communication with voters for registration, various forms of technology are also used by EMBs for the management of various forms of data, from personal registration information to electoral results. This opens EMBs to other vulnerabilities, including the hacking of private data, which could then be ransomed or sold (Canadian Communications Security Establishment, 2017). EMBs should also be concerned about the spread of information, especially about voting procedures or electoral results. Voters could be misled as to the location of their polling station, the hours of voting, or any other aspects of the electoral process, causing them to be actively denied the opportunity to vote, or simply give up on the process. Likewise, the publication of false results has occurred, for example in the 2016 election in Ghana, where the electoral commission's website was hacked (BBC News, 2016). These issues with communication with voters have the potential to degrade the trust in electoral management and the electoral process more generally. In sum, new technological threats to elections have recently become a prime concern for practitioners and scholars of electoral management.

Conclusion: Designing Election Laws

The study of elections has traditionally focused on either voter behavior or the design of electoral laws. Once laws have been written, however, there is the challenge of implementing them. The study of electoral management has seen a rapid growth in recent years to respond to this pressing gap between law and praxis.

As a result, there are now frameworks available for identifying who runs elections, for measuring electoral management quality and identifying the determinants of electoral management quality. Ironically, although the electoral management is about implementing laws, the new research shows how the design of laws is also important for good implementation. Election law, therefore, needs to be written to support high quality electoral management.

What does this mean, in practice, for writing law? Drawing from the research covered in this chapter, several lessons can be suggested. First, there are limitations to using international agreements and standards as measures of best practice because there is the risk that they are grounded in power politics and not in democratic ideals. Law should be written in such a way that promotes the achievement of democratic ideals such as promoting participation, inclusiveness, probity, and accountability, rather than following international practices *per se*.

Second, research consistently demonstrates that both legal (*de jure*) and *de facto* independence for the EMBs is important. This validates the traditional focus of the international community in the immediate post-Cold War period, which pushed for elections to be outside of the control of elected officials.

Third, resource sufficiency shapes electoral management quality, so laws that require all necessary funds to be given to electoral officials could be promoted. This includes funding for high-quality personnel and the physical resources necessary to implement these crucial activities.

Fourth, rapid changes in technology mean that laws need be regularly reviewed. Legal provisions built for traditional newspaper and broadcast media need to be updated for the digital age of social media. Additionally, as election platforms, including registration and voting, adopt new technologies, security concerns from both foreign and domestic actors must be addressed, perhaps requiring new partnerships and legal provisions for investigation and dispute resolution.

Finally, laws should also be written with the practitioner in mind. Complex, voluminous and fragmented laws should be regularly consolidated, as they can be difficult for administrators to interpret, understand, and follow in the heat of the election (James, 2014; Law Commissions, 2016).

These legal considerations must focus on helping those with the great task of implementing electoral law to conduct high-quality elections, with an aim to achieving democratic ideals.

Notes

1 The term electoral management board is sometimes used as well.
2 https://electoral.gov.mt/AboutUs.

References

Alvarez, R. M., Katz G., & Pomares, J. (2011). The impact of new technologies on voter confidence in Latin America: Evidence from e-voting experiments in Argentina and Colombia. *Journal of Information Technology & Politics*, *8*(2), 199–217.

Anderson, C. J., & Tverdova, Y.V. (2001). Winners, losers, and attitudes about government in contemporary democracies. *International Political Science Review, 22*, 321–38.
Atkeson, L. R., & Saunders, K. L. (2007). The effect of election administration on voter confidence: A local matter? *PS: Political Science and Politics, 40*(4), 655–660.
Australian Government Department of Foreign Affairs and International Trade. (2013). *Australian electoral assistance in Papua New Guinea 2000–2012: Independent evaluation.*
Bauer, R. F., & Ginsberg, B. L. (2014). *The American voting experience: Report and recommendations of the Presidential Commission on Election Administration.* Washington DC: The Presidential Commission on Election Administration.
BBC News. (2016). *Ghana election commission website hit by cyber attack.*
BBC News. (2019). *Indonesia election 2019: Why did so many officials die?.* Retrieved May 16, 2019 from https://www.bbc.co.uk/news/world-asia-48281522
Birch, S. (2008). Electoral institutions and popular confidence in electoral processes: A cross-national analysis. *Electoral Studies, 27*, 305–320.
Boyne, G. A. (2002). Concepts and indicators of local authority performance: An evaluation of the statutory frameworks in England and Wales. *Public Money & Management, 22*(2), 17–24.
Burden, B. C., & Milyo, J. (2015). The quantities and qualities of poll workers. *Election Law Journal, 14*(1), 38–46.
Canadian Communications Security Establishment. (2017). *Cyber-threats to Canada's democratic process.*
Carothers, T. (2003). *Aiding democracy abroad.* Washington, DC: Brookings Institution Press.
Carter Center. (2014). *Election observations and standards: A Carter Center assessment manual.* Atlanta, Georgia: Carter Center.
Catt, H., Ellis, A., Maley M., Wall, A., & Wolf, P. (Eds.). (2014). *Electoral management design* (Revised ed.). Stockholm: International IDEA.
Cetinkaya, O., & Cetinkaya, D. (2007). Verification and validation issues in electronic voting. *Electronic Journal of e-Government, 5*(2), 117–125.
Clark, A. (2015). Public administration and the integrity of the electoral process in British elections. *Public Administration, 93*(1), 86–102.
Clark, A. (2019). The cost of democracy: The determinants of spending on the public administration of elections. *International Political Science Review, 20*(3), 354–69.
Clark, A., & James, T. S. (2016). Why volunteer? The motivations of polling station workers on election day. In Paper for the Political Studies Association Conference, Brighton.
Elklit, J., & Reynolds, A. (2005). Judging elections and election management quality by process. *Representation, 41*(3), 189–207.
Garnett, H. A. (2017). Open election management bodies. In P. Norris & A. Nai (Eds.), *Election Watchdogs.* New York: Oxford University Press.
Garnett, H. A. (2019a). Evaluating election management body capacity. *International Political Science Review, 20*(3), 335–353.
Garnett, H. A. (2019b). Evaluating online registration: The Canadian case. *Election Law Journal: Rules, Politics, and Policy, 18*(1), 78–92.
Garnett, H. A., & James, T. S. (2020). Cyber elections in the digital age: Threats and opportunities of technology for electoral integrity. *Election Law Journal, 19*(2), 1–16.
Gerken, H. K. (2009). *The democracy index: Why our election system is failing and how to fix it.* Princeton, NJ: Princeton University Press.
Global Commission on Elections, Democracy & Security. (2012). *Deepening democracy: A strategy for improving the integrity of elections worldwide.* Stockholm: International Institute for Democracy and Electoral Assistance.
Gritzalis, D. A. (2003). *Secure electronic voting.* Springer US. doi: 10.1007/978-1-4615-0239-5
Guess, G. M. (2009). *Dysfunctional decentralization: Electoral system performance in theory and practice.* Washington, DC: Centre for Democracy and Election Management.
Hall, T. E., Monson, J. Q., & Patterson, K. D. (2009). The human dimension of elections: How poll workers shape public confidence in elections. *Political Research Quarterly, 62*(3), 507–22.
Hood, C. (1991). A public management for all seasons?. *Public Administration, 69*(Spring), 3–19.
House of Commons Public Administration and Constitutional Affairs Committee. (2017). *Lessons learned from the EU referendum.*
Hyde, S. D. (2011a). Catch us if you can: Election monitoring and international norm diffusion. *American Journal of Political Science, 55*(2).

Hyde, S. D. (2011b). *The pseudo-democrat's dilemma: Why election observation became an international norm*. Ithaca, NY and London: Cornell University Press.

Hyde, S. D., & Pallister, K. (2014). Election administration, election observation, and election quality. In J. Gandhi & R. Ruiz-Rufino (Eds.), *Routledge handbook of comparative political institutions*. New York: Routledge.

International Foundation for Electoral Systems. (2009). *Philipppines Election Reform Project*.

James, T. S. (2014). Electoral management in Britain. In P. Norris, R. Frank & F. Matinez i Coma (Eds.), *Advancing electoral integrity* (pp. 135–64). New York: Oxford University Press.

James, T. S. (2017). The effects of centralising electoral management board design. *Policy Studies, 38*, 130–148.

James, T. S. (2019). Better workers, better elections? The workforces of electoral management bodies and electoral integrity. *International Political Science Review, 40*(3), 370–390.

James, T. S. (2020). *Comparative electoral management: Performance, networks and instruments*. London and New York: Routledge.

James, T. S., & Jervier, T. (2017). The cost of elections: The effects of public sector austerity on electoral integrity and voter engagement. *Public Money & Management, 37*(7), 461–8.

James, T. S., Garnett, H. A., Loeber, L., & van Ham, C. (2019). Electoral management and the organisational determinants of electoral integrity: Introduction. *International Political Science Review, 40*(3), 295–312.

Keller, A. M., Mertz, D., Hall, J. L., & Urken, A. (2004). Privacy Issues in an Electronic Voting Machine. In Workshop on Privacy in the Electronic Society, Washington DC.

Kelley, J. (2011). *Data on international election monitoring: Three global datasets on election quality, election events and international election observation*. Inter-university Consortium for Political and Social Research (ICPSR) [distributor]. doi: 10.3886/ICPSR31461.v1

Kelley, J. (2012). *Monitoring democracy: When international election observation works, and why it often fails*. Princeton, NJ: Princeton University Press.

Kennedy, J. R., & Fischer, J. W. (2000). Technical assistance in elections. In R. Rose (Ed.), *International encyclopedia of elections* (pp. 300–5). London: MacMillian Reference.

Kerevel, Y. (2009). Election management bodies and public confidence in elections: Lessons from Latin America. In *IFES Fellowships in Democracy Studies*.

Krimmer, R., Duenas-Cid, D., Krivonosova, I., Vinkel, P., & Koitmae, A. (2019). How much does an e-vote cost? Cost comparison per vote in multichannel elections in Estonia. In *E-Vote 2018*.

Law Commission. (2012). *Electoral law in the United Kingdom: A scoping consultation paper*. London: Law Commission.

Law Commissions. (2016). *Electoral law: An interim report*. London: Law Commissions.

Leftwich, A. (1993). Democracy and development in the third world. *Third World Quarterly, 14*(3), 605–624.

Lipsky, M. (1980). *Street level bureaucracy*. New York: Russell Sage Foundation.

Lodge, M., & Hood, C. (2012). Into an age of multiple austerities? Public management and public service bargains across OECD countries. *Governance, 25*(1), 79–101.

Loeber, L. (2017). The use of technology in the election process: Who governs?. Paper presented at the Building Better Elections Workshop, organised by the Electoral Management Research Network at the ECPR Conference, Oslo, September 2017.

Lopez-Pintor, R. (2000). *Electoral management bodies as institutions of governance*. Washington DC: United Nations Development Programme.

López-Pintor, R., & Fischer, J. (2005). *Cost of Registration and Elections (CORE) Project*. New York: UNDP.

Lührmann, A. (2018). United Nations electoral assistance: More than a fig leaf?. *International Political Science Review*, 40(2), 181–96.

Manafe, D., & Yasmin, N. (2019). What kills Indonesian election officials? Jakarta Globe. Retrieved from https://jakartaglobe.id/context/what-kills-indonesian-election-officials

McCormack, C. B. (2016). Democracy rebooted: The future of technology in elections. *Atlantic Council*.

MEDSL. (2018a). *Election management in the U.S. is improving*. Boston, MA: MEDSL.

MEDSL. (2018b). *Elections performance index: Methodology report MEDSL*. Boston, MA: MEDSL.

Mohr, Z., Pope, J. V., Kropf, M. E., & Shepherd, M. J. (2019). Strategic spending: Does politics influence election administration expenditure?. *American Journal of Political Science, 63*(2), 427–38.

Mozaffar, S., & Schedler, A. (2002). The comparative study of electoral governance – Introduction. *International Political Science Review, 23*(2), 5–27.

Nelson, S. 2015. *Electoral assistance provided within the Romanian ODA programme*. United Nations Development Programme.

Norris, P. (2013a). Does the world agree about standards of electoral integrity? Evidence for the diffusion of global norms. *Electoral Studies, 32*(4), 576–88.
Norris, P. (2013b). The new research agenda studying electoral integrity. *Electoral Studies, 32*(4), 563–75.
Norris, P. (2015). *Why elections fail.* New York: Cambridge University Press.
OSCE/ODIHR. (2008). *Italy parliamentary elections 13–14 April 2008: OSCE/ODIHR election assessment mission report.* Warsaw: OSCE.
Pastor, R. A. (2004). America observed. *The American Prospect,* 20 December 2004.
Pastor, R. A. (2006). The US Administration of Elections: Decentralized to the point of being dysfunctional. In A. Wall, A. Ellis, A. Ayoub, C. W. Dundas, J. Rukambe, & S. Staino (Eds.), *Electoral management design: The international IDEA handbook.* Stockholm: International IDEA.
Piccolino, G. (2016). Infrastructural state capacity for democratization? Voter registration and identification in Côte d'Ivoire and Ghana compared. *Democratization, 23*(3), 498–519.
Rhodes, R. A. W., & Marsh, D. (1992). New directions in the study of policy networks. *European Journal of Political Research, 21*(1–2), 181–205.
Sabatier, P., & Mazmanian, A. (1983). Policy implementation. In S. S. Nagel (ed.), *Encyclopedia of policy studies.* New York: Marcel Dekker.
Tenove, C., Buffie, J., McKay, S., Moscrop, D., Warren M., & Cameron, M. A. (2018). *Digital threats to democratic elections: How foreign actors use digital techniques to undermine democracy.* Vancouver: University of British Columbia.
UN General Assembly. (1948). *The universal declaration of human rights.*
USAID. (2014). *Evaluation of USAID Electoral Assistance to Kenya.*
van Aaken, A. (2009). Independent electoral management bodies and international election observer missions: Any impact on the observed level of democracy? A conceptual framework. *Constitutional Political Economy, 20,* 296–322.
van Ham, C., & Garnett, H. A. (2019). Building impartial electoral management? Institutional design, independence and electoral integrity. *International Political Science Review, 40*(3), 313–334.
van Ham, C., & Lindberg, S. (2015). When guardians matter most: Exploring the conditions under which electoral management body institutional design affects election integrity. *Irish Political Studies, 30*(4), 454–81.
von Borzyskowski, I. (2016). Resisting democracy assistance: Who seeks and receives technical election assistance?. *The Review of International Organizations, 11*(2), 247–82.

6
ELECTRONIC VOTING

Robert Krimmer and Jordi Barrat i Esteve

Introduction

Over the last decades, different digital technologies have been implemented.[1] They aim at easing tasks to be carried out by electoral authorities, maximizing voter accessibility, reducing involuntary errors, and contributing to the overall electoral integrity (Krimmer, 2012). At the same time, digital technologies, which differ from the too generic term of new technologies, also carry new concerns that need to be addressed. In particular, consideration should be given to how the principles of secrecy and equality apply to new forms for exercising political rights and how citizens maintain a direct supervision over an electoral procedure that has new technological features (OSCE/ODIHR, 2013).

The next sections provide an overview of e-voting mechanisms based on the social and legal issues with which their implementation deals. Firstly, a terminological and conceptual classification is established. The term "electronic voting" is often used for different realities and sometimes its meaning is so broad that a consistent analysis becomes impossible. Secondly, e-voting real cases, both successful and discontinued ones, will be mapped and lessons learned will be discussed. As a third pillar, three challenges commonly associated to e-voting tools will be analyzed: How e-voting manages to protect the secrecy of the vote and freedom of voters, how equality is considered when e-voting is in place, and finally the extent to which compliance with a transparent and verifiable electoral procedure is met. As long as e-voting might be analyzed from different angles, it is worth recalling that the text focuses on social and legal perspectives only. The full picture will necessarily include other aspects, namely the computer-based one (Prosser & Krimmer, 2004).

What Is Electronic Voting?

Having in mind that electronic voting is a broad term that, in practice, may encompass a range of very different electoral procedures, a classification of electoral technologies is needed for a proper understanding of the mechanism. Otherwise, we risk ignoring its specificities.

Firstly, e-enabled tools can be used either within controlled or non-controlled environments. While the former is supervised by state officials (e.g., polling stations, embassies), the latter refers to any location from which a ballot can be cast (e.g., home). Such a distinction is important

 DOI: 10.4324/9780429401800-6

for some specific aspects that will be discussed below. For instance, voter identification and authentication are much easier within a controlled environment since such tasks may be performed in a traditional way (i.e., exhibition of an ID credential). Moreover, a controlled environment rends more difficult, though not impossible, (e.g., Bulgarian train, ballots' pictures) the task of potential coercers. On the other hand, such environments do not facilitate the process for some groups of voters, like expats, people with limited mobility, or other types of usual absentee voters. Thus, a fair balance is to be found between principles that can be contradictory in practice. Should regulations accept, for instance, postal voting, concerns regarding secrecy of the vote will be raised. E-voting is always implemented within these nuanced scenarios and thus any Manichean approach should be forbidden. E-voting paves the path for different advantages (e.g., usability, accessibility with remote voting, fast tallies, invalid ballots, and error reduction), and each country is supposed to assess its pros and cons for every specific implementing scenario.

When it comes to the classification of voting methods, another important factor relates to the verification of results by traditional paper-based means. At a first glance, electronic voting seems not to include any paper-based component, but the so-called Voter Verifiable Paper Audit Trail (VVPAT) has become crucial for the acceptance of some variations of e-voting channels. When a Direct Recording Machine (DRE) is used for casting and counting the ballots, a VVPAT can be helpful as a second source to be used for an alternative recount, together with the one carried out by the machine itself. However, it is worth recalling that VVPAT only checks whether electronic and manual results match, but such receipts are unable to address other concerns related to electronic voting (e.g., unbiased presentation of candidatures on the screens).

There are different forms of VVPAT depending on its implementation (e.g., allowing or not the voter to manipulate the document) or its binding effect that depend upon what is established in the legal framework in case of discrepancy between paper and electronic results. Moreover, determining when a recount is compulsory is an important issue to be assessed country by country. Unfortunately, regulations exist that declare only that VVPAT should be implemented with no further indication on how it should be used or its relevant legal effects. In general terms, the use of VVPAT grew after a first generation of voting machines that proved to have been poorly implemented, which was the case namely for the United States of America (Rubin, 2006). VVPATs was seen as a tool that would balance some downsides of electronic voting mechanisms. However, the introduction of VVPAT may also be controversial, as was the case both in Brazil and India (Driza-Maurer & Barrat, 2016).

Beyond within which environment e-voting is used and the introduction of VVPAT, a thorough classification of electronic voting mechanisms should also encompass other options and pay attention to more nuances. There are many steps involved in an electoral procedure and each one of them could be improved with computerized means. That's the reason that it is worth wondering whether the notion of e-voting covers all stages of such procedure or rather a specific range only.

In this regard, it is to note the role of the Council of Europe (CoE) in establishing intergovernmental standards for electronic voting. Although the recommendations approved in 2004 and 2017 have no binding effect and apply only to CoE's member states, the texts are very helpful from a theoretical approach. They also serve as soft law tools for determining in detail what implementations may be covered under an agreed notion of electronic voting. Significantly enough, in 2017, the new recommendations updated the definition. While the first recommendation (2004) shaped electronic voting as "an e-election or e-referendum that involves the use of electronic means in *at least* the casting of the vote" (Rec200411, emphasis added). In 2017, the same term (e-voting) was defined as "the use of electronic means to cast and/*or* count the vote" (Rec20175, emphasis added).

The new phrasing acknowledges that casting and counting could be performed by different means and, therefore, stand-alone scanners that are used only for the tally (i.e., counting ballots) – that is, with no previous interaction between voters and computers – are now covered by this text as actual electronic voting examples. Scanners that are just used for tally sheets and not for ballots would not be considered e-voting cases. The rationale behind this decision underscores the fact that certain problems are similar when ballots are cast or when votes are tallied by computerized means. In case of scanners, regardless of the use of ballot papers that open the window for subsequent recounts, the counting would have already ended and scanners could always be tampered with or misused with no direct supervision of laymen. Recounts would then simply be a reaction against a procedure already completed and finished. Scanners share such a feature with other e-voting mechanisms and that's the reason that they can be treated together. On the other hand, other electoral applications (e.g., voter registration) allow for error detections by laymen before ending the relevant electoral procedure.

The OSCE's Handbook for the observation of new voting technologies, which is another reference document in the field, refers to New Voting Technologies (NVT) as:

> the use of information and communications technologies (ICT) applied to the casting *and* counting of votes. This understanding includes the use of electronic voting systems, ballot scanners and Internet voting. The term 'electronic voting'...unless otherwise noted...should be considered synonymous with new voting technologies.
>
> *(OSCE/ODIHR, 2013, p. 4; emphasis added)*

The OSCE and the Council of Europe are now aligned, since both of them accept ballot scanners as a form of e-voting. Moreover, both institutions also exclude neighboring tools, such as results transmission systems (RTS) or biometric devices, when they are not linked to casting and/or tallying. Despite some erroneous interpretations, e-voting should not be seen as a generic word. E-voting cannot be assimilated to any use of digital technologies within the electoral procedure. It rather refers to concrete scenarios. If such a narrower notion is accepted, substantial distinctions are to be found between this specific component and other cases where digital technologies are used for electoral purposes. This red line serves as indicator for determining whether a specific tool should be treated as e-voting.

As already stated, according to the rationale behind OSCE's and CoE's definitions, such a borderline would depend on whether the relevant tool allows for a supervision to be undertaken by citizens with no specific knowledge. Despite all digital voting technologies make external controls harder, the ones that finish their tasks without providing evidence to be understood by laymen are limited to devices used for casting and/or counting.

Real-world cases show how theoretic taxonomies struggle to fit specific examples within pre-established shapes. The variety of e-voting cases used to challenge such patterns and classifications should be flexible enough for embedding all different forms of e-voting without watering down the notion of e-voting.

The new Belgian e-voting system may serve as a good reference for such a nuanced approach. The procedure implements two computer-based devices: One as a ballot marker – that is, a computer used for selecting the candidates and issuing a token (i.e., e-card) that will be inserted into the second device – that is, a ballot box that will automatically read the ballots and perform the tally. The example shows how complex and nuanced real electronic voting cases can be. Computers may be used at different stages (e.g., filling out, printing, casting, and tallying) of the voting process, different devices may be in place for each task and different options may be available even for the very same activity (e.g., controlled or uncontrolled environments).

The Belgian case raises no controversy, as long as at least two sensitive tasks are performed by computerized means. The voter needs to use a computer for selecting candidates and ballots are electronically tallied and computers themselves then deliver the relevant results. One may argue that the voter uses a traditional ballot paper for casting his/her vote, but the other factors clearly indicate that an actual e-voting solution is used.

However, some grey cases exist. As long as the voting flow involves different procedural pieces (e.g., delivering the ballots, filling out the ballots, and printing the ballots), sometimes it is not so apparent when a computerized e-voting process is in place. As stated above, what the e-voting notion would need is not just any impact on the electoral procedure. Any computer, regardless its features, would meet such a generic requirement and, therefore, the notion of e-voting would be diluted. What is really needed is an impact whose direct supervision is not feasible by laymen with no specific knowledge. That is the core of any e-voting mechanism. A couple of examples may illustrate the challenge of determining whether e-voting is in place.

In 2018, the Democratic Republic of Congo (DRC) deployed machines in every polling station (Lesfauries & Enguehard, 2018). These devices were intended to be used for marking and printing out ballot papers that would then be inserted into a traditional ballot box by the voter. However, the computers were also able to perform their own tally and transmit these results remotely to a central database. While the local legal framework explicitly forbade electronic voting mechanisms, it is worth wondering to what extent the solution should be considered just as a mere printer, as it was presented by electoral authorities, or rather an actual electronic voting case given its impact on crucial procedural steps, such as how to select candidates and what to choose between electronic and traditional results, in case of discrepancy.

Interestingly enough, regulations foresaw potential discrepancies between electronic and manual tallies, but the criteria to be applied differed depending on the procedural stage. While regulations were clear at the polling station level, stating that manual figures would take precedence, legal provisions became slightly darker whenever such discrepancies reappeared at second-level recount centers and a prioritization of electronic results was not totally excluded.

Moreover, such computerized ballot markers, even as mere printers, might raise other concerns regarding, for instance, the randomization of ballots. The lack of this feature would open the door for tracking every ballot using a chronological order to match voters that showed up and ballots that have been cast. This concern was also raised in the 2005 parliamentary elections in Venezuela, where a programming error in the voting machines was detected – one that allowed tracking the sequence in which a vote was cast and recorded on the machine (EU, 2006).

The DRC case shows how a system where ballots are cast by traditional means (i.e., ballot papers and classical ballot boxes) may also pose questions about its classification. Digital devices were used for other tasks and a nuanced analysis is necessary to determine whether such devices should be considered as e-voting mechanisms.

On a similar note, between 2006 and 2016 Slovenia facilitated the process for voters with disabilities, and a number of polling stations offered the option to fill out the ballot using a computer that also served as a printer. The relevant print-out was used as the actual ballot to be inserted by the voter into a traditional ballot box. Subsequent steps (i.e., tally and results transmission) was performed as usual. Contrary to those in the DRC, regulations did not foresee any electronic results to be delivered by the voting machine itself. In 2017, authorities abandoned the use of devices due to higher costs compared to paper ballots.

Finally, the United States' Uniformed and Overseas Citizens Absentee Voting Act (UOCAVA) establishes new forms of ballot delivery to voters, intending to ease electoral procedures for expats. In general terms, delivery is undertaken by electronic means (e.g., a PDF document with the ballot template), so that voters can download the relevant ballots and, once they have been filled out, either with electronic support or not, they are sent back using different means that include traditional postal mail, but also e-mail, web services, and other options. Again, as stated above, the notion of e-voting relies upon the actual impact over voting rights of every computerized stage, that is, the extent to which a layman is capable of supervising the procedure. Computers may be used simply to speed up the process and thus produce no real impact, at least in these terms. However, should voting rights, which encompass much more than the very moment of casting the ballot, be exercised and somehow modified due to the presence of computerized means that do not allow direct supervision by laymen, then the procedure in place should be classified as electronic voting.

Such examples may serve as indicators that the very definition of electronic voting and its relevant borders is not totally peaceful, as long as challenging real-world electoral procedures are much more nuanced than a mere theoretical framework. Any analysis should take into account this factor for a proper understanding of e-voting implementation.

Where and Why Is Electronic Voting Used?

Electronic voting machines already have a long history. They have been implemented and piloted by a significant number of countries, such that the term "new voting technologies" does not fully reflect the notion of the topic. There is a large heterogeneity of e-voting solutions. While all of them share basic features, as articulated above, other important elements may differ.

Firstly, it is noteworthy that e-voting implementation relies either on private companies or in-house developments by local electoral authorities. Such a plurality of players ends in an array of technological solutions.

Secondly, e-voting is used to address specific electoral needs that may vary from one jurisdiction to another and, therefore, machines are customized to every particular environment. Should illiteracy be a problem for understanding ballots, usable devices would be based on numbers and/or figures. Should spoiling of ballots be a problem, the software would warn the voter and provide guidance to battle over- or under-voting (meaning, selecting too many options or fewer options than allowed for by the electoral law). Other similar examples exist for almost every e-voting implementation.

Last but not least, it is worth keeping in mind that e-voting is also used beyond political elections, which is the scope of this chapter. The private sector (e.g., shareholder assemblies), civil society organizations, and professional bodies trust this technology as a tool for improving their internal decision-making.

In this regard, political parties need a specific approach, since they combine features from private associations and public entities. They started using e-voting for primary elections, as well as leadership and internal votes. But public regulations often do not foresee these e-voting procedures and, therefore, standards to be met differ from what is applied for political elections, what is not positive, if we keep in mind that fundamental political rights are exercised within political parties as well (Barrat & Pérez-Moneo, 2019).

In general terms, mapping e-voting cases may start with a basic distinction between local and remote procedures. Regarding the former, some countries use e-voting machines at a nationwide level (e.g., Brazil, India, and Venezuela), while others combine e-voting with other traditional methods (e.g., United States, Belgium, France, Peru, and Argentina). Ballot scanners are utilized, among other examples, in Latvia, Norway, Kirgizstan, and Mongolia.

Remote channels (i.e., internet voting) are used in a handful of countries, among which Estonia and Switzerland play a leading role. Estonia began using internet voting fin 2005, and it is the only country where such mechanisms are admitted nationwide and with no restrictions for any election or referendum (Vinkel, 2015). Other voting channels are also accepted.

In 2004, Switzerland implemented internet voting with three accredited systems to be used in Geneva, Zurich, and Neuchâtel. While Geneva's system was developed by a private vendor first and then insourced and maintained by local electoral authorities, the other two were outsourced to private companies. Over the last decade, other cantons also joined the project, choosing one of the three approved solutions. It is to be noted that, in Switzerland, elections or referendums take place approximately every three months and, therefore, an efficient, accessible, and nimble voting system is paramount. As postal voting had been introduced in a very successful way over a period of 30 years, internet voting appeared as a logic step forward. However, Switzerland adopted a cautious approach restricting internet voting to a maximum percentage of voters. Moreover, other traditional voting channels remain available.

The list of countries currently using internet voting also encompasses, as a non-exhaustive list, Canada and Norway, for municipalities; Australia, at a provincial level; Armenia, just for diplomats; United Arab Emirates, from supervised environments; India, in Gujarat; Pakistan; and Panama. West Virginia piloted several different forms of electronic voting over the years, including a blockchain platform in the 2018 US elections. Moreover, the Åland Islands admitted internet voting in 2019, and the Russian Federation conducted a blockchain-based internet voting pilot in fall 2019.

In 2017, France decided not to use internet voting. However, upcoming elections are supposed to re-start a project that targets expats. Voting machines are still in use in some municipalities, although a moratorium was approved after the 2007 presidential and parliamentary elections, so that no new players (i.e., municipalities) will be added.

On-going and future cases where e-voting is implemented show that the technology proves to be useful for some environments. In this regard, different goals may be considered when deciding whether to use e-voting (Barrat, 2006). Firstly, economical or environmental grounds play an important role since, at a first glance, electronic voting appears to be a positive solution for these purposes. However, in-depth research is necessary to support such premises since calculation of e-voting costs, as well as its comparison with other voting channels, is not so apparent (Krimmer et al., 2018). Similarly, from an environmental point of view, some e-voting solutions (e.g., VVPAT systems) are not paperless. Moreover, both computers and networks have their own environmental footprint, and research is needed to determine whether this impact is higher than that of a traditional voting method.

Secondly, accessibility may be improved with internet voting. Absentee voters, such as people with reduced mobility or expats, benefit from solutions that ease current burdensome mechanisms that are normally based on postal channels. Engaging citizens living abroad in domestic political life is being promoted by an increasing number of countries. Appropriate mechanisms are to be found, and internet voting may appear a good solution.

Thirdly, some electoral systems face important problems due to the time-lapse needed for results delivery. On the same logistic note, certain ballot sizes or layouts are prone to errors due to weak usability. E-voting facilitates innovative solutions that speed up the counting process and reduce unintentional mistakes.

Lastly, turnout is often mentioned as a reason for promoting e-voting. The rationale behind such an idea points out that a digital era creates digital citizens that need digital means for casting a ballot. Otherwise, voters will stay away from a procedure that is more linked to the past than to the present. Electronic voting, and namely internet voting, would provide for a smooth, comfortable, and modern mechanism to participate in public matters.

Such an approach has not been confirmed by real cases yet. Turnout figures increase when accessibility is improved (e.g., voting from abroad). However, in general terms, electronic voting alone is not capable to battle absenteeism, likely because such behavior relies upon deeper social and political grounds. When citizens decide whether to vote, a number of factors are considered, and comfortability may not be the most important one. Normally, political disengagement, which is caused by different democratic deficits, is a much more important reason for absenteeism.

Mapping e-voting worldwide shows that, together with consolidated examples, there is also a handful of discontinued cases. Such decisions were taken on the basis of different grounds related both to technical and social or legal aspects. The analysis of such cases is necessary, since they provide leads on where the weakest aspects of e-voting are.

Netherlands stopped using both voting machines and internet voting in 2006. The decision was taken after a computer expert raised concerns on the performance of e-voting machines. The report strongly contradicted what had been stated both by local authorities and the supplier so that, beyond such technical details, e-voting faced a crisis of social and political trust. An official commission decided to discontinue e-voting projects. Lessons learned in this case point out to the importance of civic activism for building up a social consensus supporting sensitive initiatives such as any implementation of new technologies within the electoral process. Ireland was a similar case, too. A number of voting machines were stocked and finally scrapped after a campaign led by civil society associations committed to a transparent and unbiased digital society.

Following the Dutch decision, there was a similar development in Germany. In 2009, the German Constitutional Court declared unconstitutional a law that allowed for the use of the (originally Dutch) e-voting machines (which did not provide for VVPAT) on the basis that their supervision needed specialized knowledge and, therefore, the public nature of the elections was damaged. The decision quickly became a leading case that shed light on the importance of transparent verifiability. However, a full and permanent prohibition of e-voting cannot be drawn as a conclusion from the German ruling, which is rather a statement on a particular type of e-voting. Machines with VVPAT, for instance, could comply with court's requirements.

The court also underscored that a decision on which voting channels are accepted should take into account all electoral principles and exceptions could be justified in light of other constitutional goals – that is, public goods that have to be considered together with the principle of publicity. For instance, the balance between the public nature of the elections and universal suffrage, which means accessibility to the right to vote might lead to remote voting. Despite obvious constraints on the principle of transparency, the court admits, for instance, postal voting "mit dem Ziel...eine möglichst umfassende Wahlbeteiligung zu erreichen und damit dem Grundsatz der Allgemeinheit der Wahl Rechnung zu tragen"/"with the goal ... to achieve the highest possible turnout and thus to take into account universality as electoral principle" (§126). To date, no activities to discuss or propose a law that would allow for e-voting machines with VVPAT in Germany have been undertaken.

Austria, Mexico, Norway, and Finland may be also referenced as discontinued cases of e-voting implementations. The Finnish case relates to a small pilot project whose implementation failed due to the lack of proper voter education. A number of voters went out from the polling stations, assuming that they had cast the ballot. But, in fact, they did not press the relevant confirmation button and thus the computer did not incorporate such votes. Again, the problem was rather operational or social than technical. Appropriated simulations, mock elections and voter education programs would likely have prevented the incident.

In Norway, after two pilot experiences in 2011 and 2013, new political parties in the cabinet did not prioritize internet voting and the government decided to stop the project. Still, on the local level, internet voting made a return to the political agenda, and local referenda are still using internet voting solutions. Furthermore, ballots are being scanned in central locations to do more complex forms of ballot counting (votes for candidates).

In Mexico, the following areas have used internet voting: Mexico City (2012), Baja California Sur (2015), and Chiapas (2015), where an incident occurred due to a corrupted electoral census. Two other Mexican States (i.e., Coahuila, from 2005 onwards, and Jalisco) developed their own voting machines as well, but the reconfiguration of electoral authorities, with a higher role of the federal commission, prevented local bodies from using such mechanisms again in 2018. Local commissions maintain the projects, however, for citizen participation initiatives.

Finally, the Austrian case relates to an internet voting pilot used for the elections of a federation of university students in 2009 (Krimmer, Ehringfeld, & Traxler, 2010; Krimmer, 2017). A decision of the Austrian Constitutional Court established legal criteria for such projects and no new initiatives have been undertaken so far (Driza-Maurer & Barrat, 2016).

International case-law on voting machines for persons with disabilities consists of contrasting decisions by the UN *Committee on the Rights of Persons with Disabilities and the European Court of Human Rights.* In *Fiona Given v. Australia*, the Committee (2018) expressed the view that authorities should provide equipment that assures independent voting and secret ballot regardless of financial burden, and even if voters do not ask for it in advance.

The European Court (2021), on the other hand, in its *Toplak and Mrak v. Slovenia* (Applications no. 34591/19, 2545/19) judgment found no violation in Slovenia's abandonment of voting devices even if this means that voter would need to disclose their choice to another person who would fill out the ballot for them.

Main Challenges of Electronic Voting Projects

This section deals with three different challenges that any voting system, including e-voting, always needs to address: How to protect secrecy of the vote and freedom of the voter, how to maintain a level playing field among voters or candidates, and how to build social trust on the electoral procedure when a meaningful supervision needs specialized knowledge.

Secrecy and Freedom

Electoral procedures are very sensitive, and legal frameworks surround them with a number of guarantees that intend to protect the freedom of every voter to determine his/her political choice. Secrecy appears as a means for such a goal, as it is assumed that contemporary societies could open the door for potential coercers and, therefore, vulnerable people could not be totally free when casting a ballot. The compulsory use of voting booths, voting envelopes, or a strict supervision of ballot delivery are commonly accepted procedures that normally manage to maintain secrecy and freedom. However, such a principle also accepts exceptions when a greater public good is to be achieved. Postal and proxy voting are good examples of this.

As a new voting channel, electronic voting should also meet basic standards like secrecy and freedom and the already mentioned distinction between e-voting mechanisms for controlled or uncontrolled environments play a crucial role. Firstly, the former can be assimilated to what already happens in a traditional polling station. If a DRE is used in polling stations, booths could also be compulsory and, in general terms, the system is able to protect both the freedom of the voter and his/her relevant choice. However, some specific concerns should be addressed as specific features of computer-based voting channels (e.g., unbiased display of candidates on the screens, randomization of votes that are stored by the relevant machine).

On the other hand, internet voting from non-controlled environments faces challenges that are already known when postal voting is in place. Wherever postal voting is accepted, as in Switzerland, where around 90% of citizens use postal channels for casting their ballots, the introduction of internet voting is likely be less challenging than the same procedure in countries where postal mechanisms are not accepted for electoral matters. In this regard, a comparison between postal and electronic voting is very helpful. The Venice Commission states that:

> for non-supervised e-enabled voting, technical standards must overcome different threats to those which exist for postal voting. This form of voting must only be accepted if it is secure and reliable. In particular, the elector must be able to obtain confirmation of his or her vote and, if necessary, correct it without the secrecy of the ballot being in any way violated. The system's transparency must be guaranteed.
>
> *(Grabenwarter, 2004, 69–70)*

Regarding the secrecy of the vote, it is noteworthy that some countries (e.g., Estonia, Norway) accept multiple voting as a functionality that would mitigate potential coercions. Electronic voting introduces, here, an added value that postal voting normally does not admit. The Estonian Supreme Court referred to such multiple voting as a ground for not admitting a complaint that put into question the compliance of e-voting solutions with the principle of secrecy. In this regard, it is to note that the court split the notion of secrecy into two dimensions. While the first relates to the voter, as already explained above, the second pays attention to the ballot and forbids any vote tracking. Such secrecy is also referred to as anonymity.

For this second dimension, electronic voting creates certain doubts since, once a vote has been cast by electronic means, a layman can no longer verify whether the ballot remains connected to any given voter. While traditional methods address this challenge with empty and sealed boxes, electronic voting needs to provide supplementary evidence proving that no men-in-the-middle have been able to see the content of ballots and correlate them to specific voters. Cryptography and other sophisticated techniques could offer all these properties, but, beyond the relevant and necessary academic discussions from that technical side, laymen would be expelled from the supervision, which is a democratic task that any electoral procedure needs. The section on transparency (below) will deal with transparency, and verifiability issues will be addressed as mechanisms to involve voters in the electoral supervision process when digital technologies are in place.

Concluding this section, the secrecy of the vote and the freedom of the voter stand as basic principles that any digital voting technology should meet. A comparison with other accepted voting channels (e.g., postal voting) serves as a good methodology for identifying what is specific to e-voting and what not. Moreover, e-voting may also propose new ways (e.g., double voting) for achieving such a compliance and a particular assessment will be needed for each added value.

Equality and Digital Divide

As with any other digital technology, social divide has to be duly considered when e-voting mechanisms are to be implemented. Moreover, as e-voting relates to elections, basic political rights are in place and, therefore, formal and substantial inequalities are totally unacceptable. In this regard, different dimensions of the principle of equality should be taken into account.

Firstly, equality means universal accessibility, which has always been an important concern when elections are implemented. That's the reason that traditional electoral systems already accept different ways for casting ballots, such as postal, proxy, and home-bound voting. These channels intend to maximize the access to the right to vote, while admitting exceptions to general principles (e.g., proxy voting for the direct vote or postal voting for the secrecy and freedom). Electronic voting, and namely internet voting, should be analyzed within this more general framework. Internet voting would provide higher accessibility, as long as different groups of people that cannot easily show up to the polling stations would be beneficial. In this regard, countries that already admit postal voting, such as Switzerland, are prone to implement internet voting.

However, it would be worth wondering whether such improvement only benefits those who are already familiar with new technologies. In this regard, internet voting, if offered as the unique voting channel, could deepen the digital divide if, in practical terms, some groups are excluded. Accessibility means the physical capability to use computers, but also the digital literacy that allows citizens to take advantage of these new options. Both indicators may vary a lot from one country to another and weak rates are likely to lead to a biased social implementation of internet voting. That's why international standards recommend that "unless channels of remote e-voting are universally accessible, they shall be only an additional and optional means of voting" (§3 / Rec(2017)5, Council of Europe).

Accessibility related to other forms of e-voting raises less concerns because citizens still need to show up at the relevant polling station where computers are deployed. However, digital literacy remains an important issue and, as an added risk, the likelihood for a complete replacement of traditional voting methods by digital ones is much higher when controlled environments are in place. Venezuela, Brazil, India, and Belgium would be good examples for a scenario where citizens are left with the only option of using new tools to exercise a basic political right. Large and long-term voter education programs are crucial for smooth transitions.

Finally, voting tools should also guarantee equality among candidates. While a level playing field is often considered when it comes to electoral campaigns and finances, other practical aspects, such as how candidates are displayed on ballot papers, should also be addressed. When e-voting is considered, screens play the role of ballots and the equality of candidates should be customized to this new format. For instance, whenever all candidates cannot be displayed on the same screen, scroll buttons will be implemented, but such options need to be considered on both technical and legal terms, since candidates on the first screen could be unfairly benefited. Again, a comparison with previous voting methods may serve as a guideline. In the Democratic Republic of Congo, for instance, the number of candidates is always a huge problem, but paper-based voting already used booklets in some constituencies and, therefore, different screens would not be such a drastic measure. In any case, voter education initiatives, together with pilot projects, are very useful for mitigating potential negative impacts.

Transparency

Genuine elections mean that contestants with very different ideological starting points must agree on procedural rules and accept final results, even when they give the victory to the rival. Transparency is paramount since hidden aspects, even when everything is fine, may create suspicions and may easily become alibis for not accepting a real defeat. When it comes to electronic voting, transparency is even more crucial because computers may lead to a technocracy where crucial decisions about the use of technology and elections are left (or delegated) to experts. Citizens (i.e., voters) are submitted to decisions that cannot be understood or supervised – what is known as a black box. Audits, certifications, and finally so-called End-to-End (E2E) verifiability intend to address this concern.

Firstly, e-voting may be submitted to an array of audits and certifications. While audits assess whether a mechanism has properly followed a pre-established set of rules, certifications take place beforehand. They assess the compliance to some parameters and issue the relevant certificates. Audits can be implemented together with e-voting certifications, since they have different goals. Moreover, the terms to be used for such tasks and their meanings may differ from one country to another (Barrat et al., 2015).

Legal provisions determine, among other aspects, what is to be certified/audited, who will assume such tasks, which criteria are to be applied, and the binding effect of the conclusions and its publicity. France, where available certifiers of voting machines are pre-selected by the government; Belgium, where there is a specialized public body (i.e., Collège des Experts); and the US, with a decentralized network of testing labs, are countries where certificates and/or audits are normally required. Internet voting, whose certification is much more difficult than other types of e-voting, may rely upon audit measures only, as happens in Estonia.

However, neither audits nor certifications intend to provide real verifiability. They may contribute to increase the level of trust on the e-voting procedure, but such perception still relies on indirect and specialized sources – that is, citizens have to believe what is said by pre-selected actors (i.e., private / public auditors or certifiers). That's the reason that a so-called second generation of e-voting mechanisms, mainly internet voting ones, pays more attention to an E2E verifiability that would be:

> a functionality of NVT systems that allows the validation of results on a universal and/or individual basis. Systems with universal verifiability provide means for an independent third party to establish that the result of an election was reported honestly and without manipulation, through either manual or mathematical checks. On an individual level, voters are provided with the ability to verify that their votes were cast as intended, stored as cast, and (ideally) counted as recorded.
>
> *(OSCE/ODIHR, 2013)*

Norway, Estonia, Switzerland, and Australia are leading countries when it comes to E2E verifiability. Regarding Norway, in the 2011 elections, a message was sent to each voter's mobile phone containing codes that s/he could compare with a list that was delivered beforehand. Such codes indicated which candidates s/he had voted for. The system intended to provide cast-as-intended, as well as recorded-as-cast, verifiability. Moreover, the tally was open to external verifications that were supposed to comply with the counted-as-recorded requirement. The source code was also made available before the election to allow public scrutiny of the voting system. In 2013, Norway again used the same system with slight updates, but internet voting was discontinued afterwards, mainly due to a change of government.

In Estonia: "a verification application was added to the system providing Internet voters with an option of verifying their vote based on information stored in a QR verification code" (OSCE/ODIHR, 2019). Moreover:

> a team of external auditors was dispatched to assist the [electoral authorities] with establishing vote secrecy during the computation of preliminary Internet voting results and the integrity of final Internet voting results by verifying the correctness of the cryptographic shuffle and decryption proofs. The team did not audit other critical operations, most notably the correct transmission of the final aggregation of the decrypted Internet votes.
>
> *(OSCE/ODIHR, 2019)*

In 2014, Switzerland modified the legal framework covering e-voting, and one of the main goals consisted of introducing both individual and universal verifications. Three accreditation levels were foreseen, depending on which security and verification measures were implemented. In this regard, it is worth underscoring that Switzerland follows a step-by-step strategy that conditions the maximum percentage of voters using e-voting on meeting specific technical standards. Should more requirements be met, a higher percentage of voters are allowed to use the system.

The three e-voting systems that had been in place over the last decade applied for a re-accreditation and only two managed to pass it (Geneva and Neuchâtel). Moreover, the solution originally used in Neuchâtel achieved level 2 (50% at the cantonal electorate and 30% at the Swiss one) and, in 2019, a first approval for level 3 (no restrictions on the percentages). However, as of July 2019, the actual implementation of the new system and even the continuation of any e-voting implementation remain uncertain. Firstly, in 2019, a moratorium was approved for this system after a controversial Public Intrusion Test (PIT) and scrutiny over the source code. Secondly, Geneva's project has been totally discontinued.

Finally, New South Wales in Australia started using internet voting in 2011 and introduced cast-as-intended verifiability in 2015. Nowadays, voters may verify their own ballot with a QR code and a specific verification app. Counted-as-recoded verifiability was introduced in 2019.

E2E verifiability appears as an improvement for the black-box burden that every e-voting mechanism has to face, but it is worth paying attention to some controversial aspects. Firstly, any individual verification raises concerns on the secrecy of the vote, as long as the voter is sent a proof of his/her vote. Multiple voting, as implemented in Norway and Estonia, may mitigate this problem. Secondly, in practical terms, universal verifiability still means that there is no direct supervision by laymen, as long as its implementation requires specialized knowledge. However, the fact that any person is allowed to carry out such assessment could emulate traditional supervisions and be accepted as a way to create a trustworthy scenario. Thirdly, legal doubts persist regarding how such verifications are submitted as evidence to court and how the judiciary can resolve discrepancies that could appear even among third independent parties carrying out all relevant tests. Last but not least, it is worth keeping in mind that E2E verifiability does not address e-voting concerns other than those related to results verification. Secrecy and anonymity, for instance, are not covered.

Note

1 The authors wish to thank comments to the draft received from Jordi Puiggalí, Alicia Ramón, and Adrià Rodríguez-Pérez, and for research assistance to Nathan Licht. Robert Krimmer's work has been supported by ETAG personal research grant PUT 1361. Jordi Barrat has received support through the R+D Project: DEMOC2017 by the Government of Catalonia (Generalitat).

References

Barrat, J. (2006). A preliminary question: Is e-voting actually useful for our democratic institutions? What do we need it for? In R. Krimmer (Ed.), *Electronic voting* (pp. 51–60). Bonn: Gesellschaft für Informatik.

Barrat, J., & Pérez-Moneo, M. (2019). *Digitalización de los partidos políticos y el voto electrónico*. Madrid: Civitas.

Barrat, J., Bravo, A., Krimmer, R., Neumann, S., Parreno, A. A., Schürmann, C., Volkamer, M., & Wolf, P. (2015). *Certification of ICTs in elections*. Stockholm: International IDEA Publishing Group.

Barrett, R., Thorgeirsdottir, H. K., Rubio, R., Vargas, J. L., Rozgonyi, K., & Ruzic, N. (2019). Joint report on digital technologies and elections. Joint report Venice Commission / Directorate General of Human Rights and Rule of Law. Council of Europe: Venice Commision. Retrieved from https://www.venice.coe.int/webforms/documents/?pdf=CDL-AD(2019)016-e

Committee on the Rights of Persons with Disabilities (2018). Fiona Given v. Australia (CRPD/C/19/D/19/2014). Retrieved August 10, 2020 from https://juris.ohchr.org/en/Search/Details/2393

Driza-Maurer, A., & Barrat, J. (2016). *E-voting case law: A comparative analysis*. London: Routledge.

Esteve, J. B., Bravo, A., Krimmer, R., Neumann, S., Parreno, A. A., Schürmann, C., Volkamer, M., & Peter, W. (2015). *Certification of ICTs in elections*. International IDEA Publishing Group.

Esteve, J. B., Roca, J. C., Gascó, M., Dueñas-Cid, D., Martin, L. A. A., & Dalmau, R. M. (2018). Votacions electròniques: una eina de gestió pública per a la millora de la qualitat democràtia i la participació política. Barcelona: Escola d'Administració Pública de Catalunya. Retrieved from http://eapc.gencat.cat/web/.content/home/publicacions/col_leccio_estudis_de_recerca_digital/17_votacions_electroniques_jordi_barrat/estudis_recerca_digitals_17.pdf

European Union: Election Observation Mission. (2006). *Final report of the election observation mission to Venezuela 2005*. Caracas. Retrieved from http://aceproject.org/regions-en/countries-and-territories/VE/reports/venezuela-2005-parliamentary-elections-final

European Court of Human Rights. (2021). Toplak and Mrak v. Slovenia (Applications no. 34591/19, 2545/19). Retrieved October 26, 2021 from https://hudoc.echr.coe.int/eng?i=001-212693

Grabenwarter, C. (2004). Report on the compatibility of remote voting and electronic voting with the standards of the Council of Europe (Report no. 260). Venice Commission. Retrieved from https://www.venice.coe.int/webforms/documents/default.aspx?pdffile=CDL-AD(2004)012-e

Krimmer, R. (2012). *The evolution of E-voting: Why voting technology is used and how it affects democracy*. Tallinn: TalTech / Tallinn University of Technology.

Krimmer, R. (2017). *Internet voting in Austria: History, development, and building blocks for the future*. Vienna: WU Vienna University of Economics and Business.

Krimmer, R., Dueñas-Cid, D., Krivonosova, J., Vinkel, P., & Koitmae, A. (2018). How much does an e-Vote cost? Cost comparison per vote in multichannel elections in Estonia. In R. Krimmer et al. (Eds.), *Electronic voting* (pp. 117–131). Berlin: Springer.

Krimmer, R., Ehringfeld, A., & Traxler, M. (2010). The use of E-voting in the Austrian federation of students elections 2009. In R. Krimmer (Ed.), *EVOTE 2010* (pp. 33–44). Bregenz: Gesellschaft für Informatik and E-Voting.CC.

Lesfauries, V., & Enguehard, C. (2018). *L'introduction de machines à voter en République Démocratique du Congo*. Bordeaux: Université de Bordeaux. Retrieved from https://hal.archives-ouvertes.fr/hal-01956117v2/document

OSCE/ODIHR. (October 1, 2013). *Handbook for the observation of new voting technologies*. Warsaw: Organization for Security and Co-operation in Europe. Retrieved from https://www.osce.org/odihr/elections/new_voting_technologies

OSCE/ODIHR. (2019). *Estonian parliamentary elections, 3 March 2019: ODIHR election expert team final report*. Warsaw: OSCE/ODIHR. Retrieved from https://www.osce.org/odihr/elections/estonia/409205

Prosser, A., & Krimmer, R. (2004). The dimensions of electronic voting: Technology, law, politics and society. In *Electronic voting in Europe: Technology, law, politics and society* (pp. 21–28). Bonn: Gesellschaft für Informatik.

Rubin, A. (2006). *Brave new ballot: The battle to safeguard democracy in the age of electronic voting*. New York: Morgan Road Books.

Vinkel, P. (2015). Remote electronic voting in Estonia: Legality, impact and confidence [Doctoral dissertation, Tallinn University of Technology??]. Retrieved from https://www.researchgate.net/profile/Priit-Vinkel/publication/281319274_Remote_Electronic_Voting_in_Estonia_Legality_Impact_and_Confidence/links/55e194ef08aecb1a7cc68462/Remote-Electronic-Voting-in-Estonia-Legality-Impact-and-Confidence.pdf

7

ELECTION LAW IN ADVANCED DEMOCRACIES

Steven J. Mulroy

Introduction

Recent years have seen several election reform controversies heat up, both in the US and around the world. Discussions of such controversies in the US often invoke global trends to either defend[1] or criticize[2] US practices. The contrasts between the US and other nations, and among nations globally, increases when the special case of democracies in the developing world is considered.

This chapter examines five election reform areas where the US is something of an outlier: (1) Voter registration; (2) voter ID; (3) felon disenfranchisement; (4) redistricting; and (5) proportional representation. It compares and contrasts, notes trends, and, in some cases, makes recommendations for change. It also surveys the state of democratic play in developing countries, noting how these election reform areas may differ between advanced democracies – e.g., democracies that are members of the Organization for Economic Cooperation and Development – and developing democratic countries.

Voter Registration

Regarding access to the franchise, there are some areas of near universality, including practices within the US. Almost all countries choose 18 as the age for voter eligibility (ACE Project).[3] A few outliers (including Brazil, Argentina, and Ecuador) go as low as 16, and a few (including Lebanon, Malaysia, Oman, and Singapore) as high as 21, but almost 90% of the world's nations use 18, including the US. Almost all countries further require voters to be citizens, and a good third require some period of residence, which again leaves the US squarely in the mainstream (ACE Project).[4]

But the US is an outlier when it comes to voter registration. It is rare among modern democracies in having a decentralized system, where each state or province creates and enforces its own rules and procedures regarding registration and voter eligibility (Rosenberg & Chen, 2009).[5] As a result, comparisons to other countries are sometimes more complicated, depending on the degree of regional variation.

More importantly, the United States is one of only a few democracies that require citizens to affirmatively register to vote. Most countries automatically register their citizens once they

DOI: 10.4324/9780429401800-7

become of age (Rosenberg & Chen, 2009; ACE Project, Comparative Data (Voter Registration). In these countries, the government has an affirmative responsibility to add people to the voting rolls as they become of age or become citizens (Rosenberg & Chen, 2009; ACE Project, Comparative Data (Voter Registration)). In many of these countries, individuals can opt out of automatic registration, but few do.

As one might expect, registration rates are vastly higher in the automatic registration countries. Over 90% of the eligible population, and often well above 90%, are registered in these countries (Rosenberg & Chen, 2009). This compares to a rate of 68% for the US.[6]

The US outlier status on this issue may be changing. Automatic voter registration (AVR) is a growing trend in the American states. Sixteen states and the District of Columbia have already approved automatic registration, and more states may join in. (Brennan Center, 2019a).[7] The typical American model has drivers' license agencies, and other government agencies with access to individuals' age and residence data, routinely transfer that data to elections officials, who verify their eligibility to vote and (where verified) add them to the voter rolls. Individuals are allowed to opt out of the automatic registration, but, absent an affirmative objection by the individual, registration occurs (Morris & Dunphy, 2019).

This is a recent development: The first US state to adopt AVR was Oregon in 2015.[8] As a result, not all states that have adopted AVR have implemented, and some have not implemented long enough yet for a comprehensive study of results. But from the data available, it seems that, consistent with the experience around the world, automatic voter registration has led to dramatically improved registration rates. A recent study by the Brennan Center for Justice of the seven states that had already implemented AVR indicated substantial increases in registration rates in all states, ranging from a 9.4% increase in registration rate in Washington, D.C. to a high of a 94% increase – in other words, almost doubling – in Georgia (Morris & Dunphy, 2019).[9] The average increase was 43%.

While AVR seems to increase registration rates significantly, this does not necessarily mean that actual voter participation is always increased. Some studies suggest that the need to voluntarily and affirmatively register to vote does not depress voter turnout, or has only a slight effect (*See* Franklin, 1996 & sources cited therein). It could be that persons added to the voter rolls do not in fact choose to vote. This is especially the case if the voter has a low perception of the election's salience – how competitive it is and how likely it is that its result will affect policy outcomes (Franklin, 1996). For this reason, AVR would be most effective when combined with other reforms increasing election salience – like, for example, switching from a winner-take-all model to proportional representation (see below the section on proportional representation). Either way, AVR would clear one definite hurdle to political participation, and experience has shown that AVR can be implemented smoothly, with little downside. It would thus appear to be a salutary reform.

On balance, AVR is a reform with great potential, and the US would do well to join the global mainstream here. To this end, the very first bill filed in the US House after the Democrats gained control in 2019, H.R. 1, provided for AVR for all federal elections (116th Congress, 2019).[10] That bill has been reintroduced in the current Congress.

Voter ID Requirements

A 2014 study by the International Consortium of Investigative Journalists (ICIJ) broke up global democracies into one of three categories regarding voter ID rules: (1) Countries accepting multiple forms of ID, (2) those requiring a standard government-issued ID, and (3) those requiring particular types of government ID that individual voters must actively obtain. The US falls into the third category (ICIJ Report, 2014).

Broadly speaking, African countries tend to be more flexible in allowing varying forms of ID, including such variants as affidavits by tribal elders in Liberia and Malawi (ICIJ Report, *supra*). European nations tend to require standard government-issued IDs (ICIJ Report, *supra*). In North and South America, it is more the norm to require individual voters to apply to obtain specified forms of ID (ICIJ Report, *supra*).

This more burdensome category tends to lead to lower rates of voter participation, but not always. Some countries in the Americas embark on a robust effort to educate voters and make obtaining the requisite IDs manageable, even for indigenous people, residents in remote areas, etc. Mexico and Belize, for example, have achieved voter registration rates of over 95% in this way. (ICIJ Report, *supra*).

In the US, the trend has been not only to require individuals to actively obtain specified forms of ID, but also, in many states, to become more restrictive regarding the types of ID that qualify. Of particular note is the rise of laws requiring photo IDs. Since 2000, the number of US states adopting voter ID laws of some kind rose from 15 (out of 50) to 33, with the pace of adoption accelerating in the last decade (NCSL, 2017). Some of them allow non-photo forms of identification, like signing an affidavit. But 11 of these states specifically call for a photo ID, and accept no substitutes. And, while many of these states claim to offer the necessary IDs free of charge, they require supporting documents (such as passports, birth certificates, etc.) that do cost money to obtain. Such states make the US unique internationally in forcing the voters to bear such costs (See Politifact).[11]

The predictable result in photo ID states has been a decline in voter participation. A 2014 US government study focusing on two US states that had recently adopted a photo ID law (Kansas and Tennessee) found that turnout among eligible and registered voters declined by somewhere between 2 to 3%. The study used a standard demographic "matching" methodology and controlled for such potentially confounding demographic factors as age, education, race, and sex.[12] While not as dramatic a drag on voter participation as the lack of AVR, the photo ID laws' reductions can determine the outcome of very close elections, which are quite common in the US (Mulroy, 2019).[13]

This is especially the case, since the reductions in participation disproportionately affect racial minorities (Fraga & Miller, 2018; Henninger, Meredith, & Morse, 2018). These minorities tend to vote for the center-left Democratic Party (Cifullo & Fry, 2019).

Indeed, there is some reason to believe that this partisan effect is a main motivation behind the enactment of these laws. They have been enacted predominately in states controlled by the Republican Party (Rocha & Matsubayashi, 2014) and supported predominately by Republican legislators (McKee, 2015). And several public comments from prominent Republican officials have suggested that the laws were passed with this hope in mind. For example, the House Republican leader in the US state of Pennsylvania famously declared in 2012 that its voter ID law "is gonna allow [Republican presidential nominee] Romney to win the state of Pennsylvania, done" (Weinger, 2012).

The decline in voter participation – even one skewed to enhance outcome-determinative effects – might be defensible if the laws were indeed necessary to serve their ostensible purpose, that of guarding against voter fraud. But exhaustive studies have shown that the type of voter fraud photo ID laws are designed to prevent – in-person voter impersonation, where a voter shows up at the polling place pretending to be another person – is vanishingly rare (Hasen, 2012; Minnite, 2010; Levitt, 2014). US courts reviewing the issue have reached similar conclusions.[14] Even when numerous federal law enforcement agencies went out of their way to find and prosecute such cases, their comprehensive efforts failed to yield more than a handful of cases (Mulroy, 2019).

Adding up all these restrictions on registrations and voting, the US is among the most franchise-restrictive nations in the world (Chavkin & Boland-Rudder, 2014). The predictable result is lower participation overall. The US has comparably low voter turnout rates. (Desilver, 2018). Part of this disparity can be attributed to the fact that the US is not among the 21 countries that make voting compulsory (World Factbook). But, even among voluntary voting countries, the US has comparably low turnout rates (Desilver, 2018). Only 56% of the voting-age population voted in the 2016 presidential election (Desilver, 2018), despite an unusually dramatic campaign.

The trend in the US on this topic is both negative and against the global trend. Unsurprisingly, the omnibus election reform bill HR1 in 2022 addressed this issue by requiring US states to allow an affidavit signature to substitute for a photo ID for all federal elections.

Felon Enfranchisement

The question of enfranchising prisoners while in prison recently made US headlines when Democratic presidential hopefuls talked about it at a nationally televised presidential debate (Ember & Stevens, 2019). Although some in the media characterized the near-unanimous support among the presidential candidates for prisoner voting as a sign of Democratic radicalism, the notion is not so radical globally. Roughly one-third of countries around the world allow prisoners to vote; one-third allow some prisoners to vote, depending on the type of prison sentence or local laws; and one-third do not allow prisoners to vote at all (Al Jazeera, 2019). Overall, nations with high incarceration rates tend to have more restrictive disenfranchisement laws for those convicted of crimes (Walmsley, 2013).[15]

And the pro-enfranchisement consensus is even stronger when one considers the voting rights of those who have left prison. Post-release restrictions on the franchise are relatively rare among the world's nations. Only eight countries deny the franchise to those who have completed their sentences (Harpster & Vaughn, 2016).[16]

Again, the US is a notable outlier here; it is one of those eight countries. Its rules are among the most restrictive globally (Harpster & Vaughn, 2016). Indeed, most US disenfranchisees are not in prison, but in their community on parole, probation, or having completed their sentences (Chung, 2019).

Most US states disenfranchise released felons for some period of time and, in some cases, indefinitely. While the policies vary greatly from state to state in terms of the number of underlying crimes that trigger disenfranchisement and how long disenfranchisements last, 48 of 50 states impose some kind of voting restrictions on those convicted of felonies, and most felonies qualify for triggering disenfranchisement. Thirty-two of those states disenfranchise non-prisoners who are on parole or probation; 11 of those 32 even disenfranchise persons after they have completed their sentences. Of those 11 post-sentence disenfranchisement states, policies vary regarding whether they can regain their voting rights, how long they must wait to attempt to do so, and how difficult the process is. But reenfranchisement normally involves waiting a substantial period of time and going through significant affirmative efforts. The percentage of the population disenfranchised by felony conviction has risen substantially over the last five decades, as the percentage convicted and incarcerated has risen due to "mass incarceration" policies (Chung, 2019).

As with photo ID laws, the felon disenfranchisement laws disproportionately burden racial minorities. Black voters are more than four times more likely than other voters to be disenfranchised, with one out of every 13 African-Americans disenfranchised. In four states, one in five black voters is disenfranchised (Chung, 2019).

To many in the US, felons seem a uniquely suitable group to disenfranchise. But it is by no means obvious that they should be so restricted, just as it is not obvious that other groups should be so restricted. Interestingly, some countries (Colombia, Egypt, Turkey, Venezuela) forbid voting by members of the military. The point of the restriction is to reinforce the apolitical nature of the military (ICIJ REPORT). Such countries have a history of military coups and other military interference in politics.[17]

But the justifications for felon disenfranchisement, in particular, ring hollow. Traditional arguments for the practice include a desire to deter crime; prevent electoral fraud and "subversive" voting; and protect the "purity" of the ballot box (Sigler, 2014). There is no persuasive evidence that disenfranchisement adds anything to deterrence that is not already achieved by the prison sentence itself; or that former felons, disenfranchised for a wide variety of crimes having nothing to do with election fraud or even fraud of any kind, are as a group likely to commit election fraud. Nor is there persuasive evidence that former felons would vote cohesively to somehow subvert the system – let alone do so in significant, outcome-determinative numbers. The states of Maine and Vermont, which have long allowed even prisoners to vote, have not seen these problems (Mulroy, 2019).

More sophisticated justifications discuss the notion that felons have "violated the civic trust that makes liberal democracy possible" (Sigler, 2014). However, this ends up being just a version of the abstract, symbolic argument regarding the "purity of the ballot box," or one sounding in an intuitive, moralistic, "just desserts" approach. Given the very real burden created by these laws, and the fact that what is being burdened is a fundamental right of democracy, it is questionable whether this justification is very compelling. This symbolic purity seems overkill particularly in the US, where the practice in the US is both severely racially disproportionate and large enough to change many election outcomes (Chung, 2019).

Perhaps for these reasons, the trend in the US has been toward liberalization, just as it has been regarding ease of registration and ID requirements. In the last 20 years, almost half of US states have either expanded voter eligibility or made it easier for persons to restore their rights. This includes ten states that either repealed or substantially liberalized their lifetime bans, and seven states that repealed disenfranchisement for those on probation or parole. Most notable and recent in this trend are New York, where in 2018, the governor began using his clemency power regularly to restore the franchise to parolees and Florida, which by referendum amended its constitution to about 1.54 million persons who had completed their sentences (Chung, 2019).[18] At the federal level, the HR1 election reform bill would guarantee the rights of felons to vote in federal elections, except for those still in prison.

Redistricting Commissions

All liberal democracies have independent commissions that draw district lines. A few nominal democracies that do not – Cameroon, Kyrgyzstan, Malaysia, and Singapore – have authoritarian governments that cannot really be considered liberal democracies. The notable exception is the United States, the only modern democracy that still allows incumbent politicians to draw their own district lines (Stephanopoulos, 2013).

Most of these democracies used to allow incumbents to draw their own lines, until court decisions or political reform moved them toward the redistricting commission model. Under this model, appointed nonpartisan judges, academics, or other experts draw redistricting plans, often supervising drawing done by professional demographers, cartographers, and statisticians on staff. Some models allow elected officials to participate. Even when that is the case, such representation is carefully balanced among major parties (Mulroy, 2018).

Australia is a good example. Its Australian Election Commission (AEC) is made up of three appointees: A retired judge, a professional statistician, and another government official. Working with other professional nonpartisan appointed officials, they decide on a first draft of a redistricting plan for the federal House elections, without using any political data. There is an ample public notice and comment period before finalizing the maps (Commonwealth Electoral Act 1918 Section 5 (Aust)). Similar state-level Election Commissions exist in each state for drawing state legislature maps. The AEC is well-respected as independent from political considerations, representing the gold standard here (Mulroy, 2018).

Unsurprisingly, the districting plans resulting from independent commissions generally have a lower partisan bias than those drawn in the US by politicians – i.e., there is a closer correspondence between the percentage of the vote that a party wins and the percentage of legislative seats that the party gets (Mulroy, 2018; Stephanopoulos, 2013). Studies of such plans before and after the switch to redistricting commissions show a marked immediate reduction in partisan bias (see, e.g., 2010; Jackman, 1994). One study showed that Australian districting plans had partisan bias about one-third lower than comparable American districting plans (Stephanopoulos, 2013). In the Australian House, the seat share of each major party has somewhat closely matched that party's share of the two-party vote (Stephanopoulos, 2013). Over the last ten years, the deviation has averaged 1.75%, never getting above 9.5% (Mulroy, 2018).

Contrast the United States. Again, practices vary markedly by state. But most US states still allow the elected members of the state legislature to draw directly the district lines for both the state legislature and the US House. They may employ professional demographers, but simply to effectuate the elected members' will, not to exercise independent judgment. As a result, the US continues to have a serious gerrymandering problem. Gerrymandered district plans are common and have become even more common in recent decades, as advances in computer map drawing have allowed ever more fine-tuned gerrymandering (Mulroy, 2018).

This, too, is changing. In recent years, a number of US states have adopted the redistricting commission model. Some have adopted truly nonpartisan commissions as in Australia. Others have moved just to bipartisan commissions, largely made up of incumbents, but balanced between major parties in such a way as to require at least a few members of each party to sign onto a plan (Mulroy, 2018).

While a salutary reform, even nonpartisan redistricting commissions are not a complete solution to the problem of gerrymandering. This is because of the phenomenon of "demographic clustering." People do not evenly spread themselves out according to political affiliation; they bunch together in like-minded clumps that can complicate the drawing of fair districts, which are supposed to be somewhat compact and equipopulous. In advanced democracies, a common situation is for left-of-center voters to overconcentrate in urban areas. Compact single-member districts drawn in such urban areas tend to "pack" leftist voters into districts with leftist supermajorities. This tends to "waste" the leftist votes (Chen & Rodden, 2013). This phenomenon allowed the Republicans to retain a 30-seat majority in the US House in 2012, even though Republican candidates nationwide received less than a majority of the vote (Mulroy, 2018).

For this reason, the US record with redistricting commissions has been mixed. One study comparing simultaneous redistricting plans drawn by commission and non-commission US states concluded that the commissions have not helped much in reducing partisan bias – at best, a slight improvement (Stephanopoulos, 2013). California's early experiment with bipartisan commissions at first seemed to sharply reduce partisan bias, but later elections showed partisan bias even above the national average (Mulroy, 2018). Similar reform efforts in Florida, which, by referendum, imposed party-neutral redistricting criteria like compactness, contiguity, and respect for political subdivision boundaries, proved unavailing because of demographic clustering (Chen & Rodden, 2013).

The natural skew of single-member districts caused by demographic clustering is not limited to the United States and does not always hurt leftists. For example, even the well-respected AEC can get it wrong. Both in 1990 and 1998, the major party winning the majority of the overall Australian vote did not control a majority of the seats, thanks to this skew, which some have called an "unintentional gerrymander." In one instance, the leftist major party benefited; in another, the rightist party. And, while recent Australian House plans have resulted in a fairly close alignment between votes and seats, the deviation has gone as high as almost 10%, more than enough to be outcome-determinative in a close election.

For these reasons, while redistricting commissions are a good idea, they are only a half-measure. What is truly needed is a system of proportional representation.

Proportional Representation

Proportional Representation (PR) is used more than any other electoral system around the world. Indeed, most countries use some form of PR to elect at least part of their national legislature. PR is the opposite of the "winner-take-all" system familiar to those in the Anglo-French tradition. Those systems tend to elect representatives from single-member districts. In plurality (or "first-past-the-post") systems like those used in England and India, whichever candidate gets the most votes wins, even if it is not a majority of the vote. In two-round systems as in France, if there is no majority winner, the top two candidates advance to a runoff election. Either way, it is a "winner-take-all" approach. With rare exceptions, the US uses single-member districts with primarily a plurality rule, although runoff elections are not uncommon (ACE Project).

Under winner-take-all, 50.1% of the vote yields 100% of the power, and a politically cohesive minority of, say, 35% takes nothing. Under PR, a slight majority of the vote yields a slight majority of the seats, and a 35% minority obtains roughly 35% of the seats.

The most popular form of PR is the "party-list" system, common in Europe and South America. Political parties compile ranked lists of candidates available to fill seats.[19] Each party gets a number of seats in the parliament proportional to its share of the national vote. Once a party's number of seats is known, one goes down the list in order by the party's ranking to fill the seats. To gain at least one seat, a party must meet a minimum threshold of the vote. This is the most common form of electoral system, with a "first-past-the-post" plurality system coming in second (ACE Project).

The party list system can either be "closed list," as in Argentina, Turkey, and Israel, where the voter just votes for parties. Or it can be "open list," as in Finland, the Netherlands, and Brazil, where the voter votes for individual candidates associated with a party. These votes count toward the party's overall share of seats, and the votes for the candidates usually help towards determining which candidates from that party will fill the allotted number of seats (Mulroy, 2018).

Still other countries use hybrid systems that combine a party list system with a plurality system. There are two main forms of these hybrids. The more common, used in Russia, Mexico, Pakistan, and many African countries, is called the Mixed Member Majoritarian system (MMM). Under MMM, some seats are filled using plurality elections held within single-member districts, while other seats are filled with a party list election. MMM is not a true proportional system, because the plurality-elected seats from single-member districts can throw off the overall total. The less common Mixed Member Proportional (MMP) system also has single-member district plurality and party list proportional seats but is a true proportional system. That is because MMP assigns each party a total number of seats corresponding to its overall vote share; it just starts to fill those slots with the individual candidates from that party who won in the single-member districts. If, after all single-member district seats are assigned, a party is still entitled to more seats based on overall vote share, extra seats are filled from the party list (Mulroy, 2018).

A final form of PR is the Single Transferable Vote (STV). This is used in Australia to elect its Senate. STV is a form of Ranked Choice Voting (RCV), which allows voters to rank order their candidate preferences. Under STV, voters can vote for candidates rather than parties, and they can rank their first, second, third, etc. preferences among candidates.

Like any PR system, STV calculates a threshold percentage of the vote needed by a party to fill one seat. If there are ten seats to be filled in an election, the threshold would be 1(10 + 1), or 1/11 (9%) of the vote. Any candidate receiving more than the threshold amount of first-place votes is seated. Any "surplus" votes above the threshold are reassigned to the remaining candidates based on voters' second choices. If, in a given round, no candidate meets the threshold, the weakest candidate is eliminated, and the votes for that candidate are redistributed among remaining candidates based on those ballots' second or third choices. This process of reassigning "surplus" votes and redistributing votes of eliminated candidates repeats until all seats are filled.

PR systems have many advantages over winner-take-all systems like those using single-member districts. They lead to a more accurate reflection of the popular will and avoid anomalous election results where a party with fewer jurisdiction-wide votes gains more seats than a party with more votes, which can and does happen under winner-take-all systems. They provide more diverse representation for racial, ethnic, partisan, and ideological minorities, including third parties, avoiding the rigid dominance of two major parties common in winner-take-all systems (Mulroy, 2018). By increasing the number of people who can say that at least one candidate they voted for won, they encourage voter engagement (Franklin, 1996; Mulroy, 2018).

Indeed, one international comparative study showed an increase of voter participation of 0.6 percentage points for every percentage point improvement in the correspondence between votes and seats occasioned by the use of PR (Franklin, 1996). It further indicated that structural factors like proportional representation were even more important in predicting high turnout than individual voter characteristics such as wealth and education.

These election schemes also have advantages over the single-member district form of winner-take-all systems. By holding the election at-large or with fewer, larger, multimember districts, PR systems eliminate or reduce the drawing of districts and, with that, the potential for gerrymandering abuses. They also tend to make elections more competitive than in single-member district races, which often are lopsidedly tilted toward one party (Franklin, 1996). This increase in competitiveness encourages voter turnout (Mulroy, 2018).

While proportional representation is designed simply to more accurately reflect voter preferences and need not necessarily lead to the election of one kind of candidate over another, PR electoral regimes do tend to produce more economic and social egalitarianism than single-member district plurality systems (Alesina & Glaeser, 2014; Beramendi & Anderson, 2008; Wilensky, 2002). They also generate less poverty (Brady, 2009). Such systems directly influence the distribution of income, leading to a wider distribution than binary systems with complete winners and complete losers.

As noted above, there are multiple means of achieving proportional representation. Some form of a party list system appropriate for, and commonly used by, parliamentary governments. In such governments, the party (or party coalition) achieving majority control selects the prime minister from among its members, usually the senior member of the party. In non-parliamentary systems using a direct election of the nation's chief executive, STV would be more appropriate.

Indeed, the Ranked Choice Voting feature of STV brings its own distinct advantages. It ensures that a majority winner without the need for a French-style top-two runoff. Splitting the election into two separate contests can lead to low turnout for one of the rounds. Moreover, the two-round approach arbitrarily limits the field to the top two candidates in the first round, even though a third-place finisher might have broader support. Ranked Choice Voting also avoids the "spoiler" problem of vote-splitting. It provides more opportunities for lesser-known, lesser-funded candidates. In winner-take-all systems, voters who might prefer such candidates may avoid supporting them for fear of "throwing away one's vote" on a candidate with little chance of electoral success.

Finally, RCV discourages negative campaigning. A candidate wishes to be the first choice of her own base, but also the second choice of a rival's base. It is thus less advantageous to run attack ads against a rival, for fear of alienating the rival's base. RCV thus leads to more cooperative campaigning and the election of consensus candidates with broad-based support. The most common objection to RCV, that it is too confusing for voters, is not in fact borne out by the experience of jurisdictions holding RCV elections (Mulroy, 2018).

Advanced Versus Developed Countries

The undeveloped world generally has been a latecomer to full electoral democracy. For much of the twentieth century, regimes in the Third World "oscillated between liberalization and repression" (Almeida, 2010 in Leicht & Jenkins). The repression often took the form of diminution of fundamental political rights, retarding political mobilization. Over the past three decades, however, and particularly in this century, many developing countries are seeing rapidly increasing political mobilization, especially as a reaction to globalization. This has occurred within a context of increasing opportunities for access to competitive elections. The democratization has been helped along by such early twenty-first century social movements as those promoting feminism, environmentalism, LGBT equality, and indigenous people's rights (Almeida, 2010).

Much of the globalization-fueled mobilization has been a reaction *against* globalization and some of its perceived negative economic effects on local economies. But globalization, along with other modernizing trends such as industrialization, automation, and a shift to service-based economies, has at least had the salutary political effect of reducing the extent of "clientelism" as a political form. That is, the political terrain has become less dominated by a patronage-based system controlled by a village or party machine boss. Such a political form historically has been associated with agriculturally based economies, which are on the decline (Clark & Harvey, 2010).

In fact, the very tenuousness of the economic situation in developing countries has a direct effect on political mobilization trends. Voters in such nations are much more likely to increase participation to vote out incumbent parties in times of economic distress (Redding, Barwis & Summers, 2010). Arguably, the need for democracy and electoral systems with low barriers to entry is greater in developing countries. The scholarship shows both that such countries suffer from greater economic inequality and that democratic elections tend to reduce that inequality and have a general egalitarian effect (Sen, 1999; Brady & Sosnaud, 2010, and sources cited therein).

For some of these developing democracies, the mobilization of women as a significant political force is a relatively recent phenomenon, with its potential not fully realized (Beckfield, 2010; Moghadam, 2010; Sen, 1999; Brady & Sosnaud, 2010, and sources cited therein). This gender gap in political participation largely diminishes once developing nations become truly post-industrial (Mogdaham, 2010). Indeed, the more developed a country, the more egalitarian it generally becomes in terms of political participation (Modgaham, 2010).

Again, the United States may buck the trend here. It has a lower percentage of women elected to higher office than many other countries, including countries less economically and technologically developed (Mogdaham, 2010). This despite the US being somewhat of a pioneer in feminism regarding social equality and sexual autonomy. One partial explanation is the presence in other nations of gender quotas affecting electoral office, either from the nation's constitution, electoral laws, or internal rules of major parties (Mogdaham, 2010). The eighteenth-century US Constitution did not provide for such quotas, and indeed, has been interpreted in such a way that any legislative attempt to impose them would be considered unconstitutional. The gender diversity caused by electoral quotas in parliamentary systems can lead to greater gender diversity among prime ministers (Mogdaham, 2010).

Another partial explanation may be the prevalence of proportional representation systems in other countries, including developing countries. PR systems and multimember districts tend to elect more female candidates than winner-take-all systems and single-member districts (Blais & Massicotte, 1996; Paxton & Hughes, 2007; Mulroy, 2018). In the former systems, the election of a woman is less likely to be seen as the displacement of a particular male candidate (Paxton & Hughs, 2007). It may also be easier for voters with more traditional, latent patriarchal attitudes to be able to vote for one or two female candidates out of a group being elected from a party list or multimember district, than it is to cast one's only vote for one female candidate in a winner-take-all election. This may further help to explain why so many supposedly less developed or advanced nations have seen female national leaders, even though the US has never had a female president.

Such developing countries have a relatively small number of true "political elites" with direct influence on public policy (Higley, 2010; Paxton & Hughs, 2007). Small enough – less than 2000 – that it would allow for political elites to largely know one another. This allows for relative ease of intra-group communication and collective action. This makes both control and reform easier.

These differences between developing and advanced democracies have some implications for electoral reform. Several of these reform consequences stem from the relative socioeconomic disadvantage experienced by residents of developing countries, disadvantages that create practical barriers to easy registration and voting. Thus, all the more reason for those countries to adopt AVR, as well as more flexible voting ID standards, such as the affidavits by tribal elders used in Liberia and Malawi.

Similarly, proportional representation systems seem especially appropriate in developing countries, because PR tends to lead to more redistributive economic policies and more egalitarian social outcomes. This is especially true in undeveloped countries with deep ethnic cleavages; PR achieves more diverse representation than winner-take-all, thus easing inter-group tensions (Blais & Massicotte, 1996; Mulroy, 1999).

One might argue that socioeconomic and educational disadvantage in developing countries might make them less viable candidates for RCV on the ground and that RCV is more confusing for voters. But, as noted above, the empirical experience of RCV elections does not suggest that this is a substantial obstacle. At most, it suggests that extra efforts at voter education occur, especially before the inaugural use of RCV in a given jurisdiction.

Finally, developing countries may be less well-situated to adopt the most cutting-edge technology regarding voting machines using a voter-verified paper trail. This reform has been much discussed for years in the advanced democracies and has been given new urgency in recent years due to reports of foreign interference in elections (Norden & Vandewalker, 2017). In fact, many developing countries already use paper ballots (Institute for Democracy & Electoral Assistance, 2015). This retro approach is actually less vulnerable to cyber-hacking. In this respect, developing countries may be ahead of advanced countries.

Notes

1 See, e.g., *Department of Commerce v. New York*, 139 S. Ct. 2551, 2596 (2019), 2019 WL 2619473 (Alito, J., concurring) (defending use of citizenship question on US Census by noting it is a common practice internationally).

2 *See, e.g.,* Michael McFaul, *Trump is right: The United States needs electoral reform* (WASHINGTON POST, October 31, 2016), available at www.washingtonpost.com/news/global-opinions/wp/2016/ 10/31/ trump-is-right-the-united-states-needs-electoral-reform/?utm term=a50098c7ccf). (criticizing, from a global perspective, US Electoral College, felon disenfranchisement, voting machine cybersecurity, and other aspects of the US electoral system).

3 The ACE Electoral Knowledge Network is a collaborative resource started by the United Nations and currently maintained by the UN and a number of other international organizations. ACE Project, at http://aceproject.org/about-en/. It is an oft-cited resource for up-to-date comparative data on electoral systems.

4 But see *Dunn v. Blumstein*, 405 US 330, 332-33 (1972) (invalidating, under Equal Protection, a state law requiring voters have a one-year residency in the state and a three-month residency in the county); Voting Rights Act, 52 USC §10502 (2012) (prohibiting in presidential elections any "durational residency requirement" of more than 30 days).

5 In the US, each state can write its own rules regarding voter eligibility for state and local elections. For federal elections, it cannot go below the "floor" of the US Constitution, which guarantees voter eligibility for all competent citizens above the age of 18. *See* US CONST. Amen. 26.

6 Actually, the 68% rate dates from 2009, and was used for comparison to the worldwide data. More recent figures put the rate lower still, at 61% (US Census Bureau, November 2018).

7 The states are Alaska, California, Colorado, Georgia, Illinois, Maine, Maryland, Michigan, Nevada, Massachusetts, New Jersey, Oregon, Rhode Island, Vermont, Washington, and West Virginia, in addition to Washington, DC. (Brennan Center, 2019).

8 The results there were dramatic. Just a year after it passed AVR, Oregon attained the highest voter registration rate in the US, almost quadrupling its rate from prior years (Joslin, 2017), at 251.

9 The study used the political science "matching" methodology. It compared new AVR states with demographically similar non-AVR states to derive a baseline registration rate for non-AVR (Morris & Dunphy, 2019, p. 2–4). The "matching" methodology was an attempt to control for natural increases in registration that may have occurred in the AVR states, even absent the adoption of AVR.

10 Although regulatory authority over US elections starts in the states, Congress has authority to alter state regulations, but only for federal elections. US CONST. Art. I §4.

11 See www.politifact.com/texas/statements/2016/jun/20/barack-obama/barack-obama-austin-says-us -only-advanced-demorac/.

12 Some studies on the effect of voter ID laws are inconclusive or point in a different direction, suggesting that the depressive effect is smaller. See Dan Hopkins, *What We Know About Voter ID Laws*, (FIVETHIRTYEIGHT, Aug. 21, 2018), available at https://fivethirtyeight.com/features/what-we-know-about-voter-id-laws/ (summarizing several recent studies). But all such studies show at least some negative effect on voter participation, and almost always skewed demographically against minority groups. Given the potential for outcome-determinative effects in especially close races, and the relative lack of justification based in voter fraud concerns (see above), it is reasonable to question the net benefit of such laws.

13 And the percentage reductions correspond to tens of thousands of otherwise eligible persons denied the franchise. (Mulroy, 2019)

14 See e.g., *Veasey v. Abbott*, 830 F.3d 216, 238 (5th Cir. 2016) (noting only two convictions for in-person voter impersonation fraud out of 20 million votes cast in a decade of Texas elections); *N.C. State Conference of the NAACP v. McCrory*, 831 F.3d 204, 235 (4th Cir. 2016) (observing that North Carolina failed to identify "even a single individual" who has ever been charged with in-person voting fraud).

15 This certainly holds true for the US, which has the highest total incarceration rate, and the highest per capita incarceration rate in the world. Roy Walmsley, *World Prison Population List*, International Center for Prison Studies (2013).

16 They are Armenia, Belgium, Cameroon, Chile, Finland, New Zealand, the Philippines, and the United States. (Harpster & Vaughn, 2016)

17 Colombia underwent a successful coup in 1953. Egypt experienced successful coups in 1952, 1954, 2011, and 2013. Turkey saw successful coups in 1913, 1960, 1971, 1980, as well as failed coups in 1962 and 1963, and substantial interference by the military in 1997. Military coups succeeded in 1948 and 1958. Venezuelan

leader Hugo Chavez both led a failed coup in 1992, and repelled failed coup attempts against him in 2002 and 2007. In 2019, the country saw yet another coup attempt against leader Nicolas Maduro.

18 Such progress does not rule out the possibility of retrenchment, however. In Florida, the conservative legislature tried to limit the scope of the reenfranchisement referendum through legislation denying reenfranchisement to those who, though completing their sentences, still owed fines or fees. A lower court has ruled that this violates the constitution. See *Jones v. DeSantis*, 410 F.Supp.3d 1284 (N.D. Fla. 2019). This order was stayed pending appeal. *Raysor v. DeSantis*, 140 S.Ct. 2600 (US 2020). The appeal is ongoing.

19 Thus, they eschew partisan primary elections common in the US American-style partisan primaries are the exception, rather than the rule around the world (Mulroy, 2018). This is not necessarily a good thing for the rest of the world (see Ober, 2015).

References

116th Cong. (2019). For the People Act of 2019.

ACE Project: The electoral knowledge network. Comparative data (voter registration). Retrieved from http://aceproject.org/epic-en/

Al Jazeera. (2019). How the world votes. Retrieved from https://interactive.aljazeera.com/aje/2019/how-the-world-votes-2019/index.html#suffrage

Alesina, A., & Glaeser, E. (2014). *Fighting poverty in the US and Europe: A world of difference.* Oxford, UK: Oxford University Press.

Almeida P. D. (2010). Globalization and collective action. In K. T. Leicht & J. C. Jenkins (Eds.), *Handbook of politics. Handbooks of sociology and social research.* New York: Springer. doi: 10.1007/978-0-387-68930-2_17

Amartya, S. (1999). *Development as freedom.* New York: Anchor Books.

Beramendi, P., & Anderson, C. J. (2008). *Democracy, inequality, and representation in comparative perspective.* New York: Russell Sage Foundation. Retrieved from http://www.jstor.org/stable/10.7758/9781610440448

Beckfield, J. (2010). Transboundary Politics. In K. T. Leicht & J. C. Jenkins (Eds.), *Handbook of politics. Handbooks of sociology and social research.* New York: Springer. doi: 10.1007/978-0-387-68930-2_8

Brady, D., & Sosnaud, B. (2010). *The politics of economic inequality.* doi: 10.1007/978-0-387-68930-2_28

Brennan Center for Justice. (June 19, 2019a). Automatic voter registration. Retrieved from https://www.brennancenter.org/analysis/automatic-voter-registration

Brennan Center for Justice. (June 19, 2019b). History of AVR & implementation dates. Retrieved from https://www.brennancenter.org/analysis/history-avr-implementation-dates

Blais, A., & Massicotte, L. (1996). Electoral systems. In L. LeDuc, R. Niemi & P. Norris (Eds.), *Comparing democracies.* London: Sage.

Chavkin, S., & Boland-Rudder, H. (May 5, 2014). *Your country, your vote: A rough guide to global voter restrictions.* International Consortium of Investigative Journalists (ICIJ Report). Retrieved from https://www.icij.org/blog/2014/05/your-country-your-vote-rough-guide-global-voter-restrictions/

Chen, J., & Rodden, J. (2013). Unintentional gerrymandering: Political geography and electoral bias in legislatures. *Quarterly Journal of Political Science, 8*, 239–269.

Chung, J. (June 27, 2019). Felony disenfranchisement: A primer. The Sentencing Project. Retrieved from https://www.sentencingproject.org/publications/felony-disenfranchisement-a-primer/

Cifullo, A., & Fry, R. (January 30, 2019). An early look at the 2020 electorate. Pew Research Center. Retrieved from https://www.pewsocialtrends.org/essay/an-early-look-at-the-2020-electorate/

Clark, T. N., & Harvey, R. (2010). Urban politics. In K. T. Leicht & J. C. Jenkins (Eds.), *Handbook of politics. Handbooks of sociology and social research.* New York: Springer. doi: 10.1007/978-0-387-68930-2_23

Desilver, D. (May 21, 2018). U.S. trails most developed countries in voter turnout. Pew Research Center. Retrieved from https://www.pewresearch.org/fact-tank/2018/05/21/u-s-voter-turnout-trails-most-developed-countries/

Ember, S., & Stevens, M. (April 27, 2019). Bernie Sanders opens space for debate on voting rights for incarcerated people. *New York Times.* Retrieved from https://www.nytimes.com/2019/04/27/us/politics/bernie-sanders-prison-voting.html

Fraga, B., & Miller, M. (2018). Who does voter ID legislation keep from voting? Evidence from Texas. Mit Election Data Science Lab. Retrieved from http://electionlab.mit.edu/sites/default/files/2019-01/fraga-miller_2017summary.pdf

Franklin, M. N. (1996). Electoral participation. In L. LeDuc, R. Niemi & P. Norris (Eds.), *Comparing democracies*. London: Sage.
Harpster, N., & Vaughn, M. S. (2016). Felon disenfranchisement laws: A review of current policies, challenges of disenfranchisement laws, and recent trends in legislative and legal change. *Criminal Law Bulletin, 52*(5), Article 4.
Hasen, R. L. (2012). *The voting wars*. New Haven, CT; London: Yale University Press. Retrieved from http://www.jstor.org/stable/j.ctt32bft8
Henninger, P., Meredith, M., & Morse, M. (2018). Who votes without identification? Using affidavits from Michigan to learn about the potential impact of strict photo voter identification laws. *SSRN Electronic Journal*. doi: 10.2139/ssrn.3205769
Higley, J. (2010). Elite theory and elites. In K. T. Leicht & J. C. Jenkins (Eds.), *Handbook of politics. Handbooks of sociology and social research*. New York: Springer. doi: 10.1007/978-0-387-68930-2_9
International Institute for Democracy and Electoral Assistance (International IDEA). (October 17, 2015). Use of E-Voting around the world. Retrieved from https://www.idea.int/news-media/media/use-e-voting-around-world
Jackman, S. (1994). Measuring electoral bias: Australia, 1949–93. *British Journal of Political Science, 24*(3), 319–357. Cambridge University Press. Retrieved from http://www.jstor.org/stable/194252
Joslin, J. N. (2017). Navigating the Post-Shelby landscape: Using universalism to augment the remaining power of the Voting Rights Act. *St. Mary's Law Journals, 19*(2), 217–252. St. Mary's University School of Law. Retrieved from https://commons.stmarytx.edu/thescholar/vol19/iss2/3
Levitt, J. (August 6, 2014). A comprehensive investigation of voter impersonation finds 31 credible incidents out of one billion ballots cast. *Washington Post*. Retrieved from https://www.washingtonpost.com/news/wonk/wp/2014/08/06/a-comprehensive-investigation-of-voter-impersonation-finds-31-credible-incidents-out-of-one-billionballots-cast/?utm_term=.396b6e0866ef
McKee, S. C. (2015). Politics is local: State legislator voting on restrictive voter identification legislation. Sage Journals. Retrieved from https://doi.org/10.1177/2053168015589804
Minnite, L. (2010). *The myth of voter fraud*. Ithaca, NY; London: Cornell University Press. Retrieved from http://www.jstor.org/stable/10.7591/j.ctt7zgg1
Moghadam, V. M. (2010). Gender, politics, and women's empowerment. In K. T. Leicht & J. C. Jenkins (Eds.), *Handbook of politics. Handbooks of sociology and social research*. New York: Springer. doi: 10.1007/978-0-387-68930-2_16
Morris, K., & Dunphy, P. (April 11, 2019). AVR impact on state voter registration. Brennan Center for Justice at New York University of Law. Retrieved from https://www.brennancenter.org/publication/avr-impact-state-voter-registration
Mulroy, S. J. (1999). Alternative ways out: A remedial road map for using alternative electoral systems as Voting Rights Act remedies. *North Carolina Law Review*, 77(5), 1867–1924. Retrieved from https://scholarship.law.unc.edu/cgi/viewcontent.cgi?referer=https://www.google.com/&httpsredir=1&article=3826&context=nclr
Mulroy, S. J. (2018). *Rethinking US election law: Unskewing the system*. Cheltenham, UK; Northampton, MA: Edward Elgar Publishing.
Mulroy, S. J. (2019). Barriers at the ballot box symposium issue. *The University of Memphis Law Review, 49*.
National Conference of State Legislatures. (May 31, 2017). Voter ID history: History of voter ID. Retrieved from http://www.ncsl.org/research/elections-and-campaigns/voter-id-history.aspx
Norden, L., & Vandewalker, I. (June 29, 2017). *Securing elections from foreign interference*. New York: Brennan Center for Justice at New York University School of Law. Retrieved from https://www.brennancenter.org/sites/default/files/publications/Securing_Elections_From_Foreign_Interference.pdf
Ober, J. (July 13, 2015). Here's why primaries are good for democracy. *Foreign Policy*. Retrieved from https://foreignpolicy.com/2015/07/13/heres-why-primaries-are-good-for-democracy/
Paxton, P. M., & Hughes, M. M. (2007). *Women, politics, and power: A global perspective*. Thousand Oaks, CA: SAGE Publications, Inc.
POLITIFACT. (June 20, 2016). Barack Obama: We're the only advanced democracy in the world which makes it harder for people to vote. Retrieved from https://www.politifact.com/texas/statements/2016/jun/20/barack-obama/barack-obama-austin-says-us-only-advanced-demorac/
Redding, K., Barwis, P. J., & Summers, N. (2010). Elections and voting. In K. T. Leicht & J. C. Jenkins (Eds.), *Handbook of politics. Handbooks of sociology and social research*. New York: Springer. doi: 10.1007/978-0-387-68930-2_27

Rocha, R. R., & Matsubayashi, T. (2014). The politics of race and voter ID laws in the States: The return of Jim Crow? *Political Research Quarterly*, *67*(3), 666–679. Retrieved from http://www.jstor.org/stable/24371900

Rosenberg, J. S., & Chen, M. (2009). Expanding democracy voter registration around the world. New York: Brennan Center for Justice at New York University School of Law. Retrieved from http://www.brennancenter.org/sites/default/files/legacy/publications/Expanding.Democracy.pdf

Sigler, M. (2014). Defensible disenfranchisement. *Iowa Law Review*, *99*(1961), 1725–1744. Retrieved from https://ilr.law.uiowa.edu/print/volume-99-issue-4/defensible-disenfranchisement/

Stephanopoulos, N. O. (2013). Our electoral exceptionalism. *Chicago Law Review*, *80*(2), 769–858. doi: 10.2307/41959076

U.S. Bureau of the Census. (November, 2018). Reported voting and registration, by race, Hispanic origin, sex, and age, for the United States. Retrieved from https://www.census.gov/data/tables/time-series/demo/voting-and-registration/p20-583.html

Walmsley, R. (2013). *World prison population list* (10th ed.). London: International Centre for Prison Studies. Retrieved from www.prisonstudies.org

Weinger, M. (June 25, 2012). Pa. pol: Vote ID helps GOP win state. *POLITICO*. Retrieved from https://www.politico.com/story/2012/06/pa-pol-voter-id-helps-gop-win-state-077811

Wilensky, H. L. (2002). Rich democracies: Political economy, public policy, and performance. University of California Press. Retrieved from http://www.jstor.org/stable/10.1525/j.ctt1pn955

8
CHALLENGES IN ELECTORAL INTEGRITY

Pippa Norris

Introduction

Elections provide opportunities for citizens to participate in politics and hold leaders to account.[1] When they work well, elections can ideally deepen civic engagement, inform public debate, stimulate party competition, strengthen government responsiveness, and allow the peaceful resolution of political conflict. Liberal democracies require many institutions to function well, but competitive elections are the core mechanisms of accountability and representation. All too often, however, contests fail to achieve these core objectives.

Multiparty elections for legislative office have gradually spread around the world, to all but a handful of Gulf monarchies, one-party states, and personal dictatorships. However, their quality has been frequently undermined by diverse electoral malpractices ranging from overt cases of violence and intimidation to disinformation campaigns, cybersecurity threats, barriers to voting, and the under-representation of women and minority candidates (Birch, 2011; Norris, 2015; Flores & Nooruddin, 2016).

Difficulties can occur at all stages of the electoral cycle, whether they arise from unfair laws favoring incumbents, restrictions on ballot access and party competition, bias in the news and social media coverage of election campaigns, problems of lack of a level playing field in campaign finance, fraud at the ballot box, rigged vote counts, or lack of impartial, professional, and efficient electoral officials. These types of flaws and failures matter: The consequences can exacerbate anemic voter turnout (Birch, 2010; Coma & Trinh, 2017), heighten protest politics (Tucker, 2007; Beaulieu, 2014), and fuel democratic disaffection and political mistrust (Birch, 2008; Norris, 2014). As a result, unfortunately, many contests today fail to ensure legitimate outcomes and peaceable handovers of power, potentially stoking grievances and exacerbating violence (Mansfield & Snyder, 2007).

Cases are not hard to come by; major problems were reported in a series of contests during 2018. For example, in Mexico, over 130 candidates and party workers were killed during the campaign; in Zimbabwe, the contests saw outbreaks of post-election conflict and accusations by the opposition that the poll was marred by "mammoth theft and fraud"; in Russia, President Putin face minimal effective competition after protests had been silenced and opposition leaders had been barred or incarcerated; and, in Venezuela, a rigged contest returned President Maduro to power.

DOI: 10.4324/9780429401800-8

But how extensive are malpractices in national elections around the world? Are some problems confined to a few well-known cases, or are they evident in contests around the world? What are the root causes of electoral flaws and failures? Is the digital age of social media making things worse? It remains difficult to assess the extent of any issues systematically and with any degree of reliability for many reasons (Coma & van Ham, 2015). Sore losers have an incentive to cry wolf and claim that results are unfair or fraudulent. Mass perceptions can be monitored through opinion polls, but the general public often lacks the knowledge make accurate judgments about complex technical or legal issues like the extent of partisan gerrymandering or the fairness of electoral rules. Views among partisans are also often strongly colored by the winners-losers effect and by processes of motivated reasoning (if my candidate wins, I am more likely to believe that the election process was honest and fair) (Flesken & Hartl, 2018). Reports by investigative journalism reveal problems and mobilize the reform agenda (Coffe, 2017). But illegal acts like vote-buying, fraud, and ballot stuffing are usually well-hidden from view. Many forms of manipulation may be perfectly legal. Independent reporters and the foreign press are restricted in the world's most repressive states, and press coverage in countries with freedom of expression is likely to be systematically skewed towards reporting bad news. The work of international observer missions is vital, but their reports may also suffer from biases (Hyde, 2011; Kelley, 2012, Donno, 2013) and their messages are increasingly being counterbalanced by "zombie" observer groups more friendly to authoritarian regimes, which soft-pedal criticism and drown out the voices of credible monitors (Walker & Cooley, 2013). Forensic techniques are performed on electoral autopsies of the local results in cases such as Russia and Ukraine (Myagkov, Ordeshook, & Shakin, 2009), but these statistical methods remain controversial.

To monitor the extent of the risks, the first part of this chapter discusses the concept of electoral integrity and how the Electoral Integrity Project measures it systematically through the Perceptions of Electoral Integrity expert survey. The second part examines data from the Electoral Integrity Project, which gathers data from an expert rolling survey on perceptions of electoral integrity in presidential and parliamentary contests around the world. As well as providing an overall assessment and summary index used for comparing provinces, elections, or countries, the data can also be disaggregated to examine the performance of each of the 11 stages of the electoral cycle, as well as around 50 specific indices. The third part considers several alternative theories seeking to explain the rankings, including structural, international, and institutional accounts. The fourth part focuses, in particular, upon what the evidence suggests about the campaign information environment, wherein recent concern has highlighted problems of "fake news," partisan media, foreign meddling, and cybersecurity risks. The conclusion in the fifth part summarizes the results and considers their broader implications.

What Is Electoral Integrity and How Can It be Measured?

The concept of electoral integrity refers to agreed international conventions and global norms, applying universally to all countries worldwide through the election cycle, including during the pre-election period, the campaign, on polling day, and its aftermath (Norris, 2013). These standards have been endorsed in a series of authoritative conventions, treaties, protocols, case laws, and guidelines by agencies of the international community (European Commission, 2007; Tuccinardi, 2014). Authority derives primarily from resolutions and treaties passed by the UN General Assembly, the UN Security Council, and UN human rights bodies, supplemented by agreement reaching within regional intergovernmental bodies such as the Organization for Security and Cooperation in Europe (OSCE), the Organization of American States (OAS), the African Union (AU), and the European Union (Davis-Roberts & Carroll, 2010; Carol & David-

Roberts, 2013). The Carter Center (2018) has compiled the most comprehensive and systematic set of obligations derived from international jurisprudence.

The foundation for these standards rests upon Article 21(3) in the Universal Declaration of Human Rights (UDHR 1948). This specifies that:

> The will of the people shall be the basis of the authority of government; this will shall be expressed in periodic and genuine elections which shall be by universal and equal suffrage and shall be held by secret vote or by equivalent free voting procedures.

Agreement about the norms governing the conduct of elections was further specified in Article 25 of the UN International Covenant for Civil and Political Rights (ICCPR of 1966), which came into force a decade later. International standards continued to evolve, including through international conventions on the elimination of all forms of racial discrimination (ICERD 1966) and discrimination against women (CEDAW, 1979), the UN Convention against Corruption (UNCAC, 2003), and the Convention on the Rights of Persons with Disabilities (CRPD, 2006), as well as agreements secured at the 1990 Copenhagen Document of the Conference on Security and Cooperation in Europe (CSCE) and the Venice Commission's (2002) Code of Good Practice in Electoral Matters. This framework provides the legal mandate for electoral assistance by UN agencies and bureaus, reflected in the UN General Assembly resolution 63/163 on "Strengthening the role of the United Nations in enhancing periodic and genuine elections and the promotion of democratization," which has been passed every two years since 1988.

Reflecting these notions, when monitors in the international community are asked to define what is meant by elections which are "free and fair," "genuine," or "democratic," they typically emphasize a checklist reflecting these classic principles. The International IDEA guidelines identify twenty international obligations that are regarded as key building blocks. Based on this understanding, states are obliged to protect the voting rights for all citizens, to safeguard opportunities for all candidates and parties to campaign freely, to hold contests at regular intervals, to protect candidates and citizens from threats of political violence or intimidation, to provide transparent processes of electoral administration, and to offer timely and expeditious judicial processes adjudicating complaints and disputes.

In practice, however, how these abstract principles translate into national laws and detailed administrative procedures remains a complex process. For example, the concept of a "universal franchise" is widely agreed as a basic human right, yet states continue to differ in their legal definition of "citizenship," minimal age requirements, qualifications to vote, and the exclusion of certain categories, such as prisoners or overseas populations (Massicote et al., 2014). Even greater controversy continues to surround several important issues, for which there is no global consensus and normative values clash even among Western democracies. These include the appropriate standards for guiding political finance regulations and thus the use of disclosure requirements, spending caps and donor limits, and public funding of political parties. The international obligations endorsed in international treaties, therefore, provide a *minimum* basis for electoral integrity and, while not absolutely relative, the abstract principles are open to differing legitimate interpretations when translated into national laws and practices.

There are several other ways that this notion can be understood, such as by scholars defining free and fair elections in terms of party competition and rotation of office, when drawing upon the classic theories of electoral democracy by Schumpeter, or in terms of a more expansive range of civil liberties associated with theories of liberal democracy, drawing upon Robert Dahl (Elklit & Svensson, 1997; Elklit & Reynolds, 2005). But democratic theories are not recognized as authoritative in international jurisprudence. For example, they have not been endorsed by the decisions of the UN general assembly or by inter-governmental legal treaties, and they lack legitimacy in non-democratic states. Moreover, there are many analytical advantages in keeping the distinct concepts of electoral integrity and liberal democracy separate and distinct, since the latter has many components beyond free and fair contests, including the independence of the courts, the effectiveness of the legislature, the checks and balances on executive power, and the role of civil society. Electoral integrity also draws upon ideas of good governance and human rights. By treating the conceptualization and measurement of electoral integrity and liberal democracy separately, it becomes possible to compare the relationship between these notions. In practice, they are strongly correlated – not surprisingly, since free and fair multiparty elections are at the heart of liberal democracy. Nevertheless, several outliers can be observed wherein states perform better on one or other of these dimensions. It is important to disaggregate the notion of electoral integrity to understand the workings of all its component parts.

Much data about performance indices is derived from expert evaluations, a technique widely adopted by international organizations, private actors, NGOs, and think tanks in order to generate political indicators on everything from perceptions of corruption and human rights to good governance and rule of law (Cooley & Snyder, 2015). International agencies such as Freedom House, the Committee to Protect Journalists, and Reporters without Borders use experts to monitor freedom of the press and the internet around the world, as well as to record attacks on journalists and rights to free expression, regularly publishing their national assessments in annual reports. Other agencies have long assessed the performance of liberal democracies, measuring how states rank in their political rights and civil liberties, including Polity IV, Freedom House, and the Varieties of Democracy project.[2] Nevertheless, despite widespread concern, until recently, little systematic evidence had been gathered using these types of techniques to monitor the state of electoral integrity around the globe, especially to address recent concerns in elections across a wide range of countries and diverse types of regimes around the world.

To measure this concept, the Perceptions of Electoral Integrity (PEI) expert rolling survey uses a questionnaire that includes 49 items on electoral integrity ranging over the whole electoral cycle. These positive and negative items are framed as "agree-disagree" statements, where assessments focus on the specific presidential or parliamentary election in each country, with fieldwork conducted one month after polls close. The items fall into eleven sequential sub-dimensions from the pre-election through the campaign to polling day and its aftermath, including electoral laws; electoral procedures; district boundaries; voter registration; party registration; media coverage; campaign finance; voting process; vote count; results; and electoral authorities. Most attention in detecting fraud has focused upon the final stages of the voting process, such as the role of observers in monitoring any incidents of ballot-stuffing, vote-rigging, and manipulated tallies. Drawing upon Schedler's notion of a "menu of manipulation" (2002), however, the concept of an electoral cycle suggests that failure in even one step in the sequence, or one link in the chain, can undermine electoral integrity. The PEI Codebook provides detailed descriptions of all variables and imputation procedures.

The items in the survey are recoded so that a higher score consistently represents a more positive evaluation of the quality of the election. Missing data is estimated based on multiple imputation of chained equations in groups composing of the eleven sub-dimensions. The Perceptions of Electoral Integrity (PEI) Index is an additive function of the 49 imputed variables, standardized to 100-points. Sub-indices of the eleven sub-dimensions in the electoral cycle are summations of the imputed individual variables.

The results have been tested for external validity (compared with independent sources of evidence), internal validity (consistency within the groups of experts), and legitimacy (how far the results can be regarded as authoritative by stakeholders) (Norris, Frank, & Coma, 2013, 2014a, 2014b). The analysis demonstrates not only substantial external validity, when PEI data is compared with many other expert datasets, such as the equivalent Variety of Democracy assessments, but also internal validity across the experts within the survey and legitimacy, as measured by levels of congruence between mass and expert opinions within each country (Coma & van Ham, 2015).

The release in this chapter (PEI-6.5) is drawn from a rolling survey of 3,524 expert assessments of electoral integrity across 310 elections in 165 countries around the world, excluding micro-states and others without competitive contests during this period.[3] The cumulative study covers all national presidential and parliamentary elections held from July 1, 2012 to June 30, 2018. Additional rotating batteries are added annually to the core survey to monitor specific problems each year. Given the widespread concerns about the issue of fake news, online disinformation, and foreign meddling, the 2018 survey added items focused on issues of campaign media.

Global Patterns of Electoral Integrity

Figure 8.1 presents the global map of electoral integrity, where the PEI 100-point Index is divided into five categories ranging from very low to very high levels of electoral integrity. The overall results suggest that, in general, problems are most commonly experienced in elections held in many parts of Sub-Saharan Africa, the Middle East, North Africa, and South East Asia. By contrast, not surprisingly, long-established democracies in Western societies usually scored far better, especially in Northern Europe and Scandinavia. Yet this is not always a consistent pattern, and there is considerable variation observed among states sharing similar cultural legacies and levels of human development, such as between Canada and the US, Costa Rica and Nicaragua, and Taiwan and the Philippines.

To look into the contrasts in more detail and provide a snapshot of the state of electoral integrity around the world, Figure 8.2 compares the ranking of countries by the 100-point PEI Index in states within each global region. Country scores accumulate over a series of national parliamentary and presidential elections held from mid-2012 to mid-2018.

According to the 100-point PEI scale, elections that experts evaluated as having very high integrity (over 70) include the Nordic states of Denmark, Finland, Norway, and Iceland; long-established democracies; welfare states; and affluent post-industrial knowledge societies, which are also ranked very positively in most global measures of democracy and human rights. These were ranked far more highly than contests in Greece, the UK, and Malta. It is also notable that elections in the United States are rated less positively than many other countries in the Americas and, indeed, performed the worst of any established democracy. Positive electoral integrity scores were not confined to affluent Western democracies, by any means, since very high ratings were also observed in Costa Rica and Uruguay, Estonia and Lithuania, Taiwan and South Korea, and Cape Verde and Benin. Overall, each global region varies substantially between countries seen as positive for elections and others regarded more critically.

At the bottom of the rankings were countries that experts rated with low or very low scores in the PEI Index (below 50), often (although not always) low-income developing states from diverse world regions, exemplified by Haiti and Nicaragua, Turkmenistan and Tajikistan, Afghanistan and Cambodia, Iraq and Bahrain, Equatorial Guinea and Ethiopia. Overall, all the states in Northern and Western Europe were consistently rated very high or high in the PEI Index. By contrast, in Africa, the majority of states were rated as problematic by experts.

Figure 8.1 Electoral Integrity Worldwide, 2012 to Mid-2018.

Note: The Perceptions of Electoral Integrity index summary scale ranges from 0–100. The PEI country-level mean scores cover national elections held from mid-2012 to mid-2018.

Source: The Perceptions of Electoral Integrity expert survey (PEI 6.5), country-level www.electoralintegrityproject.com.

N&W Europe		Americas		C&E Europe		Asia-Pacific		MENA		Africa	
Country	PEI Index	Country	PEI Index	Country	PEI Index	Country	PEI Index	Country	PEI Index	Country	PEI Index
Denmark	86	Costa Rica*	79	Estonia	79	New Zealand	75	Israel	74	Cape Verde	71
Finland*	85	Uruguay	75	Lithuania	78	Taiwan	73	Tunisia	67	Benin	70
Norway	83	Canada	75	Slovenia*	77	South Korea	73	Oman	61	Ghana	65
Iceland	81	Chile	71	Czech Rep.*	75	Australia	70	Morocco	56	Mauritius	64
Germany	81	Brazil	68	Slovak Rep.	75	Japan	68	Kuwait	54	South Africa	63
Sweden	81	Jamaica	67	Poland	74	Tonga	65	Jordan	49	Lesotho	62
Netherlands	80	Argentina	65	Latvia	71	Mongolia	64	Iran	49	Namibia	60
Switzerland	78	Barbados*	64	Croatia	65	Timor-Leste*	64	Turkey	47	Botswana	58
Austria	77	Peru	62	Georgia	60	Vanuatu	62	Algeria	44	Rwanda	58
France	75	United State	61	Bulgaria	58	Bhutan	61	Lebanon*	42	Ivory Coast	57
Portugal	74	Panama	61	Moldova	55	Micronesia	59	Egypt*	40	Liberia	55
Belgium	71	Grenada*	61	Romania	55	India	59	Iraq*	38	Guinea-Bissau	55
Ireland	71	Colombia*	60	Hungary*	54	Maldives	57	Bahrain	38	Sierra Leone*	53
Cyprus*	69	Mexico	57	Albania	54	Indonesia	57			Burkina Faso	53
Spain	69	Bolivia	56	Kyrgyzstan	53	Solomon Is.	57			Nigeria	53
Italy*	68	El Salvador*	54	Bosnia	52	Nepal	56			Sao Tome & Prin	53
Greece	66	Belize	54	Montenegro*	52	Myanmar	54			Central Afr. Rep.	53
UK	66	Bahamas	54	Ukraine	51	Samoa	54			Mali	53
Malta	65	Guyana	53	Serbia	48	Fiji	53			Niger	52
		Paraguay*	50	Macedonia	48	Singapore	53			Gambia	50
		Suriname	50	Armebia	47	Sri Lanka	52			Malawi	48
		Ecuador	50	Russia*	47	Philippines	51			Cameroon	46
		Guatemala	48	Kazakhstan	45	Thailand	51			Comoros	46
		Antigua and I	47	Belarus	39	Pakistan	50			Swaziland	45
		Dom. Rep.	44	Uzbekistan	38	Laos	48			Zambia	44
		Venezuela*	41	Azerbaijan*	36	Bangladesh	38			Mauritania	44
		Honduras	37	Turkmenistan*	36	Papua NG	35			Tanzania	44
		Nicaragua	36	Tajikistan	35	Malaysia*	34			Sudan	43
		Haiti	32			Vietnam	34			Kenya	43
						Afghanistan	32			Senegal	43
						Cambodia	32			Guinea	42
										Madagascar	40
										Angola	39
										Togo	37
										Uganda	37
										Zimbabwe	35
										Mozambique	35
										Gabon	34
										Chad	32
										Djibouti*	31
										Congo, Rep.	29
										Burundi	25
										Eq. Guinea	24
										Ethiopia	24
Regional mean	75		56		56		55		51		47

* = election in 2018 **Key:** = **Very High / High (60+)** = **Moderate (50–59)** = **Low / Very Low (Less than 50)**

Figure 8.2 The Perceptions of Electoral Integrity Index by Country, Mean 2012 to Mid-2018.

Note: The Perceptions of Electoral Integrity index summary scale ranges from 0–100. The PEI country-level mean scores cover national elections held from mid-2012 to mid-2018.

Source: The Perceptions of Electoral Integrity expert survey, country-level (PEI 6.5).

What Explains These Rankings?

The extensive body of research literature on processes of democratization offers several theoretical perspectives that can also help to provide insights into the general phenomena of electoral integrity, including structural, international, and institutional accounts.

Structural theories emphasize the importance of fixed (or slow-moving) conditions within each society, such as those arising from poverty and lack of economic development, deep-rooted ethnic fractionalization, geographic location and natural resources, and a legacy of inter-communal conflict. Structural accounts emphasize that these types of conditions, such as trying to hold democratic multiparty contests in the DRC, Iraq, Libya, Syria, Somalia, or Afghanistan, provide a hostile terrain for organizing competitive elections within each society, especially as part of peace-building initiatives. Debate continues about whether elections provide incentives that either exacerbate or weaken ethnic conflict (Mansfield & Snyder, 2002; Flores & Noorudin, 2016).

Structural theories emphasize the role of long-term conditions within each society that either constrain or provide opportunities for domestic actors. Thus, societies inherit colonial legacies, religious cultures, natural resources, and national borders from historical events occurring many decades or even many centuries earlier. Similarly, the spatial relationships of each country's geography are treated as fixed antecedents, including borders shared with neighboring hegemonic states, mountainous terrains, or island shores. The physical distribution of natural resources like oil, gas, gold, diamonds, and natural minerals, and thus whether economies are dependent upon these assets, are also largely fixed assets (Ross, 2012). The accumulated cultural experience of societies living for decades under brutal autocracies, and the deep-rooted values acquired from this experience, are also not likely to shift within the short duration of an election campaign. For all these reasons, fixed inhospitable structural conditions – exemplified by deep-rooted poverty and inequality, a legacy of inter-communal violence in deeply-divided multicultural societies, or the curse of natural resources – can be expected to provide opportunities for repressive rulers to manipulate the outcome and to hinder efforts by reformers to strengthen democratic regimes and facilitate free and fair contests.

Alternative accounts rooted in theories of international relations underscore the role of external forces. This includes multilateral regional organizations, bilateral donor agencies, and international NGOs supporting technical assistance, like providing capacity building, financial support, and logistical help designed to strengthen elections and processes of democratization (Norris, 2017; Lührmann, 2018). There is also the negative impact of so-called "black knight" regional hegemonic autocratic powers like China and Russia on neighboring states (Tolstrup, 2015). Levitsky and Way (2010) theorize that processes of authoritarian transition and democratic consolidation in each state are influenced by international leverage (for example, pressures like trade sanctions in Iran) and linkage (including ties such as information flows and the movement of goods, services, and peoples across national borders). Similar forces may well be at work in elections, notably the role of regional organizations and international agencies supporting electoral assistance like training and equipment with NGOs and electoral management bodies in member states.

Finally, other theories focus upon the role of institutional designs within each state. The classical liberal argument emphasizes the importance of executive constraints, suggesting that maximizing the number of veto players provides checks and balances on the power of any single actor, curbing the potential danger of governing parties and incumbents putting their thumb on the scales by manipulating the rules of the electoral game permanently in their favor. Moreover, the classic consociational democracy argument by Lijphart (1999) emphasizes that constitutional arrangements matter, like proportional representation rather than majoritarian electoral systems; parliamentary rather than presidential executives; and coalition rather than one-party governments. Power-sharing arrangements serve to maximize the number of political parties gaining elected office and broaden the number of stakeholders invested in the system, and it thus is thought to engender greater confidence and trust in the rules of the game among elites and their supporters. In particular, electoral systems are likely to influence malpractices, with single-member plurality districts heightening the incentives for parties and candidates to indulge in acts such as vote-buying and partisan gerrymandering of the district boundaries (Norris, 2017; Ruiz-Rufino, 2018). Plurality rules heighten the incentive for individual candidates to seek to win through illegal, fraudulent, or corrupt acts, especially in single-member districts with wafer-thin majorities, where even a few dozen votes could potentially determine the winner.

The type of oversight mechanisms governing the electoral process, and especially the autonomy, role, and powers of the electoral management body, are also widely believed to be important for free and fair contests (van Ham & Lindberg, 2015). Debate continues, however, about whether it is more effective to establish bodies independent of all parties, as commonly assumed (Lopez-Pintor, 2000; Wall et al., 2006; Aaken, 2009), or whether it is better to engage representatives from all the main political parties in the decision-making processes, a practice common in Latin America (Ugues, 2014). Even if the EMB is weak and ineffective, it is argued that several other agencies can also serve the oversight function, bringing malpractices to light, including an independent judiciary, the free press, and civil society organizations (Birch & van Ham, 2017).

Rather than treating these alternative approaches as rival theories, in straw-men artificial debates, they can also be understood more realistically as nested components operating within a comprehensive framework. Both structural conditions and powerful international forces can be understood to exert a direct role on the favorable or unfavorable conditions for electoral integrity, serving as constraints on the effectiveness of the constitutional arrangements.

The Campaign Media Environment

Much media attention with stories about malpractices often focus most attention on the close of polls and vote tabulation, the announcement of the official results, and the election's immediate aftermath. If the results are broken down by the stages of the electoral cycle, however, campaign finance and campaign media emerge as the ones consistently receiving the worst overall assessments in many countries, with far more positive scores for the vote count and results.

Recent years have seen growing concern about challenges to the integrity of elections arising from the decline of the legacy press and growing reliance upon online media. Developments include declining confidence in the traditional mainstream news media, populist claims of "fake news" denigrating journalists, the rise of media "bubbles" providing an echo chamber of partisan messages, the role of both misinformation and disinformation campaigns intended to mislead users of platforms such as Facebook and Twitter (Lazar et al., 2017), and the vulnerability of official electoral records and party email servers to cybersecurity attacks (Norden & Vanderwalker, 2017). Much recent apprehension about these issues has been catalyzed by intelligence reports of Russian meddling in the 2016 US election (Office of the Director of National Intelligence, 2017). The problem is not confined to America, however, as foreign interference has been reported in the Brexit referenda campaign and in parliamentary elections in Germany, Spain, and France (Rankin, 2017; Richey, 2018). In response, Facebook now employs an army of content moderators and fact-checkers, tracking 50 elections in 2018 alone, including the way that social media can be weaponized by foreign and domestic forces to manipulate undermine democratic contests, and purging thousands of fake accounts before elections in Italy, France, and Germany (Dwoskin, 2018).

In light of these concerns, the European Commission (2018) published a high-level expert study looking into disinformation, defined to include all forms of false, inaccurate, or misleading information designed, presented, and promoted to intentionally cause public harm or for profit. Other issues of long-standing concern for the quality of campaign communications include the desirability of balance and pluralistic diversity in media election reporting, avoiding highly polarized partisanship (Faris et al., 2017). Problems can also arise from the creation and dissemination online of illegal content, notably defamation, hate speech, incitement to violence, and the spread of conspiracy theories online.

The erosion of public confidence in the news media, fueled by populist claims of "fake news," are further challenges. The fake news mantra fuels a "post-truth" world (McIntyre, 2018), with populists denying the enlightenment idea that there can be such a thing as objective knowledge, scientific evidence, or impartial journalism. Declining use of legacy news media and the rise of social bubbles and echo chambers in online media reinforce dogmatism fueled by ideology, not fact (Allcott, Hunt, & Gentzkow, 2017; Fletcher et al., 2018). Where news or social media provide repeated distortions impacting citizen perceptions of events, these can give rise to deep-seated misinformed beliefs and cause significant harm. Attacks on journalistic elites as "enemies of the people" are part and parcel of authoritarian populist rhetoric, with a crack-down on mainstream media by leaders such as the Philippines' Rodrigo Duterte, Hungary's Viktor Mihály Orbán, and Turkey's Recep Erdoğan. At a joint press conference in Manila, when Duterte called the media "spies," Trump reportedly laughed.[4]

To monitor the extent of the risks, the sixth wave of the PEI expert survey included several items from a new rotating annual battery designed to capture several of these issues, including "fake news," partisan media, foreign meddling, and media monitoring. The evaluations can be compared for 26 elections held from January 1 to June 30, 2018.

The results in Figures 8.3 show that countries that generally perform poorly in elections overall, such as Egypt, Djibouti, and Venezuela, commonly have the most problems in media campaigns as well. There are several general weaknesses, even in contests that were rated very high in electoral integrity in other regards, notably in whether journalists maintain high standards and whether social media contains so-called fake news or misinformation. But it is worth highlighting that some other specific weaknesses also emerge in particular countries, such as partisan reporting in Montenegro, poor journalistic standards following government repression of the press in Hungary, and fake news on social media in Costa Rica and the Czech Republic. The partial silver lining from the results is that, despite fears, in most cases, experts reported that to date few elections have been subject to cyber-attacks on official voting records. On the other hand, this remains a stealth process that may not be apparent to election experts, and it may be that the well-publicized attacks on both major political parties in the US, as well as attempted Russian attempts to penetrate the state election office records in 21 US states (with success in a few), may inspire other hostile domestic and international hackers to attempt to follow suit.

Conclusions and Implications

Overall, therefore, the good news is that the third wave of democratization saw the spread of multiparty elections to all parts of the globe. Today, only a handful of states lack competitive contests for the national legislature. This has been a radical revolution that fueled much of the optimism common during the 1980s and 1990s about the universal spread of liberal democratic institutions and norms. The early twenty-first century saw greater recognition that many contests remain deeply flawed, or even failed, especially in electoral autocracies. Concern about democratic erosion is widespread, including growing powers by authoritarian states (Kurlantzick, 2014; Diamond et al., 2016; Levitsky & Ziblatt, 2018). The third reverse wave is a global phenomenon: Authoritarian-populist actors have destabilized long-established democracies like the US, Italy, and the UK. Human rights have deteriorated in hybrid states such as Venezuela, the Philippines, Hungary, and Turkey. Meanwhile, authoritarian regimes like Russia and China have become even more repressive at home and increasingly influential beyond their borders. Globally, values of democratic governance, rule of law, and human rights are threatened by American retreat and European divisions. China provides an alternative model of a remarkably successful market economy, despite lacking fundamental freedoms.

Moreover, recent years have also seen growing anxiety about the quality of free and fair elections even in long established democracies, such as the US and UK. America, in particular, has seen heightened controversy over Republican claims of lax security for the state procedures used for registering and casting a ballot and Democratic counter-claims of GOP attempts to

Category of Country electoral integrity		Campaign media did not spread hate speech	Campaign media allowed informed voting choices	Foreign interests did not interface in the campaign	Media watch groups monitored campaign news	Cyberattacks on official voting records did not occur during the election	Campaign news generally reflected a diversity of views and interests	Campaign news generally maintained high journalistic standards	Journalists were often not highly partisan in their campaign reporting	Social media often did not contain fake news	PEI index of electoral integrity, (0-100)
Very High	Finland	3.8	4.0	4.2	3.7	4.8	4.0	4.0	3.7	3.1	84
	Costa Rica	2.7	4.4	2.3	3.5	3.3	3.8	3.1	3.4	1.9	77
	Czech Republic	2.3	3.5	2.4	4.1	4.4	3.7	2.8	2.4	1.9	74
	Slovenia	2.8	3.4	3.2	3.4	4.6	3.2	2.8	2.5	2.6	73
High	Italy	2.4	3.2	3.4	3.5	4.1	3.3	2.6	2.3	2.1	69
	Cyprus	3.2	3.5	3.7	3.1	4.7	3.3	2.9	2.1	3.1	68
	Timor-Leste	2.4	4.0	4.4	3.2	4.8	4.1	3.3	3.7	2.3	67
	Barbados	2.1	3.5	3.5	2.7	4.8	3.4	2.9	3.6	2.3	66
Moderate	Colombia	2.4	3.8	2.3	3.1	3.4	3.7	3.1	3.3	1.9	59
	Grenada	3.6	3.5	2.8	3.0	4.0	3.0	2.8	2.3	3.0	56
	Montenegro	3.2	2.8	2.8	3.6	4.6	3.0	2.4	1.3	3.0	54
	El Salvador	3.8	3.0	2.6	3.3	4.0	3.1	2.3	2.3	2.2	54
	Hungary	1.8	2.3	3.2	3.1	4.2	2.2	1.6	1.6	2.6	52
	Sierra Leone	4.0	2.5	3.5	3.5	4.5	2.5	2.5	2.0	2.5	50
	Russia	3.0	2.8	4.0	3.4	3.9	2.6	2.2	2.8	3.0	50
Low	Antigua & Barbuda	4.0	1.0	2.0	2.5	4.0	2.0	2.5	2.0	3.5	48
	Paraguay	3.8	2.5	2.4	2.7	3.6	3.6	2.4	2.4	2.5	44
	Lebanon	2.7	3.2	1.9	3.8	4.0	3.1	2.9	1.9	3.6	42
	Turkmenistan	3.7	2.3	4.0	1.5	4.0	2.0	1.7	2.0	3.0	41
Very Low	Azerbaijan	3.2	1.8	4.4	3.4	4.7	1.6	1.8	2.5	2.5	38
	Egypt	2.5	1.3	3.6	3.0	4.3	1.2	1.2	2.2	1.5	36
	Djibouti	4.0	2.0	1.5	2.5	2.5	2.0	2.0	1.5	3.0	34
	Malaysia	2.4	3.0	3.3	3.8	3.3	2.5	1.8	2.5	2.6	33
	Iraq	2.4	2.3	1.1	3.7	2.7	2.9	1.6	2.3	1.9	32
	Venezula	3.4	2.3	2.9	2.8	3.6	3.0	1.9	2.2	1.7	27
	Toatal	**3.0**	**2.9**	**3.0**	**3.2**	**4.0**	**2.9**	**2.5**	**2.5**	**2.5**	**53**

Note: For the questions, see Table 1. Mean scores per election. All items were recoded in a positive direction to facilitate consistent comparisons across questions and the scores for each item ranged from low (1) to high (5). Countries were ranked by the overall PEI Index, ranging from 0-100.

Figure 8.3 Positive Evaluations of the Media Campaign.

Source: Perceptions of Electoral Integrity expert survey (PEI-6.5).

suppress the voting rights for legitimate groups of citizens, especially minority populations, in addition to the heavy cloud of the Mueller investigation and intelligence reports of ongoing cybersecurity threats and vulnerabilities of state election offices to foreign interference, all damaging public confidence in US elections (Norris et al., 2018). It is critical to continue to monitor the quality of electoral integrity through systematic evidence – and then the challenge is to identify effective strategies to intervene and strengthen democratic contests, a challenge made even more urgent during the era of democratic backsliding and authoritarian resurgence.

Notes

1 I am most grateful for the assistance of the Electoral Integrity Project team, including Thomas Wynter, Sarah Cameron, and Megan Capriccio, especially for their work in collecting the Perceptions of Electoral Integrity (PEI 6.5) dataset and developing the graphics. I would also like to thank previous EIP staff and all the experts who completed the survey.
2 See, for example, reports by Freedom House, the Economist Democracy Index, and the Varieties of Democracy project.
3 For details, see www.electoralintegrityproject.com.
4 www.cnn.com/2017/11/13/politics/trump-duterte-press/index.html.

References

Aaken, A.V. (2009). Independent election management bodies and international election observer missions: Any impact on the observed levels of democracy? A conceptual Framework. *Constitutional Political Economy*, *20*(3), 296–322. doi: 10.1007/s10602-008-9070-4

Allcott, H., & Gentzkow, M. (2017). Social media and fake news in the 2016 election. *Journal of Economic Perspectives*, *31*(2), 211–236. Retrieved from https://web.stanford.edu/~gentzkow/research/fakenews.pdf

Birch, S. (2010). Perceptions of electoral fairness and voter turnout. *Comparative Political Studies*, *43*(12), 1601–1622. doi: 10.1177/0010414010374021

Birch, S. (2011). *Electoral malpractice*. Oxford: Oxford University Press.

Birch, S., & Ham, C. V. (2017). Getting away with foul play? The importance of formal and informal oversight institutions for electoral integrity. European *Journal of Political Research*, *56*(3), 487–511. doi: 10.1111/1475-6765.12189/full

Carroll, D. J., & Davis-Roberts, A. (2013). The Carter Center and election observation: An obligations-based approach for assessing elections. *Election Law Journal*, *12*(1), 87–93. Retrieved from https://doi.org/10.1089/elj.2013.1215

Carter Center. (2018). *Elections obligations and standards database: A Carter Center manual*. Atlanta, Georgia: The Carter Center. Retrieved from http://www.cartercenter.org/des-search/des/Introduction.aspx

CNN Politics. (November 13, 2017). *Donald Trump laughed when Rodrigo Duterte called the media 'spies'*. Not Good. Retrieved from https://www.cnn.com/2017/11/13/politics/trump-duterte-press/index.html

Coffé, H. (2017). Citizens' media use and the accuracy of their perceptions of electoral integrity. *International Political Science Review*, *38*(3), 281–297. doi: 10.1177/0192512116640984

Coma, F. M. I., & Ham, V. C. (2015). Can experts judge elections? Testing the validity of expert judgments for measuring election integrity. *European Journal of Political Research*, *54*(2), 305–325. doi: 10.1111/1475-6765.12084

Coma, F. M. I., & Trinh, M. (2017). How electoral integrity affects voter turnout in democracies. *Australian Journal of Political Science*, *52*(1), 53–74. doi: 10.1080/10361146.2016.1238869

Davis-Roberts, A., & Carroll, David J. (2010). Using international law to assess elections. *Democratization*, *17*(3), 416–441. doi: 10.1080/13510341003700253

Diamond, L., Plattner, M. F., & Walker, C. (Eds.). (2016). *Authoritarianism goes global*. Baltimore, MD: Johns Hopkins University Press.

Donno, D. (2013). *Defending democratic norms*. New York: Oxford University Press.

Elklit, J., & Reynolds, A. (2005). A framework for the systematic study of election quality. *Democratization*, *12*(2), 147–162. doi: 10.1080/13510340500069204

Elklit, J., & Svensson, P. (1997). What makes elections free and fair? *Journal of Democracy*, *8*(3), 32–46. doi: 10.1353/jod.1997.0041
European Commission. (March 12, 2018). *Final report of the high level expert group on fake news and online disinformation*. Brussels: EC. Retrieved from https://ec.europa.eu/digital-single-market/en/news/final-report-high-level-expert-group-fake-news-and-online-disinformation
Faris, R. M., Roberts, H., Etling, B., Bourassa, N., Zuckerman, E., & Benkler, Y. (August 2017). *Partisanship, propaganda, and disinformation: Online media and the 2016 U.S. presidential election*. Berkman Center Research Publication 2017–6. Retrieved from http://nrs.harvard.edu/urn-3:HUL.InstRepos:33759251
Flesken, A., & Hartl, J. (2018). Party support, values, and perceptions of electoral integrity. *Political Psychology*, *39*(3), 707–724. doi: 10.1111/pops.12431
Fletcher, R., Cornia, A., Graves, L., & Nielsen, R. K. (2018). *Measuring the reach of "fake news" and online disinformation in Europe*. Oxford: Reuters Institute.
Flores, T. E., & Nooruddin, I. (2016). *Elections in hard times: Building stronger democracies in the 21st Century*. New York: Cambridge University Press.
Foreign Policy, Walker, C., & Cooley, A. (October 31, 2013). Vote of the living dead. Retrieved from https://foreignpolicy.com/2013/10/31/vote-of-the-living-dead/
Joseph, K., Hobbs, H., & Mattsson, C. (May 2, 2017). Combating fake news: An agenda for research and action. Retrieved from https://shorensteincenter.org/wp-content/uploads/2017/05/Combating-Fake-News-Agenda-for-Research-1.pdf?x78124
Kelley, J. (2012). *Monitoring democracy: When international election observation works and why it often fails*. Princeton, NJ: Princeton University Press.
Kurlantzick, J. (2014). *Democracy in retreat*. New Haven, CT: Yale University Press.
Lazer, D., Baum, M. Grinberg, N., Friedland, L., Joseph, K., Hobbs, W., & Mattson, C. (May 2017). "Combating Fake News: An Agenda for Research and Action". Retrieved from https://apo.org.au/sites/default/files/resource-files/2017-05/apo-nid76233.pdf
Levitsky, S., & Way, L. (2010). *Competitive authoritarianism: Hybrid regimes after the Cold War*. New York: Cambridge University Press.
Levitsky, S., & Ziblatt, D. (2018). *How democracies die*. New York: Crown.
Lijphart, A. (1999). *Patterns of democracy*. New Haven, CT: Yale.
López-Pintor, R. (2000). *Electoral management bodies as institutions of governance*. New York: United Nations Development Programme.
Lührmann, A. (2018). United Nations electoral assistance: More than a fig leaf? *International Political Science Review*, *40*(2), 181–196. doi: 10.1177/0192512117740915
Mansfield, E. D., & Snyder, J. (2007). *Electing to fight: Why emerging democracies go to war*. Cambridge, MA: MIT Press.
Massicotte, L., Blais, A., & Yoshinaka, A. (2004). *Establishing the rules of the game*. Toronto: University of Toronto Press.
McIntyre, L. (2018). *Post-truth*. Cambridge, MA: MIT Press.
Myagkov, M., Ordeshook, P. C., & Shakin, D. (2009). *The forensics of election fraud: Russia and Ukraine*. New York: Cambridge University Press.
Norden, L., & Vanderwalker, I. (2017). Securing elections from foreign interference. New York University School of Law: Brennan Center for Justice. Retrieved from https://www.brennancenter.org/sites/default/files/publications/Foreign%20Interference_0629_1030_AM.pdf
Norris, P. (2014). *Why electoral integrity matters*. New York: Cambridge University Press.
Norris, P. (2015). *Why elections fail*. New York: Cambridge University Press.
Norris, P. (2017). *Strengthening electoral integrity*. New York: Cambridge University Press.
Norris, P., Frank, R. W., & Coma, F. M. I. (2013). Assessing the quality of elections. *Journal of Democracy*, *24*(4), 124–135. doi: 10.1353/jod.2013.0063
Norris, P., Frank, R. W., & Coma, F. M. I. (2014a). Measuring electoral integrity around the world: a new dataset. *PS: Political Science & Politics*, 47(4), 789–798. doi: 10.1017/S1049096514001061
Norris, P., Frank, R. W. & Coma, F. M. I. (Eds.). (2014b). *Advancing electoral integrity*. New York: Oxford University Press.
Norris, P., Cameron, S., & Wynter, T. (Eds.). (2019). *Electoral integrity in America*. New York: Oxford University Press.
Office of the Director of National Intelligence. (January 6, 2017). *Assessing Russian activities and intentions in recent US elections (Unclassified version)*. Retrieved from https://www.scribd.com/document/335885580

/Unclassified-version-of-intelligence-report-on-Russian-hacking-during-the-2016-election#from_embed

Rankin, J. (November 25, 2017). The Guardian. EU anti-propaganda unit gets €1m a year to counter Russian fake news. Retrieved from https://www.theguardian.com/world/2017/nov/25/eu-anti-propaganda-unit-gets-1m-a-year-to-counter-russian-fake-news

Richey, M. (2018). Contemporary Russian revisionism: understanding the Kremlin's hybrid warfare and the strategic and tactical deployment of disinformation. *Asia Europe Journal, 16*(1), 101–113. Retrieved from https://doi.org/10.1007/s10308-017-0482-5

Ross, M. (2012). *The oil curse.* Princeton, NJ: Princeton University Press.

Ruiz-Rufino, R. (2018). When do electoral institutions trigger electoral misconduct? *Democratization, 25*(2), 331–350. doi: 10.1080/13510347.2017.1365057

Schedler, A. (2002). The menu of manipulation. *Journal of Democracy, 13*(2), 36–50. doi: 10.1353/jod.2002.0031

Tolstrup, J. (2015). Black knights and elections in authoritarian regimes: Why and how Russia supports authoritarian incumbents in post-Soviet states. *European Journal of Political Research, 54*(4), 673–690. doi: 10.1111/1475-6765.12079

Tuccinardi, D. (Ed.). (2014). *International obligations for elections: Guidelines for legal frameworks.* Stockholm: International IDEA.

Tucker, J. (2007). Enough! Electoral fraud, collective action problems, and post-communist colored revolutions. *Perspectives on Politics, 5*(3), 535–551. Retrieved from http://www.jstor.org/stable/20446502

Venice Commission for Democracy through Law. (2002). Code of good practice in electoral matters: guidelines and explanatory report. Venice Commission. Retrieved from https://www.venice.coe.int/webforms/documents/default.aspx?pdffile=CDL-AD(2002)023rev2-cor-e

Wall, A., Ellis, A., Ayoub, A., Dundas, C.W., Rukambe, J., & Staino, S. (2006). *Electoral management design: The international IDEA handbook.* Sweden: International IDEA.

9
ELECTIONS AS RITUALS

Graeme Orr

Ritual: The Concept and Its Role in Politics

Ritual has been conceived of as "any activity that involves its participants symbolically in a common enterprise, calling attention to their relatedness and joint interests in a compelling way" (Edelman, 1964, 16).[1] As large-scale public occasions that draw citizens together, on a cyclical basis, to form the polity, elections qualify as ritual events par excellence. Electoral democracy is as much a construct of law as it is of culture, political fashion, and changing technologies. It follows that electoral law – both in the sense of black letter rules and case law and as something given flesh by rule governed institutional players such as electoral management bodies and parties – can only be fully appreciated if we are willing to look at it through a sociological lens, informed by an understanding of ritual. This much is well understood by political historians (e.g., O'Gorman, 1989; O'Gorman, 1992). But, only in recent times, has it percolated into scholarship on modern electoral democracy.

How might we define "ritual" in the context of electoral democracy? As Kertzer (1988, 8–9) stresses, it is important to distinguish ritual, as formally structured "action wrapped in a web of symbolism," from roboticism. Mere standardized habits and customs lacking symbolization do not meet an elevated definition of what is "ritual." At the same time, that definition should not be over-determined. Especially in contemporary times, with a high level of professionalism permeating elections, it is preferable to think of ritual as any patterned behavior infused with social meaning (Orr, 2015, 12–4). This permits us to look at electoral law and practice in a technocratic age from an experiential perspective, whilst not losing sight of the forest of symbolic, social, and psychological meaning that ritual conveys, amongst the trees of low-level bureaucratic dictates that ensure smooth electoral administration.

To Edelman (1964), symbol and myth are not just epiphenomena of public affairs, they are literally the stuff of politics. This approach presents challenges to economistic, rational choice theories, as well as to liberal and deliberative accounts of electoral democracy. Electoral democracy is, of course, but one aspect of "democracy." Democracy can be understood as a set of interrelated systems of self-government and popular forms of participation and representation. Whilst Edelman's work opened (and rediscovered) ways of thinking about democratic politics in terms of elaborate theatrical and rhetorical performances, it is doubtful that "democracy" can be understood as ritual in any holistic sense. Democracy requires a teleological assessment of a

DOI: 10.4324/9780429401800-9

large, richer and heavily contested set of ideals and potential practices than do elections or even electoral democracy. Whilst aspects of democratic practice – such as the architecture or location of parliaments and their ceremonies – are obviously ripe for theorizing as rituals, democracy is not an "event" in the way that elections are.

Within the field of election studies, Hirschbein (1999), Bensel (2004), Lawrence (2009), Coleman (2013), Faucher and Hay (2015) and others have adapted the lens of ritual to yield a variety of insights, stressing in nuanced ways the inescapable and central importance of cultural practices and meanings within modern election campaigns and balloting. Elsewhere, I have tied this way of thinking to holistic understandings of electoral law as an evolving set of rules and customs (Orr, 2015).

In this vein, elections are sometimes spoken of as if they were secular rites. Such quasi-religious language, however, is apt to mislead more than it enlightens. Elections may well be a crowning moment, almost literally and certainly figuratively, for any political community. But even electoral junkies do not think of them in spiritual terms. How could they, when elections are typically times of fierce political contestation? Such electoral agonism and antagonism may be contrasted, rather than assimilated, with religion in the sense of liturgical practices designed to soothe, reassure, and unite believers in a single faith. Instead, electoral contestation can happily co-exist with religion even in mono-faith societies, each playing a distinctive integrative role at different levels of public consciousness. Elections as rituals seem to share something with the (better studied) concept of professional sport as a set of ritual practices involving players and spectators. Both spheres exhibit tribalism. And both ultimately demonstrate the tension that arises when a communally integrative endeavor is simultaneously rooted in intractable, formalized competition.

Thinking about how regulation constitutes electoral practice, through the lens of "ritual," can lead us along three paths. Down the first path lies a descriptive sociology of electoral law and institutions. In this relatively neutral approach, however, elections happen to be regulated, and interesting insights are yielded by analyzing that regulation and the practices that emanate from it, in terms of their experiential dimensions and meanings.

Take for instance how, when, and where we vote. The secret, in-person ballot cast on election day amounts to a public act, played out on a most public day in a communal location, yet within a shrouded, almost confessional space. In contrast, voting over the internet erects a more individualized and personalized transaction, played out on no particular day and on a private device rather than in a communal setting (Stromer-Galley, 2003). Here, in its descriptive guise, the ritual conception makes no necessary judgment between traditional and emerging methods of casting a ballot. Rather, it offers us a language capable of paring back the rules and technologies involved in order to better understand the essential differences between them.

Down the second path lies a more normative approach. This approach turns the core insight of rational choice theory, that voting is an irrational habit because there is precious little chance a single vote will change anything, on its head (cf. Brennan & Lomasky, 1993). In its stead is a claim that people act politically, especially at election time, because they are drawn to the social solidarity of the process more than to any external impact of their expression. From here, attending to the ritualized experience of electoral practices inevitably leads to (contested) debates about what might be valuable – or what might be improved – in electoral processes to enrich the social and personal experience of electoral democracy.

For example, traditionalists and communitarians alike defend in-person balloting. They tend to want to hang on to polling day, as the centerpiece of a tangible event, where society sees itself coming together. Election day is something to be valorized as a manifestation of the essentially civic nature of voting (Green, 2003). Others contest this, whether empirically or because they embrace the evolution of more novel values. They challenge traditionalists by asking whether people really draw satisfaction from the occasion of polling and whether it is mere nostalgia to hang on to election day in a cyberage. Examples of such debates are not hard to find, even amongst those who consciously hew to a ritual perspective. Thus, for Hirschbein (2009, 2–3), contemporary elections, especially in the US, have been losing their affective as well as effective dimension, and require a ritualistic reboot. Yet, for the British scholar Coleman (2013, viii), things are less gloomy: Elections remain constitutive events, offering an "affective…performance of who *the people* are."

Down the third and final path, ritual is neither a tool of relatively neutral observation, nor a site of contestation about desirable practices, values, and meanings. On the contrary, in this view, "ritual" conveys an alternative, pejorative connotation, in which electoral democracy has become an "empty ritual." In this negative conception, electoral campaigns and voting are not positive rituals, campaigns are not colorful opportunities for meaningful expression, and balloting is not a solemn duty. Instead, campaigning is painted as a professionalized simulacrum and voting as a bureaucratic chore. Taken as a whole, in this view, electoral democracy amounts to a hollow rather than hallowed system, with elections serving as a liberalist delusion and, worse, an elite, technocratic distraction masking a deeper, undemocratic reality.

Having given some introductory definitions, and scoped the different paths down which the language of ritual can take us, the rest of this chapter will try to elucidate and apply the ritual perspective across three fundamental aspects of elections and electoral law. One is campaigning. Another is voting. The third is the seasonal and rhythmic nature of the electoral cycle – a question intimately related to the idea of ritual as patterned, repetitive behavior. The chapter will then finish with some critique of the limits of the ritual approach by locating it within more familiar theories for understanding and informing election law and reform.

Campaigning: Then and Now

As Lefebvre (1991), foremost amongst others, has stressed, festivals were both common and vital elements of traditional agrarian societies. The importance of festivals lay in fostering communal and spiritual relationships; they acted as both a physical coming together and an homage to the powerful rhythms of nature. They were not, however, structured as grand rites, compared to say a coronation. Rather their "material and spiritual grounds [were rooted] within everyday life" (Butler, 2012, 34–5). This concept of the quotidian or everydayness of life is particularly important in any understanding of modern electoral forms and practices.

At first glance this may feel paradoxical. Surely elections are nothing if not grand political junctures that come and go every few years. They clearly serve as elite rites of passage, for candidates seeking to be elevated into the governing class. They also serve as once-in-a-lifetime, coming-of-age moments for those who vote for the first time, whether after reaching their majority or after taking out citizenship. Understood from these vantage points, elections will hardly seem like "everyday" affairs in the literal sense. But – the unique experience of voting for the first time aside – for the vast bulk of people, the experience of elections has been embedded in now familiar material practices, both institutional and social. A partial list of such practices includes: voter registration drives (signifying civic duty or opportunity, when run by electoral authorities, or signifying partisan motivation, when run by parties); the formal calling of an election and issuing of writs; the official declaration of nominations; televised leadership debates; the act of voting by post or turning out at a polling stations; and the mediated suspense of watching the tallying of results on election night. Framed within these familiar moments lies the carnival of the campaign itself.

Some electoral laws insist on modesty in campaigning, consistent with a theme of repose on election day. New Zealand, for instance, makes most kinds of last-minute electioneering an offense, to the point of empowering its electoral authorities to destroy any material not removed prior to the dawn of polling day. As Geddis (2015) argues, this can only really be understood as "a desire to inculcate a particular mood or voting experience" (p. 137). Elsewhere, such an approach extends to "dry laws," which limit or prohibit the sale of alcohol during and even leading up to election day.

Yet, there is no single approach to electoral ritual, any more than there is a single democratic culture. Polling places in New Zealand's closest neighbor, Australia, for instance, are reminders of the hustings of centuries past. They are festooned with bunting and swarm with activists making last-minute attempts to solicit votes. Such activity is subject only to a six-meter cordon sanitaire around the entrance to – and of course inside – the polling booth. Some voters appreciate this kind of color; others resent the hassle. Since such last-minute pitches have little impact on voting outcomes, their primary role seems to be to allow party activists to burn off nervous energy and feel connected to the occasion.[2]

Once we turn attention to the impact of electoral law on the experience of democracy, and through that to questions of ritual and meaning, vistas of neglected inquiry open up. Campaign finance and party regulation (and their interaction with basic electoral structures) form a case in point. In most parts of the US, primary elections are mandated. These not only open up candidate selection, so that it is not merely an internal party affair, but they also shine a public light on individual contenders for up to a year (or longer, in the case of presidential races) before election day. On top of this, thanks to first amendment, free speech jurisprudence, electioneering expenditure in the US is illimitable.[3] The net effect is to entrench a system in the US where cash is king, and the charismatic individual forms the centerpiece of a lengthy campaign season.

In contrast, in more statist systems, a greater level of control prevails and parties are accentuated over individual candidates. For example, in the UK (but also in e.g., Israel) only parties are entitled to make political broadcasts; no one else can purchase such air-time.[4] Such strictures are usually rationalized as a preferencing of political equality or deliberation over absolute liberty. But these rules also express cultural mores around campaign methods and means. Some of these distinctions are a consequence of macro or system-wide regulation, but other examples involve micro or fine-grained rules. Thus, in Japan, public funding pays not just for billboards whose size and locations are overseen by local government, but also subsidizes campaign vehicles (including boats!) whilst circumscribing other expenditure and even prohibiting door-to-door canvassing. This grows out of, but also reinforces, the very public, decorous, and decorated ritual of traditional street-corner appearances by white-gloved candidates, with megaphones on the back of vans, at Japanese elections.[5]

Voting: Who, How, When, and Where

At a very obvious level, "who" the law governing the franchise allows to vote embodies a profound symbolic meaning. The franchise creates a political, if not ethical web, differentiating (in most jurisdictions) citizens from other residents. In doing so, electors are bestowed with a privileged role, redolent with socio-political connotations. Enfranchisement divides an inner core of electors entrusted with choosing representatives from the rest of the social whole, who are left to rely on virtual representation and more tenuous political rights.[6] It also embodies a notion of incorporation: a ritual of identification with and involvement in what would otherwise be a seemingly remote, even abstract, polity (cf. Ting, 2010). However, the "right" to vote is not a one-way street. It is also properly seen as a public trust, even outside regimes that compel voting. Long-standing strictures against selling one's vote illustrate the fact that voting carries with it obligations. Being enfranchised is also usually a pre-requisite for selection for jury duty, another ancient aspect of self-governance.

Today, the franchise also embraces meanings beyond connection to local geography or national self-definition. The expansion of the right to vote amongst expatriates or permanent residents enacts a state's willingness to embrace multiple identities. Depending on the context, expatriate voting may capture the otherwise fuzzy concept of "global citizenship" as much as it may reflect nostalgia for and within diasporas. It is not just public law that performs this work: Parties do too. An illustration of this is the recent practice of the US Democratic Party in holding a "Global Presidential Primary" amongst "Democrats Abroad," even though expatriates do not form a unit in the presidential electoral college.

In electoral science, the "how" of voting is usually equated to the myriad of different voting systems that have been invented and deployed around the world. This approach makes sense if elections are just aggregative exercises to translate popular choices into electoral outcomes. But elections are much more than instruments of arithmetic. The most profound and universal innovation in electoral history has been the secret ballot. Its motivation and effects have also tended to be explained in instrumental terms, most notably in the language of electoral integrity. After all, the adoption of the secret ballot in the nineteenth century was rooted in a war against electoral intimidation and the "grosser evils" of "bribery and all those corrupt practices which consist in voting according to a bargain and understanding" (Wigmore, 1889, 1–2, 31; see also Bentham, 1818).

The coming of the law and technology of the secret ballot, however, presaged much more than an integrity mechanism. From Australia in the 1850s, it spread rapidly, such that its purest form, the untraceable, unnumbered ballot paper became known worldwide as "the Australian Ballot." The impact of the secret ballot, from its first deployment, went well beyond safeguarding electoral conscience against bribery or intimidation. It transformed the subjective and objective experiences of electoral democracy itself. An international observer, of the first general election in Victoria under the Australian ballot system, wrote that:

> In a contested election under the ballot…everything proceeds with the same tranquil placidity as if the community was undergoing a trying operation under the influence of chloroform, waking up to consciousness on the declaration of the poll…[A]ll that is wanting to render such an election a really halcyon scene…with all the peace and security of a religious ceremony, is the…abolition of the barbarous parody on bull-baiting that candidates undergo on the husting…which after all, is nothing more or less than pantomime in a frenzy.
>
> *(Kelly, 1860, 318)*

This remarkable portrait of the transformation of the ritual of elections, achieved by a single administrative reform, speaks in two voices. One is descriptive and, in one fashion or another, lives with us to this day. That is the relative quiescence of elections under the secret ballot, especially compared to the traditions that had built up around open polling over preceding centuries (Orr, 2015, 96–104). Some conservatives at the time objected to secret balloting as "unmanly" (Kinzer, 1982, 71). This view, in a curious way, is echoed today by progressives when they lament the "civic privatism" of elections (Ackerman & Fishkin, 2002, 129–30).

Bound up in all this is the question of whether elections can truly be times of communal interaction. This is reflected in moves to make election day a public holiday in some jurisdictions. In Australia, polling day has long been legislated to be on a Saturday. In large parts of Europe,

Sunday is the norm. This allows school halls to be the primary focus for voting, creating a symbolic juxtaposition given that schools are at the heart of local communities. Indeed, in Australia, just as compulsory education is an element of citizenship, substantively understood, so too does the law compel citizens to turnout to vote. Around such communal spaces, a tradition has even arisen of school and other civic groups using election day to fund raise through stalls and barbecues (Orr, 2015, 113–20). In recent years, this has led to the term "democracy sausage" becoming synonymous with election day in Australia (Brett, 2019, 155–64).

A second voice, which appears at the end of the quote above, is clearly normative rather than descriptive. The observer wants the quietism of election day to spread right across the campaign period. Within that wish we can detect a certain anti-political attitude, as much as a desire for more genuine or reflective electoral deliberation. That wish was partially granted, as campaigning has grown less face-to-face, first due to the demands of mass electioneering brought about by universal suffrage and later reinforced by the rise of mass media.

That said, as we saw in the previous section, in lightly regulated liberal electoral systems, the electoral frenzy has shifted location rather than disappeared altogether. Its locale first moved from face-to-face pamphleteering and press-fleshing to the radio broadcast of mass speeches and rallies. It then shifted to televisual presentations. Now it is most manifest in digital bombardments of puff and attack advertisements alike. Nor is the street entirely one-way. As Lawrence (2011) argues, modern elections are full of opportunities for demotic interaction, via talk-back radio, the hijacking of otherwise staged events, and ripostes to and trolling of politicians' social media accounts.

The "when" and "where" of voting is also of great significance. In centuries past (indeed until early in the twentieth century in the UK), polling could take place across multiple days in each electorate. This was to allow leeway for those travelling by horse from rural districts, but it also perpetuated the idea of the hustings as a communal festival. In a vast federal jurisdiction like India, polling unfolds over several weeks. Ostensibly, this is for integrity reasons (in particular, to ration India's security services). Yet, it also elongates what is already a festival of democracy. In many other jurisdictions a key, contemporary controversy is how election day is stretching into election week or even election month, as early voting (aka pre-polling) is not just made available but even encouraged. The ultimate extension of this trend, as noted in the introduction, pits internet voting against in-person voting, with enormous consequences for the when and where, as well as the how, of electoral participation.

Again, a debate like this presents macro and micro consequences for the ritual experience of elections. For instance, electronic voting does not permit electors to personalize a protest vote by despoiling their ballot with witty or offensive slogans. On the other hand, electronic voting allows the result of all races to be known instantaneously once the final deadline for polling passes, a development that impacts the suspenseful theatre of election night. At a practical level, technology has also opened up new, citizen driven rituals. One is the "ballot selfie" – the act of sharing an image of one's completed ballot, with friends or the world at large, via social media. Once upon a time, such an action would have been criminalized as undermining laws against vote-buying. But, as a US court recently held, there may be an expressive right to take and share ballot selfies (*Rideout v. Gardner* 838 F.3d 65, 2016). The value of citizens encouraging other citizens to vote is also recognized by more institutional practices, such as handing out "I Voted" stickers at polling stations. Wagering on elections, once a largely private affair, is also becoming a prominent affair. This is partly driven by the proliferation of online betting agencies. It is also part of a ritual, shared with sports and practiced mostly by partisans (i.e., fans of one party or another) who wish either to intensify the experience of their side winning, or to hedge the psychological impact of their side losing (Orr, 2014).

Rhythm and Seasonality

Whilst they are unique – in the sense of foundational – events in the life of any polity, elections are not unique in the strict sense. On the contrary, their very point is to be recurrent. This is obviously tied to fundamental constitutional law doctrines about the appropriate length of executive offices and legislative terms. It is also linked to constitutional principles relating to the integrity of representative government. The cyclical nature of elections allows a refreshing of the gene pool of representation and, through that, it offers a powerful, if crude, form of public accountability. To Buchler (2011), elections ideally act as periodic hiring and firing decisions.

The essentially recurrent nature of elections means that they return to greet (or haunt) us every few years, and come to serve, like comets of old, as historical place markers. Our societal and individual perspectives on time thus come to be punctuated, sometimes even defined, by major electoral races and outcomes (Orr, 2015, 31–2, and compare Cohen, 2018 on how time and timing defines politics more generally). This is especially clear in the case of presidential elections in the US (Baker, 1983, 262), which are occasions of moment around the world and not just in that country. Thompson (2004) pictures elections as marking "a moment of politics – a discontinuous phase in a continuous" political process. He analyzes their temporal properties from three vantage points. One is simultaneity, which we alluded to earlier when considering the idea of having a dedicated election day. Another is periodicity, which we just noted in terms of recurrence and cycles. The third is finality.

Finality links to a classical rule about electoral challenges. The right to petition a court to undo an election result is strictly guarded. To modern eyes, this may seem merely to be a question of institutional competence. If independent election management bodies organize each electoral race, why not trust them to oversee the process and declare the winner, instead of re-ventilating the matter before a small group of possibly unworldly judges? Yet, rules restricting electoral challenges predate professionalized electoral commissions. In restraining litigation during the election period, imposing very short time limits on post-election challenges and requiring the outcome (and not merely the vote share) to have been affected before a legal challenge can be mounted, the law has long been rooted in a desire for finality. As the top court in the British Empire put it in 1870, election disputes must "as soon as possible become conclusive" to enable the legislature or government to be "distinctly and speedily known."[7]

Elections are important, then, but life must go on. Unlike that of a referendum, an election result is not set in stone, since the cycle guarantees that new choices will, soon enough, be made. Different legal systems, of course, alight on different electoral frequencies, as well as different rules about the fixing of election dates. But the frequency of elections almost invariably falls within a range of three to five years.[8] Ultimately, the electoral cycle is not merely rhythmical in the sense of being recurrent. It also plays a defining role in the seasonality of politics. Election times see a build-up of contestation, both formal and real. After the moment of electoral choice, there is then an expectation of a certain healing, or at least a period of honeymoon for the new government or president. This hiatus is then followed by a longer period of governmental activity and opposition renewal, before the build-up to a contested election begins anew.

Anthropological approaches to modern electoral democracy go even further, and seek to identify temporality and social movement in the form of rites of passage. To Damon (2003, 53–4) elections are above all "installation rites." They first consist of a "rite of separation" in which candidates distinguish themselves from the rest of society and masquerade before it. Similarly, Kertzer (1988, 108) likens elections to a "journey" involving the "campaign as a pilgrimage" and Aguilar (2007) even calls candidates "transitional beings in a state of ambiguity," "betwixt and between" (p. 76) worlds. After the disruption of the campaign, there then transpires a transitional period of social re-incorporation (Damon, 2003, 53–62).

Rival Theories of Electoral Law and Critiques of Ritual

One objection to injecting a ritual approach to our thinking about regulating electoral democracy is that liberal political systems purport to aim for a level of neutrality. Certainly, it is easy to imagine examples of normative overreach in the name of "ritual." Totalitarian states often give priority to spectacle over liberty, and fascism, in particular, accentuates a particular aesthetic in the symbols and ceremonies of public law and governance. Liberalism, of course, is not a neutral position handed down from on high. Nor is it a singular one, as debates within liberal democracies, say about whether to ban revolutionary or racialist parties under the guise of "militant liberalism," reveal. No liberal state, therefore, occupies a truly neutral position: If it did, we might expect it to fly a blank flag or abolish its national anthem. So, ultimately, any objection to the theory of elections as rituals cannot be to the descriptive importance of the ritual perspective. At most, it acts as a warning against excesses in any normative project driven by an obsession with a particular choreographing of the ritual elements of electoral practice.

In any event, such excess is unlikely. Electoral law, especially under the common law method, has suffered from a deficit rather than a surfeit of theorizing (Schultz, 2014). The ritual approach is but one of a number of theoretical positions – and hardly a dominant approach – in debates about evaluating and reforming electoral law and practice. Elsewhere, I have attempted to map and describe the theories underlying the law of electoral politics (Orr, 2020). In that map lie four clusters, of which "ritual" is but one. The other three theoretical clusters need only briefly be explained here by way of contrast and overlap.

The first is "integrity," particularly the integrity of the basic structure of fair elections. In this view, the key role for electoral institutions and laws is to permit all who are eligible to vote, without bribery or intimidation, and to ensure the accurate aggregation of those votes. To self-described realists, this is a consciously limited but essential ambition or *sine qua non* for election law. Electoral democracy is seen as the least worst system of governance, and a base level of integrity at least allows for an ultimate form of democratic accountability, through the potential for a peaceful turnover of elites.

Second, and more questing, are theories rooted in mainstream understandings of "democracy." Notable amongst these are the values of political liberty and equality. (Deliberative democrats would add another value, namely quality information and discourse.) Obviously, these values are sometimes in creative tension, as is the case with political freedom, on the one hand, and efforts to treat citizens or parties substantially equally on the other. Each of these values is commonly invoked in discussions about election law. Along with integrity, they form the core, normative criteria invoked in both judicial review of existing laws and in evaluating proposals for law reform. They aim to ensure a system that is reasonably open and not so unequal that incumbents are entrenched through manipulating election law.

Third are more cynical approaches that revolve around a metaphor of elections as a mask. In this, typically outsiders' view, elections all too often act as a mere game. Not a game in the sense of a robust competition, but in the sense of insubstantial rigmaroles, obscuring the fact that real power and its legitimation lie elsewhere within society. This view is remarkably widespread, embraced by voices as diverse as populists, Marxists, anarchists, and even by some neo-conservative critiques of liberal proceduralism (Kristol, 1983, 50–1).

These four theoretical approaches – ritual, integrity, democratic values, and mask – are not watertight. On the contrary, they may interrelate in any given issue or problem. For instance, something as fundamental as the secret ballot implicates integrity, liberty, and equality, as well as ritualized experiences and meanings.[9] None of these debates is resolvable in the abstract either: Context matters. Take early voting, as but one example. In the US, with elections held on a Tuesday and subject to long queues in poorer communities, early voting becomes essential on grounds of equal access to participation. Whereas in Australia, with election day on a Saturday and queues rare, early voting is largely a convenience for the educated middle class that eats away at the ritual value of polling day.

It remains then to consider the limits and boundaries of a theory of elections as rituals. As a sociological insight, the theory is far from culturally invariant. On the contrary, even within liberal-egalitarian electoral democracies, as we have seen, there are significant differences in electoral practice that inform and are reinforced by culturally dependent rules. This is most obvious in the discussion of campaigning above.

Ritualized practices cannot, as a result, be expected to carry a single, objectively condensed meaning. As well as culture and context, subjectivity matters. Hence. for one person, queuing at a polling station may be a waste of time, an act of complicity with a charade; yet. for another. it may be an ultimate marker of active citizenship. To Edelman (1985, 195–6). this subjectivity renders politics more like art and literature than a quantifiable science. That is true, and any respondent-dependent social science also must weed out social desirability bias in surveys of experiences and beliefs. Coleman's recent study (2013) of the affective and emotional responses of UK voters to the act of polling demonstrates that the ritualized meanings of electoral practices are not simply matters for high-level speculation. They need also to be assayed at the ground level.

The account of elections as masks or charades bears a clear relation to the conception of electoral democracy as a ritual in the pejorative sense, which we encountered in the introduction as an alternative to ritual as either a descriptive tool or a normative good. No one, for instance, would suggest that elections in, say, North Korea, are anything but a kind of elaborate performance that farcically illuminates the first word in that country's official title ("Democratic People's Republic of Korea"). But, outside authoritarian extremes, it is not helpful to think of elections as a mask in an all-or-nothing sense. In the realism of Edelman (1988), political action through voting and lobbying can help bring modest and temporary changes, but are more effective as psychological balm…because the very focus upon politics in a narrow sense takes the existing institutional framework for granted and reinforces it (p. 130).

Elections thus are a chance for "participation in a ritual act [drawing] attention to common social ties and to the importance and apparent reasonableness of accepting the public policies that are adopted" (Edelman, 1964, 3). In this sense, as long as elections are run with a reasonable degree of integrity, liberty, and equality, they also act as ritual contests that can serve to bring political legitimation and social affirmation. Indeed, it is difficult to *not* conceive of them as significant ritual occasions – recurrent and quintessentially public occasions, marking the passage and renewal of political seasons – occasions that themselves are made up of various humbler, ritualized practices and processes (Orr, 2015, 9).

Attending to the perspective of ritual can, therefore, both lend us descriptive insights into why certain rules and customs are perpetuated and open us to a broader understanding of their normative value and significance. Ultimately, this approach reminds us that election law, institutions, and norms are not merely instrumental tools in support of a governmental structure. They also help constitute and mediate the social value of electoral democracy, as well as, for better and worse, its lived experience.

Notes

1 See also Bird (1980, p. 19), who stresses ritual as "culturally transmitted symbolic codes which are stylized, regularly repeated…and intrinsically valued."

2 As one UK MP put it, keeping a single polling day as the focus of the election allows party activists to engage in "an exciting sort of programme [otherwise] there is not much point in joining up if you are not going to see any action" (Orr, 2015, p. 66).

3 That is, US electioneering cannot be subject to mandatory caps of the sort found in other parts of the world. Candidates can, at most, voluntarily agree to limit spending in return for public funding.
4 In the UK, the limitation applies at any time, not just during election periods: *Communications Act 2003* (UK) ss 319, 321, 333.
5 See *Public Offices Elections Act 1950* (Japan), art 141.
6 In some jurisdictions, only electors (or permanent residents) may make political donations. In others, parties may limit their membership to people who are enrolled to vote.
7 *Théberge v. Laudry* (1870) 2 App Cas 102 at 106.
8 Allowing for outliers like two years for the US House of Representatives, and long terms for some upper houses.
9 We have come to see secrecy as a positive experience, hence metaphors like the "polling booth [as a] closet of prayer" in the poem 'My ancestress and the secret ballot, 1848 and 1851' (Murray, 1996, p. 80). But, as noted earlier, nineteenth-century conservative opponents of secrecy saw it as cowardly and, even today, some progressives wonder what is lost if electors feel their ballot is essentially a private concern.

References

Ackerman, B., & Fishkin, J. S. (2002). Deliberation day. *Journal of Political Philosophy, 10*(2), 129–152. doi: 10.1111/1467-9760.00146

Aguilar, F.V. (2007). Betting on democracy: Electoral ritual in the Philippine presidential campaign. In C. Beng-Huat (Ed.), *Elections as popular culture in Asia* (pp. 72–93). Abingdon: Routledge.

Baker, J. H. (1983). *Affairs of party: The political culture of northern Democrats in the mid-nineteenth century*. Ithaca, NY: Cornell University Press.

Bensel, R. F. (2004). *The American ballot box in the mid-nineteenth century*. New York: Cambridge University Press.

Bentham, J. (1818). *Plan of parliamentary reform in the form of a catechism*. Bishopsgate: TJ Wooler.

Bird, F. (1980). The contemporary ritual milieu. In R. B. Browne (Ed.), *Ritual ceremonies in popular culture* (pp. 19–35). Bowling Green: Bowling Green University Press.

Brennan, G., & Lomasky, L. (1993). *Democracy and decision: The pure theory of electoral preference*. Cambridge, UK: Cambridge University Press.

Brett, J. (2019). *From secret ballot to democracy sausage: How Australia got compulsory voting*. Melbourne: Text Publishing.

Buchler, J. (2011). *Hiring and firing officials: Rethinking the purpose of elections*. New York: Oxford University Press.

Butler, C. (2012). *Henri Lefebvre: Spatial politics, everyday life and the right to the city*. Abingdon: Routledge.

Cohen, E. F. (2018). *The political value of time: Citizenship, duration and democratic justice*. New York: Cambridge University Press.

Coleman, S. (2013). *How voters feel. Cambridge*. Cambridge: Cambridge University Press.

Damon, F. H. (2003). What good are elections? An anthropological study of American elections. *Taiwan Journal of Anthropology, 1*(2), 38–82.

Edelman, M. (1964). *The symbolic uses of politics*. Urbana, IL: University of Illinois Press.

Edelman, M. (1985). *The symbolic uses of politics: With a new afterword*. Urbana, IL: University of Illinois Press.

Edelman, M. (1988). *Constructing the political spectacle*. Chicago, IL: Chicago University Press.

Faucher, F. and Hay, C (2015). Les rituels de vote en France et au Royaume-Uni. *Revue francaise de science politique, 65*, 213–236.

Geddis, A. (2015). Law and New Zealand's 2014 election campaign. *Otago Law Review, 14*, 117–245. Retrieved from http://www.nzlii.org/nz/journals/OtaLawRw/2015/9.html

Green, H. (writing as Lardy, H.) (2003). Modernising elections: The silent premise of the electoral pilot schemes. *Public Law*, 6–13.

Hirschbein, R. (1999). *Voting rites: The devolution of American politics*. Westport, CT: Praeger.

Kelly, W. (1860). *Life in Victoria or Victoria in 1853, and Victoria in 1858*. London: Chapman and Hall (1977 reprint. Kilmore: Lowden Publishing).

Kinzer, B. L. (1982). The ballot question in nineteenth-century politics. New York: Garland.

Kertzer, D. I. (1988). *Ritual, politics and power*. New Haven, CT: Yale University Press.

Kristol, I. (1983). *Reflections of a neo-conservative: Looking back, looking ahead*. New York: Basic Books.

Lawrence, J. (2009). *Electing our masters: The hustings in British politics from Hogarth to Blair*. Oxford: Oxford University Press.
Lawrence, J. (2011). The culture of elections in modern Britain. *History, 96*(324), 459–476. doi: 10.1111/j.1468-229X.2011.00529.x
Lefebvre, H. (1991). *Critique of everyday life I: Introduction*. London: Verso.
Murray, L. A. (1996). *Subhuman Redneck Poems*. Potts Point: Duffy & Snellgrove.
O'Gorman, F. (1989). *Votes, patrons and parties: The unreformed electorate of Hanoverian England, 1734–1832*. Oxford: Clarendon Press.
O'Gorman, F. (1992). Campaign rituals and ceremonies: The social meaning of elections in England 1780–1860. *Past and Present, 135*(1), 79–115. Retrieved from http://www.jstor.org/stable/650971
Orr, G. (2014). Betting on elections: Law, history, policy. *Federal Law Review, 42*(2), 309–331. doi: 10.22145/flr.42.2.4
Orr, G. (2015). *Ritual and rhythm in electoral systems: A comparative legal account*. Farnham, UK: Ashgate/Routledge.
Orr, G. (2020). Electoral law: Theory and purpose. In A. Bogg, J. Rowbottom & A. L. Young (Eds.), *The Constitution of Social Democracy* (pp. 161–177). Oxford: Hart Publishing.
Schultz, D. (2014). *Election law and democratic theory*. Farnham, UK: Ashgate/Routledge.
Stromer-Galley, J. (2003). Voting and the public sphere: Conversations on internet voting. *PS: Political Science and Politics, 36*(4), 727–731. Retrieved from http://www.jstor.org/stable/3649269
Thompson, D. F. (2004). Election time: Normative implications of temporal properties of the electoral process in the United States. *American Political Science Review, 98*(1), 51–63. Retrieved from http://www.jstor.org/stable/4145296
Ting, M. H. (2010). Ritual and identity: Elections and voting in Singapore. *Taiwan Journal of Democracy, 6*(2), 101–124.
Wigmore, J. H. (1889). *The Australian ballot system as embodied in the legislation of various countries*. Boston, MA: Charles C. Soule.

10
INTERNATIONAL ELECTION OBSERVATION AND STANDARDS

Alexander Shlyk

Introduction

Ever since the adoption of the Universal Declaration of Human Rights, democratic elections are considered a primary mechanism for the people to "take part in the government" of their country through the free expression of their will. Article 21 of the Declaration makes it clear that, for elections to serve as a link between the people and the government, the will of the voters has to be expressed in genuine and periodic elections that are universal, equal, and secret. The International Covenant on Civil Political Rights, adopted in 1966, went a step further by adding, in Article 25, a right "to be elected" and a provision stating the importance of the "*free* expression of the will of the electors."

It is not surprising that the international documents adopted in the wake of democratization of a large part of the world in the early 1990s relied on similar formulations. Similar key words were used in the Copenhagen Document adopted by the Organization for Security and Co-operation in Europe (then, a Conference) and subsequent commitments undertaken by the states participating in the OSCE. Some innovative wording was used, however, such as the requirement, in Paragraph 6 of the 1990 OSCE Copenhagen Document, of "fair electoral processes."

Importantly, the 1990 OSCE Copenhagen Document linked the quality of elections with the importance of election observation. In Paragraph 8 of the document, OSCE participating states have underscored that "the presence of observers, both foreign and domestic, can enhance the electoral process for States in which elections are taking place." This provision has since been treated as both a standing invitation for international election observers and the recognition of the exercise as a valuable peer-to-peer review mechanism.

Since then, OSCE participating states have created a specialized institution, first known as the Office for Free Elections and now called the OSCE Office for Democratic Institutions and Human Rights (ODIHR). The mandate of ODIHR was to, first, "facilitate contacts and the exchange of information on elections within participating States" (Paris, 1990, Para. XX) and, later, to "foster the implementation of paragraphs 6, 7 and 8 of the Document of the Copenhagen Meeting of the Conference on the Human Dimension of the CSCE" (Paris, Supplementary Document, 1990). This adaptation of the mandate once again reaffirmed the value that election observation brings to the conduct of elections.

DOI: 10.4324/9780429401800-10

With this mandate in mind, OSCE participating states tasked ODIHR with developing a comprehensive election observation methodology (OSCE, Budapest Document, 1994), noting the importance of observing "before, during and after election day," and later reiterating of the goal of ODIHR to further strengthen observation methodology.

ODIHR remains a leading institution in the field of international election observation, having published not only six editions of its Election Observation Handbook, but also 13 other thematic handbooks intended to assist election observers in following various thematic aspects of elections.

In 1999, OSCE participating states reaffirmed the value of election observation by recognizing "the assistance the ODIHR can provide to participating States in developing and implementing electoral legislation...We agree to follow up promptly the ODIHR's election assessment and recommendations" (Istanbul, 1999, Paragraph 25). These commitments echoed a declaration of the OSCE Parliamentary Assembly that the "monitoring of elections are not single events but part of a continuous process, including follow up actions for promotion of democracy" (OSCE PA 1993, 15).

For 20 years now, this recognition of the value of ODIHR electoral assessments and recommendations has underpinned the work of election observers. International election observation is subject to academic scrutiny and occasionally draws criticism. This not only underscores the important role election observation plays in the framework of international relations, but also raises several important questions, including whether observers should merely report on what they see or try to help improve the conduct of elections in the long run.

This essay aims to provide a short review of current research on the relevance of international election observation and corresponding criticism. This will set the premise for my key argument that recommendations by observer missions are their most valuable contribution if they link the analysis of the law and practice with standards for democratic elections rooted in the human rights. I will further endeavor to show that the impact of the work of international election observers is inseparable from their legal expertise and precise understanding of the practical conduct of elections. To do so, I will draw on the example of vote secrecy, one of the fundamental standards for democratic elections, in order to show that it can be analyzed from both practical and legal perspectives and that both long- and short-term observation is needed. I will argue that, by focusing on practice and law, observers do not neglect the political impact of their work but rather address it by formulating tangible and evidence-based recommendations rooted in human rights. I rely on the argument that thinking of human rights from the political perspective gives grounds to reform interventions. I will then conclude by outlining some of the latest practical steps that ODIHR is taking to help states implement the recommendations and, with that, derive value from being observed.

Election Observation – Still Relevant?

In the 30 years since ODIHR has been set up as the Office for Free Elections, international observation has become a norm. ODIHR deploys between 15 and 20 election observation and assessment missions every year, which vary in scope and focus. Some of them involve hundreds of short-term observers watching how polling stations operate on election day; some are limited to a handful of experts looking at specific thematic areas; and some lie in between these two distinct types of missions. Two aspects are invariable, however, no matter what type of mission ODIHR deploys. First, each mission is deployed for the benefit of the host country and its people. Second, whatever the mission type, general principles of observation enshrined in the methodology, such as a reliance on international standards and a focus on providing tangible recommendations to apply. I will argue that these two pillars of election observation are closely related and, jointly, provide for the relevance of election observation.

The fact that election observation has become the norm is evidenced by the fact that ODIHR is always invited by each OSCE participating state to observe their elections. A few exceptions when ODIHR was not able to deploy an observation mission were linked not to the absence of an invitation, but to limitations imposed by the host country that made observation impossible. In the case of Albania in 1997, the Russian Federation in 2007, and Azerbaijan in 2015, countries requested that ODIHR limit the number of deployed observers. ODIHR refused to do so and canceled the observation altogether. In all of these countries, ODIHR later deployed missions and delivered its reports. This fact, even more than routine invitations to observe, confirms the conclusion by Rich that the "rejection of foreign electoral observers has come to be taken as a signal that the country concerned is not prepared to open itself to international scrutiny and is not interested in the international legitimacy that a positive report would bestow" (2001, 26). Similarly, Hyde argues that "the decision by an incumbent government to invite observers is closely tied to the availability of international benefits for countries perceived as democracies" (2011, 209). Both arguments are premised upon the value of international benefits, political and/or economic, derived from recognition as an electoral democracy.

Hyde further argues that the fact that "negative reports from international observers have not reduced the rate of internationally observed elections" (2011, 8) derives from the intention of the "pseudo-democrats" to take a risk of "receiving a negative report when they invite observers," while realizing that "failing to invite observers signals their type with certainty" (2011, 46). These points focus on the role of observation in delivering assessments of the elections, but do not touch upon the formulation of recommendations as the essential part of the work of observers. Moreover, the signaling effect of observer reports is looked at mostly from the perspective of those in the country observed, rather than external actors, including assistance providers.

Cheeseman and Klaas recently extend Hyde's argument towards a critique of international election observers, noting that "election monitors can become compromised by geopolitical motivations" (2018, 194) and further elaborating that "despots, dictators and counterfeit democrats are able to dupe observers into legitimizing rigged elections" and are still "able to win praise from monitors pursuing their own geostrategic goals" (2018, 206). Borzel argues similarly by finding "limits of what Western democracy promoters are willing and able to do, particularly if their geostrategic interests are at stake" (2015, 529).

In my mind, these arguments lack detail with regard to the analysis of the different types of organizations involved in international election observation. While observation has become a norm throughout the world, there are several types of observer organizations involved. The most obvious distinction can be drawn regarding the premises upon which observers are deployed. On the one hand, there are international organizations operating on the basis of a mandate agreed upon by their member states, which may occasionally disagree on what constitutes a good election but nonetheless recognize the value of observation in itself. On the other hand, there are observer organizations whose activities are premised upon a more uniform understanding of their membership of what constitutes a genuinely democratic election.

Organizations falling into the first group would be the Organization of American States (OAS), OSCE, Council of Europe (CoE), African Union (AU), and the Commonwealth. The second group includes such organizations as the European Union (EU) and a range of prominent non-governmental organizations, such as the National Democratic Institute (NDI), International Republican Institute (IRI), and The Carter Center (TCC). Interestingly, this possible classification appears to overlap with whether the organizations deploy observers to their constituent member states or to third countries. [1]

One would expect that these two types of organizations may be susceptible to pressures of geopolitics to a varying degree. It goes beyond the scope of this essay to analyze specific cases or to draw comparisons between the organizations, but it is worth highlighting that all of them endorsed the Declaration of Principles for International Election Observation (DoP) in 2005. The DoP is premised upon a common recognition that "international election observation, which focuses on civil and political rights, is part of international human rights monitoring" and "plays an important role in providing accurate and impartial assessments about the nature of electoral processes" with a view to "enhance the integrity of election processes, by deterring and exposing irregularities and fraud and by providing recommendations for improving electoral processes" (DoP, 2).

Combining Politics and Expertise in Election Observation

Much in the spirit of the DoP, Davis-Roberts and Carroll ofThe Carter Center convincingly link election observation to human rights. They argue that the common ground for assessments of elections by a variety of observer organizations should be the public international law that allows them to use "assessment criteria that are objective, transparent, consistent, and applicable to all countries." They further propose that "preliminary post-election statements of election observation missions can root the assessment criteria, related standards, as well as the overall findings in international legal obligations, and can include recommendations about how the state might better achieve their obligations in the future" (Davis-Roberts & Carroll, 2010, 18).

This argument can be built upon by looking at two aspects of election observation work and the related criticism expressed towards them. First, further analysis is needed whether observers focus on the aspects of the process that really matter. Second, it is an important question if, by focusing on legal and technical aspects of elections, even when relying on international law, observers ignore the fundamentally political nature of the process. I will claim that the political developments and the technical improvements to the elections correlate closely. With this, I demonstrate that the value of observation is contingent both on the impartial analysis of and reporting on a given electoral process and on whether observation leads to concrete improvement of the elections through tangible and relevant recommendations.

Short-Term and Long-Term Findings as the Basis for Recommendations

Bjornlund argues that "many international observers still put undue emphasis on election administration on election day" which "allows autocratic regimes to manipulate other parts of the process" (2004, 305–6). In a similar manner, Eicher claims that, "because blatant election day cheating is becoming less common in the OSCE area, the relative importance of short-term, election day-focused observation is declining in comparison to long-term observation" (2009, 273).

It is rare to see policymakers, practitioners, and academics in agreement. However, they concur that election day is only one element of the electoral process and that election observers need to look beyond the quality of the voting, counting, and tabulation of results. Indeed, I am often asked whether deploying large numbers of observers on election day itself makes sense if "the elections have already been fixed."

My reply is that both are important. However, I disagree that short-term observation is not necessary because fraud shifts to another part of the process. I would instead argue that the value of election day observation actually increases if the link between election day findings and conclusions of the long-term observation is taken into account. I do not think that observing election day proceedings in a systematic manner has lost its significance. Try asking yourself a few simple questions. What is worse: Deliberate fraud or an honest mistake by polling staff? Would you be more critical if you saw voters confused by procedures or voting with pre-marked ballots? I would certainly make the distinction, and so do the observers on election day, using the forms prepared by ODIHR.

Election day observation is crucial not only for understanding *what* the shortcomings are, but also *why* they persist. Observers assess whether commission members have been well trained, whether they have understood the procedures and whether the laws and regulations are clear enough for those who are supposed to implement them.

Indeed, election day observation can validate and provide further evidence for the findings of long-term observers. Observing the performance of election commissions on election day should demonstrate not only "what" happened, but also "why" something took place. The credibility of long-term findings depends on the robustness of short-term observation. Fraud and malfeasance are not only shifting from election day to the pre-electoral period, but rather from one stage of election day to other ones, such as from voting to counting and tabulation. Hyde, for example, enumerates electoral irregularities for which election observers may face difficulties in distinguishing intentional fraud from unintentional mistakes (Hyde, 2008, 205).

Let's draw on one example of how short-term observers can help formulate recommendations that may go beyond election day. In 2013, ODIHR published an overview of findings contained in its reports on elections held in OSCE participating states between 2010 and 2012. In the section related to election day procedures, ODIHR concluded that:

> election day procedures often complied with OSCE commitments and other international standards in most States, although cases of breaches of the secrecy of the vote, and group and (illegal) proxy voting were reported on occasion. In some OSCE participating States, a tendency was observed that, while voting procedures were overall respected, the process deteriorated during the counting and the tabulation of votes, particularly with regards to transparency, indications of ballot box stuffing and tampering with results protocols.
>
> *(ODIHR, 2013a, 5)*

Noting specific irregularities, the document specifically highlights that recommendations on further training of election commissions had been made, particularly with a view to combat group and illegal proxy voting. ODIHR reports go further and note that the occurrence of observed irregularities is related to deliberate malfeasance by election officials or poor training or understanding of procedures. Cases of ballot box stuffing and deliberate falsification of results protocols are reported as the evidence of the former, while not following the prescribed counting procedures are often linked to the latter.

Observation forms used by ODIHR short-term observers to collect election-day data allow for these conceptual links to be made. Observer responses to questions on the forms are analyzed individually, as well as in connection with overall assessment as elements of the process and of the process as a whole.

Let's take the issue of secrecy of the vote, which is provided for in a variety of international documents that contain standards and obligations for democratic elections, such as the UDHR, ICCPR, and the 1990 OSCE Copenhagen Document. It is thus one of the pillars for truly democratic elections that should be safeguarded by states. Here, I will focus on the findings pertaining to secrecy of the vote in the most recent observations in the Russian Federation and the United States.

During the 2018 presidential election in the Russian Federation, an ODIHR report noted that:

> Secrecy of the vote was problematic as it was at times compromised by overcrowding (noted in 10 per cent of polling stations observed), inadequate layout of voting premises (6 per cent of observations) or voters either not marking their ballots in secrecy or not folding the ballot before it was cast (12 and 74 per cent of observations, respectively).
>
> *(ODIHR, 2018, 21)*

The observation mission further made a following practical recommendation:

> Practical aspects of the organization of voting should be reviewed to ensure the secrecy of the vote, as provided by OSCE commitments and the law. PEC members should inform voters of their right and obligation to secrecy and the significance of ballot secrecy should be emphasized during training of election commissions and in voter education materials. Consideration could be given to introducing translucent ballot boxes.
>
> *(ODIHR, 2018, 21)*

In Russia, the forms contained several questions that fed information for the conclusion quoted above. Question G5 specifically focused on the secrecy of the vote and used a frequency scale for responses. Question D2 focused on layout in the polling stations, while question E1 was used to collect information on overcrowding in the polling stations.

Reporting by ODIHR is premised on the methodology that includes statistical analysis of the data collected by short-term observers through the observation forms. The way the conclusion was formulated in Russia in 2018 is based upon the finding of a strong correlation between violations of secrecy and overcrowding and poor layout, as well as establishing a link between violations of secrecy and the overall assessment of the voting process based on Section J of the forms.

The recommendation made in the Russian Federation is of a practical nature, as it is focused on the organization of voting, training of commissions, and voter education. The recommendation does not touch upon legal provisions, which is not necessary since secrecy of the vote is expressly provided for in the Russian electoral legislation (see Article 3 of the Federal Law on Basic Guarantees of Electoral Rights and the Right to Participate in a Referendum).

In the United States, where the findings were also based on short-term observation, the conclusions were formulated differently and the recommendation is of a legal nature. Following the observation of the 2016 general elections in the United States, ODIHR concluded, based on observation of election day, that:

> Secrecy of the vote was not always guaranteed, at odds with OSCE commitments and international obligations. In seven per cent of observations, there were cases of voters not voting in secret. This included voters not being provided with ballot sleeves to preserve the secrecy of their vote when using ballot scanners to cast their vote. In some cases, provisional ballots were not put in secrecy envelopes before being inserted

> in envelopes containing voter information. In five per cent of observations, there were indications that voters were taking photographs of their ballot.

ODIHR also recommended that "Legislation should be in place to guarantee the secrecy of the vote for in-person voting, including provisional and absentee ballots" (ODIHR, 2017, 26).

Section G of the observation forms used in the United States contained the same question as in the Russian Federation (G9 in the case of United States), while question G16 concerned voters taking pictures of their ballots. Observers additionally reported on specific instances when secrecy of the vote was not ensured through narrative reports.

Formulation of this conclusion in the United States in 2016 and the corresponding recommendation in the report signal that statistical analysis did not link violations of the secrecy of the vote to a lack of adherence to procedures or a poor understanding of them by voters. The legal focus of the recommendation is reiterated in another section of the same report from the 2016 elections. When ODIHR reported on the conduct of early voting, the report highlights that:

> Some states, however, did not provide voters with a secrecy envelope, which meant that the ballot was returned in a single envelope that contained voter information, potentially violating the secrecy of vote as provided by paragraph 7.4 of the 1990 OSCE Copenhagen Document

It also recommended that "Jurisdictions should ensure the secrecy of postal ballots are always safeguarded when received by election officials by providing secrecy envelopes" (ODIHR, 2017, 23).

Additionally, ODIHR notes that "Thirty-two states allowed electronic submission of marked ballots from out-of-country voters, which required voters to waive the secrecy of their vote, contrary to OSCE commitments" It further recommends that "Federal authorities should develop secure voting methods, including for out-of-country voters, with a view to ensuring the secrecy of the vote while allowing for the expedient return of ballots" (ODIHR, 2017, 23).

Furthermore, ODIHR highlights the legal nature of the issue of secrecy of the vote in the United States by noting that "A number of previous OSCE/ODIHR recommendations remain unaddressed in the law and certain deficiencies in the legal framework persist, such as…infringements on secrecy of the ballot" (ODIHR, 2017, 2). This makes reference to the recommendation made following the 2012 general elections that "In order to comply with international standards, consideration should be given to adopting federal legislation that guarantees the secrecy of the vote in US elections" (ODIHR, 2013b, 21).

In ODIHR reports for both the Russian Federation and the United States, it is clear that the findings of short-term observers are linked to the analysis conducted by the experts deployed for a longer period of time. But, for the experts to arrive at their conclusions, they needed to figure out whether the insufficient training and deficiencies in the organization of voting (in Russian Federation) or lack of legal provisions (in the United States) manifest themselves as shortcomings on election day. The two examples above demonstrate the attention that observers pay to the technical and legal aspects of the electoral process. This reaffirms that both the principles and the procedures should be protected by the electoral law.

Robust and statistically reliable observation of counting and tabulation requires significant numbers of observers. Even as the long-term component is strengthened, it should be further aided by the findings of the short-terms observers in those cases when electoral stakeholders see a need to follow the election day procedures closely or lack trust in how election day procedures are handled.

Human Rights as the Pillar for the Recommendations

An additional valid question would be, however, whether this focus of election observation means that observers prioritize legal and technical aspects over the fundamentally political nature of the process. In other words, should the observers be concerned with the political implications of the principles in the electoral law? Credible international observers highlight that they are not concerned with the outcome of an election, but rather focus on the process. This fact, however, does not mean that the observers are not aware of the potential political impact of their assessments. Observers should distance themselves from the results of a given election, but still need to recognize the link between greater respect of fundamental rights and the reflection of the will of the people in the election results.

One may say that observers should approach international standards for elections from an apolitical viewpoint and treat them as rooted in the human rights that belong to all by the virtue of being human. Liao and Etinson (2012), echoing Beitz (2009), term this a "naturalistic conception" of human rights. They juxtapose it with the "political conception" rooted in the thinking of Rawls. According to the latter, human rights should be thought of in terms of their function for the system of social co-operation, as per Rawls. Liao and Etinson note that Beitz argued that this "political conception" gives ground for states and international organizations to influence the internal affairs of societies where human rights are threatened and for individuals and non-governmental organizations to engage in reform-oriented political action (Liao & Etinson, 2012, 330).

The ongoing academic debate about whether the two conceptions of human rights are mutually exclusive is intriguing. It may help illuminate the extent to which international election observers and assistance providers should be concerned with the political effects of human rights violations in the countries with which they work.

In my opinion, to be successful in linking the technical and political aspects of elections, international observers should not be personally concerned with the result of a given election, but with the quality of the political process that a given election demonstrates. The latter may allow others to evaluate the legitimacy and credibility of an outcome. Providing honest assessments of legal and technical issues, as well of the level of respect of fundamental rights, contributes to the political evaluation of a given election by such other actors as political leaders in the country and abroad, as well as the media. This has previously been highlighted by Hyde, who noted that "international observers...primarily serve an informational role, and their reports matter to the extent that other actors rely on them to evaluate the quality of elections" (Hyde, 2011, 36). If observers become concerned with the results of the elections, they stop being impartial, which is the core principle enshrined in the Declaration of Principles and the Code of Conduct for observers deployed by ODIHR.

One political aspect of elections that observers should legitimately be concerned with is the political environment in which elections take place. Technical elements are also closely linked to this environment. In my experience, deliberate frauds and falsifications are more likely to occur in elections taking place in the context of poor respect for fundamental rights. Vote secrecy, for example, may be purposefully left poorly regulated or not protected by practical means for political ends. Where voters feel intimidated to disclose who they voted for, their other rights are also frequently suppressed.

It is common for ODIHR missions to evaluate such aspects of the environment as respect of fundamental freedoms of expression, association, and assembly. ODIHR observers especially focus on the level of respect of these rights from the perspective of the ability of electoral contestants to conduct their campaign activities. Beyond that, they also regularly draw upon analysis and reports by other organizations, such as the UN and its treaty monitoring mechanisms. Findings of the Committee on Civil and Political Rights give an important perspective for election observers. For example, when describing voting rights in the United States, ODIHR drew upon the committee's concluding observations on the fourth periodic report of the United States (CCPR, 2014). Similarly, when commenting on the environment in which the presidential election took place in the Russian Federation, ODIHR relied on the findings of the United Nations Special Rapporteur on the Rights to Freedom of Peaceful Assembly and of Association. References are also often made to the relevant case law of the European Court of Human Rights.

Such focus on the fundamental rights is sometimes met by criticism that international observers "go beyond their mandate" and "forget that elections are a technical process." In their responses, some states highlight that drawing conclusions based on events that take place long before the elections is contrary to the time-bound mandate of a given election observation mission. In response, election observers often stress that genuine elections cannot take place without political pluralism or in a climate of suppression. They also often demonstrate a clear link between respect of freedom of association and the opportunity for registered parties to nominate candidates, as well as between freedoms of expression and assembly and the ability to campaign. This is how the technical assessment of the elections helps others make the political assessment from the perspective of human rights.

Reporting on elections from the perspective of human rights is sometimes met with another type of criticism. We regularly hear that legality of elections should be understood as adherence of elections to domestic legislation. This is particularly evident in the statements and conclusions reached by the observers deployed by the Commonwealth of Independent States (CIS). Interestingly, despite being an international covenant, the 2002 CIS Convention is often interpreted as providing for the primary role of domestic legislation. Observers deployed by the CIS regularly refer, in their statements, to how the elections they observed fell in line with the domestic legislation of the given country. Other organizations, however, highlight the fact that assessment of the legislation itself against international commitments and standards is also an important task of election observers. They often note that international obligations do not belong to the sending organization, but rather to the states that form it. As such, OSCE commitments are not the commitments made by the OSCE or by the participating states towards the organization, but by the states towards each other.

This disagreement has a political dimension to it. By portraying international commitments or law as something external to themselves, countries aim to question the legitimacy of foreign concern with human rights violations in their society. Their goal is to discredit the critical findings of election observers and diminish the negative consequences that such reports would have. No doubt, adherence to the domestic legislation is important, but so is adherence of domestic law to international standards. This is the way in which the work of the international observers fits into the "political conception" of human rights and the way in which the legal and practical perspective of international observers meets the political nature of their work.

Follow-Up to Recommendations

As noted above, political thinking of human rights and electoral standards gives rise to the legitimacy of international assistance aimed at improving the elections and bringing them closer in line with existing international commitments and standards. As noted above, OSCE participating states have recognized the need to address ODIHR electoral assessments and recommendations. The importance of recommendations is acknowledged even by those countries that do not systematically follow up on them. Public statements by those OSCE participating

States that repeatedly question ODIHR assessments of their elections often also invoke the extent to which they have followed up on previous recommendations. With this, follow-up is becoming a norm.

From its side, ODIHR is promoting follow-up by systematically reporting on the extent to which specific legal and practical recommendations have been implemented between the elections. In 2013, ODIHR published a review of the electoral legislation and practice in the 57 participating states. This summary provides good guidance as to what aspects of elections deserve further attention. It was not intended as a quantitative or comparative assessment of the state of elections across the region. In fact, ODIHR refrains from comparing countries and even different elections in the same state. The study also merely provided a snapshot of the situation and did not link the quality of elections to the extent to which previous recommendations have been taken into account.

Next, in 2016, ODIHR published its Handbook on the Follow-up of Electoral Recommendations. This guidance document noted that election observation "is not an end in itself; it is intended to assist participating States in implementing their election-related commitments and obligations" (ODIHR, 2016, 7). It outlined the key principles of ODIHR's work to promote follow-up of the recommendations. Among these are providing support in an objective, impartial, neutral, and independent manner and only at the request of the participating state concerned, recognizing that the ultimate responsibility for organizing elections lies with the participating states, working according to the electoral cycle, encouraging political will, co-operating with other international observer organizations and citizen observer groups, and promoting public consultation and inclusion, in addition to political pluralism and the participation of under-represented groups (ODIHR, 2016, 23–4).

The next step was taken by ODIHR in 2019, when a database of electoral recommendations for several OSCE participating states was launched within the framework of a dedicated project aimed at assisting follow-up to the electoral recommendations in the Western Balkans. The searchable database contains recommendations for the past several elections in each project beneficiary, along with expert conclusions of the level of their implementation. Now, each subsequent ODIHR election observation mission is tasked with analyzing whether previous recommendations are fully, mostly, partially, or not at all implemented. This information feeds into both the database and the final report published by ODIHR some eight weeks after the conclusion of the electoral process. It is envisaged that ODIHR will extend the use of the database to all 57 OSCE participating states in the near future with a view to better inform them about the level of implementation of OSCE commitments. This will make an important contribution to further normalizing follow up on recommendations, as provided for by the commitment OSCE states made in 1999.

Reporting on the extent to which the states implement previous recommendations can help researchers and policy-makers evaluate the effectiveness of observation. Doubtless, much depends on the political will of the authorities to take up the recommendations that are formulated on the basis of the expert analysis of practical and legal aspects of an election. By focusing more efforts on assistance between the elections, ODIHR has already learned that political considerations impact the extent to which recommendations are taken up for a discussion. When political momentum exists, experts are regularly drawn in not only to provide inputs to the discussion and comparative international analysis, but also to review draft legislation and proposed practical adjustments. It is not surprising that the appetite for meaningful reforms is less prevalent where improved elections may increase the chances that those in power will be defeated at the next polls. Still, political implications of follow-up to recommendations should not detract from the value of election observation and assistance as a human rights activity.

Election observers cannot neglect the political consequences of their work. Nonetheless, they should not be guided by political considerations in providing assessments and recommendations. Instead, they should merely recognize the political impact of their work. By staying within the strict parameters of international standards and obligations for democratic elections and linking those, at all times, to universal values embodied in human rights, observers can play a vital role in maintaining the framework of international relations. Their work is not merely about signaling deviations from the accepted norm, but also about providing remedies for violations of existing standards.

Think of observers as qualified doctors who are called in for a regular check-up. If the observers see any deviations from the norm, they provide recommendations. It is up to the client to either take the advice seriously and follow up with it or dismiss it and hope that the problem disappears. By remaining impartial, basing their assessment on solid methodology and referring to the standards grounded in fundamental rights, election observers maintain their relevance and create the conditions for their recommendations to be taken seriously. If that is the case, the next check-up usually shows an improvement.

Note

1 A somewhat stand-alone case of an organization that regularly deploys observers is the Commonwealth of Independent States (CIS), whose members states do formally agree to what constitutes a good election (see, for example, the CIS Convention), but observer missions are also deployed to member states. However, the fact that the CIS Convention has not been ratified by all CIS member states and the relatively recent politically driven withdrawal of some member states do not speak in favor of cohesion or credibility of such observers.

References

Beitz, C. (2009). *The idea of human rights*. Oxford: Oxford University Press.

Bjornlund, E. C. (2004). *Beyond free and fair: Monitoring elections and building democracy*. Washington, DC: Woodrow Wilson Center Press.

CCPR (UN Committee on Civil and Political Rights). (April 23, 2014). Concluding observations on the fourth periodic report of the United States of America. (CCPR/C/USA/CO/4). Retrieved from https://www.refworld.org/docid/ 5374afcd4.html

Cheeseman, N., & Klaas, B. (2018). *How to rig an election*. New Haven, CT: Yale University Press.

Davis-Roberts, A., & Carroll, D. (2010). Using international law to assess elections. *Democratization, 17*(3), 416–441. doi: 10.1080/13510341003700253

DoP (Declaration of Principles for International Election Observation). (2005). Retrieved from https://www.osce.org/odihr/elections/215556

Eicher. (2009). Improving OSCE election observation. *Security and Human Rights, 20*(4), 264–276. doi: 10.1163/187502309789894857

Hyde, S. D. (2008). How international election observers detect and deter fraud. In M. R. Alvarez, T. E. Hall, & S. D. Hyde (Eds.), *Election fraud: Detecting and deterring electoral manipulation* (pp. 201–215). Washington, DC: Brookings Institution Press.

Hyde, S. D. (2011). *The pseudo-democrat's dilemma: Why election monitoring became an international norm*. Ithaca, NY: Cornell University Press.

Liao, S. M., & Etinson, A. (2012). Political and naturalistic conceptions of human rights: A false polemic? *Journal of Moral Philosophy, 9*, 327–352. doi: 10.1163/17455243-00903008

Lynge-Magueira, H. (2012). *Why 'professionalizing' international election observation might not be enough to ensure effective election observation*. Stockholm: International IDEA. Retrieved from https://www.idea.int/sites/default/files/publications/why-professionalizing-international-election-observation-might-not-be-enough.pdf

ODIHR. (2013a). Final report on the 6 November 2012 general elections in the United States of America. Retrieved from https://www.osce.org/odihr/elections/99573

ODIHR. (2013b). Review of electoral legislation and practice in OSCE participating states. Retrieved from https://www.osce.org/odihr/elections/107073
ODIHR. (2016). Handbook on the follow-up of electoral recommendations. Retrieved from https://www.osce.org/odihr/elections/244941
ODIHR. (2017). Final report on the 8 November 2016 general elections in the United States of America. Retrieved from https://www.osce.org/odihr/elections/usa/294196
ODIHR. (2018). Final report on the 18 March 2018 presidential election in the Russian Federation. Retrieved from https://www.osce.org/odihr/elections/383577
OSCE PA. (1993). Final Helsinki declaration of the CSCE Parliamentary Assembly. Retrieved from https://www.oscepa.org/documents/annual-sessions/1993-helsinki/declaration-22/173-1993-helsinki-declaration/file
Rich, R. (2001). Bringing democracy into international law. *Journal of Democracy*, 12(3), 20–34. doi: 10.1353/jod.2001.0056

11

ELECTION OBSERVATION

Using Law and International Standards – A Practitioner's Perspective

Hannah Roberts

Introduction

Election observation involves analyzing an electoral process, sharing findings and conclusions, and making public recommendations for future improvements. To do this fairly, observers need to have a clear framework for assessment, and thus refer to national legislation and also international standards as primarily found in treaties and political agreements committed to by a country. Observation is a challenging undertaking with missions *de facto* carrying a burden of judgement in often highly sensitive political situations. Observation is not a matter of black-and-white science, but involves consideration of context, interpretation of findings, and political sensitivity in order to be fair and constructive. The rationale, organization, complexities, and challenges of such assessments and frameworks are explored in this chapter.

The chapter also goes over some of the basics of election observation as practiced by credible international and citizen groups. Election observation is one of many ways to support a democratic process. It is fundamentally a check on an election, providing information and assessment of what has happened, and informed expert recommendations on ways forward. As election practices change, so too do the challenges of election observation.

The Rationale for Observers Using a Framework of Law and International Standards

While the practice of scrutinizing and commenting on electoral processes may be as old as elections themselves, the formal organization of observers substantively began relatively recently. At an inter-governmental level, the Organization of American States (OAS) reports deploying over 240 election observation missions since 1962. In the 1990s, the Organisation for Security and Cooperation in Europe (OSCE) established more methodical and consistent observation. Through its Office for Democratic Institutions and Human Rights (ODIHR), it moved away from *ad hoc* observation to a written methodology for its election observation missions.[1] Such methodological definition by the OSCE/ODIHR and others brought consistency, transparency, and accountability, as well as reduced subjectivity in the work of observers.

A cornerstone of any credible methodology is clarity on the framework and standards that are being used for assessment. While previously there was reference to "key criteria," or other

DOI: 10.4324/9780429401800-11

such vague phrases for home-country standards, now it is clear that the standards used should be the ones that have meaning in the country being observed and more widely amongst the international community. Thus, credible observers are not going in assessing a process according to their own view of what they think an election should be, but according to the commitments the country itself has made. Observers are looking at whether a country is holding elections in the way that the country itself has said that it wants to.

Therefore, credible international observers refer to compliance with the national legislation, and also look at how an election matches up to the international commitments that a country has made. This is vital, as often the national legislation is not sufficient and is part of the problem, containing contradictions or inadequate provisions for full compliance with a country's international human rights obligations related to elections. The international standards referred to by credible international election observation missions include the relevant binding commitments a country has made through ratification or accession to international treaties. These may be global through the United Nations, or regional through inter-governmental bodies at a continent- or sub-continent level. In addition, political commitments made by a country are also used.

There has been increasing recognition of the fundamental importance of a clear framework for assessing elections based on national legislation and international legal and political commitments. This approach became entrenched when broad agreement was reached on a framework for international election observation. In 2005, under the auspices of the United Nations, the Declaration of Principles for International Election Observation (hereafter called the "Declaration of Principles")[2] was established and is now endorsed by more than 50 organizations. The Declaration of Principles was a landmark document, as it established a framework for what international observers should and should not do and, therefore, a way to distinguish credible from non-credible observer groups (United Nations, 2005).

The first page of the Declaration of Principles states that observers assess "election processes in accordance with international principles for genuine democratic elections and domestic law, while recognizing that it is the people of a country who ultimately determine credibility and legitimacy of an election process" (United Nations, 2005). This is critical in establishing the framework for assessment, and also in being clear that observers are not there to be arbiters of an election. International observers offer their assessment but, as an election is a national process, it is up to the institutions and citizens of the state to ultimately determine whether an election is sufficiently credible with the outcome reflecting the will of the people.

Additionally, the first page of the Declaration of Principles also states that "International election observation, which focuses on civil and political rights, is part of international human rights monitoring" (United Nations, 2005). It goes on to note that in accordance with the Universal Declaration of Human Rights, the International Covenant for Civil and Political Rights, and other international instruments, everyone has the right and must be provided with the opportunity to participate in the government and public affairs of his or her country, without any discrimination prohibited by international human rights principles and without any unreasonable restrictions. Thus, a human rights-based framework is established, with international law defining the rationale for observation.

Without a clear framework for assessment, there is a risk that observing groups could use their own criteria, which might be personally influenced and/or politically motivated. There would be nothing to stop observer' benchmarks from changing during an electoral process, akin to changing the goalposts during a match, and perhaps just at one end of the pitch. For these reasons, serious international and citizen observer groups make their assessment criteria clear in advance and consistently refer to them. Failure to do this can damage the credibility of an observer mission and result in suspicion and mistrust of observers more generally, which is also detrimental to confidence in an election process. Observers need to practice what is so often preached, as well as be transparent about what criteria they are using and how a mission is assessing compliance with these criteria.

A further advantage of observers using a framework of international standards is that recommendations for electoral reform are then rooted within the country's on-going human rights commitments. Thus, recommendations from observer groups should have wider relevance, and human rights monitoring mechanisms also have the possibility to refer to them as part of their on-going dialogue with states party to a treaty. Moreover, such a framework of international standards can also be a useful starting point for opposing parties when looking to find a common way forward and undertake electoral reform.

Implementation of recommendations made by international election observation missions is self-evidently a matter of sovereign discretion. However, there is increasing interest by parts of the international community in countries showing responsiveness to following up on recommendations made in regards to electoral reform. For example, in 2012, the EU committed to "systematise follow-up use of EU election observation missions and their reports in support of the whole electoral cycle, and ensure effective implementation of their recommendations, as well as the reports of other election observation bodes (e.g., OSCE/ODIHR)."[3] EU Electoral Follow-up Missions were introduced in 2014, with the Chief Observer returning between elections to provide a check on and encouragement to election reform processes. Similarly, in 2016, the OSCE/ODIHR published a Handbook on the Follow-up of Electoral Recommendations.[4] This document details good practice for follow-up, noting the need for political will and sustainability, early reform, consultation and inclusion, an agreed framework and responsibilities, and co-ordination and cohesion.

Standards Referred to by Election Observers

The most basic principles referred to by observers are contained in international treaties and political agreements.[5] The universal international treaties, open to all countries to sign up to, are well-established and have near-global recognition. The International Covenant for Civil and Political Rights (ICCPR), a legally binding instrument, now has 172 states party to the treaty.[6] This makes it an extremely authoritative source, even if the country being observed has not chosen to ratify or accede to the treaty. A range of other universal treaties are also referred to by credible observer missions, including, for example, the Convention on the Elimination of All forms of Discrimination Against Women and the Convention on the Rights of Persons with Disabilities. These universal treaties are the bedrock of any credible observation mission.

Regional treaties are often the primary frame of reference for observer missions, given their often-greater resonance within a country, as well as their general consistency with universal instruments. Also, at times, regional treaties contain stronger obligations than are found in the universal instruments. For example, the African Charter on Democracy, Elections and Governance, which came into force in 2012, explicitly commits to "Establish and strengthen independent and impartial national electoral bodies responsible for the management of elections."[7] States also commit to "Ensure fair and equitable access by contesting parties and candidates to state controlled media" and to ensuring that there is a binding code of conduct that includes a commitment by contenders to accept the results or challenge them through exclusively legal channels.

In addition to binding treaties, observer missions refer to authoritative interpretations of treaties made by treaty monitoring bodies, such as the Human Rights Committee for the

ICCPR. Although not binding, these have authority in elaborating the broad principles contained within a treaty and, similarly, with judgments of regional courts. Political declarations often serve as a primary reference framework for those countries that have committed to an agreement, for example, the OSCE's Copenhagen Document. The Universal Declaration of Human Rights (UDHR) is also referred to, with its strong moral authority, as well as UN General Assembly resolutions.

When a matter is not covered by a treaty, related interpretation, or political agreement, then observers turn to recognized good practice. These are techniques and practices known to be the most effective means of implementing electoral processes that meet international commitments. At times, good practices, can be highly authoritative, particularly when endorsed in some way by state authorities, for example the Venice Commission of the Council of Europe.[8]

The Carter Center runs the Elections Obligations and Standards Database (EOS), which contains nearly 200 sources of public international law related to human rights and elections in a searchable format (EOS). It has also published an Elections Obligations and Standards Assessment Manual.[9] This builds on the work of earlier proponents of the use of public international law for assessing elections, as can be found in Guy Goodwin-Gill's 1994 book "Free and Fair Elections, International Law and Practice,"[10] as well as the publications of Markku Suksi.[11]

The Organization of International Observation Missions and Use of International Standards

Election observation missions have to look at the legal provisions for an election and, crucially, what they mean in practice. This is to see if citizens have both the right and the opportunity to take part in an election as is required by the ICCPR.[12] Missions need to see where there is compliance, where problems have arisen or could arise in the future, and the reasons for any shortcomings.

In order to assess the fulfilment of all the commitments related to elections, observation missions must look at more than just election day. However, a mission may not be able to be present for all stages of the process given the costs involved. For example, voter registration and delimitation of constituencies, which are cornerstones of universal and equal franchise referred to in the UDHR and ICCPR, should happen a long time in advance of election day.[13] Even if a mission is not present at the time, it should still consider how such a process was undertaken and if it has contributed to or hindered the fulfilment of electoral rights. The more time a mission has in country, the more comprehensive and rigorous it can be, directly observing different stages of the process.

After election day, it is vital that missions follow the results process and something of the complaints and appeals mechanisms. Access to remedy is a key part of any election process and is generally required under the UDHR and ICCPR.[14] However international observer missions are not always able to stay for the full duration of complaints and appeals processes, given the time involved, and the cost this would incur for extended observation. For example, in Nigeria, complainants have 21 days to lodge a petition, tribunals have 180 days to adjudicate, and then there are 60 days for appeals. Citizen observers are much better placed to undertake such detailed and extended observation.

In order to scrutinize what is happening in reality, not just what is being said in the capital, missions aim to have a broad coverage of observers around the country. This is to provide missions with a consistent picture of what is happening nationwide before, during, and after election day. They should be spread as evenly as possible, so the mission sees the full picture and not just the problem-free or problematic places. However, at times, it will not be possible to get full even coverage due, for example, to security or infrastructure limitations. Long-term observers are typically deployed in multinational teams of two in order to increase reliability and to have a balance of opinion and analysis. Long-term observers should look at all aspects of an election at a regional or local level.

Nearer election day, field coverage is typically supplemented by short-term observers who are deployed to extend observation coverage for the polling, counting, and results process. Again, short-term observers work in multinational teams of two and are deployed, as far as possible, evenly around the country, so the mission has a more complete picture.

Missions are usually led by a Head of Mission or Chief Observer, who have overall lead responsibility for the conclusions of the mission and, therefore, the assessment of a country's compliance with its commitments related to elections. He or she may be present throughout the mission, or make visits depending on other responsibilities and the organization of the mission. He or she is typically supported by a deputy, who is present throughout and has management responsibility for the political, analytical, and methodological aspects of the mission. There is a core team of experts who each assess different aspects of an election, looking at the fulfilment of specific electoral rights. This will typically include: 1) A legal analyst looking at the legislative framework, electoral dispute resolution mechanisms, and electoral offences; 2) an election analyst, looking at the election administration; 3) a political analyst, looking at the campaign, fundamental freedoms, and the actions of parties and candidates; and 4) a media analyst, looking at the freedom, performance, and access to the media. There may also be other specialist analysts, such as a campaign finance expert, depending on the country and the mission.[15]

Election observation missions are often joined by elected members of international parliamentary bodies over the election day period, which adds institutional political weight to conclusions and shows cross-party support to findings. For example, EU missions are often joined by a delegation from the European Parliament, which endorses the findings of the mission.[16] On OSCE/ODIHR missions, the preliminary statement of findings and conclusions, is typically a joint statement by various parliamentary bodies including from the OSCE, Council of Europe, EU, and the North Atlantic Treaty Organization.[17] This enables consistent and clear joint initial conclusions to be given and avoids confusing or contradictory statements from different groups. Consensus on findings and conclusions is much more easily achieved if there is agreement on the framework and standards being used for observation, with clear reference to a country's commitments.

There is a convention of international election observation missions releasing "preliminary statements" a day or two after the completion of polling, when there is intense public and political interest. This enables stakeholders to know what observers have seen and think and can also help promote an informed measured response to an election and any problems arising. However, preliminary statements are limited, as the results process is often on-going at this stage, and this is, of course, as critical as the voting itself. While a preliminary statement is often released with much media attention, what is said later by a mission may not be heard so loudly or clearly. For example, in Kenya, international election observers were subject to strong criticism for seemingly being positive about the process in preliminary statements released just after the polling on August 8, 2017. For the subsequent tabulation of results became highly problematic due to a lack of transparency, eventually resulting in the annulment of the presidential election. While observers had, in fact, called for stronger transparency in the results process, these statements, made without the fanfare of premiers and press conferences, were not remembered, leaving observers looking like they had missed the point.[18]

International observer missions usually release final reports a few months after an election, giving overall conclusions on the whole process and recommendations for improvement for future elections. Increasingly, there is emphasis on promoting national engagement on recommendations to encourage inclusive electoral reform. Some organizations, undertake return visits with the Chief Observer or Head of Mission to present the mission's conclusions and recommendations with more substantive discussions on ways forward.

Credible observation missions are increasingly emphasizing how each recommendation they make contributes to the fulfillment of election rights. Which standards and recommendations are prioritized by a mission depends on the practical and political realities in the country. Typically, the majority of recommendations made by a mission require strengthening by legal reform. This again shows that national legal frameworks are often problematic and, therefore, cannot be the leading framework for assessing an election.

To be effective, observers need to be trusted to work thoroughly and independently and to be clear about what is going well in the election process and what is not. Being critical during the process can be difficult when there is risk that negative commentary could deter voter participation, or if there are serious political or security risks. However, not commenting on issues of concern, either before or promptly after election day, can result in accusations of observers being biased, colluding with corruption, and failing in their basic task of assessing if citizens' rights to electoral participation have been upheld. This can increase agitation and such a loss of credibility can be damaging to the electoral process overall, as well as the reputation of observers and the international community more widely. Not being clear about problems can also undermine future attempts at reform.

The Work of Citizen Observers and the Use of International Standards

Citizen observation is often more comprehensive than international observation, in part due to the more modest financial costs of deployment within a country, as compared to bringing in foreign observers. Not only do citizen observers typically see far more polling and tabulation centers, but they can also bring a different quality to the work. While a team of international observers normally only stay in a polling station for 30 minutes or so, a citizen observer often stays all day from the beginning of polling to the end of the count. Citizen observers also often observe more parts of an election process – for example, voter registration, party primaries, and the petitions process – long before internationals arrive and after they leave. Citizen observers can sometimes more easily deal with large volumes of information given their greater numbers – for example, political finance data put in the public domain. Citizen observers can also provide additional information on an election, including through parallel vote tabulations of results.

Additionally, as citizens of the country, national observers are part of the process, and they can thus take a more active role in upholding people's rights as provided for in domestic legislation and international commitments. For example, citizen observers may lodge complaints and submit legal challenges, which international observers would not do so as not to become part of the process. For this reason, citizen observers may also be called monitors.

Citizen observer groups also have a critical role to play between elections in providing on-going scrutiny of any electoral activities taking place (e.g., off-cycle or by-elections), as well as in advocating for electoral reform. This is critical, as any election process can be improved, and civil society is needed in this to provide independent voices on ways forward that serve the interest of citizens, rather than those of individual parties or the political elite. Therefore, it is very important that citizen observers have the financial resources to work on electoral issues between elections.

A clear framework of law and international standards provides for more focused observation, more consistent and convincing reporting, and clearer legal challenge and advocacy. Without evident reference to a clear framework, it is harder to trust the rigor, neutrality, and conclusions of any observing organization. The importance of this framework was recognized in the 2012, Declaration of Global Principles for Non-Partisan Election Observation and Monitoring by Citizen Organizations (hereafter called the "Declaration of Global Principles").[19] It notes that non-partisan election observation and monitoring by citizen organizations makes observations, assessments, and findings based on the national legal framework and obligations concerning democratic elections that are set forth in international human rights instruments, as well as standards, principles, and commitments presented in international and regional charters, conventions, declarations, and other such documents

Citizen election observation can, therefore, be a rich source of human rights information; however, it is a challenging undertaking and is, in many ways, harder to conduct than international observation. Typically, citizen observation missions are substantially larger, with thousands of observers, sometimes tens of thousands. This presents logistical and also broader organizational challenges in maintaining professional standards amongst such a large number of people working or volunteering on a temporary basis. Citizen observers can also face challenges with trust and accusations of bias, especially given that they are working in their own country and, therefore, have a greater interest in the outcome.

In addition to these inherent challenges, citizen observers can be put under intense political pressure and subject to intimidation. While international observers have the security of leaving a country after completing their work, citizen observers stay and can be subject to greater intimidation and long-term pressure. High profile examples include the arrests and detention for more than two years of Daniel Bekele and Netsenet Demissie in Ethiopia after the 2005 elections, and the detention for over two years of Anar Mammadli in Azerbaijan from December 2013 until March 2016.[20] In addition to such personal risk, there can be organizational threats. For example, during the 2017 Kenyan elections, observing organizations lodging petitions challenging the presidential results were subject to threat of closure of programming and de-registration by state authorities (The EU Election Observation Mission, Kenya, 2017a).[21] As citizen observer groups have a critical transparency, accountability, and advocacy role, international observers must look at the opportunities available to them to undertake their work (UN Committee on Human Rights, 1996, General Comment 25, para. 20).[22]

There can be complementarity between credible international and citizen observer missions, particularly when both are using the same framework of international standards. This can help reinforce messages and reduce the risk of individual observer groups being dismissed or intimidated. Coherence between international and citizen observer groups also increases the chances of treaty bodies and other international entities referring to the findings of observers.

The Challenges in Practice of Using a Framework of Law and International Standards

Using the principles contained in treaties and political commitments can be challenging for various reasons. Firstly, observers have to identify the contributing reasons for non-compliance with obligations and principles, and then work out how harshly or leniently to assess the process. Problems can have very different meanings depending on the context and whether it was possible to avoid these issues. For example, it is understandably difficult and there are some shortcomings if it is the first time that elections are taking place, if there is insecurity in the country, if there is limited infrastructure and resources, etc. Conversely, an observation mission can be expected to be more critical if the problems could have been avoided and they are being dealt with badly without transparency or consultation with stakeholders. This grey zone of assessment involves interpretation of contextual factors and, therefore, different observer missions can sometimes come to varying conclusions.

Secondly, there needs to be consideration of the balance between different rights according to the local context. For example, maximum opportunity for enfranchisement needs to be balanced with safeguards for integrity in the process in order to protect the participation rights of all voters and candidates. So, while allowing anyone to vote who turns up at any polling station increases franchise, the lack of safeguards also increase the risk of fraud. Freedom of expression is similarly critical to an election, ensuring a level playing field for a genuine competitive process. The US puts a strong emphasis on freedom of speech with campaigning seen as part of freedom of expression, and thus there is a comparative lack of limits on campaign spending. In contrast. the European tradition puts more emphasis on promoting a level playing field, and therefore campaign spending limits are more strongly emphasized. The relative prioritization of principles depends on the specific issues and circumstances in a country.

Thirdly, the use of election principles can be delicate, as practical reality is frequently very difficult and complex, often involving compromise and sometimes political settlement. Electoral standards and principles serve as goals to work towards. However, fulfillment can take multiple electoral cycles and, in the meantime, non-compliance with some standards may be accepted as part of the political balance of the country. Indeed, it may be a political necessity in order to avoid violence and national breakdown. Observers need not only to be clear about shortcomings and identify realistic ways forward to help strengthen electoral participation in the future, but also to be mindful of the "do no harm" principle.

Fourthly, treaties contain only broad principles. Positively, this provides states with a wide margin of discretion, so that elections can be held according to the specific circumstances of each country. However, at times, such broad principles can be difficult to work with, as they can be understood in very different ways. While authoritative interpretation of treaties by treaty monitoring bodies gives specific information on how principles can be understood, this is not binding and treaty body comments do not cover all subjects.[23]

Fifthly, there are some gaps and international standards for elections are subject to development as election understanding and issues change and the human rights environment evolves. One striking example of this is the expansion of obligations related to the political participation of persons with disabilities. In 1996, General Comment 25 gave authoritative interpretation of the ICCPR, stipulating that "established mental incapacity may be a ground for denying a person the right to vote or to hold office" (UN Committee on Human Rights, General Comment 25, para. 4, 1996). However, a different approach was subsequently taken in the Convention on the Rights of Persons with Disabilities, which came into force in 2008 and, at the time of writing, has 177 states party to the treaty. Rather than removing legal capacity (and substituting decision-making), the convention focuses on access and support for persons with disabilities in order to enable participation, including in regards to elections (UN General Assembly, Convention on the Rights of Persons with Disabilities, General Comment 1, 2008).[24]

Transparency in public services is another area where there has been increased reference in international instruments. However, more is still warranted in regards to elections. Neither ICCPR article 25 nor UDHR article 21 makes reference to transparency in regards to electoral processes. This gap has been somewhat lessened with the 2011 General Comment 34 by the Human Rights Committee. This notes that "States parties should proactively put in the public domain Government information of public interest" (UN Committee on Human Rights, General Comment 34, para. 19, 2011). However, this is only authoritative interpretation and is, therefore, not binding. The 2005 Convention Against Corruption also includes some provisions; however, these are also not specifically focused on electoral transparency and somewhat discretionary language is used.[25] Without transparency from the election administration, there is risk of a lack of trust in the institution, the process, and ultimately the results and outcome.

There are various other recurring electoral issues that could, in the future, be addressed more specifically and substantially by international instruments and bodies. For example, stakeholder consultations by election administrations, as well as by parliaments, during legal reform processes.[26] The same holds true of provisions and protections for observers, and guidelines on media coverage of elections particularly state-funded media. More explicit references could also be made to political finance transparency requirements and to party functioning, given the public function that parties serve.

The role of security forces in elections has regularly been the subject of controversy and, therefore, stronger principles could be elaborated, as, for example, has been laid out in the OSCE/ODIHR Guidelines for Public Security Provides in Elections.[27] Further direction on the role and principles for judicial oversight of elections could also be useful. For example, there was extensive controversy after the surprise ruling of the Kenyan Supreme Court nullifying the August 2017 presidential elections because of inadequacies in the results process without primarily referring to the margin of victory.[28]

There are various additional new issues emerging in the digital era. These include the misuse of personal data and online threats to democratic debate and understanding. For example, insufficient transparency requirements for social media platforms are criticized for enabling material that insidiously interferes in opinion formation, perpetuates the use of hateful language and disinformation, and increases the risk of antagonism and violence.

A lack of explicit reference in international instruments to such electoral issues leaves citizen and international observers more exposed, as there is a framework gap when making an assessment and formulating recommendations. To compensate for this, observers produce guidelines, at times, so that their positions are clear in advance and there is consistency in conclusions between missions deployed.[29] More importantly, the lack of explicit reference to various issues also leaves countries with less authoritative guidance to draw upon when developing their policies, legislation, and practices. The development of standards for elections is sensitive and challenging, requiring consensus. However, it may be argued to be particularly warranted now due to the fact that elections are becoming more established in many countries in recent decades, that new issues are arising, and that there is a need to promote confidence in democratic engagement through elections that citizens trust.

Notes

1 For more information on OSCE/ODIHR election observation missions, see the 2010 OSCE/ODIHR Election Observation Handbook: Sixth Edition, OSCE/ODIHR.

2 2005, Declaration of Principles for International Election Observation and Code of Conduct, United Nations.

3 European Union. (2012). *EU strategic framework and action plan on human rights and democracy*. Similarly, the 2015 *EU Action Plan on Democracy and Human Rights* calls for elaboration of best practices and more thorough follow-up on recommendations.

4 2016, OSCE/ODIHR *Handbook on the Follow-up of Electoral Recommendations*, OSCE/ODIHR.

5 The EU's Compendium of International Standards for Elections notes "The term 'international standards…refers to the principles defined in international instruments, including political declarations, and to the clarification and interpretation that has developed within the framework of human rights bodies and courts to specify the scope of application and content of these principles." 2016, *Compendium of International Standards for Elections*, fourth edition, Election Observation and Democratic Support (EODS) for the European Union.

6 For further information, see the UN treaty status page.

7 2012, African Charter on Democracy, Elections and Governance, African Union, Article 17.

8 The Venice commission is formally called the European Commission for Democracy through Law. It is the Council of Europe's advisory body on constitutional matters. It has 61 members from the 47 Council of Europe member states and 14 other countries. The commission shares standards and best practices. It has adopted more than 130 opinions and over 60 texts. Most notably, the Code of Good Practice in Electoral Matters, adopted in 2002.

9 2014, *Election Obligations and Standards: A Carter Center Assessment Manual*, The Carter Center. Available in English, French, and Spanish.

10 Goodwin-Gill, Guy, 1994, *Free and Fair Elections, International Law and Practice*, Inter-Parliamentary Union. This was followed by an expanded edition published in 2006.

11 See, for example, Hinz, Veronica, and Markku Suksi, 2003, *Election Elements: On the International Standards of Electoral Participation*, Institute for Human Rights, Abo Akadmi University.

12 *International Covenant for Civil and Political Rights*, article 25 states: "Every citizen shall have the right and the opportunity...without unreasonable restrictions: (a) to take part in the conduct of public affairs, directly or through freely chosen representatives (b) To vote and to be elected at genuine periodic elections which shall be by universal and equal suffrage and shall be held by secret ballot, guaranteeing the free expression of the will of the electors."

13 See UDHR article 21 and ICCPR article 25.

14 See UDHR article 8 and ICCPR article 2.

15 In addition, there is typically a coordinator who is responsible for managing all field observation work by long-term and short-term observers. Some organizations also deploy dedicated press officers responsible for managing a mission's media coverage. Closer to election day, a statistics analyst typically joins a mission to process the data from observers' findings on election day when standard checklists are used during observation of polling stations and results tabulation centers.

16 For more information on EU election observation missions, see the 2016 Handbook for European Union Election Observation, Third Edition, European Union.

17 For more information on OSCE/ODIHR election observation missions, see the 2010 OSCE/ODIHR Election Observation Handbook: Sixth Edition, OSCE/ODIHR.

18 For example, on August 16, 2017, the EU Election Observation Mission to Kenya released a statement calling for *prompt publication of all results forms, rule of law to be followed and the need for space for civil society*. Also see, on August 17, 2017, "Carter Center Urges Kenyan Election Commission to Finalize Posting of Results."

19 2012, Declaration of Global Principles for Non-Partisan Election Observation and Monitoring by Citizen Organizations. See the Global Network of Domestic Election Monitors (GNDEM) for more information. GNDEM has 251 member organizations in 89 countries and territories, as well as regional network members. This Declaration of Global Principles followed on from the "Declaration of Principles for International Election Observation."

20 Many statements were made by the international community, see for example a statement by the OSCE/ODIHR Director condemning the sentencing of Anar Mammadli for five and a half years, Warsaw, May 2014. In September 2014, Mammadii was awarded the Vaclav Havel Human Rights Prize by the Parliamentary Assembly of the Council of Europe. Similarly, Daniel Bekele and Netsenet Demissie were internationally recognized as prisoners of conscience and nominated for various international awards.

21 The EU Election Observation Mission, Kenya 2017, final report notes "During the election, seven civil society organisations and networks were subject to intimidating actions by the NGOs Coordination Board just before each of the two deadlines for lodging presidential petitions (in August and November). Without a clear legal basis, the Board issued letters to them that demanded *inter alia* that they cease all political operations, including all electoral-related programmes." Pages 7 and 42.

22 Human Rights Committee, 1996, General Comment 25, paragraph 20, states "There should be independent scrutiny of the voting and counting process." The Declaration of Principles states "International election observation missions should evaluate and report on whether domestic nonpartisan election monitoring and observation organizations are able, on a non-discriminatory basis, to conduct their activities without undue restrictions or interference."

23 In particular, the Human Rights Committee monitors the ICCPR, and its general comments provide guidance, including specifically on article 25 of the treaty. Similarly, general recommendation 23 by the Committee for the Convention on the Elimination of All Forms of Discrimination Against Women elaborates on Article 7 of the treaty, which addresses women's participation in political and public life. General recommendations 5 and 25 are also relevant in covering temporary special measures.

24 The treaty body has consequently stated that the treaty does not permit the removal of legal capacity based on mental or intellectual disability. Neither general nor individualized court decisions are acceptable bases for the removal of suffrage rights. Convention on the Rights of Persons with Disabilities, 2008, General Comment 1, 2014 on equal recognition before the law.

25 For example, article 13 states: "Each State Party shall take appropriate measures, within its means and in accordance with fundamental principles of its domestic law, to promote the active participation of individuals and groups outside the public sector…This participation should be strengthened by such measures as: (b) Ensuring that the public has effective access to information." Convention Against Corruption, Article 13, 2005.

26 Positively the Convention Against Corruption in article 13 notes: "Each State Party shall take appropriate measures…to promote the active participation of individuals and groups outside the public sector, such as civil society, non-governmental organizations and community-based organizations, in the prevention of and the fight against corruption." This could be further strengthened through explicit reference on the importance of election management bodies regularly consulting with stakeholders. The OSCE and others have emphasized the value of consultation during reviews of electoral legislation. For example, the *OSCE/ODIHR Follow-up Handbook* notes that consultation and inclusion are part of five good practices listed for follow-up to electoral recommendations. *OSCE/ODIHR Handbook on the Follow-up of Electoral Recommendations*, 2016, page 31 (see also page 23).

27 2017, OSCE/ODIHR Guidelines for Public Security Provides in Elections, OSCE/ODIHR.

28 The EU election observation mission, Kenya 2017, final report, noted this was "a landmark ruling in focusing not on the *outcome* of the election but on the constitutional requirements of the results *process*…The strong emphasis on results transparency and verifiability, not just for candidates but also for citizens, appears to have contributed to increased integrity in the electoral process. This could ultimately increase confidence in future electoral processes. However, the decision for a fresh presidential election to be held within the constitutionally-stipulated 60-day limit posed immediate implementation challenges (during this period, there was also an escalation of political tensions)."

29 See, for example, some OSCE/ODIHR handbooks, and the 2016 Handbook for European Union Election Observation, Third Edition, European Union.

References

African Union. (2012). *African charter on democracy, elections and governance.*

Election Observation and Democratic Support (EODS) for the European Union. (2016). *The compendium of international standards for elections* (4th ed.).

EU Election Observation Mission to Kenya. (2017a). *Final report.*

EU Election Observation Mission to Kenya. (2017b). *Statement calling for prompt publication of all results forms, rule of law to be followed and the need for space for civil society.*

European Union. (2012). *EU strategic framework and action plan on human rights and democracy.*

European Union. (2016). *Handbook for European Union election observation* (3rd ed.).

Goodwin-Gill, G.S. (1994). *Free and fair elections, international law and practice.* Geneva: Inter-Parliamentary Union.

Goodwin-Gill, G.S. (2006). *Free and fair elections* (New expanded ed.). Geneva: Inter-Parliamentary Union.

Hinz, V., & Markku, S. (2003). *Election elements: On the international standards of electoral participation.* Turku/Abo: Institute for Human Rights, Abo Akadmi University.

OSCE/ODIHR. (2010). *OSCE/ODIHR election observation handbook* (6th ed.).

OSCE/ODIHR. (2014). *Statement by the OSCE/ODIHR Director condemning the sentencing of Anar Mammadli for 5½ years.*

OSCE/ODIHR. (2016). *OSCE/ODIHR handbook on the follow-up of electoral recommendations.*

The Carter Center. (2014). *Election obligations and standards: A Carter Center assessment manual.*

The Carter Center. (2017). *Carter Center urges Kenyan Election Commission to finalize posting of result.*

UN Committee on Human Rights. (1996). *General comment 25.*

UN Committee on Human Rights. (2011). *General comment 34.*

UN Committee on the Elimination of Discrimination against Women. (1988). *General recommendation 5.*

UN Committee on the Elimination of Discrimination against Women. (1997). *General recommendation 23.*

UN Committee on the Elimination of Discrimination against Women. (2004). *General recommendation 25.*

UN General Assembly. (1948). *The universal declaration of human rights.*

UN General Assembly. (1966). *International covenant on civil and political rights.*
UN General Assembly. (1979). *Elimination of all forms of discrimination against women.*
UN General Assembly. (2005). *Convention against corruption.*
UN General Assembly. (2008). *Convention on the rights of persons with disabilities.*
United Nations. (2005). *Declaration of principles for international election observation and code of conduct.*
Venice Commission. (2002). *Code of good practice in electoral matters.*

12
ELECTION DISPUTES, COMPLAINTS, AND APPEALS

Bob Watt

Introduction

In this chapter, we will consider the legal basis for challenging elections. Without being in the least flippant, because the matter is so serious, it should be recalled that the legal method is far preferable to the alternatives (Hatchard, 2015; 'Nyane, 2018; Omotola, 2008).[1] Denis Petit (see Petit, 2000, 5), points out that electoral disputes are both inherent to elections and proof of the vitality and strength of an electoral system.

Most of the 195 countries of the world hold some form of elections, but whether these elections offer any real choice or can be considered democratic is quite another matter. One respected source, Freedom House (2019), suggests that 44% of countries may be considered free, 30% partly free, and 26% not free.[2] Clearly, whether we are dealing with 86 (free) countries or 195 countries, a detailed consideration of the electoral laws of those included on such a list is impossible within these bounds and so we will consider only general principles. There is one further methodological point that should be made. In this chapter, we will consider election petitions mounted at a variety of levels – presidential, member of the legislature, and local government (and, briefly, challenges to referendums). This is because of the relative paucity of modern election petitions and because many legal principles are common to all types of petition; nevertheless, it should be noted that that the European regional human rights instrument applies only to elections to the legislature (see, for example *Malarde v. France* Application 46813/99).[3]

In 1948, the community of nations expressed the aspiration that "the will of the people" should be the basis of the authority of government and that will should be expressed in periodic, genuine elections held by secret ballot or equivalent free voting procedure (United Nations, 1948, Art. 21(3)). The Preamble to the Universal Declaration expressed the hope that such human rights should be protected by the rule of law, but it took a further 28 years for the legally binding Article 25(b) of the International Covenant on Civil and Political Rights to come into force in March 1976 (United Nations, 1966b). The legal right is expressed in terms similar to those found in the declaration, and the Article 25 right is expanded by the Human Rights Committee's General Comment of July 12, 1996 (United Nations, 1996).

The core right, at least for the purposes of this essay, seems to be encapsulated in General Comment 20, which provides for (*inter alia*) independent supervision of the electoral process to ensure that the election is conducted in accordance with laws that are compatible with

 DOI: 10.4324/9780429401800-12

the covenant, protection for voters from interference with their free exercise of the franchise, and access to judicial review (or equivalent process) to ensure that voters have confidence in the result of the election. It is notable that the general comment uses the word "free" or its cognates some 29 times, but it only uses the word "fair" once. If one accepts that the phrase "free and fair elections" has passed into the, at least expert, discourse[4] (and, as we shall see, some constitutions), it suggests that the main concern addressed in the covenant and the general comment is "freedom from state or official interference" rather than private interference or fairness between the parties. The right appears, thus, to be more "vertical" (between the citizen and the state[5]) than "horizontal" (between citizens) and this may – and it will be argued, does – amount to an important limitation on the right to free and fair elections. However, when one looks at the reported cases in, for example, the states of the Council of Europe (see Council of Europe, 2019) or South Africa, or Kenya, one can only easily find "vertical" cases, so these would appear to be in the majority. That does not make "horizontal" cases any less important for, as we shall see, these cases may warrant special treatment.

There are two additional important limitations to the right apart from the difficulty of applying international treaty obligations in the domestic law of some jurisdictions. General Comment 21 makes it clear that the covenant does not mandate any particular electoral system. This point is also made in at least one of the Regional Human Rights Instruments – the European Convention on Human Rights, in Article 3 of the First Protocol (P1Art3)[6] – the jurisprudence of which held that the electoral systems of the High Contracting Parties are subject to a wide margin of appreciation (see *Mathieu-Mohin & Clerfayt v. Belgium* 9267/81 at para. 52). There are other limitations on the effectiveness of P1Art3. which will be considered below, but the point is clear. Before leaving, at least for a while, the jurisprudence of P1Art3, it is essential to note that Article 6 ECHR does not apply to electoral challenges (*Pierre-Bloch v. France* 20/1996/732/938), and P1Art 3 does not apply to referendums *Moohan & Gillon v. United Kingdom* 22962/15 & 23345/15).

The other important limitation, which could be seen as an extension of General Comment 21's "wide margin of appreciation" principle was extensively analyzed by Wallis JA in the South African Constitutional Court in the local government election petition case of *Kham and Others v. Electoral Commission and Another* [2015] ZACC 37. Here the court was called upon to interpret the meaning of "free, fair, (and regular) elections" contained in Section 19(2) of the South African Constitution (1996). In the course of a long, careful, and valuable judgment, Wallis JA points out (*Kham* at para. 34, see also Notes 25 and 26) that there is no internationally accepted definition of the term "free and fair election" and that practice amongst international election observers has been to move away from the use of the term. Practice since the 1990s has been to consider the conduct of the election in its own context and to make a value judgement as to whether the election was a legitimate expression of the will of the people. Whilst Wallis JA advances a number of indicia of fairness in the context of the particular election and the extant challenge, he had already observed (in Note 26, see Bjornlund, 2004, 96–128) that such indicia are unreliable. Clearly, this difficulty over internationally applicable and consistent standards for the conduct of elections has serious consequences for the identification of substantive principles for determining election petitions. This will become clear when we consider the results obtained in particular electoral challenges; however, we will be identifying some principles that seem (mostly) to hold firm.

Amongst the substantive matters we need to consider are two important matters. We could call these "doctrinal." One was considered by Wallis AJ in *Kham* and is a matter of varying practice throughout the world. The question is the level of electoral irregularity that ought to be sufficient to warrant overturning a controverted election and forcing it, as far as possible, to be rerun. There are a number of cases from a variety of jurisdictions to consider and the leading cases in United Kingdom law (and the unusual jurisdiction here is deliberately highlighted) are strongly criticized despite their international application. The other concerns the burden of proof placed on the person who alleges wrongdoing. Do they have to prove their case on the civil standard (balance of probabilities), the criminal standard (beyond reasonable doubt), or according to some intermediate standard?

The lack of consistent substantive principles for challenge does not mean that there is a lack of procedures for challenge. The problem is that the international law basis for these standards rests (at best) in "soft law" and (at worst) in codes of practice. Denis Petit (Petit, 2000, 4–5) observes that mechanisms for the resolution of electoral disputes are not contained in international legal standards, but takes the view that, through an examination of the various soft law instruments and guidance, a set of principles can be discerned.

It seems that, from their disparate viewpoints, Wallis JA and Denis Petit are agreed that there are some core or common principles, although the application of these principles varies from country to country. The task of this short chapter is to tease these principles out; whilst it must be emphasized that it is artificial (and impossible) to draw a rigid distinction between procedural, doctrinal, and substantive matters, to do so will assist the flow and structure of their elucidation and the argument.

This brings us to the final point before entering a discussion of these matters; it applies to them all and must act as a check upon the overzealous use (or success) of electoral challenges. Weaker or stronger words to this effect appear almost ubiquitously in electoral challenges – even in those that are successful. Even when an election is so tainted by corruption that it should be overturned, it must be remembered that many or most of those voting for the tainted successful candidate did so innocently; they voted for the candidate freely and fairly because they honestly believed that s/he would prove to be the best representative of the electors. Overturning even a grossly corrupt election risks damaging the electoral process because honest voters may lose faith in voting. For that reason, it is essential that any electoral challenge must be held in open court with the greatest possible explanation and widest possible publicity for the result. Even before a case is brought, heard, or a judgment is obtained, it means that applications, procedures, evidential tests, and the law itself must fall in a narrow window between inviting casual applications and making successful challenges well-nigh impossible.

Procedures for Electoral Challenges

The United Kingdom's Electoral Commission[7] has, despite its regrettable lack of powers, produced a valuable report, showing how the UK's Election Petition[8] system falls short of the applicable international standards (Electoral Commission, 2012). The value of the work to this chapter is to provide a helpful list of the sources applicable, in the main, in wider Europe and indicate core procedural requirements.

The Electoral Commission's Report is based upon three main sources: The International Institute for Democracy and Electoral Assistance (IDEA, 2002), the Council of Europe's Venice Commission (Venice Commission, 2003) and the Organisation for Security and Cooperation in Europe's Office for Democratic Institutions and Human Rights (the OSCE / ODIHR, Petit *op. cit.*). These may be consulted for full details, but a distillation of their principles may be set out much more briefly.

Procedures for electoral challenges should be (a) established by law; (b) speedy in terms of both the application process and the delivery of a result; (c) readily available to political parties, candidates, voters, and citizens, and readily usable (both financially and procedurally)[9] by all these groups; (d) electoral officials, who are often best placed to see fraud, should have the power to bring proceedings; and (d) the outcome of the initial trial should be appealable through the courts. These provisions sound admirable and, as the Electoral Commission points out, the UK's own election petition procedures fall far short of these standards.[10] However, the international standards are all, to some extent, outdated because of the growth of social media and the phenomenon of "crowd-funding."[11] If it becomes easy (procedurally and financially) to bring an election petition, it may become possible for those dissatisfied with the result of an election on purely political grounds (their favored candidate lost the election) to mount a challenge as a political tactic and, by repeated challenges, erode faith in democracy. This potential problem is, in fact, easily surmountable. General Comment 20 to Article 25 ICCPR suggests that (some) challenges to elections should be brought by "judicial review or other equivalent procedure." Most jurisdictions operate a "leave" or "permission" stage in applications for judicial review and there should be no real difficulty in allowing for an independent or judicial determination of whether there is an "arguable case" to go before a court for a full hearing. It might be argued that this is a proper task for an independent, expert Electoral Commission. The difficulty with this last suggestion is, of course, that some election petitions are mounted against electoral commissions or other electoral authorities (*Raila Amolo Odinga & another v. Independent Electoral and Boundaries Commission and Others.* (Presidential Election Petition No 1 of 2017, Supreme Court of Kenya); *Sauvé v. A-G Canada, Chief Electoral Officer of Canada and Others* 2002 SCC 68 and *Kham* (above)).

Substantive Challenges

There are at least four types of substantive challenge to elections; clearly, the typology set out here could itself be subdivided within the postulated headings into a number of sub-classes. The first three are vertical, the fourth horizontal. The first type, which may be challenged by direct electoral challenge or, where it is available, constitutional judicial review, is where the nation's electoral law is alleged to be outside the provisions of the national Constitution or, e.g., the European Convention of Human Rights. The second type of challenge is where the state is alleged to have failed to follow the electoral law or interfered with the election. The third type of challenge may be mounted where the independent election authority (of whatever type) fails to conduct the election properly. The fourth type of challenge is where one of the parties to the election (usually, but not necessarily, the winning candidate or party) corrupts or attempts to corrupt the election. To further complicate matters, some of these classes may overlap (*In the Matter of the Parliamentary Election for Fermanagh and South Tyrone held on 7 June 2001* [2001] NIQB 36).

The first class of a constitutional challenge of an aspect of election law is well-represented in the "prisoner voting" cases where the right to vote is protected in a country's own constitution or the ECHR, e.g., in (respectively) South Africa or Canada or the UK (*August and Another v. Electoral Commission and Others* [1999] ZACC 3, *Sauvé* (above), *Hirst v. United Kingdom (No 2)*, no. 74025/01, and *Moohan v. Lord Advocate* [2014] UKSC 67, esp. para. 3.

The second class of a state acting in breach of its own established electoral law is to be found in cases such as *Upaskich v. Lithuania* 14737/08, and *Kerimova v. Azerbaijan* 20799/06. In this second case, the state wrongfully invalidated an election because of a minor breach of election rules that would not have affected the result. This draws attention to the important issue, which will be considered below, of the severity of the breach required to invalidate the election. One might also consider cases where subdivisions of a sovereign state chose to challenge or ignore national law under this heading. It is instructive to read Warren CJ's Opinion in *South Carolina v. Katzenbach* 383 US 301 (1966) (which falls between classes 1 and 2 above) for an account of the mechanisms by which some (southern) states sought to avoid the provisions of the Fifteenth Amendment to the US Constitution and the Voting Rights Act 1965.

The third class, where an error by the body supervising the election has formed the basis of a complaint, may be exemplified by cases such as *Kham* (the Kenyan Presidential Election Petition case), and the – on the one hand minor (since the electoral consequences of the successful petition were extremely limited) and, on the other hand, major (since a precedent which has been applied worldwide was established) – English case of *Morgan v. Simpson* [1975] QB 151.

The fourth class, where non-state actors such as opposing candidates and political parties interfere with the freedom of an election were historically the largest class of sources of election petitions in the United Kingdom. Between 1870 and 1925, O'Malley and Hardcastle's Reports (O'M & H) catalogue hundreds of election petitions based on allegations of personation (the English legal term for impersonation), bribery, treating (which is bribery by means of gifts of goods, food, or drink), intimidation of various sorts, breaching election spending limits, or making false allegations about a candidate's personal character. These categories recited in the English law contain many of the usual electoral offences; Wallis AJ in *Kham* (para. 86) further lists as additional potential grounds for electoral challenge:

> (denial of) the freedom to canvass; to advertise; and to engage in the activities normal for a person seeking election. Phenomena like "no go" areas; the denial of facilities for the conduct of meetings; disruption of meetings; the destruction of advertising material or the intimidation of candidates, workers or supporters.

Despite the fact that this was the largest class at the end of the nineteenth century, it has now almost faded from legal view on an international stage. It remains important domestically.

It should be clear, in any event, that there are a huge number of ways in which rival political parties and candidates can seek to unfairly disrupt each other's activities. The question for a state (in designing legislation) and for the courts (in interpreting that legislation) is to decide which activities are lawful, or ought to be lawful, and which should be unlawful.

It is surely beyond doubt that everyone would agree that personation, bribery, and any form of candidate or voter intimidation should be unlawful, but a more difficult issue is that of lying about another candidate or party's policies or character. This is particularly topical because of the vigorous public debate concerning truth in political advertising and disinformation ("fake news") in the internet age. This debate is of vital importance, but the detail is outside the scope of this chapter; a question will, however, be raised at the end.[12] A matter of this sort has arisen on three separate recent occasions (*Rowe*, *Woolas*, and *Carmichael*) in the courts in the United Kingdom.[13] One of these cases, involving the unseated MP Phil Woolas, is of particular note in the present context because it raises the important issue of the right to freedom of speech under Article 10 of the European Convention of Human Rights. particularly as applied in *Bowman v. UK* 141/1996/760/961, para. 42 and, of course, General Comments 8, 12, and 25 of the UNHRC's General Comment on Article 25 ICCPR, which emphasize the importance of freedom of expression in electoral matters.

In *R (on the Application of Woolas) v. The Election Court and Others* [2010] EWHC 3169, Woolas sought to challenge the decision of the Election Court [2010] EWHC 2702, which deprived him of the seat for the Oldham East and Saddleworth Constituency on the basis that he was held to have lied about the personal character of his opponent, Watkins, contrary to s.106 Representation of the People Act 1983 Section 106, makes it unlawful to make false assertions of fact about the personal character of an election candidate in order to affect the election result.[14] Domestic election law does not, by statute, explicitly make it unlawful to lie about your opponent's political policies, except, as we shall see, by extension in the circumstances outlines in *Rowe*. Woolas was held to have falsely claimed that Watkins had actual links with terrorists and was unseated. The important issue, however, is the link with lying about political policies. Domestic law only prohibits personal smears, and does not explicitly prohibit political lies. However, in *R (on the application of Woolas)*, which applied the *Lingens* test of striking a balance between the severity of the effect on the election with the importance of free political debate, the court said:

> 103. The right of freedom of expression does not extend to the publishing, before or during an election for the purpose of affecting the return of any candidate at an election, of a statement that is made dishonestly, that is to say when the publisher knows that statement to be false or does not believe it to be true. It matters not whether such a statement relates to the political position of a candidate or to the personal character or conduct of a candidate when the publisher or maker makes that statement dishonestly. The right to freedom of expression under Article 10 does not extend to a right to be dishonest and tell lies, but s.106 is more limited in its scope as it refers to false statements made in relation to a candidate's personal character or conduct.

This establishes an important point that, if it was endorsed by the European Court of Human Rights, would establish a valuable precedent. It is difficult to see how the Strasbourg Court could disagree with this position.

However, before this conclusion is finally endorsed, we need to consider two important issues of legal doctrine.

Doctrinal Issues

Here, we will consider the burden of proof of the evidence that needs to discharged in order to overturn an election, and then, critically, the amount or type of wrongdoing that is needed to invalidate an election.

"Burden of proof" is a concept particular to Common Law jurisdictions (Clermont & Sherwin, 2002). It seems that there is much less debate about the concept in civilian jurisdictions, where the facts simply have to be proved to an extent that satisfies the judge of the facts.[15] It would seem from the literature that the matter is of particular concern in the countries of the British Commonwealth because their legal systems are closely derivative of the British model. Hatchard's study is helpful in this respect, but may be summarized by pointing out that, in order to overturn an election in the United Kingdom, it is necessary for the plaintiff to prove to allegation of electoral wrongdoing beyond reasonable doubt (i.e., the standard of proof used in criminal trials), for authority see *R v. Rowe ex parte Mainwaring and Others* [1992] 1 WLR 1059. In other countries, statute may provide for other, lesser, standards of proof such as "on the balance of probabilities" (the civil standard of proof), as an example see *Jugnauth v. Ringadoo & Others* [2008] UKPC 50. The Court of Appeal (of England and Wales) took the view that the criminal standard of proof was appropriate because many of the ways in which elections may be disrupted by rival candidates or parties also amount to criminal offences, and it is undesirable that differing standards of proof (criminal and civil) be used on the same facts. The problem with this approach is, in those countries such as the United Kingdom, where the election petition procedure is brought not by an electoral commission or other electoral officials, the process of bringing evidence before the court may well taint it such that the police and criminal prosecutorial authorities will not use it.

This problem of the lack of agreement about the appropriate standard of evidence needed to overthrow an election is indicative of the difficulty in setting international standards in electoral law. This difficulty goes far beyond that faced by electoral law scholars trying to make sense of a confused and confusing set of decisions from a variety of jurisdictions, because it allow the legitimacy of international human rights standards to be called into doubt.[16] Where a set of differing standards applies in electoral matters, it is sometimes difficult to understand what should fall inside or outside a wide margin of appreciation.

For our final example of the issue of doctrinal problems in the law, we turn to the test that should be applied in order to decide whether an election should be overturned. The matter is – at the extremes – easy to resolve. No one would say that an election should be overturned where say, ten voters were unlawfully deprived of their right to vote where the winning Candidate A obtains one million votes and the losing Candidate B obtains one hundred thousand votes. The answer is clear but, as we shall see, problematic. This approach, as we shall see, is sometimes called "the numbers game." The alternative approach is to look at the magnitude of the wrongdoing that led to the challenge. Did it affect the fairness of the election? Both of these approaches have been used and both, as we shall see, have drawbacks.

The leading case of the "numbers game," an English case, which has been followed or replicated worldwide is *Morgan v. Simpson* [1975] QB 151. Here, the Court of Appeal overturned an election in which a small, but significant, number of ballot papers had not been validated by election staff. The procedure for validating papers, which had been designed more than 100 years before the disputed election in completely different electoral circumstances, had not been followed because improperly trained staff had been used. It was a simple, careless error and there was no intention to corrupt the election. The problem was that the number of unvalidated, and therefore void, ballot papers exceeded the margin between the two candidates. The court, led by Denning MR, had no hesitation in voiding the election. The problem is not in the result, but in the doctrine developed. The doctrine was held to be that an election should only be voided when the number of disputed votes exceeded the margin between the parties.[17] The application of this test led, in a Northern Irish case, to a quite extraordinary result. In *Fermanagh and South Tyrone*, a polling station was overwhelmed by supporters of one of the parties and forced to stay open for an extra 30 minutes beyond close of poll. The margin between the parties was some 34 votes, but the court determined, on the basis of no apparent evidence, that fewer than 34 votes had been cast in that time and so the election must stand. As a matter of pure electoral law, this cannot be correct; the decision was perhaps colored by the need to maintain the peace process in Northern Ireland and the fact that the MP elected belonged to the abstentionist, Irish Republican party Sinn Fein and would not take up her seat. If that were the case, it would be an example of political considerations operating in the judicial sphere, a suggestion that, although it sounds heretical, should not be easily dismissed.

One could argue that *Fermanagh and South Tyrone* was simply a misapplication of the law. In *Odinga & Others v. IEC*, where *Morgan v. Simpson* was applied in order to fulfill the provision of the Kenyan Constitution that a candidate should clearly obtain more than 50% of the popular vote, the full ratio of *Morgan* was set out at paragraph 647. This shows that *Morgan* should be limited (if it is applied at all) to cases in which the election was **badly conducted** (emphasis in *Odinga*), rather than in cases where the election was **corrupted** (my emphasis).

This now returns us to a consideration of *Kham*. In *Kham*, the election was, no doubt, badly conducted; the South African Electoral Commission had clearly failed in its duties.[18] However, the margin of votes between the candidates was so large that the numbers game approach[19] endorsed in Morgan would lead to the election being upheld. If the election was upheld, it would provide an endorsement to the South African Electoral Commission's sloppy and clearly unacceptable approach.[20] This would allow the commission to continue to produce defective electoral rolls that merely recorded the district in which a voter lived. This might have the advantage of being inclusive, or maximizing the number of eligible voters. This is, of course, meritorious and tends to support the aim of making the will of the people the basis of government. The problems inherent in such a careless approach are that, first, it makes checking the electoral entitlement of the putative voter difficult or impossible; second, it inhibits effective political campaigning.

Since the *Morgan* approach is flawed, we should consider the alternative. Wallis AJ in *Kham* (paras. 88–90) identifies this as the "value judgment" approach. According to this standard, the freedom and fairness of an election must be judged against "constitutional" standards. Here, of course, Wallis AJ was referring to the standards embedded in the South African Constitution, notably Sections 1(d) and 19. Equally, and with regard to other states, one might well envisage similar provisions of national constitutions, which give effect to the standards contained in Article 25 ICCPR.[21] One might also consider the important hard and soft legal standards stemming ultimately from the Universal Declaration of Human Rights, Article 25 ICCPR, and the Regional Instruments.

Clearly the overzealous (and deliberately oppressive) adoption of the "value judgment" approach by the political authorities may lead, as in the case of *Kerimova v. Azerbaijan*, to an injustice, but a court correctly exercising a constitutional function may correct the "error." In *Kerimova* (para. 44), the European Court of Human Rights said:

> It is, however, for the Court to determine in the last resort whether the requirements of Article 3 of Protocol No. 1 have been complied with. In particular, it has to satisfy itself that the conditions do not curtail the rights in question to such an extent as to impair their very essence and deprive them of their effectiveness; that they are imposed in pursuit of a legitimate aim; and that the means employed are not disproportionate. Such conditions must not thwart the free expression of the people in the choice of the legislature – in other words, they must reflect, or not run counter to, the concern to maintain the integrity and effectiveness of an electoral procedure aimed at identifying the will of the people through universal suffrage.

Clearly, Wallis AJ used very similar words in *Kham*, and one might read the judgment of the Kenyan Supreme Court upholding the 50% of votes provision of the Kenyan Constitution in the same way if one were to disregard the erroneous distraction of the Morgan "numbers game" argument. This argument would suggest that *Fermanagh and South Tyrone* was, as a matter of law (and with hindsight) wrongly decided. The political and social consequences of overturning that election result cannot be underestimated. That having been said, the "constitutional test" – was the election, all things considered, conducted in such a way as to give expression to the will of the people – appears, at least in this short and selective survey, to be the developing global standard.

Having drawn that optimistic conclusion, we should look again, in this era of "disinformation and fake news" at the phenomenon of "political lying."[22] In a range of circumstances too numerous to recount,[23] and apparently protected by constitutional protection of freedom of speech, especially the First Amendment to the Constitution of the United States, untruths have been told about political opponents. It should be noted that, in both *Woolas* and *Vitrenko v. Ukraine* 23510/02, the speech in question fell below the freedom of speech provision (Article 10) of the

European Convention of Human Rights; furthermore, it is acknowledged that it is difficult, if not impossible, to draw a dividing line between a lie and mere vulgar abuse.[24]

While it is acknowledged that abusing political opponents is popular (in both senses – frequent, and – earning public endorsement) it is surely open to question whether a public culture of political abuse or lying is compatible with either the first sentence of the Preamble to the Universal Declaration of Human Rights – the recognition of the inherent dignity and equal rights of all persons – or the derivative third paragraph of the Preamble to the ICCPR – freedom from fear where everyone may enjoy civil and political rights. For that reason, it is questioned whether the optimism that there is a developing global recognition of the standards for electoral challenge is justified.

Notes

1 Hatchard points out that, in the violence following the disputed Kenyan Presidential election in 2007, there were over 1,000 deaths and over 600,000 displaced people. 'Nyane puts part of the blame for electoral violence on the lack of an effective method for electoral challenge in Lesotho, whilst Omotola simply blames violence on a lack of democrats and/or a democratic tradition.

2 Discussion of "political freedom" is a difficult subject – it is itself "political" or contested. Freedom House detects a worldwide decline in political freedom over the past few years, whilst others (e.g., the Pew Foundation) claim that freedom and democracy are experiencing an upswing.

3 Where possible, all cases in the European Court of Human Rights referred to below are cited by their Application number. This facilitates ease of reference to the court using HUDOC and the Guide to Article 3 of the First Protocol ECHR.

4 Wallis AJ pointed out in *Kham* [2015] ZACC 37 at para. 83 that "free and fair elections" passed into the political lexicon in 1978 with UN Security Council Resolution 435 calling for elections so described in Namibia.

5 The existence of independent, executive, electoral commissions in, e.g., South Africa and Kenya complicates this distinction. These (vertical) cases against these commissions are discussed below. An "executive" electoral commission runs elections as opposed to an "advisory" electoral commission found in, e.g., the United Kingdom.

6 The High Contracting Parties undertake to hold free elections at reasonable intervals by secret ballot, under conditions which will ensure the free expression of the opinion of the people in the choice of the legislature.

7 Established by the Political Parties, Elections and Referendums Act 2000. It does not have operational authority to conduct of elections, neither can it bring electoral challenges. It seems not to have power to "supervise the electoral process" under General Comment 20 ICCPR.

8 Now contained in Part 3 of the Representation of the People Act 1983, but largely unchanged since the Parliamentary Elections Act 1868.

9 See, for a British local government case (which is not subject to P1Art3 ECHR) *Tower Hamlets* [2015] EWHC 2015 (QB) in which, at paras 665–6, these points are forcibly made. It is, at least arguable, that the high cost and procedural difficulties inherent in bringing an Election Petition in the UK (and in other countries) is not compliant with P1Art3. Clearly any challenge needs to be made in the context of an election to the legislature (see paragraph 2 of Guide on Article 3 of Protocol No. 1 to the European Convention on Human Rights: Right to free elections). *Upaskich v. Lithuania* Application 14737/08 provides authority for this proposition, and see para. 100 et seq. of the CoE guide.

10 See, e.g., the Executive Summary at pp. 4–5 the penultimate sentence of that reads: "In summary, the evidence demonstrates that the UK's petition process is outdated, complex, inaccessible and inefficient."

11 The mechanism whereby the costs of an expensive legal procedure may be spread amongst thousands of small donors by soliciting small cash donations.

12 See, for a helpful summary, the report of (UK) Parliamentary Business at https://publications.parliament.uk/pa/cm201719/cmselect/cmcumeds/1791/179104.htm#_idTextAnchor001. The Report of the Digital, Culture, Media and Sports Committee (2019). Disinformation and "Fake News" Eighth Report of Session 2017–2019. The report gives full citations to the public debate and contains Memoranda of Evidence.

13 *R v. Rowe ex pate Mainwaring & Others* [1992] 1WLR 1059; *Watkins v. Woolas*, see [2010] EWHC 2702 and *R [(on the application of Woolas)* [2010] 3169 (which arises from the same circumstances but different issues are raised in the appeal); *Morrison & Others v. Carmichael* [2015] ECIH 90. There are other cases in which these issues are raised but they are of lesser importance. *Rowe* is discussed below on the other important point which it raises. It has also been litigated in Australia in *Evans v. Crichton-Browne* (1981) 147 CLR 168 and the principle that lying in political advertising could be an electoral offence survived constitutional challenge in *Cameron v. Becker* [1995] 64 SASR 268. See also Parliament of Australia, Research Paper 13. This paper is valuable because it draws some comparisons between the situation in Australia and that in New Zealand, Canada, and the US.

14 There are a number of cases in the European Court of Human Rights that consider the effect of potential defamations in the context of elections. This are listed and analyzed in paragraphs 97–103 of *R (on the application of Woolas)*. Many of these cases are illustrative of the point which is established in *Lingens v. Austria 9815/82.*

15 A point confirmed by Wojciechowska (2018), who points out that the weakness of election petitions in Poland is due to the fact that plaintiffs have to prove their allegations to the satisfaction of the judge.

16 There was, for example, a great deal of intemperate comment in the British press following the decision in *Hirst (no2)*. Fortunately, most of this is now buried deep in the online information/comment morass. For a more recent, more measured, but equally scathing, comment, see Arnheim, 2015.

17 This decision has been strongly criticized elsewhere as an exact reversal of precedent and a misreading of the law based upon a nineteenth century handy guide to the law of elections (Watt, 2006, pp. 163–72).

18 The events detailed in *Kham* led, no doubt, to the passage of the Electoral Laws Amendment Act (no 1) of 2019.

19 Or, as Wallis AJ had it, "magic number" approach from the Canadian and US cases *Opitz v. Wrzesnewskyj* 2012 SCC 55; [2013] 3 SCR 76 at para 87. See to similar effect *Cusimano v. Toronto (City)* 2011 ONSC 7271 at para 63; *Gooch v. Hendrix* 851 P 2d 1321 (Cal. Sup. Ct. 1993) at 1327–8; *McEwing v. Canada (Attorney General)* [2013] 4 FCR 63; 2013 FC 525 at para 56.

20 The same might have been said in Kenyan Presidential Election Petition 2017. The failings and errors of the Kenyan Electoral Commission were, on the face of the court record, truly monumental. One might think that the requirements imposed on the commission with regard to validating papers and keeping an accurate tally of voters and votes were too onerous given the financial condition of Kenya, but the subsequent election proved otherwise because the rules were obeyed. Perhaps the lesson is that a price should not be put on free and fair elections.

21 See, e.g., Article 3 of the French Constitution, although reference to electoral rights is made in a number of other places in the constitution. See, too, Article 20(2) and Article 38 of the German Constitution.

22 It should be recorded that the present author tried unsuccessfully to mobilize legal action to overturn the 2016 "Brexit" Referendum on the grounds that the campaign was tainted by lying.

23 Cases include *Woolas, Carmichael, Tower Hamlets (*noted above) and *Vitrenko & others v. Ukraine* 23510/02.

24 For example, which side of that line does "Crooked Hillary" fall? Ms. Clinton may, or may not, be dishonest, but that is a matter for a court; Ms. Tymoshenko may, or may not, be a "thief," but are either of those statements, truth, lies, or just abuse?

References

Arnheim, M. (2015). *The problem with human rights law*. London: Civitas.

Bjornlund, E.C. (2004). *Beyond free and fair*. Washington, DC: Woodrow Wilson Centre Press & Johns Hopkins University Press.

Clermont, K.M., & Sherwin., E. (2002). A comparative view of standards of proof. *Am. J. Comp. Law, 50*(2), 243–275. Retrieved from https://scholarship.law.cornell.edu/facpub/222/

Council of Europe. (2019). *The guide on article 3 of protocol no. 1 to the European convention on human rights: Right to free elections*. Retrieved from https://www.echr.coe.int/Documents/Guide_Art_3_Protocol_1_ENG.pdf. Note: this guide is regularly updated and readers are advised to consult the most recent edition.

Digital, Culture, Media and Sports Committee. (2019). *Disinformation and 'fake news'*. (Eighth Report of Session 2017–2019).

The Electoral Commission. (2012). *Challenging elections in the UK*. London: Electoral Commission. Retrieved from https://www.electoralcommission.org.uk/sites/default/files/pdf_file/Challenging-elections-in-the-UK.pdf

Freedom House. (2019). *Freedom in the world*. Retrieved from https://freedomhouse.org/sites/default/files/Feb2019_FH_FITW_2019_Report_ForWeb-compressed.pdf

Hatchard, J. (2015). Election petitions and the standard of proof. *Denning Law Journal*, *27*, 291–302. Retrieved from https://heinonline.org/HOL/LandingPage?handle=hein.journals/denlj27&div=15&id=&page=

International Institute for Democracy and Electoral Assistance. (2002). *International electoral standards: Guidelines for reviewing the legal framework of elections*. Stockholm: IDEA. Retrieved from https://www.idea.int/es/publications/catalogue/international-electoral-standards-guidelines-reviewing-legal-framework

Nyane, H. (2018). A critique of proceduralism in the adjudication of electoral disputes in Lesotho. *Journal of African Elections*, 17(2), 1–24. doi: 10.20940/JAE/2018/v17i2a1

Omotola, J.S. (2008, November 16–19). Explaining electoral violence in Africa's 'new' democracies. In 27th Annual Conference of the Nigerian Political Science Association (NPSA), held at Venue State University, Makurdi, Benue State, Nigeria. Retrieved from www.ajol.info/index.php/ajcr/article/download/63320/51203

Parliament of Australia. (1996–7). *Truth in political advertising legislation*. (Research Paper 13). Retrieved from https://www.aph.gov.au/About_Parliament/Parliamentary_Departments/Parliamentary_Library/pubs/rp/RP9697/97rp13

Petit, D. (2000). *Resolving electoral disputes in the OSCE area*. Warsaw: OSCE/ODIHR.

United Nations. (1948). Universal declaration of human rights (Art. 21(3)). Retrieved from https://www.ohchr.org/en/udhr/documents/udhr_translations/eng.pdf

United Nations. (1996a, July 12). UN Human Rights Committee (HRC), CCPR general comment No. 25: Article 25 (Participation in public affairs and the right to vote). In *The right to participate in public affairs, Voting rights and the right of equal access to public service* (CCPR/C/21/Rev.1/Add.7).

United Nations. (1966b). United Nations General Assembly resolution (2200A (XXI) of 16 December 1966). Retrieved from https://www.un.org/en/development/desa/population/migration/generalassembly/docs/globalcompact/A_RES_2200A(XXI)_civil.pdf

Venice Commission. (2003, May 23). Code of good practice in electoral matters, CDLAD (2002)023rev. In *Venice Commission*. Retrieved from http://www.venice.coe.int/docs/2002/CDL-AD(2002)023rev-e.pdf

Watt, B. (2006). *UK election law: A critical examination*. London: Glasshouse Press.

Wojciechowska, J. (2018). Election petitions in Poland: The efficiency analysis of the institution. *Polish Political Science Yearbook*, *47*(3), 491–502. doi: 10.15804/ppsy2018304

13
ROLE OF MONEY IN CAMPAIGNS AND ELECTIONS

Emily Schnurr

Introduction

Elections are the means through which the people of a given nation, state, city, or region establish a government for their given area. In more democratic governmental arrangements, elections are a tool to give power to the people and to give the people a voice in the policies and laws that they will ultimately be subject to. In democracies, the consent of the governed is essential for democratic legitimacy and stability. In other types of governmental arrangements, particularly with authoritarian regimes, elections may still be held, but tend to be largely symbolic or, in some instances, merely a façade. Authoritarian dictators may engage in voter suppression and intimidation, or outright fraud, to create the appearance of popular consent in order to maintain their power. Elections can, therefore, either be a means to increase freedom and representation, or a tool of furthering oppression, depending on the historical and cultural context of a given nation.

Elections are the most common way that people participate in their government and, in order for elections to truly be free and fair, voters must be able to make an informed choice between candidates for a given office. In practice, candidates or parties develop a platform, or plan, detailing how they will tackle specific issues that matter to voters. Voters are then able to make the best choice regarding which candidate or party will address an issue. For candidates and parties, this necessitates publicizing their ideas in order to attract voters, which always requires money. Candidates and parties must produce written materials, buy television advertising time, travel, hire staff, and in other ways promote themselves to voters. For higher level offices, these costs can be exorbitant, running into the millions or billions of dollars.

Because money is an important aspect of campaigning, and the eventual result of any campaign will be placing a person into a position of power, the regulation of campaign spending has, over time, become a primary concern for government officials, regulators, and voters.

Campaign finance regulations generally come in two forms: Regulations governing how candidates or parties raise money, and regulations governing how candidates or parties spend money. In the former, regulations deal with who is allowed to donate to campaigns, how much candidates and parties are able to raise from individual donors, and the amount of disclosure required for those donations. In the latter, regulations determine what types of media candidates are allowed to purchase, the time frame during which they are allowed to purchase or distribute

DOI: 10.4324/9780429401800-13

various types of media, and whether and how private citizens are allowed to spend money in the political arena independent of political campaigns or parties. Candidates and parties must find strategic ways of working within these confines to win elections.

Across the globe, different nations have developed different means of regulating campaign finance (Pinto-Duschinsky, 2002; Casas-Zamora, 2005; Smilov & Toplak, 2008; Mendilow & Phelippeau, 2018; Nassmacher, 2019). While regulations always have intended and unintended consequences, the way a nation structures its electoral spending has important implications for the types of candidates and parties that are ultimately successful. In the end, money and elections are inextricably linked, and understanding this interaction is essential to understanding democratic governance.

Established Democracies

Democracy is often more of an ideal than an actual form of governance, and many nations around the globe seek to realize that ideal. Democracy is the most common form of government among Western industrialized nations, though democracies and developing democracies are found all over the world. Europe and the European Union feature a high concentration of democratic governments and, among these nations, only one, Switzerland, does not feature some form of campaign finance regulation.

Campaign finance regulations are generally designed to limit the potential for corruption in public figures. Money is required to run a campaign but, when money is changing hands, the potential for quid pro quos and outright bribery is high. The danger to democracy is that elected officials will be more responsive to their wealthy donors, be they private citizens, corporations, unions, or other types of organized groups, than to the citizens who elected them. If elected officials do not enact policies that are in the best interest of the mass public, and instead enact policies to benefit the wealthy few, the entire system is undermined. Therefore, the people have an interest in controlling some aspects of how candidates raise and spend money.

A chief way of combating the potential for corruption is to remove as many of the incentives for candidates to be corrupted by money through publicly funding campaigns. This is common in democracies with a multi-party, parliamentary form of government. In these nations, the available pool of election funding is put into grants and given to political parties based on their percentage of the vote in the previous election. This has the net effect of democratizing campaign finance, as the people's vote has the dual impact of electing a government and determining which parties will receive the largest grants to better enable them to support their candidates in the next election. This is particularly effective in nations with stronger parties, meaning that parties exercise a greater degree of control over their candidates. Part of this control can come from financing their campaigns, which acts to keep candidates in line with the party message.

Public financing for political parties can be a double-edged sword. On the one hand, public financing means that parties do not have to spend much time fundraising, freeing them up to provide better constituent services and generate more effective policy ideas. Furthermore, public financing has an equalizing effect in that all parties have the same opportunity to access public funds, and the ability of parties to campaign is not automatically tied to their ability to fundraise. However, on the other hand, the easy availability of public funds can mean that parties are not incentivized to seek out other forms of support, which can lead to insulation in ideas and isolation from their voters. Parties must balance these competing dynamics in order to be successful in the electoral arena.

The high costs of campaigns, particularly when elections occur more frequently, means that public funding for parties can be insufficient for effective campaigning in some nations.

Therefore, parties and candidates must still seek outside donations in order to be successful in the electoral arena. Historically, party membership dues were the main source of income for political parties. However, declining membership across the board has led parties to seek funding from other sources. This means that the potential for corruption still exists, even with public financing, and nations have had to develop ways of regulating this outside money.

In some nations, such as Australia, Germany, and the Netherlands, regulations largely focus on donor disclosure. In these nations, there are generally few restrictions on the amount that a party or candidate can raise and spend, who can donate to campaigns, and how money can be spent. Donations and spending must be disclosed, which acts as a mechanism to hold parties and candidates somewhat accountable. However, the political culture of these nations is the largest deterrent against corruption.

There are three key aspects of nations without strict regulations that act to deter wealthy individuals from having an outsized impact on elections. First, party discipline in these nations is high, which means that each individual party member is not particularly important and can easily be replaced if they are not adhering to the party standard. Therefore, there is not much incentive to try to influence an individual candidate. Second, the campaign season is short, generally around a month, which means that there is not a lot of opportunity for high spending. Finally, television advertising is closely regulated. In some nations, candidates are given free air time, or political parties own television stations (Toplak, 2019); in others, candidates may not be allowed to advertise on television; in others still, television broadcasters can only show limited amounts of particular types of advertisements. Altogether, this has the effect of disincentivizing high spending on behalf of individual candidates (International Institute for Democracy and Electoral Assistance, 2019; Waldman, 2014).

In other nations, such as Canada, France, Japan, and South Korea, restrictions are placed on both how much candidates are allowed to raise and spend. This limits the potential for corruption through placing a heavy reliance on public funding and free advertising for parties and candidates. These types of regulatory schemes are designed to accomplish two goals. First, to increase transparency in the electoral system. When parties and candidates are not reliant on private donors to fund their campaigns and initiatives, the people can feel more secure that public policy is being enacted in their best interest, rather than in the interest of wealthy individuals and corporations. And second, to make the electoral system more fair and democratic. When all parties and candidates are given equal opportunity to gain public funding and are given advertising time, voters have a greater opportunity to hear multiple perspectives on the issues of the day. This, at least in theory, gives voters the ability to make a more informed decision about how to vote (International Institute for Democracy and Electoral Assistance, 2019).

That said, there are some potential pitfalls for nations with strict regulations. When parties and candidates are not reliant on voters for funding, they may become out of touch with what the voters want. While, ultimately, public funding can help keep the political system freer from the influence of special interests, it can also insulate parties or create an ivory tower effect, whereby parties are proposing policies that are of little interest or help to the people. Moreover, shocks to the nation's economy, such as the 2008 financial crisis, can have a severe impact on the availability of public funding, which can lead to instability in the system.

Another potential regulatory scheme is to limit the amount of money that candidates and parties can spend, but not how much they can raise. Austria, New Zealand, and the United Kingdom are examples of nations with this system. In these nations, candidates and parties are able to raise as much money as they want, as long as those donations are disclosed. However, spending is limited in a variety of ways. The total amount the candidates and parties are able to spend is set in advance of the election, and parties and candidates are generally not allowed to spend electoral funds prior to the designated election period. These nations feature multi-party parliamentary systems, and the campaign period is usually between four to seven weeks. This limits the amount of spending simply through limiting the time frame that spending can occur. Further, in nations with this regulatory system, parties and candidates are often given free advertising time, or are limited in their ability to purchase advertisements, further disincentivizing high spending. Therefore, while there are technically no limits on the amount of money that can be raised or donated, there is little reason for donors to give large amounts of money to parties and candidates, as the return on investment is likely to be low (Buchanan, 2016; Feikert, 2009).

A final type of regulatory scheme is one under which donations are limited, but spending is not. Among Western democracies, this occurs in the United States and Finland. While these nations have similar rules, there are important differences that produce dramatically different effects. In Finland, parties receive public funding, and they are only allowed to spend campaign funds six months prior to the election (Hofverberg, 2016). Donation limits in Finland are also about double the limits imposed by the United States, and all parties are offered equal air time by the Finnish public broadcasting system, which prevents a single party or candidate from buying excessive airtime.

In the United States, the rules surrounding advertising are much less strict, with the net effect of the political finance system being the "worst of both worlds" (Waldman, 2014). Candidates and parties are able to spend as much as they want, meaning that election costs can run into the millions of dollars, even for low level seats. However, because individuals and groups are limited in how much they are able to give, parties and candidates must be constantly searching for new donors in order to remain financially competitive. There is always a danger of being outspent, which means that candidates never really stop campaigning, and they can end up spending an incredible amount of time raising money for their next campaign. Candidates and parties can spend as much as they want on advertising, as can outside entities not officially affiliated with the campaign. Theoretically, this allows for more ideas to enter the political marketplace, as candidates can buy as much advertising as they can afford in order to disseminate their ideas. However, the effect is often less about disseminating ideas and more about buying up as much airtime as possible to prevent one's opponent from buying airtime. This also gives a greater degree of influence to wealthy donors and corporations, which are able to buy independent advertising for their chosen candidates. This raises concerns about both the accuracy of the information being broadcast, and the ability of politicians to act independently from their donors.

A particular concern for democracies is the role of outside money in electoral systems. In order for democratic government to be legitimate, the people must ultimately be the ones to create the government through free and fair elections. This means that the people hold responsibility for making an informed decision about which candidates will represent their interests. When candidates for office are reliant on outside money to run their campaigns, the fear is that those candidates will be more responsive to their donors than to their constituents. This fear is increased when the money being donated comes from individuals or corporations based in other countries. This can mean that members of government could actively be working against the interests of their home nation, potentially delegitimizing the entire structure of government. Therefore, many democracies do not allow, or severely limit, the ability of foreign nationals and corporations to donate money to political candidates.

While any campaign finance system has loopholes that can potentially allow foreign money to enter the system, this has become a particular problem in the United States. In the United States, official candidates and parties are banned from accepting donations from foreign nationals, and money being spent within the political system is regulated. However, individuals working outside the political system are not limited in what they can spend to influence elections, and they are also not limited in what they can raise. This type of spending, known as independent expenditures, features far less regulation in terms of donor disclosure, meaning that it is fairly easy for foreign money to impact elections. While foreign money is unlikely to go directly to a candidate or campaign, candidates and campaigns can certainly benefit a great deal from advertisements purchased with money from foreign entities. But, because this type of spending is largely unregulated, it is effectively impossible to know how much foreign influence is actually impacting elections in the United States.

Overall, established democracies have developed a range of methods for regulating political finance. All of the systems have benefits and disadvantages, though all have adapted to suit their own political culture. As nations become more interconnected through globalization and the proliferation of the internet, concerns about foreign influence in elections will likely continue to plague democratic nations, and they will have to continue to work to ensure that elections are being conducted in the interests of the citizens, rather than in those of outside influences.

Communist and Former Communist Nations

Electoral finance in communist and former communist nations has taken a different path. (On campaign finance reforms and current laws and practices in post-Communist Eastern Europe, see Smilov & Toplak (2008) and Bértoa & van Biezen (2017).) While democracies have largely focused on regulation to promote fairness and legitimacy in elections, these concepts are less of a concern in other governmental arrangements. Russia, a former communist nation now ostensibly a democracy, features a parliamentary government, and both a president and a prime minister. While elections are conducted in accordance with the laws, in reality, most electoral outcomes are a foregone conclusion. United Russia, the majority party, lacks an overarching ideology, and it is widely considered to exist in order to support President Vladimir Putin and his policies. Allegations of corruption, ballot stuffing, and intimidation have been raised against United Russia since they took power in 2007. Currently, United Russia holds 53% of the seats in parliament, known as the Duma (BBC Monitoring, 2012).

While United Russia seems all but guaranteed electoral victory, there is a system of rules governing political finance. Russia regulates both campaign spending and donations. Parties are required to create campaign accounts during the campaign, and are limited in the total amount they can spend during the election. Donations are limited to individuals over the age of 18 who are registered with the party that they wish to donate to. Citizens are not limited in the number of parties that they are allowed to join. Parties are required to receive at least 3% of the vote in an election to be able to register as a party, and parties reaching this threshold are eligible to receive some state funding and free air time on state sponsored television. Parties that do not reach the 3% threshold are required to repay the state for air time and publications that they produced during the campaign (Roudik, 2007). While political finance in Russia is technically limited, it is relatively easy for those in seats of power to get around regulations, and the actual amount of money being raised and spent by politicians is difficult to track.

China adheres more closely to a communist form of government, though still carries out elections. Elections in China are conducted hierarchically: Eligible voters participate in local elections for People's Congresses, and the members of the People's Congresses then elect members to the National People's Congress and upper-level administrative positions, such as the president. While elections for local People's Congresses are conducted by secret ballot, all upper-level elected officials are elected indirectly. There are technically multiple political parties in China, though the Communist Party of China holds all of the power. Other parties are allowed to exist, but must be approved by the Communist Party, and they are extremely limited in their ability to impact national politics (Babones, 2017).

Because the Chinese Communist Party controls elections so closely, elections are more of a formality than a substantive decision-making process. As with elections in Russia, the overall outcome of the vote is a foregone conclusion, and the ability of the people to determine the composition of government is low. Within the nation of China, campaigns are funded by the government, rather than through outside donations. This gives the Communist Party not only control over the outcome of elections, but also allows them control over the information that citizens are able to access. Taken together, China is an effective illustration of how elections can be used to give greater power to the government, rather than to the people.

Both Russia and China have been at the center of international campaign finance controversies. There is some evidence that both nations have financially interfered with elections in other nations. China has sought to expand its influence throughout the Pacific region, and it is suspected of trying to influence elections in both New Zealand and Australia (Cave & Williams, 2017; Graham-McLay, 2018). China was also involved in an American campaign finance scandal in 1996. Money was funneled from the Chinese People's Liberation Army to Democratic candidates, sparking a Congressional investigation into whether policies that benefitted China were passed because of these donations (Bennet, 1998). Furthermore, China has been active in developing foreign aid projects, and now rivals the United States in terms of how much they give to developing nations each year (Hatton, 2017). For the United States, aid to developing nations often comes with requirements that the recipient nation implement democratic reforms. With China, no such strings are attached, meaning that the push toward democracy in many parts of the world has slowed. This suggests that China has an impact on global politics, even indirectly.

Russia has also sought to financially impact other nations' elections. Russia attracted attention for seeking to influence the 2016 presidential election in the United States through strategic use of social media. However, members of the Russian elite have also been linked to large donations to non-profit organizations, such as the National Rifle Association. These organizations then worked to elect candidates friendly to the organization's goals, raising serious questions about the role of foreign money in the United States electoral system (May, 2018; Nast, 2018). However, the United States also has a long history of trying to impact politics in Russia, and the USSR, which demonstrates a complicated dynamic between these nations (Beinart, 2018; Cohen, 2019).

Russia, a former communist nation, and China, the largest communist nation in existence today, both have unique local electoral conditions, and also seek to expand their global position through influencing politics in other nations.

Developing Nations

Western democracies, China, and Russia are all characterized by established economies and long-standing political systems. Other nations, particularly those in the global south, are still working to establish their economies and political systems, which can lead to instability and opportunities for foreign influence. Many of these nations have a history of colonialism and control by Western democratic nations. When the colonizing nations left, the resulting power vacuum has resulted in some developing nations descending into authoritarianism, while others have attempted to implement democratic forms of governance, with mixed results. Issues of oversight and enforcement are prominent in developing nations and, as a result, the incentives for corruption can be high in many of these nations.

Southeast Asia

India implemented a republican form of government post-colonialism, and it is now the largest democracy in the world. India uses a parliamentary system of government, and seven major parties compete for seats in the Lok Sabha, or lower legislative chamber, and the Rajya Sabha, or upper legislative chamber. Elections in India are expensive, and rules for donating and spending money in the political system are generally lax. Parties in India can receive donations from individuals or corporations, often in the form of "electoral bonds," which individuals can purchase and deposit directly into a political party's bank account. Parties are required to report how much money they receive, but the identities of donors are always kept confidential. This makes it effectively impossible to track political donations. In terms of spending, parties are able to spend as much as they wish, but individual candidates are capped on how much they can spend. In practice, the cap on candidate spending is easy to circumvent, and this rule appears to be rarely enforced. In addition to advertisements, parties and candidates spend a great deal of unaccounted money on alcohol and food, as well as outright cash payments, to attract voters (Ahmed & Ulmer, 2019). Overall, while India does attempt to regulate political finance, a lack effective oversight means that electoral spending is largely a free for all.

The 2019 election in India holds the distinction of being the most expensive election in history, with about $7 billion in total spending. The spending was largely driven by a large number of candidates – about 8,000 people ran for one of the 545 seats on the national legislature. Much of the spending resulted from candidates traveling and holding rallies, often giving food to attendees, and sometimes other gifts such as television sets and goats. However, many costs are also incurred as a result of the largely rural nature of the population, and the difficulties in establishing polling locations to allow voters to participate in difficult-to-access regions of the country (Chaudhary & Rodrigues, 2019). India has some ground to cover in terms of ensuring that campaign finance rules are enforced and applied fairly. However, on the whole, this nation does appear committed to continuing to develop democratic norms and institutions.

The Middle East and North Africa

In 2010, citizens of several Middle Eastern and North African nations participated in a series of popular uprisings collectively known as the Arab Spring. These protests were largely focused on overthrowing oppressive authoritarian regimes in favor of more democratic political arrangements, and some nations have made progress on this front. Egypt and Tunisia conducted parliamentary elections and experienced some short-term success with developing democratic institutions. Other nations, such as Libya and Yemen, were not able to turn the uprisings into meaningful change, and they have subsequently experienced instability and further unrest.

These developments illustrate the importance of incorporating political finance regulations as a foundation of establishing democratic governance. Without meaningful regulations to prevent shady financial practices, such as vote-buying or voter intimidation, the political system can become a tool for corrupt individuals to seize power. In Egypt, many rules were passed to regulate campaign finance, but mechanisms for enforcing those rules have largely failed. The fledgling bureaucracy has proven susceptible to bribery and other corrupt practices, and human rights organizations have raised serious questions about Egyptian standards for free and fair elections. In Tunisia, the post-revolution government established a system for public financing for political parties, but did not explicate how parties would qualify to receiving funding, how they could spend it, or other conditions to promote transparency (Ohman, 2013).

Other nations in the Middle East have similar issues with creating and enforcing meaningful campaign finance regulations. Many Middle Eastern and North African nations conduct elections, but the governments that are formed often work at the behest of a powerful dictator or authoritarian figure. There is often little data on what types of regulations exist, and if they are enforced. This is problematic for the citizens in these nations, as it can make it difficult to fully ascertain the inner workings of the government. There is much work to be done in this region of the world in terms of promoting transparency in government, regardless of whether more democratic forms of government are ultimately adopted.

Sub-Saharan Africa

Sub-Saharan Africa is comprised of many nations, all with distinct experiences post-colonialism. Colonizing nations often drew borders in Africa with little attention to existing cultural and ethnic divisions, and many African nations subsequently dealt with civil war and civil strife. However, in recent years, more stability has come to the continent, along with economic development and movements for more democratic governance. However, issues with bureaucracy persist. The development of post-colonial governments in Africa was often done under the auspices of the former colonial nation, meaning that there may be a framework for democratic governance in place. However, enforcement of that framework remains largely elusive (Ohman, 2016).

On the whole, information about how money is spent in elections in sub-Saharan Africa is difficult to access or simply does not exist. While some nations, such as Ghana and Rwanda, have requirements that political parties submit reports about their fundraising and expenditures, in practice, there are no real consequences for parties that ignore these requirements. This, combined with cash- and barter-based economies, makes it almost impossible to track the flow of political money in this region (Ohman, 2016). This leaves the people living there susceptible to politicians and parties more concerned with promoting the interests of their investors rather than in those of their constituents.

Nigeria has been notable for the high cost of its elections, often among the most expensive in the world. This nation has the largest economy in Africa due to a large supply of petroleum but, because of corruption and mismanagement, high levels of poverty persist. There are currently two major parties in Nigeria that win most of the seats in the House of Representatives and Senate. A lack of enforcement of campaign finance laws and easy access to public resources once in office means that politics in Nigeria can be a lucrative business. Parties are rather loosely organized, and they often lack a meaningful ideology. Candidates spend a great deal of money on rallies for supporters, and vote-buying is a significant problem. Technically, candidates are limited in what they can spend on elections but, in practice, it is all but impossible to track spending, and candidates are largely free to raise and spend as they wish. Because elections are so expensive, candidates frequently self-finance their campaigns, creating a further dynamic where, effectively, only wealthy individuals are able to run for office and, once in office, those individuals use their position to increase their own wealth. This raises concerns about the quality of democracy in Nigeria, and highlights the need for meaningful enforcement of campaign finance laws (Olorunmola, 2016).

South Africa is often cited as an example of democratization in Africa. From 1948 to 1991, the government in South Africa was characterized by Apartheid, or institutional racial discrimination that gave white citizens all of the power while black citizens were denied political rights. The first democratic elections in South Africa were conducted in 1994, and great efforts have been made there to develop democratic institutions. However, recent campaign finance scandals have demonstrated that there is more to be done, particularly in terms of promoting transparency about where political money is coming from. South Africa has historically had generally lax campaign finance laws, with no provisions barring donations from foreign or corporate entities, and no rules requiring parties or candidates to disclose how much they have raised, or how they spend those funds (Ohman, 2016). After a major scandal, largely involving bribes and selling administrative positions resulted in the ouster of President Jacob Zuma in 2018, the government has taken some action to tackle corruption in the political system (Alence & Pitcher, 2019). In January 2019, President Cyril Ramaphosa signed a bill implementing rules for increased disclosure, limits on the types of donations parties and candidates can receive, and the implementation of a commission to enforce regulations (South Africa Government News Agency, 2019). Time will tell if these regulations will be effective in promoting accountability in South Africa's electoral system.

Latin America

Nations in Latin America have largely implemented democratic forms of government post-decolonization. However, in some instances, they face similar issues with enforcement as do nations in the Middle East and Africa. Several Latin American nations have also been plagued with campaign finance scandals, undermining their ability to conduct free and fair elections. Overall, nations in Latin America struggle with the role of outside and undisclosed money in their political systems.

Brazil was rocked by the *Petrolão* scandal in 2014. In this scandal, executive members of Petrobras, Brazil's semi-public oil conglomerate, spent about $2.7 billion on bribes to public officials to ensure that Petrobras would receive government contracts (Casas-Zamora, 2016). Brazil has subsequently tried to reign in the power of corporate donations in their political system. In the 2014 election, 76% of all political donations received were from corporations (Douglas, 2015). This prompted the nation to ban corporate donations in 2015 and to attempt to implement a more expansive public financing system. While, ideally, this will reign in campaign spending, elections in Brazil remain among the most expensive in the world. Only time will tell if these changes will produce positive effects (Pearson & Trevisani, 2017).

In Mexico, elections are meant to be publicly funded, with strict regulations on both how candidates and parties raise money, and how that money can be spent. Records from the 2018 election show that no voters donated money to campaigns, and very few in-kind donations were received by any of the presidential candidates. However, enforcement of campaign finance rules is difficult, and it is easy for outside entities and individuals to make clandestine donations, or to act of their own accord in raising support for a chosen candidate. This means that there is no way to know how much is really being spent in Mexican elections and where that money is coming from (Murray & Eschenbacher, 2018).

The development of democracy in post-colonial nations has been uneven and often produced mixed results. While these nations seem, at least on the surface, committed to democratic governance, they often lack the bureaucracy necessary to hold elected official accountable. Continued efforts to limit corrupt influences on their political finance system will hopefully result in more accountable governments and more robust representation for the people.

Are Regulations Effective?

The central goal of campaign finance regulation, particularly in democracies, is limiting corruption. A government perceived as serving the interests of the wealthy few, rather than the people as a whole, can suffer from a lack of popular legitimacy over time. This raises questions about

Table 13.1 Least Corrupt Nations and Political Financing Regulations

Nation	*CPI Score*	*Regulatory Regime*	*Public Financing*
New Zealand	87	No limits on contributions, limits on spending	Yes
Denmark	87	No limits on contributions, no limits on spending	Yes
Finland	86	Limits on contributions, no limits on spending	No
Switzerland	85	No limits on contributions, no limits on spending	No
Singapore	85	No limits on contributions, no limits on spending	No
Sweden	85	No limits on contributions, no limits on spending	Yes
Norway	84	No limits on contributions, no limits on spending	Yes
Netherlands	82	No limits on contributions, no limits on spending	Yes
Luxembourg	80	No limits on contributions, no limits on spending	Yes
Germany	80	No limits on contributions, no limits on spending	Yes

Source: Corruption perceptions index annual report (2019). Transparency International, licensed under CC-BY-ND 4.0.

the effectiveness of different campaign finance regulatory regimes on perceptions of corruption in governments around the world. In other words, do campaign finance regulations work? In short, the answer is murky at best.

Table 13.1 shows the ten least corrupt nations according to the Corruption Perceptions Index (CPI). The majority of these nations feature no regulations on either contributions or spending, and have public financing for elections. However, the two nations who do not fit this mold, New Zealand and Finland, both have different regulatory regimes. New Zealand does not limit contributions, but does limit spending, while Finland limits contributions but not spending. Furthermore, two nations, Switzerland and Singapore, have no regulations on either contributions or spending, and they also do not have public financing for parties or campaigns. Denmark, Sweden, Norway, Netherlands, Luxembourg, and Germany all have no regulations on contributions or spending, and also have public financing, which suggests perhaps that these components can be an effective way to combat public sector corruption (Transparency International, 2019).

The picture gets more complicated when looking at some of the more corrupt nations in the world. The ten nations in Table 13.2 received lower scores on the CPI, indicating higher levels of corruption. Five of these nations – Yemen, Equatorial Guinea, Venezuela, the Democratic Republic of the Congo, and Turkmenistan – feature no regulations on contributions or spending and have public financing (Transparency International, 2019). This is the same general regulatory scheme featured in the majority of the least corrupt nations. Taken together, this data suggests that a combination of no regulations on contributions or spending along and public financing for political parties or campaigns may be necessary, but are clearly not sufficient to reduce corruption in government. Other factors, such as development and political culture are likely also required for fostering responsible and responsive governance.

Emerging Issues in Campaign Finance Regulation

In the internet era, social media has become an important tool for campaigns to connect with voters. Social media is an accessible and relatively inexpensive way of reaching large numbers of voters quickly, and it allows voters to obtain information about candidates easily, helping them to make a more informed choice on election day. While there are many benefits to social media, misuse and abuse of those platforms is inevitable. Social media platforms do not have the same

Table 13.2 Most Corrupt Nations and Political Financing Regulations

Nation	*CPI Score*	*Regulatory Regime*	*Public Financing*
Yemen	15	No limits on contributions, no limits on spending	Yes
Afghanistan	16	Limits on contributions, limits on spending	No
Sudan	16	No limits on contributions, limits on spending	No
Equatorial Guinea	16	No limits on contributions, no limits on spending	Yes
Venezuela	16	No limits on contributions, no limits on spending	Yes
Guinea Bissau	18	No limits on contributions, no limits on spending	No
Libya	18	Limits on contributions, limits on spending	Yes
Democratic Republic of the Congo	18	No limits on contributions, no limits on spending	Yes
Haiti	18	Limits on contributions, limits on spending	Yes
Turkmenistan	19	No limits on contributions, no limits on spending	Yes

Source: Corruption perceptions index annual report (2019). Transparency International, licensed under CC-BY-ND 4.0.

standards for accurate reporting as more traditional forms of media, creating an environment where misinformation is easily spread. There is also little external oversight of social media, allowing for a proliferation of fake accounts that work to influence voters.

Two interconnected controversies have emerged related to the use of social media to influence politics. First, nations around the world have been working to influence elections and public opinion in other nations. The most notable example of this was Russian interference in the 2016 presidential election in the United States, though this is hardly an isolated example. According to the Oxford Internet Institute (2019), over 70 nations have used computational propaganda to attempt to manipulate public opinion, and seven nations, including China, Iran, and Russia, have initiated foreign influence operations online.

Second, Facebook and Twitter are the platforms most commonly used for computational propaganda. These companies are well aware of how their platforms can be used to spread misinformation, but have come to different conclusions about their role in addressing this issue. Facebook has taken the stance that they are a neutral platform, and it is not their responsibility to police content, which could stifle free speech. In 2019, candidates for the 2020 presidential election in the United States spent tens of millions of dollars on advertisements on Facebook, some featuring blatantly false information and doctored videos (Halpern, 2019). Twitter, on the other hand, has banned all advertisements that mention a specific candidate, election, or piece of legislation in an attempt to halt the spread of propaganda and misinformation on their site (Scola, 2019). Twitter still allows for advertisements related to political issues, but these advertisements cannot call for a particular outcome, nor will the platform allow pinpoint geographic targeting of the ads for an area narrower than a state.

Social media has the potential to be a powerful tool for increasing global democracy. It also has the potential to be a powerful tool for bad actors who seek to interfere with democracy and manipulate public opinion for their own ends. It will be up to governments, candidates, and ultimately voters around the world to reconcile these competing prospective outcomes.

Conclusion

Money is an essential part of electoral politics. Every nation that conducts elections must establish rules for how money can be raised and spent by both parties and candidates in order to promote the spread of ideas, while ensuring that the ultimate role of government remains to advance the interests of the people. Nations around the world have developed unique ways of regulating electoral spending. No regulatory system is perfect, and all governments committed to democracy must continue to work to limit the negative influences of political money, while also working to encourage the spread of ideas and information.

References

Ahmed, A., & Ulmer, A. (2019, May 2). India's elections: Rules on campaign financing and spending. *Reuters*. Retrieved from https://www.reuters.com/article/india-election-spending-idUSKCN1S7397

Alence, R., & Pitcher, A. (2019, May 17). Analysis | How the ANC survived Jacob Zuma—And eked out a win in South Africa's election. *Washington Post*. Retrieved from https://www.washingtonpost.com/politics/2019/05/17/how-anc-survived-jacob-zuma-eked-out-win-south-africas-election/

Babones, S. (2017, October 21). China will be driven by 89 million votes this week, but don't call it democracy. *Forbes*. Retrieved from https://www.forbes.com/sites/salvatorebabones/2017/10/21/china-will-be-driven-by-89-million-votes-this-week-but-dont-call-it-democracy/#2c27a8393369

BBC Monitoring. (2012, March 6). How Russia's political parties line up. *BBC*. Retrieved from https://www.bbc.com/news/world-europe-15939801

Beinart, P. (2018, July 22). The U.S. needs to face up to its long history of election meddling. *The Atlantic*. Retrieved from https://www.theatlantic.com/ideas/archive/2018/07/the-us-has-a-long-history-of-election-meddling/565538/

Bennet, J. (1998, May 18). Clinton says Chinese money did not influence U.S. policy. *The New York Times*. Retrieved from https://www.nytimes.com/1998/05/18/us/clinton-says-chinese-money-did-not-influence-us-policy.html

Bértoa, F. C., & van Biezen, I. (Eds.). (2017). *The regulation of post-communist party politics*. London: Routledge.

Buchanan, K. (2016, March). Regulation of campaign finance and free advertising: New Zealand. *Library of Congress LAW*. Retrieved from https://www.loc.gov/law/help/campaign-finance-regulation/newzealand.php

Casas-Zamora, K. (2005). *Paying for democracy: political finance and state funding for parties*. ECPR Press.

Casas-Zamora, K. (2016). *The state of political finance regulations in Latin America*. International Institute for Democracy and Electoral Assistance.

Cave, D., & Williams, J. (2017, June 6). Australian politics is open to foreign cash, and China has much to gain. *The New York Times*. Retrieved from https://www.nytimes.com/2017/06/06/world/australia/china-political-influence-campaign-finance.html

Chaudhary, A., & Rodrigues, J. (2019, March 11). Why India's election is among the world's most expensive. *Bloomberg*. Retrieved from https://www.bloomberg.com/news/features/2019-03-11/why-india-s-election-is-among-the-world-s-most-expensive

Cohen, S. F. (2019, March 6). The long history of US-Russian 'meddling.' Retrieved from https://www.thenation.com/article/the-long-history-of-us-russian-meddling/

Douglas, B. (2015, September 18). Brazil bans corporations from political donations amid corruption scandal. *The Guardian*. Retrieved from https://www.theguardian.com/world/2015/sep/18/brazilian-supreme-court-bans-corporate-donations-political-candidates-parties

Feikert, C. (2009, April). Campaign finance: United Kingdom. *Library of Congress LAW*. Retrieved from https://www.loc.gov/law/help/campaign-finance/uk.php

Graham-McLay, C. (2018, October 25). Campaign contribution raises concerns about China's meddling in New Zealand. *The New York Times*. Retrieved from https://www.nytimes.com/2018/10/25/world/asia/new-zealand-china-politics.html

Halpern, S. (2019). The problem of political advertising on social media. *The New Yorker*. Retrieved from https://www.newyorker.com/tech/annals-of-technology/the-problem-of-political-advertising-on-social-media

Hatton, C. (2017, October 11). China's secret aid empire uncovered. Retrieved from https://www.bbc.com/news/world-asia-china-41564841

Hofverberg, E. (2016, March). Regulation of campaign finance and free advertising: Finland. *Library of Congress LAW*. Retrieved from https://www.loc.gov/law/help/campaign-finance-regulation/finland.php

International Institute for Democracy and Electoral Assistance. (2019). Political finance database. Retrieved from https://www.idea.int/data-tools/data/political-finance-database

Mendilow, J., & Phélippeau, E. (Eds.). (2018). *Handbook of political party funding*. Edward Elgar Publishing.
May, R. (2018, May 8). How Putin's oligarchs funneled millions into GOP campaigns. *Dallas News*. Retrieved from https://www.dallasnews.com/opinion/commentary/2018/05/08/putins-proxies-helped-funnel-millions-gop-campaigns
Murray, C., & Escehnbacher, S. (2018, June 29). Anti-corruption watchdogs wonder: Who is funding Mexico's presidential candidates? *Reuters*. Retrieved from https://www.reuters.com/article/us-mexico-election-financing-idUSKBN1JP0GG
Nassmacher, K. H. (2019). Comparing party and campaign finance in Western Democracies. In A. B. Gunlicks (Ed.), *Campaign and party finance in North America and Western Europe* (pp. 233–267). London: Routledge.
Nast, C. (2018, June 21). The N.R.A. spent $30 Million to elect Trump. Was it Russian money? *Vanity Fair*. Retrieved from https://www.vanityfair.com/news/2018/06/the-nra-spent-dollar30-million-to-elect-trump-was-it-russian-money
Ohman, M. (Ed.). (2013). *Financing politics: The Middle East and North Africa*. Washington, DC: International Foundation for Electoral Systems. Retrieved from https://www.ndi.org/sites/default/files/financing_politics_MENA.pdf
Ohman, M. (2016). *The state of political finance regulations in Africa*. Stockholm: International Institute for Democracy and Electoral Assistance. Retrieved from https://www.idea.int/sites/default/files/publications/the-state-of-political-finance-regulations-in-africa.pdf
Olorunmola, A. (2016). *Cost of politics in Nigeria*. London: Westminster Foundation for Democracy. Retrieved from https://www.wfd.org/wp-content/uploads/2017/09/Cost-of-Politics-Nigeria.pdf
Pearson, S., & Trevisani, P. (2017, October 5). Brazil's congress approves public campaign finance bill. *Wall Street Journal*. Retrieved from https://www.wsj.com/articles/brazils-congress-approves-public-campaign-finance-bill-1507204559
Pinto-Duschinsky, M. (2002). Financing politics: A global view. *Journal of Democracy*, *13*(4), 69–86.
Roudik, P. (2007, November). Russia: Parliamentary elections: Legal issues. *Library of Congress LAW*. Retrieved from https://www.loc.gov/law/help/parliamentary-elections/russia.php
Scola, N. (2019). Twitter rolls out total ban on ads from political figures. *Politico*. Retrieved from https://www.politico.com/news/2019/11/15/twitter-political-ads-071160
South Africa Government News Agency. (2019, January 23). Political party funding bill signed into law. *SAnews*. Retrieved from https://www.sanews.gov.za/south-africa/political-party-funding-bill-signed-law
Smilov, D., & Toplak, J. (Eds.). (2008). *Political finance and corruption in Eastern Europe the transition period*. Ashgate.
Toplak, J. (2019). Money and elections in Malta. *Journal of Mediterranean Studies*, *28*(1), 91–107.
Transparency International. (2019). *Corruption perceptions index annual report*.
Waldman, P. (2014, April 4). How our campaign finance system compares to other countries. *The American Prospect*. Retrieved from https://prospect.org/article/how-our-campaign-finance-system-compares-other-countries

14
POLITICAL FINANCE

Barbara Jouan Stonestreet

Introduction

The interest in the issue of political finance is a relatively recent phenomenon, and its importance has increased in the last few years. Indeed, over the past two decades, there has been growing interest in political finance and this period has seen the introduction of political finance regulation in many countries around the world. Nowadays, almost every country regulates this area, although the scope and nature of that regulation differs from country to country.

Money is a necessary component of electoral processes and, more generally, of democratic processes. Money is indeed critical to political parties to shape public debate about policy options, to promote new ideas, and to challenge existing power. Moreover, it constitutes a means for citizens to show their support of candidates or political parties through pecuniary or in-kind contributions. Money is also needed by electoral contestants to run effective campaigns and to reach out to voters. However, it can also contribute to an uneven political playing field, skewing the competition in favor of wealthy candidates and political parties.

Often described as "the mother's milk of politics" (Jesse Unruh, 1922–1987, US politician and State Treasurer of California), money undoubtedly has an impact on the conduct and quality of electoral processes. Therefore, the regulation of political finance is essential to guarantee independence of both parties and electoral contestants from the influence of generous donors, to ensure the opportunity for all parties and candidates to compete with equal opportunity, and to provide for transparency in political life.

A variety of political finance systems exist around the world, ranging from loose or vague sets of regulations to tightly regulated legal frameworks, and none of the existing systems is intended to be applied "off-the-shelf" to other countries. Indeed, each country has its own political finance regulation, which reflects the very specific nature of the electoral system, of the institutional regime, and of the combination of political, historical, economic, and societal factors. Throughout the world, the adoption of political finance regulations aims to reduce risks for corruption,[1] to level the playing field, to enhance citizen trust towards the political class and confidence in the democratic process, to increase transparency in the sources of funding, and to hold electoral and political stakeholders accountable. Developing a system of political finance transparency and accountability requires time and patience, and it is built on three main principles – i.e., equality, transparency, and accountability – that constitute the core pillars upon which the whole political finance architecture rests.

 DOI: 10.4324/9780429401800-14

In the context of political finance regulation, the term equality encompasses all regulations that aim to level the playing field in order to create conditions for all electoral contestants to run in elections with the same opportunities and under equal conditions. This set of regulations aims to ensure that the free choice of voters is not undermined by disproportionate expenditure on behalf of any candidate or political party. In order to foster transparency, electoral actors and political parties need to provide relevant institutions with financial reports containing and showing all income and expenditures pertaining to election campaigns and routine activities. The latter needs, in turn, to disclose to the public the use and the disbursement of these funds. To ensure the transparency of the whole political finance architecture, this principle also implies the need for openness of the oversight body that must make public the results of its oversight. Accountability means that all stakeholders (electoral actors, political parties, and oversight bodies) can be held responsible for the decisions that they make and for the infractions that occur relating to political finance regulations. The enforcement and implementation of existing rules by an oversight body, which is given the power and the mandate to investigate infringements and impose sanctions free from political pressure, are of the utmost importance.

What Is Political Finance?

In many parts of the world, political parties play a crucial part in election campaigns, and it is thus difficult to draw a distinct line between the costs incurred for campaign purposes by political parties and their routine expenses. Political finance is a broad term that covers both campaign finance and political party finance and encompasses all rules related to the use of funds for legitimate, irregular, or illicit political activities, including the use of state resources for political purposes and election campaigns. Political finance includes not only campaign expenses, but also costs related to a political party's day-to-day activities and regular functions. In this context, campaign finance is understood as all monetary and in-kind contributions and expenditures collected and incurred by candidates, their political parties, or their supporters for election purposes, while political party finance is defined as all monetary and in-kind transactions made by political parties in their routine activities.

To understand political finance, it is of the utmost importance to figure out the chronological imbrication of the four main political finance components – i.e., sources of funding, expenditure limits, reporting and disclosure requirements, and enforcement. To do so, one has to answer the following questions:

- Where does the money come from? *Sources of financing*;
- What is the money spent on? *Campaign expenditures and routine party activities*;
- Is the money collected and disbursed reported on and disclosed? *Reporting and disclosure*;
- Is there a supervision mechanism, coupled with a sanctioning system, in cases of infringements upon political finance regulations? *Oversight and sanctions*.

Why Does Political Finance Matter?

According to Article 25 of the International Covenant on Civil and Political Rights (ICCPR) adopted in 1966:

> every citizen shall have the right and the opportunity...to take part in the conduct of public affairs...to vote and to be elected at genuine periodic elections which shall be by universal and equal suffrage [and]...to have access, on general terms of equality, to public service in his country.
>
> *(ICCPR, Article 25)*

There are very few international standards when it comes to political finance. The main international instruments relevant for assessing political finance are Paragraph 19 of the United Nations Human Rights Committee, General Comment No. 25 to Article 25 of the International Covenant on Civil and Political Rights (ICCPR)[2] and article 7-3 of the United Nations Convention against Corruption (UNCAC) 2005,[3] which calls for reasonable limitations on campaign expenditures and for transparency in the funding of election campaigns and political parties.

The variety of legal frameworks and the frequency with which new laws concerning political finance are altered, amended, or enacted show the degree of the sensitivity of existing systems of regulations. The relationship between money and politics is very often tackled from the negative perspective of corruption, be it the improper influence of money on the democratic process as a whole, or the illegitimate personal enrichment of politicians or policy capture by narrow private interests, leading to an even deeper erosion of public trust in governments. Indeed, almost all countries have issues with money in politics, and they have used different regulations to increase transparency and counteract problems in political finance. There are frequent corruption scandals in various countries around the world that constitute reminders that difficulties endure and that continued debate and reform are needed. Indeed, these political-judicial affairs are the signal that existing political regulations are not working properly, either because they are inadequate or because they are not enforced.

One of the most famous corruption scandals occurred in 1972–1974 and relates to the story of the break-in of the Democratic National Committee (DNC) Headquarters at the Watergate office in DC in order to bug the place and the subsequent and unsuccessful attempts of the Nixon administration to cover up this crime. The investigation revealed the existence of a slush fund used by the Nixon re-election campaign committee and led to the resignation of Richard Nixon. As a result, the Federal Election Commission was created in 1974 in order to regulate the relation between money and politics.

A more recent corruption scandal occurred in the 2000s and 2010s in Spain. The ongoing "Gürtel Case" involves hundreds of businessmen and politicians from the People's Party "Partido Popular." This scandal involves accusations and suspicions of bribery, money-laundering, and tax-evasion actions that all relate to illicit political party funding, kickbacks, and the awarding of contracts by local and regional governments. Estimates of public money loss amount to some EUR 120 million.

How to Define Political Finance

In recent decades, there has been a general trend toward more political finance rules in an attempt to further regulate the relationship between money and politics. The rapidity with which legal changes relating to political finance occur in various countries and the complexity of enforcement mechanisms makes it difficult to keep track of changes.

Throughout the world, the adoption of political finance regulations aims to *enhance equality* between electoral contestants, to *increase transparency* in the sources of funding, and to hold electoral and political stakeholders *accountable*. These three main principles – i.e., equality, transparency, and accountability – constitute the core pillars of the whole political finance architecture to which are associated the main building blocks of any political finance system that consists of rules on funding sources, expenditures, transparency, oversight, and sanctions.

Equality

Generally, equality is associated with regulations pertaining to the funding sources, both the allocation of public funding and limitations or prohibitions on private funding, and to campaign expenditure limitations and/or prohibitions.

Throughout the world, there are two distinct sources of financing, which both allow for direct and in-kind contributions: Funding that can be allocated by the state, and/or funds given by individual or legal entities. Both types of funding present upsides and downsides. Public financing is often seen as a means to prevent corruption, to promote political pluralism, and to avoid undue reliance on private donors. Private funding of electoral actors through contributions is commonly seen as a form of political participation and a sign of the parties' social anchorage. However, excessive reliance on either type of funding could be detrimental. Indeed, excessive amounts of state funds could lead to the weakening of the linkage between political and electoral actors[4] and their respective electorates, while excessive dependence on private donations may bring about the capture of electoral and political processes by private interests. Public funding could also strengthen the position of governing political parties by entrenching their power.

Equality concerns two main types of regulation: Sources of financing and expenditure rules. These regulations aim to create conditions of equality between electoral and political actors by trying to level the playing field.

Sources of Financing

The allocation of public funding is one of the most common forms of political finance regulation around the world.[5] The main rationale behind the adoption of such a rule is to limit the influence of private (and interest) money on the course and outcomes of electoral processes. Most regional instruments have provisions underlying the importance of public funding as a means to put all electoral and political actors on an equal footing. Thus, the Council of Europe Committee of Ministers have stated that "The state should provide support to political parties" (Recommendation 2003/4, Art. 1). Similarly, the 2011 OSCE/ODIHR Human Dimension Seminar on the Role of Political Parties in the Political Process recommends that states consider the "importance of public financing in creating a level playing field for political parties."[6]

Public financing is not a right of political parties and electoral contestants, but rather an advantage offered to them, and it can be given directly to political parties in the form of annual subsidies in order to help them finance their political activity and/or can take the form of campaign subsidies. In most countries, the legislation sets out eligibility and allocation criteria in order to determine the quantity of public subsidies to be distributed. Those criteria are generally based on both the number of seats obtained and the percentage of votes cast, thus allowing non-parliamentary parties to be eligible for public funds if they demonstrate a minimum level of support. Public funding can also take the form of subsidies allocated to political parties and candidates before or after the holding of elections through the reimbursement of expenses deemed electoral by the political finance oversight body.

It is of the utmost importance that conditions to access public funding are unbiased, reasonably inclusive, and not unduly restrictive of the freedom of political parties to act and campaign. On the other hand, certain conditions have to be attached to the provision of such funding. Therefore, funding should not be provided unless electoral actors have provided the required financial reports and cooperated with responsible requests from the oversight bodies. In addition to direct funding, public financing may also take the form of indirect support, such as allocation of free media time, free use of billboards in order to display electoral materials, free use of public meeting halls for the purposes of campaign activities, and tax relief.

The existence of political finance regulations can also, in certain cases, be inclusive. The adoption of political finance regulations containing gendered provisions can help reduce the gender gap by ensuring the opportunity for all candidates to compete on equal footing. In order to address gender imbalance in the electoral field and the political decision-making process, as well as to contribute to the political empowerment of women, some countries have introduced gender quotas for public elections.[7] However, gender quotas have an actual and effective effect only if they are tied – directly or indirectly – to the allocation of public funding. According to International IDEA's political finance database, 27 out of the 180 countries surveyed (15%) have adopted reforms that directly target gender equality[8] by tying public funding to gender equality.[9]

The first approach is to create financial incentives for political parties that endorse a certain percentage of each gender on their lists. The second approach is to financially sanction political parties that do not comply with gender equality requirements (reducing, denying, or withholding a certain share of public funds). The third approach is to earmark funds for gender equality initiatives such as women's wings by political parties or for political parties' internal activities aimed at enhancing the participation of women and the training of women candidates.

However, public financing should not be the only source of income for political actors in order to avoid creating conditions for over-dependency on state support. The Council of Europe, in its recommendation Rec(2003)4,[10] clearly advises that:

> State support should be limited to reasonable contributions and that...states should ensure that any support from the state and/or citizens does not interfere with the independence of political parties [to avoid]...weakening of links between parties and their electorate.
>
> *(CoE, Rec 1516(2001))*[11]

All individuals have the right to freely express their support of a political party or a chosen candidate through financial and in-kind contributions. Private financing generally takes the form of membership fees, contributions from individuals or legal entities, self-funding, loans, or proceeds from party commercial activities. To ensure consistent legislation, loans taken out, and membership fees received by political parties for the purpose of election campaigning should be subject to the same restrictions and reporting requirements as donations. In order to curtail the potentially corruptive effects of private funding, relevant legislation can regulate the income flow through quantitative limitations (which cap the monetary and in-kind amounts of campaign-related contributions) or qualitative limitations (which restrict the sources of contributions).

Qualitative limitations aim to restrict the sources of contributions – i.e., foreign persons, donations from corporations with governmental contracts, donations from companies and trade unions, and anonymous donations. As stated by the Venice Commission and OSCE/ODIHR (2011):

> the banning of corporate donations exists in a number of models: France, Poland, Bulgaria, inter alia...When combined with significant state financing of political parties, the model aims to decrease the pressure exerted by big business on the political process. It is a legitimate choice for a country to make. However, it should be borne in mind that corporate bans may be circumvented in a number of ways, through channelling of corporate money through individual donations (employees of a company, for instance); donating to party-related NGOs (foundations) etc. Also, if there is no adequate level of state subsidies for the political parties, the banning of corporate funding coupled with strict disclosure provisions may create difficulties for the political parties to fundraise.
>
> *(Venice Commission and OSCE/ODIHR, 2011)*

The prohibition of foreign and anonymous contributions is the most common form of donation bans, consistent with international standards. Indeed, 61% and 49% of countries have banned foreign donations and corporate money, respectively.[12]

Quantitative limitations, which cap the monetary amounts of campaign-related contributions that people can make to a candidate or a political party, aim to minimize the possibility of corruption and the purchasing of political influence. Indeed, reasonable limits on the total amount of contributions may be imposed, so that there is not distortion in the political process in favor of wealthy interest and that corruption or purchasing of political influence is made impossible. Donation limits are in place in 55% of countries surveyed by the International IDEA political finance database.[13]

Expenditure Regulations

One common form of political finance regulations is the restriction of the total amount that electoral actors can spend in relation to election campaigns or prohibition or limitation of certain types of expenditure. The rationale behind a ceiling on expenditures is to constrain the growth of campaign expenses and to level the playing field by ensuring that electoral contestants with more financial means are not unfairly advantaged. The Guidelines on Political Party Regulation state that:

> it is reasonable for a state to determine a maximum spending limit for parties in elections in order to achieve the legitimate aim of securing equality between candidates... The maximum spending limit usually consists in an absolute sum or a relative sum determined by factors such as the voting population in a particular constituency and the costs for campaign materials and services.
>
> *(OSCE/ODIHR & Venice Commission Guidelines on Political Party Regulation, para. 196, p. 76)*

Indeed, there are different ways to calculate spending limits. The limit can consist of an absolute sum per constituency (UK), a flat fee (Afghanistan, Austria, Cyprus, Jamaica, Myanmar, Tonga), a calculation based on the minimum wage applicable in a given country (Armenia, Portugal), or a fixed number based on the number of inhabitants (France, Italy, Spain) or voters (BiH, Lebanon, Tunisia) in the constituency. Whatever methodology adopted, it is important that the spending limit be revised on a regular basis to take into account conjectural factors, such as the cost of living. Whatever approach is taken, it is important that the actual expenditure limit is a reasonable one, so that candidates and political parties can effectively campaign and reach out to voters.[14]

Moreover, there should be clarity about whether in-kind spending counts against the spending limit and whose expenditures are limited. Many countries have recently seen an increase in campaigning by interest groups and individuals who are not associated with political parties or candidates – so-called third parties or non-party campaigners. Because of the potential impact of such a campaign on the electoral process as a whole, their spending should also be regulated. For both issues could be used to circumvent existing regulations.

Campaign expenditure ceilings are relevant and enforceable only if certain conditions are met. In particular, it is necessary for a clear definition of what electoral expenditures are and for a clearly defined period that is reasonable in order to inform political actors of both types of expenditure that must be reported in the financial reports and the timeframe.

Electoral expenditures encompass both monetary and in-kind expenditures that are incurred by electoral contestants to attract votes. Therefore, unlawful practices, such as vote buying or the misuse of administrative resources (when estimated or evaluated), shall also be reported in financial reports and counted against the spending limit.

The campaign period is the span of time during which electoral contestants can campaign and incur expenses to get elector votes and must abide by regulations governing campaign expenditures. It has to be differentiated from the pre-election campaign period and the candidate nomination process. Indeed, parties, candidates, or even third-parties might attempt to circumvent political finance requirements by conducting campaign activities during the pre-campaign period.

In parallel to setting limits on campaign expenditures, certain countries have also adopted regulations aimed at strictly regulating or even forbidding certain types of expenditure. The most common restriction focuses paid political advertising and vote buying. The reason to ban or strongly regulate paid political advertising is to ensure a level playing field by avoiding the domination of public debate and electoral campaigns by wealthy and private actors. In a significant number of countries, paid political advertising is statutorily forbidden (Brazil, Chile, Denmark, France, Ireland, Mexico, Norway, Portugal, Switzerland, the UK). To counterbalance the constraint put on their freedom to campaign, electoral contestants are usually granted free or subsidized airtime, generally on public service broadcasters, to present their programs (Ethiopia, Burundi, Côte d'Ivoire, Niger, Tunisia, Argentina, Brazil, Colombia, Mexico, Peru). Other countries – such as Australia, Canada, or South Africa – do not have a blanket ban, but rather restrictions regarding the use, content, and amount of political advertising (either the amount of money spent on political advertising or the number of advertisements).

As regards the issue of paid political advertising, different views and approaches have emerged in the past years. The US Supreme Court has, little by little, deregulated the whole campaign finance system by issuing a series of decisions[15] striking down many of the main regulations on the grounds of the First Amendment enshrining the principle of freedom of speech. Since its first ruling in 1976 stating that limits on campaign expenditures were unconstitutional on the grounds that they limited speech, the Supreme Court has constantly and consistently reaffirmed the prevalence of the 1st Amendment. The court struck down the longstanding ban on corporate campaign expenditures and the aggregate limit on the amount individuals may contribute in total to political parties and federal candidates, respectively in 2010 and 2014. On the other hand, the European Court of Human Rights, has ruled, on several occasions, that a ban on paid political advertising constituted a breach of freedom of expression under Article 10[16] of the European Convention of Human Rights and that it may violate the freedom of expression of small political parties, since they receive minimal coverage in the edited media and thus paid advertising may be the only way to obtain coverage of any recently changed position. In a ruling issued in 2013, the ECtHR ruled that a ban on political advertising constitutes a permissible attempt to "protect the democratic process from distortion by powerful financial groups with advantageous access to influential media."[17]

The issue of the use and misuse/abuse of administrative resources has gained growing attention from the international community in the last few years.[18] As commonly understood, "the abuse of administrative resources" is the ability of candidates to use their official positions or connections to governmental institutions to influence the outcome of elections. While the use of administrative resources is not an issue, as long as the same resources are provided to all political and electoral forces engaged in an electoral process and as long as this equality of opportunity is not undermined by the monopolizing of such means by the governing parties for campaign purposes, it becomes problematic when such public resources are misused by incumbent candidates or their supporters during electoral campaigns in order to get votes and to get reelected.

The misuse of administrative resources during electoral processes can threaten some of the basic requirements of credible and transparent elections – i.e., equality of opportunity between electoral contestants, campaign transparency, and freedom of expression of opposition parties and candidates. The vigilance and monitoring by civil society and the media are also a good means to prevent the misuse of administrative resources that represents one of the most crucial and recurrent challenges as regards campaign finance regulation enforcement.

Transparency

Transparency relates to two main types of regulation: Reporting requirements and disclosure obligations. Those regulations, when existing, aim to create obligations for political and electoral actors to submit and disclose information about received contributions and incurred expenditures in a timely fashion. It is then critical that the political finance system provides requirements for clear and timely reporting and disclosure.

Reporting Requirements

Reporting requirements aim to enhance the accountability of political actors, third-parties included, and the legality of sources of income and expenditures. First, reporting entities must be clear about the type of required information and recordkeeping. Timely and transparent reporting is an important element for effective institutional oversight, ensuring that electoral and political actors comply with political finance regulations and establishing public confidence. To achieve these goals, it is of the utmost importance that reports be timely, detailed and exhaustive, comprehensible, and lodged with the relevant oversight body. However, it is important to avoid regulations that could place undue reporting and financial burdens on parties, candidates, and oversight bodies. This is the reason that some countries (such as Canada, the United States, and Australia) use thresholds under which resources and expenditures do not have to be reported.

The frequency and content of reporting varies across the globe. According to International IDEA's political finance database, 77% of surveyed countries have regulations in place that oblige political parties to report regularly on their finances; 59 % of the countries require political parties to report on their finances in relation to election campaigns; and 66% of countries mandate that candidates report on their campaign finances.[19] Depending on the applicable legislation, parties and candidates can be required to report on their assets and liabilities at the start of the campaign, to report regularly on their income and expenditure throughout the campaign, and to submit a final financial report to the oversight body after the elections. In any case, the deadline to submit such final financial reports should be precisely defined in the law and should not be either so short that the relevant information cannot be gathered or so long that it impedes thorough and expedient auditing by an oversight body and, where necessary, further investigations or proportional and timely sanctions.

Both types of report – i.e., political party annual financial reports and electoral contestant campaign accounts – should not only clearly distinguish between contributions and expenditures but also contain itemizations of all contributions and expenditures into standardized categories. The existence of standardized formats for all reports should be accompanied by the obligation to provide the date and amount of each transaction, as well as all supporting documents. Depending on the applicable legislation, reports have to be submitted in hard or soft copies. Some states have developed online electronic political finance platforms through which all reports have to be submitted in searchable and downloadable formats (e.g., Canada, Estonia, and the United States). As regards income, these documents pertain to donations (all data establishing the identity of the donor), membership fees, loans and credits (all data establishing the identity of the lender, the line and amount of credit, and the interest rate), and copies of checks received from donors. With regard to expenses, supporting documents are bank statements establishing all financial transactions for the whole campaign period and invoices for all expenditures with the relevant documentation (samples of electoral materials, copies of advertising spots, etc.).[20] Furthermore, in order to comply with accounting requirements, the candidate or party's financial report might be audited by an independent auditor or a chartered accountant before being submitted to the oversight body.

In many countries, regardless of the kind of elections they are standing for, political parties and candidates must open a separate bank account with an authorized institution and appoint a financial agent who is responsible for all financial matters, such as collecting contributions, paying expenditures through a specific bank account, and keeping an accurate and detailed account of all transactions made for electoral purposes. This measure aims at easing the supervisory task of the oversight body and at enhancing the transparency and comprehensiveness of financial transactions reported in the financial report.

Disclosure Obligations

Justice Brandeis once stated, "Sunlight is said to be the best of disinfectants" (Louis Brandeis, 1856–1941, American lawyer and associate justice on the Supreme Court of the United States). Indeed, disclosure of information related to the financing of both political parties and electoral campaigns is essential to enhance the transparency of the whole political finance system. In order to achieve this goal, the legal framework should clearly define:

- What has to be disclosed (electoral contestants' reports, along with the decisions of the oversight body);
- When it has to be disclosed;
- How it must be disclosed (on the internet, in media outlets);
- Who has to disclose it (political parties, candidates, or both);
- To whom electoral contestants and third-parties must disclose (to the oversight body and/or to the public).

In 60% of the countries surveyed in the International IDEA's political finance database, political parties/candidates have to disclose information contained in their reports (Question 57 of International IDEA's political finance database). However, the need for privacy could ponder the need for transparency in the field of political finance. Therefore, transparency has to be balanced with the donor's wish (or necessity) to preserve the privacy of his/her political preferences. Indeed, contributions to political parties and candidates are a form of political support, and the disclosure of donor identities might be seen as an indirect way to declare political view(s). Some countries do not make the identity of donors public due to concerns about privacy violations. In others, however, disclosure of donor identity is required either completely or above a certain threshold. For instance, in Canada, candidates have to give the full name and address of contributors who have donated a total amount of funds and goods or services greater than CAD200. In the US, reports submitted by official committees of candidates for federal office, party committees, PACs, and super PACs contain a list of all donors who donate more than USD 200, along with their address, employer, and job title. All information is then made public on the websites of the respective oversight bodies.

Accountability

Accountability pertains to regulations on oversight mechanisms and sanctioning systems. Indeed, in order to hold electoral actors responsible for the decisions that they make and for the infractions that occur, political finance regulations must be implemented and enforced by an oversight body given the power and the mandate to investigate infringements and impose sanctions, free from political pressure.

Oversight Mechanism

Strong and effective enforcement mechanisms in political finance regulation allows for the transparency and accountability of the whole regulatory system. The mandate and the autonomy of the institutions in charge of supervising political finance regulations have a clear and direct impact on the effectiveness of the executed control.

Indeed, monitoring can be undertaken by a variety of different bodies, including the Election Management Body (EMB), a competent supervisory body, or a state financial body. The independence of any control body is so important that effective measures should be taken to ensure the body's independence from political pressure and commitment to impartiality – meaning that there should not be any budgetary pressure affecting the way that it carries out its activities or any party intervention as regards the appointment of its staff.

Whichever body is tasked to monitor political finance, it is important that the legislation lays out certain rules regarding the appointment process, as well as the scope, mandate, and nature of its investigative and sanctioning powers.

Sanctions

In order to support political finance regulation, an arsenal of sanctions of varying degrees of severity must be set up in order to enable the enforcing body to apply, in each specific case, a sanction that is proportionate to the nature of the violation. Sanctions are the main tools at the disposal of the oversight body to effectively enforce campaign finance regulations. Indeed, the best conceived system is of little value, unless it is implemented and enforced effectively. As underlined by the Council of Europe:

> Any irregularity in the financing of an electoral campaign shall entail, for the party or candidate at fault, sanctions proportionate to the severity of the offence that may consist of the loss or the total or partial reimbursement of the public contribution, the payment of a fine or another financial sanction or the annulment of the election.[21]

Sanctions must at all times be objective, enforceable, effective, and proportionate to their specific purpose. Sanctions for specific offences have to be stipulated by law and respectful of the rule of law. A balance is to be struck between insufficient penalties of deterrence and excessively harsh sanctions. The gravity and recurrence of the violation should be taken into account when determining the sanction.

When sanctions are imposed, the party or candidate in question should have recourse to a fair hearing by an impartial tribunal. While regulatory authorities can determine sanctions, there should be the opportunity for a party to request that the final decision regarding sanctions should be made by the appropriate judicial body, in accordance with judicial principles. In any case, the principles of effective remedy and due process must be strictly respected.

Main Challenges

Lack/Absence of Enforcement

The core pillar upon which the whole political finance architecture lies is political finance enforcement or, put differently, the act of giving force to and executing political finance regulations. An ideal enforcement system should include not only the existence of a political finance oversight body, but also the existence of attributes allowing it to conduct and its supervision tasks – namely, investigation, prosecution, adjudication, and sanctions or the possibility to turn to law enforcement agencies. Such a system also depends on the cooperation of main institutional and non-institutional stakeholders, and it relies on the monitoring mechanisms provided by financial agents, auditors, banking institutions, civil society organizations, and the media. That is the reason it is critical that the purpose and consequences of political finance legislation be clearly set out in order to tailor the political finance components to the very unique electoral and political system of any given country.

Political finance regulation is best viewed as a comprehensive system consisting of component units. Therefore, it is difficult to enforce political finance regulation when laws contain loopholes as regards certain component units; when laws are too complex, burdensome, vague, or unrealistic to be implemented; or when oversight bodies are insufficiently resourced to carry out their duties. Therefore, it is of the utmost importance to define in the law key concepts. These include formal requirements (procedures related to bank accounts, financial agent nomination, etc.), electoral expenditures, the length of electoral campaign periods, permissible sources of financing (monetary and in-kind), calculations of spending limits, and reporting and disclosure requirements. They allow electoral contestants to comply with the rules.

A common loophole is when regulations apply to either parties or candidates, but not to both, allowing for funds to be channeled from one to the other and thus circumventing the law. Another problematic area pertains to third parties, which can, when not regulated, be used to circumvent political finance regulations and evade transparency obligations. As mentioned in the IDEA Handbook on Political Finance, "political spending by [third parties] poses serious problems in terms of the amount of corporate and interested money that can be channeled in to the political process" (IDEA's Handbook on Political Finance, p. 259). Ideally, the law should contain anti-circumvention provisions in order to anticipate and prevent this kind of situation.

In practice, the detection of possible political finance law violations is made through the monitoring and auditing of financial reports or through complaints received from individuals or organizations alleging violations supported by evidence. In order to do so, a political finance oversight body must be vested with sufficient resources and powers to carry out its tasks and must apply laws that are enforceable.

New Challenges: Social Media Campaigns

In recent years, social media has grown in importance for electoral campaigns. This new means of campaigning is very appealing due to its modest cost (compared to political advertising on traditional media outlets such as TV and radio) and its potentially wide prospects of voter outreach (as more and more people have accounts with Facebook, Twitter, YouTube, Pinterest, Instagram, and Tumblr).

The main question posed by the emerging issue of social media campaigns relates to paid advertising on social media platforms that involves targeted election-related communications. Indeed, it is critical for oversight bodies to track the amount of money spent on such ads and to trace the funding back to its source. A strict disclaimer policy in this regard would help improve the transparency of this new electioneering means.

The 2019 presidential election in Tunisia illustrates this new trend and brilliantly demonstrates how a candidate can become the frontrunner and be qualified for the run-off with a low-key campaign and massive utilization of social media.[22]

Conclusion

The general consensus in the political finance field is that, although adequately financed political parties and election campaigns are critical to a vibrant democracy, the existence of money in the political field is likely to entail risks for corruption and to contribute to citizen distrust towards the political class and lack of confidence in elections and the democratic process. There are a variety of political finance systems, with no "one-size-fits-all" method applicable in all contexts. Each country has its own political finance regulation, reflecting the very specific nature of the electoral system and of the combination of political, historical, economic, and societal factors.

While the ever-changing nature of any political finance system around the world makes it difficult for legislators and regulators to anticipate new trends and issues, the main challenge remains the enactment of comprehensive and enforceable legislation. Indeed, the best designed political finance system remains a dead letter if regulations are not enforced. Moreover, the set-up of political finance regulations must be balanced out with the need to respect fundamental freedoms and political rights, such as freedom of expression. This entails the necessity to establish a subtle balance between achieving the desired legislative outcomes and respecting political parties, candidates, and campaigners, as well as citizens' rights to freedom, expression, and association.

Notes

1 The Transparency International (2017) Global Corruption Barometer concluded that elected officials (together with the police) were found the most corrupt groups or institutions (36% of the surveyed sample).
2 Paragraph 19 of the United Nations Human Rights Committee, General Comment No. 25 to Article 25: "Reasonable limitations on campaign expenditure may be justified where this is necessary to ensure that the free choice of voters is not undermined or the democratic process distorted by the disproportionate expenditure on behalf of any candidate or party. The results of genuine elections should be respected and implemented."
3 United Nations Convention Against Corruption Article 7 (3): "Each State Party shall also consider taking appropriate legislative and administrative measures...to enhance transparency in the funding of candidatures for elected public office and, where applicable, the funding of political parties."
4 The OSCE/ODIHR (Organization for Security and Co-operation in Europe Office for Democratic Institutions and Human Rights) and Venice Commission state in their Guidelines to Political Party Regulation that "Generally, legislation should attempt to create a balance between public and private contributions as the source for political party funding. In no case should the allocation of public funding limit or interfere with the independence of a political party." (Venice Commission and OSCE/ODIHR (2010)).
5 See question 30 of International IDEA's political finance database.
6 OSCE/ODIHR Seminar in Warsaw, May 18–20, 2011. Consolidated Summary, p. 6.
7 See the International IDEA Quota Project, available at www.quotaproject.org/aboutQuotas.cfm.
8 "Quotas for women entail that women must constitute a certain number or percentage of the members of a body, whether it is a candidate list, a parliamentary assembly, a committee, or a government. The quota system places the burden of recruitment not on the individual woman, but on those who control the recruitment process. The core idea behind this system is to recruit women into political positions and to ensure that women are not only a token few in political life."

9 International IDEA Handbook on Political Finance, p. 309.
10 See question 38 of International IDEA's political finance database.
11 Recommendation Rec(2003)4 of the Committee of Ministers (Council of Europe, 2003) to member states on common rules against corruption in the funding of political parties and electoral campaigns (adopted by the Committee of Ministers on 8 April 2003 at the 835th meeting of the Ministers' Deputies).
12 Recommendation 1516 (2001)1 of the Parliamentary Assembly (2001)
13 Questions 1, 2, 7, and 8 of International IDEA's political finance database. 43% of the 28 European Union member states have banned foreign donations.
14 According to questions 41 and 43 of International IDEA's political finance database, 63% and 48% of countries surveyed have limits on the amount both political parties and candidates can spend. See also Falguera, Jones & Ohman (2014) Ohman (2013), and Ohman & Zainulbhai (2009).
15 See *"Buckley v. Valeo"* – 424 US 1 (1976); *Citizens United v. FEC*, 558 US 50 (2010); and *McCutcheon v. Federal Election Commission*, 572 US (2014).
16 Article 10 of the European Convention on Human Rights (ECHR), which states that "Everyone has the right to freedom of expression. This right shall include freedom to hold opinions and to receive and impart information and ideas without interference by public authority and regardless of frontiers... The exercise of these freedoms, since it carries with it duties and responsibilities, may be subject to such formalities, conditions, restrictions or penalties as are prescribed by law and are necessary in a democratic society."
17 *Case of Animal Defenders International v. UK*, ECtHR(GC) 48876/08 (April 22, 2013).
See also, *Bowman v. United Kingdom*, App. No 24839/94, 26 Eur. H.R. Rep. 1 (1998) and *TV Vest & Rogaland Pensjonistparti v. Norway*, ECtHR,21132/05 (December 11, 2008). See also *VgT v. Switzerland (No 2)* [GC] 32772/02 (June 30, 2009).
18 Based on the categorization of administrative resources set out by the Open Society Justice Initiative (2005) in Monitoring Election Campaign Finance, a Handbook for NGOs, 2004, the latter can be classified in four main categories: legal, financial, institutional, and coercive.
19 Questions 50, 51, and 52 of International IDEA's political finance database.
20 The OSCE/ODIHR Handbook for the Observation of Campaign Finance states "It is good practice for authorities to introduce a standard template and guidance for reporting, which enables timely analysis and meaningful comparison between different parties and candidates...Reporting formats should include the itemization of all contributions and expenditures into standardized categories as defined by the regulations. Itemized reporting should include the date and amount of each transaction, as well as copies of proof of the transaction" (p. 41).
21 Venice Commission (2001), paragraph 14, p. 4.
22 A smart scheme utilizing Facebook centered on dedicated closed groups run by the mastermind of the technical process. The young activists supporting Saied created networks at the local, regional, and national levels, which were difficult to penetrate or even find. They made them the nucleus of a project aiming at radically changing the existing regime that had been in place for more than 60 years, through the creation of groups at each administrative level of the country. The cyber-armies numbered about 600,000 people.

References

Council of Europe. (2003). Recommendation Rec(2003)4 of the Committee of Ministers to member states on common rules against corruption in the funding of political parties and electoral campaigns. Adopted by the Committee of Ministers on 8 April 2003 at the 835th meeting of the Ministers' Deputies. Retrieved from https://rm.coe.int/16806cc1f1

Falguera, E., Jones, S., & Ohman, M. (2014). *The institute for democracy and electoral assistance funding of political parties and election campaigns: A handbook on political finance*. Retrieved from https://www.idea.int/publications/catalogue/funding-political-parties-and-election-campaigns-handbook-political-finance

International IDEA (International Institute for Democracy and Electoral Assistance). (n.d.a). *Gender quotas database*. International IDEA Quota Project. Retrieved from http://www.quotaproject.org/aboutQuotas.cfm

International IDEA (International Institute for Democracy and Electoral Assistance). (n.d.b). *Political finance database*. Retrieved from https://www.idea.int/data-tools/data/political-finance-database

OECD. (2016). *The OECD report on financing democracy*. Retrieved from http://www.keepeek.com/Digital-Asset-Management/oecd/governance/financing-democracy_9789264249455-en#page1

Ohman, M. (Ed.). (2013). *TIDE political finance oversight handbook*. Retrieved from https://www.ifes.org/sites/default/files/tide_political_finance_oversight_handbook_0.pdf

Ohman, M. & Zainulbhai, H. (Eds.). (2009). *Political finance regulation: The global experience*. Retrieved from https://www.ifes.org/sites/default/files/political_finance_regulation_ the_global_experience_0.pdf

Open Society Justice Initiative. (2005). *Justice in action series: Monitoring election campaign finance: A handbook for NGOs*. Retrieved from http://www.soros.org/sites/default/ files/Handbook_in_full.pdf

OSCE. (2015). *The Organization for Security and Cooperation in Europe's Office for Democratic Institutions (OSCE/ODIHR) handbook for the observation of campaign finance*. Retrieved from https://www.osce.org/odihr/elections/135516

OSCE/ODIHR Seminar in Warsaw. (2011, May 18–20). *Consolidated summary*. Retrieved from https://www.legislationline.org/news/id/4/osce/odihr-human-dimension-seminar-on-%E2%80%9Cthe-role-of-political-parties-in-the-political-process%E2%80%9D--18-20-may-2011--warsaw

Parliamentary Assembly. (2001). Recommendation 1516(2001)1 of the Parliamentary Assembly on the Financing of political parties (adopted by the Standing Committee, acting on behalf of the Assembly on 22 May 2001). Retrieved from http://www.assembly.coe.int/nw/xml/XRef/Xref-XML2HTML-en.asp?fileid=16907&lang=en

Transparency International. (2017). *Global corruption barometer: Citizens' voices from around the world*. Retrieved from https://www.transparency.org/news/feature/global_corruption_barometer_citizens_voices_from_around_the_world

Venice Commission. (2001). *Guidelines and report on the financing of political parties*. Retrieved from https://www.venice.coe.int/webforms/documents/?pdf=CDL-INF(2001)008-e

Venice Commission & OSCE/ODIHR. (2010). The guidelines on political party regulation by OSCE/ODIHR and Venice Commission adopted by the Venice Commission at its 84th Plenary Session, Venice, October 15–16, 2010, CDL-AD(2010)024. Retrieved from https://www.venice.coe.int/webforms/documents/default.aspx?pdffile=CDL-AD(2010)024-e

Venice Commission & OSCE/ODIHR. (2011). Joint OSCE/ODIHR – Venice Commission opinion on the draft law on amendments and additions to the organic law of Georgia on political unions of citizens. Adopted by the Venice Commission at its 89th Plenary Session, Venice, December16–17, 2011. Retrieved from https://www.legislationline.org/download/id/3569/file/Joint%20VC%20ODIHR%20Opinion%20on%20draft%20Law%20amendments%20and%20additions%20to%20the%20Georgian%20Law%20on%20POLIT_Unions_22%20Dec%202011_en.pdf

15
GENDER QUOTAS IN POLITICS

Drude Dahlerup and Lenita Freidenvall

Introduction

Given the slow speed by which women's representation in political bodies has increased, there have been amplified calls for more effective measures to reach gender balance in political institutions. Gender quotas represent one such measure. In fact, since 1995, gender quotas have rapidly spread across the world (Dahlerup, 2006; Dahlerup & Freidenvall, 2005; Krook, 2009; Lépinard & Rubio-Marín, 2018). Today, more than one hundred countries have adopted gender quotas to "fast-track" women's representation in elected bodies of governments, ranging from reserved seats, legislated candidate quotas, and party quotas at national and/or subnational levels. While gender quotas vary in terms of design, where they are used, and to what extent they have achieved their objectives, they represent a major electoral reform, changing the dynamics of candidate selection and the traditional norms of politics as a male business.

This chapter addresses this global phenomenon – this gender quota revolution – by focusing on three key aspects: What are gender quotas, why are they adopted, and how have they been implemented (effect). The ways in which they have contributed to the diffusion of quotas in other arenas (spill-over) are also addressed. The chapter is based on our extensive research in the field over the past 20 years, as well as additional research by colleagues across the world. In general, gender quotas are a mounting research area and subject to scientific discussions in dissertations, journal articles, and books, as well as at numerous conferences (Dahlerup, 2019).

What Are Gender Quotas?

In principle, the idea behind gender quota systems is to recruit more women into political positions and to achieve equal participation of women and men in elected political assemblies. While different terms for equal participation have been used, such as gender equal representation, gender balance, or parity, they all refer to the idea of equal presence between women and men in political decision-making. Gender quotas in politics, also named electoral gender quotas, are thus a special measure to achieve the goal of gender balanced decision-making bodies. Gender quotas in politics can be defined as an affirmative action measure, which requires that a certain number or percentage of women – or of both sexes – be included among the candidates, or alternatively those elected (Dahlerup, 2018, p. 61 ff). The aim of gender quotas is to "reverse

 DOI: 10.4324/9780429401800-15

discrimination in law and practice and to level the playing field for women and men in politics" (IDEA, IPU & SU, 2014). While gender quotas, in general, are introduced in order to remedy women's historical underrepresentation, most quota laws, which target candidates, are in fact formulated in a gender-neutral way, thus setting a minimum/maximum for both sexes, e.g., 30–70 or 40–60%.

In countries without a constitutional affirmative action provision, gender quotas have, in some cases, for instance in France in 1982, been ruled unconstitutional – as a violation of the universal principle of equal treatment of all (Sineau, 2011). However, gender neutral quota laws have, as far as we know, not been charged on this ground. In general, we need more comparative studies of court rulings concerning gender quotas (Bjarnegård & Zetterberg, 2014). Gender quotas may target many different arenas, including politics, public administration, business, and academia, but the focus of this chapter is political institutions. Gender quotas may also be introduced at any level of the political system: Federal, national, regional, or local. This chapter focuses on the national level, specifically quotas adopted to increase the proportion of women elected in national assemblies. While many of the initial quota laws were unambitious (like the Armenian 5% quota for women) or imprecisely formulated, recent years have seen a wave of revisions, strengthening the original laws (see gender quota data bases: www.idea.int/data-tools /data/gender-quotas, www.openicpsr.org).

The three main types of gender quotas used in politics are: 1) Reserved seats (constitutional and/or legislative), 2) legal candidate quotas (constitutional and/or legislative), and 3) political party quotas (voluntary) (Dahlerup & Freidenvall, 2005; Dahlerup, 2006; Dahlerup & Freidenvall, 2010). The first type regulates the number of women elected (reserved seats), and the other two types set a minimum for the proportion of women candidates or a minimum/maximum of both sexes, either as a legal requirement (legal candidate quotas) or a measure written into the statutes of individual political parties (political party quotas).

Predominantly, gender quota regulations in politics are based on a binominal distinction between "women and men." Consequently, some quota scholars prefer the notion of "sex quotas." From an *intersectional* perspective, research has identified different ambitions behind quotas for national and ethnic minorities versus those for gender quotas. While quotas for national minorities aim to increase the autonomy of ethnic groups through separate or overlapping constituencies, the intension to adopt gender quotas is to integrate women (Htun, 2004; Bjarnegaard & Zetterberg, 2014). Looking at the actual difference between quotas regulation based on gender, ethnicity – and more seldom class (Egypt) – one finds that even if these groups overlap, there are usually separate and different quota types applied for genders and for ethnic national minorities. A large-scale exception is the Indian quota regulations from 1993–1994, where the 33% reservation for women at the local councils, the *Panchayats*, were combined with the already existing reservations for the scheduled castes. Such an integrated model will no doubt become more widespread in the future, since many political parties today discuss how to recruit more immigrants and ethnic minorities through quotas, alongside their quotas for women, with the purpose of integrating both groups.

Two Dimensions of Quota Systems

In scrutinizing the character of quota systems, a distinction can be made between two separate dimensions: 1) Where is the gender quota mandated and 2) what level of the candidate selection process does the gender quota target (Dahlerup, 2006, 19–21). See Table 15.1 below.

As for the first dimension, where the gender quota is mandated, gender quotas may be mandated in law (legal candidate quotas) or mandated by political parties themselves (voluntary

Table 15.1 Two Dimensions of Electoral Quotas Systems

At What Stage in the Candidate Selection Process/Mandated by	*Aspirants*	*Candidates*	*Elected Representatives*
Legal quotas (constitution or/ and electoral law)	Primaries	Candidate quotas	Reserved seats
Voluntary party quotas (party statutes or programs)	Aspirant quotas (short lists)	Candidate quotas	Informal reserved seats

Source: Dahlerup, 2006, p. 21, updated.

party quotas). Legislated gender quotas are mandated either by the constitution (like in Burkina Faso, France, Nepal, Tunisia, and Uganda) or by the electoral law or party law (as in many parts of Latin America, as well as, for example, in Belgium, Bosnia-Herzegovina, Spain, Poland, and Slovenia). In general, quota regulations may be described in detail in constitutions, while, in other cases, the constitutional formulations are quite vague, like Article 46 of the 2014 Tunisian Constitution, which states that "The state works to attain parity between women and men in elected Assemblies." Hereafter, the actual regulation is formulated the electoral law.

Voluntary party quotas are introduced by political parties themselves, most often by green, left, and social-democratic parties. In some countries, including Germany, Norway, and Sweden, several political parties have introduced quotas for their own lists, while, in other countries, only one or two parties have opted to use quotas. However, if the leading party in a country has adopted a party quota, such as the ANC in South Africa or the Social Democratic Party in Sweden, this adoption may have a momentous impact on the overall rate of female representation.

As for the second dimension, quotas may target the first, second, or third stage of the candidate selection process. Quotas that target the *first stage* focus on selecting *aspirants*, i.e., those willing to be considered for nomination, either by a primary or by the candidate selection committee and other parts of the party organization. Gender quotas at this stage are regulated by voluntary party rules that require a specific number or percentage of women or either sex be represented in the pool of candidates that are up for discussion. This system has been used in countries with plurality-majority electoral systems, like the controversial "All-Women Short Lists" used for some elections by the British Labor Party, and which gave priority to women in selecting candidates for vacant seats. Quotas that target the *second stage* of the candidate selection process focus on the actual nomination of *candidates* to be placed on the ballot by the party. This "candidate quota" system is frequently used and implies that a formalized rule (legislated or voluntary) is installed, according to which a certain percentage (for instance, 20, 30, 40, or even 50%) of the candidates must be women or formulated as a minimum-maximum in a gender-neutral way. Quotas that target the *third stage* of the candidate selection process focus on those *elected*. The type of gender quotas that target this stage are reserved seats. Here, it is decided that a certain percentage or number among those elected must be women. Reserved seats for national or ethnic minorities are well-known historically and have even previously been applied to women in some rare cases such as Pakistan after 1956 and Bangladesh after 1972, with some interruptions. Increasingly, gender quotas are being introduced by applying reserved seat systems, and women selected for reserved seats are increasingly not appointed, but elected like in Jordan, Uganda, Morocco, India (local), and Rwanda. Reserved seats are mandated in the constitution, since they require changes of the very frames of the electoral system (see the data base: http://constitutions.unwomen.org/en). An irregular exception was the Moroccan elections of 2002 and 2007, where the reservation of 30 women elected on a special National List with only women candidates was introduced by an "agreement" between the political parties in order to bypass the Constitutional Court. However, this arrangement was later legalized through a constitutional reform and a new electoral law. Reserved seats come in the following three main formats:

1. *A special nation-wide tier for female candidates only*: This system takes three major forms. (1) The election of a set number of women from districts designed for electing female parliamentarians only (in Rwanda, where women are elected in 24 provinces, through a specially designated electoral college); (2) a separate tier of female MPs directly elected in single-member districts (in Uganda); and (3) a separate tier reserved for women to be elected from a special all-women national lists (such as the 60 reserved seats for women in Morocco elected through a women-only list PR system/closed list and, in Mauritania, which elects 20 women through a women-only nationwide list) (Dahour & Dahlerup, 2013; Gender Quota Database);
2. *Specific constituencies reserved for women only*: This system ensures that specific districts will return only female candidates. It is used at the sub-national level in India by rotating reserved wards from one electoral cycle to another in order to avoid eliminating male candidates from the contest in a given district/ward for a long period of time (see Gender Quota Database);
3. *The "best loser system"*: This system reserves seats for women who garnered the most votes in their districts (as compared to other women), but did not win. For example, in Jordan, where 15 seats are reserved for women, the election commission calculates the percentage of votes for unsuccessful women candidates in district elections by dividing the number of votes they obtain by the total number of votes cast in their constituency. The 15 women candidates who obtain the highest percentage of votes nationwide are declared elected on the condition that no governorate/district obtains more than one reserved seat for women (Gender Quota Database).

Why Are Gender Quotas Adopted?

The adoption of gender quotas can be interpreted as a reaction against the persistent under-representation of women in elected bodies and the growing awareness of the need to redress this problem with the help of special measures, such as gender quotas. Despite the introduction of suffrage reform, which provided women and men equal rights to vote and stand for election more than 100 years ago in many older democracies, men continue to be over-represented in politics, whereas women constitute a small or large minority of elected representatives. In 1995, the world average was 11% women in the world's parliaments (single or lower house). In 2021, the figure has increased to 26% (www.ipu.org/wmn-e/world.htm). One may say, with Lépinard & Rubio-Marín (2018), that women's political participation in elected bodies has remained dismal.

Research has shown that the dominant citizenship model of a country is a key factor in explaining why (or why not) gender quotas have been adopted. Corporatist-consociational and hybrid (social-democratic) models have shown to be more amenable to gender quotas, as compared to liberal and republican citizenship models (Krook, Lovenduski, & Squires, 2009). For instance, Belgium's model of consensus democracy and tradition of integrating linguistic groups into public administration has offered a good starting point for the inclusion of women in politics (Meier, 2000; Meier, 2004; Meier, 2018), while France's republican model, based on an abstract citizenship and universalism, has traditionally been seen as a barrier to gender quotas claims (Murray, 2004). In recent years, however, significant nuances have been added to these claims. For instance, like its Belgian neighbor and despite its different conception of citizenship, France has emerged as a "true land of gender quotas" in many spheres of public life (Lépinard & Rubio-Marín, 2018; Lépinard, 2018). What is more, in the hybrid/social democratic models of citizenship in Scandinavia, which is considered a favorable context to advance equal representation of women and men, no legal quotas for political bodies have been adopted (Freidenvall, 2018; Rolandsen Augustin, Siim, & Borchorst, 2018). However, in Norway, legal quotas for corporate boards have been introduced (Teigen et al., 2018). As noted by Lépinard and Rubio-Marín, conceptions of citizenship may play a key role in framing the debates on quotas, but a minor role in predicting "if and what type of quotas will be adopted" (2018, p. 24).

Research has shown that the rapid diffusion of gender quotas may be explained by at least four factors, including the mobilization of the women's movement (Bruhn, 2003; Kittilson, 2006), the support of political elites for strategic reasons (Caul, 1999; Caul, 2001; Meier, 2004; Davidson-Schmich, 2006; Chowdhury, 2002; Baldez, 2004), the embeddedness of quotas in country-specific values of equality and representation (Inhetveen, 1999; Meier, 2000; Opello, 2006), and the transmission of international norms via transnational networks (Krook, 2006; Norris, 2007; Bush, 2011). As Mona Lena Krook has argued, "women mobilize for quotas to increase women's representation; political elites recognize strategic advantages for pursuing quotas; quotas are consistent with existing or emerging notions of equality and representation; and quotas are supported by international norms and spread through transnational sharing" (2007a, 369). A study of the driving forces behind the adoption of gender quotas, country by country, points to the importance of the *regional factor*, e.g., the important inspiration from neighboring countries and to the fact that gender quotas have been adopted by all kinds of societies, be they democratic, semi-democratic, or authoritarian (Dahlerup, 2018). Hence, gender quotas have been promoted by several actors that have seen a need for their introduction, albeit with different arguments and motives.

Coalitions that include women's organizations, male political elites, and international organizations or their transnational counterparts, and transnational feminist movements have been instrumental in passing electoral gender quota reforms (Krook, 2009; Dahlerup, 2018). Following the Arab Uprisings, several countries in North Africa and the Middle East have adopted gender quotas, partly to ease revolutionary movements. However, referring to international experiences, especially from the "West," could be counterproductive in contemporary Arabic contexts (Darhour & Dahlerup, 2019). In Central and Eastern Europe, as well as in the Balkans, gender quotas were in the start controversial because of the communist/socialist legacy (Dahlerup & Antíc Gaber, 2017).

Recent European research has added important new insights. For instance, broad coalitions of women, within and outside of political parties and cutting across the political spectrum, have been important in promoting gender quotas in Belgium, France, Greece, Slovenia, and Poland. However, quotas have also been adopted where women's movements have been week or internally divided, or where cross-partisan coalitions of women have been absent. In Italy and Portugal, for instance, the influence of European norms and standards, as well as other key actors, have been key, not women's mobilization (Donà 2018; Espírito-Santo, 2018).

The influence of the international community has also been an important additional factor in explaining the adoption of gender quotas (Krook, 2007b, 2009; Lépinard & Rubio-Marín, 2018). Mobilization for gender quotas has been helped by international norms, including hard law, soft law, policies, and programs, in which special measures (including affirmative action) have been promoted to increase the number of women in politics or even achieve gender-balanced representation. For instance, the international community recommends that measures should be taken to promote a more balanced representation of women and men in decision-making bodies. The Convention of the Elimination of All Forms of Discrimination against Women of 1979, which advocates "temporary special measures"[1] and Beijing Platform for Action[2] (adopted at the United Nation's Fourth World Conference for Women, 1995) have both been important policies in this area for legitimating the demand for gender balance in politics put forward by women's organizations and for calling on governments to implement special measures (including affirmative action) to ensure the equal participation of women and men in decision-making "in order to strengthen democracy and promote its proper functioning." In one of the 12 objectives of the Platform for Action, women's equal access to and full participation in power structures and decision-making is included, and there is a clearly stated aim to achieve gender balance in the nomination process, as well as in all decision-making processes. The conceptualization of "equal access," "full participation," and "gender balance" sends imperative signals to the world that there is a problem to be fixed, although the controversial word "gender quotas" is not mentioned. Usually, the UN Beijing Platform for Action in 1995 is pointed out as the starting point for the introduction of gender quotas, although voluntary party quotas were introduced in the Scandinavian countries in the 1970s, and legalized candidate quotas was adopted by Argentina, as the first country in the world, in 1991, in the recent wave of quota adoption.[3]

In addition to these international norms, further transnational sources have been important for the adoption of gender quotas, including regionally adopted human rights treaties such as the American Convention of Human Rights (1969); the African Charter on Human and People's Rights (1981), its Protocol on Women (2003), and the African Charter on Democracy, Elections and Governance (2007); and the European Convention on Human Rights (1950), as well as various declarations adopted at the international, regional, and sub-regional levels. In Europe, European Council Recommendation 96/694 has had an impact on quotas adoption among countries in Europe, including Belgium, France, Greece, Italy, Portugal, Spain, Slovenia, and Poland.

Implementation and Effects of Gender Quotas

Quotas have spread rapidly across the world in recent years, to countries and territories of varied political/institutional, socio-economic, and cultural backgrounds. Their form and design vary, as do their implementation and effects.

Out of the 50 countries that, as of August 2019, have more than 30% or more women in the lower houses of parliament, 42 (84%) countries use some type of gender quota system. Among these, 20 countries (40%) use legislated candidate quotas, 16 countries (32%) use voluntary party quotas, and 6 countries (12%) use reserved lists. Only 8 out of the 50 countries (16%) do not apply any type of quota system. In 2013, only 37 countries had passed the 30% threshold and, of them, 81% made use of gender quotas.

Partly because of unambitious and vague quota laws or lack of implementation, a little over 40% of the countries (43.6%) experienced no increase or less than five percentage points increase in the first election after the quota provision took effect. Additional causes, such as defeat of parties with higher women's representation, may have contributed to the actual decrease in ten countries. However, in a little less than 40% of the elections (37.2%), the result was an increase of 5 to over 20 percentage points in the proportion of women in parliament. Great leaps occurred in countries such as Rwanda (number one on the world rank order), Senegal, and Bolivia. Reserved seats quota systems did a little better than legislated candidate quotas, following the more decisive format of the latter.

As mentioned earlier, we have seen a wave of quota revisions, usually strengthening the laws, for instance, by raising the quota percentage or introducing effective sanctions for non-compliance. Note the three countries that have raised their quota provisions further, even though the increase after the first law exceeded 20% as was the case in Mexico (Dahlerup, 2018, 81 ff).

In addition, many political parties experienced considerable increases after their first adoption of voluntary party quotas. Take the example of the large Social-Democratic parties in Europe: In the Netherlands from 19 to 31% (1987), Germany from 16 to 27% (1988), and Sweden from 41 to 48% (1993). In the United Kingdom, as noted above, the Labour Party went from 14 to 24% women in their parliamentary group in 1994, after the first introduction of the All-Women Short Lists (Lovenduski, 2005; Dahlerup, 2018).

In some countries, the percentage of women elected has increased rapidly following the adoption of quotas (Bauer & Britoon, 2006; Kittilson, 2006; Nanivadekar, 2006) but, in other countries, the development has been slower or even non-existent (Murray, 2004; Htun, 2002). The reason for this varied result depends on many factors, including the electoral system into which the quota has been applied, the existence of rank-order, and sanctions for non-compliance. Informal norms involved in the selection process, such as the perceptions of women as politicians and the political will to change women's historical under-representation, also impact the implementation of gender quotas.

Quotas work differently under different electoral systems. In the analysis of electoral systems, the district magnitude (the number of representatives elected in one electoral district); the party magnitude (the average size of parties winning seats in each district); the electoral formula by which the winner of a seat is chosen; and the ballot structure, which determines whether the voter votes for a candidate or a party, as well as whether the voter makes a single choice or expresses a series of preferences, are three key components that have all shown to be important factors for women's representation. Indeed, all research has shown the importance of electoral systems for women's representation. In general, systems of proportional representation return more women than plurality/majority systems, since most of the latter are based on single-member districts. The major reason for this is that PR-systems offer multiple seats per districts, allowing parties to balance the ticket in terms of gender (Matland, 1998). Intervening variables such as the size of the district (district magnitude), legislative turnover, and party rules of candidate selection also need to be accounted for (Schwindt-Bayer, 2005; Tremblay, 2008; Matland, 1993; Jones 2009; Schwindt-Bayer et al., 2010; Kittilson & Schwindt-Bayer, 2012). Yet, today, the presence of an effective gender quota system may challenge most older theories of variations in women's representation. Larserud and Taphorn (2007) sketch the "best-fit-medium fit-and-non-favorable-combinations," and an updated version on these combinations and their prevalence can be found in *Atlas of Electoral Gender Quotas* (IDEA et al., 2014). Quotas are more easily introduced in PR systems than in majoritarian systems, since parties usually have several seats (multi-member districts) to "play with" in contrast to the zero-sum game in majoritarian systems, where there is only one seat available (single-member districts), meaning that the inclusion of a woman candidate means the exclusion of the incumbent candidates (predominantly men). But, even in PR-systems, some political parties may, in all or some constituencies, have difficulties in implementing quotas because they might only conquer one seat. Party magnitude is, therefore, another key intervening variable to consider when analyzing the implementation and effects of gender quotas (Schwindt-Bayer et al., 2010).

Rank-Order Rules

For gender quotas to be effective, rank-order rules, also called placement mandates, are crucial, since there is a need to specify where on the party list (in PR-systems) or in which constituencies (majority systems) women are to be placed. If a 40% quota for women means that these women candidates are placed at the bottom of the list, or in unwinnable constituencies, the objective of the quotas will not be reached. Hence, a rank-order system is needed, requiring parties to place women in winnable positions on party ballots or in winnable constituencies. Various types of rank-order rules (both vertical and horizontal) have therefore been adopted, such as the zebra or zipper system (a vertical rule), where women and men are placed on alternate seats on the party ballot (e.g., Bolivia, Costa Rica, Tunisia, and Ecuador). This type of alternation is also used by many Social Democratic parties and Green parties. In some countries, there is a requirement that the top two candidates are not of the same sex (e.g., Belgium). Other countries require a 40:60 ratio for every five posts on the list (e.g., Spain) or that one out of every group of three candidates must be a woman (e.g., Albania, Argentina, Indonesia, Northern Macedonia, Serbia, and Timor-Leste). In plurality/majority systems with single-member districts, horizontal quota rules may be applied. In France, for example, each party is required to field equal numbers of male and female candidates across all single-member electoral districts. For quotas to be effective, however, parties need to place women and men candidates equally in safe and unsafe constituencies. Most recently, however, some countries with single member districts have moved to solve this problem. In Mexico, the electoral authorities have, in some states, ruled that women shall be nominated in half of the "winnable seats," defined as districts where the party won a seat in the previous election.

Sanctions for Non-Compliance

For quota regulations to be effective, sanctions for non-compliance have proved to be crucial. Both rejection of the list and financial sanctions have been adopted. The most effective sanction is when the electoral management body has the legal mandate – and uses it – to reject non-compliant lists. This type of sanction is used, for instance, in Poland, Costa Rica, Northern Macedonia, and Belgium. In many countries, parties that do not comply with quota rules have a week, 48, or 24 hours to amend their lists (IDEA et al., 2014). Financial sanctions may be divided into two types: Financial penalties and financial incentives. Financial penalties imply that non-compliance with the legislated candidate quota is penalized financially. In Portugal, for instance, any party list that violates the quota law is made public and punished with a fine (IDEA et al., 2014), which is calculated according to the level of noncompliance. In France, non-compliance (in elections to the National Assembly) is punished by a fine that depends on the grade of the violation; however, the biggest parties have not found the fine sufficiently large to change their recruitment practices. In Albania, there is a fixed fine for non-compliance. In Ireland, political parties lose an important 50% of their state funding unless the quota requirement is met (a minimum of 30% women candidates and a minimum of 30% men candidates to be increased to 40% in future elections). In some countries, for instance, in Columbia, Croatia, and Georgia, financial incentives have been introduced to encourage political parties to nominate more women. In Georgia, parties that nominate at least 30% candidates of a different sex from each group of ten candidates on party lists receive a 30% bonus from the state budget; however, this has had little effect, especially in one of the largest parties, which has had a billionaire as its formal, later informal, leader.

Quota Spill-Over

Recent research shows that adoption and diffusion of gender quotas in politics has also taken place in other sectors, such as public administration and the corporate sector. However, the adoption of gender quotas unfolds differently in different scenarios and a certain sequence in the adoption of quotas in different sectors cannot be found. In their study of the adoption and diffusion of gender quotas in Europe, Lépinard and Rubio-Marín (2018) find the timing and sequencing of quotas differ greatly across their case studies. They also find that the adoption and diffusion, but also rejection, of gender quotas has followed four different paths in Europe: 1) Gender quotas as accessory equality measures, 2) gender quotas as transformative equality remedies, 3) gender quotas as symbolic equality remedies, and 4) gender quotas as corrective equality remedies (Lépinard & Rubio-Marín, 2018). The first scenario, *gender quotas as accessory equality measures*, comprises the Nordic dual-breadwinner welfare state countries Denmark, Sweden, and Norway, characterized by a relative paucity of quota schemes. Despite an early interest in gender equality, as shown by the early adoption of voluntary party quotas (but also rejection in Denmark and Finland), there has been a reluctance to use quotas and other top-down measures (maybe except for in Norway). Rather, bottom-up processes and self-regulation have been preferred, in line with their egalitarian culture and consensual democratic tradition. The second scenario, *gender quotas as transformative equality remedies*, consists of France, Belgium, Slovenia, and Spain, which are characterized by mixed gender regimes with relative high labor market participation of women but low participation in politics until the 1990s. A quota revolution is unfolding in these countries, having adopted not only voluntary party quotas followed by legislated candidate quotas but also quotas for public administration and corporate boards (Belgium, France, and Spain). The adoption of quotas is linked to transforming the gender regime and to making the democratic system more inclusive. The third scenario, *gender quotas as symbolic equality remedies*, comprises Italy, Greece, Portugal, and Poland, countries with a mixed or conservative domestic gender regime. Despite resistance to quotas, legislated candidate quotas have been adopted, often following a period the use of voluntary party quotas by some important parties. However, the introduction of quotas has been symbolic, and the discourse on gender equality has not translated into gender balance or transforming the conservative gender relation. The fourth scenario, *gender quotas as corrective equality remedies*, comprises Germany and Austria, two conservative countries with strong male breadwinner models that have rejected the adoption of legislative gender quotas. However, voluntary party quotas have been adopted, as well as public administration quotas and corporate gender quotas (for publicly owned companies), in a system of gradual correction. The adoption of one type of quota has paved the way for the adoption of another, despite resistance from conservative forces (Lang, 2018). Taken together, the four scenarios of quota adoption in Europe show that the paths toward the adoption of gender quotas vary.

The adoption of voluntary part quotas has paved the way for the adoption of legislative candidate quotas in some countries (France, Spain, and Slovenia, 2nd scenario; and Greece, Portugal, and Poland, 3rd scenario), other countries have resisted legislative candidate quotas (all five Nordic countries, 1st scenario) and even abandoned voluntary party quotas in the name of gender equality (Denmark and Finland, partly because quotas do not fit their open-ballot formats). But other countries introduced quotas for the public administration as far back as the 1980s, while first Norway, later Iceland, has included gender quotas in the corporate sector. In other countries the adoption of voluntary party quotas has paved the way for the adoption of public administration quotas and corporate board quotas, but not legislative candidate quotas (Austria and Germany, 4th scenario). In all countries, however, the actors that push for quotas remain the same: Women's rights organizations, women's sections in political parties, and women's policy agencies (Lépinard & Rubio-Marín, 2018). When the commitment of political parties and women's movements have been missing, the gender quota revolution has been limited in scope and reach.

Conclusion

This chapter has addressed a major electoral reform of recent years – the adoption of gender quotas in politics, by focusing on three key aspects: What are gender quotas, why are they adopted, and how have they been implemented. It has shown that, even if gender quotas do not solve all the many obstacles women meet in politics, gender quotas have contributed to increase in women's political representation, when constructed with high ambitions, clearly formulated rules, rank-order provisions, and sanctions for non-compliance. Out of the 50 countries that, as of August 2019, have more than 30% or more women in the lower or single houses of parliament, 42 (84%) countries use some type of gender quota system. It also shows that gender quotas in politics have started to contribute to the diffusion of quotas to other sectors (spill-over). However, the gender quota revolution that we have witnessed the last 20 years or so unfolds differently in different scenarios. Taken together, the chapter shows that there is indeed a need for more comparative studies on the adoption, diffusion, implementation, and spill-over effects of gender quotas, including the reactions from the court system to gender quotas.

Notes

1 Convention of the Elimination of All Forms of Discrimination against Women: www.un.org/womenwatch/daw/cedaw/.
2 Beijing Platform for Action: www.un.org/womenwatch/daw/beijing/platform/.
3 Gender quotas were used in politics by most Communist countries, however, utilizing a variety of quotas types (in contrast to the post-Communist myth of a unified 30% quota for women during Communism). Further, Pakistan applied gender quotas after 1956, Bangladesh after 1972 with some interruptions, and Egypt 1979–1984 – all, however, quite unpopular.

References

Bauer, G., & Britoon, H. E. (2006). *Women in African parliaments*. Lynne Rienner Publishers.
Baldez, L. (2004). Elected bodies: The gender quota law for legislative candidates in Mexico. *Legislative Studies Quarterly*, *29*(2), 231–258. Retrieved from http://www.jstor.org/stable/3598632
Bjarnegård, E., & Zetterberg, P. (2014). Why are representational guarantees adopted for women and minorities? Comparing constituency formation and electoral quota design within countries. *Representation*, *50*(3), 307–320. doi: 10.1080/00344893.2014.951171
Bruhn, K. (2003). Whores and lesbians: Political activism, party strategies, and gender quotas in Mexico. *Electoral Studies*, *22*(1), 101–119. doi: 10.1016/S0261-3794(01)00039-7
Bush, S. N. (2011). International politics and the spread of quotas for women in legislature. *International Organization*, *65*(1), 103–137. doi: 10.1017/S0020818310000287
Caul, M. (1999). Women's representation in parliament: The role of political parties. *Party Politics*, *5*(1), 79–98. doi: 10.1177/1354068899005001005
Caul, M. (2001). Political parties and the adoption of candidate gender quotas: A cross-national analysis. *Journal of Politics*, *63*(4), 1214–1229. doi: 10.1111/0022-3816.00107
Chowdhury, N. (2002). The implementation of quotas: Bangladesh experience. Paper presented at the IDEA Workshop, Jakarta, Indonesia, September 25.
Dahlerup, D. (2018). *Has democracy failed women?*. Oxford: Polity Press.
Dahlerup, D. (2019). Gender quotas in politics. In *Oxford Bibliographies in Political Science*. Retrieved from www.oxfordbibliographies.com
Dahlerup, D. (Ed.). (2006). *Women, quotas and politics*. New York: Routledge.
Dahlerup, D., & Freidenvall, L. (2005). Quotas as a 'fast track' to equal representation for women. Why Scandinavia is no longer the model. *International Feminist Journal of Politics*, 7(1), 26–48. doi: 10.1080/1461674042000324673
Dahlerup, D., & Freidenvall, L. (2010). Judging gender quotas: Predictions and results. *Policy & Politics*, *38*(3), 407–425. doi: 10.1332/030557310X521080

Dahlerup, D., & Garber, M. A. (Eds.). (2017). Gender quotas in politics in Central East Europe. *Teorija in Praksa*, *54*(2), 307–412. Retrieved from https://www.fdv.uni-lj.si/docs/default-source/tip/tip_02_2017_dahlerup_gaber.pdf?sfvrsn=2

Darhour, H., & Dahlerup, D. (2013). Sustainable representation of women through gender quotas: A decade's experience in Morocco. *Women's Studies International Forum*, *43*(2), 132–142. doi: 10.1016/j.wsif.2013.04.008

Darhour, H., & Dahlerup, D. (2019). *Double-edged politics on women in the MENA region*. Mounting View: Palgrave Macmillan.

Davidson-Schmich, L. (2006). Implementation of political party gender quotas: Evidence from the German länder 1990–2000. *Party Politics*, *12*(2), 211–232. doi: 10.1177/1354068806061338

Dona, A. (2018). Epur si muove: The tortuous adoption and implementation of gender quotas in conservative Italy. In E. Lépinard & R. Rubio-Marín (Eds.), *Transforming gender citizenship. The irresistible rise of gender quotas in Europe* (pp. 186–215). Cambridge: Cambridge University Press.

Espírito-Santo, A. (2018). From electoral to corporate board quotas: The case of Portugal. In E. Lépinard & R. Rubio-Marín (Eds.), *Transforming gender citizenship. The irresistible rise of gender quotas in Europe* (pp. 216–244). Cambridge: Cambridge University Press.

Freidenvall, L. (2018). Gender equality without legislated quotas in Sweden. In E. Lépinard & R. Rubio-Marín (Eds.), *Transforming gender citizenship. The irresistible rise of gender quotas in Europe* (pp. 366–399). Cambridge: Cambridge University Press.

Freidenvall, L., Dahlerup, D., & Skjeie, H. (2006). The Nordic countries. An incremental model. In D. Dahlerup (Ed.), *Women, quotas and politics* (pp. 55–82). New York: Routledge.

Goetz, A. M., & Hassim, S. (Eds.). (2003). *No shortcuts to power. African Women in politics and policy making*. New York: Zed Books.

Htun, M. (2002). Puzzles of women's rights in Brazil. *Social Research*, *69*(3), 733–751. The Johns Hopkins University Press. Retrieved from http://www.jstor.org/stable/40971571

Htun, M. (2004). Is gender like ethnicity? *Perspectives on Politics*, *2*(3), 439–458. doi: 10.1017/S1537592704040241

Inhetveen, K. (1999). Can gender equality be institutionalized? The role of launching values in institutional innovation. *International Sociology*, *14*(4), 403–422. Retrieved from https://journals.sagepub.com/doi/10.1177/0268580999014004002

International IDEA, Inter-Parliamentary Union, & Stockholm University. (2014). *Atlas of electoral gender quotas*. Stockholm: IDEA.

Jones, M. (2009). Gender quotas, electoral laws, and the election of women: Evidence from the Latin American vanguard. *Comparative Political Studies*, *42*(1), 56–81. doi: 10.1177/0010414008324993

Kenworthy, L., & Malami, M. (1999). Gender inequality in political representation: A worldwide comparative analysis. *Social Forces*, *78*(1), 235–269. doi: 10.2307/3005796

Kittilson, M. C. (2006). *Challenging parties, changing parliaments*. Columbus, OH: Ohio State University Press.

Kittelson, M. C., & Schwindt-Bayer, L. A. (2012). *The gendered effect of electoral institutions: Engagement and participation*. Oxford: Oxford University Press.

Krook, M. L. (2006). Reforming representation: The diffusion of candidate gender quotas worldwide. *Politics & Gender*, *2*(3), 303–327. doi: 10.1017/S1743923X06060107

Krook, M. L. (2007a). Candidate gender quotas: A framework for analysis. *European Journal of Political Research*, *46*(3), 367–394. doi: 10.1111/j.1475-6765.2007.00704.x

Krook, M. L. (2007b). National solution or model from abroad? Analyzing international influences on the Parity Movement in France. *French Politics*, *5*(1), 3–19. Retrieved from http://citeseerx.ist.psu.edu/viewdoc/download?doi=10.1.1.1065.7708&rep=rep1&type=pdf

Krook, M. L. (2009). *Quotas for women in politics: Gender and candidate selection reform worldwide*. New York: Oxford University Press.

Krook, M. L. (2010). Women's representation in parliament: A qualitative comparative analysis. *Political Studies*, *58*(5), 886–908. doi: 10.1111/j.1467-9248.2010.00833.x

Krook, M. L. (2013a). Electoral institutions. In G. Waylen, K. Celis, J. Kantola & S. L. Weldon (Eds.), *The Oxford handbook of gender and politics* (pp. 554–578). New York: Oxford University Press.

Krook, M. L. (2013b). Gender quotas and comparative politics: Past, present, and future research agendas. *Politics and Gender*, *9*(3), 299–303. doi: 10.1017/S1743923X13000160

Krook, M. L., & Childs, S. (Eds.). (2010). *Women, gender and politics: A reader*. New York: Oxford University Press.

Krook, M. L., Lovenduski, J., & Squires, J. (2009). Gender quotas and models of political citizenship. *British Journal of Political Science, 39*(4), 781–803. doi: 10.1017/S0007123409990123

Lang, S. (2018). Quota contagion in Germany: Diffusion, derailment, and the quest for parity democracy. In E. Lépinard & R. Rubio-Marín (Eds.), *Transforming gender citizenship. The irresistible rise of gender quotas in Europe* (pp. 279–307). Cambridge: Cambridge University Press.

Larserud, S., & Taphorn, R. (2007). *Designing for equality: Best-fit, medium-fit and non-favourable combinations of electoral systems and gender quotas*. Stockholm: International Idea.

Lépinard, E. (2018). The French parity reform: The never ending quest for a new gender equality principle. In E. Lépinard & R. Rubio-Marín (Eds.), *Transforming gender citizenship. The irresistible rise of gender quotas in Europe* (pp. 62–93). Cambridge: Cambridge University Press.

Lépinard, E., & Rubio-Marín, R. (Eds.). (2018). *Transforming gender citizenship. The irresistible rise of gender quotas in Europe*. Cambridge: Cambridge University Press.

Lovenduski, J. (2005). *Feminizing politics*. Cambridge: Polity Press.

Matland, R. E. (1993). Institutional variables affecting female representation in national legislatures. The case of Norway. *Journal of Politics, 55*(3), 737–755. Chicago, IL: The University of Chicago Press. doi: 10.2307/2131998

Matland, R. E. (1998). Women's representation in national legislatures. Developed and developing countries. *Legislative Studies Quarterly, 23*(1), 109–125. doi: 10.2307/440217

Matland, R. E., & Studlar, D. T. (1996). The contagion of women' candidates in SMD and PR electoral systems. Canada and Norway. *Journal of Politics, 58*(3), 707–733. Chicago, IL: The University of Chicago Press. doi: 10.2307/2960439

Meier, P. (2000). The evidence of being present: Guarantees of representation and the Belgian example. *Acta Politica, 35*(1), 64–85.

Meier, P. (2004). The mutual contagion effect of legal and party quotas. A Belgian perspective. *Party Politics, 10*(5), 583–600. doi: 10.1177/1354068804045389

Meier, P. (2018). Gender quotas in Belgium: Consolidating the citizenship model while challenging the conception of gender equality. In E. Lépinard & R. Rubio-Marín (Eds.), *Transforming gender citizenship. The irresistible rise of gender quotas in Europe* (pp. 41–61). Cambridge: Cambridge University Press.

Murray, R. (2004). Why didn't parity work? *French Politics, 2*(4), 347–362. doi: 10.1057/PALGRAVE.FP.8200063

Navidekar, M. (2006). Are quotas a good idea? *Politics and Gender, 2*(1), 119–128. doi: 10.1017/S1743923X06241011

Norris, P. (1985). Women's legislative participation in Western Europe. *West European Politics, 4*, 90–101. Retrieved from http://www.jstor.org/stable/1037889

Norris, P. (2007). Opening the door: Women leaders and constitution building in Iraq and Afghanistan. In B. Kellerman (Ed.), *Women who lead* (pp. 197–226). New York: Jossey-Bass.

Opello, K. A. R. (2006). *Gender quotas, parity reform and political parties in France*. New York: Lexington Books.

Rolandsen, A., Siim, B., & Borchorst, A. (2018). Gender equality without gender quotas: Dilemmas in the Danish approach to gender equality and citizenship. In E. Lépinard & R. Rubio- Marín (Eds.), *Transforming gender citizenship. The irresistible rise of gender quotas in Europe* (pp. 400–423). Cambridge: Cambridge University Press.

Schwindt-Bayer, L. A. (2005). The incumbency disadvantage and women's election to legislative office. *Electoral studies, 24*(2), 227–244. doi: 10.1016/j.electstud.2004.05.001

Schwindt-Bayer, L. A., Malecki M., & Crisp, B. F. (2010). Candidate gender and electoral success in single transferable vote systems. *British Journal of Political Science, 40*(3), 693–709. doi: 10.1017/S000712340999010X

Sineau, M. (2011). Case study France: Legislated 'parité'. In D. Dahlerup & L. Freidenvall (Eds.), *Electoral gender quota systems and their implementation in Europe* (pp. 69–81). Brussels: European Parliament, PE 435.210.

Teigen, M., Lépinard, E., & Marin, R. R. (2018). *The 'natural'prolongation of the Norwegian gender equality policy institution* (pp. 341–365). Cambridge: Cambridge University Press.

Tremblay, M. (Ed.). (2008). *Women and legislative representation. Electoral systems, political parties and sex quotas*. New York: Palgrave Macmillan.

Verge, T. (2018). Gender quotas in Spain: Broad coverage, uneven treatment. In E. Lépinard & R. Rubio-Marín (Eds.), *Transforming gender citizenship. The irresistible rise of gender quotas in Europe* (pp. 126–156). Cambridge: Cambridge University Press.

Websites

The Gender Quota Database. (n.d.). *Shows gender quota provisions world-wide. Issued by International IDEA in cooperation with Department of Political Science, Stockholm University and the Inter-Parliamentary Union, IPU.* www.quotaproject.org

Global Gender Equality Constitutional Database. (n.d.). *UN Women's database of the world's constitutions, quoting all the specific articles related to women and gender equality (in English, as well as the respective original language).* http://constitutions.unwomen.org/en.

Inter-Parliamentary Union. (n.d.). *Issued by the Inter-Parliamentary Union, showing women's parliamentary representation worldwide, country by country, since 1997, including the world rank-order: archive* [http://archive.ipu.org/wmn-e/classif.htm]. www.ipu.org

Quota Adoption and Reform Over Time (QAROT) (1947–2015). *Provides longitudinal data on adoption, implementation, and later reform of national gender quotas worldwide. Includes new measures of quota effectiveness.* www.openicpsr.org

16

ELECTION PARTICIPATION OF PERSONS WITH DISABILITIES

Enira Bronitskaya

Concept of Disability

One billion of people, or 15% of the world's population, experience some form of disability. Between 110 million and 190 million people experience significant disabilities (The World Bank). The Preamble to the Convention of the Rights of Persons with Disabilities (CRPD) defines disability as "an evolving concept" and stresses that "disability results from the interaction between persons with impairments and attitudinal and environmental barriers that hinder their full and effective participation in society on an equal basis with others." Article 1 of CRPD continues this definition as "Persons with disabilities include those who have long-term physical, mental, intellectual or sensory impairments which in interaction with various barriers may hinder their full and effective participation in society on an equal basis with others" (CRPD, Article 1). Disability is a characteristic of a person and, with elimination of different kinds of barriers, this characteristic should disappear or be minimized. Such a human rights approach towards disability took quite a long time to be elaborated and accepted. However, it is always important to remember that persons with disabilities are not a homogenous group. Persons with different types of disabilities may require different forms of assistance and support in order to enjoy their rights on an equal basis with others. Nevertheless, they have the same rights.

Electoral Rights

Many persons with disabilities do not have access either to education, health care, and employment, or to political life and election participation. The granting and implementation of political rights to persons with disabilities have always been very sensitive issues. This situation is still far from being good in the world. Typically speaking, electoral rights include the right to vote and right to stand for office. Out of 190 countries, 128 countries have exceptions in their constitutions, legislation, or laws that could restrict the right to vote for persons with disabilities, out of which 94 countries have exclusions targeting persons with mental or intellectual disabilities. Only 62 countries legally give all citizens including persons with disabilities the right to vote with no exception. On the right of persons with disabilities to be elected for office, 161 out of 176 countries have exceptions, out of which 104 countries include exclusions targeting persons with mental or intellectual disabilities. Only 15 countries give all citizens including persons with

DOI: 10.4324/9780429401800-16

disabilities the right to be elected for office without exception (Realization of the Sustainable Development Goals, for and with Persons with Disabilities. UN Flagship Report on Disability and Development, 2018, 303–4).

It should be noted that practical implementation of legal norms is another problem and requires separate evaluation. When we are speaking about persons with disabilities, it is especially important not just to prescribe the right but also to ensure true opportunity for its realization. Furthermore, persons with disabilities could find it challenging to exercise not only the rights to vote and rights to stand for office but also to participate in organizing and conducting elections (to be a member of election commission), to obtain information, to be a campaign member, or even just to be present at campaign events.

The global tendency to move forward in this area has been recognized by experts as beginning with CRPD acceptance. The CRPD was adopted in 2006 and came into force in 2008. As of 2020, 181 states were parties to the treaty, meaning that it enjoys near-universal recognition. However, before the CRPD, there were already positive examples. First of all, the 1965 Voting Rights Act (VRA) in the US required election officials to allow a voter who is blind or has another disability to receive assistance from a person of the voter's choice (other than the voter's employer or its agent or an officer or agent of the voter's union). The VRA also prohibits conditioning the right to vote on a citizen's ability to read or write, a particular level of education, or the passing of an interpretation "test." Later, the 1984 Voting Accessibility for the Elderly and Handicapped Act (VAEHA) required accessible polling places in federal elections for elderly individuals and people with disabilities. Where no accessible location is available to serve as a polling place, voters must be provided an alternate means of voting on Election Day (VRA, 1965). The 1990 Americans with Disabilities Act (ADA) requires state and local governments ("public entities") to ensure that people with disabilities have a full and equal opportunity to vote. The ADA's provisions apply to all aspects of voting, including voter registration, polling station selection, and the casting of ballots, whether on Election Day or during an early voting process (ADA, 1990). The 1993 National Voter Registration Act (NVRA) requires all offices that provide public assistance or state-funded programs that primarily serve persons with disabilities to also provide the opportunity to register to vote in federal elections (NVRA, 1993). The 2002 Help America Vote Act (HAVA) required jurisdictions responsible for conducting federal elections to provide at least one accessible voting system for persons with disabilities at each polling place in federal elections. The accessible voting system must provide the same opportunity for access and participation, including privacy and independence that other voters receive (HAVA, 2002).

Key Elements for Election Participation of Persons with Disabilities

Devoted to the political participation of persons with disabilities, Article 29 of the CRPD requires state parties to guarantee that persons with disabilities have political rights and the opportunity to enjoy them on an equal basis with others (CRPD, Article 29). The convention specifies certain measures – although it does not limit state parties to these measures alone – to be taken to ensure that persons with disabilities can effectively and fully participate in political and public life on an equal basis with others, including the right and opportunity to vote and to be elected. These measures involve:

- Ensuring that voting procedures, facilities, and materials are appropriate, accessible, and easy to understand and use;
- Protecting the right of persons with disabilities to vote by secret ballot;

- Protecting the right of persons with disabilities to stand for elections and to hold office and perform all public functions at all levels of government, including facilitating the use of supportive technologies, where relevant; and
- Ensuring equal and effective access to voting procedures and facilities in order to exercise their right to vote, including the provision of reasonable accommodations.

Article 29 further requires state parties to promote an environment in which persons with disabilities can effectively and fully participate, without discrimination, in the conduct of public affairs and to encourage their participation in public affairs (Article 29).

Beyond Article 29 there are several elements – such as equality and non-discrimination, legal capacity, accessibility, and awareness raising – that are crucial in order for Article 29 to be fully implemented and to ensure that persons with disabilities possess electoral rights and are able to realize them (CRPD, Article 29). We are going to describe these key elements and international standards explicitly, as well as existing international and some prominent national case law.

Equality and Non-Discrimination

The first elements are equality and non-discrimination. These ensure general protection of any rights for vulnerable groups including persons with disabilities. Article 2 of the CRPD defines discrimination as:

> Any distinction, exclusion or restriction on the basis of disability which has the purpose or effect of impairing or nullifying the recognition, enjoyment or exercise, on an equal basis with others, of all human rights and fundamental freedoms in the political, economic, social, cultural, civil or any other field. It includes all forms of discrimination, including denial of reasonable accommodation.

States that have ratified or acceded to the treaty are obliged to "take all appropriate measures, including legislation, to modify or abolish existing laws, regulations, customs and practices that constitute discrimination against persons with disabilities" (Article 4.1(b)). They are also further obliged to "take all appropriate measures to eliminate discrimination on the basis of disability by any person, organization or private enterprise" (Article 4.1(e)).

Article 29 (a) of CRPD prescribes that states are obliged, without any exception, based on disability type to "ensure that persons with disabilities can effectively and fully participate in political and public life on an equal basis with others" (Article 29 (a)).

In 1991, OSCE participating states made explicit commitments regarding disability. In Moscow, states committed themselves to "ensure protection of the human rights of persons with disabilities" and, importantly, to "take steps to ensure the equal opportunity of such persons to participate fully in the life of their society."

Countries should have general antidiscrimination legislation that already give persons with disabilities serious protection in cases of violations of their election rights. Even good anti-discrimination legislation and practices could solve all following issues. This is also noted in Committee for the Rights of Persons with Disabilities General Comment No. 6 (United Nations, 2008) paragraph 70 on equality and non-discrimination exclusion from electoral processes and other forms of participation in political life are frequent examples of disability-based discrimination. They are often closely linked to denial or restriction of legal capacity. States parties should aim to:

- Reform laws, policies, and regulations that systematically exclude persons with disabilities from voting and/or standing as candidates in elections;

- Ensure that the electoral process is accessible to all persons with disabilities, including before, during, and after elections; and
- Provide reasonable accommodation to individual persons with disabilities and support measures based on the individual requirements of persons with disabilities to participate in political and public life.

Legal Capacity

The next element is legal capacity. Persons with disabilities can be deprived of their rights based simply on fact of their disability. There is a long-standing stereotype that persons with disabilities (all or some) can't cast a "rational vote." Various terms are used to stipulate the exceptions, such as "incapacity," "incapacitated," "inability," "incompetence," "incapable," "under guardianship or curatorship," "infirmity of body or mind," "unsound mind," "insanity," "officially ordered into an institution," "committed to an institution," "mentally or physically incompetent to perform official duties," or having a "sound mind," "working ability," or "business capacity" to vote or be elected. However, Article 12 of CRPD obliges states to "recognize that persons with disabilities enjoy legal capacity on an equal basis with others in all aspects of life" (Article 12, CRPD). The article does not provide for any exceptions, including with regard to electoral participation. It instead specifies that states "take appropriate measures to provide access by persons with disabilities, to the support they may require in exercising their legal capacity" (Article 12, CRPD).

In 2010, the European Court of Human Rights (ECtHR) heard the case *Alajos Kiss v. Hungary* (application no. 38832/06), which related to the removal of voting rights based on mental disability. The court's decision narrowed the basis for the removal of voting rights based on mental disability by making it contingent on an individualized court decision, rather than on a blanket ban. The court stated that "an indiscriminate removal of voting rights, without an individualized judicial evaluation and solely based on a mental disability necessitating partial guardianship, cannot be considered compatible with the legitimate grounds for restricting the right to vote."

In 2014, the ECtHR heard a similar case, *Harmati v. Hungary* (application no. 63012/10). The applicant suffered from an intellectual disability. On October 4, 2000, he was placed under plenary guardianship (*Harmati v. Hungary* (application no. 63012/10). As an automatic consequence flowing from Article 70(5) of the Constitution, as in force at the material time, he was deleted from the electoral register. Consequently, he could not vote in the general elections held in Hungary on April 11, 2010. The court considered that the circumstances of the present application are virtually identical to those of the *Alajos Kiss* judgment, and it found no reason to reach a different conclusion in the present case. It thus followed that there had been a violation of Article 3 of Protocol No. 1.

The case law of the ECtHR does not fully reflect the approach of the CRPD on the matter of legal capacity. The ECtHR permits the limitation of legal capacity with respect to the right to vote, if the limitation is imposed by a court following an individual assessment. This contrasts with the CRPD, which affirms the right of people with disabilities to legal capacity on an equal basis with others and considers any limitation as discrimination.

In 2011, in *Bujdosó and five others v. Hungary* (CRPD/C/10/D/4/2011), the Committee on the Rights of Persons with Disabilities considered a case in which people with intellectual disability were placed under partial or full guardianship and their names automatically were removed from the electoral register. The committee noted that:

> Article 29 does not provide for any reasonable restriction or exception for any group of persons with disabilities. Therefore, an exclusion of the right to vote on the basis

> of a perceived or actual psychosocial or intellectual disability, including a restriction pursuant to an individualized assessment, constitutes discrimination on the basis of disability, within the meaning of article 2 of the Convention...States parties have a positive duty to take the necessary measures to guarantee to persons with disabilities the actual exercise of their legal capacity...Having found the assessment of individuals' capacity to be discriminatory in nature, the Committee holds that this measure cannot be purported to be legitimate. Nor is it proportional to the aim of preserving the integrity of the State party's political system...State party is required to adapt its voting procedures, by ensuring that they are "appropriate, accessible and easy to understand and use," and, where necessary, allowing persons with disabilities, upon their request, assistance in voting. It is by so doing that the State party will ensure that persons with intellectual disabilities cast a competent vote, on an equal basis with others, while guaranteeing voting secrecy.

In December 2011, the Venice Commission (European Commission for Democracy through Law, an advisory body of the Council of Europe in constitutional matters) amended its position on the electoral participation of people with disabilities, by adding a revision to its earlier Code of Good Practice in Electoral Matters (originally issued in 2002). The original Code of Good Practice had allowed for people judged by a court of law to have mental incapacity to be deprived of their voting rights. The original Code of Good Practice stated that deprivation of the right to vote and to be elected based on a finding of mental incapacity may only be "imposed by express decision of a court of law" (Council of Europe 2002). The 2011 Revised Interpretative Declaration to the Code of Good Practice in Electoral Matters on the Participation of People with Disabilities in Elections takes a different position, albeit still with some ambiguity related to ECtHR. It states that "Universal suffrage is a fundamental principle of the European Electoral Heritage. People with disabilities may not be discriminated against in this regard, in conformity with article 29 of the CRPD and the case-law of the ECtHR" (Council of Europe 2011).

Furthermore, in Committee for the Rights of Persons with Disabilities General Comment No. 1 (2014) on Equal Recognition Before the Law, the committee states that:

> Denial or restriction of legal capacity has been used to deny political participation, especially the right to vote, to certain persons with disabilities. In order to fully realize the equal recognition of legal capacity in all aspects of life, it is important to recognize the legal capacity of persons with disabilities in public and political life.
>
> *(Article 29)*

This means that a person's decision-making ability cannot be a justification for any exclusion of persons with disabilities from exercising their political rights, including the right to vote, the right to stand for election, and the right to serve as a member of a jury. States parties have an obligation to protect and promote the right of persons with disabilities not only to access the support of their choice in voting by secret ballot but also to participate in all elections and referendums without discrimination. The committee further recommends that state parties guarantee the right of persons with disabilities to stand for election, to hold office effectively, and to perform all public functions at all levels of government, with reasonable accommodation and support, where desired, in the exercise of their legal capacity.

Positively legal capacity has been a focus of reforms at the national level linked to ratification of the CRPD. For example, in December 2018, Spain removed the provision stating that people declared "incapable" by a final court judgment shall not have the right to vote. In its place, the revised article states that "every person may exercise their right to vote, consciously, freely and voluntarily, whatever their method of communication and with the means of support they require." As well as applying to new rulings on legal incapacity, the amendments also reinstate the right to vote of those currently under guardianship. The reforms followed a long-running legal case culminating in a 2016 Constitutional Court ruling that lower courts' decisions depriving a woman with intellectual disabilities of the right to vote on the basis of her lack of knowledge of basic aspects of the political and electoral systems did not violate the constitution.

In Germany in January 2019, the Federal Constitutional Court took a decision (2 BvC 62/14) that exclusion from voting rights of persons placed under full guardianship and of offenders confined in a psychiatric hospital, based on exemption from criminal responsibility, is unconstitutional. The Federal Elections Act prescribes that the right to vote may be deprived from certain group of persons who are "considered not sufficiently capable of participating in the communication process between the people and state organs." However, the court order states that the act:

> fails to satisfy the constitutional requirements regarding statutory categorisation, since the group of persons affected by the exclusion from voting rights is determined in a manner that runs counter to the right to equality without sufficient factual reasons. The law is not suitable for identifying persons who are generally incapable of participating in the democratic communication process.

The court stated that existing legislation contradicts the principle of universal suffrage and the prohibition of discrimination on grounds of disability.

The European Union has ratified the CRPD, but to date, its bodies have refused to initiate infringement procedures against member states that have not implemented principles outlied in the *Bujdosó* decision in their legal *systems* (Toplak 2020).

The African Commission on Human and Peoples Rights has also addressed the issue of legal capacity in the context of political participation. In the Gambia, the constitution provides that "[e]very citizen of the Gambia of full age and capacity" may vote, stand for election, and have equal access to public service (Constitution of Gambia, Article 26). In *Purohit & Moore v. The Gambia,* the African Commission on Human Rights interpreted Article 13 of the African Charter in relation to persons with disabilities in the Gambia, finding that the right to political participation for persons with disabilities is not subject to arbitrary exclusion. The case, which was brought by mental health advocates on behalf of patients detained at Campama, a Psychiatric Unit of the Royal Victoria Hospital in the Gambia, included a complaint that patients detained in the unit were not allowed to vote. In its judgement, the commission noted that:

> [i]n its earlier submissions, the Respondent State admits that persons detained at Campama are not allowed to vote because they believe that allowing mental health patients to vote would open the country's democratic elections to much controversy as to the mental ability of these patients to make an informed choice as to which candidate to vote for. Subsequently, the Respondent State in its more recent submissions suggests that there are limited rights for some mentally disabled persons to vote; however, this has not been clearly explained.
>
> *(African Commission on Human and Peoples' Rights,* Purohit and Moore v. The Gambia, *para. 74, Communication No. 241/2001)*

The commission went on to interpret Article 13 of the Charter, drawing also on clarifications provided by the UN Human Rights Committee regarding ICCPR Article 25, to find that there were no objective and reasonable criteria established by law which would provide grounds for excluding mentally disabled persons from voting.

However, issues of legal capacity are still, despite all international standards, the biggest legal challenge worldwide for full and equal participation of persons with disabilities in elections.

Accessibility

Typical obstacles reported by persons with disabilities in casting their ballots include difficulties in reading the ballot, waiting in line, finding and getting into the polling place, writing on the ballot, and communicating with election officials. All these could be solved by next key element, accessibility. Accessible environments, infrastructure, and media are often recognized as preconditions for the exercise of other rights prescribed by the CRPD (Committee for the Rights of Persons with Disabilities, General Comment No. 2, 2014). The requirement of accessibility is unconditional, so does not depend on circumstances or individual requests.

The concept of accessibility is much broader than a simple ramp. Article 9 of CRPD requires accessibility as "appropriate measures to ensure to persons with disabilities access, on an equal basis with others, to the physical environment…to information and communications…and to other facilities and services open or provided to the public" (CRPD, Article 9). "Communication" is comprehensively defined in Article 2 as including "languages, display of text, Braille, tactile communication, large print, accessible multimedia as well as written, audio, plain-language, human-reader and augmentative and alternative modes, means and formats of communication, including accessible information and communication technology" (CRPD, Article 2).

Here, we should also mention that Article 21, related to access to information, is also important for electoral participation, requiring states to provide "information intended for the general public to persons with disabilities in accessible formats and technologies appropriate to different kinds of disabilities in a timely manner and without additional cost" (CRPD, Article 21); to accept and facilitate "the use of sign languages, Braille, augmentative and alternative communication, and all other accessible means modes and formats of communication of their choice by persons with disabilities in official interactions;" and to encourage "the mass media, including providers of information through the Internet, to make their services accessible to persons with disabilities" (CRPD, Article 21).

Two key concepts connected to the accessible environments are universal design and reasonable accommodation. Universal design is defined as "the design of products, environments, programmes, and services to be usable by all people, to the greatest extent possible, without the need for adaptation or specialized design." The Committee's for the Rights of Persons with Disabilities General Comment No. 2 (2014) elaborates that "All new objects, infrastructure, facilities, goods, products and services have to be designed in a way that makes them fully accessible for persons with disabilities, in accordance with the principles of universal design." A very simple example would be ballot booths and boxes that are universal and convenient for everyone.

The second key concept is "reasonable accommodation," which is related to individuals who may have needs in a particular setting that go beyond general accessibility standards. This is defined as the

> necessary and appropriate modification and adjustments not imposing a disproportionate or undue burden, where needed in a particular case, to ensure to persons with disabilities the enjoyment or exercise on an equal basis with others of all human rights and fundamental freedoms.

For example, subtitles on campaign debate would be a measure of general accessibility while providing an individual sign language interpreter for a deaf member of the election commission would constitute reasonable accommodation.

With regard to elections, the Committee's General Comment No. 2 specifically notes that:

> Persons with disabilities would be unable to exercise those rights equally and effectively if States parties failed to ensure that voting procedures, facilities and materials were appropriate, accessible and easy to understand and use. It is also important that political meetings and materials used and produced by political parties or individual candidates participating in public elections are accessible. If not, persons with disabilities are deprived of their right to participate in the political process in an equal manner. Persons with disabilities who are elected to public office must have equal opportunities to carry out their mandate in a fully accessible manner.

So, procedures, facilities, and materials should be exactly accessible, meaning that states should proactively ensure this accessibility without waiting for some individual request (as it can be in case of reasonable accommodation) and should not depend on state resources or other excuses. In other words, accessibility is an obligation.

The Revised Interpretative Declaration to the Code of Good Practice in Electoral Matters also refers to accessibility of voting procedures and facilities, availability of information in alternative formats, and assistance technologies.

In 2016, EU issued the Directive on the Accessibility of the Websites and Mobile Applications of Public Sector Bodies (Web Directive). This sets out accessibility requirements of the websites and mobile applications of public-sector bodies to make them more accessible to users in EU Member States, in particular to persons with disabilities. In addition, there is a European Parliament resolution on the use of sign language interpretation, which "emphasises that public and government services, including their online content, must be made accessible via live intermediaries such as on-site sign language interpreters, but also alternative internet-based and remote services, where appropriate." It also refers to "making the political process as accessible as possible, including through the provision of professional sign language interpreters;" and "notes that this includes elections, public consultations and other events, as appropriate."

The 1991 OSCE Moscow document states a commitment to "encourage favorable conditions for the access of persons with disabilities to public buildings and services, housing, transport, and cultural and recreational activities" (OSCE, 1991), which includes access to polling stations, campaign venues, and other premises in the course of elections.

International case law on accessibility issues in elections has developed in recent years both by the Committee on the Rights of Persons with Disabilities and European Court of Human Rights. A promising case was *Fiona Given v. Australia* (CRPD/C/19/D/19/2014), considered by the Committee on the Rights of Persons with Disabilities in 2018. The plaintiff had cerebral palsy, and, as a result, she had limited muscle control and dexterity and no speech. She used an electric wheelchair for mobility and an electronic synthetic speech device for communication. On September 7, 2013, federal elections were held by means of postal voting, polling stations, and electronically assisted voting for persons with visual impairments. Fiona Given wanted to vote with the use of electronically assisted voting, but was refused, as it was limited only to the visually impaired. Under Article 29 of the CRPD, the state party is required to adapt its voting procedures by ensuring that they are appropriate, accessible, and easy to understand and use. The committee recalls that accessibility is related to groups, whereas reasonable accommodation is related to individuals. This means that the duty to provide accessibility is an ex-ante duty. States parties, therefore, have the duty to provide accessibility before receiving an individual request to enter or use a place or service. The obligation to implement accessibility is unconditional. This means that the state can't excuse itself from implementation of this obligation by limited resources, for example. In this case, the committee reaffirmed that election procedures should be unconditional and accessible to persons with disabilities on an equal basis with other people (CRPD, Article 29).

Assistance

This element, in theory, should be eliminated by accessibility and reasonable accommodation or should receive new meaning connected to personal assistance and/or supporting decision-making. But, historically, many international documents prescribed the element of assistance to persons with disabilities in voting.

The 1966 International Covenant on Civil and Political Rights (ICCPR) provides for the right to electoral participation "without unreasonable restrictions" (United Nations, 1966a, Article 25). In 1996, the ICCPR treaty body, the Human Rights Committee, prepared General Comment 25, an interpretation of Article 25. This stated that "Assistance provided to the disabled, blind or illiterate should be independent" (United Nations, 1996b). Article 29 of the CRPD also explicitly prescribes the right for assistance in voting procedure "where necessary, at their request, allowing assistance in voting by a person of their own choice" (CRPD, Article 29).

Classical understanding of assistance is related to physical help at polling stations, usually for persons with physical or sensory impairments. As for persons with mental, intellectual, or other disabilities that prevent them from easy and clear expression of their will, we need to mention another very important assistance: Supported decision-making. This is a series of relationships, practices, arrangements, and agreements designed to assist an individual with a disability to make and communicate to others decisions about their life, including when exercising the right to vote. Each person may need an individual approach, and some may need plain language materials or information in visual or audio form, some extra time to discuss choices, and some to bring a supporter into campaign event to take notes and help the person remember and discuss their options. Supporters should ensure that the person with a disability remains involved in all decisions concerning his or her life and that the identified supports match the person's abilities as he or she progresses across life. Unfortunately, today there is a tendency in some countries to not provide equal capacity to persons with disabilities (mental and intellectual), unless working mechanisms of supported decision-making are in place.

Another important note that should be mentioned in this section is that the concept of independent living means that "individuals with disabilities are provided with all necessary means to enable them to exercise choice and control over their lives and make all decisions concerning their lives," as it defined by General Comment No. 5 (2017) on living independently and being included in the community. This refers to personal, individualized support in everyday life, which also include electoral participation, as well as to the fact that moving towards full independent and inclusive living persons with disabilities simultaneously moves in realization of their electoral rights. General Comment No. 5 specifically states that:

> In order to influence and take part in decisions impacting the development of their community, all persons with disabilities should enjoy and exercise their rights to participation in political and public life (art. 29) personally or through their organizations. Appropriate support can provide valuable assistance to persons with disabilities in

exercising their right to vote, to take part in political life and to conduct public affairs. It is important to ensure that assistants or other support staff do not restrict or abuse the choices that persons with disabilities make in exercising their voting rights

Assistance Raising

Last but not least is an element related to awareness raising. As it was mentioned in the very beginning the concept of disability is also about attitude barriers for persons with di, and the area of electoral rights is not an exception.

The 1991 OSCE Moscow document encourages participants to "promote the appropriate participation of such persons in decision-making in fields concerning them" (OSCE, 1991), which includes in election-related laws, regulations, and policies.

Article 8 of the CRPD is fully devoted to awareness raising and requires:

- Awareness be raised throughout society, including at the family level, regarding persons with disabilities and respect for the rights and dignity of persons with disabilities be fostered;
- Stereotypes, prejudices, and harmful practices be combated relating to persons with disabilities, including those based on sex and age, in all areas of life; and
- Awareness of the capabilities and contributions of persons with disabilities be promoted (CRPD, Article 8).

In general, CRPD obligations specifically highlight the importance of educating those who, by their work duties, are obliged to guarantee the rights of persons with disabilities – namely "To promote the training of professionals and staff working with persons with disabilities in the rights recognized in the present Convention so as to better provide the assistance and services guaranteed by those rights." In case of electoral rights, we are speaking first of all about specific education for election administration and other relevant stakeholders. One good practice is to conduct regular training for election commissions members on how to communicate with persons with disabilities.

References

Bazalová, V. (2021). Accessibility of polling stations is at discretion of states, says european court of human rights. *Equinet Europe*. 29 November 2021. Retrieved February 20, 2022 from https://equineteurope.org/accessibility-of-polling-stations-is-at-discretion-of-states-says-european-court-of-human-rights/

Bundesverfassungsgericht. (2019). *Federal constitutional court (2 BvC 62/14)*. Retrieved August 10, 2020 from https://www.bundesverfassungsgericht.de/SharedDocs/Entscheidungen/EN/ 2019/01/cs20190129_2bvc006214en.html

Caballero-Perez, A. (2022). Toplak and Mrak v. Slovenia (ECtHR, 34591/19 and 42545/19): Positive obligations so that persons with disabilities can effectively vote. *European human rights cases updates*. Retrieved February 20, 2022 from https://www.ehrc-updates.nl/commentaar/211897?skip_boomportal_auth=1

Committee on the Rights of Persons with Disabilities. (2013). *Bujdosó and five others*.

Committee on the Rights of Persons with Disabilities. (2014a). General comment No. 1 on equal recognition before the law. Retrieved August 11, 2020 from https://documents-dds-ny.un.org/doc/UNDOC/GEN/G14/031/20/PDF/G1403120.pdf?OpenElement

Committee on the Rights of Persons with Disabilities. (2014b). General comment No.2 on accessibility. Retrieved August 11, 2020 from https://documents-dds-ny.un.org/doc/UNDOC/GEN/G14/033/13/PDF/G1403313.pdf?OpenElement

Committee on the Rights of Persons with Disabilities. (2017). General comment No. 5 on living independently and being included in the community. Retrieved August 11, 2020 from http://docstore.ohchr.org/SelfServices/FilesHandler.ashx?enc=6QkG1d%2fPPRiCAqhKb7yh snbHatvuFkZ%2bt93Y3D%2baa2q6qfzOy0vc9Qie3KjjeH3GA0srJgyP8IRbCjW%2fiSqmYfmDq3ksxwLkOg4ah20l9gIdTLftrM9hYrdwAJtQTlzP

Committee on the Rights of Persons with Disabilities. (2018a). Fiona Given v. Australia (CRPD/C/19/D/19/2014). Retrieved August 10, 2020 from https://juris.ohchr.org/en/Search/Details/2393

Committee on the Rights of Persons with Disabilities. (2018b). General comment No. 6 on equality and non-discrimination. Retrieved August 11, 2020 from http://docstore.ohchr.org/SelfServices/FilesHandler.ashx? enc=6QkG1d%2fPPRiCAqhKb7yhsnbHatvuFkZ%2bt93Y3D%2baa2qtJucAYDOCLUtyUf%2brfiOZckKbzS%2bBsQ%2bHx1IyvGh6OYrTkKW94%2bbftZyA2qp1n6CSHPkid5oppX5B7PWy3A7N

Council of Europe. (2011). *Venice Commission revised interpretative declaration to the code of good practice in electoral matters on the participation of people with disabilities in elections*. Retrieved August 8, 2020 from http://www.venice.coe.int/webforms/documents/CDL-AD%282011%29045.aspx

Council of Europe. (2002). *Venice commission code of good practice in electoral matters*. Retrieved August 8, 2020 from https://rm.coe.int/090000168092af01

EUR-Lex. (n.d.). *Directive (EU) 2016/2102 of the European Parliament and of the Council of 26 October 2016 on the accessibility of the websites and mobile applications of public sector bodies*. Retrieved August 10, 2020 from http://eur-lex.europa.eu/legal-content/EN/TXT/?uri= CELEX:32016L2102

European Court of Human Rights. (2010). *Alajos Kiss v. Hungary (Application no. 38832/06)*. Retrieved August 10, 2020 from http://hudoc.echr.coe.int/eng?i=001-98800

European Court of Human Rights (2014). *Harmati v. Hungary (application no. 63012/10)*. Retrieved August 8, 2020 from http://hudoc.echr.coe.int/eng?i=001-147275

European Court of Human Rights. (2021). *Toplak and Mrak v. Slovenia* (Applications no. 34591/19, 2545/19). Retrieved October 26, 2021 from https://hudoc.echr.coe.int/eng?i=001-212693

European Parliament. (2016). *European Parliament resolution of 23 November 2016 on sign languages and professional sign language interpreters (2016/2952(RSP))*. Retrieved August 10, 2020 from http://www.europarl.europa.eu/sides/getDoc.do?pubRef=-//EP//TEXT+TA+P8-TA-2016-0442+0+DOC+XML+V0//EN

Global Health & Human Rights Database. (n.d.). *Purohit & Moore v. The Gambia (Communication No. 241/2001)*. Retrieved August 8, 2020 from https://www.globalhealthrights.org/africa/purohit-and-moore-v-the-gambia/

Grad, F., Sovdat, J., & Zagorc, S. (2021). *Volilno pravo*. Ljubljana: University of Ljubljana Faculty of Law.

Norton, H. (2021). EU court ruling fails to remove obstacles for voters with disabilities. *Euractiv*. 15 November 2021. Retrieved February 20, 2022 from https://www.euractiv.com/section/non-discrimination/news/eu-court-ruling-fails-to-remove-obstacles-for-disabled-voters/

OSCE. (1991). Document of the Moscow meeting of the Conference on the Human Dimension of the CSCE. Retrieved August 8, 2020 from https://www.osce.org/files/f/documents/2/3/14310.pdf

Realization of the Sustainable Development Goals for and with Persons with Disabilities. (n.d.). *UN flagship report on disability and development 2018*. Retrieved August 8, 2020 from https://www.ohchr.org/Documents/HRBodies/CRPD/UN2018FlagshipReportDisability.pdf

The World Bank. (n.d.). *Disability inclusion*. Retrieved August 8, 2020 from https://www.worldbank.org/en/topic/disability

Toplak, J. (2020). Voting is every EU citizen's right, regardless of disability. *Euractiv*. 7 September 2020. Retrieved February 20, 2022 from https://www.euractiv.com/section/eu-elections-2019/opinion/voting-is-every-eu-citizens-right-regardless-of-disability/

Vikash Kumar. Dignity and disability rights at the Indian supreme court. *Oxford Human Rights Hub*. Retrieved February 20, 2022 from https://ohrh.law.ox.ac.uk/vikash-kumar-dignity-and-disability-rights-at-the-indian-supreme-court/

United Nations (1966a). International covenant on civil and political rights (ICCPR). Retrieved February 21, 2022 from https://www.ohchr.org/en/professionalinterest/pages/ccpr.aspx

United Nations. (1996b). International covenant on civil and political rights (ICCPR), General Comment 25, Committee on Human Rights.

United Nations (2008): Convention of the Rights of Persons with Disabilities. Retrieved August 10, 2020 from https://www.un.org/development/desa/disabilities/convention-on-the-rights-of-persons-with-disabilities/convention-on-the-rights-of-persons-with-disabilities-2.html

United States Department of Justice. (n.d.). *The Americans with Disabilities Act of 1990 and revised ADA regulations implementing Title II and Title III.* Retrieved August 11, 2020 from https://www.ada.gov/2010_regs.htm

Vrancken, M. (2022). (Not) applying CRPD standards and the question of fair referencing: Toplak and Mrak v. Slovenia. *Strasbourg Observers.* 8 February 2022. Retrieved February 20, 2022 from https://strasbourgobservers.com/2022/02/08/not-applying-crpd-standards-and-the-question-of-fair-referencing-toplak-and-mrak-v-slovenia/

17

PERSONALIZATION OF ELECTIONS

In Search of the Sound Conception

Klemen Jaklič[1] *and Maša Setnikar*[2]

Introduction

In the most abstract sense, the idea of the personalization of elections is about making elections more about individuals and less about political parties. This is important, as many citizens feel it easier to entrust decision-making in their own affairs to concrete individual persons, as opposed to the relatively more abstract entities of political parties. Beyond this highest level of generalization, the meanings of the concept of personalization begin to diverge.

In this chapter, we argue that the primary purpose of personalizing elections is to enhance the decisive influence of voters over the issue of which individual candidates – competing flesh and blood individuals – are to be elected. In a democracy, it is the people, the voters, who are both the ultimate addressees and themselves the authors of any legal norm. It is therefore imperative that the question of personalization of elections be viewed and assessed through this even more fundamental background principle of the decisive (as opposed to irrelevant) influence of voters. According to this understanding, the systems with the greater degree of personalization are those that unleash the greater extent of the decisive influence of voters over the said issue. Because it does not take seriously enough the background principle of the decisive influence of voters, we will argue that the other major understanding of the concept of personalization of elections – the idea of whether or not some electoral system is cultivating the personal reputations of individual candidates as the decisive factor in elections versus the reputations of the parties to which they belong – may not be the better understanding of the concept.

To make the discussion more graphic, we will introduce the topic with the example of the Slovenian electoral system, which was recently subjected to a close judicial scrutiny before the Slovenian Constitutional Court, but only in order to extrapolate from that and make broader points, relevant for the scholarship on personalization generally. We will indicate three different, but crucial, meanings of the decisive influence of voters and show some ways in which proportional electoral systems can frustrate this background principle. At the core of such frustrations is precisely the improper understanding of the concept of personalization of elections – the one assuming that the requirement of personalization is met already, or met best, when an electoral system cultivates the personal reputations of individual candidates instead of the reputation of the parties to which they belong.

DOI: 10.4324/9780429401800-17

In the first section, we present these two majors, but also competing, understandings of the concept of personalizing elections. There we also explain how the "personal reputations" version has been implemented in Slovenian election law. In the following section, we then proceed to show the weakness of such a concept of personalization – although masquerading itself as a personalization-enhancing feature, it does not serve well the central principle of the equality of vote ("one person one vote") or, what is crucial, the background principle of the decisive influence of voters. This is followed by an identification of the sound conception and meanings of the personalization of elections, which must not only be compatible with the equality of vote, but must also be favorably assessed against the three different meanings of the decisive influence of voters as the background value that the idea of the personalization is supposed to secure and enhance. Through the scrutiny of the concrete case, the analysis draws broader lessons for reviewing, drafting, and reforming electoral systems, in general, so that they may genuinely further the goal of personalizing elections.

Personalization of Elections

The focus of electoral scholarship has long been on the inter-party aspects of election systems. This is concerned with the distribution of seats across parties. More recently, however, this focus has been joined also by the intra-party dimension – more in-depth studies into the question of the distribution of seats among individual candidates within parties.[3] While this scholarship has produced several different sub-variants of understanding the idea of personalizing elections, two are major conceptual meanings. They are, in part, also conflicting.

The most widely recognized early analysis of the intra-party dimension was carried out by Carey and Shugart (1995). It suggests that some electoral systems "encourage candidates to cultivate their personal reputations, whereas others give candidates an incentive to rely on the reputations of the parties to which they belong" (Renwick & Pilet, 2016, 18). The first type electoral systems lead to elections dominated by individual candidates, while the second type systems to party-dominated elections. Carey and Shugart (1995) then used several sub-criteria to classify electoral systems along this line of personalization/non-personalization. They distinguished, for instance, among the systems where one can cast one's vote only for a party, the systems in which one can vote for multiple individual candidates, and the systems where one can vote for only one individual candidate. From the perspective of their above-defined notion of personalization, they concluded that it is the third type of electoral system (where one can vote for only *one* candidate) that unleashes the greatest incentive for the candidates to cultivate their personal reputations; for, it is in these kinds of systems that the candidate most needs to be the voters' first preference (Renwick & Pilet, 2016, 19). This "personal reputation" approach thus represents the first major conceptual meaning of personalization.

The other understanding of personalizing elections is less candidate-focused. It is instead more voter-centered and thus concentrated on the question of the openness/closure of the choice that the voter has in choosing which of the individual candidates of the same party should be elected (Renwick & Pilet, 2016, 19). The more open the voter's choice among the individual candidates of the same party, the more personalized the electoral system. And the other way around: The more this choice is reserved to the parties themselves, as opposed to being left to the voter, the more the electoral system is de-personalized (party-centered). We suggest that the deeper principle of the decisive influence of voters (over the question of which individual candidate is to be elected) underpins this second major understanding of the idea of personalization.

In the spirit of the idea of personalizing elections, Slovenia introduced an electoral system,[4] according to which each political party could delegate one – and only one – individual candidate per voting district in a proportionate system of party lists. The typical proportional system, therefore, also incorporated this personalization dimension. In this system, the voter casts a vote for an individual candidate, a real person with a name and record of personal reputation. Moreover, the voter casts her vote only for one candidate in her voting district; each party, as mentioned, is only permitted to delegate one candidate for each district. At the same time, the vote cast for the individual candidate also counts as the vote for the political party of this individual candidate in the proportional electoral system. The candidates are elected according to the classical proportionate formula, assigning first the total number of sits won by each party on the national level. These seats would then be filled by the individual party candidates who, in their respective districts, won the greater percentage of votes than did their competitors from the same party in their own districts. And so on, until the total number of seats won by each party is exhausted.

It is obvious from this description that the Slovenian election law quite straightforwardly adopted the first conception, or meaning, of personalization – the idea that personalization is about the electoral system's ability to cultivate the personal reputations of individual candidates, which allegedly was most effectively secured in those systems in which the voter could vote only for *one* candidate. At the same time, this is just as clearly not the second understanding of the personalization idea; indeed, we will see that it leaves little to no choice to the voter herself as to which individual candidate of the candidates from same party is to be elected.

Improper Implementations

The Equality of Vote

It is characteristic of majority electoral systems to insist on roughly equal-sized voting districts. This is, of course, in order to ensure the equality of vote by each voter across the different voting districts. Proportional electoral systems, by contrast, do not usually divide their voting districts to equal-sized units. Nor do they need to. The equality of vote is not compromised by the different-sized districts because the distribution of seats to candidates from different parties, just as the total number of seats won by the parties themselves, is determined at a larger level – either the national level or one common level above the district level – where the unit size is equal.

Yet, we are about to see that this general rule becomes problematic when such a typical proportional system is enriched by the element of personalization, more precisely by the first of the two types of personalization described in the previous section. This is exactly the type also employed by the Slovenian election law. The problem is that, in the case of this first type personalization-enriched proportional system, the district size suddenly matters. It does so not in terms of the equality of vote (one person one vote) with respect to the candidates of different parties (the inter-party dimension), but rather with respect to the candidates of the same party (the intra-party dimension).

A recent constitutional challenge to the national election law before the Slovenian Constitutional Court included the claim that, due to the radically different sizes of the voting districts, such a system of personalization violated the fundamental constitutional principle of the equality of vote, or "one person one vote." The majority of the Constitutional Court refused to consider this major substantive challenge, brushing it gently under the carpet, and then decided instead to overrule the election law on much more formal grounds that are irrelevant to the topic of this article. A more straightforward dissenting opinion, however, did go further and addressed the mentioned challenge (Judgment of the Constitutional Court of Slovenia, 2018. Separate opinion, concurring in part and dissenting in part, by Judge Dr. Jaklič). In so doing, it exposed some relevant insights.

The difference in size among different voting districts in Slovenia was one to approximately four, which is a ratio not untypical for proportional system.[5] In proportionate systems, the difference in district size does not normally pose any problem, as the parliamentary seats are distributed among the party lists at the national or similar larger level that is of the same size to all. Yet, due to the second type of personalization adopted by the Slovenian electoral code, such difference in district sizes was nonetheless problematic. Although the number of seats won by each political party and the distribution of seats across competing parties was distributed at the national level, the question of which individual candidate from the same party list was going to be elected (get to occupy one of the seats within the number won by each party) was inevitably resolved at the lower, district level (Toplak, 2006).[6] This means that, as to the decisive personalization question – which of the candidates from the same party gets to get in? – the law that assumed different district sizes in proportion of 1:4, in effect, gave some voters one vote, while some other voters an equivalent of four. This is because, in determining the power of the vote, the district size obviously matters: When you are casting your vote within a group of ten, your vote carries four times more weight than it does when you are doing so in a group of 40. Thus, in Slovenia, the voter in the smallest district had about four times greater weight (an equivalent of four votes) over which individual candidate from the same party list was going to be elected than the voter from the largest district, whose vote's weight, as to this intra-party question, was four times weaker (an equivalent of one vote).

This election law has been in place since Slovenian independence. The dissenting opinion was therefore critical of the fact that the Slovenians, for almost 30 years now, have been electing their representatives through a system that gravely violated the fundamental democratic principle of "one person one vote," which is considered one of the preconditions to democracy:

> This is an obvious and, indeed, an appalling violation of the equality of vote, which should not happen in any democratic state. By nature of things, a state with such a fundamental violation of the democratic process could hardly be characterized as a democracy. It does not respect the fundamental principle of democracy stating that, regardless of the social, economic, racial, gender, or any other status, including the place of residence, every person should have no more votes than another ("one person one vote").[7] This appalling violation of the basics of democracy and of voting rights has been going on in Slovenia for more than twenty years. For a state in the 21st century that characterizes itself as democratic, this is impermissible and, unfortunately, also disgraceful…I understand the discomfort of the majority of my colleagues, who preferred to brush the issue under the carpet. The Slovenian politics, as well as its scholarship that had helped prepare and push such a law through the parliament without even making this type of critique, have in my view both failed on this issue. It is likewise true that even the Constitutional Court itself in subsequent years, but before this composition, ruled in favor of constitutionality of this law no less than twice. Yet that was never on the specific ground that I have been mentioning right now. The parties before the Court back then always mistakenly presented the argument from inequality as being about the allocation of the numbers of sits between different political parties. The Constitutional Court correctly rejected that argument, explaining that it was not sound because the numbers of seats among the parties were allocated on the national level, where there

was only one calculating unit size, the national, and that one was equal for all. But the Court back then did not, unfortunately, think further than that: it did not also look into the different issue of the allocation of *individual candidates* to those numbers of the party sits, which, in the Slovenian version of personalization, happens in the parallel race between the candidates of *the same* party. That race, however, is decided on the level of the voting districts, and there the districts' unequal size is fatal for the equality of vote. Up to this case, no party before the Constitutional Court has ever made that argument. It would not have been entirely clear in this case either, if it was not for the public hearing, at which I expressly clarified with the party that this, too, is what it was meant with its challenge.

(Judgment of the Constitutional Court of Slovenia, 2018. Separate opinion, concurring in part and dissenting in part, by Judge Dr. Jaklič)

This is indeed a serious violation. Once exposed, it became inevitable that it would have, sooner or later, been subject to the scrutiny of the European Court of Human Rights in Strasbourg. At issue is its obvious (in)compatibility with the minimum common European standards in the electoral field, as codified by the European Commission for Democracy Through Law (the Venice Commission) in its Code of Good Practice in Electoral Matters (The Venice Commission, 2018). Moreover, it represents a rather radical departure from the comparatively accepted minima in this area. In the US, for instance, ever since the 1960s, even the smallest departures from "one person one vote" (above 1% in district size) are declared violations of the equal protection of the laws and thus held unconstitutional.[8] In the European context, the mentioned Code of Good Practice in Electoral Matters, issued by the Venice Commission, explains that the district size difference may be up to 10%, not 15, except in truly exceptional circumstances, such as when the protection of minorities so requires.[9] In Australia, Belarus, Italy, and Ukraine, departures are permitted up to 10%,[10] with Australia requiring an additional constraint limiting the district difference to no more than 3.5% in the period of three years and six months after new corrections. In Germany and the Czech Republic, one finds the greatest departures still tolerated in the scholarly literature,[11] i.e., 15%.[12] In the UK, a standard of as high as a 25% difference was set in 1944. It was, however, declared impermissible only two years later. The current rule in the UK permits for no more than the 5% difference.[13] We see, therefore, the placement in this comparative landscape of the Slovenian case, where the difference in district size and the corresponding difference in the votes' weights, is almost 400%!

In contrast to the court's majority, the dissent insisted that such a violation be presented to the public openly and with no reservations:

The Constitutional Court decides cases in the name of the people and for the people as the sovereign of this country. By what right, then, could we keep them in the dark – be it for the sake of defending scholarship, politics, or the illusionary legitimacy of the Parliament's personal compositions thus far – and thus hide from them the fact that in all these years since the break with the old regime their democratic rights nonetheless remained fundamentally curtailed, and the promise of democracy unfulfilled. Now that the violation is known and has been exposed, the legislature will have no alternative but to fix the problem. It will not be enough for it to remedy just the formal aspects the majority of my colleagues invoked as the reason for invalidating the law. Whether it likes it or not, it will need to find a remedy also for this fundamental violation of the "one person one vote" axiom. Or else, sooner or later the country will face a

> serious difficulty before the European Court of Human Rights as the guardian of the European Convention on Human Rights and Fundamental Freedoms. The common European standards on the question of the permitted degree of departure from "one person one vote" are clear and even codified.

Although presenting itself as a personalization-enhancing feature, we see that, in proportional electoral systems, the improperly understood concept of personalization can lead to a conflict even with the fundamental axiom of a democratic electoral system, the equality of vote ("one person one vote"). In what follows, we will observe how such a conception of personalization not only can, but does, harm the other major ideal of a democratic electoral system – the principle of the decisive influence of voters.

The Decisive Influence of Voters

The Slovenian Constitution explicitly stipulates an electoral system that guarantees "a decisive influence of voters over the distribution of parliamentary sits." This is, at the same time, one of the core general principles, or ideals, of a democratic order. Being undisputed as an ideal, the question remains as to what exactly the principle means in more concrete terms.

We suggest that it could be understood in at least three different, but mutually complementary and reinforcing, ways. They all are very important – separately, as well as together in their cumulative effect. We will argue, however, that each of these, and thus all together, are frustrated by the improper (the first) type of personalization. This is paradoxical, as the point of personalization is to secure and enhance the decisive influence of voters on the concrete distribution of parliamentary seats to individual candidates, and not the other way around. Such an analysis will, in the end, also pave the way to identifying the soundest understanding of the personalization of elections, which is the only one fully compatible with all of the three meanings, both individual and collective, of the decisive influence of voters.

Vis-à-vis Other Voters

The first meaning of the decisive influence of voters already flows from the discussion on the equality of vote from the previous subsection. This meaning sees the decisive influence as a measure among voters, i.e., as an influence of a voter vis-à-vis another voter's influence. We saw in the previous subsection that, as to the distribution of seats among the candidates from the same party list, some voters (those casting their votes in the smallest voting districts) have a truly decisive influence when compared to some other voters (those casting their votes in the largest districts). In the given example, the difference in the influence was 400%, which was a reflection of a typical difference in district size in proportional systems. It is obvious that, in such an electoral system, some of the voters enjoy a decisive influence over the concrete distribution of sits to individual candidates from the same party, while some other voters, by definition, have an insignificant influence over that same issue. We see that the first conceptual meaning of personalization (personalization as mere cultivation of personal reputations of individual candidates, irrespective of the openness of the system to the voter's choice among several candidates of the same party) tends to compromise this important initial meaning of the decisive influence of voters. At the minimum, the first conceptual meaning of personalization does not by itself guarantee this first meaning of the decisive influence of voters. Only a richer concept of personalization would be able to do that.

Vis-à-vis Political Parties

The second meaning of the decisive influence of voters is the central one. It concerns the question of whether the decisive influence over which individual candidates from the same party list get elected is in the hands of the political parties or, alternatively, in the hands of the voters themselves. This meaning of the decisive influence amounts exactly to the second major conceptual meaning of personalization, as defined at the inception of our contribution in the first section. From the comparative perspective, there are electoral systems that leave this type of decisive influence to political parties (less or no personalization), as well as electoral systems that try instead to grant it to the voters themselves (more personalization).

A comparative survey demonstrates that an electoral system that adopts the first conceptual meaning of personalization, such as in the example of the Slovenian electoral law, is highly restrictive of this central meaning of the decisive influence of voters and thus of the second conceptual meaning of personalization. It does not even allow for the voter to choose among different candidates of the same party. In the district in which the voter casts his or her vote, the voter is instead presented with only one name from each political party and even that candidate is delegated by the party itself. While this kind of a system may encourage the cultivation of personal reputation of individual candidates (the first concept of personalization), it undermines the second conceptual meaning of personalization (the voter's open choice among different individual candidates of the same party). Yet, in a large part of scholarship, the question of whether the voter can or cannot choose among different candidates of the same political party is one of the main criteria for judging the decisive influence of voters (and thus the degree of personalization of a system), as opposed to the influence of the political parties, over who are to be the voters' representatives (Renwick & Pillet, 2016; Gallagher & Mitchell, 2005; Toplak, 2017).

Curiously, the majority of the Slovenian Constitutional Court did not find that this rather severely limited influence of voters constituted a breach of the explicit constitutional provision that the electoral system be such as "to guarantee the decisive influence of voters," as opposed to political parties. It ruled instead that the decisive influence of voters was already secured by the existing proportional system because the voter was able to cast her vote for an individual candidate (the first meaning of personalization). It was not, in other words, that the cast vote counted only as the vote for a political party, as such, but also as the vote for that individual candidate delegated to the district by the party. The dissent, however, disagreed and argued that a large part of the comparative scholarship assumes the decisive influence of voters (personalization in the proper sense) to be potentially secured only in systems allowing the voters the choice among *several* candidates from each party (our second conceptual meaning of personalization).

What is more, many electoral scholars complain that even some of these open systems that leave the choice to the voters themselves in practice then put hidden hurdles against the decisive influence of voters, so that the party's influence (as opposed to the voters') is nonetheless ultimately decisive.

In the open Austrian system, for instance, the same voter is presented with the choice among about 12 candidates from the same political party, in Denmark among about seven candidates from the same party, in Finland among about 20, in the Netherlands among about 30, and in Belgium among a number that ranges from 4 to 22 (Gallagher and Mitchell, 2005).[14] In systems like these, it is the voter herself who, by casting the preferential vote, makes her choice between different candidates of the same party. Such systems clearly allow for an incomparably greater influence of voters vis-à-vis political parties than do closed proportional systems, like the Slovenian one, where each voter is faced with only party-imposed lists or single candidates from each party.

Yet, even for such a group of open proportional systems to satisfy "the decisive influence of voters," an important strand of comparative scholarship seems to demand more than the mere nominal choice by the voter among different candidates from the same political party. Analyzing the Belgian electoral system, Lieven De Winter, for instance, observes that, at the point of the introduction of the preferential voting in 1919, only 15% of the voters made use of that option. This number grew steadily up to the 60% and more, where it is today (De Winter, 2005).[15] Nevertheless, as the author explains, for various reasons, in practice the influence of the preferential vote is oftentimes not significant. One reason is that the Belgian voter is able to choose between casting her preferential vote and casting her vote in favor of the fixed lists as prepared by the political parties (the so-called alternative vote).[16] Given that even 60% of preferential votes cast is sometimes not enough for characterizing the system as one that guarantees the decisive influence of voters (as opposed to the parties), what would one say about classical closed proportional systems, such as the Slovenian and many others, where not even the precondition to such an influence – the choice among different candidates, whether one uses it or not – is secured?

Most scholars would agree that the Danish and Finnish electoral systems are more inclined towards the decisive influence of voters than is the described Belgian one. Just like in the Belgian case, in the Danish system, the voter can use her preferential vote to decide among several candidates from the same political party. However, the difference is that there is no "alternative vote" option here. Since only the option of the preferential vote is given, this means that only those individual candidates with the greatest numbers of the preferential votes can be elected the voters' representatives. As Jørgen Elklit describes, on the Danish voting sheet, candidates appear according to the alphabetical order. Unlike the case of the alternative vote in Belgium, the political party thus cannot by itself rank-order the candidates. This means that, unlike in Belgium, the voter necessarily must choose an individual candidate *by herself* by casting her preferential vote. The consequence is that those elected are only the candidates with the greater number of preferential votes cast than their competitors from the same party list (Elklid, 2005, 463–5). This means that the decisive influence of voters is secured in this system in practice.

An expert on the Finnish electoral system, Tapio Raunio, makes a similar observation about the decisive influence of voters as constituted in that system (Raunio, 2005, 474–84). It follows from his elaboration that it would be difficult to speak of the decisive influence of voters without the voters' option to choose between several candidates from the same party, whereby this option should also have the decisive effect in practice. Moreover, the Finnish system even makes another important step further in the direction of the voter's decisive influence than do the Belgian and Danish systems. More specifically, it requires that the prior question of which individual candidates from the same party are going to appear on the ballot is, to a significant degree, determined by the voters themselves (members of the party residing in that district), and not by the official political party organs or elites. Only up to about one-fourth (depending on a party) of the chosen candidates may then be replaced by the party organs, primarily in order to meet the required or most appropriate geographical, socio-economic, gender, and demographic balance. Raunio adds that such replacements are, however, rare in practice, which only confirms that the decisive influence of voters, as opposed to that of the political parties, is realized in Finland both at the conceptual and the practical level (Raunio, 2005, 474–8).

These, then, are examples of electoral systems satisfying the second meaning of the decisive influence of voters (our personalization in the second conceptual sense). Given that, even in these systems, scholars warn about it not being enough that the conceptual option is given to the voters, but that the decisive influence should then also not be frustrated in practice, what does this mean for closed proportional systems in which the voter does cast her vote for an individual candidate and not just a party, like in the example of the Slovenian electoral system (the first conceptual meaning of personalization)? There, the voter is not presented even with the conceptual option of choosing among different candidates from the same party, but the party itself instead delegates a single candidate to the voter's district. It is obvious that, judging by the standard evolving from the comparative scholarship, the first understanding of personalizing elections disables the possibility of the decisive influence of voters already at the start, even before the question of its realization/frustration in practice occurs. This kind of a system thus cannot be said to guarantee the decisive influence of voters as measured vis-à-vis the influence of political parties. This was also the conclusion of the dissenting opinion in the Slovenian case that criticized the majority for not considering seriously enough the voice from the comparative scholarship on this theme.

In addition to this almost complete exclusion of the decisive influence of voters, as opposed to that by the parties, an electoral system that assumes only one individual candidate from each party per district (e.g., the Slovenian system) also hides another related anomaly. This delegation (imposition) by the party of just one individual candidate per voting district creates a paradoxical situation in which some voters strongly supporting a particular political party votes for an individual candidate from this party whom, however, she might dislike and would never have voted for, if it were about this particular person and not the party. The voter is not only unable to vote for another individual candidate from this same party, whom she really admires personally as a great candidate, since he was delegated by the party to some neighboring district, where the voter cannot vote (voters can vote only in the district of their respective residence). What is much more, by casting her vote for the candidate from her district, whom she dislikes, but votes for because of the preferred party to which he belongs, she is thereby actually casting her vote *against* the truly personally preferred candidate from this party who runs in the neighboring district. The candidates from the same party, as we saw above, compete for the parliamentary seats won by their party with each other, so that the one with the relatively greater number of votes between them takes the next of the party's won seats. This means that, as far as the personalization of elections is concerned, such an electoral system actually – and here is the paradox, the perversion – translates the genuine will of the voter into its opposite. By voting for the individual candidate she strongly dislikes, but from the party she supports, her vote counts *against* the individual candidate from the same party (running in the neighboring district) whom she truly supports and would like to see in the parliament. In other words, the electoral system, as far as personalization is concerned, perverts the will of the voter into its opposite, so that the voter's vote actually counts against her true and genuine will. The result becomes a distribution of seats that is the opposite of the voter's own will. The decisive influence of voters on the distribution of seats to individual candidates (a key aspect of the personalization of elections) is thus disabled, and the will of the voters ultimately skewed to an extent that makes one wonder if the result of elections under such a system could at all be characterized as the will of the people.

Vis-à-vis Candidates

The third meaning of the decisive influence of voters can be observed from the perspective of the question of whether or not the voter has the chance of exerting her electoral pressure on individual candidates striving to be (re)elected. This influence is closely related to the issue of whether or not at least one candidate is elected in the district where the voter was eligible to cast her vote. If, from the voter's district, no individual candidate is elected to parliament, then such a voter's influence is less than the influence of the voter from whose district one, or perhaps even more, individual candidate is elected to parliament. It could be said that the first voters' influence is insignificant, while the second voter's influence is decisive. Moreover, if large numbers of voters do not have a representative elected from their districts, this means that a large segment of the electorate is left without decisive influence.

The "decisive influence" of voters cannot be understood as a mere empty phrase, as the voter's openness of choice among several candidates of the same party, but openness that is irrelevant in practice. Instead, it should be understood as serving its real purpose, that is, the constitutional value of the voter's effective influence over their own lives within a representative form of government. The voters lead their lives more by themselves (though correctly and properly not fully by themselves within the system of representative form of government) when they do have the effective power to both "vote in" and "vote out" an individual elected representative who they feel is not serving their interest, which they express in the direct relationship of the voters and their representative/candidate. Only when a (re)election of a candidate is effectively dependent upon the voter's vote can one speak of the decisive influence of the voter as being fulfilled and serving its purpose. The problem is that, in many proportional systems, like the Slovenian, where numerous districts are left with no elected representatives in the parliament, this direct link between the respective voters and the elected representatives who all come from other districts is severed. The elected representatives, if they want to be (re)elected, tends to be more responsive to the interests and needs of the voters in their own districts. Moreover, since the voters from the neighboring districts, even if from their own political parties, can cast their vote within the same party only in favor of their competing candidates and thus always only against, and never for, the elected candidates from the other districts (candidates from the same parties, but from different districts, compete with each other for the seats won by their party), these elected representatives tend to disregard the expressions of interests of such voters from the other districts. Ironically, the representatives increase their chance of being personally reelected by increasing the support for their party in their own districts, while decreasing that same support in their competing nearby districts. This situation, leading to large numbers of voters who are left with no elected representatives, creates an inequality as to the voters' influence among different groups of voters in the country.

From a quick comparative survey,[17] it appears that this third meaning of the decisive influence tends to be secured in at least some electoral systems with proportional representation. The criterion is that, from each district in which the voter is eligible to vote, at least one or more candidates should actually be elected. In this case, the above-described deficit as to the third meaning of the decisive influence of voters is significantly alleviated or even cured. In Austria, for instance, from four to five candidates per district are elected, in Denmark about eight in seventeen districts are elected (at least two and at most sixteen), in Finland about 13 candidates are elected in 14 districts, in Belgium from 4 to 22 candidates from a total of 11 districts are elected, and in the Netherlands and Israel all the candidates are elected by all the voters from the single, nation-wide electoral district. At first glance, the third meaning of the decisive influence of voters can successfully be secured even in proportional electoral systems. If so, our argument is that those electoral systems that fail to secure it, like the Slovenian (where, in one of the last elections, 21 districts were left without elected representatives) and several others, should be reformed so as to meet this important principle and the constitutionally mandated value underlying it. In order to secure this third meaning of the decisive influence of voters, one easy way of reforming the Slovenian electoral law would, for instance, be to replace the current 88 districts with 44 districts, which means that, mathematically, *each* of the 44 districts would elect two representatives. Similarly, reducing the current 88 districts with 22 would lead to *each* district electing four candidates, while reducing the number of districts to 11 or to 8 would lead to, respectively, 8 or 11 elected candidates from *each* district. In light of the explicit provision of the Slovenian Constitution, guaranteeing "the decisive influence of voters," some such reform, despite the ruling by the Constitutional Court majority, seems to be necessary.

The Sound Meanings of Personalization

The above analysis enables us to draw some conclusions. They also lead us to the contours of the sound conception and meanings of personalization.

The first observation is that the systems with a conception of personalization that looks solely into the system's ability to cultivate personal reputations of candidates, as opposed to the reputation of parties, is not yet a sufficient conception of personalization. Yet, even these systems do present a degree of personalization; the voter's vote is cast not just for the parties, but also for an individual candidate delegated by the parties, one per party for each district. On the one hand, this is different from pure proportional systems, wherein a vote is cast only for parties and not for individual candidates. A degree of personalization is, therefore, clearly there. On the other hand, this degree is far too small. Such a system that incorporates only our first conceptual understanding of personalization still does not take into account the need to secure the three meanings of the decisive influence of voters, which are behind the sound idea of personalization in a democracy. It does not guarantee any of them and is even antithetical to the central (the second) meaning of the decisive influence of voters, which is about the system's openness to the voter's choice among several candidates of the same party, i.e., the second conceptual meaning of personalization.

The further stage of personalization is thus reached only by those electoral systems that go beyond the first meaning of personalization and adopt our second conception of personalization. We saw several examples of such systems above. Yet, at this level as well, the sound variant of personalization is not yet fully secured. As we saw, some systems do provide the open choice to the voter among different individual candidates of the same party. Rather, they function so that, in practice, open choice has little to no effect. In Belgium, this was reportedly because the voter's choice was not simply about individual candidates alone, but also included the alternative possibility of confirming the pre-arranged party lists as such. Moreover, one can imagine proportional electoral systems that are based on the second conception of personalization and thus satisfy the second meaning of the decisive influence of voters but simultaneously fail to fulfill also the first and the second meaning of the decisive influence of voters. This would, likewise, not yet be enough to characterize such a system as following the fully sound conception of personalization. We saw, for instance, that, without the third meaning of the decisive influence of voters (voters from each district should have the effective power to vote in or out of office the candidates they able to choose from in elections), the voter's choice among different candidates would be an empty choice. Similarly, by violating the first meaning of the decisive influence of voters (the weight of influence by one voter vis-à-vis another voter), such a system would pervert the idea of personalization and make it inconsistent with the central democratic principle of "one person one vote." Only when the interplay between the concept of personalization and the three different meanings of the decisive influence of voters (including the one embodying the idea of one person one vote) is harmonious can the concept of personalization be sound and serve its imperative democratic purpose.

The fully sound conception of personalization is thus the one that follows the second conceptual meaning of personalization but then also makes sure that it is consistent with and secures all the three meanings of the decisive influence of voters. We saw above that, while some systems do not meet this requirement, others do. Examples of those that do include the Danish and Finnish electoral systems, wherein the problem from the Belgian system (the reported insufficient functioning of personalization in practice) is systemically avoided, as is the danger of compromising the three meanings of the decisive influence of voters. Moreover, it should also be concluded that, even within the group of systems with this sound notion of personalization, further differentiations in the degree of personalization are possible. For instance, the Finnish system is even more personalized than is the Danish; unlike the latter, the former provides that the voters themselves, as opposed to the parties, appoint a large number of individual candidates who are to appear on party voting lists in the first place. These different variants would then represent different sound meanings of personalization within the general sound concept of personalization.

We suggest that the personalization dimension in all electoral systems can be properly assessed through these criteria. That was recently the case with the Slovenian electoral law that was challenged before the Constitutional Court. Yet, the defined assessment framework and its criteria are general, so any electoral law can be subjected to its scrutiny. They prompt rethinking some other electoral laws, potentially leading to similar challenges in their own domestic contexts, or/and further improvements of electoral policies along these lines.

Notes

1 Judge of the Constitutional Court of Slovenia, Full Professor of Constitutional Law, LL.B. (Ljubljana), LL.M. and S.J.D. (Harvard), D.Phil. (Oxford).

2 Research Assistant to Prof. Jaklič and law student at the University of Ljubljana.

3 For an account of the shift in the focus and the evolution of the scholarship, see A Renwick and J-B Pilet, *Faces on the ballot, The personalization of electoral systems in Europe*, OUP 2016.

4 After the fall of communism in the early 1990s.

5 By "size," we mean the number of registered voters per voting district.

6 Even in a proportional system, each candidate from the same party inevitably competes against other candidates from the same party who run in the other districts. Either the absolute number of votes or the relative percentage of them then determines the prevailing candidates who are assigned the parliamentary seats from the quota of the seats won by their party. This means that the weight of the voter's vote at the district level matters for the question of which candidate from the same party is elected, while the other is not, and that this weight must be roughly equal among all the voters across all the districts if the principle of one person one vote is to be respected.

7 Only in rare cases, e.g., the case of positive discrimination for the sake of preserving national minorities, exceptions are sometimes permitted, when a smaller number of citizens, e.g., members of the national minority, can enjoy the privilege of having two votes: One for parliamentary elections in general and the other for the election of the minority representative within that parliament. Note that this exception does not, of course, embrace the cases of specific electoral systems, such as the so-called "split voting," when all the voters may cast more than one ballot or an electoral system that allows for separate voting in two districts. As the Venice Commission explains, in these cases the principle of "one person, one vote" remains fully intact; it only means that all electors should have the *same number* of votes (The Venice Commission, *Code of Good Practice in Electoral Matters*, 2018).

8 See *Karcher v. Daggett*, 462 U.S. 725 (1983): "Congressional districts must be mathematically equal in population, unless necessary to achieve a legitimate state objective."

9 "The maximum admissible departure from the distribution criterion adopted depends on the individual situation, although it should seldom exceed 10% and never 15%, except in really exceptional circumstances (a demographically weak administrative unit of the same importance as others with at least one lower-chamber representative, or concentration of a specific national minority)" (The Venice Commission, 2018, 16, para. 15).

10 Study conducted by the Department of Analyses and International Cooperation, the Constitutional Court of Slovenia. The study is part of the case file cited under note 1; see also *The ACE Encyclopedia: Boundary Delimitation*, available at: http://aceproject.org/ace-en/topics/bd/onePage.

11 Ibid. and Toplak. 2000, 68–9, 90–3.

12 Study conducted by the Department for Analyses and International Cooperation, the Constitutional Court of Slovenia, part of the case file, cited under note 1; see also *The ACE Encyclopedia: Boundary*

Delimitation, available at http://aceproject.org/ace-en/topics/bd/onePage, p. 44, 122; and also *Delimitation Equity Project: Resource Guide*, p. 251–60, available at www.ifes.org/ publications/delimitation-equity-project-resource-guide.

13 Ibid.

14 See also examples of the ballot papers from the mentioned countries, which were obtained for the purposes of the comparative study on the case cited in Note 1, part of the case file U-I-32/15 at the Constitutional Court of Slovenia.

15 There are similar findings for Slovenia – e.g., the study of the use of preferential voting by Slovenian voters in the case of local elections (where, unlike at national elections, the Slovenian voter has the option to choose among different candidates from the same political party). See Toplak, 2003.

16 Some other arrangements, however, while allowing the choice of different candidates from the same political party (preferential voting), later reduce the influence of voters in relation to political parties in other ways, e.g., by introducing different thresholds for taking preferential votes into account. At such a threshold, preferential votes are taken into account only if the candidate collects them enough. See Toplak, 2017.

17 Due to the limited space and scope, we have not completed a comprehensive comparative analysis on this issue, which will need to await further studies. We nonetheless think that the introduction and definition of this third meaning of the voters' decisive influence is conceptually important and deserves such further studies. Assuming that, at least some, or perhaps even many, electoral systems suffer from this weakness (in a similar way as does the Slovenian), this third conceptual meaning of the decisive influence can serve as a sound measure for such systems' further improvement.

References

Carey, J. M., & Shugart, M. S. (1995). Incentives to cultivate a personal vote: A rank ordering of electoral formulas. *Electoral Studies*, 14(4), 417–439. doi: https://doi.org/10.1016/0261-3794(94)00035-2

De Winter, L. (2005). Belgium: Empowering voters or party elites?. In M. Gallagher & P. Mitchell (Eds.), *The politics of electoral systems*. Oxford: Oxford University Press. doi: 10.1093/0199257566.003.0020

Elklid, J. (2005). Denmark: Simplicity embedded in complexity (or is it the other way round?). In M. Gallagher & P. Mitchell (Eds.), *The politics of electoral systems*. Oxford: Oxford University Press. doi: 10.1093/0199257566.003.0022

Gallagher, M., & Mitchell, P. (Eds.). (2005). *The politics of electoral systems*. Oxford: Oxford University Press. doi: 10.1093/0199257566.001.0001

Judgment of the Constitutional Court of Slovenia U-I-32/15. (from 8. 11. 2018). Separate opinion (concurring in part and dissenting in part) by Judge Dr. Klemen Jaklič, from 30. 11. 2018.

Karcher v. Daggett, 462 U.S. 725 (1983).

Raunio, T. (2005). Finland: One hundred years of quietude. In M. Gallagher & P. Mitchell (Eds.), *The politics of electoral systems*. Oxford: Oxford University Press. doi: 10.1093/0199257566.003.0023

Renwick, A., & Pilet, J. B. (2016). *Faces on the ballot, The personalization of electoral systems in Europe*. Oxford: Oxford University Press.

The Venice Commission. (2018, October). *Code of good practice in electoral matters*. Retrieved from https://www.venice.coe.int/webforms/documents/default.aspx?pdffile=CDL-AD(2002)023rev2-cor-e

Toplak, J. (2000). *Volilni sistem in oblikovanje volilnih enot*. Ljubljana: Nova revija.

Toplak, J. (2003). Preferenčni glas in njegova uporaba v Sloveniji. *Lex Localis*, 1(2), 15–43. Retrieved from http://www.lex-localis.info/files/346e6f6e-ce13-4228-bb13-f505c68cf501/632897183329062500_2003_02_02.pdf

Toplak, J. (2006). The parliamentary election in Slovenia, October 2004. *Electoral Studies*, *25*(4), 825–831.

Toplak, J. (2017). Preferential voting: Definition and classification. *Lex Localis*, *15*(4), 737–761.

18

EUROPEAN COURT OF HUMAN RIGHTS AND THE ELECTION LAW

Jurij Toplak

Introduction

This chapter provides an overview of the law governing elections in Europe and focuses on the standards set by the European Court of Human Rights. It begins by describing the relationship between the three levels of the law governing elections in Europe: The law of European Convention of Human Rights (ECHR), the law of the European Union (EU) and the national law of individual member-states. It then presents the principles set out by the European Convention of Human Rights, as interpreted by European Court of Human Rights (ECtHR). It emphasizes the issues that are at the center of political debate and academic research.

Council of Europe, the European Union, and the States' National Law

In addition to the election principles set out by the United Nations[1] and other international organizations,[2] there are three levels of law governing elections in Europe. The first level is that of the Council of Europe – set out in the European Convention of Human Rights and interpreted by the European Court of Human Rights – to guarantee basic election principles. Article 3 of the First Protocol of the Convention assures "free elections," the "right to vote," and a "secret ballot."

Twenty-seven of the convention parties have united in the European Union. The European Union has its own rules on election procedures, and these constitute the second level of law. For the most part, European Union law regulates local elections and elections to the European Parliament, but only slightly addresses national parliamentary elections. European Union election law is regulated by EU treaties and directives, as well as by the jurisprudence of the European Court of Justice.

The third level of election law is national law. Naturally, this must conform to the wording of the convention, the decisions of the ECtHR in 47 of the Council of Europe member states, and to European Union election rules in 27 EU member states.

There is considerable variety in the type of elections held in these European democracies. At the national level, every country runs parliamentary elections and some conduct presidential or other types of election. Every country also conducts elections at either one or two local levels – the regional and the municipal. The federations usually have three. But, in addition to

DOI: 10.4324/9780429401800-18

these national and local elections, voters in 27 EU member states choose representatives to the European Parliament.

The European Convention of Human Rights and Its Jurisprudence

The Council of Europe plays an active role in setting electoral standards. It does so through three of its bodies: The Parliamentary Assembly, the Venice Commission, and the European Court of Human Rights.

The European Commission for Democracy through Law, better known as the Venice Commission, is the Council of Europe's advisory body on constitutional matters.[3] Since its creation, the Venice Commission has been particularly active in the electoral field through the adoption of opinions on draft electoral legislation. The Venice Commission has also taken part in drafting the wording of electoral legislation for various European democracies. The resolutions of the Parliamentary Assembly have further played an important role in influencing the electoral legislation in the Council of Europe's 47 member states. But the European Court of Human Rights in Strasbourg has been the most influential of the three bodies when it comes to setting electoral and voting standards. It does so by interpreting the European Convention of Human Rights and, in particular, the convention's first protocol.

While the Council of Europe member states agreed on the convention wording regarding most rights, they had considerable difficulty agreeing on the words guaranteeing rights to property, education, and free elections. Consequently, these rights were later included in a protocol to the convention. Article 3 of the first protocol reads:

> The High Contracting Parties undertake to hold free elections at reasonable intervals by secret ballot, under conditions which will ensure the free expression of the opinion of the people in the choice of the legislature.

This wording was carefully tailored after the United Kingdom ruled out the phrase "free and fair elections," since this could entail the institution of some form of proportional representation to ensure a fair balance of representation (Andrews, 1984, 463, 478). During the preparation process [i]t has been held repeatedly that, whilst this means that electors must be free from any form of duress or influence, and political parties must be free to mount campaigns and put up candidates, there is no guarantee that every vote will be equal (Andrews, 1984, note 9, 478).[4] Consequently, the protocol does not guarantee any principle of equality in elections or anything similar to the American principle of "one person, one vote."

Many member states have chosen to ratify the protocol later than they ratified the basic text of the convention and, as mentioned, three of the convention parties still have not ratified the protocol (Andrews, 1984, note 6).

Scope of the "Free Elections" Article

One should take notice of the wording of the Article P1-3, which differs from the formulation of many of the other rights in the convention:

> While most of the other rights in the Convention say that "[e]veryone has the right to..." or that "[n]o one shall be...," and thus clearly describe individual rights of non-interference from state activities, Article P1-3 stipulates that "[t]he High Contracting Parties undertake to hold..." The difference was reflected in the Commission's initial

> position according to which Article P1-3 did not contain any individual rights, for example the individual's right to vote or to stand for election, but exclusively an "institutional" right to the holding of free elections.
>
> *(Lindblad, 2005, 60)*

This initial approach, which resulted in the commission's declaration of inadmissibility in cases concerning individuals' complaints that they had been denied their individual right to vote,[5] changed in 1967 (*X v. the Federal Republic of Germany*, 1967, 10 YB 336; Lindblad, 2005).

When the court faced the article for the first time in 1987,[6] it deliberately went far beyond the case and explained the meaning of the article in considerable detail. The court recognized that the protocol protects citizens' right to vote and right to stand for election, even where the protocol does not explicitly mention them. It further recognized an individual's right to complaint under this section. The court defined the protocol's term, "legislature," and determined the types of elections covered by the protocol. Moreover, it stressed that the protocol does not require any specific electoral system to be utilized by the member states.

Although this was not at all the issue in the Mathieu-Mohin case, the court explained that the article does not create any "obligation to introduce a specific system," such as proportional representation or majority voting with one or two ballots (*Mathieu-Mohin & Clerfayt v. Belgium*, 1987, Series A no. 113, §54).[7]

The court held that the article "applies only to the election of the 'legislature,'" but that "the word 'legislature' does not necessarily mean only the national parliament" and "it has to be interpreted in the light of the constitutional structure of the State in question" (*Mathieu-Mohin & Clerfayt v. Belgium*, 1987, Series A no. 113, §53).

The term "legislature" has been further defined in a number of court decisions. In federal states such as Germany, Austria, Belgium, and Switzerland, the parliaments of the federated states (the Länder, regions, and communities or cantons) are also considered legislatures in the sense of Article 3 (*Timke v. Federal Republic of Germany*, 1995, 158ff).[8] In contrast, local authorities' deliberative assemblies are not considered legislators, since they are endowed only with statutory powers.[9] Equally, the scope of Article 3 does not extend either to elections for Head of State or to participation in referendums.[10] In two recent decisions, the court has, however, left the possibility that the presidential elections could be subject to the ECtHR review, if the president possesses powers usually regarded as legislative powers.[11] In regards to Italian regional councils, it was initially left open as to whether these organs might be deemed to be part of the legislature in Italy,[12] but it later ruled that they are in a subsequent decision (*Vito Sante Santoro v. Italy*, no. 36681/97, §52, ECHR 2004-VI).

While member states of the European Union are parties of the convention, the European Union itself is not. It has thus been held that European Union legislation cannot be subject to review by the European Court of Human Rights. Until 1999, when asked to decide on matters related to European Parliament elections, the court consistently held that the European Parliament was not a legislature because it lacked legislative powers. In the *Matthews v. United Kingdom*[13] decision, however, the court extended its jurisdiction over cases concerning European Parliament elections.

Electoral Thresholds

In systems that employ proportional representation, it is common for electoral law to include a legal threshold, below which a party is awarded no seats. "This is a cut-off point which is designed to reduce the number of tiny, splinter parties in the system" (Farrell, 2001, 81). Electoral thresholds, also called "thresholds of exclusion," are often implemented with the intention of bringing stability to a political system.

Thresholds are usually expressed as a minimum percentage of the vote or a minimum number of seats won. Slovenia is among those democracies that has used both kinds of thresholds over the past decade. In the Slovenian parliamentary elections of 1992 and 1996, the threshold was set at three parliamentary seats. In practical terms, this meant that a party needed to win about 3.2 to 3.4% of the votes in order to exceed the threshold. In 2000, the threshold was raised to 4% of the votes cast. In Denmark the threshold is set at 2%, in Ukraine 3%, and in Germany 5%. In Sweden, a party must win either 4% of the national vote, or 12% of the vote in a single constituency, in order to be eligible for seats (Farrell, supra note 131, at 17). In Poland, the threshold is set at 5%, but ethnic minority parties do not have to reach this threshold to reach parliament. The number now stands at two percent in Israel's Knesset (it was 1% before 1992, and 1.5% from 1992 to 2003). Turkey's 10% threshold is considered to be the highest threshold applied at the national level. At the same time, there are countries such as Portugal, Finland, the Netherlands, and Republic of Macedonia that have proportional representation systems without a threshold.

If the electoral threshold is set too high, a large number of votes may be cast that do not produce any actual representation (so-called "wasted votes"). Such a high threshold is thus often considered to be unjustified and contrary to democratic principles. Turkey's threshold of 10% caused over 45% of votes (cast for below-threshold parties) to be unrepresented in the Turkish parliament in the wake of the 2002 elections. Similarly, in Ukraine, with a 3% threshold during the March 2006 elections, 22% of voters voted for minor parties that did not win any seats. In some cases, thresholds may be deliberately used in order to exclude ethnic minority parties from representation.

The commission and the European Court of Human Rights have evaluated electoral thresholds in several different countries. In all of the three most recent cases – brought against Italy, Spain, and Turkey – the commission evaluated complaints filed by regional parties that enjoyed strong local support, but were having trouble reaching the national threshold. As we shall see, the commission tended to find in favor of the existing laws.

In 1996, the commission ruled on the compliance of the Italian electoral threshold of four percent with the convention.[14] The Italian province of Bozen-Südtirol/Bolzano-Alto Adige has 420,000 inhabitants, of which 72.35% belong to the German-speaking and Ladin-speaking populations. The German-speaking population predominantly votes for the party called Südtiroler Volkspartei (SVP). Before the law was changed, the party generally gained more than 80% of the votes of the German-speaking and Ladin-speaking minority in all the elections to the Chamber of Deputies in Rome, and it was represented by three or four deputies in the parliament. Members of the Chamber of Deputies were elected by a party-list system of proportional representation.

In accordance with the provisions of a new electoral law,[15] 75% of the seats were distributed by a majority system and 25% by a system of proportional representation. Under this system, the threshold set for the allocation of a seat in the Chamber of Deputies was 4% of the votes cast on the national level.

In the autonomous region of Trentino-Alto Adige/Trentino-Südtirol (which consists of two provinces: The province of Trento and the province of Bozen-Südtirol/Bolzano-Alto Adige, mentioned earlier), eight seats of the Chamber of Deputies were allocated by majority vote and two by proportional representation.

Under this new electoral law, the minority SVP was unable to obtain at least 4% of the national vote. "In the parliamentary elections of March 1994, the SVP gained three seats under the system of simple majority in the electoral district of Trentino-Alto Adige and no seat in respect of the system of proportional representation."[16]

The applicants complained that, under the new electoral law and its system of proportional representation, they were in effect excluded from having a seat in the Chamber of Deputies because, in order to obtain the required four percent of the votes cast, a party must poll approximately 1,600,000 votes nationwide.[17]

The commission rejected the arguments of the applicants.[18] According to the commission,

> [e]ven a system which fixes a relatively high threshold, e.g. as regards the number of signatures required in order to stand for election or, as in the present case, a minimum percentage of votes on the national level, may be regarded as not exceeding the margin of appreciation permitted to States in the matter...Moreover, similar provisions concerning the minimum threshold for the allocation of seats exist in other European legal systems.[19]

Five years later, in the 2001 case of *Federación Nacionalista Canaria v. Spain*,[20] the court considered electoral thresholds in the elections to the legislative assembly of the Autonomous Community of the Canary Islands. The law[21] laid down two alternative conditions under which a party could win representation: Either at least 30% of all valid votes must be obtained in an individual constituency or at least 6% of all valid votes must be obtained in the Autonomous Community as a whole.

The court considered "that a system of that kind, far from hindering election candidates such as those put forward by the applicant federation, affords smaller political groups a certain degree of protection" (*Federación Nacionalista Canaria v. Spain*, no. 56618/00, ECHR 2001-VI). It thus found no violation of the convention.

In the most recent and probably most interesting case – the case of *Yumak and Sadak v. Turkey*[22] – the court evaluated the national 10% threshold of the Turkish parliamentary elections.

According to the Turkish law in force until 1995, the National Assembly was elected by a proportional representation system[23] with two electoral thresholds: The provincial threshold (the number of electors divided by the number of seats to be filled in each constituency) and the national threshold of 10%. In 1995, the Constitutional Court declared the provincial threshold null and void.[24] Moreover, Turkish law expressly forbade the formation of electoral coalitions of two or more parties. Consequently, each party had to obtain at least 10% of the votes nationally in order to win parliamentary seats.

In the November 2002 elections, 18 political parties had taken part, but only two succeeded in passing the threshold. One of the parties, DEHAP, is of a markedly regional nature, strong particularly in the Kurdish areas of Turkey. Turkey is a large country, and even regional parties may be supported by millions of voters. DEHAP won 45.95% of votes in the province of Şırnak, but fell short of passing the national 10% threshold. Two DEHAP candidates filed complaints to the Strasbourg Court. They claimed that the 10% threshold was undemocratic and contrary to the right to free elections, as guaranteed by Protocol One.

The Turkish government argued that the threshold was set as a result of several decades of political instability in Turkey and prevented fragmentation of the parliament. The government put forward two arguments in seeking to persuade the court that, although the 10% threshold was high in relation to the thresholds generally adopted, the system as a whole was "proportionate":

(a) The applicants could have been elected if they had been independent candidates; and
(b) The applicants could have been elected if their party had entered into a coalition with larger parties before the election.

The court concluded that neither argument was persuasive, and the second was even incorrect: Coalitions were expressly forbidden by Turkish law.

Yet, in a 5-2 decision, the court found no violation of the convention and justified the decision based on the political instability of Turkey in the 1970s. The electoral threshold of ten percent was accepted as a measure "to prevent excessive and debilitating parliamentary fragmentation and thus strengthen governmental stability" (*Yumak and Sadak v. Turkey*, no. 10226/03). The court stressed, however, that "rules that would be unacceptable in the context of one system may be justified in the context of another." In other words, the same threshold may well not be acceptable in states with a long democratic tradition.

Judges Cabral Barreto and Mularoni delivered a dissenting opinion. They were of the opinion that "the Turkish electoral system, which lays down a national threshold of ten percent without any corrective counterbalances, raises such a problem under Article 3 of Protocol No.1 that there has been a violation of the provision"[25]

They relied, in the first place, on the fact that 45.3% of the voters received no representation in the Turkish parliament since their votes were cast for parties that did not pass the threshold. Second, they relied on the decision of *Federación nacionalista Canaria v. Spain*.[26] In this decision, the court emphasized that it found no violation because any political party had a chance to win parliamentary seats by passing at least one of the two alternative thresholds – either a 30% constituency threshold or a 6% threshold in the region as a whole. In the *Canaria* case both types of parties – local and national – had a chance to be elected. In the case of Turkey, there were no such alternatives, but only a single, national threshold of 10%. The dissenting judges also took note of the Parliamentary Assembly of the Council of Europe, which had declared the threshold to be manifestly excessive and invited Turkey to lower it (Council of Europe Resolution 1380, 2004).[27] Finally, they repeated the majority's conclusion that all the arguments put forward by the government in regards to the proportionality of the Turkish electoral system were either unpersuasive or incorrect.

The Test Used for the Protocol 1, Article 3 Review

When examining compliance with the Article 3 of Protocol No. 1, the court does not use the same test used for examining compliance with other political rights protected by the convention. When pronouncing on cases involving the rights to private and family life (Art. 8); freedom of thought, conscience, and religion (Art. 9); freedom of expression (Art. 10); and freedom of assembly and association (Art. 11), the court constantly utilizes its proportionality test. For the examination of P3-1 cases, however, the court employs "less stringent" standards, which it explained in the Ždanoka judgment.

The court delineated that, in P3-1 cases, it applies the concept of "implied limitations," which "means that the Court does not apply the traditional tests of 'necessity' or 'pressing social need' that are used in the context of" other individual rights. As the court explained,

> In examining compliance with Article 3 of Protocol No. 1, the Court has focused mainly on two criteria: whether there has been arbitrariness or a lack of proportionality, and whether the restriction has interfered with the free expression of the opinion of the people. In this connection, the wide margin of appreciation enjoyed by the Contracting States has always been underlined...For a restrictive measure to comply with Article 3 of Protocol No. 1, a lesser degree of individualisation may be sufficient, in contrast to situations concerning an alleged breach of Articles 8-11 of the Convention.
>
> *(*Ždanoka v. Latvia *[GC], no. 58278/00, §115, ECHR 2006)*

Active and Passive Suffrage – Different Standards of Review

In Europe, the right to vote is often referred to as an "active electoral right," "active aspect of the right to vote," or "active suffrage." The right to stand as a candidate for election is referred to as a "passive electoral right" or a "passive aspect of the right to vote."[28]

It is acknowledged that the standards applied for establishing compliance with the protocol are less stringent when the court examines cases involving the right to be elected than when it examines cases involving the right to vote. In both the *Melnychenko* and *Ždanoka* judgments cited above, the court observed that stricter requirements may be imposed on eligibility to stand for election than on eligibility to vote. While the test relating to the "active" aspect of the Article 3, Protocol No. 1 has usually included a wider assessment of the proportionality of the statutory provisions that disqualify a person or a certain group of persons from the right to vote, the court's test in relation to the "passive" aspect of the above provision has been limited largely to a check on the absence of arbitrariness in the domestic procedures leading to disqualification of any individual from standing as a candidate.[29]

The European Court of Human Rights and United Nations Law

In three judgments issued in 2021, the Strasbourg-based court cited the United Nations Convention on the Rights of Persons with Disabilities (CRPD) but departed from case-law established by the Committee on the Rights of Persons with Disabilities. In its Toplak and Mrak v. Slovenia judgment, the court departed from the CRPD standards on accessibility, secret ballot, access to courts, and voting devices.[30] Vrancken (2021) called court's use of international law "unfair" (Vrancken 2021). In two judgments, the court did not follow CRPD's position that states should recognise voting rights of all persons regardless of their disabilities.[31]

Notes

1 Article 21 of the Universal Declaration of Human Rights (UDHR) of December 10, 1948, as well as Article 25 of the International Covenant on Civil and Political Rights (ICCPR) of December 16, 1966 contain provisions dealing with elections. For excellent overviews of the case-law and standards set by the above-cited provisions, see two publications published by Markku Suksi (Hinz & Suksi, 2003; Lindblad & Suksi, 2005).

2 The OSCE 1990 Document of the Copenhagen Meeting of the Conference on the Human Dimension of the Conference on Security and Co-operation in Europe (known as the "Copenhagen Document"), adopted on June 29, 1990, enlists numerous democratic rights, freedoms, and principles relevant to elections and the exercise of voting rights. Constitutional and Supreme courts, the European Court of Human Rights, the Venice Commission, and other bodies often rely on the Copenhagen Document. See, for example, the Venice Commission (2004) claiming that Moldova's ballot access legislation could be in odds with the Copenhagen Document.

3 The Council of Europe's Venice Commission's reports and opinions are not binding, but the European Court of Human Rights often relies on them in its decisions. See, for example, the judgment of *Hirst v. the United Kingdom (no. 2)* [GC], no. 74025/01, ECHR 2005.

4 See also *The Liberal Party and Others v. United Kingdom* (dec.), no. 8765/79, December 18, 1980. However, the court held that this article contains an implicit recognition of an individual right to "equality of treatment of all citizens in the exercise of their right to vote and their right to stand for election." Case of *Mathieu-Mohin and Clerfayt v. Belgium*, judgment of March 2, 1987, Series A no. 113, §54.

5 See, for instance, the commission's decisions *X v. Belgium*, Decision of the Commission of September 18, 1961, 4 YB 324 and *X v. Others v. Belgium*, Commission Decision of May 30, 1961, 4 YB 260. According to the commission, Article P1-3 does not guarantee the right to vote, to stand for election or to be elected...but solely the right whereby Contracting States hold 'free elections at reasonable

intervals by secret ballot under conditions which will ensure the free expression of the opinion of the people in the choice of the legislature.'" *X v. Belgium*, Decision of the Commission of September 18, 1961, 4 YB 324, cited in Lindblad, (2005, at 61).

6 *Mathieu-Mohin and Clerfayt v. Belgium*, judgment of March 2, 1987, Series A no. 113.

7 The court cites "Travaux Préparatoires," vol. VII, pp. 130, 202, and 210, and vol. VIII, p. 14.

8 See also *Cherepkov v. Russia* (dec.), no. 51501/99, ECHR 2000-I and *X v. Austria*, no. 7008/75, Commission decision of July 12, 1976, DR 6, pp. 120–21, on the application of Article 3 of Protocol No. 1 to regional parliaments – *Landtag* – in Austria.

9 *Molka v. Poland* (dec.), no. 56550/00, ECHR 2006; *Salleras Llinares v. Spain* (dec.), no. 52226/99, ECHR 2000-XI; *Cherepkov v. Russia* (dec.), no. 51501/99, ECHR 2000-I; European Commission of Human Rights, decision of July 5, 1985, *Booth-Clibborn et al.*, DR 43, pp. 236, 247, and onward)

10 See *Baskauskaite v. Lithuania*, no. 41090/98, Commission decision of October 21, 1998 and *Habsburg-Lothringen v. Austria*, no. 15344/89, Commission decision of December 14, 1989, DR 64, p. 211; *Hilbe v. Liechteinstein* (dec.), no. 31981/96, ECHR 1999-VI; *Bader v. Austria*, no. 26633/95, Commission decision of March 15, 1996; *Ž v. Latvia* (dec.), no. 14755/03, ECHR 2006.

11 "The Court does not exclude, however, the possibility of applying Article 3 of Protocol No. 1 to presidential elections...Should it be established that the office of the Head of the State had been given the power to initiate and adopt legislation or enjoyed wide powers to control the passage of legislation or the power to censure the principal legislation-setting authorities, then it could arguably be considered to be a 'legislature' within the meaning of Article 3 of Protocol No 1." *Boškoski v. the former Yugoslav Republic of Macedonia* (dec.), no. 11676/04, ECHR 2004-VI. See similar wording in *Guliyev v. Azerbaijan* (dec.), no. 35584/02, ECHR 2004.

12 See *Luksch v. Italy*, no. 21614/95, commission decision of May 21, 1997, DR 89, pp. 76–8.

13 *Matthews v. the United Kingdom* [GC], no. 24833/94, ECHR 1999-I.

14 *Silvius Magnago and Südtiroler Volkspartei v. Italy*, no. 25035/94, Commission decision of April 15, 1996, DR 85.

15 *Law No. 277* of August 4, 1993.

16 *Silvius Magnago and Südtiroler Volkspartei v. Italy*, no. 25035/94, Commission decision of April 15, 1996, DR 85.

17 They also complained that the SVP as such, its candidate and the electors, belonging to the German-language and Ladin-language groups, are the victims of a difference of treatment amounting to discrimination on grounds of language and membership of a national minority. The commission rejected this argument by noting that the electoral law in issue applies to all candidates and the convention does not compel the contracting parties to provide for positive discrimination in favor of minorities. *Silvius Magnago and Südtiroler Volkspartei v. Italy*, no. 25035/94, commission decision of April 15, 1996, DR 85.

18 The SVP also contested the new electoral law at the Constitutional Court of Italy, but without success. "A constitutional appeal was declared inadmissible by the Constitutional Court on 14 December 1993. The Constitutional Court pointed out that the Parliament had rejected the proposal not to apply the 4% threshold in the region of Trentino-Alto Adige as well as other proposals made in that context. It found that where, as in the present case, the legislature had chosen one of several possibilities in respect of the electoral system, the Constitutional Court was prevented from substituting itself for the legislature." *Silvius Magnago and Südtiroler Volkspartei v. Italy*, no. 25035/94, commission decision of April 15,1996, DR 85.

19 *Silvius Magnago and Südtiroler Volkspartei v. Italy*, no. 25035/94, commission decision of April 15, 1996, DR 85. Through the decision, the commission relied on two previous decisions in which it considered electoral thresholds in the context of the margin of appreciation left to the member states. In both of these decisions, it noted that, in this sphere, states enjoy considerable latitude. *Etienne Tête v. France*, no. 11123/84, Commission decision of December 9, 1987, Decisions and Reports (DR) 54, p. 52; *Marcel Fournier v. France*, no. 11406/85, commission decision of March 10, 1988.

20 *Federación Nacionalista Canaria v. Spain*, no. 56618/00, ECHR 2001-VI.

21 Statute of Autonomy of the Canary Islands (as amended by Institutional Act no. 4/1996 of December 30, 1996), First transitional provision, §2.

22 *Yumak and Sadak v. Turkey*, no. 10226/03.

23 On the electoral system, see primarily Law no. 2839 on the election of members of the National Assembly, published in the Official Gazette on June 13, 1983. See some of the law's relevant provisions in *Yumak and Sadak v. Turkey*, no. 10226/03, §22–28.

24 Judgement of the Constitutional Court of Turkey of November 18, 1995 (E. 1995/54, K. 1995/59). See more in *Yumak and Sadak v. Turkey,* no. 10226/03, §29–31.

25 Joint dissenting opinion of Judges Cabral Barreto and Mularoni. *Yumak and Sadak v. Turkey,* no. 10226/03.

26 *Federación Nacionalista Canaria v. Spain,* no. 56618/00, ECHR 2001-VI.

27 See some parts of the Resolution in *Yumak and Sadak v. Turkey,* no. 10226/03, §34.

28 See, for instance, *Ždanoka v. Latvia* [GC], no. 58278/00, §105–106, ECHR 2006 ("the right to vote, i.e. the so-called 'active' aspect of the rights under Article 3 of Protocol No. 1…individual's right to stand as a candidate for election, i.e. the so-called 'passive' aspect of the rights"). A quick check of how frequently and in which contexts these different terms are used shows that terms "active voting right" (106 matches on Google), "passive voting right" (137 matches on Google), "active right to vote" (140 matches), "passive right to vote" (217 matches), "active electoral right" (96 matches), and "passive electoral right" (112 matches) are used almost exclusively by authors coming from the areas where English is not the official language. In many different languages, the terms "active" and "passive" are used in connection with voting, but not in English. The above terms are thus only a result of unfortunate word-for-word translations. Terms like "active suffrage" (550 hits) and passive suffrage (942 hits) are used slightly more often, but the terms like "right to run for office" (67,100 hits), "right to be elected" (43,900 hits), "the right to stand for election" (21,200 hits), "right to stand as a candidate" (18,000 hits), "right to be a candidate" (10,300 hits), and, in particular, the term "ballot access" (934,000 hits) are commonly used in the English-speaking environments, although the term "ballot access" is sometimes distinguished from the above terms.

29 Compare *Ždanoka v. Latvia* [GC], no. 58278/00, §106–108, ECHR 2006, with the *Melnychenko v. Ukraine*, no. 17707/02, ECHR 2004. On this issue see also *Ždanoka v. Latvia* [GC], no. 58278/00, §115, ECHR 2006.

30 *Toplak and Mrak v. Slovenia*, no. 34591/19, 42545/19, 26 October 2021.

31 *Strøbje and Rosenlind v. Denmark*, no. 25802/18 27338/18, February 2, 2021, and *Caamaño Valle v. Spain*, no. 43564/17, May 11, 2021.

References

Hinz, V. U., & Suksi, M. (2003). *Election elements: On the international standards of electoral participation.* Turku/Åbo: Institute for Human Rights, Åbo Akademi University.

Lindblad, J. (2005). The right to free elections according to the European convention on human rights. In *Lindblad and Suksi* (pp. 49–126).

Lindblad, J., & Suksi, M. (2005). *On the evolution of international election norms: Global and European perspectives.* Turku/ Åbo: Institute for Human Rights, Åbo Akademi University.

Venice Commisssion. (2004). European commission for democracy through law. In Draft Recommendations on the Electoral Law and the Electoral Administration in Moldova: Opinion No. 272/2004. CDL-EL(2003)015, Strasbourg, March 3, 2004.

Vrancken, M. (2022). (Not) applying CRPD standards and the question of fair referencing: Toplak and Mrak v. Slovenia. *Strasbourg Observers.* 8 Feb 2022. Retrieved February 20, 2022 from https://strasbourgobservers.com/2022/02/08/not-applying-crpd-standards-and-the-question-of-fair-referencing-toplak-and-mrak-v-slovenia/

19

POST-ELECTION DISPUTES IN EUROPE

Mathieu Leloup

Introduction

Democracy rests on the idea that all citizens have the right to participate in government, either directly or via representatives, through genuine and fair elections. However, even in the strongest democracies, disputes concerning the electoral process can arise. The swift and fair resolution of such disputes is an essential part of democracy and crucial for voter trust in the electoral process.

All over the world, election dispute resolution is an increasingly prevalent topic. As a recent and notable example, President Trump indicated that the 2020 elections might ultimately be decided before the Supreme Court. In Europe, as well, there has been a recent surge in election disputes, sometimes with far-reaching consequences. In Austria, for example, the Constitutional Court annulled the 2016 presidential elections. Similarly, in Serbia, the Republic Electoral Commission ruled that the voting in over 200 polling stations was invalid, thereby giving more than 200,000 citizens the right to go vote again. In Belarus and Poland, appeals of the election results were brought before their respective Supreme Courts, but were ultimately dismissed.

Besides this surge in the number of election disputes, European-wide standards have recently evolved on the topic. International organizations like the Office for Democratic Institutions and Human Rights (ODIHR) and the Venice Commission routinely issue opinions and recommendations to European countries regarding their legislative framework on elections, including election disputes (Fasone & Piccirilli, 2017). Moreover, international courts and tribunals like the European Court of Human Rights (ECtHR) and the UN Human Rights Committee are increasingly imposing standards to which the domestic election dispute resolution system should adhere. Even though the ECtHR has consistently held that the right to a fair trial, safeguarded in Article 6 ECHR, is not applicable in an election context,[1] it has had an undeniable impact on the systems of election dispute resolution. It has done so mainly via the principle that the effective examination of individual complaints and appeals in matters concerning electoral rights is one of the essential guarantees of free and fair elections, enshrined in Article 3 of the First Additional Protocol.[2]

These evolutions make election dispute resolution in Europe a welcome topic to address in this volume. This chapter will provide a comparative overview of the existing standards for election disputes in Europe. As such, it will focus on institutional and procedural aspects, rather than on more substantive issues of electoral law, like electoral thresholds.[3] It will focus on the

DOI: 10.4324/9780429401800-19

standards that are set out in the opinions and recommendations by the Venice Commission and the ODIHR, as well as in the jurisprudence of the ECtHR.

European Standards on Election Disputes

When talking about election disputes, a distinction can be made based on when the dispute itself arises (ODIHR, 2019d). First, there are pre-election disputes, which as the word indicates take place before election day itself. These are, for example, disputes about candidate or voter registration, or about campaign financing. Second, there are disputes on election day itself, mostly relating to voter identification or alleged violations of election day procedures. Third, there are post-election disputes, which concern the final election results, including the counting and tabulation of votes. It could be argued that each of these types of election disputes is different and may, therefore, have to adhere to different standards.

However, when the case law of the ECtHR and the opinions and recommendations of the Venice Commission and the ODIHR are examined in more detail, it becomes apparent that they do not impose different standards based on the moment in which the dispute takes place. Rather, the only concern of these bodies seems to be the question of whether the domestic legislative framework prevents arbitrary decisions and allows for the effective protection of electoral rights by establishing an effective system for the examination of election disputes.

For this reason, this article will focus on specific issues of election dispute resolution, rather than on distinctions based on the timing of the dispute. The first of these issues is which type of body can be in charge of election dispute resolution. Then, the article will turn to the question what powers this body must have. Afterwards, it will examine any requirements concerning standing and time limits before this body. The final issue concerns the procedural safeguards that must be respected by the domestic bodies. For each of these issues, the prevailing European standards will be examined.[4]

Which Type of Body Is Competent?

Without a doubt the most important institutional issue concerning election dispute standards is the question of what kind of body should ultimately decide them. There is an incredible variety among European countries in this area, as different countries have opted for different institutional avenues to decide on election disputes. This is often a result of historical and political factors specific to each state. In some, mainly Central and Eastern European, countries, such disputes are dealt with by election commissions. In others, courts and tribunals are the competent actors. In a minority of states, for example Belgium and the Netherlands, parliament itself is competent to rule over certain election disputes. This institutional diversity is further compounded by the fact that, in many countries, the competent body varies depending on the topic of the complaint.

To a certain extent, this institutional variety reflects the principle of separation of powers (Romainville, 2020, 156; Verdussen, 2014, 461). In many European countries, election disputes, especially the validation of election results, have long been the exclusive domain of parliament itself. The original intention was to safeguard the independence of parliament by preventing any interference in its composition by the other branches of power (Muylle, 2010, 728; Philip, 1961, 5–6). The predominant position of election commissions in some countries can also be seen as an attempt to keep the politically sensitive issue of election disputes away from the courts (Tushnet, 2018, 115–23). Nonetheless, this political mechanism of dispute resolution has gradually lost favor in Europe. More and more countries have felt the need to take this competence away from the parliaments themselves and to instead entrust it to impartial and independent actors. France decided, for example, in 1958 to give the last word over the verification of election results to the *Conseil Constitutionnel*, instead of to parliament. In this sense, the Venice Commission has noted that there has been an evolution in Europe during the twentieth century, in which election disputes have been assigned to a judicial body, at least at the last instance (Venice Commission, 2019, para 20).

The idea that election disputes should – at least, at last instance – be subject to judicial review is also the point of view of the relevant international institutions. The Venice Commission has clearly held in its Code of Good Practice in Electoral Matters that an effective system of appeal requires that the appeal body in electoral matters should be either an electoral commission or a court. An appeal to parliament may be provided for in first instance. In any case, however, final appeal to a court must be possible (Venice Commission, 2002, II.3.3.a.). The ODIHR is equally of the opinion that disputes in electoral matters should be subject to judicial review. It relies on article 5.10 of the 1990 Copenhagen document, which holds that everyone must have an effective means of redress against administrative decisions, so as to guarantee respect for fundamental rights and to ensure legal integrity. From this provision, it has derived a general principle that all decisions by the election administration or other administrative bodies in an electoral context should be subject to judicial review (ODIHR, 2019d, 27). In many of its country reports, the ODIHR has recommended that the state in question amend its legislative framework in such a way that all decisions concerning elections are amenable for judicial review (ODIHR, 2020b, 21; ODIHR, 2019h, 21; ODIHR, 2017a, 16; ODIHR, 2017f, 19). This is the case, even if there already is some form of review, for example, by a hierarchically higher election commission (ODIHR, 2019i, 18; ODHIR, 2018b, 18–9).

Thus, the Venice Commission and the ODIHR are clear in their requirement that election disputes should – at least in last instance – be subject to judicial review. The same point of view has been adopted by the UN Human Rights Committee (1996, para 20). A purely political system, wherein the domestic parliament is the sole judge of its own elections, is therefore clearly not allowed. The ECtHR's standpoint on this issue is less clear. In the 2010 judgment of *Grosaru*,[5] the Court had held that the Romanian system of post-election dispute resolution, which did not allow for judicial review, but only for an appeal to a commission that was composed for a large majority of members of parliament, violated the right to free elections. Many commentators interpreted this judgment in such a way that the court equally required a review by a court or other independent body in (post-)election disputes (Leloup, 2019, 416; Gaudin, 2019, 80; Van Drooghenbroeck, Van der Hulst, & Caboor, 2018, 575; Van Drooghenbroeck & Belleflamme, 2010, 17–26).

In the recent judgment of *Mugemangango* of July 2020, the court – in its Grand Chamber formation – explicitly addressed the question of what kind of body should decide post-election disputes.[6] In this case, Mugemangango, a Belgian politician, had lost the race for a seat in the Walloon Parliament by only a handful of votes. He subsequently asked for a recount of the ballots that had been declared blank, spoiled, or disputed. According to Belgian law, the Walloon Parliament itself, as constituted by the outcome of the elections Mugemangango was disputing, was in charge of this decision and ultimately denied his request. Subsequently, Mugemangango appealed to the ECtHR, claiming that the fact that the parliament had to decide on the election dispute violated his right to stand as a candidate in free elections (Article 3 of the First Additional Protocol) and his right to an effective remedy (Article 13 ECHR).

In its judgment, the Grand Chamber unanimously came to the conclusion that the Belgian system violated both convention rights. It held that the parliamentary system of election dispute resolution did not offer Mugemangango an effective examination of his complaint. Importantly, however, this violation was not based on the mere fact that it was parliament itself that had decided on the complaint. On the contrary, the court explicitly held that the Convention does not require a judicial authority. It held that

> in a case concerning a post-election dispute about the election results and the distribution of seats, it is necessary and sufficient for the competent body to offer sufficient guarantees of impartiality, for its discretion to be circumscribed with sufficient precision by provisions of domestic law and for the procedure to afford effective guarantees of a fair, objective and sufficiently reasoned decision.

In *Mugemangango*, the court thus stated unequivocally that a judicial review is not required and that an appeal to parliament can also be seen as an effective remedy. Even though the court makes mention of the fact that it concerns a post-election dispute, there is not immediately any sign in the case law to suggest that the principle set forth in *Mugemangango* cannot be extended to other kinds of election disputes. In other cases that concern (pre-)election disputes, the fact that there was no possibility for judicial review did not automatically lead the court to find a violation.[7]

It can thus be concluded that the court, as opposed to the Venice Commission and the ODIHR, does not require a final judicial review when it comes to election disputes. A review by a non-judicial body, like an election commission or the parliament itself, can suffice. This is, however, on the condition that this body fulfills the three requirements that were mentioned above. Among these requirements is the fact that the body in question is sufficiently impartial. One can wonder how this requirement is supposed to work in practice when it is parliament that decides on election disputes. The court itself has indicated that members of parliament cannot by definition be impartial.[8] How then can a body existing exclusively of parliamentarians ever be considered impartial? This question remains, even if measures are taken to improve the situation, such as excluding direct competitors for the seat at issue from the voting process. It is almost unavoidable that there is at least an appearance of partiality when parliament has to rule over its own elections.

To a certain degree, the *Mugemangango* judgment thus seems to be contradictory. On the one hand, it explicitly states that members of parliament are by definition not impartial. On the other, it implicitly indicates that parliament, a body which is composed exclusively of members of parliament, can be seen as an impartial body if certain procedural or institutional requirements are met (Leloup, 2020, 392). This apparent contradiction is also lamented in two concurring opinions attached to the judgment. These opinions argue that, even though the judgment in theory leaves the states the option to choose either a parliamentary or a (quasi)-judicial remedy, the latter is the only viable option in practice. One can indeed wonder what measures could be taken in practice to ensure the impartiality of parliament in such cases. The most prudent choice for the European states would thus appear to be to establish a judicial review in election disputes, as is also required by the Venice Commission and the ODIHR.

Another question that relates to the broader issue of what type of body may be competent for election disputes concerns the composition of election commissions. In several, mostly Central and Eastern European, countries such commission are widely used and are often competent to take important decisions, for example, with regard to candidate registration. Hierarchically higher election commissions are usually competent to hear an appeal against a decision of a lower election commission and can, therefore, act as a body of election dispute resolution.

Given these wide powers, their composition is important. The way in which these commissions are composed varies among countries, but it is generally some mixture of members of the majority and opposition, possibly with some additional independent members. In some countries, complaints have been raised about the composition of these commissions, based on the argument that the members of the political majority constitute a dominant majority. Such a composition would not allow for an effective and independent examination of election disputes. In its opinions, the Venice Commission has pointed to the crucial importance of an equitable composition of election commissions, stressing that this should be guided by principles of maximum impartiality and independence from politically motivated manipulation (Venice Commission, 2020b, para 26; Venice Commission, 2002, paras 74–6). The ODIHR as well has denounced the imbalanced composition of the election commissions in some states (ODIHR, 2020a, 8; ODIHR, 2019b, 9; ODIHR, 2004, 2) or noted that all members exclusively voted along party lines (ODIHR, 2019a, 22).

Occasionally, complaints about the composition of election commissions also reach the ECtHR. A string of cases against Azerbaijan is indicative of the way in which the court's jurisprudence on this issue may evolve. Whereas the court has held that it is important for the authorities to be in charge of electoral administration to function in a transparent manner and to maintain impartiality and independence from political manipulation,[9] it took a while before it actively engaged with complaints concerning the composition of election commissions. In the earlier cases, the court avoided these complaints completely by finding a Convention violation on different grounds.[10] In later cases, however, it increasingly dealt with this issue. In a first step, it referred to the observations in a report of the ODIHR (ODIHR, 2010), which drew attention to the serious concerns that had arisen regarding the impartiality, openness, and transparency in the Azerbaijani election commissions.[11] A few months later, it substantively addressed the issue itself. It held that

> [a]lthough there can be no ideal or uniform system guaranteeing checks and balances between the different State powers or political forces within a body of electoral administration, [it] shares the view that the proportion of pro-ruling-party members in all electoral commissions in Azerbaijan is currently particularly high.[12]

Immediately, it added that the *raison d'être* of an electoral commission is to ensure the effective administration of free and fair voting in an impartial manner, which is achievable by virtue of a structural composition that guarantees its independence and impartiality, but which would become impossible to achieve if the commission were to become another forum for political struggle between various political forces.

It then noted, however, that the case at hand, in isolation, did not require it to determine, *in abstracto*, whether the way in which the Azerbaijani election commissions are composed is in itself compatible with the Convention. In its report on this string of cases, the Committee of Ministers stressed that Azerbaijan should take general measures with regard to the composition of the election commissions to make sure they can function independently (Committee of Ministers, 2013). As of yet, the Azerbaijani Government has not introduced any structural changes. Given that no concrete steps have been taken to mitigate the problems indicated by the court, it is not impossible that it will give a stronger signal in future cases and expressly rule that the current composition is in violation of the right to free elections. Even if it does not do this in the particular case of Azerbaijan, the court has made clear in this string of cases that it is willing to examine the composition of election commissions in the light of the right to free and fair elections and that it is conscious of the importance of equitable distribution between majority and opposition members in these bodies.

The Issue of Jurisdiction

The previous section pointed out that, within one and the same country, many different bodies can be tasked with some aspect of election dispute resolution. Even the Venice Commission and the ODIHR, which require a judicial review in the last instance, allow for a prior appeal to another body like an election commission. Furthermore, as was already mentioned, the competent appeal body often varies depending on the issue at stake. The resulting panoply of bodies and procedures may hinder the effectiveness of the system of dispute resolution. Especially in the field of election disputes, marked by its very short time-limits (see below), it is crucial that a person can immediately find out with which body he or she must lodge a certain appeal. A clear domestic system of jurisdiction is therefore key.

This concern has also been raised in many reports by the ODIHR and the Venice Commission. Both organizations have stressed the need to avoid conflicts of jurisdiction between election administration bodies and courts (ODIHR, 2019d, 27; Venice Commission, 2020b, para 238). Neither the appellants nor the authorities should be able to choose the appeal body. In other words, the possibility of forum shopping must be avoided (Venice Commission, 2002, II.3.3.c.)

Both institutions have also repeatedly addressed this issue in their country-specific reports and opinions. The common thread throughout these texts is that the legislative framework must be harmonized in such a way that the law clearly indicates which domestic body has jurisdiction over each complaint (ODIHR, 2019g, 21; Venice Commission, 2013, para 39). Laws that offer a choice on where to submit a complaint, for example, by making an appeal against a decision of an election commission possible with either a hierarchically higher election commission or with the courts, should be abolished (Venice Commission, 2018a, para 88; Venice Commission, 2014b, para 121; ODIHR, 2019j, 28; ODIHR, 2019e, 19). However, both the Venice Commission and the ODIHR do allow such concurrent complaint procedures, if there is a clear and effective mechanism in the law to prevent the simultaneous use of both avenues, for example, by explicitly stipulating in the law that the judicial route has precedence in case of parallel proceedings (Venice Commission 2020a, para 29; ODIHR, 2020c, 20).

Which Decision-Making Powers Must the Competent Body Have?

As noted by the Venice Commission, a successful system of election dispute resolution relies on the effectiveness of the decision-making powers of the competent body (Venice Commission, 2020a, para 124). Election disputes would, indeed, be deprived of all usefulness, if the competent body were not in a position to rectify any irregularities.

In this regard, it is important firstly that an appeal body can act not only against specific actions of election administration bodies, but also against inactions (Venice Commission, 2018a, para 89; Venice Commission, 2014a, para 76; ODIHR, 2019d, 48). A second important consideration is that public authorities that are charged with executing electoral legislation do not act outside the law, but instead exercise their powers in accordance with the applicable legal rules.[13] Third, in the case that legislation does allow some room for discretion to the election administration, it is crucial that this discretion is not extraordinarily wide. The discretion must be circumscribed with sufficient precision by the law.[14]

Importantly, if an appeal procedure is open to domestic courts, their powers of review may not be limited in such a way that makes this review ineffective. The courts must have a sufficiently wide power of review in order to prevent arbitrary decisions.[15] Furthermore, if the courts render a judgment in a complaint procedure, it is crucial that the election authorities feel bound by this decision. The effective protection of the rights in an election context presupposes an obligation on the part of the electoral authorities to comply with a final judgment against them.[16] The ECtHR's judgment in *Petkov* provides a good example of this. In this case, Petkov appealed a decision that refused to put him on the list of candidates. Even though he won this appeal before the Bulgarian Supreme Court, the election authorities refused to add him to the list of candidates. The court found this to be a violation of the right to an effective remedy, as it essentially allowed the authorities to arbitrarily deprive candidates of their electoral rights.[17] The ODIHR also has indicated that domestic courts should be empowered to order the performance of a specific duty by election commissions, rather than to only quash their decisions (ODIHR, 2017d, 20). Thus, generally speaking, the competent body must be able to effectively remedy the situation that is being appealed.[18]

Time Limits

One of the aspects that sets election law, in general, and election dispute resolution, in particular, apart from other fields of law is the extremely short time-limits that must be adhered to. By definition, election disputes only occur during the electoral process, where time is of the essence. This urgency is irrespective of whether the dispute in question concerns pre-election or post-election proceedings; a person who has been refused to stand for election has just as much interest in the rapid resolution of this dispute as someone who challenges the final election results. This is not to say that all forms of election disputes must have identical time limits (for example: ODIHR, 2019f, 18). A state is free to modify the time-limit according to the topic of the dispute.

This need for swift dispute resolution must be contrasted with the need for due process and the importance of granting the deciding body sufficient time to assess each complaint. Election disputes are often factual and very complex issues, which take time to adequately examine. The need for short time limits should, therefore, not stand in the way of procedural guarantees, like the right to be heard, or lead to decisions that do not address the substance of the complaint.

The ECtHR has acknowledged this difficult balance as follows:

> considerations of expediency and the necessity for tight time-limits designed to avoid delaying the electoral process, although often justified, may nevertheless not serve as a pretext to undermine the effectiveness of electoral procedures or to deprive the persons concerned by those procedures of the opportunity to effectively contest any accusations of electoral misconduct made against them.[19]

In this regard, the court has lamented the situation in which the applicant was afforded only a day to prepare for the hearing,[20] but has equally criticized a system for which the entire system of election dispute resolution could take up to 18 days.[21]

Both the ODIHR and the Venice Commission have taken a clear stance on the topic of time limits in election dispute resolution. The ODIHR has held that there should be expedited deadlines for filing and adjudicating all election-related disputes (ODIHR, 2019f, 18; ODIHR, 2019c, 17). These deadlines must, moreover, be expressly established in domestic legislation (ODIHR, 2017e, 15). The Venice Commission has, like the ECtHR, stressed that time limits must be short, but should nonetheless be long enough to make an appeal possible and to guarantee the exercise of the right of defense and a reflected decision (Venice Commission, 2002, para 95). It makes a distinction between the time limit to lodge a complaint and the time limit for adjudicating this complaint (Venice Commission, 2020a, para 76). For both stages, it suggests a time limit from three to five days.

Both institutions have, moreover, been very active on this topic in their recommendations to the European states. In almost all reports or opinions, mention is made of the issue of time limits, often coming to the conclusion that the domestic legislative framework establishes a time limit that is too short (Venice Commission, 2018b, para 54; Venice Commission, 2014b, para 125; ODIHR, 2019h, 20; ODIHR, 2018b, 19) or too long (Venice Commission, 2017, para 78; ODIHR, 2018e, 16; ODIHR, 2018c, 13). However, irrespective of these recommendations, the Venice Commission has concluded in a recent study that it is difficult to determine a positive or negative trend among the European states regarding time limits and that, in many of them, explicit legal provisions regarding time limits are still lacking (Venice Commission, 2020a, para 105).

Standing

Another important issue concerning election disputes is standing. A system of election dispute resolution would be deprived of much of its effectiveness if the domestic legislation unduly limited the people who are entitled to file complaints on perceived irregularities or inaccuracies.

The Venice Commission and the ODIHR support a very wide interpretation of standing when it comes to election disputes. In its Code of Good Practice in Electoral Matters, the Commission holds that all candidates and all voters registered in the constituency concerned must be entitled to lodge an appeal. However, for the voters a reasonable quorum may be imposed for appeal of the results of elections (Venice Commission, 2002, II.3.3.f.). In later reports, it also expressly mentions the right of appeal for political parties (Venice Commission, 2020a, para 59). Similarly, the ODIHR has stated that every voter, candidate, or political party should have the right to lodge a complaint on every aspect of the electoral process (ODIHR, 2019d, 71; ODIHR, 2016a, 19).

Both institutions have applied this extensive interpretation of standing to their recommendations to specific countries. Many examples can be found in which they criticize the domestic legal framework for limiting the right to lodge a complaint for specific groups (Venice Commission, 2018a, paras 91–2; Venice Commission, 2014a, para 72; Venice Commission, 2011, para 58; ODIHR, 2019j, 27; ODIHR, 2019e, 19–20; ODIHR, 2019f, 17–8).

As opposed to this very broad interpretation of standing by the Venice Commission and the ODIHR, the ECtHR follows a much more restrictive interpretation. In fact, it has expressly held that the right of individual voters to appeal against the results of voting may be subject to reasonable limitations in the domestic legal order.[22] The court is of the opinion that it should be cautious about conferring unrestricted standing on individual participants in the electoral process and affords the domestic authorities a very wide margin of appreciation in this regard.[23] While there is a clear tension between this approach and that of the Venice Commission and the ODIHR, it is arguably in line with the recent stress on the Court's subsidiary position (Lemmens, 2020, 684).

Procedural Guarantees during Election Disputes

The previous sections discussed questions that were related to the domestic body that is competent to rule on election disputes and to how this body could be reached. Nevertheless, questions could also arise on what procedural guarantees this body should afford to the individuals or groups of people who lodge a complaint. It is to this question that we now turn.

All three institutions that form the focus of this article have stressed the importance of due process and procedural guarantees during election disputes and this at the level of both election commissions and courts alike (Venice Commission, 2020a, paras 106–23; ODIHR, 2019f, 19).[24] For this reason, this section will not make a distinction between the court and the Venice Commission and the ODIHR, as it has in several previous sections, but instead will examine the various procedural guarantees that these institutions require.

First of all, a person who lodges a complaint has the right to be heard (Venice Commission, 2002, II.3.3.h; ODIHR, 2018f, 18).[25] This presupposes that the person in question is informed about the timing and the place of the hearing (ODIHR, 2017b, 21).[26] This information must, moreover, be conveyed in a timely manner, allowing sufficient time to prepare for the hearing.[27] In this regard, the court did not accept the situation in which the applicant was informed about the hearing 15 minutes before it took place.[28]

Secondly, the applicant has a right to submit evidence (Venice Commission, 2020a, para 90). For one, this implies that the applicant may submit written conclusions.[29] The person involved should also receive any documents that are relevant for his or her complaint.[30] Moreover, there must be a possibility to challenge any evidence against him or her.[31] Finally, the right to submit evidence would be completely ineffective if the domestic authorities could choose to ignore it. Therefore, there is a procedural obligation on both election commissions and courts to adequately assess the available, pertinent evidence, while disregarding irrelevant evidence.[32]

Thirdly, as regards the eventual decision of the body in question, this decision must be reasoned (Venice Commission, 2020a, para 88; ODIHR, 2018g, 22–3).[33] This reasoning may also not be overly formalistic,[34] but should instead assess the applicant's complaint in substance (ODIHR, 2017c, 22).[35] This means that the domestic institutions are required to adequately assess any pertinent argument that is submitted.[36]

Finally, it is crucial that the proceedings before the election commissions and the courts take place in a manner that respects the principles of impartiality and transparency (Venice Commission, 2020a, para 116).[37] This presupposes that hearings should, in principle, be public and decisions should be published (Venice Commission, ODIHR, 2019e, 19; ODIHR, 2019a, 21; ODIHR, 2018d, 18).

Analysis

The previous title examined the European standards on election dispute resolution by making a distinction between several substantive topics. This section will take a look at all of these topics together and aims to provide some overarching points of analysis.

The first and clearest conclusion is that the prevailing European standards are geared towards the protection of non-state actors in the electoral process: The voters and the candidates. The relevant standards concern standing and time limits, the prohibition on formalistic decision-making, and the duty to apply admissibility rules mildly (ODIHR, 2019j, 29–30), and they all clearly stem from a concern to make the system of election disputes as accessible and effective as possible. In this vein, the Venice Commission and the ODIHR have stipulated that states should avoid unnecessary obstacles to lodging a complaint (Venice Commission, 2020a, para 110; ODIHR, 2016b, 22). Whereas this "applicant-centered" point of view is in line with the fact that the right to free elections is a fundamental right, it can nonetheless not be denied that it puts a lot of pressure on the domestic authorities that are tasked with election administration.

Secondly, it is apparent that, in many of its cases concerning the right to free elections, the Strasbourg Court refers to reports by the Venice Commission and the ODIHR (Suksi, 2016). The court may, for example, use these reports as evidence of irregularities during the election process (Bodnár, 2017, 57). Importantly, the court also looks at these instruments for guidance on the standards that the domestic system of election dispute resolution should adhere to. In this way, these soft law standards get somewhat of a hard edge and the international institutions' recommendations may be transformed into obligations (Úbeda de Torres, 2017, 38). Given the very active role that these institutions play in this field, the effects of this may be far-reaching.

However, it should be pointed out – and this is the third conclusion – that the court does not do this in all circumstances. It does not indiscriminately adopt the position of these international organizations but, at times, also chooses not to follow them. One important example of this is the judgment of *Mugemangango*, where the Grand Chamber of the Court made clear that election disputes do not have to be decided by a (quasi-)judicial body, thereby derogating from the clear stance of the Venice Commission and the ODIHR. The court, referring to its subsidiary position and the diversity in electoral systems in Europe, stated that it was not its place to indicate what type of remedy should be provided. This was a question closely linked to the separation of powers that fell within the wide margin of appreciation afforded to the European states.[38] Another example can be found on the topic of standing, where the court indicated that a very low level of scrutiny would apply to the more technical stages of vote counting and expressed caution about conferring unrestricted standing to challenge this stage of elections on individual participants in the electoral process.[39] These examples show that, on some topics concerning the right to free elections, the court attaches significant importance to its subsidiary position and is wary of imposing standards that would have a considerable impact on European states (Bodnár, 2017, 59). This echoes the conclusion of other scholars that the court has not interpreted the right to free elections as dynamically as many other Convention rights (Dickson & Hardman, 2017, 5).

Nevertheless, it must be concluded that the combined effect of the recommendations by the Venice Commission and the ODIHR and the case law of the ECtHR is slowly, but surely, leading to a convergence among European countries in the field of election dispute resolution. The best example may be found on the issue of which body is competent to rule on post-election disputes. As was mentioned above, whereas there has been a general evolution towards establishing judicial review in this field throughout the twentieth century, a few countries have kept parliament as the sole competent body. Nonetheless, several of these countries have recently initiated a process to move away from such a parliamentary system. For example, both Luxembourg and Ireland have included a provision allowing for final judicial review over such disputes in their newly proposed constitutions. In Norway, a joint expert and political commission has recently recommended the introduction of a new judicial body to decide on election disputes. In Belgium, the 2020 coalition agreement makes mention of a revision of the current election dispute system as well. Thus, the few countries that still have a purely parliamentary system of post-election dispute resolution are taking steps to move away from this system and to follow suit in establishing judicial review. Though not the only reason, these countries do mention the Venice Commission and the ECtHR as reasons for making this transition. This shows that the Venice Commission, the ODIHR, and the ECtHR are contributing to what can be described as a Europeanization of the systems of election dispute resolution. This is not to say that they do not leave room for differences between countries or that they require uniformity across Europe. Yet, the fourth and final conclusion must be that these three actors can be seen as a driving motor for a convergence among European states in the field of election dispute resolution.

Conclusion

The ODIHR report on the 2018 presidential elections in Azerbaijan mentions that no formal complaints had been filed at any level of the election administration or the courts, either before or after election day. Some individuals specifically mentioned that they had not filed a complaint because they had no faith in the election commission and the courts to handle it in an impartial and professional manner (ODIHR, 2018a, 19).

Such a state of affairs is clearly unacceptable and inevitably works to the advantage of the incumbent majority. In a well-functioning democratic system based on the rule of law, there must be room for disputes at all stages of the electoral cycle in order to verify whether these took place in a free and fair fashion. In an election context, fairness means that voters and candidates must be afforded a reasonable opportunity to take part in the election and that all votes validly cast must be taken into account in order to accurately calculate the result of the election (Lemmens, 2020, 676). If election law is to be more than words on paper, any person who has the feeling that this has not been the case must have the opportunity to raise these complaints in front of a body that can effectively remedy the situation and offer sufficient safeguards. Only under such conditions can the electoral system keep the faith of the electorate and can the idea of democracy truly be respected.

This chapter looked into the formation of European-wide standards of election dispute resolution in Europe due to the work of the Venice Commission, the ODIHR, and the ECtHR. It has examined the standards that these three bodies have set on several specific issues of election dispute resolution, and it has indicated that these standards are geared towards the protection of the non-state actors in the election process. Furthermore, it has shown that the combined effect of these three bodies is a driving force of convergence among the European states that may lead to a certain Europeanization of the domestic systems of election dispute resolution.

Table 19.1 Overview of Electoral Standards and International Organizations

	Venice Commission	*ODIHR*	*ECtHR*
Competent Body	Judicial review in final instance	Judicial review in final instance	No specific type of body, but 1) Guarantees of impartiality; 2) Discretion circumscribed by law; 3) Guarantees of fair decision
Decision-Making Powers	Review of both action and inaction; can cancel election results partly or fully	Review of both action and inaction; can cancel election results partly or fully; empowered to order the performance of a duty	Discretion circumscribed by law; appeal body able to effectively remedy complaint
Standing	Every voter, candidate, and political party	Every voter, candidate, and political party	Wide margin of appreciation, no clear standards
Time Limits	Three to five days for lodging complaint and three to five days for adjudication	No clearly established standard. Recommendations point to two to five days	No clearly established standard. Question whether any given time limit is long enough for effective complaint
Procedural Guarantees	Right to be heard; right to adequate time to prepare for hearing; right to submit evidence; right to reasoned decision; right to impartial and transparent proceedings		

Notes

1 ECtHR (GC) July 10, 2020, Case No. 310/15, *Mugemangango v. Belgium*, §96; ECtHR October 21, 1997, Case No. 24194/94, *Pierre-Bloch v. France*, §51.
2 ECtHR October 8, 2015, Case No. 36503/11, *Gahramanli a.o. v. Azerbaijan*, §69.
3 See Jurij Toplak's chapter in this volume.
4 An overview of the standards imposed by the Venice Commission, the ODIHR, and the ECtHR on the various topics can be found in Table 1.
5 ECtHR March 2, 2010, Case No. 78039/01, *Grosaru v. Romania*.
6 ECtHR (GC) July 10, 2020, Case No. 310/15, *Mugemangango v. Belgium*.
7 ECtHR May 21, 2019, Case No. 58302/10, *G.K. v. Belgium*; ECtHR December 15, 2015, Case No. 16732/05, *Ofensiva Tinerilor v. Romania*.
8 ECtHR July 8, 2008, Case No. 9103/04, *Georgian Labour Party v. Georgia*.
9 ECtHR April 8, 2010, Case No. 18705/06, *Namat Aliyev v. Azerbaijan*, §73; ECtHR July 8, 2008, Case No. 9103/04, *The Georgian Labour Party v. Georgia*, §101.
10 ECtHR September 25, 2014, Case No. 12535/06, *Karimov v. Azerbaijan*, §51; ECtHR April 8, 2010, Case No. 18705/06, *Namat Aliyev v. Azerbaijan*, §92.
11 ECtHR June 11, 2015, Case No. 31953/11, *Tahirov v. Azerbaijan*, §60.
12 ECtHR October 8, 2015, Case No. 36503/11, *Gahramanli a.o. v. Azerbaijan*, §78.
13 ECtHR September 25, 2014, Case No. 12535/06, *Karimov v. Azerbaijan*, §42.
14 ECtHR (GC) July 10, 2020, Case No. 310/15, *Mugemangango v. Belgium*, §70; ECtHR May 21, 2019, Case No. 58302/10, *G.K. v. Belgium*, §57; ECtHR December 15, 2015, Case No. 16732/05, *Ofensiva Tinerilor v. Romania*, §56; ECtHR October 13, 2015, Case Nos. 48555/10 and 48377/10, *Riza a.o. v. Bulgaria*, §143; ECtHR February 7, 2008, Case No. 39424/02, *Kovach v. Ukraine*, §54.
15 ECtHR March 24, 2020, Case No. 25560/13, *Cegolea v. Romania*, §64.
16 ECtHR June 11, 2009, Case No. 77568/01, 178/02 and 505/02, *Petkov a.o. v. Bulgaria*, §65.
17 ECtHR June 11, 2009, Case No. 77568/01, 178/02 and 505/02, *Petkov a.o. v. Bulgaria*, §79.
18 ECtHR May 24, 2016, Case No. 41683/06, *Paunović and Milivojević v. Serbia*, §48.
19 ECtHR December 5, 2019, Case No. 8513/11, *Abil v. Azerbaijan (No. 2)*, §75; ECtHR April 8, 2010, Case No. 18705/06, *Namat Aliyev v. Azerbaijan*, §90.
20 ECtHR July 26, 2011, Case No. 4508/06, *Orujov v. Azerbaijan*, §56.
21 ECtHR July 11, 2019, Case Nos. 28508/11, 37602/11 and 43776/11, *Abdalov a.o. v. Azerbaijan*, §99.
22 ECtHR May 30, 2017, Case No. 75947/11, *Davydov a.o. v. Russia*, §335.
23 ECtHR May 30, 2017, Case No. 75947/11, *Davydov a.o. v. Russia*, §287.
24 ECtHR February 21, 2012, Case No. 16511/06, *Abil v. Azerbaijan*, §39; ECtHR September 30, 2010, Case No. 20799/06, *Kerimova v. Azerbaijan*, §45.
25 ECtHR May 21, 2019, Case No. 58302/10, *G.K. v. Belgium*, §61; ECtHR October 8, 2015, Case No. 36503/11, *Gahramanli a.o. v. Azerbaijan*, §81; ECtHR February 21, 2012, Case No. 19554/06, *Khanhuseyn Aliyev v. Azerbaijan*, §39.
26 ECtHR May 30, 2017, Case No. 75947/11, *Davydov a.o. v. Russia*, §313; ECtHR February 21, 2012, Case No. 16511/06, *Abil v. Azerbaijan*, §39.
27 ECtHR February 28, 2012, Case No. 18469/06, *Atakishi v. Azerbaijan*, §48.
28 ECtHR August 4, 2020, Case Nos. 5113/15 a.o., *Political Party "Patria" a.o. v. Republic of Moldova*, §37.
29 ECtHR May 21, 2019, Case No. 58302/10, *G.K. v. Belgium*, §61.
30 ECtHR June 11, 2015, Case No. 319553/11, *Tahirov v. Azerbaijan*, §68.
31 ECtHR December 5, 2019, Case No. 8513/11, *Abil v. Azerbaijan (No. 2)*, §75.
32 ECtHR December 5, 2019, Case No. 8513/11, *Abil v. Azerbaijan (No. 2)*, §77; ECtHR February 28, 2012, Case No. 18469/06, *Atakishi v. Azerbaijan*, §47; ECtHR February 21, 2012, Case No. 16511/06, *Abil v. Azerbaijan*, §38; ECtHR January 10, 2012, Case No. 6984/06, *Hajili v. Azerbaijan*, §56; ECtHR July 26, 2011, Case No. 4508/06, *Orujov v. Azerbaijan*, §48.
33 ECtHR June 11, 2015, Case No. 319553/11, *Tahirov v. Azerbaijan*, §70; ECtHR February 28, 2012, Case No. 18469/06, *Atakishi v. Azerbaijan*, §46.
34 ECtHR April 8, 2010, Case No. 18705/06, *Namat Aliyev v. Azerbaijan*, §85.
35 ECtHR May 30, 2017, Case No. 75947/11, *Davydov a.o. v. Russia*, §315 and §333; ECtHR June 11, 2015, Case No. 319553/11, *Tahirov v. Azerbaijan*, §61.
36 ECtHR August 4, 2020, Case Nos. 5113/15 a.o., *Political Party "Patria" a.o. v. Republic of Moldova*, §37.

37 ECtHR April 8, 2010, Case No. 18705/06, *Namat Aliyev v. Azerbaijan*, §73; ECtHR July 8, 2008, Case No. 9103/04, *Georgian Labour Party v. Georgia*, §101.
38 ECtHR (GC) July 10, 2020, Case No. 310/15, *Mugemangango v. Belgium*, §138.
39 ECtHR May 30, 2017, Case No. 75947/11, *Davydov a.o. v. Russia*, §287.

References

Bodnár, E. (2017). The level of protection of the right to free elections in the practice of the European Court of Human Rights. In H. Hardman & B. Dickson (Eds.), *Electoral rights in Europe: Advances and challenges* (pp. 49–66). London: Routledge.

Committee of Ministers. (2013). *Notes of the 1179th meeting of 24–26 September 2013.*

Dickson, B. & Hardman, H. (2017). Introduction. In H. Hardman & B. Dickson (Eds.), *Electoral rights in Europe: Advances and challenges* (pp. 1–13). London: Routledge.

Fasone, C. & Piccirilli, G. (2017). Towards a *ius commune* on elections in Europe? The role of the code of good practice in electoral matters in "harmonizing" electoral rights. *Election Law Journal, 16*(2), 247–254.

Gaudin, T. (2019). À propos de l'arrêt G.K. c. Belgique et de la vérification des pouvoirs: reculer pour mieux sauter?. *Revue Trimestrielle des Droits de l'Homme, 4*, 979–996.

Leloup, M. (2019). G.(emiste) K.(ans)/België: het EHRM ontwijkt een uitspraak over de bestaanbaarheid van artikel 48 van de Grondwet met het EVRM. *Tijdschrift voor Bestuurswetenschappen en Publiekrecht, 74*(7), 414–418.

Leloup, M. (2020). Kroniek van een aangekondigde verdragsschending: het onderzoek van de geloofsbrieven getoetst aan de Europese mensenrechtenstandaarden. *Tijdschrift voor Bestuurswetenschappen en Publiekrecht, 75*(8), 383–407.

Lemmens, P. (2020). The right to fair elections under article 3 of protocol no. 1 to the European Convention on Human Rights. In R. Leysen, K. Muylle, J. Theunis, & W. Verrijdt (Eds.), *Semper Perseverans: Liber Amicorum André Alen* (pp. 657–668). Antwerp: Intersentia.

Muylle, K. (2010). L'autonomie parlementaire à l'abri des droits de l'homme? *Revue Trimestrielle des Droits de l'Homme, 3*, 705–731.

ODIHR (2004). *Georgia, Extraordinary Presidential Election*, 4 January 2004: Final Report.

ODIHR (2010). *Azerbaijan, Parliamentary Elections*, 7 November 2010: Final Report.

ODIHR (2016a). *Belarus, Parliamentary Elections*, 11 September 2016: Final Report.

ODIHR (2016b). *Georgia, Parliamentary Elections*, 8 and 30 October 2016: Final Report.

ODIHR (2017a). *Austria, Early Parliamentary Elections*, 15 October 2017: Final Report.

ODIHR (2017b). *Bulgaria, Early Parliamentary Elections*, 26 March 2017: Final Report.

ODIHR (2017c). *Georgia, Local Elections*, 21 October and 12 November 2017: Final Report.

ODIHR (2017d). *Kyrgyzstan, Presidential Election*, 15 October 2017: Final Report.

ODIHR (2017e). *Netherlands, Parliamentary Elections*, 15 March 2017: Final Report.

ODIHR (2017f). *Turkey, Constitutional Referendum*, 16 April 2017: Final Report.

ODIHR (2018a). *Azerbaijan, Early Presidential Election*, 11 April 2018: Final Report.

ODIHR (2018b). *Bosnia and Herzegovina, General Elections*, 7 October 2018: Final Report.

ODIHR (2018c). Cyprus, Presidential Election, 28 January and 4 February 2018: Final Report.

ODIHR (2018d). *The former Yugoslav Republic of Macedonia, Referendum*, 30 September 2018: Final Report.

ODIHR (2018e). *Italy, Parliamentary Elections*, 4 March 2018: Final Report.

ODIHR (2018f). *Montenegro, Presidential Election*, 15 April 2018: Final Report.

ODIHR (2018g). *Turkey, Early Presidential and Parliamentary Elections*, 24 June 2018: Final Report.

ODIHR (2019a). *Albania, Local Elections*, 30 June 2019: Final Report.

ODIHR (2019b). *Belarus, Early Parliamentary Elections*, 17 November 2019: Final Report.

ODIHR (2019c). *Greece, Early Parliamentary Elections*, 7 July 2019: Final Report.

ODIHR (2019d). *Handbook for the observation of election dispute resolution.*

ODIHR (2019e). *Kazakhstan, Early Presidential Election*, 9 June 2019: Final Report.

ODIHR (2019f). *Lithuania, Presidential Election*, 12 and 26 May 2019: Final Report.

ODIHR (2019g). *Moldova, Parliamentary Elections*, 24 February 2019: Final Report.

ODIHR (2019h). North Macedonia, Presidential Election, 21 April and 5 May 2019: Final Report.

ODIHR (2019i). *Romania, Presidential Election*, 10 and 24 November 2019: Final Report.

ODIHR (2019j). *Ukraine, Presidential Election*, 31 March and 21 April 2019: Final Report.

ODIHR (2020a). *Azerbaijan, Early Parliamentary Elections*, 9 February 2020: Final Report.

ODIHR (2020b). *Poland, Presidential Election*, 28 June and 12 July 2020: Final Report.
ODIHR (2020c). *Tajikistan, Parliamentary Elections*, 1 March 2020: Final Report.
Philip, L. (1961) *Le contentieux des élections aux assemblées politiques françaises*. Paris: LGDJ.
Romainville, C. (2020). Quel contrôle post-electoral?. *Administration Public (Trimestriel)*, *1*, 150–157.
Suksi, M. (2016). The use of election observation reports in regional human rights jurisprudence. *Nordic Journal of Human Rights*, *34*(4), 229–246.
Tushnet, M. (2018). *Advanced introduction to comparative constitutional law* (2nd ed.). Cheltenham: Edward Elgar.
Úbeda de Torres, A. (2017). Between soft and hard law standards: The contribution of the Venice Commission in the electoral field. In H. Hardman & B. Dickson (Eds.), *Electoral rights in Europe: Advances and challenges* (pp. 30–48). London: Routledge.
United Nations Human Right Committee. (1996). *General Comment No. 25 on the right to participate in public affairs, voting rights and the right to equal access to public service*, CCPR/C/21/Rev.1/Add.7.
Van Drooghenbroeck, S., & Belleflamme, F. (2010). Assemblées, juges du contentieux postélectoral: Une institution en sursis? In A. Rezsöhàzy & M. Van der Hulst (Ed.), *Droit parlementaire et les droits fondamentaux* (pp. 1–39). Brussels: La Charte.
Van Drooghenbroeck, S., Van der Hulst, M. & Caboor, P. (2018). Le contentieux post-électoral. In F. Bouhon & M. Reuchamps (Eds.), *Les systèmes électoraux de la Belgique* (2nd ed., pp. 565–584). Brussels: Larcier.
Venice Commission (2002). *Code of good practice in electoral matters: Guidelines and explanatory report*, CDL-AD(2002)23.
Venice Commission (2011). *Joint opinion on the election code of Bulgaria*, CDL-AD(2011)013.
Venice Commission. (2013). *Joint opinion on the electoral code of the Former Yugoslav Republic of Macedonia*, CDL-AD(2013)020.
Venice Commission. (2014a). *Joint opinion on the draft election code of Bulgaria*, CDL-AD(2014)001.
Venice Commission. (2014b). *Joint opinion on the draft electoral law of the Kyrgyz Republic*, CDL-AD(2014)019.
Venice Commission. (2017). *Joint opinion on amendments to the electoral code in Bulgaria*, CDL-AD(2017)016.
Venice Commission. (2018a). *Joint opinion on the draft election code of Uzbekistan*, CDL-AD(2018)027.
Venice Commission. (2018b). *Joint opinion on the law for amending and completing certain legislative acts in Moldova (electoral system for the election of the parliament)*, CDL-AD(2018)008.
Venice Commission. (2019). *Amicus curiae brief for the European Court of Human Rights in the case of Mugemangango v. Belgium on the procedural safeguards which a state must ensure in procedures challenging the result of an election or the distribution of seats*, CDL-AD(2019)021.
Venice Commission. (2020a). *Report on election dispute resolution*, CDL-AD(2020)025.
Venice Commission. (2020b). *Report on electoral law and electoral administration in Europe*, CDL-AD(2020)023.
Verdussen, M. (2014). Prendre au sérieux le contrôle des élections. *Revue belge de droit constitutionnel*, *3*, 461–473.

20

THE ELECTION LAW IN LATVIA, ESTONIA, AND LITHUANIA

Inese Druviete and Ēriks Kristians Selga

Introduction

This chapter provides an overview of the Baltic election law framework, broadly outlining its main characteristics and legal topicalities. While Latvia receives a more in-depth investigation of its electoral system, the election law-related judicature and practice are explored for all three Baltic states. They have very similar historical origins, and they place significant weight on protecting their right to enjoy democratic and fair elections. This has also manifested in difficult grappling with how far such protection should go, as will be elaborated upon later in the chapter.

The rest of the chapter proceeds as follows. First, the Latvian electoral framework will be outlined, followed by a focus on candidature and party formation. Second, the Latvian jurisprudential practice connected to voting will be outlined. A similar format then follows for Lithuania and Estonia. The piece concludes with an outline of the function of the European Union Parliamentary elections, in which all three states participate.

The Latvian Electoral Framework

The Latvian electoral framework, like much of the state's legal system, draws its roots from its period of independence in the inter-war period (Kerikmäe et al., 2017). In 1991, after regaining independence from the Soviet occupation, the Constitution of 1922 was reinstated to manifest the continuity of the Latvian nation (Ziemele, 2005). The constitution is inspired by the Westminster model and stipulates a strong parliament, an executive body responsible to the parliament, and a figure-head president (Taube, 2001). Derived from the Weimar constitution, the constitution also provides means of direct democracy. The 70-year hiatus, however, came with significant anachronisms that have been amended (Peniķis, 2010).[1] The first parliamentary elections in 1992 ran on the novel Law on Parliamentary Elections, which directly mirrored the 1922 electoral law on various points. Many of the particularities derived from the twentieth-century legal originator are still present in the Latvian electoral system, and they are responsible for forming an altogether unique electoral system.

Since 1992, the Law on Parliamentary Elections has stipulated a proportional representation party list system, with a preference voting scheme and a total of a hundred members of parliament. For the purpose of parliamentary elections, the Constitution of Latvia requires the

DOI: 10.4324/9780429401800-20

country be split into areas proportional to the number of voters in each area. Latvia is split into five major constituencies, with seats allocated according to a population census four months prior to the elections. Voters residing abroad are included in the Riga constituency.[2] Generally, this has resulted in two constituencies accounting for more than half of the total amount of seats, compounded in recent years by the migration from the regions of Latvia to Riga and emigration trends (Davies & Ozolins, 2001, 2004; Pryce, 2012).[3]

The Law on Financing Political Organizations and Law on Pre-election Campaign are the primary statutes covering party and campaign financing. Parties can be financed through membership fees, donations for individuals, and income collected through economic activity conducted by the party. Illegal, anonymous, or foreign entities cannot donate. Donations per individuals are capped per party and per year. The state provides public funds from the state budget that are proportional to the results of the party in the previous elections. The expenditure ceilings of electoral candidates are also limited by law.

The Law on Central Election Commission establishes a three-tier election administration composed of the Central Election Commission, 119 Municipal Election Commissions, and 1078 Polling Station Commissions. The Central Election Commission is a parliament-appointed body of nine members, with each appointment lasting for four years. One member is nominated by the Supreme Court from the judiciary. The commission is responsible for the general conduct of elections.

Municipal Election Commissions are made up of between seven to fifteen members who serve four-year terms based on appointments by respective municipal councils, which originate in nominations by individuals on the council, political parties, or groups of at least ten voters. They oversee the conduct of elections in their respective municipalities. Meanwhile, Polling Station Commissions are comprised of five to seven members appointed by their respective Municipal Election Commissions, and they are responsible for overseeing voting and counting procedures on election day.

Candidates and Parties in Latvia

To be a candidate in parliamentary or local elections, as well as to hold a position in state service, a person must hold Latvian citizenship. A person who was active in the Communist Party or the Working People's International Front of the Latvian Soviet Socialist Republic after January 12, 1991 is not allowed to run for elected office. Past collaboration with the KGB also precludes candidacy. The latter has presented a few difficulties in practice, which will be investigated later in the chapter.

To become a candidate, one must become a member of a party. Parties must be formed at least a year before parliamentary elections and contain at least 500 members, or be an alliance of various such parties with a total of 500 members.[4] The party submits a candidate list in each constituency, on the condition of a monetary deposit.[5] The list contains some basic information about the candidates, as well as their sign-off on a statement acknowledging their capacity to use the Latvian language at a professional level and a party program that cannot exceed 4000 characters.[6]

Several changes were made immediately within the first election (Davies & Ozolins, 1994). More specifically, obstacles were placed to prevent party fragmentation by changing the formula for allocating seats from a Hare quote to a highest average Sainte Lague formula using odd divisors 1, 3, 5, 7, etc. with the threshold set to 5% in 1995 (Millard, 2011). This was done as the former seat formula allowed dozens of parties from an equally large amount of interest groups to prevent the functioning of parliament and government in Latvia's inter-war period (Jungerstam-

Mulders, 2006; Millard, 2011). The voting age was reduced from 21 to 18 years of age in order to reflect the modern trends and higher education standards. In 1997, the term of parliament was changed from three to four years. The voting period was shortened from two days to one.

Voters must also hold Latvian citizenship. When entering a voting booth, voters are presented with a list of the party and their candidates. Within this open-list system, voters can place the list in the ballot box, or place a plus sign next to the names of as many candidates as they wish, concurrently striking out the candidates they are against. The ballots are counted by taking the total sum of votes cast for the party, starting with those not expressing a preference and those expressing at least a single preference. Each candidate then receives the total vote for his or her party in the respective constituency, with the votes for the party alone being allocated equally to all candidates in the party list. The sum of positive preferences expressed for a candidate, minus the sum of negative preferences, are added, and candidates are elected in the order of their combined totals.[7] While parties decide the order of candidate in the list, they're not formally important, as voter preference is the deciding factor for which candidate is elected to the seats gained by the party.

The preferential voting scheme exists as a compromise between the requirement for candidates to run under parties and that for parties to submit full lists to election areas. Voters can exert their preference for individual candidates, which ought to serve as a counterweight to the mandatory party selection. This has resulted in the paradigm of parties becoming leader-based parties, where list leaders have a clear advantage due partly to the visibility at the top of the list and partly to name recognition.[8] When lists have multiple dozens of candidates, it is not uncommon for voters to be uninformed about the majority of their merits, especially as campaign resources and advertising are generally spent on the party as a whole and on party-leaders.

Concurrently, as candidates can be placed on the list of multiple constituencies, but can only win in one, the following candidates in the list would move up one, taking their position, in a sense wasting the preference of the voter. There is also no way of predicting where and how the winning candidate is selected, and who takes their place in the candidate list depends upon the relatively rare voters that would adduce preferences to candidates lower down the list. To remedy this trend, a reform was instituted in 2010 to limit the number of constituencies where a candidate's name can appear to just one (Liepiņš, 2009). To a lesser extent, voter frustration also seeps into the Cabinet of Ministers, which is made up of elected parliamentarians. The convention, which is not mandated by the constitution or any other norm, is to give up one's seat when taking up a ministerial post. This allows several additional candidates to move up the list, rotating into the position of an elected political representative.

Until 2012, parties did not receive state financing and requirements on party and campaign funding and campaigning transparency – though increased in 2004 through regulatory amendments – were deemed generally ineffective. Political scientists have highlighted that the influence of wealthy patrons has been a core challenge to securing fair elections, especially in Latvia's tradition of many parties with trivial membership (Millard, 2011). Better funded parties were significantly more successful than others, regardless of other factors (Īkstens, 2019).

Latvian Judicature

The Latvian election law domain is characterized by the consistent reappearance of cases regarding the rights of certain individuals to run in elections, with cases regularly being taken to the Constitutional Court or the European Court of Human Rights.[9] Two strains of cases are outlined below.

In 2006, the European Court of Human Rights delivered its judgment in the case ofTatjana Zdanoka v. Latvia.[10] The applicant was denied the right to stand for election after the first elections of 1993, when the Municipal Election Act provided that candidacy was not allowed for those who had been members of the Communist Party of the Soviet Union or the Communist Party of Latvia and its affiliated organizations after January 13, 1991, which fit the applicant's case.

Therefore, the applicant was not allowed to run in the 1998 parliamentary elections, which rose through instances to the Latvian Supreme Court, which judged that, as the applicant had been a member of the Community Party of Latvia after the set deadline, her claim to her rights to election being violated were unfounded. A Supreme Court Senate upheld the decision in year 2000. After being refused to run in the parliamentary elections of 2002, the case was heard by the European Court of Human Rights on the basis of the applicant's right to election.

The court admitted that taking into account and ruling on the activities of members in connection with the Communist Party of Latvia was reasonable, as was presuming that their leading officials held anti-democratic stances. On that basis, the applicant's exclusion from parliamentary election was reasonable. Though this measure would be unjustifiable in countries where democratic traditions had existed for many decades or centuries, it was acceptable given Latvia's historico-political context and the need to restrict threats to newly established democracy.

The court thus found such mechanisms to be fair, as long as they are not arbitrary, are constantly reviewed, and do not exist indefinitely. It posited that the Latvian Parliament should constantly review such statutory restrictions, with a view of cancelling it in the near future. If progress is not made to such an end, the European Court of Human Rights might deliver opposite rulings in similar cases in the future.

In a continuation of the matter of the same applicant, the Latvian Constitutional Court in 2018 upheld its previous decision,[11] finding that, due to various external threats to democracy that have emerged since 2014, the rules disallowing the candidacy of individuals working with the Communist Party of Latvia or the Communist Party of the Soviet Union and its affiliated agencies beyond January 13, 1991 are still necessary and proportional to protect the Latvian state and its democratic institutions.

The Constitutional Court has previously stated that restrictions on electoral rights as exceptions should be interpreted narrowly, yet the more recent decision interprets the 1995 rule in a way that does not conform to the principle of legal certainty.[12] For example, we can examine the interpretation of Section 5 (6) stipulating the freedom for the Central Election Commission to assess whether a person with his or her actions still threatens the independence of the State of Latvia and the principles of a democratic state without any demonstrable requisites or remedies. The dissenting opinion points out the line of cases and the rules depended on in the judgment ultimately exist to limit the right to political candidature for "one or two" people, especially without a recurring objective and founded justification.

In a 2008 case, the European Court of Human Rights[13] upheld a challenge against a person's candidacy on the grounds that the legal provisions under which he had been disqualified were too broad. The person in question was an officer of the Border Guard Forces of the former Soviet Union, where he was promoted to the rank of commander. In 1992, he left the forces and returned to Latvia, where he was appointed to and eventually became commander of the newly restored Latvian Border Guard Forces. In 1994, he abandoned his military career to enter politics, where he became Minister of the Interior, and remained a member of parliament until 2002. The court noted that the person had held important posts since 1991 without engaging in anti-democratic activities.

In 1998, a parliamentary record office took measures to record the individual as having collaborated with the KGB and a national judgment found that he had served as an officer of the KGB Border Guard Forces and not a KGB officer as maintained by the prosecution. As the Parliamentary Elections Act disqualified citizens "who are or have been serving officers of organs of public security or intelligence or counter-espionage services" of foreign states, he was struck off the 2002 election candidate list. The plaintiff then brought the case to the Court of Human Rights, relying on the right to free elections and prohibition of discrimination.

The court found that, in general, the Parliamentary Elections Act was too broad in targeting former officers of the KGB, specifically with regard to the wide functions of the agency, and that a case-by-case basis should be employed instead. As for the applicant, the court could not find anything in his past to suggest an opposition or hostility to the recovery of Latvia's independence and democratic order, especially due to being disqualified from standing in elections only after a ten-year long military and political career in Latvia, which should have served as ample evidence of loyalty to the Latvian state and democratic values.

Estonian Election Framework

The Estonian parliament is made up of 101 members, elected through a proportional open-list system for a four-year term from 12 multi-member constituencies. Parties are required to obtain at least 5% of valid votes nationwide to cross the threshold. Personal mandates are distributed among candidates based on a simple quota, dividing the number of votes by the number of mandates in a district. Parties that attain a 5% threshold nationwide can participate in extended distribution of seats, with the order of candidates in district lists altered to represent the number of votes received per candidate. Parties receive district mandates for candidates exceeding the simple quota, and remaining seats are distributed at national levels using an alternative D'Hondt method.

As of the 2017, amendments to the Election Act, elections are administratively managed by the National Electoral Committee, an autonomous body responsible for general electoral management that issues decisions regarding the electoral legal framework. The National Electoral Committee heads the execution of elections and is responsible for operational functions in elections. It supervises election officials and organized internet voting, working together with 79 municipal secretaries. There are 451 Voting District Committees appointed by municipal councils. They organize elections at the polling-station level.

Estonian law is generally well-developed in the sphere of e-government services, with detailed legislation on digital identification, data protection, and public information.[14] This allows many services with traditionally paper-based documentation to be handled electronically.[15] Estonia is distinctive by holding "e-elections" – providing its citizens a method of distance voting with binding results through the use of the internet. Voters vote on the basis of state-issued digital identities initially used for e-banking and digital contracts. E-elections have been run since 2005 for parliamentary, local, and European elections on the basis of the Local Government Council Election Act Amendment Act. Though e-elections were once considered a national and legal experiment, they have become regular a portion of their election framework.

The Estonian State Electoral Office conscientiously worked to mitigate various risks to the system by bolstering the integrity and secrecy properties via technical and operational means. Digital signature-based authentication policies have been introduced to allow operators and auditors to effectively assess the authenticity of input and output data in the voting systems. While particular care has been taken to strengthen the system against external attacks, international stakeholders have pointed to certain weaknesses internally, like individuals with privileged access to digital ballots being able to break vote secrecy. Notwithstanding the persistence of certain security risks, internet voting has widely been considered a success by international stakeholders (OSCE, 2019).

The Political Parties Act regulates party and campaign finance. Parliament allocates funding to parties, with an additional sum divided among parties with seats proportional to the number held. As of 2015, Estonia has limited the amount and sources that can be donated to parties, capped per year and per individual. Legal entities and anonymous donors are not allowed. Parties are not allowed to engage in commercial enterprise, but may take loans.

Candidates and Parties in Estonia

Parties can be registered upon collecting at least 1000 members. They can submit their members, if they are citizens over the age of 21, to run for elections, with the exception of serving members of the military. Candidates can run as independent or registered on the lists of political parties. Long-term residents with undetermined citizenship cannot vote or become candidates in national elections, but they can vote for office in local elections.

Estonian Judicature

The implementation of e-elections was not a frictionless process. In 2005, the President of Estonia refused to promulgate the relevant Local Government Council Election Act Amendment Act, which would have instituted e-voting due to an opined conflict with the principle of uniformity of local government council elections, as established in the Constitution of Estonia, as not all voters are guaranteed equivalent possibilities of voting.[16] The president objected to the system in which voters have the possibility to alter their vote, if they vote by electronic means, by either voting electronically again or via ballot paper, whereas voters who do not utilize electronic voting cannot alter their vote at all. The Supreme Court opined on the constitutionality of the acts, in particular on the principle of uniformity of local government council elections established in the constitution. The principle of uniformity necessitates equal access to the voting, and the president argued that not everyone may have access to electronic voting and thus the proposed amendment infringed on the principle.

However, the Supreme Court found that "equal treatment" in the context of electing representative bodies does not denote absolute equal possibilities in performing the act of voting. Electronic voting is compared to other methods like advance polls, voting in custodial institutions, home voting, and voting in a foreign state. In fact, the use of new technology is supported by the growing number of internet users and the spread of services offered through the internet, which would increase the total participation of voters. However, the court found that the possibility of changing the vote through electric means during the advance polls is in itself an "essential supplementary guarantee" to the principle of free elections, as well as that there is no infringement of the right to equality and uniformity.

Several other Supreme Court cases have presented obiter dicta on the basis of cases brought by, but not directly related to, the plaintiff. In one case, the Supreme Court highlighted the fact that a person who is convicted of a crime and is serving a sentence in prison may not be able to participate in voting may be a contradiction between the Convention for the Protection of Human Rights and Fundamental Freedoms and the acts regulating elections in Estonia.[17] Though it was not "procedurally able to establish" the particular contradiction to several prisoner's right to vote cases of the European Court of Human Rights, they did demand that the Riigikogu react to the possibility.[18]

The safety of e-voting has been questioned in two cases. In one, a plaintiff evidenced how certain groups of individuals voting, like prisoners, can easily be traced and their votes monitored. In another, the plaintiff proved that a virus can be placed into the computer of the voter without his or her awareness, changing the transmission and result of the vote.[19] The plaintiff alleged that because the voter using the e-voting system cannot be certain that a third party will not record or change his or her vote, unlike voting in a booth in a poll division, the electronic votes case in the elections of 2011 should be annulled. Though the court acknowledged the possibility for a virus to be on the voter's computer without his or her awareness, it dismissed the complaint of the plaintiff on the basis of the hypothetical possibility not satisfying the prerequisite for declaring the voting results invalid, as no voter's rights were actually shown to be violated.

In another case, it was not possible to cast a vote for a certain candidate during e-voting because it was not fully compatible with certain settings chosen in an operating system, at times concealing the entire lower part of the voting application. These technical impediments thus prevented the voters from casting their vote for a particular candidate. The court stated that it is the responsibility of the state to ensure compatibility of the software; however, the onus is on the voter to seek advice from e-voting technical support and, in case such problems cannot be eliminated during the e-voting, voting should be made by means of a paper ballot.

Lithuanian Election Framework

The Lithuanian parliament consists of 141 members, elected for a term of four years on the basis of universal suffrage in a secret ballot, as set by the 1992 Constitution and the 1992 Law on Parliamentary Election. As a political compromise from the first free elections in 1990, the electoral system is mixed majority-proportional (Clark & Wittrock, 2005). Out of the total, 71 members are elected in single-member districts, and, if no candidate gets an absolute majority, the first two contenders proceed to a second round during which majority votes choose the victor. The other 70 are elected in a nationwide multi-candidate party list-based under proportional representation with preferential voting. The threshold for political parties is 5% for political parties and 7% for coalitions. The structure, procedures, and functions of the Seimas are regulated by the statutes of the parliament.

Campaign financing rules are set by the Law on Funding of Political Campaign and Control of Funding. The laws set limits for membership fees in political parties, and they allow for the financing of campaigns from party funds, loans, donations from citizens, and interest received on funds kept in banks. Donations from individuals are capped, as are donations from candidates' own funds. The limit on campaign spending is tied to the number of voters in a constituency. The law specifies that no more than half of the accorded spending limit can be used on televised campaigning.

Elections are administered at three levels. The Central Election Commission is the primary election oversight body, and appointments combine professional and party representation for four-year terms. The commission establishes boundaries for constituency to reflect changes in population prior to elections. As of 2015, the deviation on the basis of numbers of voters should be less than 10% of the nationwide average. There are 71 Constituency Election Commissions also comprised of nominees from various professional associations, local administrations, and parties that won proportional seats in the previous elections and are appointed temporarily for each election. There are currently 1996 Precinct Election Commissions appointed prior to every election, and they are composed of members nominated by political parties with seats in parliament or the respective municipal council.

Candidates and Parties in Lithuania

For individuals to become candidates, they must be over the age of 25 and nominated by a registered political party.[20] Membership requirements for parties were increased from 1000 to 2000 in 2015. In single-mandate constituencies, potential candidates can nominate themselves. Individual candidacies must be supported by at least a thousand signatures from registered voters in the respective constituency. A candidate must receive an absolute majority to be elected in a majoritarian contest, if the voter turnout is above 40%. If the turnout is lower than 40%, the candidate receiving the most votes must still have received votes from a minimum of 20% of possible voters. In case of no victor in the first round, a run-off round is organized between the two highest-voted candidates. In the proportional contest, candidates win based on who received the most votes, if at least 25% of the turnout was secured.

Lithuanian Judicature

The Constitutional Court has significantly revised election legislation in the past few years, in line with modern practices and recommendations from international organizations. In particular, several amendments were made following the court's decision in 2004 related to the conduct of campaigns to equate the giving of any good or benefit of material value to a voter by a party or related member to qualify as vote-buying, as well as reducing early voting and postal voting opportunities and introducing morality standards into campaigns.[21] A 2015 Constitutional Court case also recognized that a rule allowing the number of voters in each electoral district to differ from the national average by 20% conflicted with the constitution, remedying a long-term grievance to preserving the equality of voting rights (Jastramskis, 2018).

Two cases have been particularly noteworthy for their connection and ultimate impact on Lithuanian election law. The case of *Uspaskich v. Lithuania*,[22] in the European Court of Human Rights, centered on how Lithuania interprets the duty of an elected politician, as well as how a candidate acts in good faith and how a system of immunities can be abused. The case was based on a complaint brought by a well-known former Lithuanian politician about his house arrest, pending an investigation of political corruption by the national authorities.

The applicant argued that placing him under house arrest interfered with his electoral rights during the elections of October 2007. However, the government argued that the house arrest had been imposed without arbitrariness, granted that it was set only after the applicant's arrest in Russia and return to Lithuania. It further argued that the house arrest was a lighter measure and that media and outdoor advertising could have been used for his candidature. The state further presented that the applicant had held a number of posts during his political career, which granted him immunity from prosecution, and sought to move on once immunity was lost by regularly participating in municipal, parliamentary, and European Parliament elections, which allowed him to enjoy immunity for a certain time period.[23] The applicant's political party itself was also able to change its legal personality and reorganize in order to discontinue a criminal case against it.[24]

The court highlighted that, while guarantees of parliamentary immunity service to ensure the independence of parliament and performance of its tasks, states are encouraged to limit that immunity for the purpose of ensuring a democratic society. As the applicant had been provided with multiple instances and forms of appeal, the court found that Lithuania had not violated the right to free elections under the European Convention of Human Rights.

The other case in the European Court of Human Rights regarded the attempt of a former impeached national president to register as a candidate for the 2012 elections.[25] The

Constitutional Court was asked by members of parliament to examine whether a newly placed amendment to the Presidential Elections Act in 2004 limiting the period banning an impeached person from office for a period of five years was constitutional and whether there was a violation of the right to free elections under the European Convention for the Protection of Human Rights and Fundamental Freedoms. The court found that, while there was a violation to the person's right to stand for election, the right to election did not exclude the possibility of imposing restrictions on the electoral rights of a person who has seriously abused his position.

While the court found the restrictions understandable, it was not sufficiently convinced that reversible disqualifications were proportionate to satisfying the requirements of preserving democratic order. In obiter dicta, the court noted that Lithuania's position was an exception among its peers in Europe, in that the restriction in question was not subject to a time limit, but derived from a constitutional rule. The relevant legal provision was also found to be strongly influenced by the circumstances related to the individual.

European Parliament Elections

The European Parliament has 751 members, as laid down in the Lisbon Treaty. Each member is elected from the European Member states by direct universal suffrage for a five-year period. Each country decides the form of the elections, but must guarantee the equality of sexes, a secret ballot, and uniformity of elections. Beyond these rules, there are various differences in how the European member states handle them, and, while the Baltic States are relatively homogenous, differences also persist between them. Latvia and Lithuania, for example, enforce a 5% threshold for candidates to begin competing for a seat. Estonia has no such threshold. The three states have in common a system of constituency for the elections and a minimum age of 21 for candidates (2019 European elections: National rules, 2019).

As European Union elections are conducted by proportional representation, each country has a different number of members of parliament allocated on the basis of the D'Hondt formula. The principle of degressive proportionality employed results in smaller amounts of representatives from smaller countries and vice versa. Hence, respective to the size of their populace, Estonia has six seats in the European Parliament, Latvia has eight, and Lithuania has eleven. Though voters elect members of parliament from their own national parties, once elected, they are organized by political affiliation instead of nationality. There are currently eight parties, as well as a group of non-attached Members of Parliament (The European Parliament, 2019).[26]

Members of the European Parliament have several powers. They co-legislate European Union rules with the Ministers of the European Union member states, adopt and amend legislative proposals, and decide on the European Union budget. They supervise the work of the European Union executive branch, the commission, and other European Union bodies. The European Parliament has been slowly gaining power over concerns of lack of democratic accountability in the European Union, with significant expansion of its role in the Lisbon (Hix, Noury, & Roland, 2007; Schmidt, European Commission, & Directorate-General for Economic and Financial Affairs, 2015). Elections in the European Parliament are not considered an indication of party support at the national level (Īkstens, 2019). Latvia has seen discussion of choosing the next European Union Commissioner on the basis of respective party performance in the elections, but the approach has not received much support (Īkstens, 2019).

In the Baltic States, the European Parliamentary elections conform to the second-order theory, according to which voters select their candidates on the basis of national-level actualities and sympathies, rather than their fit against European-level issues (Īkstens, 2019; Reif & Schmitt, 1980). However, all three countries have increased in the importance of the European

Union dimension for voters making their decision in European Parliament elections, with previous experience at the European level making notable difference in their preferences (Ehin & Talving, 2019; Īkstens, 2019; Jastramaskis, 2019).

Conclusion

The Baltic States, notwithstanding their geographical proximity and similar historical development until the early 1990s, have diverged significantly in their electoral regimes. In each country, the electoral framework differs in mechanism and procedure at both the party and candidate level. Estonia has kept building its proportional open-list system; Latvia has embraced a proportional system; and Lithuania has bolstered a rare mixed majority-proportional system of voting. Together with their differing national priorities, the regimes, together with their unique challenges, have also been evolving divergently, and surprisingly quickly. Estonia has been challenged by the experiment of electronic voting and the guarantees it can provide for it. Latvia has toiled to tame political financing rules, while Lithuania has faced gerrymandering challenges.

There are equally important threads that unite the three countries, as classical remnants of a shared history under the Soviet Union. Voting rights for long-term residents without a declared citizenship are highly politicized matters that have repeatedly been challenged in courts. Though all three countries have faced the issue, their response has not been monolithic. Similarly, the national legal systems have had to handle exceptions from the electoral systems against certain individuals. In these cases, the legal frameworks have held steadfast to support the stances of the polity upon which they are based. While the Baltic stances have been more clearly understood in the past few decades by international stakeholders, the nations have also attuned much more effectively Western standards, particularly, with the European Parliamentary Elections – a melting pot for all the European Union.

Notes

1 The lack of human rights provisions, various numerical thresholds in the constitution, and the lack of provisions for decentralized governance in, for example, municipal government.

2 There have been debates on the possibility of splitting voters residing abroad in a different manner.

3 As of 2019, the capital city of Riga houses 633,000 inhabitants, or approximately 33% of the total. See the Central Statistics Bureau.

4 The electoral alliance is not an uncommon mechanism in Central and Eastern Europe, with the exception of being banned in Estonia. In Latvia, it has been used as a mechanism to counter oligarch-sponsored parties and become a form of conglomerating fractions or creating new identities. This has also been identified as a risk, as rebranding folk that had lost internal or voter favor in a different cowl. Numerous alliances have formed over the past two decades, though often not to the pleasure of the public. However, alliances have had the most success in gaining party seats.

5 The current amount set in law is EUR 1400.

6 The list must also contain information on the domicile and additional citizenships or residencies candidates hold, as well as their current employment or titles. Until 2014, the law also stipulated that candidates must disclose title to or other forms of dominion of vehicles and real estate, securities, and any other monetary savings if they, individually or collectively, are worth more than 20 minimum monthly salaries. Until 2005, candidates had to disclose their marital status and, until 2002, a notarized certificate of the highest Latvian language proficiency. The latter was removed due to concerns from the Organization for Security and Cooperation in Europe and the European Union.

7 Up until 2010, parties participating in the elections were able to place candidates in more than a single constituency. The candidate winning a seat in more than a single area would be removed from the ballot count elsewhere. This was removed to increase the turnover of candidates, as well as clarify and more directly link voter choice to particular candidates.

8 As well as a general behavioral preference to select the tops of lists. While, in theory, a rational voter should.

9 It bears mentioning that, while the applicants were limited in participating in national elections, they could still run for European Parliamentary seats, where similar restrictions did not apply.

10 See case *Ždanoka v. Latvia*, European Court of Human Rights, Judgement of the Grand Chamber, Application no. 58278/00.

11 See decision in Satversmes Tiesas lieta Nr. 2017-25-01 "Par Saeimas vēlēšanu likuma 5. Panta 6. Punkta atbilstību Latvijas Republikas Satversmes 1., 9. Un 981. Pantam."

12 See the separate opinion in Atsevišķās domas Satversmes Tiesas lieta Nr. 2017-25-01 "Par Saeimas vēlēšanu likuma 5. Panta 6. Punkta atbilstību Latvijas Republikas Satversmes 1., 9. Un 981. Pantam."

13 See case *Ādamsons v. Latvia*, European Court of Human Rights, Judgement of the Grand Chamber, Application no. 3669/03.

14 Commonly referred to as "e-signatures."

15 E-services are also available in the procedures under administrative, criminal, intellectual property, and consumer protection laws.

16 See the case 6SC 3-4-1-13-05, Petition of the President of the Republic in 2005. Available at www.nc .ee/?id¼823 1

17 See the Supreme Court case 3-4-1-7-11. Available at https://www.riigikohus.ee/en/constitutional -judgment-3-4-1-7-11

18 The cases referred to, in particular, are Chamber judgment *Greens and M.T. v. the UK*, November 23, 2010 and Grand Chamber judgment *Hirst v. United Kingdom (No. 2)*, October 6, 2005. Both cases touched upon the validity of the disenfranchisement of voters, highlighting that any exceptions to the convention should require a case-by-case investigation in front of a judge, even for prisoners.

19 It bears noting that the plaintiff set out several arguments challenging the safety of e-voting. While the electronic voting project manager opined that the Estonian Cyber Emergency Response Team, Cyber Defence League, and other organizations responsible for cyber security would identify the spreading virus and advise the National Electoral Committee regarding the need to annul electronic voting results, the plaintiff argued that viruses are generally not detected for up to a year and that Estonia, as of yet, lacks a system that would quickly detect such a virus.

20 Certain caveats apply: the candidate's residence must be in Lithuania, and judges, active military personnel, and certain officials, among others, cannot apply.

21 See case *Paksas v. Lithuania*, European Court of Human Rights, Judgement of the Grand Chamber, Application no. 34932/04.

22 See case *Uspaskich v. Lithuania*, 2016, European Court of Human Rights, Judgement of the Grand Chamber, Application no. 14737/08.

23 The applicant was elected to a municipal council in 2007 and, after finding out that the post did not grant immunity from prosecution, the applicant refused the mandate, choosing to run for parliament a few months later. After his immunity was lifted by parliament, he ran for European Parliament and resigned from the Lithuanian Parliament. There, however, his plea to be shielded from prosecution in Lithuania was rejected. He was re-elected to the European Parliament two years later, where the institution again lifted his immunity in 2015.

24 The party used the same name and same logo, but under a different legal entity.

25 The president had been found unlawfully granting Lithuanian citizenship to a Russian businessman, disclosing state secrets, and exploiting his own status to exert undue influence on a private company. See *Uspaskich v. Lithuania*, 2016, European Court of Human Rights, Judgement of the Grand Chamber, Application no. 14737/08.

26 The oldest required candidate age is 25, valid in both Greece and Italy.

References

2019 European elections: National rules. (2019). Retrieved July 1, 2019 from https://www.europarl .europa.eu/RegData/etudes/ATAG/2018/623556/EPRS_ATA(2018)623556_EN.pdf

Clark, T. D., & Wittrock, J. N. (2005). Presidentialism and the effect of electoral law in postcommunist systems: Regime type matters. *Comparative Political Studies*, *38*(2), 171–188. doi: 10.1177/0010414004271076

Davies, P. J., & Andrejs, V. O. (1994). The Latvian parliamentary election of 1993. *Electoral Studies*, *13*(1), 83–86. doi: 10.1016/0261-3794(94)90012-4

Davies, P. J., & Andrejs, V. O. (2001). The 1998 parliamentary election in Latvia. *Electoral Studies, 20*(1), 135–141. doi: 10.1016/S0261-3794(00)00023-8

Davies, P. J., & Andrejs, V. O. (2004). The parliamentary election in Latvia, October 2002. *Electoral Studies, 23*(4), 834–840. doi: 10.1016/j.electstud.2004.02.004

Ehin, P., & Talving, L. (2019). Estonia: A scene set by the preceding national election. In L. de Sio, M. N. Franklin, & L. Russo (Eds.), *The European Parliament Elections of 2019* (pp. 128–133). Roma: Luiss University Press.

Hix, S., Noury, A. G., & Roland, G. (2007). Democratic politics in the European Parliament by Simon Hix. *Cambridge Core*. Retrieved July 1, 2019 from /core/books/democratic-politics-in-the-european-pa rliament/03F83F400698CFD0009107FBFC78B98C

Ījkstens, J. (2019). Latvia: European expertise matters. In L. de Sio, M. N. Franklin, & L. Russo (Eds.), *The European Parliament elections of 2019* (pp. 181–185). Roma: Luiss University Press.

Jastramskis, M. (2018). Effects of mixed parallel electoral system in Lithuania: The worst of all worlds? *Parliamentary Affairs, 72*(3), 561–587.

Jastramaskis, M. (2019). Lithuania: Defeat of Eurosceptic parties. In L. de Sio, M. N. Franklin, & L. Russo (Eds.), *The European Parliament elections of 2019* (pp. 187–191). Roma: Luiss University Press.

Jungerstam-Mulders, S. (Ed.). (2006). *Post-Communist EU member states: Parties and party systems*. Aldershot; Burlington, VT: Ashgate.

Kerikmäe, T., Joamets, K., Pleps, J., Rodiņa, A., Berkmanas, T., & Gruodyte, E. (Eds.). (2017). *The law of the Baltic States*. Springer International Publishing. Retrieved July 2, 2019 from https://www.springer.com /gp/book/9783319544779

Liepiņš, V. (2009). Vēlēšanu sistēmas evolūcija, nevis revolūcija. *Juristavards.lv*. Retrieved July 1, 2019 from https://juristavards.lv/doc/187397-velesanu-sistemas-evolucija-brnevis-revolucija/

Millard, F. (2011). Electoral-System change in Latvia and the elections of 2010. *Communist and Post-Communist Studies, 44*(4), 309–318. doi: 10.1016/j.postcomstud.2011.10.002

OSCE. (2019). *Estonia parliamentary elections 3 March 2019 ODIHIR election expert team final report*. Warsaw: OSCE Office for Democratic institutions and Human Rights. Retrieved from https://www.osce.org/ odihr/elections/estonia/424229?download=true

Peniķis, J. (2010). Par saeima vēlēšanām: Skats atpakaļ un uz priekšu. *Akadēmiskā Dzīve, 47*. 2–5.

Pryce, P. (2012). The 2011 parliamentary election in Latvia. *Electoral Studies, 31*(3), 613–616. doi: 10.1016/j. electstud.2012.05.006

Reif, K., & Schmitt, H. (1980). Nine second-order national elections: A conceptual framework for the analysis of European election results. *European Journal of Political Research, 8*, 3–44. doi: 10.1111/j.1475-6765.1980.tb00737.x

Schmidt, V. A., European Commission, & Directorate-General for Economic and Financial Affairs. (2015). The Eurozone's crisis of democratic legitimacy: Can the EU rebuild public trust and support for European economic integration? Luxembourg: Publications Office.

Taube, C. (2001). *Constitutionalism in Estonia, Latvia & Lithuania: A study in comparative constitutional law*. Uppsala: Lustu Forlag.

The European Parliament. (2019). *The political groups*. Retrieved July 1, 2019 from http://www.europarl .europa.eu/about-parliament/en/organisation-and-rules/organisation /political-groups

Ziemele, I. (2005). *State continuity and nationality: The Baltic States and Russia: Past, present and future as defined by international law*. Retrieved July 1, 2019 from https://brill.com/view/title/11582

21
ELECTION LAW IN TURKEY

Ali Çarkoğlu

Introduction

As part of late nineteenth-century reform initiatives, the first general election for the Chamber of Deputies (Meclis-i Mebusan) of the Ottoman Empire was held in 1877. This followed the adoption of the new constitution a year earlier, which had turned the empire into a constitutional monarchy. The upper house members or the senate of the parliament, the General Assembly, were appointed notables in the Ottoman government. General elections for the Chamber of Deputies were subject to various restrictions that included suffrage for only propertied males. Even with limited suffrage, however, these elections still played a significant role in socializing large masses into a new governance system via representative elections into assemblies. Moreover, these elections legitimized a new constitutional citizenship and mobilized large segments of the population, expanding the public sphere via rallies, journalism, petitions, and other campaign activities (Kayalı, 1995, 282). In total, six general elections were held between 1877 and 1919. Following the dissolution of the Chamber of Deputies during the Allied occupation of the then capital city of Istanbul, the national movement against the Allied occupation held, in 1920, another election of deputies for the new Turkish Grand National Assembly (Türkiye Büyük Millet Mecklisi, TBMM), which provided the institutional umbrella for the conduct of the war of liberation in Anatolia that culminated in the founding of the Republic of Turkey in 1923 (Kalaycıoğlu, 2010; Kydyralieva, 2019; Tunaya, 1963).[1]

Although a representative assembly provided the foundation of political legitimacy for the new republic, several attempts at a multiparty competition in elections failed until the May 1950 election that led to the defeat of the Republican People's Party (Cumhuriyet Halk Partisi, CHP), which had remained in power as the founding party of the young Republic.[2] Numerous changes in the electoral system were subsequently introduced.[3] There were two primary motivations behind these changes: 1) Representational distortions and 2) instability due to weak coalitions. Typically, distortions in favor of the winning parties reduced the electoral representation of the opposition parties, or the election system contributed to the acute fragmentation of the party system that resulted in governmental instability via weak coalition governments.

The current constitution recognizes these historical experiences with the election systems adopted in the country. Article 67 sets a rugged ideal to achieve: "The electoral laws shall be drawn up to reconcile the principles of fair representation and stability of government." A

DOI: 10.4324/9780429401800-21

paragraph added in 2001 also states that "Amendments to the electoral laws shall not apply to the elections to be held within one year from the entry into force date of the amendments." Hence, legislators reflect an awareness of the manipulative character of impending changes to the election system that favor the incumbent majority in the TBMM, aiming to maintain this status via changes in the election law. This stipulation is only binding by the elites' unwritten political culture that controls a large majority to change the constitution.

In fact, the particular stipulation that aimed to deter the short-term manipulative changes in the electoral laws was waived for the next general elections by the constitutional amendments approved by the April 2017 referendum. These amendments aimed to turn the parliamentary regime of the country into an executive presidential system. In the new presidential system, the president's executive powers were emboldened, while those of the TBMM declined significantly.[4] Hence the dynamics of the elections were expected to change. The referendum results showed a slim margin of victory for the presidential system supporters. Given the 10% threshold, the opposition group, including the main opposition party, the Republican People's Party (Cumhuriyet Halk Partisi, CHP), and the ethnic Kurdish Peoples' Democratic Party (Halkların Demokratik Partisi, HDP) could satisfy the threshold. However, the presidential system's critical supporting parties, such as the Nationalist Action Party (Milliyetçi Hareket Partisi, MHP), which had inner-party turmoil, risked remaining out of the parliament. This waiver of the stipulation is, perhaps, evidence of the expectation that an early election could be necessary or unavoidable after the constitutional referendum of 2017 and that arrangements in the election system were deemed necessary to maintain the new presidential system's sustainability.

These election system arrangements came about a year later, on March 13, 2018. The substantive series of changes adopted had two main impacts on the election system that, in turn, transformed the nature of Turkish politics at large. First, these changes created a new electoral system and effectively rendered the restrictive nature of the 10% threshold mostly obsolete. Second, several significant changes demolished the principles established in the founding years of the multiparty elections concerning the administration of elections.

In the following sections, I will argue that the Turkish electoral system still struggles to achieve the constitution's unfeasible task. I will briefly go over the election system's central legal tenets, note a few important reflections of these legal arrangements in the party system, and lay down the current reform challenges and their implications for Turkish politics.

Constitutional Foundations of the Election System

Article 67 of the constitution clarifies the right to vote, to be elected, and to engage in political activity:

> Elections and referenda shall be held under the direction and supervision of the judiciary, in accordance with the principles of free, equal, secret, direct, universal suffrage, and public counting of the votes. However, the law determines applicable measures for Turkish citizens abroad to exercise their right to vote. All Turkish citizens over eighteen years of age shall have the right to vote in elections and to take part in referenda...Privates and corporals at arms, cadets, and convicts in penal execution institutions, excluding those convicted of negligent offenses, shall not vote. The necessary measures to be taken to ensure the safety of voting and the counting of the votes in penal execution institutions and prisons shall be determined by the Supreme Board of Election; such voting is held under the on-site direction and supervision of an authorized judge.

Given the large draft-based armed forces, the restriction on low-ranking army personnel restricts young male voters' participation. Professionalization and reduced reliance on drafted soldiers are expected to reduce this restriction. However, given the sensitivity around armed forces influencing civilian politics in the country, such restrictions are not likely to be lifted.

There is a large population of Turkish citizens living abroad. The exact size is not known, since the official government data is based only on voluntary registration of Turkish citizens in their local embassies or consulates. However, the Turkish Ministry of Foreign Affairs reports that more than 6.5 million Turkish citizens live abroad, with 5.5 million in Western Europe.[5] Only in 1995 did Turkish citizens living abroad gain the right to vote. However, to exercise this right, they needed to travel back to Turkey and cast their votes by physically being present at custom offices, airports, or country borders. Since 2014, these procedures have become more accessible since expatriates could make an appointment in the diplomatic representative office closest to their registered international addresses in order to cast their votes. While the appointment condition was lifted in 2015, expatriates had to be physically present in consulates or embassies to cast their votes. As of 2017, registered voting-age citizens could vote at any embassy, consulate, or border polling station. Despite these facilitating arrangements, the turnout rate remains significantly lower than domestic turnout. However, expatriate vote choice is reported to be similar to domestic vote choice.[6] If the turnout rate reached similarly high levels abroad, would we still observe a similar vote choice? The answer to this question is mostly unknown. However, we know that, given the low turnout, the influence of the votes abroad remains limited on the election outcome. Facilitation of registration procedures and expansion of the number of polling stations abroad could raise the turnout. However, online or mail voting is more likely to raise the participation of citizens abroad in elections.

The Electoral Law

There are 600 seats available in the TBMM, for which elections are held using the d'Hondt method. In order to win a seat in the TBMM, a party needs to obtain 10% of the valid nationwide votes. Available seats are distributed to 87 electoral districts.[7] Turkey inherited an administrative system from the Ottoman Empire that is based on the geographic boundaries of provinces. These provinces each have a provincial governor (vali) appointed by the central government in Ankara. Each province is also sub-divided into districts with district governors (kaymakam), and then into villages in the rural sector and neighborhoods in the urban areas, each having a headman or muhtar. While the central government appoints valis and kaymakams, the muhtars are elected by their local constituencies. In addition, provinces and districts also have an elected executive mayor working with provincial assemblies. Larger metropolitan greater-city and district mayors, municipal and provincial councilors, neighborhood and village muhtars, and their village councils are elected by a simple plurality first-past-the-post election system.

At the national level, the seat distribution across provinces or the apportionment system for the TBMM introduces a significant bias into the election system that favors the smaller central and eastern Anatolian provinces at the expense of the larger metropolitan provinces of the coastal regions. According to the apportionment method, each of the 81 provinces first gets one seat, irrespective of its population, and then the remaining 519 seats are distributed in accordance with provincial population figures and the largest remainder, or Hamilton method. If, for instance, a province has 10.3% of the total population, then 519 x 0.103 = 53.46 seats are due to be allocated to that province. This province, based on its population, "deserves" 53 seats and a partial 0.46 of a seat. The provinces are then ranked based on the fractional remainders, and the provinces with the largest remainders are each allocated one additional seat, until all the seats have been allocated.

There are at least two analytical problems here. One concerns the first round of distributing seats without reference to provincial populations. Some provinces do not have a population that would guarantee a single seat or, simply put, 1/600 of the total population, which represents approximately 135,000 people. If a province does not have this population, it nevertheless gets one guaranteed seat from this first round. Then the remaining seats are distributed in accordance with the provincial population. Assuming that a small province has, let us say 110,000 people, the result is only (110,000/81,000,000) x 600 = 0.814, or 81.4% of a seat. Then this province may get an additional second seat in the second round of undistributed seat allocations. In this way, a small province with only a population that justifies about 81% of a single seat may get two seats in the TBMM. Hence smaller provinces get over-represented.

The second issue is due to the zero-sum nature of apportionment biases; i.e., if some provinces receive seats that they do not deserve based on their population, some other provinces must lose seats that should have been allocated to them. Indeed, smaller central and eastern Anatolian provinces receive seats at the expense of large coastal metropolitan provinces. The political meaning of this bias in the system is that these over-represented smaller Anatolian provinces are also relatively less competitive electoral markets, wherein conservative and ethnic issues mobilize voters relatively more easily. Hence this apportionment bias creates an advantage for the conservative and ethnic parties at the expense of more centrist and left-wing parties with relatively more progressive agendas.[8]

A List System of Proportional Representation

Once the seats are allocated to provinces, then each province constitutes a large electoral district with multiple seats available, and a proportional representation (PR) system with the d'Hondt formula translates party votes to seats in the TBMM. Each party forms a list of candidates to fill the number of available seats in each electoral district or province. If, in a given district, there are ten seats available, each party typically forms a list of ten candidates. Given the party votes shares, each party sends the top so many candidates from their list who win, according to the d'Hondt formula, in proportion to their vote shares.

The 1980 military regime imposed a minimum of 10% nationwide electoral support for winning any seats in the TBMM. Even if a regional party wins a substantial majority in several provinces of the country, unless that party's vote constitutes at least 10% of the valid votes nationwide, it will not get any seats from those provinces. This arrangement was designed to create majorities in the TBMM, hence avoiding any coalitions due to small party votes fragmenting the parliament's seat distribution.

Over the last two decades, this arrangement principally worked to keep regional Kurdish ethnic parties out of the parliament. However, minor right-wing pro-Islamist, as well as Turkish nationalist parties, were also constrained by the same threshold, which rendered the founding of new parties difficult. Consequently, smaller ideological or issue-based constituencies were grouped under larger umbrella parties, which rendered inner-party politics all the more difficult to manage. In a sense, coalitions were brought into the party organizations. The real party politics came to be played in the shaping of party lists to be offered for elections in the sizeable multi-member district PR elections.

The nationwide electoral threshold only applies to parties that run in the national elections. To win a single seat, independent candidates who run in a given district are only constrained by the d'Hondt formula requirement. Parties may support multiple independent candidates. As long as each of these candidates receives a level of support that qualifies for a seat, he or she can all get elected as an independent from a multi-member district. However, if an independent candidate receives more votes than necessary to win a seat, those excess votes are, in a sense, "wasted."

Such a large number of independent candidates from a party who cannot pass the national threshold, with each running separately in different provinces, requires a great deal of coordination and voter mobilization. There are various ways to make this more complicated such as the ban of independent candidates using candidate-printed name ballots, thereby forcing voters to find the right candidate on centrally printed ballots.

For the 2007 and 2011 elections, the Kurdish parties supported independent candidates to bypass the 10% threshold limitation and, since 2015, they have run on a national platform and successfully passed the threshold. Hence, by supporting independents to bypass, the threshold can be said to have served the Kurdish parties to grow and nationalize their original regional bases of support. There have also been a few independent candidates who have run in their hometowns based on their name recognition, family, or tribal ties, which has rendered their election easier.

March 2018 Amendments

As noted earlier, the constitutional referendum of 2017, which turned the country's parliamentary system into an executive presidential system, inherently shifted the political dynamics focused on the presidential elections. However, no matter how secondary the role of the TBMM was rendered in the new system, it still necessitated a comfortable majority of support therein to smoothly sustain the new presidential system function. Hence, the election system for the representatives in the TBMM continues to be a challenge for the new executive presidential system.

As a significant shift in the system, the March 2018 amendments instituted pre-election coalitions or alliances (*ittifaklar* in Turkish) via shared lists.[9] The 10% threshold was now to be applied to the total vote of the alliance, so that individual parties that formed the alliance, no matter how small their share of the vote, could effectively enjoy seats from the alliance lists. All alliances and single parties had to surpass the threshold, but the threshold did not apply to independent candidates. If a minor party could get into an alliance that could surpass the threshold, no matter how small its vote contribution to the alliance vote share, it could gain seats from winning positions in the alliance lists. As such, the minor parties deemed critical for the success of an alliance stood to earn disproportionate seat gains, while other parties not included in an alliance that surpasses the threshold stood no chance of gaining any representation. Those parties that are ideologically marginal or unacceptable to mainstream alliances are likely to suffer from this arrangement, while others, no matter how small an electoral gain they can bring to the alliance, can obtain some representation according to their negotiations for electable positions on alliance lists.

The new opportunity to join alliances appeared to help many minor parties that stood no chance of winning a seat due to their inability to surpass the 10% threshold. Two alliances were formed prior to the June 2018 general election. The Justice and Development Party (Adalet ve Kalkınma Partisi, AKP) joined with the MHP and the Grand Unity Party (Büyük Birlik Partisi, BBP) to form the People's Alliance (Cumhur İttifakı). The RPP joined with the Good Party (İyi Party), Felicity Party (Saadet Partisi, SP), and the Democrat Party (Demokrat Parti, DP) to form the counter Nation Alliance (Millet İttifakı). While the opposition alliance brought together an ideologically diverse group of opposition parties whose main objective was to weaken the incumbent AKP's alliance, the People's Alliance projected an ideologically more coherent stance. The ethnic Kurdish HDP was not part of any alliance and took the risk of remaining below the threshold, therefore standing alone in the election. Hence the threshold remained binding only for the HDP, though it eventually also surpassed the threshold. As such, the threshold remained ineffective for all parties.

The referendum of April 2017 witnessed a major legal row between the opposition and the Supreme Election Board (Yüksek Seçim Kurulu, YSK). On the referendum evening, YSK declared that ballots without the seal of the election boards inscribed on the back of the ballot papers would still be counted as valid. Apparently, a significant number of such ballot papers were used in this referendum, casting doubt on the outcome if such a questionable late decision were not taken. To render this practice legal, the March 2018 amendment to the election law allowed the counting of ballot papers without the inscription of the seal of the election board as valid, so long as the Supreme Election Board (Yüksek Seçim Kurulu, YSK) watermark and logo appeared on the back of the ballot papers and envelopes. The opposition claims that such a double standard for valid votes with or without the proper seal renders diagnosis of vote-rigging attempts difficult.

The other changes introduced by the March 2018 amendments primarily concern the administration of elections. One significant change was lifting the requirement for the removal of potentially biased ministers of justice, transportation, and internal affairs from their posts and for the appointment, in their stead, of an independent non-political or bureaucratic figure for the campaign and election period. These ministries are critical in running the election process (preparation of the ballots, safe and correct counting, and preparation of the final tally), and rendering this process fair by replacing partisan figures with unbiased non-partisan appointments was deemed essential in the aftermath of the 1961 Constitution. Given the recent complaints by the opposition parties, especially during the 2017 constitutional referendum, concerning partisan decisions taken during the administrative phase by the Supreme Election Council (Yüksek Seçim Kurulu), such a shift towards a more partisan administration of the election process is puzzling.

Equally critical in the administration of the election process is the formation of election boards responsible for the hands-on running of the election at each polling station. Since the first competitive multiparty elections of 1950, the administration of elections has remained under the judiciary's control as an impartial mediator. The new change allowed the provincial and district governors (*vali*s and *kaymakams*) to appoint public officials as members of the election boards at each polling station. As such, the incumbent government, its ministers, and appointed bureaucrats, rather than non-partisan members of the judiciary, became the primary administrators of the whole election process.

The March amendments also allowed anyone amongst the voters who feels that some groups or people are disrupting the order at the ballot box by force or threats to invite the police or other law enforcement personnel to the polling stations during the course of the voting process. Such an authority previously only resided in the members of the election board. Partisan animosities amongst the voters in different polling stations could thus lead to disruption of the voting process. Since law enforcement is also under the control of the incumbent government, such further limitation of the election boards' authority is perceived by the opposition as a potential partisan disruptive power that could work against the election process.

The March 2018 amendment also allowed the casting of votes via mobile ballot boxes. As such, the elderly, sick, and disabled voters could cast their votes in their homes. Although this amendment expands access to voting by disadvantaged groups, the opposition complained about the possibility of moving ballot boxes strategically in order to impede some groups from voting.

Conclusion and Issues for Electoral System Reform

Electoral dynamics are continually shifting in Turkey due not only to the young and dynamic population, but also to the global Covid-19 pandemic and its consequent economic crisis. One additional factor that complicates Turkey's electoral scene is due to the major systemic shift resulting from the long tenure of the incumbent AKP and the acceptance of its project to create an executive presidency in Turkey in April 2017. The experience of this referendum and the anticipation of discomforting electoral dynamics in future elections under the new presidential system led to major changes in the electoral system. One significant result of these changes was the formation of new electoral alliances that further fragmented the party system. Another result concerned the centralization of the election administration by the executive branch at the expense of the judiciary. The opposition and the ruling alliance parties are likely to keep their uneasiness with the new election administration, especially given the consequent experience in the local elections in Istanbul, which got canceled and repeated in 2019 due to electoral irregularities and fraud claims.

Two electoral reform issues continue to be on the public agenda. The first and foremost among these focuses on the nationwide threshold of 10%, which remains amongst the highest in the world. However, this threshold's restrictive nature has been diminished, given the new electoral alliance arrangement made before the 2018 general elections. Given the electoral developments since 2015, which pushed the Kurdish electoral tradition represented by the Peoples' Democratic Party (Halkların Demokratik Partisi, HDP) comfortably above the threshold, only about 2% of the valid votes do not receive representation in the TBMM. Since the June 2018 general elections, two new splinter parties have been founded by two leading figures from the AKP. Ahmet Davudoğlu, the ex-minister of foreign affairs and prime minister of the AKP founded the Future Party (Gelecek Partisi, GP). Ali Babacan, the former deputy prime minister of AKP founded the Democracy and Progress Party (Demokrasi ve Atılım Partisi, DEVA). The electoral appeal of these parties is yet unknown. However, the uneasiness amongst conservative constituencies is likely to have fueled their split from the AKP. Critical questions for the future of electoral politics in the country. remain about their respective futures: Will they form a separate alliance in the next general elections and put forth a candidate for the presidential race, or will they join the opposition alliance is a critical question.

As long as alliances continue to be allowed in the election system, any group that can mobilize some electoral support that can be helpful for any alliance is likely to split away from existing parties of electoral significance, such as the ruling AKP or the main opposition CHP. Other parties that remain around 10 to 15% electoral support are also likely to find it difficult to control groups within their parties that may be tempted to use alliances for guaranteed seats in the TBMM via splinter parties. These splinter parties are likely to negotiate their support for existing alliances or an alliance of their own. Lowering the still existing 10% threshold would further fragment the party system and likely render a coordinated single opposition alliance more difficult. However, the first and foremost challenge is still the presidential race. If a first-round winning strategy can be created for the ruling People's Alliance, then risking the fragmented TBMM by lowering the threshold will not be followed.

Once alliances allow for different parties to enter into the TBMM, they can also form their parliamentary groups and exert their influence over the policymaking process. Managing such rising plurality may be difficult. Hence, a proposal to divide up the large constituencies even further is circulating in public debates. For huge metropolitan provinces like İstanbul, Ankara, İzmir, Bursa, and others, with 10 to 15 seats available, the proposal is to create electoral districts with six to seven seats.

AYSK decision taken in 2011 stipulates that, if a province has 1 to 18 seats, a single provincial election district is used; for provinces with 19 to 35 seats, there are two election districts within the province in question; and, for provinces with 36 or more seats, there are three provincial election districts. As such, as of today, Istanbul and Ankara each have three election districts. Bursa and İzmir each have two election districts. This decision reduces the district sizes in large metropolitan provinces with serious electoral consequences.

With 98 total seats available in Istanbul, the first election district has only 35 seats, the second election district has 28, and the third election district has 35. The d'Hondt formula applied for a total of 98 seats would reduce the number of votes necessary to win a seat to a number considerably lower than that in a district where only 35 seats are available. Hence, larger district size renders smaller parties or independent candidates' chances of winning a seat higher.

Consider the hypothetical example below, where four parties (A, B, C, and D) receive 45.1, 32, 12, and 7%, respectively. Independent candidate 1 gets 2% of the total valid votes, while independent candidates II and III receive 1 and 0.9%, respectively. If only 12 seats are available, Party A gets six, B gets four seats, and parties C and D get one seat each. For Independent I to obtain one seat, there should be at least 48 seats available; for independent candidate II to win a seat, there should be 98 seats; and for independent candidate III to win a seat, there should be 108 seats.

In other words, in a province like Istanbul, where there are nearly 10.5 million voters, an independent candidate with slightly more than a hundred thousand votes could win a seat if all 98 seats are available in a single district. However, when the province is divided into three electoral districts with about 30 seats each, the minimum support level for an independent candidate rises by nearly threefold.

This example illustrates the fact that district size can also be used as a *de facto* threshold. In the above example, by setting the district size to 12, the minimum support level for winning a seat is effectively 7%. However, if the district size is reduced further to, say, ten, given the distribution of electoral support, the effective threshold rises towards 10%.

Dividing large electoral constituencies into smaller parts will seriously constrain the smaller parties and lead to an over-representation of larger parties from the metropolitan constituencies. However, as we observed earlier in Turkey, such a forceful constraint upon smaller parties may push their elites and mass support base towards larger parties, making it difficult to contain and control them after the elections. In other words, every adjustment in the election system creates reactionary forces that will play out in accordance with the country's political culture and electoral dynamics. Hence, any new design, such as the lowering of the national threshold or

Table 21.1 A Hypothetical Example under the Electoral Formula in Turkey

	Vote %	*Seats Won*			
Party A	45.1	6	22	45	50
Party B	32	4	16	32	35
Party C	12	1	6	12	13
Party D	7	1	3	7	7
Independent I	2		1	1	1
Independent II	1			1	1
Independent III	0.9				1
	100	12	48	98	108

the division of large constituencies into smaller parts, is likely to result in reactions that may be entirely unanticipated. Changes in the election system may create a winning alliance. However, maintaining this alliance in support of a newly elected and all-powerful president may still prove to be complicated. Hence, the constitution's objective to create a stable and representative election system continues to be challenging for Turkey.

Notes

1 For Ottoman and early Republican elections, see Koçu (1950), Khalidi (1984), and Tuncer (2002).
2 For the opposition parties during the one-party era of the Republic, see Ahmad (2008, 2016), Celep (2014), Emrence (2000), İpek (2018), and Zurcher (1991).
3 See Hale (1980, 2008) for a review of the historical evolution of the Turkish election system in the multiparty era.
4 See Aytaç et al. (2017) and Esen & Gümüşcü (2018) on the new presidential system in Turkey.
5 See the official website of the Ministry of Foreign Affairs: www.mfa.gov.tr/the-expatriate-turkish-citizens.en.mfa (retrieved in October 2020).
6 See Sevi et al. (2020) on the voting behavior of Turks living abroad.
7 There are a total of 81 provinces. Istanbul and Ankara are divided into three electoral districts, and Bursa and İzmir into two, hence totaling 87 districts.
8 Çarkoğlu and Aksen (2019, 49) report that, for the November 2015 elections, when the TBMM had 550 seats, 53 (or 9.6%) of the seats in the TBMM were shifted between provinces. "Of the 81 provinces five suffered 2-seat losses and 43 suffered 1-seat loss. Of the 17 provinces that gained a seat or more, Istanbul gained 20, Ankara 7, İzmir 4, and Antalya and Bursa 3 seats each." Those which gained seats are large metropolitan cities, and those which lost seats are smaller Anatolian provinces. Çarkoğlu and Erdoğan (1998) also conducted a similar analysis and showed which parties stand to gain or lose from these apportionment shifts across provinces.
9 For a more in-depth discussion of March 2018 changes in the election administration, see Kalaycıoğlu (2021).

References

Ahmad, F. (2008). Politics and political parties in Republican Turkey. *The Cambridge History of Turkey*, *4*, 226–265.

Ahmad, F. (2016). The progressive Republican Party, 1924–1925. In: Jacob M. Landau, and Heper Metin (Eds.). *Political Parties and Democracy in Turkey*, 65–82.

Aytaç, S. E., Çarkoğlu, A., & Yıldırım, K. (2017). Taking sides: Determinants of support for a presidential system in Turkey. *South European Society and Politics*, *22*(1), 1–20.

Çarkoğlu, A., & Aksen, D. (2019). Partisan and apportionment bias in creating a predominant party system. *Political Geography*, *69*, 43–53.

Çarkoğlu, A., & Erdoğan, E. (1998). Fairness in the apportionment of seats in the Turkish legislature: Is there room for improvement?. *New Perspectives on Turkey*, *19*, 97–124.

Celep, Ö. (2014). The political causes of party closures in Turkey. *Parliamentary Affairs*, *67*(2), 371–390.

Emrence, C. (2000). Politics of discontent in the midst of the Great Depression: The Free Republican Party of Turkey (1930). *New Perspectives on Turkey*, *23*, 31–52.

Esen, B., & Gumuscu, S. (2018). The perils of "Turkish Presidentialism." *Review of Middle East Studies*, *52*(1), 43–53.

Hale, W. (1980). The role of the electoral system in Turkish politics. *International Journal of Middle East Studies*, *11*(3), 401–417.

Hale, W. (2008). The electoral system and the 2007 elections: Effects and debates. *Turkish Studies*, *9*(2), 233–246.

Ipek, Y. (2018). Autobiography and conservative-nationalist political opposition in Early Republican Turkey. *Turkish Studies*, *19*(1), 139–165.

Kalaycioğlu, E. (2010). The Turkish Grand National Assembly: New challenges and old problems. In *Turkey's engagement with modernity* (pp. 119–141). London: Palgrave Macmillan.

Kalaycıoğlu, E. (forthcoming 2021). A new national legislative election system? An assessment of the breakdown of consensus on the administration of elections. In A. Çarkoğlu & E. Kalaycıoğlu (Eds.), *Elections and public opinion in turkey: Through the prism of the 2018 elections*. London: Routledge.

Kayali, H. (1995). Elections and the electoral process in the Ottoman Empire, 1876–1919. *International Journal of Middle East Studies*, *27*(3), 265–286.

Khalidi, R. I. (1984). The 1912 election campaign in Syria. *International Journal of Middle East Studies*, *16*, 461–74.

Koçu, R. E. (1950). Türkiye'de seçimin tarihi, 1887–1950 (History of elections in Turkey, 1887–1950). *Tarih Dünyası*, *1*, 181–82.

Kydyralieva, S. (2019). Turkish parliamentary experience review of the parliamentary experience of Turkey from Ottoman to Republic periods. *Journal of Universal History Studies*, *2*(2), 239–250.

Landau, J. M., & Heper, M. (2016). *Political Parties and Democracy in Turkey*. Routledge.

Sevi, S., Mekik, C. S., Blais, A., & Çakır, S. (2020). How do Turks abroad vote?. *Turkish Studies*, *21*(2), 208–230.

Tunaya, T. Z. (1963). The establishment of the government of the Turkish Grand National Assembly and its political character. *Annales de la Faculté de Droit d'Istanbul*, *13*(19), 47–76.

Tuncer, E. (2002). *Osmanlı'dan günümüze seçimler, 1877–1999 (Elections from the Ottoman Era to present day, 1877-1999)*. Ankara: TESAV Yayınları.

Zürcher, E. J. (1991). *Political opposition in the early Turkish Republic: The progressive Republican Party, 1924–1925 (No. 44)*. Leiden; New York: EJ Brill.

22

ELECTION LAW IN LATIN AMERICA

Daniela Urosa

Introduction

Election law refers to the set of principles and rules that explain and guarantee the fundamental political rights of citizens, through the election of their representatives and the exercise of direct citizen participation (Nohlen & Sabsay, 2007, 27-30).[1] Principles and rules may have a different hierarchy, as they may be provided for in the constitution, laws, administrative regulation, and even supranational or international rules and principles that define the sense and scope of local election laws. Therefore, in theory, we could not speak about a Latin American election law. Rather, we should study the legislation of each country individually.

However, considering the common history of Latin American countries for many centuries, the transition towards democracy experienced by most of these countries in the last decades of the twentieth century, as well as the presidential system, which is common denominator thereof, it is possible to establish a set of sociopolitical and electoral values that are common and general among them and which that be deemed as fundamental principles of the Latin American election law. Likewise, the comparative study of the electoral systems implemented in this region reveals several aspects or matters that have special relevance within the Latin American context, whether for historical, political, or sociological reasons, which are worthy of special consideration (Tuesta, 2005, 211-13).

The following pages focus on the analysis of these common principles and the most relevant electoral matters in Latin America, emphasizing the fact that it is not a detailed study of each national electoral legislation but, instead, of the fundamental characteristics that are a common denominator of the Latin American countries.

Latin American Election Law Principles

In Latin America, there is no supranational system similar to that in Europe through the European Union, for example, which involves a true legal system superior to national ones. Certainly, there are a few sub-regional legal systems, such as Mercosur and the former Andean Community of Nations. However, in matters of democracy and human rights, we may find certain regional instruments in Latin America that let us establish the common Latin American election law that we are looking for.

DOI: 10.4324/9780429401800-22

The Charter of the Organization of American States (OAS),[2] the American Convention on Human Rights[3] and, especially, the Inter-American Democratic Charter[4] are multilateral instruments of regional scope that set forth fundamental principles that are binding upon member states in each electoral legislation.

The American Convention on Human Rights or the Pact of San José recognizes, in its 23rd Article, the following political human rights: (i) To take part in the conduct of public affairs, either directly or through freely chosen representatives; (ii) to be elected in genuine periodic elections, which shall be by universal and equal suffrage and by secret ballot that guarantees the free expression of the will of the voters; (iii) to have access, under general conditions of equality, to the public service of his country; and (iv) to have the right to equal political rights. Therefore, each country's laws may only regulate or limit them, "only on the basis of age, nationality, residence, language, education, civil and mental capacity, or sentencing by a competent court in criminal proceedings."

The Inter-American Democratic Charter is a commitment undertaken by its subscribing states through which they recognize that "representative democracy is indispensable for the stability, peace, and development of the region, and that one of the purposes of the OAS is to promote and consolidate representative democracy, with due respect for the principle of nonintervention." Even though the Charter is not an international treaty, it is a multilateral instrument binding upon its subscribing states (Perina, 2012, 7).

As essential elements of such representative democracy, Article 3 of the Charter sets forth that

> respect for human rights and fundamental freedoms, access to and the exercise of power in accordance with the rule of law, the holding of periodic, free, and fair elections based on secret balloting and universal suffrage as an expression of the sovereignty of the people, the pluralistic system of political parties and organizations, and the separation of powers and independence of the branches of government.

Therefore, according to Article 23 of the Charter, member states shall organize and guarantee "free and fair electoral processes" and may request the advice or assistance of the OAS for the strengthening of their electoral institutions and processes, including sending preliminary missions for that purpose.

Therefore, such supranational instruments provide several fundamental principles of election law in Latin America which are reflected, with greater or lesser intensity, in all Latin American countries.

The principle of *constitutional democracy* involves (i) the rule of law, by which government is exercised pursuant to the law; and (ii) the principle of representative democracy that prevails through the election of representatives, as a complement to participatory democracy.

The principle of recognition of *political rights* encompasses (i) the right to universal, direct and secret vote; (ii) the right to be elected; (iii) the right to exercise public office duties; and (iv) the right to citizen participation in public matters, whether directly or indirectly, through elected representatives and referendums, among others.

The principles of *political alternation and pluralism* provide that elections must be held on a regular basis, both freely and fairly, and that their results must be a reflection of popular sovereignty.

The principles of *equality and electoral competitiveness* must be reflected in several aspects, including (i) a system of political parties and organizations, including political pluralism and equality of conditions during the entire electoral cycle, especially during electoral campaigns and financing of parties; and (ii) gender equality on electoral matters, not only regarding the qualifications for candidacy, but also regarding the exercise of their respective duties.

In addition are the following principles. The principle of *election observation* stands as a means of assistance for member states to strengthen their electoral institutions and processes. Further guaranteed are the principles of independent, impartial, and professional *electoral authorities* during the organization and control of electoral processes, as well as the principle of *electoral justice*, which can be accessed through autonomous and impartial electoral courts.

Such principles shall be analyzed in depth below. It is also important to draw attention to the aspects that will not be considered in this study. We will not study Latin American electoral systems – i.e., government election methods existing in Latin America (one- or two-round presidential or semi-presidential systems with limited or unlimited reelection) – or parliamentary election methods (d'Hondt method and electoral circuit methods, among others). Likewise, the purpose of this work is not an exhaustive analysis of each legal system, but rather a glimpse of the fundamental principles that are common among them.

Finally, this is a study on election law and not on Latin American politics or an empirical analysis of the electoral practice of this region. Therefore, we will not make reference either to the vicissitudes and flaws that Latin American electoral systems may have in practice, or to the electoral integrity challenges tackled by the region, specifically in certain countries that are dealing with electoral and political crisis situations, such as Venezuela and Nicaragua.

Political Rights, Especially the Right to Vote

Latin American constitutions grant special relevance to the recognition and guarantee of political rights, which are exhaustively regulated, to a greater extent than are those in European and North American constitutions. Such constitutional regulation is also provided for and complemented by election laws, which define the manner in which political rights are exercised and protected.

In Latin American constitutional democracies, the quintessential political right is the right to active suffrage or the right to vote (Aragon, 2007, 165). Essentially, all Latin American constitutions are emphatic in recognizing the right to vote as a fundamental right, which shall be exercised in a free, universal, direct, and secret election (in Argentina, Bolivia, Brazil, Chile, Venezuela, Colombia, Costa Rica, Ecuador, Mexico, Guatemala, and Honduras, among others).

Those who have voter status and, therefore, may vote are also regulated by constitutions in Latin America. Generally, constitutions set forth that the only requirement for national elections (presidential and legislative) is that voters must be citizens and be over 18 years old.[5] In addition, each election law sets forth certain formal conditions for exercising this right, such as being previously registered in the electoral register and not being subject to disqualification.

A matter of interest within the Latin American election law is the fact that the right to vote is both a right and a duty. In this sense, most constitutions and electoral laws recognize it as a right-duty and even expressly set forth its mandatory exercise (Argentina, Bolivia, Brazil, Ecuador, Honduras, and the Dominican Republic), a matter that has been widely criticized, since a right may only be such when it is free and the person may autonomously decide whether to exercise it. Moreover, when voting is considered a duty, there is an excess in its functionality, and it is deemed as a means for achieving popular expression and democracy, rather than as an individual right, which is its primary essence. Perhaps that is the reason for a shift in certain countries of the region from vote-obligation to vote-right (Venezuela in 1999; El Salvador in 2004; the Dominican Republic in 2010; Chile in 2012; and Peru in 2013).

But the right to vote is evidently not the only political right recognized in the Latin American region. As mentioned above, its countries tend to be prolific when recognizing and guaranteeing fundamental rights. All constitutions from the region include the right to be eligible for public office (right to passive suffrage), and many countries also include the right of access to electoral information (Venezuela and Argentina), the right to association for political purposes (Mexico, Costa Rica, El Salvador, Nicaragua, and Venezuela, among others) and the right to peaceful protest (Venezuela and Costa Rica).

Consequently, it may be said that political rights, especially the right to vote, are the cornerstone of election law in Latin America, since the guarantee of their exercise involves the guarantee itself of representative democracy.

The Right to Citizen Participation and Direct Democratic Institutions

The right to citizen participation is also a fundamental political right that grants citizens the power to get actively involved in public matters beyond the mere exercise of the right to vote.

This right has been recognized in many Latin American legal systems, especially and exponentially since the 1990s, as a reaction to the crises of political parties (Ramirez, 2011, 11), and it has been understood as a basis for a participatory or direct democracy that, in contrast to representative democracy, is focused on the taking of certain political decisions directly by citizens.

It is important to clarify that, in my opinion, direct democracy is by no means incompatible or distinct from representative democracy. On the contrary, representation is essential for any democracy and, therefore, cannot be replaced by new forms of direct participation that complement it, facilitating the taking of decisions in certain and specific public matters. Fortunately, this seems to be the criterion accepted by Latin American election law as well.

According to Zovatto, since the end of 2004, 16 Latin American countries have included different direct democracy institutions in their constitutions and, hence, the right to citizen participation may be deemed as a common principle of Latin American electoral legislation. Consequently, despite using different terms when referring to similar institutions, direct democracy mechanisms are recognized by the constitutions of Argentina, Bolivia, Brazil, Colombia, Costa Rica, Chile, Ecuador, El Salvador, Guatemala, Honduras, Paraguay, Peru, Uruguay, and Venezuela, while Panama provides such in its electoral legislation (Zovatto, 2007b, 141).

The direct democracy mechanisms in Latin America are diverse. Some are of consultative nature – popular referendums, open council meetings, and plebiscites – while others have a binding nature, emphasizing, in this case, the approval of abrogative and recall referendums, as well as legislative initiatives. Such citizen participation mechanisms vary in each country according to their local, regional, or national scope of application, as well as regarding those matters that may be submitted to popular referendum, the procedures to be followed, and the majority required for considering the approval or rejection of the matter submitted to vote. Likewise, there has been an increase in the development of participation mechanisms derived from popular initiative, rather than those promoted or called by the government. Uruguay has been a pioneer in the use of citizen participation means derived from popular initiative (Welp, 2010, 27–8).

Undoubtedly, direct democracy mechanisms are an essential feature of Latin American election law; however, these have been a matter of political and academic debate in regards to their convenience or inconvenience. For, on one hand, as expressed by Welp, "direct democracy instruments have been efficient for institutionally and democratically channeling the demands of citizens, generating greater consensus and governability" (2010, 42) in the region. However, on the other hand, these same mechanisms have been occasionally used as instruments for the development and consolidation of populist and authoritarian governments, distorting their true nature, which is direct citizen participation in public matters (Urosa, 2018, 29-31). Specifically, this has been the experience in Venezuela, Bolivia, Ecuador, and, recently, in Nicaragua.[6]

The Electoral Authorities or Electoral Arbitrators

The electoral authority is the institution or set of institutions that organize, direct, and monitor electoral processes during all the electoral cycle phases and guarantee the effective exercise of the right to vote and other political rights. As a result, the electoral authority is the institutional or organizational element of election law.

The electoral authority has fundamental relevance in Latin American election law since it is responsible for the organization of elections and, jointly with electoral courts, for the electoral conflict resolution throughout the region. Therefore, they have been created as competent entities, granted functional and budgetary autonomy, in order to guarantee their impartiality and objectivity.

Decades ago, the electoral authorities had the status of a provisional body or agency, which was only established just before the elections and would be dissolved right after their end. Nowadays, they are permanent institutions in every Latin American country and do not depend on calls for elections since, as previously mentioned, they perform duties that require constant activity, such as the electoral register, resolution of conflicts, and regulation of political parties.

In two countries, Venezuela and Nicaragua, the electoral authority has the same status and autonomy of the legislative, executive and judicial branches. It is called Electoral Power. In other countries, it is an administrative institution having autonomy from the Executive Power (functional autonomy) or it is part of the Judicial branch, such as in Argentina, Brazil, and Paraguay. In all these cases, this highest electoral authority is a federal or centralized institution, which may have regional offices.

In most Latin American countries, the electoral authority and its main duties are established by the constitution and provided for by the law. Only in Argentina is the electoral authority not established by the constitution; in Guatemala, the constitutional reference to such authority is very brief; and, in Cuba, it was recently included in the Constitution of 2019.

The electoral authorities' powers are gradually increasing and diversifying and may be classified as follows:

- *Administrative powers*. (i) Administrations of the electoral processes; (ii) making calls for elections (except for Argentina, Bolivia, and Peru, where the call is made by the Executive Power); (iii) approval of candidates' nominations; (iv) counting and casting votes; (vi) making proclamations of winning candidates; (v) creating electoral regulatory standards; (vi) legalizing political parties and administering public funds for financing electoral campaigns; (vii) imposing sanctions in the event of illegal electoral activities; and (viii) processing complaints and implementing administrative remedies against electoral acts.
- *Registration powers*. These provide for new voters' registration and the regular updating of the electoral register.
- *Jurisdictional powers*. In some Latin American countries, the electoral authority has a dual nature: Administrative (for the elections' organization and monitoring and for administrative complaints resolution) and jurisdictional (for electoral conflict resolution). As a result, in some countries (Nicaragua and Bolivia), the electoral authority is considered an electoral court that decides jurisdictional conflicts, unlike most countries (Mexico, Venezuela, and Colombia), in which the electoral authority exclusively has an administrative nature and has the authority to organize elections and resolve administrative complaints, although its proceedings may be submitted to the electoral judicial review.

In conclusion, electoral authorities are a key element of Latin America election law, as they are involved in all phases of the electoral cycle and must guarantee the efficiency, impartiality, and transparency of electoral processes.

Political Pluralism, Gender Parity, and Electoral Competitiveness

Equality, political pluralism, and electoral competitiveness are essential principles of Latin American democracy and, therefore, of Latin American election law. The Inter-American Democratic Charter sets forth that political pluralism is essential for representative democracy and, thus, Latin American electoral laws must guarantee that citizens' votes reflect the plurality of political parties and society, avoiding at all costs the hegemonic and totalitarian thinking imposed by the ruling party, such as recognized by all Latin American constitutions as well.

Regarding equality, Latin America election law includes gender quotas in order to have equal access for men and women to public office positions, candidate nominations, and the internal organization of political parties.

In order to achieve such equality, it is necessary to promote and facilitate women's exercise of political rights, especially through political representation quotas in parliaments. Gender parity has been a fundamental matter of comparative election law, and Latin America is not an exception in this aspect.

In this sense, after the subscription of the Inter-American Convention on the Prevention, Punishment, and Eradication of Violence against Women ("Convention of Belém Do Pará") in 1994, the recognition of women's political rights and gender equality has been intensified in the exercise of political rights, not only the right to vote, but also the right to be elected and the exercise of public office, especially through the inclusion of gender quotas in the nomination of candidates in most Latin American countries.

Since then, most Latin American legal systems have included gender parity as a fundamental principle; in some countries, such as Argentina,[7] Ecuador, and Mexico, the constitution itself sets forth a minimum representation for women. In other countries, such as Bolivia, Costa Rica, Nicaragua, Guatemala, and Panama, election laws regulate this matter. In turn, Panama and Honduras have also included gender parity regulations in the political parties' internal election processes for candidate nominations. Moreover, in several Latin American countries, such as Bolivia, Costa Rica, Ecuador, Honduras, Mexico, Nicaragua, Panama, and Argentina, mandatory gender quotas have increased from 30% to 50%.

The special consideration granted by Latin American election law to this matter has led the region to a leading position in terms of female parliamentary representation through participation quotas. According to the International IDEA Global State of Democracy Report 2019,

> Latin America and the Caribbean is the region with most advances in political gender equality in the past decades. Together with Europe, the region has the highest representation of women in parliament, averaging 27 percent, which is above the world average of 24 percent.[8]

Quotas and gender parity rules have undoubtedly played an essential role in this increase. Nevertheless, there are still certain discrimination and electoral violence issues that affect gender equality and inclusion in the political scenario (Alanis, 2017, 231).

Electoral Campaigns

Electoral campaigns may be understood, in general, as the set of activities carried out by political parties and candidates to present their political offer to the voters and to encourage voting intention to their favor. The electoral campaign is an essential step of every election process, and its proper development is indispensable for guaranteeing competitiveness and equality among candidates and the integrity of elections (Dimino, Smith, & Solimine, 2017, 141).

In Latin America election law, the electoral campaign is one of the most relevant matters. The deepening of democracy in Latin America during the last decades, as well as the rehabilitation of the election as a mechanism for improving public office positions' exercise, has increased the importance of political parties and political-electoral competition, giving rise to a greater focus on electoral campaigns as a decisive factor of electoral success (Zovatto, 2007, 745–6).

The regulation of campaigns, their financing, mechanisms, limitations of electoral publicity, political proselytism, ballot buying, prohibitions, and penalties in the event of noncompliance with the electoral campaign rules are all matters of constant analysis, debate, and special regulation in Latin American countries. A better performance of the election campaign is also one of the matters to be addressed in the Inter-American region in order to improve the level of electoral integrity.

Most Latin American constitutions include basic principles on electoral campaign matters that are consistent with the Inter-American Democratic Charter's general guidelines and other Inter-American System regulatory instruments. Such principles are further developed by different election laws, either in a systematic manner, by devoting an entire election law chapter (such as in Bolivia, Brazil, Nicaragua, the Dominican Republic, and Honduras), or dispersed in several legislative instruments, such as in Argentina, Colombia, Chile, and Ecuador. In other cases, such as Venezuela, even though the law sets forth general principles in a single chapter, the electoral authority has extensive discretion regulating the election campaign, causing legal uncertainty and frequent arbitrary modification of rules for partisan purposes (Alarcón, Trak, Torrealba, & Urosa, 2016, 95–6).

A common feature in Latin America is an exhaustive and detailed regulation of electoral campaigns, their limitations, prohibitions, and penalties, and, in many cases, the constant amendments of these matters prior to election day.

Regarding campaign conditions, Latin American electoral systems commonly set forth freedom and equality during electoral campaigns and advertising (except for Argentina, Mexico, and Uruguay). Likewise, they expressly set the impartiality of public officials during the campaign. All countries from the region have detailed regulation of the use of public resources for campaign purpose, except for Bolivia, Guatemala, and Paraguay, which have not yet included provisions regarding such limitations in their respective laws. The most frequent bans include the prohibition of electoral campaigns and electoral advertisements in public buildings and urban facilities, the prohibition of anonymous and disrespectful campaigns, and the prohibition of the promotion of governmental acts for electoral purposes during the campaign period.

Likewise, there is a general tendency in Latin America to regulate the electoral campaign's length and dates. However, it may vary. In some cases, the campaign can only last 30 days and, in others, it can last up to six months (Lauga & Garcia, 2007, 736).

A matter of special relevance is the influence of cyberpolitics, social media, and fake news during electoral campaigns in Latin America. It is a new aspect that has not yet been regulated by Latin American legal systems. However, it has been considered a relevant problem in the region for negatively contributing to misinformation and polarization among voters, with a clear impact on recent electoral results in Latin America, such as the case of Mexico, Venezuela, and Brazil in 2018 (Fernández, 2018, 147). The cyber campaigns' regulation and control is, therefore, a pending task of Latin American election law.

Electoral Financing

Previously, we mentioned that political parties and electoral campaigns have a special leading role in elections in Latin America. However, there has been a gradual increase in campaign costs due to the increasing sophistication of advertising media, causing, therefore, the exponential growth of electoral expenses. At the same time, there has been an unwanted increase in illegal financing of campaigns in the region, the predominance of strong economic groups, influence peddling, and even narco-financing. For these reasons, electoral regulations in Latin America are more vigilant on electoral financing and the control of electoral corruption (Zovatto, 2007, 746).

We found the following general features of Latin American legal systems on electoral financing matters: (i) All countries, except for Venezuela, set forth a mixed financing system in which political parties receive contributions from public funds and private funds for electoral campaigns; (ii) public financing is allocated according to several criteria – in some countries, the contribution is proportional to the electoral strength of each party (Bolivia, Colombia, Costa Rica, Chile, and Guatemala, among others), i.e. according to the percentage of votes obtained during prior elections; (iii) other countries apply a mixed criterion in which all parties are equally allocated a fixed-percentage contribution and a variable percentage is allocated according to the electoral strength thereof (Argentina, Brazil, Ecuador, Mexico, and Peru, among others).

Regarding private financing, most countries set certain limitations, such as the ban of financial support from foreign governments or institutions, financial support from state contractors, and anonymous contributions. The countries with the most prohibitions are Argentina, Bolivia, Chile, Honduras, Mexico, and Paraguay, among others, in order to avoid electoral corruption and electoral financing through illegal activities. Only El Salvador, Panama, and Uruguay have no limitations on this matter. In addition, it has become more and more common to establish limitations to the contributions made from private financing, maximum limit of expenses, and limits over the length of campaigns in order to encourage expense reduction.

A matter of special relevance in Latin American electoral laws is the control of electoral financing. Most Latin American countries have included the principle of transparency and accountability in their laws. Venezuela has even included it in the constitution in order to emphasize the citizens' right to know the funds' origin and use granted for electoral purposes.

In most countries of the region, such control over electoral financing is exercised by the electoral authority or, otherwise, by a special control authority. There is also a complete system of administrative and criminal penalties in the event of noncompliance (almost all countries, except for El Salvador and Uruguay, set multiple controls on this matter) by parties, candidates, and contributors.

Finally, according to Zovatto, one of the matters that still requires careful regulation in Latin America is equal access to the media, especially audiovisual media, which is an indirect form of public financing and which is only regulated in a few countries such as Mexico, Chile, and Brazil, thereby encouraging electoral competitiveness (Zovatto, 2007, 7936).

Election Observation

Election observation is included among the electoral integrity fundamental guarantees in order to provide assistance by specialized organizations that legitimize the impartiality and transparency of electoral processes in their different phases, generate trust among voters, and contribute to the proper development of the elections.

Election observation missions in Latin America began during the decade of the 1980s, which coincided with the peak of Latin American democratic transitions. Since then, these have become a widespread practice (Boneo, Carrillo, & Valverde, 2007, 1076), especially through the Organization of American States (OAS) observation missions, to the extent that, nowadays, election observation has reached a particularly relevant progress and has become indispensable throughout elections in Latin America (Thompson, 2008, 37–8).

However, election observation acquires several dimensions in Latin America. It may be carried out by international, regional, and local organizations. Even though they all have the same final goal – to achieve more transparent elections – each of them has a different legal and political essence. International and regional observation seeks regional democratic strengthening based on agreements subscribed to by member countries, while local observation is carried out by the civil society as an expression of its political rights, specifically the fundamental right to citizen participation in public matters.

Latin American election law regulates both regional observation and local observation. Regional observation, led by OAS, finds a common basis in Articles 23 to 25 of the Inter-American Democratic Charter, which not only promote observation missions to strengthen and develop elections, but also set basic parameters for their applicability.

However, neither regional observation nor local observation are regulated by Latin American constitutions, despite the fact that, in my opinion, election observation is an expression of the right to citizen participation in electoral matters, as well as a fundamental guarantee of electoral integrity. Instead, their development has been assigned to legislators and has been treated as an administrative matter. Only the constitution of Ecuador makes a slight reference to election observation in Article 223, which states that "electoral authorities shall be subject to social control."

Therefore, observation requirements and procedures vary from one country to another. Nevertheless, in general, Latin American election laws are highly favorable towards local, regional, and international observation and grant electoral authorities the duty of authorizing electoral observers prior to the corresponding election. In some countries, such as Mexico, election observation is recognized as the political right to witness and monitor the electoral process.

In exceptional cases such as Venezuela, electoral observation is restrictively regulated. It is the electoral authority, rather than the law, that regulates this matter, limiting in an excessive manner the election observation's scopes and limits, considering it as a mere electoral "accompaniment" in which organizations cannot issue an opinion or comment. Therefore, in the last few years, some relevant electoral observation missions have been rejected in Venezuela, such as those of the OAS and UN, and only those organizations that are affiliated to the ruling party have been authorized (Alarcón, Track, Torrealba & Urosa, 2016, 48).

Finally, even though electoral observation is fundamental in Latin America, it is a matter that requires greater and better constitutional and legislative provisions based on the criterion that there is a right to electoral observation and, therefore, there must be a clear definition on the observers' powers and duties and the legal value of their reports, as well as a reduction in the electoral authority's discretionary power.

Electoral Justice

Another fundamental condition of electoral integrity is electoral justice to achieve effective and impartial resolution mechanisms for electoral conflicts, an effective electoral judicial review, and an effective protection of citizens' rights regarding elections. Electoral justice is the final custodian of the electoral cycle: Any failure in the electoral integrity conditions may, and must, be reestablished by electoral justice.

Electoral justice is a condition of electoral integrity because: (i) It guarantees the rule of law and constitutional democracy; (ii) it guarantees the exercise of political rights; (iii) it guarantees the fundamental right to effective judicial protection, especially the right of access to justice and due process, from the point of view of both individual and collective or diffuse rights, such as those recognized by Article 25 of the American Convention on Human Rights and Latin

American Constitutions; and (iv) it guarantees the principles of transparency, competitiveness, and electoral process compliance.

Moreover, electoral justice is a key element of Latin American election law. Additionally, the Latin American electoral justice model is very specific and distinguishable from those existing in other countries to the extent that, according to Orozco, the Latin American electoral justice model is one of the most relevant regional contributions to comparative election law, upon becoming a major factor for the recent re-democratization and democratic consolidation processes in Latin America (Orozco, 2012, 114).

Thus, every country in this region has authorities (named electoral tribunals, courts, juries, court divisions, or councils) possessing the power to resolve electoral conflicts pursuant to the election law, annulling electoral results, if applicable, and protecting any fundamental rights that may be infringed upon during elections (Sobrado, 2006, 161-3). Therefore, the resolution of electoral conflicts in Latin America is carried out through jurisdictional means, pursuant to the law, rather than through political means based on discretional criteria or negotiations between political parties. For this reason, reference is frequently made to the *judicialization of electoral conflicts in Latin America* (Fix-Zamudio, 2001, 11).

In turn, such Latin American electoral courts may vary in nature and structure:

(i) In some cases, these courts are part of the judicial power, such as the Electoral Tribunal (Mexico), the Electoral Chamber of the Supreme Tribunal of Justice (Venezuela), and the Contentious-Administrative Courts (Colombia) having power over electoral matters.
(ii) In other cases, there are autonomous electoral courts, i.e., tribunals that are not part the judiciary, such as those in Costa Rica, Chile, Ecuador, El Salvador, Guatemala, Honduras, Panama, Peru, the Dominican Republic, and Uruguay.
(iii) Finally, in some countries, the electoral court is an administrative authority that decides on electoral conflicts pursuant to the applicable law on specific cases (in Nicaragua and Bolivia).

In any case, it is important to mention that, in most Latin American countries, except for Nicaragua, there are two mechanisms for controlling the legality of electoral proceedings: (i) An administrative mechanism, exercised by the electoral authority or electoral agency, that rules on administrative electoral complaints; and (ii) a jurisdictional mechanism that, as mentioned above, corresponds to an electoral court, whether or not it is part of the judiciary.

Likewise, in some cases, electoral court decisions are final and may not be reviewed by another administrative agency or higher court (in Costa Rica, Ecuador, Mexico, Nicaragua, Peru, the Dominican Republic, Uruguay, and Venezuela[9]). In other countries, the decisions of electoral courts may be appealed before the Supreme Court of Justice (in Argentina, Brazil, El Salvador, Honduras, Panama, and Paraguay), before a Contentious-Administrative Court (in Colombia), or before the Constitutional Court (in Bolivia, Guatemala, and Chile).

Regardless of the model, the common principle in Latin America is, as previously mentioned, the resolution of electoral controversies through special electoral jurisdiction. Such special electoral courts have, in general, the following duties or powers:

(i) Judicial review over elections during any phase of the electoral cycle (before, during, and after election day) and over electoral results. Such control allows the total or partial annulment of electoral results, the issue of precautionary measures during any phase of the electoral process, and the resolution of conflicts between political parties.[10] Likewise, in many countries, the electoral court has the power to protect political rights, which may be exercised through a special brief and summary proceeding, such as Peru, Venezuela, Brazil, El Salvador, and Mexico, among others.

(ii) Electoral administrative powers, in those countries in which the electoral court also has competence to organize elections (Nicaragua and Costa Rica, among others). In this case, the court shall also have duties related to the organization of elections, counting of votes, the proclamation of winning candidates, and authority for the imposition of penalties.

Finally, regarding the procedures to be followed for the resolution of electoral complaints before the electoral court, it is common in Latin American countries to establish brief and expeditious means that allow for the rapid resolution of electoral conflicts, as well as flexibility in the submission of evidence and effective precautionary and enforcement mechanisms.

Conclusion

In conclusion, it may be asserted that there is a Latin American election law based on the fundamental principles of constitutional democracy and the rule of law, recognition of the fundamental right to vote and other political rights, political alternation, political pluralism, and electoral integrity, as included in multilateral Inter-American treaties and instruments.

Such principles are included and reiterated in several Latin American constitutions and electoral laws and, therefore, despite the differences in certain regulations of each one, the fundamental principles are generally the same.

Special relevance is granted by Latin America election law to the recognition and guarantee of political rights, which are the basis for both representative and direct democracy, electoral authority, gender equality and electoral participation quotas, electoral campaigns, electoral financing, election observation, and electoral justice.

However, there are still aspects that require better legislative regulation, especially on matters related to cyber campaigns and cyberpolitics. Likewise, it would be convenient to avoid making frequent amendments to electoral laws, which would undoubtedly strengthen the electoral legal framework and electoral integrity in the region, since such amendments are usually made for political and partisan purposes arising from upcoming electoral processes.

Notes

1 Regarding the definition of election law, see Nohlen, Dieter and Sabsay, Daniel, Derecho Electoral in *Tratado de derecho electoral comparado de América Latina*, Inter-American Human Rights Institute and others, Economic Culture Fund, Mexico, second edition, 2007, pp. 27 & 162 respectively.

2 Subscribed in Bogota in 1948 and amended by the Protocols of Buenos Aires (1967), Cartagena de Indias (1985), Washington (1992), and Managua (1993).

3 Subscribed in San José, Costa Rica, in 1969.

4 Approved on September 11, 2001, at the General Assembly of the OAS.

5 The constitutions of Brazil and Nicaragua allow 16-year-olds to vote.

6 We refer, in this sense, to the use and abuse of popular referendums during the governments of Chavez in Venezuela, Morales in Bolivia, Correa in Ecuador, and Ortega in Nicaragua.

7 In fact, Argentina was the first country in the world to set gender quotas in 1991. Its constitution sets forth the gender parity principle as follows: "Real equality of opportunities between men and women for having access to elective office and party positions shall be guaranteed by positive actions in the regulation of political parties and in the electoral system."

8 International IDEA report *The Global State of Democracy 2019. Addressing the Ills, Reviving the Promise*, 2019, p. 115. www.idea.int/sites/default/files/publications/the-global-state-of-democracy-2019.pdf.

9 It has been exposed, both in Venezuela and Peru, how, in practice, the decisions of the Constitutional Court directly influence electoral trials, to the extent of modifying decisions of the Electoral Court, even though, in theory, these are unappealable.

10 In some countries, such as Venezuela, the Electoral Chamber of the Supreme Tribunal has been granted authority to control internal elections of private entities, such as unions, companies, and even social clubs. This has been an object of criticism, since it exceeds the functions that should naturally correspond to an electoral court and represents an inappropriate interference in the internal affairs of such private organizations (Urosa 2014, 388).

References

Alanis, M., & Carmen, M. (2017). Violencia política hacia las mujeres, respuesta del Estado ante la falta de una ley en México. In Freidenberg & Valle (Eds.), *Cuando hacer política te cuesta la vida. Estrategias contra la violencia política hacia las mujeres en América Latina* (pp. 231–248). México, DF: UNAM.

Alarcón, B., Trak, J., Berrios, J., Torrealba, M., & Urosa, D. (2016). *Propuestas para una reforma electoral. Buscando la integridad electoral en Venezuela*. Caracas: UCAB.

Aragón, M. (2007). Derecho Electoral: sufragio activo y pasivo. In D. Nohlen, D. Zovatto, J. Orozco, & J. Thompson (Eds.), *Tratado de derecho electoral comparado de América Latina* (2nd ed., pp. 162–173). México, DF: Inter-American Institute of Human Rights.

Boneo, H., Carrillo, M., & Valverde, R. (2007). La Observación (internacional y nacional). In D. Nohlen, D. Zovatto, J. Orozco, & J. Thompson (Eds.), *Tratado de derecho comparado de América Latina* (2nd ed., pp. 1072–1109). México, DF: Inter-American Institute of Human Rights.

Dimino, M., Smith, B., & Solimine, M. (2017). *Understanding election law and voting rights*. Durhman, NC: Carolina Academic Press.

Fernández, C. (2018). Ciberpolítica 2018: Tendencias en Latinoamérica. In Wesemann (Ed.), *Nuevas campañas electorales en América Latina* (pp. 147–162). Montevideo: Konrad Adenauer Foundation.

Fix-Zamudio, H. (2001). Justicia constitucional y judicialización de la política. In J. Orozco (Ed.), *Sistemas de justicia electoral: evaluación y perspectivas* (pp. 11–38). México, DF: IFE.

Lauga, M., & García, J.R. (2007). La campaña electoral: publicidad/propaganda, período, prohibiciones. In D. Nohlen, D. Zovatto, J. Orozco, & J. Thompson (Eds.), *Tratado de derecho electoral comparado de América Latina* (2nd ed., pp. 709–743). México, DF: Inter-American Institute of Human Rights.

Nohlen, D., & Sabsay, D. (2007). Derecho electoral. In D. Nohlen, D. Zovatto, J. Orozco, & J. Thompson (Eds.), *Tratado de derecho electoral comparado de América Latina* (2nd ed., pp. 27–38). México, DF: Inter-American Institute of Human Rights.

Orozco, H.J. (2012). Evolución y perspectivas de la justicia electoral en América Latina. *Revista Mexicana de Derecho Electoral, 1*, 107–131.

Perina, R. (2012). Los desafíos de la carta democrática interamericana. *Estudios Internacionales, 173*, 7–36.

Ramírez, F. (2011). Nuevas instituciones participativas y democráticas en América Latina. *Revista de Ciencias Sociales, 40*, 11–20.

Sobrado, G.L. (2006). Tendencias de la justicia electoral latinoamericana y sus desafíos democráticos. *Revista de Ciencias Jurídicas, 109*, 155–184.

Thompson, J. (2008). La observación electoral en el Sistema Interamericano. *Diálogo Político, 4*, 37–67.

Tuesta, S.F. (2005). Sistemas electorales en América Latina. *Revista IIDH, 42*, 211–226.

Urosa, D. (2014). Resolución de conflictos electorales. Revisión administrativa y judicial de actos electorales. In B. Alarcón & J. Casal (Eds.), *Proyecto integridad electoral Venezuela: Las reformas impostergables* (pp. 380–409). Caracas: UCAB.

Urosa, D. (2018). Autoritarismo judicial electoral. *Revista Electrónica de Derecho Administrativo, 14*, 28–46.

Welp, Y. (2010). El referendo en América Latina. Diseños institucionales y equilibrios de poder. *Revista Nueva Sociedad, 228*, 26–42.

Zovatto, D. (2007a). El Financiamiento electoral: subvenciones y gastos. In D. Nohlen, D. Zovatto, J. Orozco, & J. Thompson (Eds.), *Tratado de derecho electoral comparado de América Latina* (2nd ed., pp. 744–820). México DF: Inter-American Institute of Human Rights.

Zovatto, D. (2007b). Las instituciones de democracia directa. In D. Nohlen, D. Zovatto, J. Orozco, & J. Thompson (Eds.), *Tratado de derecho electoral comparado de América Latina* (2nd ed., pp. 134–161). México DF: Inter-American Institute of Human Rights.

23

CONTESTED ELECTIONS IN AFRICA

The Roles of Courts in Electoral Processes

Ugochukwu Ezeh

Introduction

In 1979, Nigeria's democratic transition process, designed to terminate 13 years of military rule, was nearly aborted by an impassioned legal dispute over the presidential election result. The statutory framework governing the 1979 presidential election required the successful candidate to score "the highest number of votes at the election" and "not less than one-quarter of the votes cast at the election in each of at least two-thirds of all the states in the Federation."[1] Given that the country comprised nineteen states at the time, it was most significant that the candidate who won the majority vote in the presidential election had also obtained a quarter of the votes in 12 states, but narrowly missed the stipulated minimum threshold in the 13th. The Federal Electoral Commission adopted a literal interpretation of the relevant statutory provisions in a bid to avert an imminent impasse. On this interpretive approach, a successful candidate would then be required to obtain a quarter of two-thirds of the total votes cast in the 13th state. When the commission subsequently declared the election results, on the strength of this interpretation, its decision was challenged in a celebrated election petition[2] that ultimately reached the Supreme Court.

On one plane of analysis, the central issue before the court in *Awolowo v. Shagari*[3] involved the proper legal interpretation of what two-thirds of 19 states amounted to for the purpose of determining the winner of a historic presidential election. Yet, the election petition also catapulted the Supreme Court to the center of the ongoing transition process. In the decade leading up to the petition, the military regime had progressively consolidated power by relegating the court to a marginal role in the political process.[4] However, in *Awolowo v. Shagari*, the court was fortuitously presented with a salient adjudicatory opportunity to influence the trajectory of the Second Republic and rehabilitate its own status within the incipient democratic constitutional order.

In its majority decision,[5] the court sought to resolve the electoral dispute by dismissing the petition and upholding the interpretative approach adopted by the Federal Electoral Commission and Presidential Election Tribunal.[6] The court further justified its decision by suggesting that the presidential election had been conducted substantially in accordance with the relevant legal frameworks and that any case of non-compliance had no material effect on the election results.

DOI: 10.4324/9780429401800-23

Obaseki JSC, who decided with the majority, albeit on different grounds, reasoned that, on a proper interpretation of the extant electoral laws, "no tribunal in any petition by a weak presidential opponent, can justifiably invalidate any election for non-compliance on a minimal scale."[7] *Awolowo v. Shagari* has been characterized as an expedient decision aimed at safeguarding the democratic transition and averting political crisis in a volatile context (Nwabueze, 1982b, 200; Adediran, 1982, 54–6).[8] Yet, the case is also significant for its canonical formulation of the substantial effect[9] doctrine in African electoral jurisprudence, as well as for having foreshadowed the issue of contested presidential election results now prevalent across the continent.

This chapter contributes to the discourse on democratic decline in nascent democracies by thematizing a significant phenomenon: The increasing judicialization of highly charged electoral politics in Africa. Courts, election candidates, pro-democracy activists, and other politico-constitutional actors in a range of African jurisdictions have sought – with varying degrees of success and failure – to invoke judicial power as a remedial mechanism against the onslaught of electoral malpractices and other forms of democratic decline (Kaaba, 2015; Azu, 2015).[10] Indeed, the "African" presidential election petition has particularly emerged as a critical terrain of democratic struggle. Against this backdrop, the chapter discusses key judicial decisions from the recent comparative African electoral jurisprudence in order to frame insights on the normative roles municipal courts can play in confronting the incidence of democratic decline.

Accordingly, the chapter discusses three normative functions that courts may fulfill within the electoral processes of nascent democracies on the continent. Within the limits of judicial authority, courts may: Invalidate electoral malpractices; facilitate the independence of core democratic institutions (such as electoral management bodies); and edify democratizing polities by signaling constitutional norms and disseminating democratic values.

Judicial Invalidation of Electoral Malpractices

Courts can exercise practical remedial functions by refusing to sanction irregularities and malpractices that compromise the integrity of the electoral process. In exceptional cases, this may entail judicial invalidation of sham elections. To discharge this normative function, however, courts may need to evolve progressive interpretations of the prevalent "substantial effect" doctrine applied in election petitions.

In basic terms, African courts confronted with the task of determining election petitions have grappled with tensions between qualitative and quantitative standards of validity under the overarching rubric of the substantial effect doctrine (Kaaba, 2015; Nyane, 2019).[11] Qualitative standards emphasize the substantive quality and credibility of the electoral process and insist on meaningful compliance with applicable constitutional and statutory frameworks. In contrast, the quantitative standard generally upholds a presumption of validity in favor of impugned elections, unless petitioners establish that electoral irregularities have substantially affected the numerical results of an impugned election.[12] Although the distinction between both standards of validity seems artificial, it has nonetheless served as a useful heuristic device in several election petitions.

The prevalent adjudicatory approach has been to treat both standards as a conjunctive two-pronged test, although the quantitative standard has generally been regarded as the determining factor. As such, petitioners have been required to establish, first, that an impugned election was not conducted in accordance with relevant electoral rules and, second, that the non-compliance substantially affected the numerical election results.

In some variants of the substantial effect doctrine, encapsulated by the Nigerian case of *Awolowo v. Shagari* (1979), petitioners were required to further establish that they would have won the impugned election "but for" substantial noncompliance with applicable electoral rules.[13] Although the prevalent approach is not without its merits, it imposes onerous evidentiary burdens on petitioners in circumstances that often shield deficient and fraudulent elections from effective legal scrutiny (Sekindi, 2017, 164; Nkansah, 2016, 117; Kaaba, 2015, 345–9).[14]

Insights from Recent Cases

Within the limits of judicial authority, courts may draw inspiration from progressive adjudicatory approaches adopted in recent cases from Kenya and Malawi. In *Raila Odinga & Anor. v. Independent Electoral and Boundaries Commission & Ors. (Presidential Petition No. 1 of 2017)*,[15] the majority decision of the Supreme Court of Kenya nullified the disputed August 2017 presidential elections for non-compliance with the constitution and applicable statutory frameworks.

The majority opinion in *Odinga* tempered the rigor of the substantial effect doctrine by decoupling the two standards of validity.[16] On the disjunctive test applied by the court, it was sufficient for the petitioner to establish that "the conduct of the election violated the principles in [the] Constitution" (para 203) and other applicable electoral laws – although the majority opinion noted obiter that the noncompliance had, in any case, also affected the election results (para 379). With respect to its democratic legitimacy to determine the case, the court stated that its judicial powers – "including that of invalidating a presidential election" – were neither "self-given nor forcefully taken" (para 399), but flowed from the authority of the Kenyan Constitution.

In justifying its decision to order fresh presidential elections, the court further emphasized its constitutional obligations to ensure that the democratic will of the Kenyan people was not subverted through elections conducted in violation of the electoral principles enshrined in the constitutional text (para 399).

The example set in *Odinga* was recently followed in the celebrated case of *Peter Mutharika & Electoral Commission v. Lazarus Chakwera & Saulos Chilima*[17] decided in May 2020. There, the Malawian Supreme Court of Appeal declared that Peter Mutharika had not been duly elected as President of Malawi and affirmed the decision of the Constitutional Court to order fresh elections. The court faulted previous adjudicatory approaches for emphasizing the quantitative standard and relegating concerns about the integrity of the electoral process. The court reasoned that such quantitative conceptions of elections had unwittingly reinforced "increased electoral malpractices over the years," resulting in "the focus being on maximizing the numbers [of votes] by whatever means, without complying with the law" (p. 89).

Echoing the principle earlier enunciated in *Odinga*, the court rejected the notion that a presidential election was a mere "event" or a simple numerical exercise in vote-counting. Such a notion, the court reasoned, would not adequately address cases where the numerical results may have been affected by "inaccurate counting, intimidation, fraud or corruption" and other forms of electoral malpractice (p. 84). In the final analysis, the court reasoned that a sound adjudicatory approach would be to focus on the electoral process and evaluate its quality by reference to its substantive (non)compliance with applicable constitutional and statutory rules (p. 84).

Adjudicatory Dilemma – Political Backlash or Damaged Credibility

Notwithstanding the foregoing, African judicial actors seem trapped within an adjudicatory dilemma: Courts seriously undermine their legitimacy when they validate sham elections, yet they risk significant political backlash if they make assertive interventions in the electoral process.

Contemporary African electoral history demonstrates that incumbents threatened by assertive judicial decisions have typically taken retaliatory measures to neutralize the political risks posed by independent electoral courts.[18] Forms of political backlash engendered by judicial activism essentially aim at weakening the capacity of courts to exhibit meaningful independence within the electoral process. In some jurisdictions, incumbents have deployed targeted sanctions – including suspensions, forced retirements, and dismissals – against judges at the highest echelons of the judiciary in order to signal the adverse consequences of activist decision-making to lesser-ranked judicial officers.[19] Beyond the weaponization of disciplinary procedures, other forms of political backlash have involved attempts to delegitimize the courts through intemperate criticism (Okubasu, 2018, 168),[20] as well as structural measures that seek to reconfigure legal systems so as to constrict the jurisdiction of courts over electoral causes (Amoah, 2020, 82).[21]

Political interference has also taken pre-emptive and retaliatory dimensions. In the latter case, the regime – whose political interests have already been impacted by assertive or adverse judicial decisions in the electoral sphere – targets retributive measures against the judiciary as a whole or specified judicial officers. After the Malawian Supreme Court of Appeal delivered its celebrated decision to order fresh presidential elections, the Mutharika government took retaliatory measures by attempting to force the premature retirement of Chief Justice Andrew Nyirenda and Justice Edward Twea, the next judge in line in the judicial hierarchy.[22] However, this attempt failed due to widespread protests by civil society groups, pro-democracy activists, and members of the legal profession.[23] High Court judges also weighed in by issuing decisions invalidating the purported retirements.[24] The fresh presidential election thus proceeded, as ordered by the courts – resulting in a historic victory for the opposition candidate, Lazarus Chakwera.[25]

The outcome was less salutary in Kenya, where the government introduced legislative proposals to constrict the scope of judicial jurisdiction in electoral causes following the *Odinga* decision (Amoah, 2020, 82). Whilst the Supreme Court was preparing to hear arguments in another petition, seeking to postpone the re-run election, there was a suspicious armed attack on the bodyguard of one of the judges. The court subsequently failed to achieve a quorum at the hearing, and the re-run went ahead, culminating in the re-election of the incumbent president, Uhuru Kenyatta.[26] Thus, the court was caught up in a vortex of intrigue and political conflict in the wake of its historic decision.

Other cases are illustrative of pre-emptive political interference with the courts. For instance, in the period leading up to the 2019 presidential polls in Nigeria, there were strong indications that the elections would be contested, thereby raising the real prospect of eventual electoral adjudication by the Supreme Court. The Buhari regime, in a brazenly unconstitutional move, then swiftly announced the suspension of the Chief Justice, reportedly for failing to declare his personal assets.[27] An acting Chief Justice, widely perceived as more sympathetic to the regime, was subsequently installed. The suspicious timing of Chief Justice Walter Onnoghen's suspension – barely a few weeks to the presidential election – raised widespread local[28] and international[29] concerns about democratic backsliding and attacks on judicial independence in Nigeria. After the re-election of the president was announced, an election petition was filed challenging his eligibility to contest for office and alleging pervasive electoral malfeasance. When the election petition wound its way up to the Supreme Court, presided over by the newly appointed Chief Justice, it was unanimously dismissed.[30]

Similarly, in Zimbabwe, the government's apprehensions about the political risks of independent electoral adjudication shaped pre-emptive measures against the courts. It is instructive that the judiciary, under the progressive leadership of Chief Justice Anthony Gubbay, had increasingly clashed with the Mugabe regime over its authoritarian character and repeated assaults on the rule of law (Karekwaivanane, 2017, 215–32; Roux, 2018, 193–228). In *Movement for Democratic Change v. Chinamasa*,[31] the Gubbay Supreme Court valiantly struck down a statutory instrument, enacted by the Mugabe regime, that purported to prohibit judicial determination of several pending parliamentary election petitions. Shortly after this landmark decision, the regime forced Chief Justice Gubbay out of office (Karekwaivanane, 2017, 231–2).[32] The Supreme Court was subsequently packed with partisan judges (Roux, 2018, 228–9), and the pending election petitions were never completely resolved (Solidarity Peace Trust, 2005, 5).[33]

How should African courts seek to resolve this adjudicatory dilemma? While the complex issues involved hardly admit of totalizing answers, there are cogent grounds for arguing that the capacity of courts to surmount political backlash against judicial activism in the electoral sphere will likely be conditioned by contextual factors such as the political context, legal culture, historical factors, and the existence of durable judicial support networks. The Malawian model, however, suggests that a major part of the survival strategy of an electoral court should include cohesive and coordinated responses by supportive stakeholders in civil society, the judicial system, and the legal profession.[34] Furthermore, in an increasingly globalized world, successful countermeasures against retaliatory backlash may also depend on the capacity of embattled courts to mobilize support from international pro-democracy partners. Conversely, judicial activism may prove unsustainable or less feasible in jurisdictions where courts are highly risk-averse. Similarly, when assertive decision-making in electoral causes is contested within the judiciary itself, or when stakeholders are unable to articulate principled and unified responses to political interference with the courts, activist electoral adjudication may be successfully suppressed.[35]

Courts and Core Democratic Institutions: The Case of Electoral Management Bodies

In response to patterns of democratic decline, courts can help open up juridical space for core democratic institutions, like electoral management bodies, to assert their independence with a view to strengthening the democratic process. As institutions vested with crucial functions of electoral administration, election management bodies are central to the consolidation of democratic governance and the development of credible electoral processes in transitional societies. Yet, as Omotola (2010) has rightly observed, the "weak institutionalization of core institutions in the governance of electoral processes" (p. 536) militates against democratization in such societies.[36] The need to facilitate institutional empowerment of electoral management bodies thus assumes practical significance (Jinadu, 1997; Maphunye, 2017).[37]

Courts may strategically utilize opportunities presented by election petitions to uphold constitutional provisions guaranteeing the institutional independence of electoral management bodies. Within the context of electoral dispute resolution, courts may also resolve complex legal issues; highlight defects in regulatory frameworks applicable to electoral bodies; and make recommendations for institutional reforms. Courts may also contribute to the institutional empowerment of electoral management bodies by safeguarding their jurisdictional spheres from encroachment by other politico-constitutional actors.

Facilitating Independence through Positive Intervention and Strategic Restraint

The case of *Amartey v Electoral Commission of Ghana* (2012)[38] provides a positive example of judicial invalidation of efforts to infringe on the functions of electoral management bodies. There, the Minister of Local Government encroached on the constitutional powers of the Electoral Commission to delineate electoral boundaries to be used for elections at the national and local government levels.[39] Subsequently, the plaintiff challenged certain subsidiary legal instruments that purported to confer jurisdiction on the minister to delimit electoral areas for municipalities, metropolises, and districts in the country. In a unanimous decision, the Supreme Court of Ghana held that the Electoral Commission could not be deprived, by subsidiary legislation enacted by the minister, of its constitutional authority to create electoral areas. The court thus preserved the scope of the commission's authority by declaring the impugned subsidiary enactments void and unconstitutional.

Beyond safeguarding the jurisdictional spheres of electoral management bodies, courts have also sought to facilitate the independence of such institutions through strategic non-intervention in the electoral process. The well-known South African case of *New National Party v. Government of the Republic of South Africa* (1999)[40] particularly exemplifies this adjudicatory approach. The appellant, the New National Party, challenged certain provisions of the Electoral Act that stipulated possession of some identification documents, to the exclusion of others, as preconditions for voter registration. The appellant further contended, inter alia, that the ANC-led South African government had taken several measures that compromised the impartiality and curtailed the independence of the Electoral Commission. Furthermore, the appellant averred that the views of the commission had been unduly side-lined in governmental decisions on critical issues of electoral administration, and that its operational efficiency was seriously hampered by inadequate funding.

Following an extensive consideration of the issues, the Constitutional Court found that, on the facts of the case, there had been no infringements on the independence of the Electoral Commission. However, the Constitutional Court strategically seized the opportunity to explicate the normative significance of constitutional provisions guaranteeing the financial and administrative autonomy of the Electoral Commission. Leveraging its powers of constitutional interpretation, the court also clarified the status of the Electoral Commission vis-à-vis other constitutional organs. To this end, the court observed that the Electoral Commission possessed substantial duties of electoral administration that were not "merely supervisory or monitoring" (para 76), but denoted an "active, involved and detailed management obligation over a wide terrain" (para 76).

Remarkably, the court affirmed that other constitutional organs possessed positive constitutional obligations to ensure the effectiveness, dignity, impartiality, and independence of the commission (para 78).[41] The practical implications of these obligations, the court reasoned, may require other constitutional actors to make adjustments in their institutional practices and operations in order to accommodate the interests of the commission (para 78). Against this backdrop, the court faulted the Minister of Finance and other government departments for generally failing to grasp the implications of the commission's autonomy, as well as its crucial role in the democratic system established by the post-apartheid legal order (para 100).

More pertinently, Langa DP held that the commission had demonstrated a sound awareness of its legal rights and interests in its dealings with constitutional actors and government departments concerning the disputes that formed the subject-matter of the case (para 107). Accordingly, the court saw "no reason to believe that the Commission will fail to take appropriate action to protect its interests, should it be necessary for it to do so" (para 106). It is also noteworthy that the court deferred to the commission's decision to opt for negotiation, as opposed to litigation, in resolving its disputes with governmental departments in the case. In this regard, the court noted that the commission was not merely a helpless institution requiring judicial protection, but had commendably "asserted its independence and impartiality" (para 104). Fowkes (2016) persuasively argues that the court's perceptive grasp of the peculiar dynamics of the case informed its decision not to recognize the New National Party's locus standi to seek judicial reliefs on the commission's behalf.[42] By reposing faith in the commission's capacity to determine appropriate methods for resolving the particular dispute in *New National Party*, the Constitutional Court's demonstrated, as Fowkes put it, that "[p]art of building institutions is letting them exercise their authority" (p. 69).

Insights from Recent Presidential Election Petitions

The relationship between courts and electoral management bodies has taken more complicated turns in the more recent African electoral jurisprudence as is apparent from the facts of *Odinga* (2017).[43] In the course of litigation, tensions arose between the Supreme Court of Kenya and the Independent Electoral and Boundaries Commission (IEBC), when the latter failed to comply with judicial orders to grant experts, appointed by the court, access to its ICT logs and servers for the purpose of verifying the petitioners' claims about a major breach of the IEBC's IT system. The majority decision of the Supreme Court famously decried the "contumacious disobedience" (para 280) displayed by IEBC officials and made adverse inferences against the electoral body concerning the particular facts in issue.

The court held that the IEBC bore the onus of establishing "that it had complied with the law in the conduct of the presidential election especially on the transmission of the presidential election results" (para 276) due to the fact that it "had the custody of the record of the elections" (para 276). In the circumstances, however, the court was satisfied that the IEBC had "failed to discharge that burden" (para 276). The Supreme Court further stated that the IEBC ought to have conceptualized the judicial order to permit scrutiny of the electoral technology system[44] as a valuable opportunity to assure aggrieved election candidates and the general public of its credibility and independence as an electoral management body (para 279).

Accordingly, the court found it worrisome that the "IEBC strenuously opposed the petitioners' application for access to its servers" (para 277) in circumstances that indicated a substantial misapprehension of the importance of independent and impartial electoral administration. In light of the flagrant disobedience of its orders, the court felt constrained to conclude that the IEBC officials had either unlawfully manipulated the electoral technology system themselves or exhibited considerable negligence in failing to protect the system from infiltration by third parties (para 280). Indeed, the violations of statutory provisions stipulating synchronized electronic transmission of election results, as well as other electoral principles enshrined in the Kenyan Constitution, formed a major part of the court's decision to invalidate the August 2017 presidential election (para 299). In the final analysis, there are good grounds for inferring that the Supreme Court conceptualized the conduct the IEBC officials in *Odinga* as indicative of a troubling disregard for its own role as major oversight institution in the Kenyan electoral process (para 299). However, it is doubtful whether conflictual interactions between courts and electoral management bodies, as exemplified by *Odinga*, will conduce to democratic consolidation in the long term.[45]

The recent case of *Mutharika v. Chakwera*[46] provides further insights into other potential loopholes in the relationship between courts and electoral management bodies. An important issue that arose in that case concerned the Malawi Electoral Commission's establishment of Constituency Tally Centres (CTCs) in the absence of express statutory authorization. From the facts of the case, stakeholders had designed the CTCs to transmit results to the National Tally Centre "in a bid to improve the conduct of the elections" (p. 60). Although the Supreme Court of Appeal conceded that the CTCs "were created to enhance operational efficiency,"[47] the court reasoned that they were nonetheless illegal. The court framed the CTCs as a usurpation of legislative authority to alter the organizational structures of the Malawian electoral system and held that the functions performed by the CTCs were unlawful "as no effectual delegation could have been made to an illegal entity" (p. 60).

Although this decision is defensible, there are good grounds for leveling alternative angles of critique beyond the court's legalistic framing of the issues. It is plausible to argue, for instance, that the CTCs raised interesting issues concerning rule adaptation – a significant feature of institutionalization – on the part of the MEC. Facilitating the institutional autonomy of electoral management bodies, in certain contexts, may involve affirming the competence of stakeholders, acting in good faith,[48] to adapt and modify organizational procedures in order to ensure more efficient electoral administration. While the *Chakwera* decision rightly underscores the need to ensure that electoral institutions operate within the parameters of applicable legal frameworks, it nonetheless raises critical questions concerning the margin of discretion available to such institutions.

Edificatory Roles – Disseminating Constitutional Norms and Democratic Values

In several African jurisdictions, presidential election petitions have generated considerable public interest in circumstances that often propelled courts to the center stage of national discourse.[49] In *Hakainde Hichilema v. Edgar Chagwa Lungu*,[50] the majority judgment of the Constitutional Court of Zambia controversially dismissed a petition brought by Hakainde Hichilema, a candidate in the 2016 presidential election, on the grounds that the prescribed timeline for hearing election petitions had lapsed.[51] In the circumstances, the petitioners had been unable to conclude their arguments within the constitutionally stipulated 14-day period for hearing election petitions in the Constitutional Court.[52]

In a trenchant dissenting judgment, Justice Munalula faulted the majority opinion for failing to adopt a purposive and holistic reading of the Zambian constitution.[53] Justice Munalula reasoned that, in failing to decide the petition on the merits, the court had missed an invaluable opportunity to edify the polity by affirming the cardinal principle of fair hearing enshrined in the constitution. "The issue of a presidential election petition," she declared, "is too heavy for a mechanical response by the Court and a well-reasoned decision would have helped to heal this nation" (p. 7).[54] Beyond its nebulous aspects – it is unclear how judicial review would have healed the polity – Justice Munalula's dictum nonetheless suggests that judicial resolution of electoral disputes may involve certain edificatory functions.

Edifying through Transparency: Open Justice in Presidential Election Petitions

Courts may perform edificatory functions, within the context of electoral dispute resolution, by disseminating democratic values and signaling the importance of constitutional norms. As such, courts may make positive contributions towards the promotion of democratic values by clarifying the normative content of citizens' rights of political participation, as well as the scope of the legal interests and obligations of other stakeholders in the electoral process. By the same token, courts can edify democratizing polities by foregrounding the need for peaceful resolution of electoral disputes through constitutional channels. Emerging trends in the African electoral jurisprudence indicate that municipal courts are already articulating and performing certain edificatory roles in the course of determining presidential election petitions.

In some recent cases, courts have signaled the importance of transparency as year a tenet of democratic governance by thematizing the normative relationship between open justice, judicial transparency, and electoral dispute resolution. This was encapsulated by the decision of Ghana's former Chief Justice, Georgina Wood, to permit live radio and television broadcasts of the proceedings of the country's historic presidential election petition in 2013. The live broadcasts of judicial proceedings in *Akufo-Addo & Ors v. Mahama & Anor*[55] were unprecedented in Ghana at the time,[56] and they served to underscore the significance of normative values of probity and accountability enshrined in the Ghanaian constitutional order.

The example set by the Ghanaian Supreme Court in *Akufo-Addo*, concerning the role of transparency as a democratic adjudicatory practice, served as a precursor to similar approaches in other jurisdictions. Thus, in *Chamisa v. Mnangagwa*,[57] the Constitutional Court of Zimbabwe extensively considered the normative significance of judicial decisions to permit live streaming of courts proceedings in its recent judgment on the 2018 presidential election petition. The applicant, Nelson Chamisa, had petitioned the Constitutional Court for judicial orders to, inter alia, invalidate the presidential election results announced by the Zimbabwe Electoral Commission and set aside the declaration of Emerson Mnangagwa as the President of the Republic of Zimbabwe. Although the court ultimately dismissed the application, it strove to clarify the relationship between transparency and electoral justice, treating this issue as an important preliminary matter in its reasoned decision.

Accordingly, the court noted that objections to live broadcasts of judicial proceedings could be anchored on justifiable concerns about the risks of sensationalism and populism in the judicial system. In this respect, the court observed that such broadcasts could unduly sensationalize court proceedings and reduce them to the level of "media circuses," thereby diminishing the solemnity of the judicial process.[58] On the other hand, live broadcasts could also undermine principled judicial decision-making; inject populist considerations into judicial reasoning; and incentivize judges to pander to the vagaries of public opinion.[59]

Following a detailed discussion of the issues, the court held that "the principle of transparency" was "the overriding consideration" in its decision to adopt televised recordings of the proceedings of the presidential election petition.[60] According to the court, transparent proceedings could be justified by reference to two alternative analytical paradigms. On the one hand, such proceedings served to promote public confidence in the judicial process as well as incarnate constitutional values such as "transparency, accountability, responsiveness and justice."[61] Alternatively, transparent adjudicatory procedures could be justified on the basis of rights-based arguments that foreground the rights to freedom of expression and freedom of the media, as well as the rights of access to information and access to justice.[62] By conceptualizing judicial power as a form of constitutional authority ultimately "derived from the people,"[63] the court pointed out that a rights-based approach accentuated the role of judicial accountability in democratic societies.

Against this backdrop, the court concluded that the live broadcasts were justified in the interests of justice given that the presidential election petition, as a matter of utmost constitutional significance, raised polycentric issues implicating the rights of all citizens to a credible electoral process. As Malaba CJ put it:

> Once it is accepted that the proceedings before the Court were not only limited to the parties' interests but extended to those of all citizens to a free, fair and credible Presidential election, it is clear that it was in the interests of justice to allow the live streaming through national television of the proceedings. Members of the public had an interest in having knowledge of the evidence produced by the disputants. They had an interest in witnessing how the Court handled the matter and what decision it reached. They had an interest in deciding whether, in their own objective assessment, the decision of the Court was fair and just.[64]

Election Petitions and the Uses of Judicial Transparency

These recent decisions seem to indicate an emerging norm of adjudicatory transparency in the African electoral jurisprudence. Significantly, invocations of open justice in *Akufo* and *Chamisa* rest on underlying normative assumptions that link transparency to other democratic values such as accountability, public trust, and civic engagement.

First, transparent adjudicatory practices may be conceptualized as fulfilling crucial accountability functions in transitional societies characterized by diminished public confidence in governmental institutions.[65] As Dikgang Moseneke (2018), former Deputy Chief Justice of South Africa cogently observed, albeit in a non-electoral context, open justice in transitional societies can powerfully symbolize a juridical rupture with a repressive political order characterized by governmental secrecy and impunity.[66] By opening up judicial proceedings to public scrutiny, courts in transitional societies therefore signal a willingness to be held accountable in ways that affirm the significance of constitutional values enshrined in the democratic legal order.[67]

The public scrutiny facilitated by transparent judicial proceedings also furthers judicial accountability by providing a basis for courts to clarify the appropriate boundaries of judicial authority in a democratic system of government. Alluding to the widespread interest that the court proceedings in *Akufo-Addo* had generated among the Ghanaian public, Akoto-Bamfo JSC noted that it was the "preserve of the citizens" as opposed to the courts, "to determine who occupies the highest office of the land."[68] While recognizing the role of "effective judicial oversight" in guaranteeing a credible electoral process, she nonetheless emphasized the need for electoral adjudication to uphold the genuine democratic will of the citizenry.[69] The Zimbabwean Constitutional Court echoed similar normative concerns about judicial accountability in *Chamisa* when it suggested that the live broadcasts adopted during the proceedings enabled the public to make independent and informed evaluations about the fairness of its decision in the presidential election dispute.[70] As such, the cases signal the notion that disclosing the form and content of judicial decision-making, in the volatile context of electoral adjudication, may render courts more accountable to the public.

Second, the resort to transparent judicial procedures also aims at building public trust in the judicial system and electoral process. Presidential election petitions, arising from events that generate considerable national attention, provide courts with strategic opportunities to present themselves to the public as impartial and independent arbiters deserving of public confidence. According to Birchall (2011),[71] institutions may be incentivized to adopt transparent procedures in some cases in order to accrue "transparency capital" given that "[t]ransparency has become a sign of cultural (as well as moral) authority" (p. 8–9). In this respect, transparency practices may be constitutive of the legitimacy of a given institution and the respect its decisions enjoy. In *Chamisa*,[72] for instance, the Constitutional Court symbolically positioned itself as a transparent institution earlier on during the proceedings by permitting the live broadcasts. In its subsequent reasoned judgement, the court strenuously sought to justify its decision to dismiss the petition as an impartial and objective verdict. Courts have thus instrumentalized transparency in order to construct institutional legitimacy, articulate moral claims to constitutional authority, and encourage public confidence in legal channels for resolving electoral disputes.

Third, courts have adopted transparent adjudicatory practices in order to promote civic engagement as a democratic value. Recent scholarship on popular reactions to the 2012 presidential election petition in Ghana, indicates considerable civic engagement with the judicial determination of the electoral dispute in *Akufo-Addo*. According to Atengble (2014),[73] the transparency that characterized the Supreme Court hearings catalyzed broad civic engagement with the electoral process. As such, remarkable events, personalities, and idioms from the court proceedings formed the basis of narratives that both circulated widely within social media platforms and permeated public discourse in Ghana.[74]

Other commentators have argued that judicial transparency in *Akufo-Addo* facilitated "greater democratic learning among the population" (Bob-Milliar & Paller, 2018, 16)[75] by creating public awareness about the workings of electoral and judicial processes in the country (Aggrey-Darkoh & Asah-Asante, 2017, 141).[76] The idea is that courts may edify democratizing polities by promoting a sense of inclusion in processes of electoral dispute resolution.

The Limits of Adjudicatory Transparency

Whilst upholding open justice in electoral cases, courts should, however, avoid overestimating the practical value of judicial transparency within the context of a broader project of democratic consolidation. First, courts may need to acknowledge that the assumption of edificatory roles in election petition cases may also imply corresponding obligations to render judicial decisions and proceedings in more intelligible forms.[77] This issue maps on to questions of constitutional literacy in the African context. In this respect, constitutional literacy refers to the capacity of citizens to effectively grasp the meaning, implications, and normative content of their rights, freedoms, and obligations within the context of a constitutional democracy (Fombad, 2019, 2).[78] Constitutionally literate citizens would, therefore, exhibit better proficiency in the register of rights and obligations that inform the status of citizenship in genuinely democratic societies. Transparent adjudicatory practices may thus have to be wedded to cognate normative projects of constitutional literacy in order to produce more tangible and sustainable results.[79]

Second, courts may need to recognize that there are hardly fixed causal relationships between transparency and institutional legitimacy that may entitle institutions deploying transparent procedures to assume that their decisions will routinely enjoy legitimacy and respect. As transparency scholars, such as Roelofs (2019) remind us, "transparency and its effects on trust are fluid, constructed, and context specific" (p. 566).[80] Indeed, the pathways linking legitimacy and transparency are often circuitous, rather than rectilinear (Adams, 2020, 3–5).[81] Thematizing the contextual effects of transparency thus provides a sound basis to account for differences in outcome in the jurisdictions where electoral courts have deployed transparent adjudicatory practices. Again, Ghana and Zimbabwe make for an interesting contrast in this regard.

There is broad consensus in the scholarly discourse on democratization in Africa that Ghana witnessed a progressive institutionalization of the tenets of democratic governance in the wake of its transition from military rule in the early 1990s.[82] Accordingly, the restoration of democracy led to greater respect for the rule of law and other constitutional norms. By the same token, the scope of judicial independence in post-authoritarian Ghana expanded due to the convergence of several factors. These included the formal empowerment of the judiciary by the 1992 Constitution; the evolution of a political milieu more favorable to the exercise of judicial power; and the agency of individual judicial actors who adopted assertive approaches in defense of human rights and other democratic values in politically salient cases (Quashigah, 2016).[83]

Progressive democratic consolidation was, however, endangered in the aftermath of the 2012 presidential election, which proved to be one of the most contentious electoral contests of the Fourth Republic.[84] After John Mahama was returned as president, opposition groups vehemently rejected the election results declared by the Electoral Commission. Nana Akufo-Addo, the leading opposition politician, petitioned the Supreme Court, alleging a raft of electoral malpractices including incidents of voting in illegal polling centers; widespread cases of unverified and ineligible voters; over-voting (in which total votes cast exceeded the number of registered voters at certain polling stations); and the announcement of results unattested by presiding officers. The volatile circumstances that formed the background of the *Akufo-Addo* petition thus amounted to a "democratic rupture" (Bob-Millar & Paller, 2018) defined as "an infraction in the democratization process during competitive elections that has the potential to cause a constitutional crisis" (p. 8).[85]

However, several scholars have argued that the Supreme Court's authoritative intervention in this electoral dispute facilitated democratic renewal in the country (Adams & Asante, 2020)[86] by underscoring the importance of peaceful resolution of political conflicts (Owusu-Mensah & Rice, 2018).[87] Furthermore, as Bob-Milliar and Paller (2018)[88] have also contended, the transparency that characterized judicial proceedings in *Akufo-Addo* inspired institutional reforms by uncovering deficiencies in the electoral process. Judicial transparency also enlightened the citizenry by democratizing access to information about the workings of electoral and judicial processes in the country. Although the Supreme Court ultimately dismissed the election petition, by a 5-4 majority decision, its legitimacy within the Ghanaian political process was, nonetheless, consolidated when Nana Akufo-Addo, the unsuccessful petitioner, publicly declared his acceptance of the adverse verdict.[89]

Another positive outcome of adjudicatory transparency in *Akufo-Addo* was that it helped motivate opposition political parties to hone their organizational structures in a bid to improve their performance in future electoral cycles (Oppong, 2016).[90] It is noteworthy, in this regard, that Nana Akufo-Addo, the unsuccessful petitioner, subsequently won the 2016 presidential election in a peaceful electoral contest that is widely regarded as having deepened Ghanaian democracy.[91] The Ghanaian experience would then suggest that in some jurisdictions where meaningful progress towards democratization has already occurred – and where judicial institutions enjoy political legitimacy and possess a track record of independent decision-making – courts may, nonetheless, fulfill important edificatory functions, even when they do not directly overturn the results of impugned elections.

Conversely, in Zimbabwe, where judicial independence has been more checkered in recent times,[92] the Constitutional Court's decision to dismiss the petition in *Chamisa* was pointedly rejected by the opposition (Krönke, 2018, 1).[93] More so, there is little indication that the resort to transparent adjudicatory procedures significantly raised public confidence in the judiciary (Mwonzora & Xaba, 2020, 11–3).[94] Beyond affirming judicial transparency, certain aspects of the court's decision were also controversial. For instance, the court failed to accord fair consideration to some of the applicant's normative concerns about the lack of independence of the Zimbabwean Electoral Commission, as well as the disproportionate access to media coverage enjoyed by the incumbent president during the electioneering campaign.[95]

To this extent, it appears that the court failed to appreciate that judicial institutions can help open up space for marginalized groups to inscribe counternarratives in the legal archive of a country's democratic struggle (Karekwaivanane, 2017, 237) – even in jurisdictions where the political context is unfavorable to intrepid displays of judicial independence in highly charged election petitions. As such, the criticism that the judiciary lacks real autonomy in politically salient cases and disputes implicating the core interests of the regime is not unjustified (Magaisa, 2019).[96] Thus, there are good grounds for arguing that adjudicatory transparency in election petitions may not always compensate for flaws in the substantive judicial decision itself.

Conclusion

Building on insights derived from comparative African electoral jurisprudence, this chapter thematized and discussed three key normative roles courts can play within electoral processes. As such, courts may leverage judicial power as a remedial mechanism against the onslaught of election malpractices by invalidating flawed elections and defending the integrity of the electoral process. Through positive intervention in the electoral process, as well as by strategic judicial restraint, courts may also facilitate the institutional empowerment and independence of core democratic institutions like electoral management bodies. Finally, courts can contribute towards democratic renewal and consolidation by signaling the importance of constitutional values and democratic norms. However, the capacity of African electoral courts to meaningfully discharge the aforementioned normative functions is conditioned by the complex interaction between the structural contexts in which courts in various jurisdictions are embedded, as well as by the agency of judicial actors themselves.

Notes

1 Electoral Decree No. 73 of 1977 (as amended), s 34A (1) (c) (i)–(ii).
2 *Obafemi Awolowo v. Shehu Shagari & Ors* (1979) 6-9 SC 51-152. The petitioner, Obafemi Awolowo, contended, inter alia, that Shehu Shagari had not been lawfully elected as president, and that on a correct interpretation of the electoral laws, two-thirds of 19 states was 13 states. On the petitioner's averment, the 13 state had to be regarded as a whole entity and could not be fractionalized for the purpose of determining the results of the presidential election. See also Peter Koehn, "Prelude to Civilian Rule: the Nigerian Elections of 1979" (1981), Africa Today, 28(1), 17, 42–5; Surinder S. Boparai, *Chief Awolowo v. Alhaji Shagari* (1981), "Verfassung und Recht in Übersee/Law and Politics in Africa," Asia and Latin America, 14(4), 387–99; James S. Read, *Awolowo v. Shagari and Others* (1979), Journal of African Law, 23(2), 175–82.
3 *Obafemi Awolowo v. Shehu Shagari & Ors* (1979) 6-9 SC 51-152.
4 See *Lakanmi v. Attorney-General (West) & Ors.* (1970) 6 NSCC 143: Where the Supreme Court boldly asserted judicial power to strike down decrees and other legislative enactments of the military regime, and the Federal Military Government (Supremacy and Enforcement of Powers) Decree No. 28 of 1970 (in which the regime retaliated by abrogating the *Lakanmi* decision). For the background to these developments, see Nwabueze, B. *A Constitutional History of Nigeria* (1982), London: C. Hurst & Co, pp. 170–5.
5 *Obafemi Awolowo v. Shehu Shagari & Ors* (1979) 6-9 SC, 51-72.
6 *Obafemi Awolowo v. Shehu Shagari & Ors* (1979) 6-9 SC, 68-69.
7 *Obafemi Awolowo v. Shehu Shagari & Ors* (1979) 6-9 SC, 110.
8 Nwabueze, B. *The Presidential Constitution of Nigeria* (1982), New York: St. Martin's Press; M. Olu Adediran "*Awolowo v. Shagari* – A Case of Compromise Between Law and Political Expediency" (1982), Journal of the Indian Law Institute, 24(1), 41–56.
9 M. Olu Adediran "*Awolowo v. Shagari* – A Case of Compromise Between Law and Political Expediency" (1982), Journal of the Indian Law Institute, 24(1), 70, where the majority opinion affirmed, obiter, that the substantial effects doctrine could have served as an alternative basis for its decision to dismiss the appeal.
10 O'Brien Kaaba (2015), "The Challenges of Adjudicating Presidential Election Disputes in Domestic Courts in Africa," African Human Rights Law Journal, 15, 329; Miriam Azu (2015); "Lessons from Ghana and Kenya on why Presidential Election Petitions Usually Fail," African Human Rights Law Journal, 15, 150; Pal Ahluwalia (2017), "The Saga of the 2017 Kenyan Elections: Can They Really Be Free and Fair?" African Identities, 15(4), 351.
11 O'Brien Kaaba (2015), "The Challenges of Adjudicating Presidential Election Disputes in Domestic Courts in Africa," African Human Rights Law Journal, 329, 343–5; H. Nyane (2019), "The Role of Judiciaries in Presidential Electoral Disputes Resolution in Africa: The Cases of Zambia and Zimbabwe," Fourth Annual International Conference on Public Administration and Development Alternatives (IPADA), 11–9. Available at http://ulspace.ul.ac.za/handle/10386/2687.
12 See *Peter Mutharika & Electoral Commission v. Lazarus Chakwera & Saulos Chilima* (MSCA Constitutional Appeal No. 1 of 2020) [2020] MWSC 1 (May 8, 2020), 77–92: for a discussion of quantitative and qualitative standards of validity and their recent application in comparative African electoral jurisprudence. Available at https://malawilii.org/system/files/judgment/supreme-court-appeal/2020/1/Prof%20Arthur%20Peter% 20Mutharika%20and%20Electoral%20Commission%20Vs%20Dr%20Saulos%20K%20Chilima%20and%20Dr%20Lazarus%20M%20Chakwera%20MSCA%20Constitutional%20Appeal%20No%2001%20of%202020.pdf.
13 *Obafemi Awolowo v. Shehu Shagari & Ors* (1979) 6-9 SC, 111.
14 Fred Sekindi (2017), "Presidential Election Disputes in Uganda: A Critical Analysis of the Supreme Court Decisions," Journal of African Elections, 16(1), 154–79; Lydia A. Nkansah (2016), "Dispute Resolution and Electoral Justice in Africa: The Way Forward, Africa Development," 41(2), 97, 117;

O'Brien Kaaba (2015), "The Challenges of Adjudicating Presidential Election Disputes in Domestic Courts in Africa," African Human Rights Law Journal, 329, 345–9.

15 [2017] eKLR Presidential Petition 1 of 2017. Available at http://kenyalaw.org/caselaw/cases/view/140716/.

16 It is noteworthy that the disjunctive wording of section 83 of the Elections Act provided a cogent statutory basis for this aspect of the majority decision. See also Harrison Otieno (October 18, 2017), The Fulcrum for the Invalidation of Kenya's 2017 Presidential Election: Section 83 of the Elections Act, OxHRH Blog. Available at https://ohrh.law.ox.ac.uk/the-fulcrum-for-the-invalidation-of-kenyas-2017-presidential-election-section-83-of-the-elections-act/

17 [2020] MWSC 1 (May 8, 2020). Available at https://malawilii.org/system/files/judgment/supreme-court-appeal/2020/1/Prof%20Arthur%20Peter%20Mutharika%20and%20Electoral%20Commission%20Vs%20Dr%20Saulos%20K%20Chilima%20and%20Dr%20Lazarus%20M%20Chakwera%20MSCA%20Constitutional%20Appeal%20No%2001%20of%202020.pdf.

18 Olabisi D. Akinkugbe & James T. Gathii (2020), "Judicial Nullification of Presidential Elections in Africa: Peter Mutharika v. Lazarus Chakera and Saulos Chilima in Context," 1, 4. https://papers.ssrn.com/sol3/papers.cfm?abstract_id=3642709; see also George H. Karekwaivanane (2017), *The Struggle Over State Power in Zimbabwe: Law and Politics Since 1950* (Cambridge: Cambridge University Press), 224–5.

19 Al Jazeera (June 17, 2020), "Malawi Lawyers Protest Chief Justice's Pre-Vote Forced Retirement." https://www.aljazeera.com/news/2020/6/17/malawi-lawyers-protest-chief-justices-pre-vote-forced-retirement.

20 Duncan Okubasu (2018), "Kenya: The State of Liberal Democracy" in R. Albert et al (eds.), *2017 Global Review of Constitutional Law*, (I.CONnect & The Clough Center, 2018), 166–71.

21 Michael Amoah (2020), "Sleight is Right: Cyber Control as a New Battleground for African Elections," African Affairs, 119(474), 68–89.

22 Charles Pensulo (June 16, 2020), "Forced Retirement of Malawi's Chief Justice Before June Election Blocked," The Guardian. www.theguardian.com/global-development/2020/jun/16/forced-retirement-of-malawis-chief-justice-before-june-election-blocked.

23 The regime's attempt to force Chief Justice Andrew Nyirenda into early retirement was firmly resisted by the Malawi Law Society. See Owen Khamula (June 14, 2020), "Malawi Law Society Slams Muhara Over Forcing Chief Justice to Retire: Assault on Judiciary," Nyasa Times. www.nyasatimes.com/malawi-law-society-slams-muhara-over-forcing-chief-justice-to-retire-assault-on-judiciary/.

24 See *State obo HRDC and Others v. President of Malawi and Others* (Judicial Review Case Number 33 of 2020) [2020] MWHC 26 (August 27, 2020). https://malawilii.org/mw/judgment/high-court-general-division/2020/26.

25 Wanga Gwede (June 28, 2020), "Chakwera Describes His Election as a 'Win for Malawi, Democracy and Justice,'" Nyasa Times. www.nyasatimes.com/chakwera-describes-his-election-as-a-win-for-malawi-democracy-and-justice/.

26 Ed Cropley (October 31, 2017), "Exclusive: Kenyan Supreme Court Judges Denied Extra Security After Shooting," Reuters. www.reuters.com/article/us-kenya-election-judges-exclusive/exclusive-kenyan-supreme-court-judges-denied-extra-security-after-shooting-source-idUSKBN1D02LO.

27 BBC News (January 26, 2019), "Nigerian Chief Justice's Suspension Raises International Concerns." https://www.bbc.com/news/world-africa-47015698.

28 The Nigerian Bar Association (NBA), in a public statement, denounced the suspension of Chief Justice Onnoghen as both an "attempted coup against the Nigerian Judiciary and evident suspension of the Nigerian Constitution by the Executive arm of the Federal Government"; See Evelyn Okakwu (January 25, 2019), "Onnoghen's suspension coup against judiciary, unacceptable," NBA, Premium Times. www.premiumtimesng.com/news/headlines/308039-onnoghens-suspension-coup-against-judiciary-unacceptable-nba.html.

29 Commonwealth Lawyers Association (CLA) (January 28, 2019), "Joint Statement on the Chief Justice of Nigeria." www.commonwealthlawyers.com/statement/cla-joint-statement-on-the-chief-justice-of-nigeria/.

30 *Atiku Abubakar v. Independent National Electoral Commission* [2020] 12 NWLR (Part 1737), 37.

31 SC. 7/2001 Const. Application No. 383/2000.

32 See also Human Rights Watch (2008), "A Compromised Judiciary." www.hrw.org/reports/2008/zimbabwe1108/5.htm.

33 Solidarity Peace Trust (March 2005), "The Role of the Judiciary in Denying the Will of the Zimbabwean Electorate since 2000," http://solidaritypeacetrust.org/download/report-files/subverting_justice.pdf;

Theunis Roux (2018), "The Politico-Legal Dynamics of Judicial Review: A Comparative Analysis," Cambridge: Cambridge University Press, 2018, 230.

34 Al Jazeera (June 17, 2020), "Malawi Lawyers Protest Chief Justice's Pre-Vote Forced Retirement." www.aljazeera.com/news/2020/6/17/malawi-lawyers-protest-chief-justices-pre-vote-forced-retirement. See also the joint public statement issued by several international legal scholars in defense of judicial independence in Malawi: (June 15, 2020) "World's Law Professors and Academics Condemn Executive Assault on Malawi Judiciary," Nyasa Times. www.nyasatimes.com/worlds-law-professors-and-academics-condemn-executive-assault-on-malawi-judiciary/.

35 In contrast to the Malawian courts, the Supreme Court of Kenya did not reach a unanimous decision to nullify the August 2017 election. It is also noteworthy that the Nigerian legal profession failed to organize a sustained and cohesive opposition to the unconstitutional suspension of Chief Justice Onnoghen. Furthermore, attempts by the leadership of the Nigerian Bar Association (NBA) to organize a nationwide boycott of the courts in protest against the suspension were resisted by some lawyers. See Halima Yahaya (January 29, 2019), "Onnoghen: Why we ignored NBA Boycott Order – Nigerian Lawyers," Premium Times. www.premiumtimesng.com/news/top-news/308730-onnoghen-why-we-ignored-nba-boycott-order-nigerian-lawyers.html.

36 J. Shola Omotola (2013), "Elections and Democratic Transition in Nigeria Under the Fourth Republic (2010)," African Affairs, 109(437), 535–53.

37 Adele L. Jinadu (1997), "Matters Arising: African Elections and The Problem of Electoral Administration," African Journal of Political Science, 2(1), 1–11; Kealeboga J. Maphunye (2017), "Straining Without Training? Capacity-Related Problems Facing African Election Executives and Officials," International Journal of African Renaissance Studies – Multi-, Inter- and Trans-disciplinarity, 12(1), 55–75.

38 (J1/25/2012) [2012] GHASC 48; https://ghalii.org/gh/judgment/supreme-court/2012/48.

39 1992 Constitution of Ghana, Art 45(b).

40 1999 5 BCLR 489 (CC); www.saflii.org/za/cases/ZACC/1999/5.html.

41 1999 5 BCLR 489 (CC); www.saflii.org/za/cases/ZACC/1999/5.html.

42 James Fowkes (2016), *Building the Constitution: The Practice of Constitutional Interpretation in Post-Apartheid South Africa*, Cambridge University Press, 2016, 68–70.

43 [2017] eKLR Presidential Petition 1 of 2017; http://kenyalaw.org/caselaw/cases/view/140716/.

44 The controversy touched on s 39(1)(c) of the Elections Act, which imposed obligations on the IEBC to ensure, inter alia, electronic transmission, in the prescribed form, of tabulated results of the presidential election.

45 Courts and electoral management bodies will need to demonstrate a more acute awareness of their respective roles as institutional stakeholders and team-players engaged in a collaborative – as opposed to conflictual – project of enhancing the credibility of the electoral process.

46 (MSCA Constitutional Appeal No. 1 of 2020) [2020] MWSC 1 (May 8, 2020).

47 (MSCA Constitutional Appeal No. 1 of 2020) [2020] MWSC 1 (May 8, 2020).

48 The court could, perhaps, have recommended that future electoral law reform efforts should take the viewpoints of Malawian electoral officials and stakeholders into greater consideration with a view to creating more efficient structures and procedures of electoral administration.

49 For instance, see the apt observation of Adinyira JSC noting, with respect to Ghana's contested 2012 presidential election, that elections implicate the rights of political participation of the citizenry, and as such the election petition "arising out of the exercise of those rights, has caught the imagination of all Ghanaians." *Akufo Addo v. Mahama* [2013] (J1/6/2013) GHASC (August 29, 2013) at p. 570. https://ghalii.org/gh/judgment/supreme-court/2013/5.

50 (2016/CC/0031) [2016] ZMCC 4 (September 5, 2016). https://zambialii.org/node/12445.

51 (2016/CC/0031) Ruling No. 33 of 2016 at pp. 1217–8. https://zambialii.org/zm/judgment/2016//election-petition-majority-ruling.pdf.

52 (2016/CC/0031) Ruling No. 33 of 2016 at pp. 1217–8. https://zambialii.org/zm/judgment/2016//election-petition-majority-ruling.pdf. See also Dunia P. Zongwe (2017), "*Hichilema and Another v. Lungu and Another* (2016/CC/0031) [2016] ZMCC 4 (September 5, 2016)," Minority Judgement, SAIPAR Case Review, 1(1), 19–26.

53 (2016/CC/0031) 1-8; https://zambialii.org/zm/judgment/2016//election-petition-dissenting-munalula.pdf.

54 (2016/CC/0031) 1-8; https://zambialii.org/zm/judgment/2016//election-petition-dissenting-munalula.pdf.

55 [2013] (J1/6/2013) GHASC (August 29, 2013). https://ghalii.org/gh/judgment/supreme-court/2013/5. The petition was filed following the declaration of John Mahama as winner of the December 2012 election. The petition, brought pursuant to Art 64(1) of the 1992 Constitution, marked the first presidential election petition since the restoration of democratic government in Ghana in 1993.

56 [2013] (J1/6/2013) GHASC (August 29, 2013), p. 123: "The Court began taking evidence on 17 April 2013 with live television and radio broadcast which was unprecedented."

57 Judgment No. CCZ 21/19 Constitutional Application No. CCZ 42/18; www.veritaszim.net/sites/veritas_d/files/Nelson%20Chamisa%20and%2024%20Ors%20v%20Emmerson%20Mnangagwa.pdf. The petition was brought pursuant to s. 93(1) of the Constitution of Zimbabwe Amendment (No. 20) 2013.

58 Judgment No. CCZ 21/19 (Constitutional Application No. CCZ 42/18) at p. 9.

59 Judgment No. CCZ 21/19 (Constitutional Application No. CCZ 42/18) at p. 9.

60 Judgment No. CCZ 21/19 (Constitutional Application No. CCZ 42/18) at p. 10.

61 Judgment No. CCZ 21/19 (Constitutional Application No. CCZ 42/18) at p. 3.

62 Judgment No. CCZ 21/19 (Constitutional Application No. CCZ 42/18) at p. 7; the court formulated the issue in terms of facilitating "easy access to justice."

63 Judgment No. CCZ 21/19 (Constitutional Application No. CCZ 42/18) at p. 7.

64 Judgment No. CCZ 21/19 (Constitutional Application No. CCZ 42/18) at p. 13.

65 Dikgang Moseneke (2018), "The Courtroom as TV Studio: The Case of the Oscar Pistorious Trial," International Journal of Law in Context, 14, 493, 495-496.

66 Dikgang Moseneke (2018), "The Courtroom as TV Studio: The Case of the Oscar Pistorious Trial," International Journal of Law in Context, 14, 493, 495–6.

67 Dikgang Moseneke (2018), "The Courtroom as TV Studio: The Case of the Oscar Pistorious Trial," International Journal of Law in Context, 14, 493, 495–6.

68 *Akufo Addo v. Mahama* [2013] (J1/6/2013) GHASC (August 29, 2013) at p. 570.

69 *Akufo Addo v. Mahama* [2013] (J1/6/2013) GHASC (August 29, 2013) at p. 570.

70 Judgment No. CCZ 21/19 (Constitutional Application No. CCZ 42/18) at p. 13.

71 Clare Birchall (2011), "Introduction to 'Secrecy and Transparency': The Politics of Opacity and Openness," Theory, Culture & Society, 28(7), 7–25.

72 Judgment No. CCZ 21/19 (Constitutional Application No. CCZ 42/18).

73 Kirchuffs Atengble (2014), "Social Media and Ghana's 2012 Election Petition: A Discussion," Advances in Journalism and Communication, 2(3), 121–6.

74 Kirchuffs Atengble (2014), "Social Media and Ghana's 2012 Election Petition: A Discussion," Advances in Journalism and Communication, 2(3), 122–3.

75 George M. Bob-Milliar & Jeffrey W. Paller (2018), "Democratic Ruptures and Electoral Outcomes in Africa: Ghana's 2016 Election," Africa Spectrum, 53(1), 5–35.

76 Evans Aggrey-Darkoh & Kwame Asah-Asante (2017), "Supreme Court Ruling on 2012 Electoral Dispute in Ghana: A Recipe for Chaos or Deepening of Ghana's Democracy?" in B. E. Asare & A. K. D. Frempong (eds.), Selected Issues in Ghana's Democracy Vol. 1 (Tema: Digibooks Ghana Ltd., 2017).

77 Cf. Joseph Goldstein (1992), *The Intelligible Constitution*, Oxford: Oxford University Press, 1992, Ch. 6, particularly p. 112–4. Goldstein makes an extensive normative case, inter alia, for rendering judicial decisions more accessible and intelligible to non-specialist audiences and groups in the US context. However, as normative values, accessibility and intelligibility are also of acute importance in emerging democracies and transitional societies.

78 Charles Manga Fombad (2019), "Constitutional Literacy in Africa: Challenges and Prospects," Commonwealth Law Bulletin, 44(3), 492.

79 Even in jurisdictions like Ghana, where the role of electoral courts in signaling democratic values is relatively more established, the jargon and prolixity that characterizes judicial decisions may render them largely unintelligible and inaccessible to few outside the legal profession. Commentators like Fombad [(2019), "Constitutional Literacy in Africa: Challenges and Prospects," Commonwealth Law Bulletin, 44(3), 492] have argued, in another context, that African countries should recognize a constitutional right to constitutional literacy, which would impose positive obligations on governmental actors to establish, inter alia, civic education programs and cognate public enlightenment schemes.

80 Portia Roelofs, (2019). "Transparency and Mistrust: Who or What Should be Made Transparent?", Governance, 32(3), 565–80.

81 Rachel Adams (2020), *Transparency – New Trajectories in Law* (Oxford: Routledge), 3–5.

82 Richard Asante (2020), "Democratic Civil-Military Bargain: Examining the Ghanaian Experience," Civil Wars, 22(2–3), 333–52; Peter Arthur (2010), „Democratic Consolidation in Ghana: The Role and Contribution ofThe Media, Civil Society and State Institutions," Commonwealth & Comparative Politics, 48(2), 203–26; Sarah Brierley & George Ofosu (2014), "The Presidential and Parliamentary Elections in Ghana, December 2012," Electoral Studies, 35, 382–5. This narrative, however, is by no means uncontested. For alternative accounts, see Abdulai, A., & Crawford, G. (2010), "Consolidating Democracy in Ghana: Progress and Prospects?," Democratization, 17 (1), 26–7.
83 Kofi Quashigah (2016), "Defying Assumptions About the Nature of Power Relations Between the Executive and Judiciary: An Overview of Approaches to Judicial and Executive Relations in Ghana" in C. Fombad (ed.), Separation of Powers in African Constitutionalism, Oxford: Oxford University Press, 2016, 226–38.
84 J. Shola Omotola (2013), "The Election Commission of Ghana and the Administration of the 2012 Elections," Journal of African Elections, 12(2), 34–55.
85 George M. Bob-Milliar & Jeffrey W. Paller (2018), "Democratic Ruptures and Electoral Outcomes in Africa: Ghana's 2016 Election," Africa Spectrum, 53(1), 5–35.
86 W. Asante & E. B. Asare (2016), "Ghana's 2012 Election Petition and its Outcome: A Giant Leap Towards Democratic Consolidation," Journal of Political Sciences & Public Affairs, 4(1), 5.
87 Isaac Owusu-Mensah & Joanna Rice (2018), "The Judiciary and Democracy in Ghana's Fourth Republic," Journal of African Elections, 17(2), 44–65.
88 Supra (n 68).
89 Chrispin Mwakideu (August 29, 2013), "Ghana's Supreme Court upholds election result," Deutsche Welle. www.dw.com/en/ghanas-supreme-court-upholds-election-result/a-17054771.
90 Nelson Oppong (December 21, 2016), "Ghana's 2016 Election Results: The Story of a Presidential Petition," ROAPE Blog. https://roape.net/2016/12/21/ghanas-2016-election-results-story-presidential-petition/. See also, Anon (October 18, 2017), "President Akufo-Addo Commends Mrs. Wood for Restoring Confidence in Judiciary," Ghana Broadcasting Corporation. www.gbcghana.com/1.11143482.
91 Nic Cheesman et al. (2017), "Ghana: The Ebbing Power of Incumbency," Journal of Democracy, 28(2), 92–104; see also George M. Bob-Milliar & Jeffrey W. Paller (2018), "Democratic Ruptures and Electoral Outcomes in Africa: Ghana's 2016 Election," Africa Spectrum, 53(1), 9.
92 See Solidarity Peace Trust (2005), "The Role of the Judiciary in Denying the Will of the Zimbabwean Electorate Since 2000;" Anthony R. Gubbay (2009), "The Progressive Erosion of the Rule of Law in Independent Zimbabwe," Bar of England and Wales Third International Rule of Law Lecture (London). www.barcouncil.org.uk/uploads/assets/73146293-cc62-4a62-b1c697d378f8464e/The-progressive-erosion-of-the-Rule-of-Law-in-Independent-Zimbabwe-1.pdf; Daniel Compagnon (2013), *A Predictable Tragedy: Robert Mugabe and the Collapse of Zimbabwe*, Philadelphia, Pennsylvania: University of Pennsylvania Press, 2013, Chap 5.
93 Matthias Krönke (December 2018), "Bounded Autonomy: What Limits Zimbabweans Trust in Their Courts and Electoral Commission?," Afrobarometer Policy Paper No. 52. https://afrobarometer.org/sites/default/files/publications/Policy%20papers/ab_r7_policypaperno52_bounded_autonomy_of_zimbabwes_electoral_commission_and_courts.pdf; see also MacDonald Dzirutwe (August 25, 2018), "Zimbabwe's Chamisa Rejects Court Judgment Confirming Mnangagwa as President," Reuters. www.reuters.com/article/us-zimbabwe-election-politics/zimbabwes-chamisa-rejects-court-judgment-confirming-mnangagwa-president-idUSKCN1LA0BZ.
94 Gift Mwonzora & Mzingaye Brilliant Xaba (2020), "From the Booth to The Dock: 2018 elections in Zimbabwe and The Elusive Search for Electoral Integrity," Commonwealth & Comparative Politics, 58(4), 433–51.
95 See, for instance, Judgment No. CCZ 21/19 (Constitutional Application No. CCZ 42/18), p. 113 of the reasoned judgment where the court, using dismissive language, appeared to trivialize the contentions of the applicant: "The allegation that the Commission lacked independence was without foundation. It was made for the sake of making it."
96 Alex Magaisa (2019), "Zimbabwe: An Opportunity Lost," Journal of Democracy, 30(1), 143–57.

References

Abdulai, A., & Crawford, G. (2010). Consolidating democracy in Ghana: Progress and prospects?. *Democratization*, *17*(1), 26–27.

Adams, R. (2020). *Transparency: New trajectories in law*. Oxford: Routledge.
Adediran, M. O. (1982). *Awolowo v. Shagari*: A case of compromise between law and political expediency. *Journal of the Indian Law Institute, 24*(1), 41, 54–56.
Aggrey-Darkoh E., & Asah-Asante, K. (2017). Supreme court ruling on 2012 electoral dispute in Ghana: A recipe for chaos or deepening of Ghana's democracy?. In B. E. Asare & A. K. D. Frempong (Eds.), *Selected Issues in Ghana's Democracy* (Vol. 1). Tema: Digibooks Ghana Ltd.
Ahluwalia, P. (2017). The saga of the 2017 Kenyan elections: Can they really be free and fair?. *African Identities, 15*(4), 351.
Akinkugbe, O. D., & Gathii, J. T. (2020). *Judicial nullification of presidential elections in Africa: Peter Mutharika v. Lazarus Chakera and Saulos Chilima in Context*. Retrieved from https://papers.ssrn.com/sol3/papers.cfm?abstract_id=3642709
Amoah, M. (2020). Sleight is right: Cyber control as a new battleground for African elections. *African Affairs, 119*(474), 68–89.
Arthur, P. (2010). Democratic consolidation in Ghana: The role and contribution of the media, civil society and state institutions. *Commonwealth & Comparative Politics, 48*(2), 203–226.
Asante, R. (2020). Democratic civil-military bargain: Examining the Ghanaian experience. *Civil Wars, 22*(2–3), 333–352.
Asante, W., & Asare, E. B. (2016). Ghana's 2012 election petition and its outcome: A giant leap towards democratic consolidation. *Journal of Political Sciences & Public Affairs, 4*(1), 5.
Atengble, K. (2014). Social media and Ghana's 2012 election petition: A discussion. *Advances in Journalism and Communication, 2*(3), 121–126.
Azu, M. (2015). Lessons from Ghana and Kenya on why presidential election petitions usually fail. *African Human Rights Law Journal, 15*, 150.
Birchall, C. (2011). Introduction to 'secrecy and transparency': The politics of opacity and openness. *Theory, Culture & Society, 28*(7), 7–25.
Bob-Milliar, G. M., & Paller, J. W. (2018). Democratic ruptures and electoral outcomes in Africa: Ghana's 2016 election. *Africa Spectrum, 53*(1), 5–35.
Boparai, S. S. (1981). Chief Awolowo v. Alhaji Shagari. Verfassung und Recht in Übersee / Law and Politics in Africa, Asia and Latin America, *14*(4), 387–399.
Brierley, S., & Ofosu, G. (2014). The presidential and parliamentary elections in Ghana, December 2012. *Electoral Studies, 35*, 382–385.
Cheesman, N. et al. (2017) Ghana: The ebbing power of incumbency. *Journal of Democracy, 28*(2), 92–104.
Compagnon, D. (2013). *A predictable tragedy: Robert Mugabe and the collapse of Zimbabwe*. Philadelphia, PA: University of Pennsylvania Press.
Fombad, C. M. (2019). Constitutional literacy in Africa: Challenges and prospects. *Commonwealth Law Bulletin, 44*(3), 492.
Fowkes, J. (2016). *Building the constitution: The practice of constitutional interpretation in post-Apartheid South Africa*. Cambridge: Cambridge University Press.
Goldstein, J. (1992). *The intelligible constitution*. Oxford: Oxford University Press.
Gubbay, A. R. (2009). The progressive erosion of the rule of law in independent Zimbabwe. In Bar of England and Wales Third International Rule of Law Lecture, London. Retrieved from https://www.barcouncil.org.uk/uploads/assets/73146293-cc62-4a62b1c697d378f8464e/The-progressive-erosion-of-the-Rule-of-Law-in-Independent-Zimbabwe-1.pdf
Human Rights Watch. (2008). *A compromised judiciary*. Retrieved from https://www.hrw.org/reports/2008/zimbabwe1108/5.htm
Jinadu, A. L. (1997). Matters arising: African elections and the problem of electoral administration. *African Journal of Political Science, 2*(1), 1–11.
Kaaba, O. (2015). The challenges of adjudicating presidential election disputes in domestic courts in Africa. *African Human Rights Law Journal, 15*, 329.
Karekwaivanane, G. H. (2017). *The struggle over state power in Zimbabwe: Law and politics since 1950*. Cambridge: Cambridge University Press.
Koehn, P. (1981). Prelude to civilian rule: The Nigerian elections of 1979 *Africa Today, 28*(1), 42–45.
Krönke, M. (2018, December). *Bounded autonomy: What limits Zimbabweans' trust in their courts and electoral commission?* Afrobarometer Policy Paper, No. 52. Retrieved from https://afrobarometer.org/sites/default/files/publications/Policy%20papers/ab_r7_policypaperno52_bounded_autonomy_of_zimbabwes_electoral_commission_and_courts.pdf
Magaisa, A. (2019). Zimbabwe: An opportunity lost. *Journal of Democracy, 30*(1), 143–157.

Maphunye, K. J. (2017). Straining without training? Capacity-related problems facing African election executives and officials. *International Journal of African Renaissance Studies - Multi-, Inter- and Trans-disciplinarity*, *12*(1), 55–75.
Moseneke, D. (2018). The courtroom as TV studio: The case of the Oscar Pistorious trial. *International Journal of Law in Context*, *14*, 493.
Mwonzora, G., & Xaba, M. B. (2020). From the booth to the dock: 2018 elections in Zimbabwe and the elusive search for electoral integrity. *Commonwealth & Comparative Politics*, *58*(4), 433–451.
Nkansah, L.A. (2016). Dispute resolution and electoral justice in Africa: The way forward. *Africa Development*, *41*(2), 97, 117.
Nwabueze, B. (1982a). *A constitutional history of Nigeria*. London: C. Hurst & Co.
Nwabueze, B. (1982b). *The presidential constitution of Nigeria*. New York: St. Martin's Press.
Nyane, H. (2019). The role of judiciaries in presidential electoral disputes resolution in Africa: The cases of Zambia and Zimbabwe. In 4th Annual International Conference on Public Administration and Development Alternatives (IPADA) (pp. 11–19). Retrieved from http://ulspace.ul.ac.za/handle/10386/2687
Okubasu, D. (2018). Kenya: The state of liberal democracy. In R. Albert et al. (Eds.), *2017 global review of constitutional law* (pp. 166–171).
Omotola, J. S. (2010). Elections and democratic transition in Nigeria under the Fourth Republic. *African Affairs*, *109*(437), 535–553.
Omotola, J. S. (2013). The Election Commission of Ghana and the administration of the 2012 elections. *Journal of African Elections*, *12*(2), 34–55.
Oppong, N. (2016, December 21). Ghana's 2016 election results: The story of a presidential petition. *ROAPE Blog*. Retrieved from https://roape.net/2016/12/21/ghanas-2016-election-results-story-presidential-petition/
Otieno, H. (2017, October 18). The fulcrum for the invalidation of Kenya's 2017 presidential election: Section 83 of the Elections Act. *OxHRH Blog*. Retrieved from https://ohrh.law.ox.ac.uk/the-fulcrum-for-the-invalidation-of-kenyas-2017-presidential-election-section-83-of-the-elections-act
Owusu-Mensah, I., & Rice, J. (2018). The judiciary and democracy in Ghana's Fourth Republic. *Journal of African Elections*, *17*(2), 44–65.
Quashigah, K. (2016). Defying assumptions about the nature of power relations between the executive and judiciary: An overview of approaches to judicial and executive relations in Ghana. In C. Fombad (Ed.), *Separation of powers in African constitutionalism* (pp. 226–238). Oxford: Oxford University Press.
Read, J. S. (1979). Awolowo v. Shagari and Others. *Journal of African Law*, *23*(2), 175–182.
Roelofs, P. (2019). Transparency and mistrust: Who or what should be made transparent? *Governance*, *32*(3), 565–580.
Roux, T. (2018). *The politico-legal dynamics of judicial review: A comparative analysis*. Cambridge: Cambridge University Press, 2018.
Sekindi, F. (2017). Presidential election disputes in Uganda: A critical analysis of the supreme court decisions. *Journal of African Elections*, *16*(1), 154–179.
Solidarity Peace Trust. (2005, March) *The role of the judiciary in denying the will of the Zimbabwean electorate since 2000* (p. 5). Retrieved from http://solidaritypeacetrust.org/ download/report-files/subverting_justice.pdf
Zongwe, D. P. (2017). Hichilema and another v. Lungu and another (2016/CC/0031) [2016] ZMCC 4 (5 September 2016), minority judgement. *SAIPAR Case Review*, *1*(1), 19–26.

24
ELECTION LAW IN INDIA

M. V. Rajeev Gowda and Varun Santhosh

Introduction

Since its independence in 1947, India has established a vibrant multi-party democracy featuring universal suffrage, high voter participation, and competitive elections from the village to the national level.[1] Over seven decades, India has conducted 17 national elections with peaceful transfers of power. Nearly a billion voters were on the rolls for the 2019 general election that witnessed a voter turnout of 67% (Election Commission of India, 2019).

An elaborate and robust framework of election-related laws and institutions enable the successful conduct of elections. We provide an overview of this framework and its evolution. We first examine the overarching role of the Constitution of India. Next, we elaborate on the institutions that derive their authority from the constitution. After we examine the laws that govern elections of different types, we examine the deepening of democracy through elections to local government and affirmative measures that empower historically disadvantaged groups. We then discuss laws pertaining to political parties, before examining laws that affect candidates. In the following section, we discuss laws to combat "defection" and the criminalization of politics. Finally, we describe laws pertaining to media.

The Constitution

India's Constitution came into effect in 1950 and established a sovereign democratic republic. In the landmark *Kesavananda Bharati*[2] judgement, the Supreme Court of India (SC) ruled that the basic structure of the constitution cannot be amended by parliament. The SC also held that democracy is a key element of the basic structure of the constitution.

India's electoral history began in November 1947 with the preparation of a draft electoral roll to implement the principle of universal adult suffrage (Shani, 2017) codified in Part XV of the constitution. Article 326 lays down that every Indian citizen 18 years of age and older shall be eligible to register as a voter, provided that he or she is not disqualified by law on grounds of non-residence, unsoundness of mind, crime, or corrupt or illegal electoral practices.[3]

Granting the vote to every citizen was a bold move in a newly-emerging nation with tremendous linguistic, ethnic, and religious diversity, as well as high illiteracy, poverty, and social stratification. The SC has held that the right to vote is a statutory right,[4] though interpretation

DOI: 10.4324/9780429401800-24

of Articles 325 and 326 has led to debates about whether it is actually a constitutional right (Jain, 2012).

The second foundational principle laid down by the constitution is secularism, which the SC held as protected by Article 325.[5] No person may be excluded from the electoral roll, or claim inclusion on any special electoral roll, on the grounds of religion, race, caste, or sex.

The constitution further empowers parliament to legislate on matters connected with elections to parliament or state legislatures. Article 328 confers similar powers to state legislatures,[6] with respect to states, on matters not provided for by the parliament. The Representation of the People Act of 1950 and 1951 (RPA) and the Delimitation Commission Act of 1952 were enacted accordingly under Article 327. However, such laws are subject to the provisions of the constitution, which remains the supreme law on all election-related matters (Kafaltiya, 2003).

Institutions

Election Commission

Article 324 established the Election Commission of India (ECI) as a permanent body independent of the executive and in charge of elections to parliament, state legislatures, and the presidency and vice-presidency of India. The SC has ruled that: "Holding periodic, free and fair elections by the Election Commission are part of the basic structure" of the constitution[7] (Quraishi, 2014). Changes to the ECI's structure and functioning require a constitutional amendment, which requires supermajority support in parliament. This makes the ECI more authoritative and independent than if it were only a statutory body subject to ready amendment by parliament. Once an election is underway, Article 329 protects the ECI from judicial interference. The RPA of 1950 and 1951 provide the legislative framework for the conduct of elections and allow petitioners to challenge the electoral process in the courts.

Given the formidable challenge of conducting elections with nearly a billion voters, the ECI has a remarkably small permanent staff at its headquarters (Sridharan & Vaishnav, 2017). It operates in states through Chief Electoral Officers drawn from state governments. For the preparation of electoral rolls and the conducting of elections, the ECI draws on personnel from state and local governments who are temporarily assigned to it. During elections, the ECI has the power to transfer any government official whose behavior it considers detrimental to the fairness of the electoral process (Quraishi, 2014).

The ECI undertakes the mammoth exercise of creating and updating electoral rolls periodically by conducting house-to-house surveys to register eligible voters (Quraishi, 2014). Moreover, it now has provisions for voters to register online subject to physical verification. In the aftermath of controversies about illegal immigration, the SC enjoined the ECI to ensure that only citizens of India are enrolled as voters.[8]

The ECI is granted the authority by the RPA of 1951 to register and recognize political parties, allot them election symbols (to assist illiterate voters), and grant them national or state party status. The addition of Section 29A to the RPA in 1988 further required parties to submit their respective constitutions to the ECI. It granted the ECI enforcement powers, e.g., requiring parties to hold internal elections or face possible de-recognition.

The ECI has a history of asserting its regulatory powers to ensure free and fair elections in the face of "increasing election-related violence, instances of outright vote rigging ('booth-capturing')" and a steady inflow of undeclared "'black money' used for elections" (Sridharan & Vaishnav, 2017). However, the SC has observed that, while the distribution of free goods by political parties does not constitute bribery, it does have sway over voters and is therefore against the spirit of free and fair elections.[9]

The ECI enforces a Model Code of Conduct (MCC) that commences when the ECI announces the election calendar and that regulates all aspects of campaigns. The MCC is not backed by statute and relies on voluntary compliance. While the ECI has limited powers to punish violations of the MCC, it arguably has acquired a law-like character. Once the MCC is in force, incumbent governments at all levels within that jurisdiction are prohibited from announcing new policies or programs (thus affecting the continuity of government activity when elections stretch over months).

The ECI introduced Electronic Voting Machines (EVM) to replace ballot papers, which had been vulnerable to "ballot box stuffing" and "booth capturing" (Election Commission of India, 2018c). Initially the SC ordered a re-poll with paper ballots in a state legislative election in 1982 in Kerala, where it had been introduced,[10] accepting the contention that the RPA did not envisage the use of EVMs. The addition of Section 61A to the RPA of 1951 in 1989, however, legitimized the use of EVMs and was upheld by the SC. Since 2001, all elections to state legislative assemblies and parliament (since 2004) utilize EVMs. India's EVMs are non-networked, standalone machines that are programmed to jam if they are tampered with or used multiple times in a short period, thus preventing rigging.

Delimitation Commission

Article 82 authorizes parliament to enact a Delimitation Act after every population census (conducted decennially). Under these acts, the federal government periodically constitutes a Delimitation Commission to demarcate the boundaries of parliamentary and legislative assembly constituencies in order to ensure broadly equal representation for equal populations (the principle of "One Vote, One Value").[11] The decisions of the Delimitation Commission cannot be challenged in a court of law. The most recent delimitation of constituencies was conducted in 2008, under the Delimitation Act of 2002, on the basis of the 2001 Census.

The first delimitation exercise was carried out in 1950–1951 by the President of India, in coordination with the ECI, after which the Delimitation Commission Act of 1952 came into force. Thereafter, the Delimitation Commission conducted the exercise in 1963, 1973, and 2002. There was no delimitation following the 1981 and 1991 censuses due to a dispute over the provision that "the ratio between the number of Lok Sabha seats in a state and the population of the state is, as far as practicable, the same for all states" according to the 31st Constitutional Amendment. There were concerns that states with higher population growth would be "rewarded" with more seats in parliament, as compared with states that had already better implemented the national priority of family planning and thus had lower population growth. This dispute was resolved by the 42nd Constitutional Amendment of 1976, which suspended delimitation until 2001, further extended to after 2026 by the 84th Constitutional Amendment of 2001. These required intra-state equalization of constituency size by population without altering the number of seats that each state had in parliament.

The Judiciary

Courts have issued landmark orders, including in response to public interest litigations initiated by civil society organizations (Devi & Mendiratta, 2014). Simultaneously, courts have followed restraint in law-making, citing the principle of separation of powers as the rationale for not directing parliament to legislate on electoral reforms. Key judicial interventions are discussed under the relevant sections in this chapter, except for the following unique innovation.

Nota

In 2013, the SC recognized that the fundamental right to freedom of speech and expression includes the right to not vote, i.e., to express a negative opinion.[12] To operationalize this right, while protecting the secrecy of voters, the SC directed the ECI to include a "None of the Above" (NOTA) option on all EVMs. The NOTA option serves only a symbolic function as, even if a majority of votes are cast for NOTA, the candidate who obtained the second-highest votes is declared the winner. Between 2013 and 2017, in 261 assembly constituencies and 24 Lok Sabha constituencies, the number of votes cast for NOTA was higher than the margin of victory (Roy & Vachana, 2017).

Governor

Article 153 of the constitution provides for the appointment of a governor in every state (and a lieutenant governor or an administrator in the Union Territories) by the president of India (Article 155, Id.), who is bound by the advice of the Central Council of Ministers. Executive power in states is formally vested in the governor, who is constitutionally bound to act on the advice of the state's Council of Ministers, except where the constitution expressly confers discretion.

The governor plays a crucial role in the formation of governments after elections (Article 164, Id.) and their possible dismissal (Article 356, Id.). After an election, the governor has discretion over whom to invite to form the government, particularly when multiple parties stake claims in the absence of a party and/or alliance obtaining a majority. When no party/alliance is able to form a government, a state can be brought under President's Rule where the governor effectively administers the state until an elected government is sworn in.

In the case of "hung assemblies," where no single party has a majority, conventions have evolved for the governor to invite: (i) The pre-poll alliance with the largest number of seats; (ii) a single, usually largest, party claiming support from others; or (iii) a post-electoral coalition. Since these have not been codified, these issues have given rise to multiple court cases.[13] As the governor is appointed by the president at the instance of the federal government, on occasion, governors are alleged to have acted in a partisan manner to favor the ruling party at the center (Dubey, 2018).

Article 356 allows the president to dismiss an elected state government in case of a failure of "constitutional machinery." This power can be exercised if the president receives a report from the governor recommending such an action or is otherwise satisfied on the need for the drastic step. The SC, in the landmark *S. R. Bommai* case in 1994,[14] held that the power to dismiss governments was conditional and subject to judicial review. This ruling has brought down the instances of President's Rule in states, especially in cases pertaining to the failure to form governments. President's Rule was invoked 91 times between 1951 and1993, but only 20 times between 1994 and March 2016 (Ministry of Home Affairs, 2016).

Election Laws and Types of Elections

Representation of People Acts

Before the first general elections, India's Provisional Parliament enacted the RPA of 1950 and 1951[15] to govern electoral processes. These cover the qualifications and disqualifications of those who contest elections; registration of political parties; financing of parties; election expenditures; details of the administrative machinery, including functions of the ECI and other officers;

provisions for resolving disputes regarding elections; and penalties for electoral offences and corrupt practices. The RPA of 1951 has undergone numerous amendments and its interpretation has been shaped by both SC judgements and ECI actions.

Major Amendments to the RPA

1. Booth Capturing: In the 1980s, as the involvement of criminals in electoral politics became rampant, incidents of booth capturing and intimidation of voters increased, and money and muscle power played a major role in affecting electoral outcomes. An amendment in 1989 inserted Section 58A of the RPA of 1951, which allowed the ECI to countermand an election or declare the poll null and void and to call for a fresh poll, if it was convinced that the election had been compromised. Section 135A of the RPA of 1951, inserted in 1989, made booth capturing an offence punishable with imprisonment. It gave a detailed definition of booth capturing and also included it as a corrupt practice under the Act in Section 123(8). It further allowed the ECI to deploy EVMs to prevent the rigging of elections. In a 1996 amendment, under Section 20B, the ECI could appoint observers to supervise elections, empowered to stop the counting of votes if they felt that booth capturing had taken place.
2. Election Funding: In 2003, section 29C was added to the RPA of 1951, requiring the treasurer of a political party to prepare a report in each financial year that records contributions in excess of Rs 20,000 from any person and any company other than government companies. These reports must be submitted to the ECI within a certain time limit (The Election and Other Related Laws (Amendment) Act, 2003).
3. Proxy voting or postal ballot: In 2003, certain classes of people were allowed to vote through proxy votes or postal ballots. Armed police forces of a state serving outside that state and employees of the Government of India serving outside the country are allowed to vote by postal ballot, and members of the armed forces can vote either through proxies or postal ballots (The Election and Other Related Laws (Amendment) Act, 2003).
4. Voting Rights for Non-Resident Indians: In 2010, the RPA of 1950 was amended to remove restrictions that prevented Non-Resident Indians from exercising their right to vote. However, such voters are still required to be physically present at the voting booth. A bill to enable them to vote through proxy was proposed in 2017, but it has not yet been enacted.

Different Types of Elections

India's multi-tiered democratic system features a complex tapestry of electoral mechanisms.

Direct and Indirect Elections

Direct elections are employed to elect the lower house of parliament, the Lok Sabha, the lower house of state legislatures, the Vidhan Sabha, and local governments. They utilize the simple and easily understandable "First Past the Post" system, in which the winner is the candidate who obtains the highest number of votes.

Indirect elections are used to elect the upper house of parliament, the Rajya Sabha, state legislative councils, and the president and vice president, each through specified electoral colleges. Indirect elections employ a system of proportional representation with a single transferable vote. In order to win, a candidate must obtain a fixed quota of votes, usually determined by a formula in which the total number of votes is divided by the number of positions to be filled, plus one.

Open Ballot Voting

Members of the Rajya Sabha are elected by members of legislative assemblies. In 2003, to check cross-voting, the RPA was amended to establish an open ballot system for Rajya Sabha elections. Voters are now required to show their marked ballot to their party's designated agent prior to casting their votes. If a voter refuses to do so, his or her vote can be invalidated.

However, this does not necessarily prevent legislators from cross-voting, as it is not a ground for disqualification under the anti-defection law. The SC ruled that the open ballot cannot be seen to violate the freedom of expression of a legislator and, hence, is not a ground for disqualification.[16]

Simultaneous Elections

Until 1967, India held elections simultaneously to parliament and state legislative assemblies. Following the early dissolution of some state assemblies in 1968 and 1969, as well as the early dissolution of the Lok Sabha in 1970, this synchronization ceased to exist.

Several reports and commissions have examined the idea of simultaneous elections. These include the Law Commission of India, which prepared a Report on Reform of Electoral Laws (1999); Parliamentary Standing Committees on Personnel, Public Grievances, Law and Justice (2015); and the NITI Aayog (Debroy & Desai, 2017).

However, returning to simultaneous elections would entail prematurely terminating a number of elected state governments, as their legislative assemblies would need to be dissolved to enable simultaneous elections. This would run afoul of the SC's judgment[17] that Article 356 is to be used only when there is a breakdown of constitutional machinery in the state. Simultaneous elections would also raise a number of other practical challenges to parliamentary practice (e.g., the ability of governments to dissolve parliaments and call for early elections) and require substantial amendments to the constitution.

Moreover, people vote differently and in response to different issues at different tiers of democracy. Conducting elections together could endanger this plural and varied expression by voters, and allow national issues to overshadow state and regional issues, which goes against the spirit of federalism (Kumar, 2018).

Promoting Inclusion and Deepening Democracy

Reservations for Scheduled Castes and Scheduled Tribes

In order to affirmatively redress the historic and prevailing discrimination faced by certain communities categorized as Scheduled Castes (SC) and Scheduled Tribes (ST), the constitution provided for time-bound reservations of seats in state legislative assemblies (Article 332) and in the Lok Sabha (Article 330). The number of such reserved seats is determined on the basis of the ratio of the SC and/or ST population within the state or Union Territory to its total population.

If a constituency is reserved for SCs, then the candidate must belong to an SC community. The case is similar for ST seats. All voters within reserved constituencies are eligible to vote for these candidates. At present, 84 Lok Sabha seats are reserved for SCs, and 47 for STs. SC and ST candidates can also contest in unreserved constituencies. Constituencies reserved for SCs are to be geographically distributed around a state. Those reserved for STs must be located where their populations are concentrated.

Originally, Article 334 stated that these provisions would be applicable for a period of ten years, i.e., up to 1960, but amendments have extended their applicability every ten years. The

104th Constitutional amendment of 2019 extended these reservations up to 2030. (It also abolished the reservation of two seats, filled by government nomination, in the Lok Sabha, and one in state legislative assemblies, for the Anglo-Indian community.)

Panchayati Raj

Gandhian ideals of self-governance at the village level inspired Article 40 of the constitution (DeSouza, 2002). Part of the non-enforceable Directive Principles of State Policy, Article 40 states that: "The state shall take steps to organize village panchayats and endow them with such powers and authority as may be necessary to enable them to function as units of self-government."

In 1993, the 73rd and 74th Constitutional Amendment Acts provided constitutional status to Urban and Rural Local Self Government Bodies.[18] A three-tier system for Panchayati Raj Institutions (PRI) was established at the village, intermediate block/taluk/mandal, and district levels. These acts established State Election Commissions and State Finance Commissions in order to ensure that adequate financial resources are available for panchayats and municipalities.

Reservations in Panchayati Raj Institutions

The 73rd and 74th Constitutional Amendments expanded the scope of reservations by extending them to the offices of chairpersons and introduced the rotation of reservations. One-third of the seats were reserved for women. Many states have increased the reservation for women to 50%. States have also legislated to provide reservation of seats in PRI for other historically neglected classes. The SC has ruled that all reserved seats in PRI cannot exceed 50% of the total.[19] This led many states to reduce the number of seats previously reserved. In Karnataka, the seats reserved for other backward classes went down by nearly half between the 2010 and 2015 gram panchayat elections (Desai, 2015).

However, the project of deepening democracy through devolution and representation has arguably been reversed through laws in the states of Haryana and Rajasthan. The Haryana Panchayati Raj (Amendment) Act of 2015 introduced exclusionary conditions for eligibility to contest elections including educational qualification, failure to repay loans taken from cooperative societies, electricity bill arrears, and absence of a functional toilet at one's residence. The Rajasthan government imposed similar conditions in 2014. These state laws were challenged, but were upheld by the SC in December 2015. These educational criteria alone rendered ineligible an average of 67.52% of the electorate who were otherwise eligible to contest. This exclusionary measure has been criticized as militating against the inclusive spirit behind the 73rd Constitutional Amendment (Singh, 2016).

Political Parties and Their Financing

Political parties, though recognized in the RPA of 1951, were formally recognized in the constitution only through the 52nd Constitutional Amendment in 1985, which inserted the 10th Schedule, commonly termed the Anti-Defection Law. Political parties raise and expend resources within a restrictive legal framework. Their reported expenditures do not include amounts spent by individual activists, candidates, or at events and on campaigns underwritten by ad hoc fundraising. Indian politics is also suffused with cash, typically "black" or unaccounted funds (Gowda & Sridharan, 2012; Quraishi, 2014). However, political parties need to account formally for a range of official expenses and thus need to raise resources in an auditable manner.

Corporate contributions are a major source of party funds. Their regulation in India can be organized into two phases – 1947 to 2003, and 2003 to date (Sridharan & Vaishnav, 2017; Gowda & Sridharan, 2012). During the first phase, corporate contributions were permitted, albeit with restrictions on amounts, along with reporting requirements. Corporate donations were banned in 1969, ostensibly to combat corruption, but allegedly to restrict funding to right-wing opposition parties (Sridharan & Vaishnav, 2017). The ban on corporate donations was lifted in 1985, subject to a maximum of 5% of the company's average profit of the last three years. A 2013 amendment to the Companies Act increased this limit to 7.5%. Such contributions must be approved by the board and reported in companies' accounting statements.

The second-phase of party financing regulation commences with the enactment of the Election and Other Related Laws (Amendment) Act of 2003 (Sridharan & Vaishnav, 2017; Gowda & Sridharan, 2012; Quraishi Ed., 2019). Amendments to the RPA of 1951 and Income Tax Act incentivized corporate (and individual) donations by making them 100% tax deductible. New reporting requirements for political parties were introduced under the RPA of 1951 for donations greater than Rs. 20,000. Donations below this amount were considered too small to be accounted formally, and this exception was also intended to facilitate smaller donations from individuals. Political parties have regularly reported that the bulk of their finances have come from such "unknown" sources. In the financial year 2018–2019, funding from unknown sources reportedly accounted for 67.02% of the resources raised by all parties in total (Association for Democratic Reforms, 2020), raising questions about whether this provision serves as a loophole to convert unaccounted cash into accountable resources.

In 2013, the Central Information Commission ruled that political parties are public authorities accountable under the Right to Information Act of 2005 (Central Information Commission, 2014). Parties have contested this ruling and are yet to comply as of March 2020.

In recent years, the Finance Bill, a part of the annual budget, has been utilized to bring in changes to party financing laws. Being an integral part of the budget, finance bills are assured of passage in the Lok Sabha, where the government has a majority. They only need to be considered and returned by the upper house of parliament, the Rajya Sabha, which does not have authority over money bills.

The Finance Act of 2017 brought about multiple changes in political funding laws. It introduced a new instrument for funding parties called electoral bonds. These can be purchased from the State Bank of India during designated time periods and donated to the political party of one's choice. Since electoral bonds are purchased through a bank, this measure was touted as an electoral reform that promoted the use of "clean money" (Jaitley, 2017). However, electoral bonds have been criticized for being opaque, as the donor does not need to disclose either the donation or the recipient, and the recipient only needs to disclose the amount received and not the source. It was claimed that anonymity would incentivize corporates and others to donate to political parties, whereas earlier they hesitated to do so openly for fear of retaliation by non-recipient political parties (Vaishnav, 2019; Kak, 2017).

The Finance Act of 2017 also abolished the cap on corporate donations, along with reporting requirements. Far from reforming the system, critics argue that "the floodgates are now open for limitless, anonymous political giving" (Vaishnav, 2018). According to one estimate, electoral bonds constituted 78.02% of party funding from unknown sources in financial year 2018–2019, and the bulk of this (64%) went to the ruling BJP (Association for Democratic Reforms, 2020).

It also reduced the cap on cash donations from Rs. 20,000 to Rs. 2,000. However, no changes were made to the RPA's corresponding reporting requirements, thus essentially permitting anonymous donations up to Rs. 20,000 (Vaishnav, 2019). This does little to make the party funding system more transparent.

The Delhi High Court held that the BJP and the Indian National Congress (INC), the largest national parties, had accepted funds from entities operating in India, but which actually were "foreign" companies.[20] The court determined these donations to be violative of the Foreign Contributions (Regulation) Act of 1976 and the RPA of 1951. This order was circumvented by using the Finance Bills in 2016 and 2018 to amend the relevant laws to provide retrospective protection to these political parties, by redefining foreign companies with a retrospective date of application going back to 1976 (Vaishnav, 2018).

Candidates

Actions Attracting the Disqualification of Candidates

Section 123 of the RPA of 1951 defines corrupt electoral practices that are civil in nature and that attract disqualification from voting and contesting elections. These include bribery; undue influence; appeal on the ground of religion, race, caste, community, or language; publication of false statements; the hiring of vehicles and vessels; excessive expenditure; procurement of the assistance of government servants; and booth capturing practices. Some of these offences have supplementary penal provisions.

Electoral offences enumerated in Chapter III, part VII of the RPA of 1951, as well as the Indian Penal Code of 1860 (Chapter IXA), attract liabilities that are criminal in nature, including imprisonment or fine or both, in addition to the civil disabilities. Further, electoral offences under the Indian Penal Code are applicable to all elections held in the country. However, electoral offences and corrupt practices under the RPA of 1951 are specifically applicable to elections to parliament and state legislatures.

A voter or defeated candidate can file an election petition to challenge an election result in the High Court and/or SC by establishing electoral offences committed by in-charge authorities and/or corrupt practices adopted by the winning candidate. Historically, the most momentous such case in India's constitutional and political history is *Indira Nehru Gandhi v. Raj Narain*, 1975. Raj Narain, who had lost to Prime Minister Indira Gandhi in the 1971 Lok Sabha election, challenged her victory on grounds that included the allegation that a government servant had been involved in her campaign. This was upheld by the Allahabad High Court, which set aside the result of the election. This verdict triggered a series of developments, including constitutional amendments and the proclamation of an internal emergency that led to the arrest of opposition politicians and the suspension of fundamental rights, the only such instance in India's democratic history (Austin, 1999; Mody, 2013).

Candidate Expenditures

Section 77 of the RPA of 1951 requires all candidates to maintain an account of their election campaign expenditures. If this amount exceeds the prescribed cap, that candidate's election can be annulled. However, no cap was placed on third-party expenditure on behalf of the candidate. The candidate's party and supporters could, therefore, provide for the expenses of a candidate. This loophole was brought before the SC several times and, in 1975, it finally considered party expenditure as part of the candidate's expenditure and disqualified the election of a member of parliament (MP) for breaching the prescribed expenditure ceiling.[21] The court observed that the disparity in party resources could produce anti-democratic effects and provide an unfair advantage to some candidates/parties over others.

This judgement was overturned by a 2003 amendment to the RPA of 1951, whereby an explanation was added to Section 77 that expenditure incurred by a party for propagating its political program would not be considered as part of a candidate's expenditure (Election and Other Related Laws (Amendment) Act, 2003).

In 2007, the ECI categorized party expenditure into three heads: General party propaganda without reference to a particular candidate, direct support for a candidate, and promotion of the prospects of a particular candidate. Only the first of these is not included as part of the candidate's expenditure (Election Commission of India, 2007).

The federal government last revised candidate expenditure limits in 2014. The caps stood at between Rs. 5 and 7 million for Lok Sabha elections, depending on the state from which the candidate contested, and between Rs. 2 and 2.8 million for state legislative assembly elections.

In October 2020, the ECI set up a panel to look into revising the candidate expenditure limit, given that there has been a substantial increase in the size of the electorate, as well as in the Cost Inflation Index. As a temporary measure, the government approved a 10% increase in expenditure limits to meet the expenses of conducting digital campaigns during the Covid-19 pandemic (Election Commission of India, 2020).

Gowda and Sridharan (2012) argue that the caps on election expenditure are impractically low compared to the actual amounts spent by candidates during the polls. They argue that the EC's efforts to police overt election expenditures have had the effect of driving expenditures underground. This has favored the rise of candidates with black money and the networks to expend such resources, thus providing an impetus to corruption. Gowda and Santhosh (2020), therefore, advocate the creation of public funding avenues to level the electoral playing field.

Transparency and Candidate Disclosures

In 2002, the SC upheld the Delhi High Court's decision that the ECI should collect and disclose certain information about election candidates.[22] It held that the fundamental right to freedom of speech and expression, guaranteed under Article 19(1) (a) of the constitution, extends to the right of electors to know about the details of persons contesting for public office. The SC directed the ECI to require all candidates to disclose their criminal charges and records (if any), assets (including those of their spouse and dependents), liabilities, and educational qualifications. Accordingly, in 2002, parliament added Section 33A to the RPA of 1951.

In 2015, the SC ruled that suppression or non-disclosure of information, particularly relating to serious offences, is tantamount to undue influence over voters and is a corrupt practice under the RPA of 1951.[23] The SC has further mandated[24] that political parties must share details of candidates' criminal antecedents on their respective websites, and candidates and parties must publish notices of criminal antecedents in local newspapers.

Challenges to the Integrity of Election Defections and Criminalization

Anti-Defection Law

Defections pose a unique challenge to the democratic system. When an elected representative deserts his or her political party, it can be considered a breach of their social contract with voters. Defections have led to the fall of governments and political instability.

The 33rd Constitutional Amendment of 1974 was enacted to provide that a resignation by a representative would be valid only if the Presiding Officer of the House was satisfied that the resignation was voluntary and genuine. This amendment did not provide sufficient deterrence and elected representatives continued to defect and vote against the instructions of their parties.

For instance, 36 MPs belonging to the Janata Dal shifted to the Indian National Congress (INC) in 1980 (Chawla, 1980).

The 52nd Constitutional Amendment of 1985 sought to combat "the evil of political defections," which was "likely to undermine the very foundations of our democracy and the principles which sustain it." The Tenth Schedule was inserted in the constitution to disqualify elected representatives, among other grounds, if they voluntarily resigned from their political parties or voted or abstained from voting contrary to the party's directions.

These provisions are not applicable in cases of splits and mergers or when the adverse voting has been condoned by the political party. The Tenth Schedule of the Constitution defined a split as at least one-third of the representatives of the political party resigning or voting adversely. This provision was abolished by the 91st Constitutional Amendment of 2003. A merger is where at least a two-thirds of the representatives agree to merge the political party with another. The Tenth Schedule's prohibition on voting against the party whip has been criticized as taking away the right (and duty) of representatives to take conscientious stands on issues.

In cases of disputes, the Presiding Officer of the House was to be the final adjudicating authority with no appeal lying to the decision. The SC has held this proviso unconstitutional[25] and decisions of Presiding Officers can be appealed in the relevant High Courts or SC.

Presiding Officers' powers are vulnerable to abuse and can give rise to disputes. Since the Tenth Schedule does not provide for a time frame to dispose of disqualification proceedings, representatives defecting to the majority party have escaped disqualification proceedings, if the Presiding Officer delayed decisions on disqualification applications, thereby frustrating the application of the anti-defection law. Defectors to ruling parties in states have sometimes been rewarded with cabinet positions, instead of being disqualified. Thus, the SC ordered that all applications for disqualification must be decided within three months save for exceptional circumstances.[26] It also exhorted parliament to consider amending the Tenth Schedule to allow disqualification proceedings to be decided by a permanent tribunal.

Laws Related to Criminals and Elections

A report by the Association of Democratic Reforms (ADR) shows that, compared to 34% in 2014, nearly 43% of MPs in the 2019 Lok Sabha have self-declared criminal cases[27] against them; 29% of MPs have serious criminal cases against them, including for offences like assault, murder, kidnap, crimes against women, etc. (ADR, 2019).

The Law Commission's 244th Report identified trial delays and low conviction rates among the reasons for the ineffectiveness of laws to combat the criminalization of politics. A sample of affidavits filed by candidates for the general election in 2009 showed that a majority had criminal cases pending against them for more than six years, with some spanning more than 20 years (Law Commission of India, 1999). In 2009, 30% of sitting MPs had criminal charges framed against them (Vaishnav, 2014).

To address these problems, the SC, in 2014, ordered that all pending trials against sitting MPs and Members of Legislative Assemblies (MLAs) for specified offences should be concluded within one year of the framing of such charges. Trial judges would be required to submit a report containing reasons for not meeting the deadline to the Chief Justice of the relevant high court.[28]

In 2013, the SC struck down Subsection 8(4) of the RPA of 1951, which allowed sitting MPs and MLAs disqualified under the RPA to remain in office for three months from sentencing and also if any appeals against their sentencing were pending in courts.[29] The SC declared this provision unconstitutional and mandated immediate disqualification of any sitting MP/MLA, if convicted for an offence and sentenced to more than two years' imprisonment. Disqualification could be deferred only if the defendant obtained a stay on conviction, which previous judgements had held could be issued only in exceptional circumstances.[30]

Media

India's diverse and vibrant media plays an important role in affecting electoral outcomes, but faces only a few regulatory constraints. Expenditures on media during elections have grown enormously. During the 2014 election, the BJP reported spending Rs. 3,045 million on media advertisements (Election Commission of India, 2018a), in contrast to INC's expenditure of Rs. 2,078 million in 2009 (Election Commission of India, 2018b). The 2019 general election has been described as "the first national election contested within a truly digital consumption society, wherein approximately half the voting population had access to digital pathways, and another one-third had access to social media." Between February and May 2019, Google and Facebook declared total political online advertising of $7.94 million (Mehta, 2019).

Free Air Time

Since 1977, the ECI has allocated parties limited, but free and equitable, broadcast time on state-owned television and radio to appeal to voters. This scheme was updated in 1998 and, thereafter, guidelines were evolved for their content and requirements that transcripts be pre-approved (Devi & Mendiratta, 2014). These were formalized through the Election and Other Related Laws (Amendment) Act of 2003, which inserted a new section 39A in the RPA of 1951. In 2019, the BJP got almost 160 hours of broadcast time, and INC 80 hours, which led the ECI to reprimand the news house in question (Election Commission of India, 2019). The ECI was also given the power to formulate a new code of conduct for cable operators and electronic media. However, no scheme has been devised for privately-owned electronic media as proposed in section 39A(4) of the RPA, 1951 (Devi & Mendiratta, 2014).

Political Advertising

The ECI, on the basis of an interim order by the SC in 2004,[31] laid down rules under the provisions of the Cable Television Networks (Regulation) Act of 1995 on the content, review, and certification of political advertisements for television. During election campaigns, powers of certification are delegated to a media certification committee constituted by state Chief Electoral Officers. In 2013, the ECI laid down guidelines on the usage of social media in election campaigns (Devi & Mendiratta, 2014). Section 126 of the RPA of 1951 prohibits election campaigning for a period of 48 hours before polling on television, but not in print media.

Paid News

"Paid news" has allegedly become a lucrative source of income for media houses. The Parliamentary Standing Committee on Information Technology's report on "Issues Related to Paid News" in 2013 recommended stricter penal provisions to deter the practice. The ECI has advocated making paid news an electoral offence.

In 2011, the ECI banned an MLA from contesting elections for three years for failing to disclose expenditures on paid news amounting to election advertisements (Election Commission of India, 2011). The disqualified MLA, who had to vacate her seat with four months still left on her term (Balaji, 2011), challenged the ECI's order by questioning its jurisdiction and the constitutionality of Sec. 10A of the RPA of 1951 related to disqualification for failure to disclose election expenses. The Allahabad High Court dismissed her submissions for lacking in substance and upheld the constitutionality of Sec. 10A and the powers of the ECI to exercise suo moto powers under this section.[32]

Coverage of Opinion and Exit Polls

Section 126A was added to the RPA of 1951 in 2009 to prohibit the publication of exit poll results for any period as may be notified by the commission, along with a penalty for contravention. Opinion polls are, as yet, unregulated. Concerned about opinion and exit polls influencing voters, the ECI has banned media coverage of exit polls until the last phase of polling has been completed.

Social Media

Social media has emerged as the primary platform for fake news and propaganda that influences voters during elections (and which can also ignite communal violence and riots). Ahead of the 2019 General Elections, the ECI urged major social media platforms to devise a Voluntary Code of Ethics. The Internet & Mobile Association of India, along with social media platforms Facebook, WhatsApp, Twitter, and Google created and adopted this Voluntary Code (Press Information Bureau, 2019). The code included provisions for pre-certified political advertisements, observing the 48-hour silent period, and taking action against violations. 909 violations of the code were reported during the election (Id., 2019).

Conclusion

A responsive legislative framework and empowered, independent institutions such as the Election Commission and the judiciary have played a crucial role in the sustained success of Indian democracy. The ability of these institutions to resist pressures from the government of the day and to ensure free and fair elections are constantly put to the test, e.g., currently by how parties and political actors are using media and social media, as well as by the rising influence of corporate donations in politics.

Some election laws have had counterproductive effects. Gowda and Sridharan (2012) discuss how unrealistic election expenditure limits drive spending underground, thus favoring corrupt and criminal politicians and thereby undermining governance. The anti-defection law has been criticized for concentrating power in the hands of a party's leadership and of stifling freedom of representatives to express their views. These challenges are yet to be addressed.

The representativeness of the electoral system can be questioned on the basis of whom it excludes. For instance, women, who comprise half of India's population, have never held even 15% of Lok Sabha seats. A Women's Reservation Bill to redress this imbalance by reserving a third of these seats for women was passed in the Rajya Sabha in 2010, but subsequently lapsed as it was not passed by the Lok Sabha.

Similarly, representation of Muslims, India's largest religious minority, in the Lok Sabha, has always been below their share of the population. This is partly the result of how the Muslim population is distributed geographically, a factor that also affects the representation of numerous other communities. Political parties have attempted to address this underrepresentation by electing Muslims to the Rajya Sabha (Farooqui, 2020).

Overall, how India continues to evolve and implement its framework of election laws to address these and future challenges will be crucial to the health of its democracy.

List of Cases

A.C. Jose v. Sivan Pillai (1984) 2 SCC 656
Association of Democratic Reforms v. Union of India. (2014) W.P.(C) 131/2013
Chandrakant Kavlekar v. Union of India. (2017) 3 SCC 758
In Re: Special Reference No. 1 of 2002 (2002) 8 SCC 237
Inderjit Barua and Ors. v. Election Commission of India (1984) 1 SCC 21
Indira Nehru Gandhi (Smt.) v. Raj Narain and Anr. (1975) 2 SCC 159
K. Krishnamurthy and Ors. v. Union of India and Anr. (2010) 7 SCC 202
Kanwar Lal Gupta v. Amar Nath Chawla (1975) 2 SCR 259
Keisham Meghachandra Singh v. The Hon'ble Speaker Manipur Legislative Assembly and Ors. (2020) SCC Online SC 55
Kesavananda Bharati v. State of Kerala (1973) 4 SCC 225
Kihoto Hollohan v. Zachillhu and Ors. (1992) 2 SCC Supl. 651
Krishnamoorthy v. Sivakumar (2015) 3 SCC 467
Kuldip Nayar v. Union of India and Ors. (2006) 7 SCC 1
Lily Thomas v. Union of India (2013) 7 SCC 653
N.P. Ponnuswami v. Returning Officer, Namakkal Constituency (1952) 1 SCR 218
People's Union for Civil Liberties v. Union of India (2013) 10 SCC 1
Public Interest Foundation and Ors. v. Union of India (2015) 11 SCC 433
Public Interest Foundation and Ors. v. Union of India and Anr. (2018) 3 SCC 224
R.C. Poudyal v. Union of India (1993) 1 SCR 891
Rambabu Singh Thakur v. Sunil Arora and Ors. (2020) SCC Online SC 178
Rameshwar Prasad v. Union of India AIR (2006) SC 980
Ravikant S. Patil v. Sarvabhouma S. Bagali (2007) 1 SCC 673
S. Subramaniam Balaji v. Govt of Tamil Nadu (2013) 9 SCC 659
S.R. Bommai v. Union of India (1994) 3 SCC 1
Secretary, Ministry of Information and Broadcasting v. M/s Gemini TV Pvt. Ltd and Ors. (2004) 5 SCC 714
Umlesh Yadav v. Election Commission of India and Ors. (2011) HC 6921
Union of India v. Association for Democratic Reforms (2002) 5 SCC 294

Legislations

Cable Television Networks (Regulation) Act, 1995 (Ind.)
Companies Act, 2013 (Ind.)
Constitution of India, 1949 (Ind.)
Constitution (Thirty-first Amendment) Act, 1973 (Ind.)
Constitution (Thirty-third Amendment) Act, 1974 (Ind.)
Constitution (Forty-second Amendment) Act, 1976 (Ind.)
Constitution (Fifty-Second Amendment) Act, 1985 (Ind.)
Constitution (Sixty-first Amendment) Act, 1988 (Ind.)
Constitution (Eighty-fourth Amendment) Act, 2001 (Ind.)
Constitution (Ninety-First Amendment) Act, 2003 (Ind.)
Constitution (One Hundred and Fourth Amendment) Act, 2020 (Ind.)

Delimitation Act, 2002 (Ind.)
Delimitation Commission Act, 1952 (Ind.)
Election and Other Related Laws (Amendment) Act, 2003 (Ind.)
Finance Act, 2017 (Ind.)
Foreign Contributions (Regulation) Act, 1976 (Ind.)
Indian Penal Code, 1860 (Ind.)
Representation of the People Act, 1950 (Ind.)
Representation of the People Act, 1951 (Ind.)
Representation of People (Amendment) Act, 2003 (Ind.)
Representation of the People (Second Amendment and Validation) Bill, 2013 (Ind.)
Right to Information Act, 2005 (Ind.)

Notes

1 The authors thank Pradeep Chhibber, M.R. Madhavan, S.Y. Quraishi, Chakshu Rai, E. Sridharan, Rahul Verma, and Gilles Verniers for their valuable suggestions and Himani Bhatt, Akash Satyawali, Fathima Shakir, Fiza Thakur, Shonali Thangiah, and Saumya Varma for their research assistance.
2 *Kesavananda Bharati v. State of Kerala*, 1973.
3 The voting age was initially 21 years. It was lowered to 18 years by the Constitution (61st Amendment) Act (1988). Non-resident Indians are now permitted to enroll as voters, but must cast their votes in person.
4 *N.P. Ponnuswami v. Returning Officer, Namakkal Constituency*, 1952.
5 *R.C. Poudyal v. Union India*, 1993.
6 State legislatures consist of a directly-elected legislative assembly called the Vidhan Sabha. Six states (Andhra Pradesh, Bihar, Karnataka, Maharashtra, Telangana, and Uttar Pradesh) also have an indirectly-elected legislative council called the Vidhan Parishad. State legislative assemblies have the power to create or abolish legislative councils.
7 *In Re: Special Reference No. 1 of 2002*, 2002.
8 *Inderjit Barua and Ors. v. Election Commission of India,* 1984.
9 *S Subramaniam Balaji v. Govt of Tamil Nadu*, 2013.
10 *A. C. Jose v. Sivan Pillai*, 1984.
11 In the first two general elections, some constituencies were dual member constituencies and were represented by two candidates, one of which was to belong to the particular category for which that constituency was also reserved. This system was abolished in 1961. Thereafter, each constituency has elected only one representative. Dual member constituencies are gaining attention again as a possible solution to resolve the deadlock on the reservation for women in parliament and legislative assemblies. Women's organizations have proposed amendments to the (lapsed) Women Reservation Bill, which would double the number of existing members by converting all seats of the Lok Sabha and assembly constituencies into dual-member constituencies that would elect a man and woman each.
12 *People's Union for Civil Liberties v. Union of India*, 2013.
13 *S.R. Bommai v. Union of India*, 1994; *Rameshwar Prasad v. Union of India*, 2006; *Chandrakant Kavlekar v. Union of India*, 2017.
14 *S.R. Bommai v. Union of India*, 1994.
15 The RPA of 1950 did not contain all the provisions relating to elections, but merely provided for the allocation of seats in and the determination of constituencies for the purpose of elections to parliament and state legislatures, the qualifications of voters, and the preparation of electoral rolls. Provisions for the actual conduct of elections to parliament and state legislatures, the qualifications for the membership of these Houses, the definition of corrupt and illegal practices and other offences, and the resolution of election disputes were all made in the RPA of 1951.
16 *Kuldip Nayar v. Union of India*, 2006.
17 *S. R. Bommai v. Union of India*, 1994.
18 Rural local government bodies at the village level are termed gram panchayats. The institutions of local self-government, both rural and urban, are together termed Panchayati Raj institutions.
19 *K. Krishnamurthy and Ors. v. Union of India and Anr.*, 2010.

20 *Association of Democratic Reforms v. Union of India*, 2014.
21 *Kanwar Lal Gupta v. Amar Nath Chawla*, 1975.
22 *Union of India v. Association for Democratic Reforms*, 2002.
23 *Krishnamoorthy v. Sivakumar*, 2015.
24 *Public Interest Foundation v. Union of India*, 2018.
25 *Kihoto Hollohan v. Zachillhu and Ors*, 1992.
26 *Keisham Meghachandra Singh v. The Hon'ble Speaker Manipur*, 2020.
27 These include cases arising from political activities such as conducting demonstrations in violation of statutory orders, etc.
28 *Public Interest Foundation v. Union of India*, 2014.
29 *Lily Thomas v. Union of India*, 2013.
30 *Ravikant S. Patil v. Sarvabhouma S. Bagali*, 2007.
31 *Secretary, Ministry of Information and Broadcasting v. M/s Gemini TV Pvt Ltd and Ors*, 2004.
32 *Umlesh Yadav v. Election Commission of India and Ors.*, 2011.

References

Association for Democratic Reforms. (2019). *Lok Sabha elections 2019 analysis of criminal background, financial, education, gender and other details of winners.* Retrieved from https://adrindia.org/content/lok-sabha-elections-2019-analysis-criminal-background-financial-education-gender-and-other

Association for Democratic Reforms. (2020). *Analysis of sources of funding of national parties of India, FY 2018–19.* Retrieved from https://adrindia.org/content/analysis-sources-funding-national-parties-fy-2018-19

Austin, G. (1999). *Working a democratic constitution: A history of the Indian experience.* New Delhi: Oxford University Press.

Balaji, J. (2011, October 21). "Paid news" claims first political scalp as EC disqualifies MLA. *The Hindu.* Retrieved from https://www.thehindu.com/news/national/paid-news-claims-first-political-scalp-as-ec-disqualifies-mla/article2556366.ece

Central Information Commission (2014, November). (Notification No: CIC/SM/C/2011/001386). Retrieved from https://adrindia.org/sites/default/files/CIC-notice-to-6-Political-Parties-3rd-Nov-2014.pdf

Chatterjee, S. (2012). *Campaign finance reforms in India: Issues and challenges (Issue Brief No.47).* Observer Research Foundation. Retrieved from https://www.orfonline.org/wp-content/ uploads/ 2013/02/ IssueBrief_47.pdf

Chawla, P. (1980, February 15). Bhajan Lal, 35 Janata MLAs join Congress (I). *India Today.* Retrieved from https://www.orfonline.org/wp-content/uploads/2013/02/ IssueBrief_47.pdf

DeSouza, P. R. (2002). Decentralization and local government: The second wind of democracy in India. In Z. Hasan, E. Sridharan, & R. Sudarshan (Eds.), *India's living constitution: Ideas, practices, controversies.* Delhi: Permanent Black.

Debroy, B., & Desai, K. (2017). Analysis of Simultaneous Elections: The "What," "Why" and "How". *NITI AAYOG discussion paper.* Retrieved from https://niti.gov.in/writereaddata/files/document_publication/Note%20on%20Simultaneous%20Elections.pdf

Desai, R. B. (2015, May 23). OBC seats reduced by half in gram panchayats this time. *The Hindu.* Retrieved from https://www.thehindu.com/news/national/karnataka/obc-seats-reduced-by-half-in-gram-panchayats-this-time/article7237461.ece

Devi, V. S. R., & Mendiratta, S. K. (2014). *How India votes: Election laws, practice and procedure.* New Delhi: LexisNexis.

Dubey, A. K. (2018). Presidential takeover of state government. *ILI Law Review Summer Issue.* Retrieved from http://ili.ac.in/pdf/akd.pdf

Election Commission of India. (1998, January 21). *Guidelines for publication and dissemination of results of opinion polls/exit polls. No. ECI/PN/98/09 [Press Note].* Retrieved from https://eci.gov.in/files/file/1614-guidelines-for-publication-and- dissemination-of-results-of-opinion-pollsexit-polls/

Election Commission of India. (2007, March 29). *Section 77 of the Representation of the People Act, 1951: Election Expenditure of candidates: Regarding. No. 76/2007/JS-II.* Retrieved from https://eci.gov.in/files/file/69-section-77-of-the-representation-of-the-people-act-1951-election-expenditure-of-candidates-regarding/

Election Commission of India. (2011, October 21). *Disqualification of Smt. Umlesh Yadav, MLA from Uttar Pradesh for filing incorrect account of election expenditure: Suppression of expenditure incurred on "Paid News." No. ECI/PN/57/2011 [Press Note]*. Retrieved from https://eci.gov.in/files/file/2625-disqualification-of-smt-umlesh-yadav-mla-from-uttar-pradesh-for-filing-incorrect-account-of-election-expenditure-suppression-of-expenditure-incurred-on-%E2%80%9Cpaid-news%E2%80%9D/

Election Commission of India (2018a, September 7). *Bharatiya Janata Party election expenditure statement: Lok Sabha 2014*. Retrieved from https://eci.gov.in/files/file/7806-bharatiya-janata-party/

Election Commission of India. (2018b, September 7). *Indian National Congress election expenditure statement: Lok Sabha 2009*. Retrieved from https://eci.gov.in/files/file/7721-inc/

Election Commission of India. (2018c, September 20). *Status paper on electronic voting machine* (3rd ed.). Retrieved from https://eci.gov.in/files/file/8756-status-paper-on-evm-edition-3/

Election Commission of India. (2019, April 9). *Political coverage on DD News Channel*. Retrieved from https://eci.gov.in/files/file/9853-political-coverage-on-dd-news-channel/

Election Commission of India. (2020, October 9). *General Election to Legislative Assembly of Bihar 2020: Allotment of broadcast/telecast time to national/state political parties -regarding. No. ECI/PN/75/2020/ Communication [Press Note]*. Retrieved from https://eci.gov.in/files/file/12389-general-election-to-legislative-assembly-of-bihar-2020-allotment-of-broadcasttelecast-time-to-nationalstate-political-parties-regarding/

Farooqui, A. (2020). Political representation of a minority: Muslim representation in contemporary India. *India Review, 19*(2), 153–175.

Gowda, R. M.V., & Santhosh, V. (2020). Public funding of elections and political parties. In Pai, S. (Ed.), *Constitutional and democratic institutions in India: A critical analysis* (pp. 343–370). Delhi: Orient Blackswan Private Limited.

Gowda, R. M. V., & Sridharan, E. (2012). Reforming India's party financing and election expenditure laws. *Election Law Journal, 11*(2), 226–240. Retrieved from https://casi.sas.upenn.edu/sites/default/files/upiasi/Reforming%20India%27s%20Party%20Financing%20and%20Election%20Expenditure%20Laws.pdf

Jain, M. P. (2012). *Indian constitutional law*. Haryana: LexisNexis Butterworths Wadhwa.

Jaitley, A. (2017, March 30). *Debate on Finance Bill 2017. India. Parliament. Lok Sabha. Uncorrected Debate. 16th Lok Sabha, Session XI*. Retrieved from http://loksabhadocs.nic.in/debatestextmk/16/XI/30.03.2017.pdf

Kafaltiya, A. (2003). *Democracy and election laws*. New Delhi: Deep and Deep Publications.

Kak, S. (2017, February 9). Electoral bonds will protect donors' identity: FM Jaitley in Lok Sabha. *Hindustan Times*. Retrieved from https://www.hindustantimes.com/india-news/electoral-bonds-will-protect-donor-identity-fm-jaitley-in-lok-sabha/story-IzyGtjGUUNw2CibZ1BfszO.html

Kumar, S. (2018, August 23). Simultaneous polls will be a blow to federalism. *The Asian Age*. Retrieved from https://www.asianage.com/opinion/oped/230818/glamming-up-the-ramp.html

Law Commission of India. (1999). *Reform of electoral laws (Report No. 170)*. Retrieved from http://lawcommissionofindia.nic.in/lc170.htm

Mehta, N. (2019). Digital politics in India's 2019 general elections. *Economic and Political Weekly, 5*(51). Retrieved from https://www.epw.in/engage/article/digital-politics-indias-2019-general-elections

Ministry of Home Affairs (2016, May 03). Response to right to information application. Retrieved from https://factly.in/wp-content/uploads//2018/06/MHA-Presidents-Rule.pdf

Mody, Z. (2013). *10j that changed India*. New Delhi: Penguin Random House.

Parliamentary Standing Committee on Personnel, Public Grievances, Law and Justice. (2015). *Feasibility of holding simultaneous elections to the House of People (Lok Sabha) and State Legislative Assemblies (Report No. 79)*. Retrieved from http://164.100.47.5/newcommittee/reports/EnglishCommittees/Committee%20on%20Personnel,%20PublicGrievances,%20Law%20and%20Justice/79.pdf

Press Information Bureau. (2019, September 26). *"Voluntary code of ethics" by social media platforms to be observed in the general election to the Haryana & Maharashtra Legislative Assemblies and all future elections [Press Release]*. Retrieved from https://pib.gov.in/PressReleaseIframePage.aspx?PRID=1586297#:~:text=Internet%20%26%20Mobile%20Association%20of%20India,bye%20elections%20being%20held%20simultaneously

Quraishi, S.Y. (2014). *An undocumented wonder: The making of the great Indian election*. New Delhi: Rupa.

Quraishi, S. Y. (2019). *The great march of democracy: Seven decades of India's elections*. New Delhi: Penguin Random House.

Roy, M., & Vachana, V. R. (2017, February 28). NOTA and the Indian voter. *The Hindu*. Retrieved from https://www.thehindu.com/opinion/op-ed/nota-and-the-indian-voter/ article17378495.ece

Shani, O. (2017). *How India became democratic: Citizenship and the making of the universal franchise*. Cambridge: Cambridge University Press.

Singh, I. (2016). Haryana's panchayati raj: Excluding the deprived. *Economic and Political Weekly, 51*(16). Retrieved from https://www.epw.in/journal/ 2016/16/commentary/haryanas-panchayati-raj.html

Sridharan, E., & Vaishnav, M. (2017). Election commission of india. In D. Kapur, P.B Mehta, & M.Vaishnav (Eds.), *Re-thinking public institutions in India*. New Delhi: Oxford University Press.

Vaishnav, M. (2014). *Crimes but no punishment in Indian elections*. Carnegie Endowment for International Peace. Retrieved from https://carnegieendowment.org/2014/01/24/crime-but-no-punishment-in-indian-elections-pub-54310

Vaishnav, M. (2018, January 8). Electoral bonds prize anonymity, you won't know who's bought them. *The Indian Express*. Retrieved from https://indianexpress.com/article/opinion/ electoral-bonds-prize-anonymity-you-wont-know-whos-bought-them-5015810/

Vaishnav, M. (2019). *Political finance in India: Déjà vu all over again*. Carnegie Endowment for International Peace. Retrieved from https://carnegieendowment.org /2019/01/31/political-finance-in-india-d-j-vu-all-over-again-pub-78280

25
ELECTION LAW IN MALAYSIA

Mohd Azizuddin Mohd Sani

Introduction

Malaysia recently saw quite an extraordinary political development, a change in government for the first time since independence in 1957. In May 2018, the Barisan Nasional (BN) government was defeated in the 14th General Election by the opposition Pakatan Harapan (PH). An opposition alliance led by Malaysia's former ruler Mahathir Mohamad, then 92 years old, won a majority in parliament, a shock victory that ended the ruling BN coalition's 60-year grip on power.

The PH won 113 seats – one more than required for simple majority – while the BN held 79 seats in the 222-member parliament. The opposition also swept state elections, including those in Johor, where the erstwhile dominant Malay party BN was founded. Its rout was made possible by a "Malaysian tsunami," in which all major ethnic groups turned out to vote against the ruling coalition. John Sifton, Human Rights Watch's Asia advocacy director said in *Aljazeera* that: "Nothing less than a historic political earthquake is under way in Malaysia right now" (Aljazeera, 2018, 1). Though the new PH promised to bring reforms, particularly in electoral system and processes in Malaysia, it did not last a full term. Instead, the coalition collapsed due to infighting, which led to Mahathir resigning as prime minister on February 24, 2020.

A new government, Perikatan Nasional (PN), was formed. It was led by Muhyiddin Yassin, President of Parti Peribumi Bersatu Malaysia (PPBM), who decided to bring PPBM to leave PH and form a new government with Barisan Nasional (BN), Islamic Party (PAS), Sarawak Coalition Parties (GPS), and several parties from Sabah, including Parti Bersatu Sabah (PBS) and a splinter group of People Justice Party's (PKR) leaders after consulting with the Yang di-Pertuan Agong (the King of Malaysia) in March 2020.

This paper, however, will not focus on this political tussle within Malaysian politics. Instead, it will give special attention to politico-legal discourse on election in the country. As we know, there is quite a debate regarding whether Malaysian election law upholds free and fair elections. In general, the Malaysian government has previously admitted the need for reform in Malaysian election laws because of the concerns about many issues, including representatives, constituencies, election financing, and election systems. As announced by the PH government, the Electoral Reform Committee (ERC) was established in 2018 and tasked with improving the electoral system and processes in Malaysia (Chung, 2018). However, this paper will look at

DOI: 10.4324/9780429401800-25

current election law in Malaysia and examine the possibilities for electoral reform that could make Malaysian politics more democratic. Focus will be given to three main issues crucial to ensuring free and fair elections in Malaysia: The electoral system, political financing, and media freedom.

The Electoral System

Elections in Malaysia are governed by three main laws or acts: The Election Act of 1958 (Act 19), the Election Commission Act of 1957 (Act 31), and the Election Offences Act of 1954 (Act 5). Through these acts, the governing body of the election, the Election Commission, was established to oversee the conduct of elections. Political parties, however, are governed under the Societies Act of 1966 and registered with the Registrar of Societies (ROS), a body under the Ministry of Home Affairs that may refuse any registration of any political party if it is deemed to be "used for unlawful purposes or any purpose prejudicial to or incompatible with peace, welfare, security, public order, good order or morality in Malaysia." Party elections are conducted based on their party constitutions by following the guidelines set up through the Societies Act of 1966 (Rahman, 1994).

Because Malaysia is a federation, it has two levels of elections, the federal (or national) and the state levels. The federal level election concerns the 222 members of the *Dewan Rakyat* (House of Representatives), or the lower house of parliament. The upper house of parliament, or *Dewan Negara*, does not have elections to determine its 70 members. Rather, it is filled through nominations, with 26 nominated by the state legislative assemblies, with two senators for each state, and 44 members appointed by the Yang di-Pertuan Agong (the King) from names proposed by the government, including four appointed to represent the federal territories. Members are elected from single-member constituencies utilizing First-Past-The-Post (FPTP) voting. Traditionally, the party with the majority in the House of Representatives forms the federal government. However, since the establishment of the Perikatan Nasional (PN) government in March 2020, the federal government has been formed by members of parliament (MPs), as long as they reach the majority threshold of 112 seats. (The PN government managed to get 113 MPs.) The general election is held at least once every five years as stipulated in the Federal Constitution of Malaysia. The prime minister may ask the Yang di-Pertuan Agong to dissolve the parliament at any time before the five-year period has expired. Besides general and state elections, Malaysia also has by-elections that occur when a member of the parliament or state assembly dies, resigns, or is disqualified from holding a seat. However, the vacancy can be allowed to fill during the half-term, or first two-and-a-half years after the general election. The seat is otherwise left vacant until the next general election (Harding, 1996).

Since independence in 1957, Malaysia has been governed by a coalition of political parties, namely the BN (previously known as Perikatan), until it was defeated in the 2018 general election. It strives to promote the multi-ethnic nature of the coalition, but it is dominated by the most prominent ethnic Malay party, the United Malays National Organization (UMNO). Previously, the BN held a coalition of 13 parties representing specific ethnic groups. However, there were accusations that the BN's tight control over the election process limited the ability of opposition parties to successfully contest elections. The Election Commission (EC) is seen as one of the primary instruments through which the BN has allegedly manipulated the election process for its own political gain. For instance, Malaysia favored malapportioned districts and over-representation of rural communities by utilizing a simple plurality first-past-the-post (FPTP) or majoritarian electoral system modeled on the British Westminster System, with 222 single-member constituencies (SMCs) used for electing representatives to the House of Representatives or Lower House of the Parliament. However, there were many demands, particularly from the opposition, to replace the FPTP system with another system that was more representative and reflected the popular votes during elections. For example, during the general elections of 2013, the BN gained only 47.38% of the popular vote but still managed to win 133 out of the 222 (60 percent) of the parliament seats. On the other hand, the opposition Pakatan Rakyat (PR) gained more than 50.87% of the popular vote but received only 89 (40 percent) of the seats. Clearly, if FPTP had worked to magnify BN's parliamentary majority in the past, it strangely failed to work for PR in 2013. Indeed, had it worked equally well for both sides, PR would now lead the government of Malaysia (Ng, 2015).

The Federal Constitution, through Article 114, establishes the Election Commission (EC) and the criteria governing it. The EC is charged with conducting elections for the House of Representatives and state legislatures. The EC is also charged with recommending changes to constituency boundaries, which are then implemented by the federal government, as well as with the planning and oversight of all of the technical aspects of voter registration and elections. It further acts as a judicial body, hearing grievances from both candidates and electors about any aspect of the election process. Under Article 5(1) of the Elections Act of 1958, entitled "General powers and duties of the Election Commission," the EC shall:

(a) Exercise control and supervision over the conduct of elections and the registration of electors on the electoral rolls, and shall enforce on the part of all election officers fairness, impartiality, and compliance with Part VIII of the Constitution and this Act and any regulations made under it;
(b) Have power to issue to election officers such directions as may be deemed necessary by the Commission to ensure effective execution of Part VIII of the Constitution and this Act and any regulations made under it;
(c) Have power to administer any oath required to be taken under this Act and any regulations made under it; and
(d) Execute and perform all other powers and duties which are conferred or imposed upon it by this Act and any regulations made under it.

The EC has a chairman, a deputy chairman, and five members, all appointed by the Yang di-Pertuan Agong after consulting the Conference of Rulers. All members may serve until the mandatory retirement age of 65, and they may be removed from office only by a special tribunal called by the prime minister. Parliament members may not serve on the commission. The EC is not a fully autonomous body, as stipulated by the Federal Constitution under Article 113(5) on Conduct of Elections, "so far as may be necessary for the purposes of its functions under this Article the Election Commission may make rules, but any such rules shall have effect subject to the provisions of federal law." Therefore, federal law can reverse any provision created by the EC (Lim, 2002).

In fact, any recommendations proposed by the EC for changes to the constituency boundaries must get approval from the prime minister, who later submits the proposal to the Lower House in seeking approval for the delimitation plan. All criteria for the delimitation of electoral boundaries are contained in the Article 113 of the Federal Constitution, and these include the following:

1) Delimitation may not take place more frequently than once every eight years;
2) No single delimitation exercise may take longer than two years to complete; and

3) The recommendation of the commission is submitted to the prime minister, who must then present it to the House of Representatives with or without amendment for a simple-majority vote of at least 112 votes.

The last redelineation exercise was approved just before the 2018 General Election on May 9, 2018. The EC started a delineation review on September 15, 2016, and then submitted its final report to Prime Minister Najib Razak on March 9, 2018. This process was rushed and controversial because it was allegedly done in favor of the ruling BN party. For instance, the Selangor state government controlled by the PH government filed a legal challenge in October 2016 seeking to nullify the EC's notice of redelineation, arguing that it violated the Federal Constitution in drawing new electoral boundaries. The redelineation proposal, covering both federal and state constituencies, received approval with a simple majority votes (Ooi, 2018).

Another big election issue has been malapportionment, which is a manipulation of electorate size. It not only violates the moral democratic principle of "one person, one vote," but it also violates the constitutional principle spelled out in Thirteenth Schedule 2(c), which states that "the number of electors within each constituency in a State ought to be approximately equal." The typical example used to showcase the violation of this "equal apportionment" rule is the comparison between the electorate sizes of two federal constituencies: Kapar's 146,317 voters and Putrajaya's 17,627 voters. It happens that big constituencies tend to be won by the opposition, rather than small constituencies by the BN. With the huge gap in number of electorates, it is clearly in violation of the Thirteenth Schedule 2(c) of the Federal Constitution, which specifically mentions that the number of electors within each constituency, particularly in the same state, ought to be approximately equal (Ooi 2018).

Lim Wei Jiet, Deputy Chairman of the Bar Council Constitutional Law Committee and Secretary General of the National Human Rights Society, became concerned about the proposal to lower the age of voting from 21 to 18, known as "Vote 18." He said that enabling youth to vote would worsen the country's "one person, one vote" principle. He explained that

> In (the state of) Selangor, most youths aged between 18 and 21 are found in under-represented parliamentary constituencies, such as Bangi (178,790 voters), instead of over-represented ones, like Sabak Bernam (40,863)...When politicians say (it is a) historic amendment...(and that) the youth will no longer be ignored or the youth (would be given a) greater political voice, they are not very accurate...The worth of an urban youth in Selangor is only one-fifth the vote of a rural youth in Pahang.
>
> *(Povera, 2019, 1)*

Lim argued that, if issues of gerrymandering and malapportionment of parliamentary constituencies remain unresolved, the constitutional amendment would only effectively empower rural youth in over-represented states. On the other hand, youth in under-represented urban states would not be empowered and would likely continue to be ignored if issues with the constitutional amendment were not addressed. He concluded that, if the authorities were keen on empowering youth, they should address problems with the electoral system. These flaws in the election led the people to demand reform of the electoral system.

Political Financing

The Federal Constitution of Malaysia provides resources for all agencies and laws. However, as the supreme law of the country, it does not have a specific clause on political funding. The

Societies Act of 1966, on the other hand, regulates the act of political funding in Malaysia. Critics have argued that the act mainly regulates the movements of political parties, which must register with the ROS. The party elections are held in accordance with the Societies Act and their respective party constitution. This election is carried out entirely by the management of the political parties themselves. They all need to submit their financial statement and annual report that has been audited by the ROS. This can be said to be the only annual responsibility for the political parties. The implementation of the act can be considered as "loose" because the rules governing the committee are very basic and no proper supervision is carried out by authorized bodies. Hence, problems arise due to the lack of supervision of party election processes by the ROS or other appropriate monitoring bodies. Now, it is imperative to take further steps, such as legislation on financing, in order to reform the partisan system in dealing with corruption and money politics (Sani et. al, 2019).

Another law that can be said to exist as an "almost law" for political financing issue is the Election Offences Act of 1954. The act covers various issues, from punishment for corruptions practices and restrictions on feasts and bribes during the campaign period, to the process of submitting financial statements to the authorized bodies during the campaigning processes (Malaysian Law Journal, 2006). From Sections 8 to 24, the act does mention all the dos and don'ts. There are several other provisions regarding administrative matters, including the steps to submit election petitions, the establishment of enforcement teams, and other administrative issues. Section 19 of the act also provides spending limits for each candidate during the campaigning period: RM200,000 for a parliamentary seat, RM100,000 for a state assembly seat, RM10,000 for a local authority seat, and RM3,000 for a local council seat (Gomez, 2018).

The drafting process for a special law on political financing has been discussed for years, and most political parties and the new government assume that the law can combat corruption and illegal practices among political parties. In fact, in 2015, the BN government established the National Consultative Committee on Political Financing and this committee managed to produce a report on August 26, 2016, setting forth recommendations to enact a new law on political funding and spending. However, it is not clear what happened to the report. According to Abu Kassim Mohammed, the Head of Directors for Governance, Integrity and Anti-Corruption Centre (GIACC), the process of making the political funding act as a reality is one of the most crucial agendas in the National Anti-Corruption Plan (NACP) that had been launched in January 2019 by Prime Minister Mahathir Mohamad, under the PH government. Mohammed also added that the government may take time in preparing the act, up to two years, depending on how far they can engage with all related parties involved with elections (Buang, 2019a).

The most highlighted element in the act regards the transparency of political funding. Taking an example from a most controversial case, in 2015, Malaysia's then prime minister, Najib Razak, was accused of channeling over MYR2.67 billion (approximately USD700 million) in political donations from 1Malaysia Development Berhad (1MDB), a government-run strategic development company, to his personal bank accounts (The Guardian, 2015). People were somehow enlightened about the existence of political funding, and they were eager to know the persons behind the funds. This shows that the government itself needs to be transparent and expose every single transaction that had been made, especially during elections. Furthermore, transparency is very crucial because it can avoid any attempt to abuse power, especially in managing funds and financing political parties.

It is obvious that it is time to amend current laws because they are partially weak. So far, there are no clear guidelines in managing campaigning funds, particularly acts that are considered non-biased in administrating elections. In addition, the enforcement of existing laws can also be considered futile because there are loopholes in political financing that can be manipulated by politicians either from the ruling government or from the opposition. The government and EC, as an autonomous entity, should impose new regulations that specifically cater to political financing. Indeed, Malaysia definitely needs a new law or laws that can govern and regulate political financing.

Freedom of the Media

Malaysians obviously saw major changes in the way that the Malaysian media reported on certain issues, as the PH government pledged to ensure media freedom in Malaysia. Previously known to be politically linked to the BN, the mainstream media – such as TV3, RTM, and the New Straits Times – were free to report unbiased news across the political spectrum. Another media organization, Astro Awani, for instance, had the freedom to dedicate its airtime to broadcast the extremes on both sides of the Malaysian political spectrum, i.e., on PH leaders and opposition leaders. In fact, for the first time, UMNO had its presidential debate televised live in July 2018 (The Sun Daily, 2018). Previously, the media, including the press, would have showcased the former BN government in a very favorable light. Instead, it openly provided limited and negative coverage to the opposition, the PH.

Indeed, the PH government seemed to urge the media to play a key role in providing a check-and-balance in any reported news. In this new paradigm, the media was expected to revert to investigative journalism and the responsible exposure of wrong-doings in order to ensure that those in power would not abuse the trust given to them by the people. In fact, the PH government had promised to implement the right of expression, which included whistleblower protections and the freedom to impart information in order to fight abuses of power and graft. Accountability and integrity seemingly became paramount to safeguard public interest.

Mahathir obviously sent a signal that he would uphold free speech in a "New Malaysia" under the PH government. For instance, Mahathir instructed the police not to prosecute a man who had insulted him, after the police in Langkawi had arrested him on charges of insulting the Prime Minister (Ramzy, 2018). During the campaign period, PH released a manifesto pledging to review and potentially abolish regulations that undermine freedom of the media (Palatino, 2018). These include the Prevention of Terrorism Act of 2015, Prevention of Crime Act of 1959, Sedition Act of 1948, Communications and Multimedia Act of 1998, and Anti-Fake News Act of 2018. Deputy Minister Hanipa Maidin, in the Prime Minister's Department, reiterated the commitment of the PH to repeal those laws, but asked for patience as the government prepared for broader reforms in the bureaucracy:

> I only hope the people can be a little more patient with us, just as we have been very patient with BN over the past 60 years... This is because there is far too much damage left by the previous regime for us and for you. This is not an excuse, but a sincere request from us.
>
> *(Palatino, 2018, 1)*

Tommy Thomas, the attorney general, said that repealing "oppressive laws" such as the Anti-Fake News Act, the Universities and University Colleges Act (UUCA), and the Security Offences Special Measures Act (SOSMA), was one of the government's first legal priorities. He specifically named the fake news law and a national goods and services tax, adding that "the list of such laws is pretty long." Thomas also declared his support for freedom of the media by saying: "I am happy for everybody to criticize me; it's part of free speech…In fact, I'd rather listen to criticism than praises" (Ramzy, 2018, 1).

Initially, the Malaysian Communications and Multimedia Commission (MCMC) used its broad powers to block websites reporting on the 1MDB corruption scandal, including the UK-based Sarawak Report and the regional news outlet, The Asia Sentinel. However, on May 17, 2018, the MCMC decided to unblock Sarawak Report and The Medium (Article 19, 2018). In his recent address to the 73rd United Nations General Assembly on September 28, 2018, Mahathir pledged that Putrajaya would ratify all remaining core UN instruments related to the protection of human rights, including freedom of the media (Rosli, 2018). Mahathir gave the statement in the wake of the riots in the vicinity of the Seafield Sri Maha Mariamman Temple in USJ 25, near Subang Jaya, from Monday November 26, 2018 to Tuesday November 27, 2018 (Bernama, 2018). He said that "No one can act as one likes in violation of the law and cause anxiety among the people and chaos in the country" (Bernama, 2018, 1). The riot incidents near the temple resulted in the death of firefighter Muhammad Adib Mohd Kassim, several injuries, 23 torched cars, and damage to both public and private property. After an investigation into the riots, the police arrested 30 people. This incident raised concerns about hate speech and potential laws to eliminate hate speech in Malaysia.

Salleh Buang said that:

> Free speech is the freedom to voice out our thoughts and expressions without restrictions, whilst hate speech is the abuse of this freedom to harm others, or speech intended to cause violence. Put differently, free speech means we can say whatever we want. Hate speech is when we say things that are offensive or harmful, targeted at a particular person or group of people.
>
> *(2019b, 1)*

In July 2018, minister in the Prime Minister's Department, Mujahid Yusof Rawa proposed three new laws to criminalize hate speech – the Anti-Discrimination Act, National Harmony and Reconciliation Commission Act, and the Religious and Racial Hatred Act. In September 2018, Communications and Multimedia Minister, Gobind Singh Deo, stated there was a need to push ahead for laws on hate speech. He said that such a law must have an "extra-territorial reach" to facilitate the prosecution of persons who reside abroad. Gobind was referring to a "turban remark" by a London-based blogger against a senior Bukit Aman police officer, Amar Singh, which the minister regarded as an attack, not just against the police officer, but against the entire Sikh community (Salleh, 2019b).

Since GE14, Malaysian media is clearly more open than before. Coverage has been given to all ruling and opposition parties, even though the media has prioritized official government statements and messages in the public sphere. However, not all have been convinced that freedom of the media is fully implemented. For instance, Eric Loo argued that Malaysia's political system and race-based society pose barriers to true media freedom. Although media editors can be independent, even if their papers are owned by a political party, in reality, the mainstream media have for decades generally favored the ruling party (Tan, 2018). Moreover, Steven Gan of the Malaysiakini stressed that there are still about 35 laws that impinge on media freedom in Malaysia. Gan wants to see these laws amended. He also wants the independence of government institutions like the anti-graft agency and election commission. Gan welcomed the government's effort to set up a council for media independence. He said that "Therefore, even if new people come into power, they would not be able to inflict too much damage (on media freedom)" (Tan, 2018, 1). In my personal conversation with two media practitioners from Radio and Television

Malaysia (RTM), just after the change of government in March 2020, they expressed a different reality of media freedom under the PH government. According to them, the PH government did impose a directive to blacklist many people, including academic scholars who are critical of them, from appearing in media, particularly the RTM. If this is true, it means that the Ministry of Communications and Multimedia had previously imposed censorship against dissent, which is against the spirit of free media advocated by the PH government itself. Yet, it is clear that media freedom is important in the "New Malaysia." Indeed, the media must be free to write about issues affecting the country, so that Malaysians can understand the steps taken by the government to resolve them (Zainal, 2018).

Transforming the Electoral System

With regard to the electoral system, the Electoral Reform Committee (ERC) established by the PH government proposed the proportionate representation (PR) system to be adopted in the Malaysian electoral system for parliamentary seats, as it is in some Commonwealth countries such as New Zealand. Chairman of ERC, Abdul Rashid Abdul Rahman, said that the system was seen as an improvement to the existing FPTP system. He explained that

> If we change the system to another system, such as the proportionate representation (PR) system, the voters will not vote for the candidate, they will vote for the party. The party will then select the person who will represent it...However, the ERC thinks the FPTP needs to be maintained at least for the state elections as state assemblymen have close ties with the voters.
>
> *(Bernama, 2019a, 1)*

The ERC held nationwide engagement sessions to get feedback from the people on election matters in Malaysia. For instance, in addition to several sessions earlier in 2019 in Putrajaya, Pahang, Johor, Melaka, and Negeri Sembilan, engagement sessions were held in Kota Bharu, Kelantan on August 8, 2019; Ipoh, Perak (August 15, 2019); Kangar, Perlis (August 19, 2019); Alor Setar, Kedah (August 20, 2019); Miri, Sarawak (August 26, 2019); and Kuching, Sarawak (August 28, 2019) (Bernama, 2019b). The ERC also held discussions with various parties to coordinate policy and technical issues related to elections, as well as to conduct comparative studies of the electoral performance of other countries such as Australia, the United Kingdom, New Zealand, Canada, and Germany.

Abdul Rashid also argued that the registration and regulation of political parties should be managed by the EC, rather than by the Registrar of Societies (ROS), in order to ensure transparency. The EC is an independent body that is not controlled by any political party, unlike the ROS, which is a government department under the Ministry of Home Affairs. On the redelineation of electoral boundaries, Abdul Rashid said that a special commission for that purpose should be set up to reduce the workload of the EC, enabling it to focus on its main role of conducting elections (Bernama, 2019a).

Among the recommendations by the ERC is the transformation of the electoral system from a FPTP to a PR system on the federal level. On the state level, the FPTP system is to be maintained in order to ensure that all constituencies in state assemblies are represented in order to address the people's needs on the grassroot level. In parliament, the PR system would be applied to ensure that members of parliament play their specific roles as policy makers. Moreover, the PR system would be able to avoid defections that can bring instability to the government. For example, the formation of the PN system was rooted in the defection of parliament members who withdrew themselves from the PH to join the PN. By having PR system with party lists, the same party who wins the election is guaranteed to maintain power because people vote for political parties, not representative of the party as they do in the FPTP system. For example, consider a party that wins 51% of the seats. If one of the names chosen to be an MP decides to leave the party or passes away, the percentage and number of seats won by that party would remain unaffected because the vacant seat can be filled by a new member of parliament from the same party. The PR option is considered essential for electoral reforms because it gives a choice for electorates to choose the government directly through elections, unlike the FPTP system, where people only choose the representative of their constituencies, not the government, and the representative or member of parliament can collaborate among themselves to form a majority government, sometimes without the consent of people who voted for the political parties of these representatives.

Although the ERC advocates the PR system to bring free and fair elections, it is nonetheless concerned about the survivability of state parties and small parties, particularly in the East Malaysian states of Sabah and Sarawak. Parties like Warisan are only established in Sabah, not in any other state. Therefore, it is difficult for this party to get enough representation on the federal level. For this reason, the ERC favors applying the PR system through the formation of three corridors – namely Peninsular, Sabah, and Sarawak. One thing not mentioned by the ERC is whether each corridor would receive an equal number of seats. In response to ERC's proposal of these corridors, Abang Johari Tun Openg, Chief Minister of Sarawak, demanded that electoral reforms must include giving Sarawak and Sabah more than one-third of the seats in parliament. One of the state proposals to the ERC, according to Abang Johari, would give both states, Sarawak and Sabah, a say in amendments to the Federal Constitution, which require a two-thirds majority to be passed. As of right now, Sarawak has 31 parliamentary seats and Sabah 25 parliamentary seats, for a combined 56 seats, or 18 short of one-third of the total seats (Ling, 2020).

Another concern about changing the electoral system involves issues of ethnicity and religion. P. Ramasamy (2019), Deputy Chief Minister of Penang, said that the electoral system in Malaysia is heavily weighted in favor of ethnic and religious issues, so the focus of the electoral competition is on these issues and not on policy matters. He argues that

> Over the years, this system was reinforced by delimitation exercises that further strengthened the FPTP system in Malaysia. While I am not sure whether we can intelligently copy the mixed-member proportional system (MMP) of countries like Germany or New Zealand, there is nothing wrong with learning from the electoral systems in these countries.
>
> *(Ramasamy, 2019, 1)*

He further argues that

> reforms that we need to bring to the electoral system must be based on the country's unique history and experience. This would be the most difficult part to do, rather than to copy the system of another country or countries. There is no such thing as supplanting one electoral system with another. This might not be even possible, as there are too many high stakes in the present electoral system. Both the ruling coalition and the opposition, having tasted the success of the system, might want the FPTP to continue. Again, the electoral systems in Germany and New Zealand might not have been instituted to address racial or religious issues in the first place. Rather,

> their systems in place might be more favorable to discuss policy matters, rather than matters of ethnicity or religion.
>
> *(Ramasamy, 2019, 1)*

Therefore, Ramasamy (2019) believes that the reform of the electoral system is one way of moving beyond the confines of ethnicity and religion.

The ERC believes that the PR system would allow better representative among ethnic, religious, and gender groups in the political parties and parliament. In the party list, all ethnicities are represented. The foreseeable concern is that political parties in Malaysia are not multiethnic in nature. Many are still ethnic-based political parties with long traditions since independence, including UMNO, Malaysian Chinese Association (MCA), and Malaysian Indian Congress (MIC). In fact, some multiethnic parties like the PKR, DAP, and PAS are also clearly dominated by one ethnic group. There are many who are still concerned about this situation because it could cause the abolishment of ethnic-based political parties in favor of a multiethnic one. Obviously, many parties would resist this idea.

Furthermore, the National Professorial Council of Malaysia (MPN) rejected the move to change the system from FPTP to PR because it could lead to a wider divide between urban and rural voters (Zain, 2020). According to Statista.com, in 2019, 76.61% of Malaysia's total population of 32 million lived in urban areas and cities (Plecher, 2020). This could make political parties focus more on urban issues during the election, rather than on rural ones, unlike now when rural issues are still important because electorates go back to their home towns in rural areas to vote. For, if the PR system is applied, they would not have to go back to rural areas to vote, but could instead vote anywhere close to their home in urban areas. Therefore, there is a concern that rural issues would be sidelined by the political parties because the electorate is primarily from urban areas, the party list would come from urbanites, and urban issues would dominate the public sphere and government policy.

UMNO, on the other hand, welcomed any reasonable amendment to the electoral system, though it requested that the ERC retain the FPTP system. Deputy President of UMNO, Mohamad Hasan, explained that, in the PR system, no by-election would be permitted if a seat is vacant, just to replace with someone from the same party (UMNO Online, 2019). This would then replace the right of people to choose their own representative in an election. The PR system also is not people-friendly, but party-friendly, because elections would no longer be contested by people independently like the FPTP system that allows non-party or independent candidates to contest. The PR system would only allow party members on the list. Hasan also remained uncertain if the PR system would be applied in Sabah and Sarawak, while state elections on the peninsula would still maintain FPTP system. Two systems at the same time could be very confusing. Thus, he urged that any new electoral system should be suitable to the Malaysian context and not just a copy of a system from another country.

The biggest challenge for reforms is not only political will, but also amendments to the constitution and laws in order to embed this transformation of the electoral system. The process of amending the constitution is not easy because it requires a two-thirds majority in parliament. As we know, the current PN government does not have a two-thirds majority. This is going to be a significant hurdle to pass any constitutional amendment because any change of electoral system requires amendment to the constitution. Furthermore, Khoo Ying Hooi (2020) argues that electoral reforms alone cannot be effective unless other institutional reforms are also addressed. She wants Malaysia to

> repeal oppressive laws such as the Sedition Act and laws that allow detention without trial such as the Security Offences (Special Measures) Act (SOSMA). Reforms must

> also ensure a clear separation of powers between the three branches of government: the executive, the legislature, and the judiciary. Furthermore, these reforms must be comprehensive to be effective.
>
> *(Khoo, 2020, 1)*

However, one successful reform effort done by the PH government is "Vote 18." With this reform, Malaysia has managed to lower the voting age and eligibility to contest in election from 21 to 18 years. Furthermore, voters are also automatically registered in the electoral roll. The Constitution (Amendment) Bill 2019 to lower the voting age to 18 was approved in the parliament with more than a two-thirds majority, by 211 members of parliament, on July 16, 2019. This brings the prospect of about 7.8 million new voters in the electoral roll by 2023 (Daim & Radhi, 2019). This amendment is waiting to be gazetted before it can be applied in future elections. The main worry of "Vote 18" is the issue of political literacy among young voters. Indeed, there is a tendency for young Malaysians to become politicized by political parties for votes. One major anxiety is that Malaysia's education system will be politicized by political parties influencing the syllabus and curriculum at the school level. This issue needs to be addressed by the government in order to avoid any manipulation that is detrimental to the education system. Moreover, if Malaysia introduces the PR system, it would force the EC to urgently promote electoral education because voters in Malaysia should be aware and educated about the new electoral system. This definitely takes time to implement. Therefore, it requires systematic strategy to educate Malaysia in order to make its citizens aware of the new electoral system before they can be allowed to vote in elections.

Conclusion

According to Rashid, the Chairman of the ERC, one of the main priorities for electoral reforms is to eradicate corruption in the electoral system. This is in line with the government's goal for a corruption-free administration and transparency. For him, it is important to have a free and fair election and to abolish corrupt practices. He argued

> We were lucky to have good administrative practices in place in spite of the fact that there were corrupt incidences. We have been managing the country well. I believe the government elected after GE14 (14th General Election), too, would continue the practice of good governance, perhaps better than before, minus some of the bad practices. Mahathir recognizes that, and I always talk to him about it and advise him on how we cannot go on with laws that no longer keep up with the times. You have to change.
>
> *(Othman, 2019)*

The ERC was working towards the creation of a law for elections, which might oppose separate legislation for electoral practices. It was a law that covers an act and regulations. In August 2020, ERC submitted 49 recommendations for electoral reforms to the government without disclosing the details about these recommendations. The PN government has yet to make any policy on whether to proceed or not with the ERC's recommendations.

Another major aspect that the PN government needs to examine is the introduction of a law that regulates political financing. Political financing, or money politics, has become a big concern for Malaysians, particularly during the general election. Democratic countries, such as our neighboring countries, Singapore and Indonesia, have enacted laws to regulate political financing. Surprisingly, Malaysia has yet to take any steps to regulate political parties and campaign financing, let alone establish a body that can regulate political financing. Political financing is a term to explain political contributions and spending of political parties and politicians. Previously, the BN and PH government had pledged to introduce a law on political financing, but failed to do so. Now, it is the job of the PN government to fulfill the need to enact a law on political financing. Indeed, such a law is vital in order to avoid vote-buying during elections and, worse still, political trade-offs and foreign interventions in domestic affairs. For instance, foreign political donations may fuel foreign imperialism, which could influence the country's political process in a negative way. Obviously, there will be possible dangers if the government refuses to regulate political financing.

In my opinion, electoral reforms need political will and efforts from the current PN government. Facing the Covid-19 pandemic and uncertainties in politics and economy may distract the government from electoral reforms. However, only electoral reforms can make Malaysia more mature in democracy and ensure that people's votes are not wasted but counted for the benefit of democracy. Although changing electoral system could be somewhat controversial and, perhaps, need further in-depth study before implementation, reforms that address political financing and freedom of the media are definitely essential for democracy. Though I am not yet sure how the current government will respond to proposals from the ERC, I hope that there is a light at the end of the tunnel for electoral reforms. The most important issue is that the government should have a main policy that includes the propagation of electoral reforms for the common good.

References

Aljazeera. (2018, May 10). Malaysia's opposition pulls off shocking election win. Retrieved from https://www.aljazeera.com/news/2018/05/malaysia-opposition-pulls-shocking-election-win-180509184811723.html

Article 19. (2018, May 22). Reform laws restricting freedom of expression. *Malaysiakini*. Retrieved from: https://www.malaysiakini.com/news/426155

Bernama. (2018, November 30). Mahathir warns free speech abusers. *Daily Express*. Retrieved from: http://www.dailyexpress.com.my/news.cfm?NewsID=129064

Bernama. (2019a, October 2). Electoral Reform Committee proposes proportionate representation system for parliamentary seats. *The Sun Daily*. Retrieved from https://www.thesundaily.my/local/electoral-reform-committee-proposes-proportionate-representation-system-for-parliamentary-seats-KX1440804

Bernama. (2019b, August 3). ERC holds six engagement sessions in August. *The Sun Daily*. Retrieved from https://www.thesundaily.my/local/erc-holds-six-engagement-sessions-in-august-DJ1209371

Buang, S. (2019a). *Akta dana politik: Bersediakah?* Kuala Lumpur: Utusan Malaysia.

Buang, S. (2019b, January 2). Freedom of speech: Do not cross the line. *New Straits Times*. Retrieved from https://www.nst.com.my/opinion/columnists/2019/01/446413/ freedom-speech-do-not-cross-line

Chung, C. (2018, August 30). 15 reforms on the table for ERC. *The Star Online*. Retrieved from https://www.thestar.com.my/news/nation/2018/08/30/15-reforms-on-the-table-for-erc-committee-to-study-proposals-for-two-years-before-submitting-it-to-t

Daim, N., & Nor, A. M. R. (2019, July 16). Dewan Rakyat approves 'Vote 18'. *New Straits Times*. Retrieved from https://www.nst.com.my/news/government-public-policy/2019/07/504855/dewan-rakyat-approves-vote-18

Gomez, E. T. (2018). *Financing politics and the 14th General Election*. Kuala Lumpur: The Star.

The Guardian. (2015, July 6). Malaysian taskforce investigates allegations $700m paid to Najib. Retrieved March 24, 2018 from https://www.theguardian.com/world/72015/jul/ 06/malaysian-task-force-investigates-allegations-700m-paid-to-pm-najib

Harding, A. (1996). *Law, government and the constitution in Malaysia*. Kuala Lumpur: Malayan Law Journal Sdn Bhd.

Kamal, S. M. (2018, May 15). Ambiga, Shad Saleem members of newly-formed Institutional Reforms Committee. *Malay Mail.* Retrieved from https://www.malaymail.com/news/malaysia/2018/05/15/ambiga-shad-saleem-members-of-newly-formed-institutional-reforms-committee/1631086

Khoo, Y. H. (2020, March 21). People matter in electoral reforms. *Aliran.* Retrieved from https://aliran.com/newsletters/people-matter-in-electoral-reforms/

Lim, H. H. (2002). Electoral politics in Malaysia: 'Managing' elections in a plural society. In A. Croissant (Ed.), *Electoral Politics in Southeast and East Asia* (pp. 101–148). Singapore: Friedrich Ebert Stiftung.

Ling, S. (2020, February 6). Abang Johari: Electoral reforms must give Sarawak, Sabah one-third of parliament seats. *The Star Online.* Retrieved from https://www.thestar.com.my/news/nation/2020/02/06/abang-johari-electoral-reforms-must-give-sarawak-sabah-one-third-of-parliament-seat

Malaysiakini. (2019, March 30). Daim, Jomo setuju dedah laporan CEP tapi terserah k'jaan. Retrieved from https://www.malaysiakini.com/news/470153

Malaysian Law Journal. (2006). *Undang-Undang Malaysia: Akta 5 akta kesalahan pilihan raya 1954.* Kuala Lumpur: Percetakan Nasional Berhad.

Ng, C. N. (2015). The influence of electoral laws on the conduct of elections in Malaysia. *Tindakan Malaysia.* Retrieved from https://www.academia.edu/5270000/ The_Influence_of_Electoral_Laws_On_The_Conduct_Of_Elections_In_Malaysia

Ooi, K. H. (2018, March 19). How Malaysia's election is being rigged. *New Naratif.* Retrieved from https://newnaratif.com/research/malaysias-election-rigged/

Othman, A. F. (2019, October 9). Electoral reform vital to ensure level playing field. *New Straits Times.* Retrieved from https://www.nst.com.my/news/nation/2019/ 10/528264/electoral-reform-vital-ensure-level-playing-field

Palatino, M. (2018, August 9). The jury's still out on freedom of expression in 'New Malaysia.' *Asian Correspondent.* Retrieved from https://asiancorrespondent.com/2018/08/freedom-of-expression-malaysia/

Plecher, H. (2020, July 9). Urbanization in Malaysia 2019. *Statista.com.* Retrieved from https://www.statista.com/statistics/455880/urbanization-in-malaysia/

Povera, A. (2019, July 18). Real flaws are gerrymandering, malapportionment. *New Straits Times.* Retrieved from https://www.nst.com.my/news/nation/2019/07/505239/real-flaws-are-gerrymandering-malapportionment

Rahman, A. R. (1994). *The conduct of elections in Malaysia.* Kuala Lumpur: Berita Publishing Sdn. Bhd.

Ramasamy, P. (2019, November 14). Racial, religious politics can't be reduced by electoral reform alone. *Malaysiakini.* Retrieved from https://www.malaysiakini.com/news/499742

Ramzy, A. (2018, June 18). Hopes for new era of Malaysian free speech are high, but pending. *New York Times.* Retrieved from https://www.nytimes.com/2018/06/18/world/ asia/malaysia-mahathir-free-speech.html

Rosli, J. (2018, October 1). There must be limits to freedom, Dr M says of human rights. *Malay Mail Online.* Retrieved from https://www.malaymail.com/news/malaysia/2018/10/01/ there-must-be-limits-to-freedom-dr-m-says-of-human-rights/1678304

Sani, M. A. M., Shabudin, N. A. S., Zakuan, U. A. A., Ahmad, N. S. Y., Pandian, S., & Kasim, A. (2019). Political financing in Malaysia: The weakest link in Malaysian politics. *Journal of Advanced Research in Dynamical and Control Systems, 11*(5), 1120–1128.

Tan, C. K. (2018, December 4). Malaysia media spreads its wings as Mahathir promises free speech. *Nikkei.* Retrieved from https://asia.nikkei.com/Spotlight/Asia-Insight/Malaysia-media-spreads-its-wings-as-Mahathir-promises-free-speech

The Sun Daily. (2018, June 30). Umno elections showdown: Three presidential candidates lay out why the party lost out big in GE14. Retrieved from https://www.thesundaily.my/archive/umno-elections-showdown-three-presidential-candidates-lay-out-why-party-lost-out-big-BUARCH560234

UMNO Online. (2019, December 21). Pembaharuan pilihan raya: Jangan langgar hak asasi dalam berdemokrasi – tok mat. Retrieved from https://umno-online.my/2019/12/21/pembaharuan-pilihan-raya-jangan-langgar-hak-asasi-dalam-berdemokrasi-tok-mat/

Zain, H. (2020, February 12). Sistem perwakilan berkadar untungkan DAP. *Malaysiakini.* Retrieved from https://www.malaysiakini.com/news/510578

Zainal, H. (2018, June 2). Anwar: Media freedom truly important in the new Malaysia. *The Star Online.* Retrieved from https://www.thestar.com.my/news/nation/2018/06/02/anwar-media-freedom-truly-important-in-the-new-malaysia/#G9hJU0dE5YD0hhD8.99

26

LEGAL REFORMS FOR ELECTORAL INTEGRITY IN PAKISTAN

Hassan Nasir Mirbahar[1]

Introduction

Concerns over electoral integrity are ubiquitous globally. While many such concerns are reported from emerging or new democracies, older democracies are not immune to electoral malpractices (Amar, 2017; Birch, 2007, 2011; Norris, 2011, 2012, 2013a, 2017c; Norris, Frank, & Coma, 2014; Norris, Nai, & Grömping, 2016). Such malpractices depress voter turnout, reduce confidence in elections, and make them contentious, resulting in protracted regime instability and often in violent actions (Birch, 2010, 2011; Norris, Frank, & Coma, 2015). These malpractices can be addressed by applying international electoral integrity standards to both electoral laws and the conduct of elections (Mirbahar, 2019; Norris, 2014, 2017b). As a necessary first step, the electoral legislation must be reformed in line with international election standards.

However, scholarly research on electoral reforms has mostly been focused on changes within electoral systems: The so-called major electoral reforms. For a long time, several early scholars considered the major reforms to be the only reforms that were worthy of intellectual attention (Celis, Krook, & Meier, 2011; Jacobs & Leyenaar, 2011; Katz, 2011; Leyenaar & Hazan, 2011; Norris, 2011). Later scholars have widened their electoral reforms research to include technical and minor reforms, examining such topics as the introduction of gender quotas, campaign finance and voting rights (Birch, 2005; Celis et al., 2011; Leyenaar & Hazan, 2011; Massicotte, Blais, & Yoshinaka, 2004; Norris, 2004). Despite such advancements, authors have pointed out several shortcomings in the previous scholarly research on electoral reforms, such as inconsistently and inadequately defining minor and technical reforms, too great a focus on national-level reforms, and a general tendency to overlook reforms in new and emerging democracies. Such narrow attention poses methodological challenges as well (Bowler & Donovan, 2013; Jacobs & Leyenaar, 2011; Katz, 2011; Leyenaar & Hazan, 2011). Taking on the agenda of the reconceptualization of electoral reforms, Jacobs and Leyenaar (2011) have tried to develop a conceptual framework for major, minor, and technical reforms. While their approach has some strengths, it faces archetypal problems. Firstly, it still focuses heavily on electoral systems as major reforms. Secondly, its differentiation of technical, minor, and major reforms is blurry, as the so-called major and minor reforms involve many technicalities (such as the definitions of electoral systems). Hence "technical reforms" cannot be separated from so-called major or minor reforms. Thirdly, scholars do not define the word "reform," which ordinarily means an improvement.

DOI: 10.4324/9780429401800-26

Table 26.1 Typologies of Electoral Reforms Based on Electoral Integrity Standards

Reform Category	*Definitions*
Major	If improvements are made to at least six electoral processes
Minor	If improvements are made to fewer than six electoral processes
Non-reform	Electoral changes that do not impact electoral integrity, i.e., they neither improve it nor reduce it
Regressive changes	Changes in electoral legislation that reduce electoral integrity
No Change/Reform	When reform efforts failed, and no changes were made

Since no electoral system is perfect, a change of electoral system cannot be considered a reform. Fourthly, it limits its focus to five aspects of elections without fully justifying the selection; thereby, it ignores the full electoral cycle. Finally, it does not include any standards that can be applied to study reforms across countries.

Therefore, the present chapter departs from the existing scholarly research on electoral reforms and proposes a new framework for studying them. The proposed framework uses the electoral integrity standards and electoral cycle approach to define electoral reforms as legislative changes that improve electoral integrity. It also defines typologies of major and minor reforms while dropping the category of technical reforms. The paper also describes what can be called "non-reform" and what legal change should be considered "regressive" (see Table 26.1). The framework is then applied to explain Pakistan's electoral reforms through the Elections Act 2017.

Pakistan made headlines globally in 2017 as its bicameral federal parliament enacted the Elections Act 2017, improving transparency, accountability, and inclusion in its electoral processes. This was an outcome of deliberations of a 33-member committee, which held some 120 meetings during the three or so years of its operation. The Elections Act consolidated Pakistan's scattered election laws into one law and introduced several reforms (N. A. o. Pakistan, 2017). Most of these reforms were in line with electoral integrity standards, thereby helping to diffuse many electoral integrity standards in Pakistan's new electoral framework (Mirbahar & Simm, 2018). While not perfect, the electoral reform process and the Elections Act 2017 set a good example that many old and new democracies can adapt to their respective situation.

What Is Electoral Integrity?

This paper defines electoral integrity based on standards grounded in international public law (Davis-Roberts & Carroll, 2010; Mirbahar, 2019; Norris, 2013b, 2014). This framework is chosen as it provides a universal and relatively comprehensive approach for measuring electoral integrity.

Several international human rights declarations and treaties form the sources of these standards. Notable among these are the Universal Declaration of Human Rights (UDHR) (UN, 1948) and its Article 21, the International Covenant on Civil and Political Rights (ICCPR) (UN, 1966) Article 25, the Convention on the Elimination of All Forms of Discrimination against Women (CEDAW) (UN, 1979) Article 7, and the Convention on the Rights of Persons with Disabilities (CRPD) (UN, 2007), which in Article 29 includes political rights. The International Convention on the Elimination of All Forms of Racial

Discrimination (ICERD) (UN, 1965) and the Convention against Corruption (CAC) (UN, 2003) are also highly relevant for elections.

The standards contained in these declarations and treaties have been reinforced through several political commitments (Meyer-Resende, 2011; Norris, 2013a). Together with these, the Human Rights Committee's General Comment 25 on ICCPR's Article 25 unpacks the standards and provides authoritative guidelines for applying them to elections.[2] General Comment 34 on the ICCPR and CEDAW Committee's General Recommendation 23 are also relevant (Commission, 2008; TCC, 2015).

The relevance and usefulness of these standards are further supported by their widespread use in international aid and domestic practices. The core human rights treaties have been ratified by over 160 countries, which also signifies their universal application and acceptability. Almost all international election observation groups use these standards as part of their methodology for assessing electoral laws and elections (Davis-Roberts & Carroll, 2010; Mirbahar, 2019; Norris, 2013a, 2014). Many domestic actors, including election observers, increasingly draw on these standards as a framework for their work.

Scholars, practitioners, and media often focus mostly on the polling day itself to make a judgement on elections. However, elections are a process involving several steps across an electoral cycle, which is often divided into three broad phases, namely, pre-polling days, polling-day, and post-polling day processes. Ergo, a full assessment of the integrity or quality of elections requires investigation into all elements across the electoral cycle. Together the cycle and standards constitute a way of assessing the quality of electoral laws and the conduct of elections that is more transparent, comprehensive, and accessible than other approaches.

International law requires that countries incorporate the treaty provisions within their domestic legislation:

> Where *not already provided for by existing legislative or other measures*, each State Party to the present Covenant undertakes to take the necessary steps, *in accordance with its constitutional processes* and with the provisions of the present Covenant, *to adopt such laws or other measures* as may be necessary to give effect to the rights recognized in the present Covenant. (emphasis added)
>
> *(See Article 2.2. of ICCPR UN, 1966)*

While international law comes into effect automatically in the countries following the monist legal tradition, countries with the dualist legal tradition have to provide for it expressly in the election legislation (Marian, 2007). Notwithstanding legal traditions, incorporation of electoral standards should cover several aspects in the election legislation, including the administration of elections, election system, candidacy rights and procedures, the right to vote, voters' registration, and boundary delimitation. It should also include voting, and election-day procedures, the secrecy of the ballot, and provisions for counting, tabulation, and compilation of results, transparency and accountability requirements, campaign rights and obligations, dispute resolution, women voting rights and non-discrimination, and consideration of persons with disabilities and accessibility.

International electoral standards do not favor any election system or political system; they only require that the election system should be defined in the legal framework while respecting universal and equal suffrage and other standards (Meyer-Resende, 2011).

Therefore, electoral integrity framework applies to assessing laws as well as electoral reforms when measuring electoral integrity.

Redefining Electoral Reforms

Unpacking Existing Electoral Reform Studies

Scholarly research has long focused on electoral reforms. Monique Leyenaar and Reuven Hazan (2011) identify three waves of such studies. The first two of these waves mainly focused on the so-called major reforms. Arend Lijphart, as one of the founders of these studies, defined major reform as "wholesale replacement of the electoral formulae of national electoral systems," focusing on the proportionality of the system, district magnitudes and thresholds for translating votes into seats (Lijphart, 1994, 51). For many years, scholars only focused on major reforms, studying such changes purely at the national level, while also covering the motives behinds the reforms and their political outcomes (Ferrara et al., 2006; Grofman & Lijphart, 1986; Moser & Scheiner, 2012). Some of the later studies started including minor reforms, albeit without adequately defining them. Leyenaar and Hazan argue that the third wave was more comprehensive and inclusive, as it focused on major, minor, and technical reforms covering such changes as compulsory voting, gender quotas, and several other electoral processes. The third wave also covered different actors that triggered reforms, such as courts, civil society organizations, and the public, unlike earlier studies which only considered politicians. However, scholars could not agree on definitions of major, minor, or technical. For example, some considered minor reforms to be minor changes to operative details of electoral systems, whereas others thought minor reforms should include reforms at the subnational or local level (Bowler & Farrell, 2009; Jacobs & Leyenaar, 2011; Katz, 2011; Leyenaar & Hazan, 2011). Major reforms, on the other hand, were reforms at the national level and only deemed "major" if they entirely or significantly changed the electoral system. Other scholars tried to distinguish minor from major based on the degree of impact of the reforms. For them, a significant impact on the electorate or representation meant a major reform. In contrast, a minor impact was considered minor reform.

Kristof Jacobs and Monique Leyenaar (2011) filled the definitional gap by providing a new conceptualization framework that could be used to define major, minor, and technical electoral reforms. In their framework, they use five dimensions to break down the term "electoral" in the electoral reforms. These five dimensions are:

1. Proportionality: Changes to different aspects of the electoral system;
2. Electoral levels: Levels at which changes are made;
3. Inclusiveness: How far changes promote inclusiveness of elections;
4. Ballot Structure: Including candidate choices and inclusion of gender quotas;
5. Electoral Processes: The operative details on the election management and conduct of polling.

Jacobs and Leyenaar (2011) take a qualitative assessment of content and quantitative measurement of the degree of reform using these five dimensions for defining the major, minor, and technical reforms. Using this framework, they define electoral reforms as any change in the legislation on the several electoral processes. While they provide a more robust way of conceptualizing major, minor, and technical reforms, they still assign higher weighting to electoral system changes at the national level and label such changes as major reforms. So, in a way, they do not address some of the problems that Leyenaar and Hazan point out when reinvigorating the need for a reconceptualization of electoral reforms and broadening of their scope. Besides, there are several other shortcomings within this approach, as follows.

Firstly, while Jacobs and Leyenaar (2011) make a good start by using "electoral" as the basis for defining electoral reforms, they do not fully define the term "electoral" and limit themselves to five dimensions of elections. Such an approach is problematic because as the paper contends above, elections are a process, and they involve several steps. These are best explained by the electoral cycle, which divides an electoral process into pre-polling day, polling day, and post-polling day phases, each incorporating multiple steps and factors as set out earlier in this paper. All these aspects have to be defined in law together with the electoral system, and therefore any changes to the law should consider the entire spectrum of the electoral cycle. Jacobs and Leyenaar do not fully justify why they pick their five aspects over others, nor why multiple aspects are lumped together under criterion number five.

Secondly, an election system is only one part of the electoral processes or laws. There are at least eleven other key electoral processes, which need to be defined (TCC, 2015). Scholars rightly point out that an election system is the most lethal weapon of election manipulation, and that is perhaps the reason why Jacobs and Leyenaar and others attach most importance to it (Grofman & Lijphart, 1986; Jacobs & Leyenaar, 2011). Nevertheless, in practice, it is equally possible to use other aspects of the electoral design to manipulate electoral outcomes. Take the example of gerrymandering in boundary delimitation, banning opposition parties by law, or imposing one-party rule.

Thirdly, Jacobs and Leyenaar (2011) treat as technical only those matters in elections that deal with election processes, barring four first criteria in their framework (proportionality, electoral levels, inclusiveness, and ballot structure). In a way, they do not consider an election system as technical. This treatment is untenable as election systems are also highly technical, like other aspects of the electoral process such as voter registration, boundary delimitation, counting processes, or candidate scrutiny. A lot of electoral technicalities flow from electoral systems, such as: How do we determine winners? How do votes translate into seats? Must electoral boundaries be drawn and, if so, how can those boundaries be drawn? In short, the definition of electoral systems requires provisions on various technical aspects of an election system.

Otherwise, another problem with most scholarly research is that it does not define the word "reform" – indeed that is the case with Jacobs and Leyenaar. Cambridge, Oxford, and Merriam-Webster dictionaries define reform as a change that improves something. If we apply this definition, then a change in the electoral system does not always translate into an improvement in the elections. Why is this?

Firstly, studies point out that no election system is perfect; each has its promises and perils (Bowler, Farrell, & Pettitt, 2005; Reynolds, Reilly, & Ellis, 2005). A mere change of election system is not a reform. Even if one considers that one election system is better than another, countries have switched back and forth from one system to another repeatedly. So which instance is a reform – switching from a majoritarian system to a proportional system or vice versa?

Secondly, the impact of change in the election system on improving or reducing electoral integrity also deserves some attention. A mere textbook-based application of most election systems has limited or no impact on electoral integrity. However, some regimes do use election systems in a manipulative way, to discriminate against some groups; this goes against the electoral integrity standards. A party block vote system or panel system, for example, may be used in this way. Such limited exceptions aside, an election system may not impact electoral integrity all the time. However, changes to most other aspects of the electoral cycle do improve or reduce electoral integrity.

Therefore, a change in the electoral system does not itself amount to reform or improvement. One has to see whether the proposed change improves electoral integrity or not.

Defining Electoral Reforms and Their Typologies

To address the above problems, for the purpose of the present paper and future studies, this paper proposes to use the following definition of electoral reforms:

> A change to election legislation that improves the quality or integrity of elections is an election reform.

Here, the term legislation is used in its broad sense. It could include a constitution, primary laws (acts of parliament), and regulations or administrative rules (Clegg et al., 2016). Different countries incorporate definitions of electoral processes at different levels of law,[3] therefore study of electoral reforms may have to assess changes at all these three hierarchies of laws. From the international standards perspective, the most essential aspects should at least be defined within primary laws.

This paper also proposes to use the electoral cycle approach to measure electoral reforms, i.e., to assess reforms across all aspects of an election.

The paper proposes five categories for labelling legal reforms (see Table 26.1). Firstly, the approach can be used to define major and minor reforms more transparently, both qualitatively and quantitively. This paper has identified above at least 12 aspects of elections that need legal definitions. If at least six of these aspects are improved, we should consider this to constitute major reform. Legislative changes that improve fewer than six aspects should be considered minor reforms.

Secondly, any legal change that does not improve or reduce electoral integrity will be considered a non-reform.

Thirdly, a change that reduces electoral integrity will be regarded as a regressive amendment. In relation to this, some changes need more in-depth analysis to see whether they violate or promote electoral integrity, or whether they constitute non-reform. While all such examples cannot be covered in this short paper, one case is discussed to give an example.

The introduction of voting technology, which some consider a significant reform. The voting machines help improve vote casting and counting processes. However, they compromise both secrecy of ballot and transparency of elections (DRI, 2011), which are core tenets of electoral standards. Therefore, the introduction of voting machines can be a regressive change, warranting a closer assessment.

Finally, if a reform effort was undertaken, but no changes were made to the electoral legislation or the effort failed, such an effort will be categorized as no change/reform.

As pointed out above, the author considers the technical category unhelpful as almost all electoral processes, including the election system, involve several technical details.

Assessing the Elections Act 2017 Based on the Proposed Framework

The Elections Act 2017 introduced several reforms long demanded by political parties and civil society and suggested by the international observers. The ECP also made several improvements to the rules and conduct of elections (DRI, 2018; FAFEN, 2018; Union, 2018),[4] but owing to limited space, this paper focuses its analysis on the Elections Act 2017. However, many of the ECP's endeavors were a result of reforms introduced in the Elections Act 2017.

As Table 26.2 summarizes, the Elections Act improved at least nine aspects of elections. Six of these are registered as significant reforms, namely: The administration of elections, transparency and accountability, dispute resolution, results processes, women's participation, and the

Table 26.2 Summary of Reforms Introduced through Pakistan's Elections Act 2017

Election Process Aspect	*Change*	*Degree of Change*	*Overall Reform Type*
1. The administration of elections	ECP's financial and administrative powers enhanced, including measures for its accountability	Significant improvements	Major
2. Election system	No change	None	
3. Candidacy rights and procedures	No change	None	
4. Right to vote and voter registration	Voter registration simplified, while a regressive provision was maintained	Improvements	
5. Boundary delimitation	Criteria for equality of suffrage established	Improvements	
6. Voting/election-day procedures, the secrecy of the ballot	Security of ballot improved	Improvements	
7. Provisions for counting, tabulation, and compilation of results	Transparency of process increased	Significant Improvements	
8. Transparency and accountability requirements	Several provisions increased transparency and accountability of the electoral process	Significant improvements	
9. Campaign rights and obligations	No change	None	
10. Dispute resolution, including complaints and petitions, using the due process of law	Right to remedy and due process of law expanded	Significant improvements	
11. Provisions with regards to women's participation, including non-discrimination and affirmative action as may be required	Several measures introduced to increase women's participation as voters and candidates	Significant improvements	
12. Provisions with regards to persons with disabilities, including universal accessibility	Postal ballots introduced for persons with some disabilities	Significant improvements	

rights of persons with disabilities. The right to vote and voting procedures were improved, but the act retained one regressive provision in this regard, and these are therefore categorized as a minor improvement. Minor improvements were also made to the boundary delimitation provisions.

No changes were made to three electoral aspects: The election system, candidacy rights, and campaign rights. Pakistan's candidacy criteria remain problematic as they contain subjective provisions and needed reform. The committee did not touch them, partly because some of the criteria are allegedly based on religious interpretations.

Based on the reform typologies framework defined above, the author categorizes the act's provisions as constituting major electoral reform as nine electoral aspects were improved.

A brief overview of some of the key reforms contained in the law is presented below. Where relevant, analysis is also presented on reforms not undertaken or on where the new law falls short in meeting the election standards.

Empowerment of the ECP

International electoral standards require that an election management body should be autonomous and charged with adequate financial and administrative powers to conduct credible elections (Commission, 2008; TCC, 2015). While the Constitution of Pakistan provides for an independent election commission, the ECP previously lacked several administrative and financial powers, which limited its ability to manage some aspects of elections (DRI & RSIL, 2017). The Elections Act 2017 increased the autonomy of the ECP to help it fulfil its constitutional mandate. In particular, it empowered the ECP to initiate disciplinary measures against election officials. Before 2017, the ECP had no explicit authority to take actions against election officials seconded from other government departments. As a result, if an official did not follow the law or the ECP directions, the ECP was helpless to undertake corrective measures. All it could do was to write to the department responsible for taking appropriate action (Union, 2013b). However, the incumbent or winning government could easily influence such proceedings in their favor, especially if they benefited from the deliberate or indeliberate wrongdoings of election officials. Having been granted these powers, the ECP can directly initiate proceedings and make decisions as per the law. The act, however, falls short of defining the ECP's mandate over the staff seconded from the judiciary.

Similarly, under the past electoral laws, the ECP was required to seek presidential approval for formulating administrative rules for the conduct of elections. This requirement compromised the ECP's independence, as the president was associated with the ruling government, and often the approval was sent through the government. The arrangement resulted in delays in the approval of rules ahead of the 2013 elections, which affected the ECP's ability to move ahead with some core electoral operations (DRI & RSIL, 2017; Union, 2013b). The ECP can now formulate election rules without presidential approval. To further boost the ECP's independence, the act also gave the ECP full financial and administrative authority. It does not require the executive's approval for its budget, nor for creating staff positions that it deems necessary for the operations of the elections. The commission was also given powers equal to a high court of Pakistan.

Accountability of the ECP

The international electoral standards call for the right to information and the accountability of state institutions, including election management bodies. The enforcement of these provisions during Pakistani elections has, however, been limited in the past (DRI & RSIL, 2017). The Elections Act 2017 increased the accountability of the ECP. Although it is a constitutionally independent body, it continues to operate using taxpayers' money. It should be accountable before the people and their representatives. The Elections Act requires the ECP to develop and submit its annual reports to the parliament and provincial assemblies and publish the same on its websites. Furthermore, the ECP is also required to develop an action plan at least four months before a general election. Additionally, the law requires the ECP to publish election rules on its website and seek stakeholder input during their formulation (DRI, 2018). Such a requirement is vital because, in the past, the ECP did not consult political parties or civil society when formulating administrative rules under the election legal framework.

Improvements to the Complaints and Tribunal Processes

The ICCPR stipulates that any citizens whose rights are violated should have the right and opportunity to file complaints (DRI, 2010b; UN, 1966). However, Pakistan's electoral legal framework did not allow every citizen to do so. The right to complain was limited to candidates, who could do so regarding results and candidacy, and it was extended to voters only in regard to voter registration. This meant that Pakistan's legal framework was not compliant with the election standards (DRI & RSIL, 2017). The Elections Act 2017 addressed the issue, in part, and afforded the citizens the right and opportunity to file complaints to the ECP on any aspect of an election. The law requires the ECP to address complaints received within 30 days and to publish on its website the orders issued to address complaints. The right to complain has one limitation in place, however. It does not allow voters or citizens to challenge results before electoral tribunals. Future reforms could consider extending the scope of complaints to cover this as well, which would further improve Pakistan's compliance with the electoral integrity framework.

The act retains the provisions that limited the right to appeal on boundary delimitation. It states that no delimitation can be challenged in a court once finalized by the ECP. This provision does not comply with the due process of law provided under international electoral standards (Mirbahar, 2017).

The act also improved election tribunal processes by requiring the filing of petitions on results directly with election tribunals. In the past, the ECP used to receive and process such petitions, which blurred the judicial and executive lines (DRI & RSIL, 2017; Union, 2013b).

Easy Registration of Voters and Extending Voting Rights to Overseas Pakistanis

The 2017 law simplified the voter registration process in Pakistan. Before the enactment of the law, voters were required to secure a computerized national identity card from the citizen registry. Once they had secured the identity card, they had to go to an ECP office and register with the ECP (DRI & RSIL, 2017). The act requires that voters are automatically registered when they apply for an identity card or renew one. It also requires the citizen registry to share its database with the ECP, so that it can regularly update its voters list. As Pakistan's law requires advance registration of voters, this simplification of the process enfranchises millions of voters.

The act requires the ECP to explore possible ways of extending the right to vote to overseas Pakistanis. The ECP has thus far conducted some pilots. However, the act does not define several key factors related to this aspect. Absence of such details could prove problematic for this high-risk exercise – for a general discussion see DRI's paper on out of country voting (DRI, 2012).

The Election Act falls short of addressing one regressive provision on voting rights. Historically, Ahmadis[5] were placed on a separate electoral roll. As Ahmadis face severe discrimination and, in many cases, violent attacks, they often do not exercise their right to vote as the separate electoral rolls put them at risk (DRI & RSIL, 2017). Although an earlier version of the Election Act, passed in October, repealed this provision of maintaining separate electoral rolls for Ahmadis, this change was reversed in November 2018 following a backlash from some religious groups (Mirbahar & Simm, 2018). The provision sits against the right to non-discrimination as stipulated in the ICCPR and ICERD (DRI & RSIL, 2017).

Transparency of Electoral Governance and Processes

Transparency during every aspect of the electoral process is clearly established within the international electoral standards. Together with the right to information, the standards require the provision of all necessary information throughout the electoral cycle (DRI & RSIL, 2017; TCC, 2015; Union, 2013b). During past elections in Pakistan, even the most essential information about the elections – such as results tallies, candidate nomination papers, and data on the electoral register – was not always available publicly (DRI, 2016; Union, 2013b). The act introduced several measures for improving the transparency of electoral processes. It requires the ECP to publish full tallies of the results on its website. There was previously no such requirement in the law. This had hindered the ability of the political parties, candidates, and citizens to audit the veracity of the results, thereby reducing confidence in the results. It is believed that the unavailability of full results tallies contributed significantly to the challenges made to the election results in 2013 and the political instability that followed them.

Additionally, the election officials are required to paste copies of the results sheets at polling stations, while making certified copies of the results available to the candidates or their designated agents. While the ECP had followed such practices in the past, they were not required to do so by the law. As a result, they were inconsistently applied.

Women's Political Participation

Women's right to political participation under CEDAW requires that state parties ensure full political participation for women as voters and candidates during an election (DRI & RSIL, 2017; TCC, 2015). While Pakistan has made some improvements in this regard by having around 16% of seats reserved for women in the national parliament and provincial assemblies, it still falls short of meeting the global target of ensuring at least 30% in the elected houses at all levels (Naz & Mirbahar, 2018). When it comes to voting, 11.67 million women were estimated to be unregistered ahead of the 2018 elections (FAFEN, 2016), while in several parts of the country women were forcibly disenfranchised. Neither state of affairs fulfils electoral integrity standards.

Measures for enhancing women's political participation and addressing the above problems were also included in the new law. Firstly, the act empowered the ECP to cancel the results of a constituency if the women's turnout was less than 10% or where agreements were made to disenfranchise women voters (Mirbahar & Simm, 2018). Such measures were necessary because, in previous elections, political parties or their candidates made agreements in some constituencies not to allow voters to cast their ballots. In other cases, such operations were done covertly. However, the law gives the ECP full discretion to apply this provision, without defining criteria for its operationalization.

Nonetheless, the provision also indirectly meant that political parties and candidates had more incentive to increase women voters' participation during polling. In addition, the ECP was required to make every effort to increase women's registration on the electoral rolls. This provision is aimed at addressing the gender gap in electoral rolls.

Furthermore, the ECP is required to record and release sex-disaggregated data for voter turnout. Sex-disaggregated turnout data are required under CEDAW, helping to target voter and registration education drives in the areas where women's participation remains the law. However, this requirement is only on an annual basis and such data should be disclosed after every election.

Participation of Persons with Disabilities

The act made it easier for people with some disabilities to participate in elections, as it introduced a postal ballot for them. Many persons with disabilities are unable to travel polling stations, so this was an essential provision for increasing their inclusion. Furthermore, the ECP was also required to make proactive efforts to increase registration of persons with disabilities as voters.

Security Features in the Ballot Paper

International standards require the security of ballot papers for electoral credibility. During the 2013 elections, several parties alleged, controversially, that ballots were printed privately by some groups. The act requires the ECP to build a unique watermark into ballot papers. This measure was considered necessary to increase the security of ballot papers and prevent fraud and controversy.

Improving the Scrutiny of Electoral Processes

International electoral standards require that the opportunity exists for independent scrutiny of electoral processes (DRI & RSIL, 2017). Election observers provide a useful check on electoral processes by providing an independent assessment of various aspects of elections (Norris & Nai, 2017). As most observers these days use international electoral standards, their work also helps assess the conduct of elections against these standards. While the ECP had facilitated the accreditation of election observers in the past, this area was unregulated and was therefore dealt with on an ad hoc basis. For the first time in the history of Pakistan, the Elections Act 2017 enshrined the rights and duties of election observers. It falls short of giving them full access, however, as observer access is limited to polling, counting, and consolidation of results (Mirbahar & Simm, 2018). Additionally, the act requires observers to gain security clearance from the government, which further restricts their ability to scrutinize electoral processes.

Equality of Suffrage in Boundary Delimitation

International standards require universal and equal suffrage. Equal suffrage is understood to mean that every voter has equal votes (Commission, 2008; TCC, 2015). As Pakistan follows the first-past-the-post electoral system, electing one candidate from each of 272 national assembly constituencies, the concept of equal suffrage also applies to the delimitation of constituencies, in that each constituency should have roughly the same population size. However, in the case of Pakistan, electoral constituencies have historically remained massively skewed. Data from the 2013 election showed that Pakistan's largest constituencies are approximately 500% bigger than the smallest constituencies.[6]

The Election Act 2017 requires no more than 15% population variation across the constituencies. While the international standards do not stipulate exact limits, the widely respected Venice Commission has suggested 10–15% population variation across constituencies. This limit is considered good practice among practitioners and has also been reinforced by Pakistan's higher courts in the context of local elections in Sindh. However, the application of these new criteria remains problematic. Based on the analysis of interim boundary delimitation, over 94 constituencies were found to contain more than 15% variation in population (Mirbahar & Serrato, 2018).

Conclusion

The case of electoral reforms in Pakistan shows the strengths of applying international electoral standards to strengthen and assess electoral integrity. As contended by the author, here and elsewhere, incorporating electoral integrity standards is a necessary first step in ensuring electoral integrity during the conduct of elections. Using these electoral integrity standards and the election cycle approach, this paper helps redefine electoral reforms and creates new definitions for typologies of major reform, minor reform, non-reform, and regressive legal changes. It suggests dropping the technical category, as all electoral details are technical in one way or another. The proposed approach helps address many methodological problems identified by scholars in previous electoral reform studies, while helping to advance the field in a more comprehensive way.

The case of Pakistan shows several ways in which the electoral integrity standards were translated into the Elections Act 2017, where political parties, civil society organizations, the election management body, election observers, and courts played different roles. At least nine aspects of electoral processes were improved through the Elections Act, while three aspects did not register any change. Regressive provisions regarding the separate electoral list of Ahmadis were maintained. Overall, the reforms are categorized as major reforms. Many of these reforms also helped improve several aspects of the 2018 elections (FAFEN, 2018; Union, 2018).

Issues similar to those identified in Pakistani elections have been reported elsewhere in the world. The 2019 Electoral Integrity Report assessed 103 elections as having low or very low electoral integrity scores. The electoral integrity of 56 contests was ranked as moderate. These elections were spread across all the continents and included elections in even so-called established democracies (including the US, the UK, Malta, and Greece). Observers and commentators have used the electoral integrity standards to point out the integrity shortcomings in these elections, while also recommending legal reforms to address them. Meanwhile, as in Pakistan, 25 Latin American and Caribbean member states of the Organization of American States (OAS) have addressed at least half of the recommendations made by OAS observer missions, which were also based on the electoral integrity standards and covered the entire electoral cycle. With several democracies needing and undertaking reforms to strengthen electoral integrity, the framework proposed here provides a useful methodology for assessing the reforms, strengthening the electoral legislation, and expanding electoral reforms scholarship to cover all aspects of elections.

Notes

1 The author is a democratic governance expert with expertise in electoral assistance, parliament strengthening, and human rights promotion. The current paper, and opinions and analysis contained in it, are produced in his personal capacity and do not in any way reflect the views or opinions of his present or previous employers. For communication, please write to him at: hnmirbahar@gmail.com, Twitter: @hassannasir, website: https://www.mirbahar.net/.

2 The full understanding and application of these treaties also involves the use of General Comments or General Recommendations issued by the treaty bodies. Treaty bodies are established by the United Nations and have a mandate for monitoring the implementation of human rights treaties. Each treaty has a corresponding treaty body. The bodies also provide official interpretation on the different provisions of relevant law; these are called General Comments or General Recommendations.

3 International standards require that core electoral processes are defined at least in primary legislation, with operational definitions left to administrative or secondary legislation.

4 EU EOM 2018, some Pakistani civil society organizations and many political parties nonetheless raised concerns over the overall political environment in which elections were held.

5 Ahmadis are a religious group in Pakistan who are constitutionally declared non-Muslims.

6 NA-41 (Tribal Areas VI) comprised 92,719 voters whereas NA-19 (Haripur) had 531,685 registered voters. The National Democratic Institute (NDI) and Asian Network for Free Elections (ANFREL) highlighted this point in their observation report for Pakistan's 2013 general election. Democracy Reporting International's paper on Delimitation in Pakistan highlights further issues: https://democracy-reporting.org/wp-content/uploads/2016/03/dri-pk_ip3_briefing_paper_on_delimitation_en.pdf, accessed on October 12, 2020.

References

Amar, V. D. (2017). The stakes of electoral reform at home and abroad. *Election Law Journal: Rules, Politics, and Policy, 16*(2), 211–212. doi: 10.1089/elj.2017.0451

Anis, M. (2017). *Election Reforms Bill 2017 passed by NA*. Retrieved April 10, 2021 from https://www.thenews.com.pk/print/225349-Election-Reforms-Bill-2017-passed-by-NA

Birch, S. (2005). Establishing the rules of the game: Election laws in democracies. *Representation, 41*(3), 238–239. doi: 10.1080/00344890508523314

Birch, S. (2007). Electoral systems and electoral misconduct. *Comparative Political Studies, 40*(12), 1533–1556. doi: 10.1177/0010414006292886

Birch, S. (2010). Perceptions of electoral fairness and voter turnout. *Comparative Political Studies, 43*(12), 1601–1622. doi: 10.1177/0010414010374021

Birch, S. (2011). *Electoral malpractice*. Oxford; New York: Oxford University Press.

Bowler, S., & Donovan, T. (2013). *The limits of electoral reform*. Oxford: Oxford University Press.

Bowler, S., & Farrell, D. M. (2009). Approaches to the study of electoral system design: Devils, details and "experts". Paper presented at the ECPR Joint Sessions, Lisbon, April 2009, Lisbon.

Bowler, S., Farrell, D. M., & Pettitt, R. T. (2005). Expert opinion on electoral systems: So which electoral system is "best"? *Journal of Elections, Public Opinion and Parties, 15*(1), 3–19. doi: 10.1080/13689880500064544

Celis, K., Krook, M. L., & Meier, P. (2011). The rise of gender quota laws: Expanding the spectrum of determinants for electoral reform. *West European Politics: Understanding Electoral Reform, 34*(3), 514–530. doi: 10.1080/01402382.2011.555981

Clegg, M., Ellena, K., Ennis, D., & Vickery, C. (2016). The hierarchy of laws: Understanding and implementing the legal frameworks that govern elections. Retrieved October 3, 2020 from https://www.ifes.org/sites/default/files/2016_ifes_hierarchy_of_laws.pdf

CP No 5098/2013, Sindh High Court (Sindh High Court 2013).

Davis-Roberts, A., & Carroll, D. J. (2010). Using international law to assess elections. *Democratization, 17*(3), 416–441. doi: 10.1080/13510341003700253

Donno, D. (2013). *Defending democratic norms: International actors and the politics of electoral misconduct*. New York: Oxford University Press.

DRI. (2010a). The 18th Amendment to the Constitution and Electoral Reform in Pakistan. Retrieved October 2, 2020 from https://democracy-reporting.org/wp-content/uploads/2016/02/dri_briefing_paper_5_-_comments_to_the_18th_amendment.pdf

DRI. (2010b). *International covenant on civil and political rights: Pakistan's new international obligations and election reform*. Retrieved October 2, 2020 from https://democracy-reporting.org/wp-content/uploads/2016/02/dri_042010_briefingpaperno2_pakistan.pdf

DRI. (2011). *Electronic voting machines: Promise and perils*. Retrieved October 2, 2020 from https://democracy-reporting.org/ur/dri_publications/briefing-paper-11-electronic-voting-machines-promise-and-perils/

DRI. (2012). Out of country voting: Principles and practices. Retrieved October 2, 2020 from https://democracy-reporting.org/wp-content/uploads/2016/02/dri_bp_23_out-of-country_voting_principles_and_practices.pdf

DRI. (2016). Fix it before it breaks: Local election lessons for 2018 elections in Pakistan. Retrieved April 10, 2021 from https://democracy-reporting.org/dri_publications/fix-it-before-it-breaks-what-the-local-elections-tell-us-for-improving-the-2018-general-election/

DRI. (2018). *From legislation to action: Next steps for implementing electoral reforms in Pakistan*. Retrieved October 2, 2020 from https://democracy-reporting.org/wp-content/uploads/2018/02/DRI_PK_DE_FROM-LEGISLATION-TO-ACTION_2018-01-30_Final.pdf

DRI, & RSIL. (2017). *Pakistan election laws and international standards: A reference guide on legislative gaps and vulnerabilities*. Islamabad: Democracy Reporting International & Research Society of International Law.

DRI, & TCC. (2013). *Strengthening international law to support democratic governance and genuine elections.* Retrieved August 23, 2020 from https://democracy-reporting.org/ur/?dri_publications=report-strengthening-international-law-to-support-democratic-governance-and-genuine-elections

European Commission. (2008). *Handbook for European Union election observation.* Retrieved August 23, 2017 from http://eeas.europa.eu/eueom/pdf/handbook-eueom-en-2nd-edition_en.pdf

European Commission. (2017). *Beyond election day: Best practices for follow-up to EU election observation missions.* Brussels: EU.

FAFEN. (2011). *A unification of Pakistan's election legislation including model provisions for electoral reform.* Retrieved October 2, 2020 from https://fafen.org/wp-content/uploads/2014/04/105_502_696.pdf

FAFEN. (2016). *11.67M women await registration as voters.* Retrieved October 3, 2020 from https://fafen.org/11-67m-women-await-registration-as-voters/

FAFEN. (2018). *FAFEN general election observation 2018: Election day process: Observation and analysis.* Retrieved October 2, 2020 from https://fafen.org/wp-content/uploads/2019/04/FAFEN-General-Election-Observation-2018-Election-Day-Process-Analysis-Pakistan.pdf

Ferrara, F., Herron, E. S., Nishikawa, M., & Palgrave, C. (2006). *Mixed electoral systems: Contamination and its consequences.* Basingstoke: Palgrave Macmillan.

Grofman, B., & Lijphart, A. (1986). *Electoral laws and their political consequences.* New York: Agathon Press.

Ham, V. C. (2015). Getting elections right? Measuring electoral integrity. *Democratization, 22*(4), 714–724. doi: 10.1080/13510347.2013.877447

Jacobs, K., & Leyenaar, M. (2011). A conceptual framework for major, minor, and technical electoral reform. *West European Politics, 34*(3), 495–513. doi: 10.1080/01402382.2011.555977

Katz, R. S. (2011). Democracy as a cause of electoral reform: Jurisprudence and electoral change in Canada. *West European Politics, 34*(3), 587–606. doi: 10.1080/01402382.2011.555985

Kelley, J. G. (2012). *Monitoring democracy: When international election observation works, and why it often fails.* Princeton, NJ: Princeton University Press.

Leyenaar, M., & Hazan, R. Y. (2011). Reconceptualising electoral reform. *West European Politics, 34*(3), 437–455. doi: 10.1080/01402382.2011.555974

Lijphart, A. (1994). *Electoral systems and party systems: A study of twenty-seven democracies, 1945–1990.* Oxford: Oxford University Press.

Marian, B. (2007). The dualist and monist theories. International law's comprehension of these theories. Curentul Juridic, The Juridical Current, *Le Courant Juridique, 1–2*, 16–27.

Massicotte, L., Blais, A., & Yoshinaka, A. (2004). *Establishing the rules of the game: Election laws in democracies.* Toronto; Buffalo; London: University of Toronto Press.

Meyer-Resende, M. (2011). *International consensus: Essential elements of democracy.* Retrieved April 10, 2021 from https://democracy-reporting.org/wp-content/uploads/2016/02/essential_elements_of_democracy_2.pdf

Mirbahar, H. N. (2017). *Election Bill 2017: An appraisal and way forward. Parliamentary research digest.* Pakistan Institute for Parliamentary Services (PIPS).

Mirbahar, H. N. (2019). Flawed laws, flawed elections: Local elections in Pakistan. *Election Law Journal: Rules, Politics, and Policy, 18*(1), 1–15. doi: 10.1089/elj.2017.0479

Mirbahar, H. N., & Kiani, S. (2016). Electoral conflicts in Pakistan: Setbacks in democratic stability. Paper presented at the Contentious Elections, Conflict and Regime Transitions, Poznan, Poland.

Mirbahar, H. N., & Serrato, R. (2018). *Pakistan's 2018 delimitation of electoral districts: Analysis of preliminary results.* Retrieved October 3, 2020 from https://democracy-reporting.org/pakistans-2018-delimitation-of-electoral-districts-analysis-of-preliminary-results/

Mirbahar, H. N., & Simm, A. (2018). Pakistan's Elections Act 2017: What you need to know. Retrieved October 3, 2020 from https://democracy-reporting.org/pakistans-elections-act-2017-what-you-need-to-know/

Moser, R. G., & Scheiner, E. (2012). *Electoral systems and political context: How the effects of rules vary across new and established democracies.* Cambridge: Cambridge University Press.

Naz, R., & Mirbahar, H. N. (2018). *Making gender quota meaningful: Implementing 5% general seat quota.* Islamabad: Heinrich Boll Stiftung.

Norris, P. (2004). *Electoral engineering: Voting rules and political behavior.* Cambridge, UK; New York: Cambridge University Press.

Norris, P. (2011). Cultural explanations of electoral reform: A policy cycle model. *West European Politics, 34*(3), 531–550. doi: 10.1080/01402382.2011.555982

Norris, P. (2012). *Why malpractices generate pressures for electoral reform: An agenda-setting model.* Electoral Integrity Project.

Norris, P. (2013a). Does the world agree about standards of electoral integrity? Evidence for the diffusion of global norms. *Electoral Studies*, *32*(4), 576. doi: 10.1016/j.electstud.2013.07.016

Norris, P. (2013b). The new research agenda studying electoral integrity. *Electoral Studies*, *32*(4), 563. doi: 10.1016/j.electstud.2013.07.015

Norris, P. (2014). *Why electoral integrity matters*. New York: Cambridge University Press.

Norris, P. (2017a). Chapter 5: *Reforming electoral laws. Strengthening electoral integrity*. Cambridge: Cambridge University Press.

Norris, P. (2017b). *Strengthening electoral integrity*. Cambridge: Cambridge University Press.

Norris, P. (2017c). *Why American elections are flawed (and how to fix them)*. Ithaca, NY; London: Cornell University Press.

Norris, P., & Grömpin, M. (2019). *Electoral integrity worldwide*. Retrieved October 3, 2020 from https://www.dropbox.com/s/csp1048mkwbrpsu/Electoral%20Integrity%20Worldwide.pdf?dl=0

Norris, P., & Nai, A. (Eds.). (2017). *Election watchdogs: Transparency, accountability and integrity*. New York: Oxford University Press.

Norris, P., Frank, R. W., & Coma, F. M. (2014). Measuring electoral integrity around the world: A new dataset. *PS: Political Science & Politics*, *47*(4), 789–798. doi: 10.1017/S1049096514001061

Norris, P., Frank, R. W., & Coma, F. M. (2015). *Contentious elections: From ballots to barricades*. New York: Routledge.

Norris, P., Nai, A., & Grömping, M. (2016). *Perceptions of electoral integrity - US 2016 (PEI_US_1.0)*. Retrieved from: https://doi.org/10.7910/DVN/YXUV3W

Pakistan, E. C. o. (2013). *Report on the General Elections 2013* (Vol. I).

Pakistan, J. C. (2014). *Pakistan Judicial Commission on 2013 General Elections Judicial Commission*.

Pakistan, N. A. o. (2017). *The report of the Parliamentary Committee on Electoral Reforms on The Elections Bill 2017: National Assembly of Pakistan*.

Renwick, A. (2010). *The politics of electoral reform: Changing the rules of democracy*. Cambridge: Cambridge University Press.

Renwick, A. (2011). Electoral reform in Europe since 1945. *West European Politics: Understanding Electoral Reform*, *34*(3), 456–477. doi: 10.1080/01402382.2011.555975

Reynolds, A., Reilly, B., & Ellis, A. (2005). *Electoral system design: The new International IDEA handbook*. Retrieved October 3, 2020 from https://www.idea.int/sites/default/files/publications/electoral-system-design-the-new-international-idea-handbook.pdf

Roberts, H., Aranceta, I., Blanchet, D., & Gomez, C. (2017). *Evaluation of EU election observation activities*. Retrieved April 10, 2021 from https://eeas.europa.eu/topics/election-observation-missionseueoms_en/25845/Evaluation%20of%20EU%20Election% 20Observation%20Activities

Schauer, F. (Forthcoming, 2020). Lon Fuller and the rule of law. In M. Sevel (Ed.), *Routledge handbook of the rule of law*. London: Routledge.

TCC. (2015). *Election obligations and standards*. Retrieved October 3, 2020 from https://www.cartercenter.org/resources/pdfs/peace/democracy/cc-oes-handbook-10172014.pdf

UN. (1948). *Universal Declaration of Human Rights (UDHR)*. United Nations.

UN. (1965). *International convention on the elimination of all forms of racial discrimination (ICERD). United Nations, treaty series*, (20th ed.,Vol. 660, pp. 195). United Nations.

UN. (1966). *International Covenant on Civil and Political Rights (ICCPR). U.N.T.S.* No. 14668 (Vol. 999 (1976)). United Nations General Assembly.

UN. (1979). *Convention on the elimination of all forms of discrimination against women (CEDAW). United Nations, treaty series*, (Vol. 1249, pp. 13). United Nations.

UN. (2003). *Convention against corruption (CAC). A/58/422, (Vol. 58/4 of 31 October 2003)*. United Nations General Assembly.

UN. (2007). *Convention on the Rights of Persons with Disabilities (CRPD). A/RES/61/106* (6th Session ed.). United Nations General Assembly.

Union, E. (2013a). *Election observation mission to Pakistan*. Retrieved April 10, 2021 from https://eeas.europa.eu/sites/eeas/files/pakistan_eom_final_report_eng_1.pdf

Union, E. (2013b). *Election observation mission to Pakistan*. Retrieved October 3, 2020 from https://eeas.europa.eu/sites/eeas/files/pakistan_eom_final_report_eng_1.pdf

Union, E. (2018). *Final reportL European Union election observation mission to Islamic Republic of Pakistan - General elections*, 25 July 2018. Retrieved October 3, 2020 from https://eeas.europa.eu/sites/eeas/files/final_report_pakistan_2018_english.pdf

27

DEEP ELECTION LAW IN SOUTH KOREA

Erik Johan Mobrand

Introduction

Election law is serious business in South Korea. Modes of electoral mobilization are profoundly linked to laws on elections and political parties. Laws on campaigning, organizing, and political speech are at least as important as the electoral system in shaping the country's electoral politics. Violators face fines, and scandals regularly bring down winning candidates. The relevant bureaucracies take election law so seriously that they have spearheaded the formation of the Association of World Election Bodies (A-WEB), which has its secretariat just outside Seoul (Association of World Election Bodies, 2020).

In this context, election law is not simply legislation or a set of institutions. Just because it is written down does not make the legal code matter. Rather, election law is situated in and expresses a disciplined form of electoral mobilization. Over decades, candidates and political parties have adapted their activities in ways that relate to election law. These adaptations have shaped the types of people who become politicians and the sorts of interests that gain representation. A powerful normative framework underpins the system of election law even as it has critics. At the same time, surveillance and control enforce compliance with the system. Together, these features mean that South Korea has what might be called *deep* election law. That is, the law goes well beyond what is written.

The depth of election law in South Korea makes it different from many other contexts. Elsewhere, election laws can appear acceptable, but poor enforcement means they relate only indirectly to what happens. Yet, in South Korea, it cannot be said simply that enforcement is better. Rather, election law itself is implicated in a web of activities that include the enforcement of rules. Powerful actors appeal to the legitimacy of the law. These claims help induce discipline and make enforcement easier. If we were to separate the laws from issues of compliance, then we would miss a lot of the ways that election law operates in South Korea.

Because the position of election law in South Korea's political system dates to the authoritarian period, the country's experience points to questions about the connection between election law and regime type. When is election law authoritarian and when is it not? Scholars tend to view election law in authoritarian regimes in terms of manipulation. In democracies, election law is seen in other ways, including as a strategic design of politicians. But, when a thriving democracy has an election law that became deeply rooted under an earlier period of authoritarian rule,

DOI: 10.4324/9780429401800-27

then the authoritarian-democratic distinction gets blurred. For this reason, South Korea offers a fascinating view into the relationship between election law and political engagement.

The Context of Election Law

Much of the political science scholarship on East Asia views political systems through an American lens. This lens finds electoral systems and encourages a focus on them. They assume open competition reigns and a secondary position of election law, possibly to make campaign finance fairer. The American influence on constitutional orders, especially in Japan and South Korea, is some justification for this view. However, this viewpoint obscures more than it reveals.

The state in South Korea plays a significant role in setting the boundaries of electoral competition. A few considerations lie behind this point. One is that South Korea's electoral politics has its origins in an illiberal period of counter-revolutionary state-making and proto-Cold War politics. Parties and elections began in the years after liberation from Japan in 1945, which also brought about division of the peninsula. During three years of rule by a US army government, priority was placed on eliminating or marginalizing forces that might have leftist tendencies (Cumings, 1981). The Americans, sensing rivalry with the Soviets, were concerned about communists finding support in southern Korea. Therefore, anticommunism infused the creation of public political space. The result was a set of serious constraints on who could participate in electoral and party politics. This pattern continued with the establishment of the Republic of Korea in 1948. While the constitution guaranteed many rights, the anticommunist imperative put brackets around those rights (Ch'oe, 2005). The National Security Law emerged as a primary mechanism for that bracketing. Under the law, suspected enemies of the state could be detained without due process. For decades, leaders used the National Security Law to harass and destroy competitors, as well as those perceived as critics. The experience of war on the peninsula made it easier for leaders to cite security concerns in order to put limits on democracy (Paik, 2013). These considerations meant that electoral politics was a regulated affair.

Another source of the state's role in shaping electoral politics was the kind of public order that emerged in South Korea. Even though American influence was tremendous, South Korea was a civil law jurisdiction. Prussian legal thought had a profound impact, in part indirectly through experience under Japanese colonial rule. The first generations of South Korean lawyers and legal scholars had German if not Japanese training. The state loomed large in the vision of public order. Later, West German ideas also made their way to Korea. In particular, Koreans seized on ideas developed in West Germany regarding the position of political parties in the political system. The idea of "militant democracy," articulated in the West German basic law, informed a constitutional revision in South Korea in 1960. This clause allows the state to disband parties that threaten the "basic democratic order" (Song, 2010). South Korean lawmakers also picked up on the West German notion that separate legislation could be written to regulate political parties. For these reasons, there is a deep history of state regulation of, or interference in, electoral politics.

But surely it might be claimed that the democratic transition implied a resetting of patterns of electoral mobilization. After all, politicians were now operating in a new environment, one with fewer threats and in which no single grouping could control election laws. South Korea surged toward democracy in 1987, when the regime announced immediate constitutional reforms that included a return to direct presidential elections (Saxer, 2002). Even if some of the old election laws were retained, they would take on new significance in this changed context. Laws would then be more a reflection of the strategic interests of legislators who could re-write them than of any continuity. However, these claims underestimate the depth of election law in

South Korea's context. Again, law was not simply legislation; it was instead disciplined behavior. The same forces that make compliance high are those that keep authoritarian-era patterns relevant.

Legislation on Parties and Elections

Three pieces of legislation form the key laws that are relevant for party and electoral politics. These are the Law on Election of Public Officials, the Political Donations Law, and the Political Parties Act. Each is subject to constant revision. The Law on Election of Public Officials was previously a set of three separate laws covering presidential elections, National Assembly elections, and local elections. In 1994, these three laws were merged into one. The three laws are often revised together, with possible amendments considered together by a National Assembly committee.

Among the stated priorities in these laws are the fighting of corruption and prevention of excessive conflict in elections. There is fear that unbridled electoral mobilization will bring rapacious candidates or cause underlying tensions to boil over. Reference to these concerns is found throughout proposed legislation and in court decisions related to the laws (Mobrand, 2015). These concerns support laws that limit campaigning and participation. Imposing such limits is a primary means of accomplishing the stated tasks. A few examples can help sketch out these limits.

An important group of limits written into the Law on Election of Public Officials concerns restrictions on campaign periods. Each type of election has a fixed number of days in which candidates may campaign. This period is set at 13 days for local and National Assembly elections, while it is about three weeks for presidential elections. Before the campaign period, candidates must be cautious not to engage in activities that could be construed as campaigning. These limits mean that candidates have very few opportunities to make themselves known to voters. Similarly, candidates who are already well-known have an advantage in this situation.

Another set of restrictions is in the electoral thresholds that parties must meet. Previously, if a threshold was not met, the party could be disbanded according to article 44 of the Political Parties Act. The threshold was set at 2% of the vote in National Assembly elections. At the same time, if a party did not nominate a candidate in any election over a four-year period, it would also be disbanded. Although a Constitution Court ruling in 2014 stopped this practice, parties were regularly disbanded according to the procedures of this threshold. After the 2004, 2008, and 2012 National Assembly elections, for example, 35 parties were dissolved for failing to win enough votes (Mobrand, 2019b, Ch. 5). In an especially cruel turn, the law stated that any party that had been disbanded could never again register under the same.

The effort to limit contact between politicians and voters went even further in a bizarre revision to the Political Parties Act made in 2004. The Political Parties Act sets out parameters within which parties can operate. Until 2004, the basic unit of a party was a legislative district. The leader of this unit was called the "branch party head." A concern that had been raised was that branch heads could manipulate their positions to embezzle money or interfere improperly in candidate selection processes. For instance, it was reported that branch heads would register friends or associates as party members and use them to influence results on polls on candidates (Kim, 2003). Their control over party finance made them too powerful, it was charged. In response, in 2004, legislators proposed a bill that declared that "In order to improve the high-cost, ineffective party structure, the branch party system is to be completely eliminated" (Chŏngch'i Kaehyŏk T'ŭkpyŏl Wiwŏnjang, 2004, 2). The bill passed. The main local unit of the party was abolished, and parties then consisted of a party headquarters and provincial party chapters.

The elimination of branch parties points to a particular use of election law. If party leaders were concerned about branch party offices, then they might have taken action within their parties. They could have rewritten party rules to disempower branch party offices, or made adjustments to party finance. Instead, they opted to cooperate across party lines and legislate a solution. The labour party, which held a small number of seats in the National Assembly, opposed the reform. Like labour parties elsewhere, the Democratic Labour Party was strong on local organizing and the branch party was the main site of member participation – including in voting on party leadership and on candidates for elected office. Incumbents also gained an advantage. Sitting legislators could use the offices in their districts to run campaigns. However, representatives of other parties could not set up a campaign office until 120 days before an election. The consequences of the reform to the Political Parties Act were thus distributed unevenly across parties (Mobrand, 2019b, Ch. 5).

Election Law and Political Mobilization

These laws provide a guide to electoral mobilization. Election law helps explain the sharp divergence that can be observed between the political culture of demonstrations and the political culture of election campaigns in South Korea. A glance at a newspaper or a visit to downtown Seoul is enough to see the high level of political awareness and engagement in the country. Commuters tune into political podcasts. Street protests are part of everyday life. Workers regularly strike. Leaders of civic groups pour boundless energy into an array of causes. This engagement fits within a history of ordinary people having little choice but to press demands on frustrating or unresponsive governments. Mass movements punctuated the march out of authoritarian rule. These movements, in turn, have become memorialized as sacred moments for the nation.

A set of norms has formed around gatherings in connection with mass movements in South Korea. They are peaceful affairs. Participants often join as families, and so all ages can be seen represented. There is often singing and dancing. Volunteers distribute snacks and drinks. The atmosphere is positive, communal, and festive. The Candlelight Movement of 2016–2017, which responded to wrongdoing by then president Park Geun-hye, involved gatherings with these characteristics. Participants contributed in a range of spontaneous ways, from preventing violence to cleaning up at the end of the evening.

Election campaigns invite a culture that is entirely foreign to what is seen at rallies. There is so little room for creativity that every campaign looks just like the next. Candidates and their supporters distribute business cards at metro station entrances (but not in the stations – that is illegal). Lorries pass by with pop music blaring and a loudspeaker repeating the name of the candidate. Campaign staff wear baseball caps and jackets in the color of the party they represent. Staff working for the major political parties repeat the name of the party and candidate, but have nothing to say about a political program. These staff are given a nominal compensation per day and are usually connected personally to the candidate. They are not committed activists. Above all, campaigns are devoid of the passion that can be found in more organic modes of political mobilization.

The electoral system cannot predict these outcomes. Most seats in the National Assembly are allocated to winners of district races that follow first-past-the-post rules. On paper, then, parties have incentives to nominate candidates who have strong support bases in their districts. Given the high level of political and civic activism in South Korea, there is a deep pool of leaders with strong local reputations and networks. One would expect these individuals to be the preferred candidates of parties. Alternatively, running as independents, local notables might challenge party representatives. In reality, however, these local organizers have skills and resources that fit poorly with what is permitted. Civic activists excel at holding rallies, making speeches, and mobilizing supporters to pound pavements. Such activities get the word out about the candidate. Yet, these activities are either banned or severely restricted under the election law. The limited numbers of rallies and speeches give candidates few opportunities to reach voters. Since the size of the team helping a given candidate is also fixed, they cannot demonstrate a show of force on the streets. And they certainly cannot have committed supporters knocking on doors to speak directly with citizens about the issues.

It is election law, and not the broader political culture or the electoral system, that molds the formulaic style of electoral mobilization. A mode of political engagement all of its own has grown up around heavily restricted elections. With candidate-voter contact discouraged in the name of fighting corruption, election campaigns struggle to tap into the meanings that make Koreans passionate about public issues in other contexts.

Election Law before Democracy

The discouragement of contact between voters and candidates was not introduced to South Korea with the democratic transition. This approach to regulation was equally prominent in the authoritarian era. What changed was the justification for the approach. While today battling corruption is the main given reason, before democratization such restrictions were announced more frequently in terms of preventing popular movements. In particular, the concern was that politicians with mass bases would succeed with more open electoral arrangements (Mobrand, 2019b, Ch. 1). This possibility, in the context of the Cold War and a divided peninsula, could be linked to threat to the public security. Politics had to be kept cool in order to keep communists out.

A key moment in the development of South Korea's election law was the so-called "negotiated election law" of 1958 (Sŏ, 2013). This legislation represented an inter-party bargain to introduce legal measures to keep out a popular third party. The background to the legislation lies in the perceived threat of a left-leaning Progressive Party and its leader, Cho Pong-am. In the 1956 presidential election, the Democratic Party – the main opposition party – saw its candidate pass away suddenly weeks before polling. Instead of fielding another candidate, the party announced support for Cho as a candidate under the Progressive Party. While Cho hardly came close to defeating president Syngman Rhee, he still earned 30% of the vote. That performance made opposition lawmakers, as well as those within Rhee's own Liberal Party, concerned that Cho could challenge them further.

The Liberals and the Democrats attempted to find a solution that would be mutually beneficial. The Democrats feared their position as the main opposition party would be threatened. The fear was not the Progressive Party itself but any force that was able to use elections to mobilize popular support. In any case, Cho was charged under the National Security Law and later executed for treason. The Progressive Party was forcibly disbanded. Still, his example unnerved the political establishment. Looking for restrictions, legislators turned to election laws from militarist-era Japan (Sŏ, 2013; Song, 2005). In the 1934 election law, they found heavy restrictions on campaigning and found these attractive. Many of the clauses today that limit contact between voters and politicians can be traced to the 1958 election law. Strict rules on campaigning were imposed through the law. It introduced brief campaign periods, banned door-to-door campaigning, limited campaign speeches, and regulated campaign material.

The new election law was followed immediately by a National Assembly election. The law succeeded in all but eliminating third parties (Sŏ, 2013). Five years later, another major piece of legislation was introduced with the similar aims of exclusion. By then, politics had changed a great deal. The Rhee regime collapsed in 1960 in the wake of electoral fraud; a coup the following year put military figures into power. In 1963, as the junta prepared to make way for the return of civilian rule, the regime introduced the Political Parties Act. This law was among the first in the world on political parties specifically. The idea had come from West Germany, but that country did not adopt a party law until 1967. The Political Parties Act was, of course, aimed at smoothing the transition to civilian rule and helping Park Chung Hee win power as president.

The approach was to demobilize possibly threatening forces. The act stipulated what parties could and could not do, as well as how they must organize. Through the setting of registration requirements, the Political Parties Act provided a blueprint for party organization. Parties were required to have legislative districts as the basic unit with the headquarters in Seoul. A party had to have a presence across the county – in the first version of the Political Parties Act, parties needed to have offices in five provinces and in 30% of all legislative districts. A party could not, therefore, be established only in one part of the country (Mosler, 2014). With this rigid formula for what a party could be, the regime worked to keep popular movements at bay.

Exclusion was a technique of control in South Korea before democratization, and law was frequently a tool for that purpose. Election law is deeply tied to exclusion; those deep ties are both long-lasting and wrapped up in an elite agreement on using election law to exclude. Accustomed to the rules, politicians clung to them even as the democratic transition unfolded (Mobrand, 2015). The architecture of election law remained intact through the democratic transition. In some areas, election laws became even more restrictive on political activities.

Controversial Articles

Specific articles of election law have prompted criticisms that illustrate the approach to regulating elections. Two articles that legal scholars have criticized are articles 90 and 93 of the 1994 Integrated Election Law. Article 90 reads as follows:

> Between 180 days before election day and election day, in seeking to influence the election in ways other than those stipulated in this law, nobody can install, display, post, or distribute garlands, balloons, signs, banners, ad balloons, gadgets, propaganda towers, other advertising products or fixtures, nor can they wear or distribute stickers or other indicators, nor can they produce or sell dolls, mascots, and other icons that stand for candidates (including those who pledge to become candidates).
>
> *(Election Law of South Korea, 1994, Article 90)*[1]

The detailed list of prohibited items is, perhaps, most striking in this passage. Two other parts are equally significant. First, the concept of "influence" raises questions of meaning. When might something be a source of influence? This concept has been criticized. One scholar, for example, notes that the "concept of behaviour that influences elections is unclear and vague" (Yu, 2012, 116). These qualities could discourage participation.

Another important part of Article 90 is the introduction of a time period of 180 days before an election. Election law imposes a division in time between ordinary time and the six months prior to an election. Ordinary freedoms for speech apply only outside these six months. During the half year before an election, though, a wide range of restrictions on speech come into force. Aspiring candidates and their supporters must refrain making statements, no matter how true, lest they influence the election. Even publicizing one's legislative record in this period could be illegal, even as such information would seem to be useful to voters. Violations of Articles 90 and 93 have prompted punishments, including both fines and jail time. A party member who took to the party website to criticize a corruption scandal in the party was charged with violating the equality of opportunity to campaign. He was found guilty of inappropriate influence under Article 93. When the case came to the Constitutional Court, it found nothing unconstitutional in the articles (Yun, 2010, 580–2).

As these examples suggest, the election law places overwhelming emphasis on limiting political communication. Speech itself becomes a potential threat to proper procedure. Such rules are certainly surprising to find in a liberal democracy. Election law is largely silent on other values that might be associated with electoral democracy: Participation, competition, diversity, pluralism, and so on. An examination of another area of election law, gender imbalance in politics, illustrates that law can be used to expand representation – within certain bounds.

The Gender Quota

An increase in women in the legislature is tied directly to changes in election law. Activists for women's representation had hoped that democratization would expand opportunities in politics for women. It did not. Very few women made it into the National Assembly in the 1990s. Local elected offices had an even smaller proportion of women. Campaigns by activists included requests to parties to introduce quotas on women as candidates in elections (Park, 1999). In the early 2000s, versions of proposed quotas were accepted and put into law. With parties required to nominate more women, the proportion of women in the National Assembly grew steadily. Furthermore, the quota had amplifying effects. A portion of women who at first benefited from the quota built reputations that allowed them to successfully contest elections without support from the quota (Mobrand, 2019a). Women elected as officials have now gone on to serve as ministers. Election law can be credited with this shift.

Even the example of the gender quota, though, points to the limiting nature of election law in South Korean politics. Research on gender quotas worldwide finds that inter-party competition is a primary mechanism driving the widespread adoption of a gender quota (Dahlerup, 2007). The process usually begins with a progressive party introducing an internal target or quota for women candidates. As this approach proves popular or successful, other parties follow suit. This contagion leads either to a norm or law that support should be in place to encourage the nomination of women as candidates. In South Korea, too, progressive parties were quicker to endorse the nomination of more women as candidates. Yet, before any major party declared a gender quota within the party, legislators across parties consulted each other to work out an acceptable form of the gender quota (Mobrand, 2019a). They then proposed the quota as legislation, which took form between 2000 and 2004.

The version that they proposed and that became law has, as its most important component, a "zipper" system for nomination by gender: For party lists in the National Assembly, parties are required to alternate men and women as candidates. Soon after, the norm in the largest parties became to place a woman at number one and then every second place on the party list. This ensured that half the women elected on the party list won places in the National Assembly. The trouble is that, in the period since the quota's introduction, only one-sixth to one-fifth of the seats are allocated by party list. There is no stipulation that parties must nominate more women in district races, which account for the vast majority of seats in the national assembly (Yoon & Shin, 2015). Neither was there a requirement in local politics. While the law provides marginal incentives to parties for supporting women's political careers, these have failed to encourage parties to nominate more women in districts.

The quota as it stands, then, does little to reorganize parties around women. It instead encourages the parachuting of a nationally prominent women onto party lists. Both in terms of the numbers of women in the National Assembly, as well the modes of political recruitment and contestation, women as politicians benefit relatively little from this arrangement. Instead of gaining greater opportunities, women are simply granted seats in almost reservation-like fashion.

What parties did was circumvent the logic of contagion through inter-party competition. Instead of allowing competition across parties to increase the commitment to a quota with higher expectations, legislators stepped in to prevent competition from ramping up the commitment. They then agreed on a solution that brought a limited number of women into high politics. While this result led to more women entering politics, it is still not optimal. This experience followed the pattern seen in other aspects of regulation of politics in South Korea (Mobrand, 2019a). Parties collaborated to prevent competition from taking away some of their power. The point here is not that the gender quota is irrelevant, but rather that the opportunity to press for increased opportunities for women was partially subverted by the exclusionary politics of deep election law.

The Central Election Management Commission

A major force behind election law is the Central Election Management Commission (CEMC). The body has wide-ranging responsibilities. One of its primary tasks is, of course, to carry out the administration of elections, which is done through this centralized authority. The agency is also involved in proposing legislation. Its staff advise legislators on election law and make recommendations. The CEMC claims credit for the 1994 Integrated Election Law. The agency runs visible campaigns around election time to encourage people to follow the rules. Celebrities are hired to serve as ambassadors for the CEMC and help with this work. CEMC campaigns have high visibility around the country, as well as online.

Monitoring is also handled by the CEMC. The organization oversees all aspects of campaigning. For example, it assists in the arrangement of campaign banners and posters. In any given election, these mostly appear suddenly overnight when the campaign period begins. Where posters have not been approved by the CEMC, its staff are quick to remove them. Before elections, the CEMC mobilizes extra personnel to watch for illegal activity. Special attention is paid to settings where illegal campaigning is feared to occur, such as churches. While candidates are not permitted to campaign in religious or other community-based contexts, the CEMC enters churches in order to spread the message of clean elections. In the 1990s, military styles informed CEMC surveillance operations: Police and bureaucrats would be deployed briefly with the organization and put into squads for "crackdowns" and intensified monitoring for illegal behavior (Chungang Sŏn'gŏ Kwalli Wiwŏnhoe, 2009, 583–5).

The CEMC also has the power to issue punishments in certain cases. Where voters have received money or goods from a candidate, the CEMC is authorized to charge a fine 50 times greater than the amount in question. In other cases, the CEMC refers suspects to the police and prosecution. That election laws are taken seriously is due, in no small part, to the clout of the CEMC.

Areas of monitoring by the CEMC have grown over time. As laws were introduced to regulate balloting within parties, the CEMC was empowered to both manage and investigate intra-party votes. While parties had previously taken charge of these activities, they now permitted the CEMC to exercise authority.

The CEMC has been involved in the most controversial decisions on election law cases. In 2004, a month before a National Assembly election, President Roh Moo Hyun made a speech in which he mentioned his support for one political party. Critics accused him of violating the election law for interfering in an election. The National Assembly impeached him. The CEMC's nine commissioners held a meeting to determine whether Roh had broken the law.

Proceedings of the meetings are secret, so the public in unable to scrutinize the decision-making process. The commissioners determined that Roh had engaged in early election campaigning and had, therefore, indeed broken the election law. This decision was extremely unpopular. Ordinary Koreans took to the streets, upset that an elected president had been removed. When the National Assembly election came, voters punished the parties that had impeached Roh (Mobrand, 2019b, Ch. 4).

In 2013, the CEMC helped launch the Association of World Electoral Bodies (A-WEB). The organization has states as members. The presidency rotates, but a large proportion of the funding comes from South Korea. CEMC officials, seconded, staff the organization's secretariat. Their offices are located in a gleaming tower in Songdo, a new city developed on reclaimed land. A-WEB concerns itself largely with technical advice around electoral management (Association of World Election Bodies, 2021). It sells voting machines in Africa and central Asia. The ethic and discipline of the CEMC, core components of South Korea's deep election law, find an international platform in A-WEB.

Conclusion

A-WEB showcases the orderliness of South Korea's elections to new democracies and other places that struggle to keep elections civil. To people in many societies, the strict rules and strong enforcement can make the country's election law attractive. Where elections invite violence or politicians give gifts or money to voters, the example of South Korea's calm elections can be powerful. While there might be lessons to be drawn and shared, it is important not to form these too quickly. South Korea did not simply write laws and then build enforcement capacity. The effectiveness of election law relates rather to a discipline first instilled under profoundly illiberal regimes. That is what has been meant here by thinking of South Korea as having deep election law.

A lesson here is that discipline linked to exclusionary election laws can be a covert conduit for illiberal practices to seep into a democracy. That is what is at risk with deep election law. Rule of law and the need to fight corruption can mask practices that undermine democratic principles, even as they seem to express them. The shift to multiparty elections is no guarantee that forms of domination practiced under authoritarian rule through election law will disappear. For these forms can be appropriated and redeployed. Indeed, under conditions of deep election law, exclusionary practices can linger while taking on a neutral, legalistic guise. As the examples of the gender quota and regulation of political parties demonstrate, deep election law can have far-reaching consequences long after a democratic transition has occurred. The phenomenon of deep election law should give observers pause when examining democratic transition. It is important to examine the position of election law in political struggle, not simply in formal or technical terms.

Today, South Korea struggles with a problem that has mostly been overlooked in research on new democracies. If a system of election law grows roots under authoritarian rule, then people must fight against it later. This fight is a difficult one, in part because the problems can be difficult to describe. In South Korea's experience, the language of corruption emerged to offer powerful justification for continuing exclusionary election laws. Finding symbolic resources to use in a battle against that language is not easy.

A small number of people in South Korea have advocated thorough election law reform. These include a greater number of legal scholars than political scientists. One lawyer criticizes the Constitutional Court for supporting strict election campaign laws (Hong, 2013). The problem, he notes, is that strict campaign laws make the National Assembly weaker and the

Constitutional Court stronger. Values of freedom and participation lose out to concerns over fairness and corruption prevention. Sustained criticism of the deep election law might spur public discussions about how election law can be re-thought to better serve and represent South Koreans in a democratic context.

Note

1 *Election of Public Officials and Election Violations Prevention Act*, Article 90, enacted March 16, 1994. Some parenthetical remarks have been omitted.

References

Association of World Election Bodies. (2021). *2020 Annual report*. Incheon: A-WEB.

Ch'oe, C. (2005). *Minjuhwa ihu ŭi minjujuŭi: Han'guk minjujuŭi ŭi posujŏk kiwŏn kwa wigi (Democracy after democratization: The conservative origins and crisis of Korean democracy)* (Rev. ed.). Seoul: Humanit'asŭ.

Chŏngch'i Kaehyŏk T'ŭkpyŏl Wiwŏnjang (Chair of the Special Committee on Political Reform). (2004). *Chŏngdangbŏp chung kaejŏng pŏmnyuran (Proposal for a partial revision to the Political Parties Act)* (Sixteenth assembly, bill no. 3169).

Chungang Sŏn'gŏ Kwalli Wiwŏnhoe (2009). *Taehan Min'guk son'gŏsa (History of elections in the Republic of Korea)* (Vol. 5). Kwach'ŏn: Chungang Sŏn'gŏ Kwalli Wiwŏnhoe.

Cumings, B. (1981). *The origins of the Korean War, Vol. 1: Liberation and the emergence of separate regimes, 1945–1947*. Princeton, NJ: Princeton University Press.

Dahlerup, D. (2007). Electoral gender quotas: Between equality of opportunity and equality of result. *Representation*, *43*(2), 73–92. doi: 10.1080/00344890701363227

Hong, S. (2013). Sŏn'gŏ undong ŭi chayu wa kyuje e kwanhan hŏnpŏpchŏk koch'al: Hŏnpŏp chaep'anso p'allye e taehan p'yŏngga rŭl chungsim ŭro (A constitutional study of freedom and restrictions on election campaigning: An evaluation of Constitutional Court decisions). *Hŏnpŏphak yŏn'gu (Constitutional Studies)*, *19*(4), 123–156.

Kim, Y. (2003). Han'guk chŏngdang ŭi kukhoe ŭiwŏn kongch'ŏn chedo: Chisok kwa pyŏnhwa (Korean parties' systems for nominating National Assembly members: Continuity and change). *Ŭijŏng yŏn'gu (Legislative Studies)*, *9*(1), 6–29.

Mobrand, E. (2015). The politics of regulating elections in South Korea: The persistence of restrictive campaign laws. *Pacific Affairs*, *88*(4), 791–811. doi: 10.5509/2015884791

Mobrand, E. (2019a). On parties' terms: Gender quota politics in South Korea's mixed electoral system. *Asian Studies Review*, *42*(4), 114–131. doi: 10.1080/10357823.2018.1512554

Mobrand, E. (2019b). *Top-down democracy in South Korea*. Seattle, WA: University of Washington Press.

Mosler, H. (2014). Judicialization of politics and the Korean Constitutional Court: The "party chapter abolition case." *Verfassung und Recht in Übersee*, *47*(3), 293–318.

Paik, N. (2013). South Korean democracy and Korea's division system. *Inter-Asia Cultural Studies*, *14*(1), 156–169. doi: 10.1080/14649373.2013.753853

Park, K.A. (1999). Political representation and South Korean women. *Journal of Asian Studies*, *58*(2), 432–448. doi: 10.2307/2659403

Saxer, C.J. 2002. *From Transition to Power Alternation: Democracy in South Korea, 1987–1997*. New York: Routledge.

Sŏ, P. (2013). Chehanjŏk kyŏngjaeng ŭi chedohwa: 1958-yŏn sŏn'gŏbŏp ch'eje (The institutionalization of limited competition: The system of the 1958 election law). *Sŏn'gŏ yŏn'gu (Electoral Studies)*, *3*(1), 109–138.

Song, S. (2005). Sŏn'gŏ undong kyuje ippŏp ŭi yŏnwŏn: 1925-yŏn Ilbon pot'ong sŏn'gŏbŏp ŭi sŏngnip kwa Han'guk pundan ch'eje ŭi yuip" (The origins of legislation on election campaign regulations: The establishment of the 1925 Japanese common election law and its entry into Korea's divided system). *Sŏul Taehakkyo pŏphak (Seoul National University Legal Studies)*, 46(4), 28–53.

Song, S. (2010). Chŏngdang haesan simp'an ŭi silch'ejŏk yogŏn: Chŏngdang haesan simp'an chedo ŭi chwap'yo wa kwallyŏn hayŏ" (The actual conditions for ruling that a political party should be dissolved: Guidelines for the system of ruling on the dissolution of political parties). *Sŏul Taehakkyo pŏphak (Seoul National University Legal Studies)*, *51*(1), 27–65.

Yoon, J., & Shin, K.-Y. (2015). Mixed effects of legislative quotas in South Korea. *Politics & Gender, 11*(1), 186–195.

Yu, C. (2012). *Sŏn'gŏ undong kyuje kaep'yero chŏngch'i ch'amyŏ pojang (Preserving political participation through adjusting restrictions on election campaigning). Kukhoe po* (National Assembly bulletin).

Yun, Y. (2010). Sŏn'gŏ ŭi kongjŏngsŏng e kwanhan kŏmt'o: Kongjik sŏn'gŏbŏp che 93-cho che 1-hang munsŏ tŭng paebu kŭmji kyujŏng e taehan kwadohan kwangbŏmsŏng pŏmni e ttarŭn wihŏnsŏng kŏmt'o rŭl chungsim ŭro (An examination of the fairness of elections: The unconstitutional status, due to excessive scope, of Article 93, clause 1, of the Law on Election of Public Officials, which prohibits distribution of documents). *Hŏnpŏphak yŏn'gu (Constitutional Law), 16*(3), 573–612.

INDEX

For Product Safety Concerns and Information please contact our EU representative GPSR@taylorandfrancis.com
Taylor & Francis Verlag GmbH, Kaufingerstraße 24, 80331 München, Germany

www.ingramcontent.com/pod-product-compliance
Ingram Content Group UK Ltd.
Pitfield, Milton Keynes, MK11 3LW, UK
UKHW050232200926
475702UK00020B/2987
* 9 7 8 1 0 3 2 1 8 3 0 5 3 *